Proxy Militias

The Taliban, Daesh, Pakistani and
Central Asian Terrorist Organizations

Proxy Militias

The Taliban, Daesh, Pakistani and
Central Asian Terrorist Organizations

Musa Khan Jalalzai

Vij Books India Pvt Ltd

New Delhi (India)

Published by

Vij Books India Pvt Ltd
(Publishers, Distributors & Importers)
2/19, Ansari Road
Delhi – 110 002
Phone: 91-11-43596460
Mobile: 98110 94883
e-mail: contact@vijpublishing.com
www.vijbooks.in

ISBN: 978-93-93499-45-5 (Hardback)

ISBN: 978-93-93499-46-2 (Paperback)

ISBN: 978-93-93499-47-9 (ebook)

Contents

Introduction

The Taliban misrule, their collaboration with ISIS and Pakistan based terrorist groups in extra judicially killing former Afghan army, intelligence and police officers, and their war against women and girls' education have ultimately pushed Afghanistan to the brink. They are enemies of education, scientific aggrandisement, and technological development. Their protection of the ISIS, Central Asian and Pakistani terrorist groups, and their shaggy-dog story and old chestnut against the Holy Quran and Islamic traditions of Afghanistan have raised several questions, including the misuse of Hadiths and the Holy Quran to justify their takfiri jihadism against the people of Afghanistan. They are selling everything such as minerals, military weapons and national assets to Pakistan. With their arrival in August 2021, they immediately attacked women and young girls and forced them to marry their mountainous goats. The role of Foreign Minister Amir Khan Mottaqi is more audacious, shameless, barefaced and outrageous who advocated a suchlike culture of forced marriage of innocent Afghan women and girls to terrorists and extremists of different nationalities. According to the Counter Extremism Project report: "Amir Khan Motaqi is a U.N.-sanctioned Taliban leader who served as Minister of Education during the Taliban's first regime. Following the Taliban's takeover of Afghanistan in August 2021, Motaqi was named Foreign Minister of the Taliban government on September 7, 2021. Given Motaqi's prominent role within the Taliban, the United Nations Security Council sanctioned Motaqi on January 25, 2001, with the U.K. Office of Financial Sanctions Implementation also enforcing sanctions on Motaqi on April 2, 2001".

On 01 July 2022, Human Rights Council held an urgent debate on the Human Rights of Women and Girls in Afghanistan. In its report, the Human Rights Council warned that since the Taliban took power, women and girls in Afghanistan were experiencing the most significant and rapid roll-back in enjoyment of their rights across the board in decades. Federico Villegas, President of the Council, warned that discrimination against women was one of the oldest violations of human rights, and it affected more than half of humanity. Women have been incarcerated, tortured, raped and transported to different destinations. Girl's schools were closed and women from Hazara communities were kidnapped and forced to marry terrorists. The culture of suicide brigades was promoted, and suicide bomber and war criminals were adorned with medals and rewards. Pakistani terrorists were allowed to establish check posts across Afghanistan, extort money, and purchase weapons in order to wage jihad against India and Central Asia. During the first half of 2021, Taliban were responsible for killing 699 civilians, according to United Nations Assistance Mission in Afghanistan and Afghan Independent Human Rights Commission. The Taliban were responsible for the destruction and looting of private homes and civilian infrastructure during May and June 2021, UNAMA noted. In July 2021, in Malestan District, Taliban forces killed civilians, looted private properties, set them on fire, and destroyed and looted shops. During the Panjshir conflict, the Taliban were accused of extrajudicial executions and blocking food supplies.

On 20 July 2022, the United Nation in its report (Human rights in Afghanistan: 15 August 2021–15 June 2022), noted Taliban atrocities in Afghanistan. The report documented extrajudicial killing, torture, and kidnapping, arbitrary arrests and detention of men, women and young girls by the Taliban regime: "Despite an overall, significant reduction in armed violence, between mid-August 2021 and mid-June 2022, UNAMA recorded 2106 civilian casualties (700 killed, 1406 wounded). The majority of civilian casualties were attributed to targeted attacks by the armed group self-identified "Islamic State in Iraq and the Levant–Khorasan Province" against ethnic and religious minority communities in places where they go to school, worship and go about their daily lives. "It is beyond time for all Afghans to be able to live in peace and rebuild their lives after 20 years of armed conflict. Our monitoring reveals that despite the improved security situation since 15 August, the people of Afghanistan, in particular women and girls, were deprived of the full enjoyment of their human rights," said Markus Potzel, Acting Secretary-General's Special Representative for Afghanistan. Torture and harassment of women and girls and kidnapping have become a routine business of terrorist groups in Afghanistan. The UN report also noted the difficulty of women and young girls and their confinement in homes:

"The decision not to allow girls to return to secondary school means that a generation of girls will not complete their full 12 years of basic education. At the same time, access to justice for victims of gender-based violence has been limited by the dissolution of dedicated reporting pathways, justice mechanisms and shelters. "The education and participation of women and girls in public life is fundamental to any modern society. The relegation of women and girls to the home denies Afghanistan the benefit of the significant contributions they have to offer. Education for all is not only a basic human right, it is the key to the progress and development of a nation," said the UN envoy. On 17 August 2021, the de facto authorities announced an amnesty for former government officials and Afghan National Security and Defence Force members. This amnesty does not, however, appear to have been consistently upheld, with UNAMA recording at least 160 extrajudicial killings of former government and security officials by members of the de facto authorities between 15 August 2021 and 15 June 2022". The UN report also documented killing, torture of former ANA officers, police officers, and harassment of civilian population by the terrorist regime:

"2106 civilian casualties (700 killed, 1406 wounded) predominantly caused by improvised explosive device (IED) attacks attributed to ISIL-KP and unexploded ordnance (UXO). 160 extrajudicial killings, 178 arbitrary arrests and detentions, 23 instances of incommunicado detention and 56 instances of torture and ill-treatment of former ANDSF and government officials carried out by the de facto authorities. Fifty-nine extrajudicial killings, 22 arbitrary arrests and detentions and seven incidents of torture and ill-treatment by the de facto authorities of individuals accused of affiliation with self-identified "Islamic State in Iraq and the Levant–Khorasan Province". Eighteen extrajudicial killings, 54 instances of torture and ill-treatment and 113 instances of arbitrary arrest and detention and 23 cases of incommunicado detention of individuals accused of affiliation with self-identified "National Resistance Front". Two hundred seventeen instances of cruel, inhuman and degrading punishments carried out by the de facto authorities since 15 August 2021 118 instances of excessive use of force by the de facto authorities between 15 August 2021 and 15 June 2022".

With the establishment of Taliban government in Afghanistan in 2021, mentally and physically tortured civilians experienced every mischance and stroke of bad luck. The proxy militia inflicted deep pain and torment on minorities by attacking mosques and religious places, and protecting Pakistani and Central Asian terrorist organizations. Women were tortured, humiliated and incarcerated, girls were deprived from education and their schools were shamelessly closed. After taking control of Ghazni province on 21 August 2021, they used inhuman and illegal strategies and policies that resulted in huge barriers to women's health and girls' education. Afghan women experienced collapsed human rights and risk of basic rights, and were treated like goats and dogs. Human Rights Watch (HRW) and SJSU interviewed women in Ghazni province and documented their spiralling prices for food, transportation, and schoolbooks. The poorer and hungry parents sold their girls and sons for a piece of bread. Taliban kidnapped women, sexually abused and tortured transgender then killed them. Some women felt heightened risk because of gender, ethnicity and religious sect. Human Rights Watch in its recent report (Afghanistan: Taliban Deprive Women of Livelihoods, Identity: Severe Restrictions, Harassment, Fear in Ghazni Province -18 January, 2022), noted intimidation of villagers by Taliban fighters: "Taliban authorities have also used intimidation to extract money, food, and services. 'When the Taliban visit a village, they force the households to feed them and collect food items from people,' a woman from a village said. 'The Taliban and their fighters call us in the middle of the night to cure and give special treatment to their patients and families,' a health worker said. They enter the hospital with their guns, it's difficult for the doctors and nurses to manage." HRW noted.

The concept of suicide attacks, or dying in order to kill in the name of religion become supreme ideal of Taliban and IS-K groups that have been carrying out suicide attacks against the innocent civilians of Afghanistan and Pakistan. After the US invasion of Afghanistan, Taliban resorted to suicide terrorism to force the United States and its NATO allies to withdraw their forces from the country and restore Emirate Islami of Taliban. Taliban and the IS-K became dominant forces in suicide terrorism to internationalise and justify it. Modern suicide terrorism emerged in Afghanistan after 9/11, but it was introduced in different shapes. Over the past two decades, the tactic of suicide terrorism in Afghanistan and Pakistan were modified and justified by religious clerics. According to expert, Assaf Moghadam (Suicide Terrorism, Occupation, and the Globalization of Martyrdom: A Critique of Dying to Win, published in 2006), "the growing interest in suicide terrorism in recent years has generated a steep rise in the number of books that address a topic that is inherently fascinating—a mode of operations that requires the death of its perpetrator to ensure its success".

Analyst and writer, Florian Weigand has noted (Afghanistan's Taliban: Legitimate Jihadists or Coercive Extremists?) that Taliban wants to introduce sharia and prohibit music and suppress women: "The Taliban are usually depicted as ideological fighters – religious extremists who want to introduce harsh rules in Afghanistan, including the prohibition of music and the suppression of women. Their mode of governance stands in stark contrast to Western ideals, with the fall of the Taliban government in 2001 being portrayed as a victory against terrorism and human rights abuses. However, the influence of the Taliban and other armed opposition groups is steadily growing again throughout Afghanistan. They describe themselves as 'jihadists' that fight against the government and its foreign supporters. According to a report for the United States (US) Congress, not even 60 percent of the country's districts were under Afghan government control or influence in 2017 (SIGAR 2017, 87). At the same time the US is welcoming direct peace talks with the Taliban (Tolo News, February 24, 2016). This development raises the question as to what the affected people – rather than the foreign interveners – think about the Taliban".

The Looting and ransacking of Afghanistan's natural resources by NATO and the United States and their criminal militias; suchlike the ISIS and Taliban terrorist groups, caused a misunderstanding between the Afghans and the International Coalition that they all were involved in the looting of mineral resources of their country. The IS-K controls a large amount of territory in Afghanistan, and that includes parts of the country's rich mineral wealth, especially talc, chromite and marble. According to the Global Witness research report, several insurgents' groups, militias, Taliban and ISIS are deeply involved in the plunder of these resources: "The Islamic State in Afghanistan (ISKP) controls major mining sites in eastern Afghanistan and has a strategic interest in the country's rich mineral resources, new Global Witness research shows–a powerful example of the wider threat posed by armed groups and corrupt actors in Afghan mining. The Islamic State in Afghanistan (ISKP) controls large talc, marble and chromite mines in the Islamic State stronghold of Achin district in the Nangarhar province of eastern Afghanistan–the same area where in April 2017, the US military dropped the 'Mother of All Bombs' against ISKP-held caves. Nangarhar was the deadliest Afghan province for US troops in 2017. An estimated 380,000 tons of talc was imported into the United States in 2017. On average, around 35 percent of US imports are from Pakistan, according to the US Geological Survey. From our research we also estimated that around 80 percent of Pakistan's 2016 exports of talc actually originated in Afghanistan. Of those exports, 42 percent went to the US, and another 36 percent went to EU countries, especially the Netherlands and Italy".

The perception that Taliban are ideological fighter is totally wrong, the reason for that they are terrorists and act like terrorists, carrying out suicide attacks against civilians and destroy everything they don't like. They have committed war crimes, beheaded innocent Muslims, kidnapped women and children and used them for sexual exploitation. They are proxies of Pakistan's military establishment, barking for the American Army and ISI equally. They have established suicide brigades and threatened Afghanistan's neighbours. The Taliban's relationship with al Qaeda and the IS-K further generated fear and consternation. As Afghanistan remained a top destination for foreign terrorist groups, Taliban entered into alliances with different groups.

The fall of Afghanistan to the Taliban generated a news terror threat in South and Central Asia. The Taliban's close relationship with several Pakistani terror groups and its inability to govern the whole country may turn Afghanistan into a nest of terror militias. In Afghanistan, close cooperation between Daesh and some disgruntled Taliban groups added to the pain of the Taliban Government. The Khorasan terrorist group, which emerged with a strong military power in 2015, is in control of important districts in Jalalabad province. The group's military tactics include beheading, public prosecution, kidnapping, and torture, looting and raping, and also forcing families from their homes. Due to the weakness of Taliban and local administration, the IS-K expanded its networks to all districts of Jalalabad. In Kunar, Nuristan and Jalalabad provinces, more than 13 terrorist groups were operating with their strong networks. Some of the groups including Quetta Shura, Tora Bora Jihadi group, Gul Buddin Hekmatyar group, Salafi group, Fidayee Karwan, Sia Pushan groups (identified as black-clad and masked terrorists) were in clandestine collaboration with the Khorasan group, TTP, and Lashkar-e-Islam group. In Mohmand Agency, Jamaat Al Ahrar and TTP were operating in collaboration with ISKP.

Afghanistan is still run by proxy militias of different internal and external stakeholders. In October 2015, Kunduz was destroyed by these militias which looted banks, markets and houses. After the Soviet invasion of Afghanistan, and the emergence of Mujahideen's militias in Pakistan and Iran, regional powers, US, NATO and the Arab world's military experts arrived in Pakistan to train, support, and arm every terrorist and extremist group to defeat the Soviet army in Afghanistan. All these private militias era are still dancing to different tangos in all provinces of Afghanistan. They receive financial support from the different channels-challenging the territorial authority of the national army of the country.

Pakistan based extremist and terrorist group are now sponsored by the United States to use their suicide units against Central Asia and Russian Federation. These groups have been professionally trained and adorned with sophisticated biological weapons. A new addition to the list of terrorism organizations is Tablighi Jamaat which has established a strong intelligence network in Pakistan, India and Bangladesh. Tablighi intelligence and its units recently exhibited their power and professional capabilities by organising sarcastic elements against Kazakhstan in January 2022. Those recruited in Africa, South Asia and Central Asia are invited to participate in its congregation in Riwand Lahore, in order to receive new guidance from the Pakistani establishment. Majority members of intelligence agencies of the country belong to different sectarian groups. This illegal affiliation also directed intelligence operations on sectarian bases against Pakistani citizens. Poor data collection with regard to the activities of militant sectarian organisations and their networks across the country is a challenging problem. Many criminals who joined terrorist groups are not tracked and profiled effectively.

The nexus of jihadists, wealthy individuals, religious organizations, serving and retired bureaucrats, as well as opportunistic politicians, have lent their support to the invisible forces of disorder so that the deep state is able to preserve and continue a lucrative business enterprise. To punish Afghanistan's National Army, Pakistan's intelligence agencies provided sophisticated weapons to the terrorist Taliban and other extremist organisations to make the war in Afghanistan disastrous and unfavourable to Kabul since 2001. Pakistan's military establishment continues to train, arm, and transport terrorist groups inside Afghanistan and India to target civilian and military installations, and make the lives of civilians, including women and children, the hell. The ISI has often been accused by the former Afghan Army and Government of playing a role in major terrorist attacks. Pakistan has long been a vigorously troublesome state for Afghanistan, and India and is struggling to limit India's political influence there.

Moreover, Afghans understand that Pakistan Army pursued its own agenda in Afghanistan by providing funds and sanctuaries to Taliban and the ISIS terrorist group. Its support to the Haqqani terrorist Network, and the IS/Daesh prolonged the catastrophic Afghan war. These and other concerns have caused greater diplomatic and foreign policy challenges for Islamabad. Today, the country's leadership feels isolated, and no one is willing to dance to its beat. These and other afflictions and suffering have forced civilian leadership to attempt reconceptualization of foreign policy. Furthermore, the military-madrasa-mullah nexus has deliberately manipulated and encouraged jihadism by favouring a tactical deployment of jihadi groups in Kashmir and Afghanistan to expand Pakistan's regional influence. The internal conditions within Pakistan have also deteriorated over the past decades because of the focus on building up militancy and grooming Islamist extremist groups as weapons, in Rawalpindi's eternal and obsessive struggle against India. The military-militant cabal is the core problem of Pakistan today.

The miltablishment and the ISI view the Afghan Taliban as the 'Good Taliban', and support the latter's fight in Afghanistan as a welcome development. Regarding the issue of the Good and Bad Taliban, the Pakistan Army views all such Afghan groups, including the Quetta Shura in Balochistan, and the Haqqani Network, in Waziristan, as 'strategic assets'. The Afghan Taliban is supported by the ISI to maintain influence over Afghanistan, particularly in a scenario after the American drawdown of forces from the area, as many in Pakistan's military establishment continue to think of the Afghan landmass as Pakistan's backyard and an area which will offer them 'strategic depth' in the event of hostilities with India. Pakistan has also encouraged and promoted terrorist organisations such as the LeT, JeM, and HuM which it views as strategic assets to be used against India. These terrorist groups have been waging a proxy war against India over the past three decades in Kashmir at very little cost to Pakistan – a policy of bleeding India with a thousand cuts, but keeping the conflict below perceived levels of India's threshold of response. Terrorist organisations including al Qaeda, LeT, Taliban, a range of Arab extremists and Takfiri jihadists in Pakistan and Afghanistan pose a threat to regional and world security. They train suicide bombers across Asia and the Middle East.

The shameless role of the British army, specifically, the role of Gen Sir Nick Carter who issued a statement to BBC on 05 September 2021 that "Everybody got it wrong" on how quickly the Taliban would take over Afghanistan, the head of Britain's armed forces has said". In fact he joked with the Afghan nation by taking the Afghan President in a helicopter to Rawalpindi to sign the deal of handing over Afghanistan to the Pakistan army and its proxies. The war crimes of the British army committed in Afghanistan was also reported by BBC and other media outlets. The BBC probe suggested Afghanistan war crimes by UK special forces. The UK Special Forces killed 54 Afghans in suspicious circumstances during the 2010-11 in Helmand. The Al Jazeera report exposed British commandos or Special Air Service (SAS) corps killing unarmed Afghan men routinely "in cold blood" during night-time raids, and weapons were planted on them to justify the crimes, the four-year inquiry found. Al Jazeera reported. Senior officers, including General Mark Carleton-Smith, who headed the UK Special Forces at the time, were aware of concerns within the SAS about the operations but failed to report them to military police, the BBC reported. Responding to the BBC investigation of repeated killing of unarmed men in suspicious circumstances in Afghanistan between 2010 and 2011 by the UK Special forces, Zaman Sultani, Amnesty International's South Asia Researcher, said: "Amnesty International demands an effective and transparent investigation into the allegations made against the UK Special forces in Afghanistan, that delivers justice for victims and holds the perpetrators accountable." This book highlights different terrorist militias in Afghanistan, Central Asia and Pakistan, and documents the atrocities of Taliban and Pakistan army against the people of Afghanistan.

The US and NATO new Jihad in Central Asia against Russia and China has raised many questions including the deployment of sarcastic extremist forces near the border of Tajikistan. The United States has trained dozens of terrorist groups, including Taliban and the Islamic State of Khorasan in Afghanistan, and tested their operational capabilities and suicidal tactics consecutively in the country that killed thousands of innocent women and children during the past 20 years long so-called war on terrorism. Ministers, MPs, bureaucrats and commanders of Afghan army within the Governments of Hamid Karzai and Ashraf Ghani helped the US and NATO forces to facilitate Taliban, and IS-Khorasan terrorist group, and transport their suicide bombers to their destinations. They secured their live by lurking in their houses in cities and towns, and shared with their networks military information of Afghan army, and its geographical stretch-out. In his analysis of working partnership of Russia and China on security threat in Central Asia, Asim Kashgarian (China, Russia Working Together on Security Threats in Central Asia-VoA, October 27, 2021) has highlighted security threats in Central Asian states:

"Moscow has been the dominant security partner for the countries within the Russia-led Collective Security Treaty Organisation framework and has been the largest supplier of arms. Russia remains the main security backer of Central Asia, accounting for 62 percent of the regional arms market, while its economic dominance dropped from 80 percent of the region's total trade in the 1990s ($110 billion) to just two-thirds that of Beijing ($18.6 billion). "Lately there has been a trend of China becoming a security player, too,"Avdaliani told VOA. "First, there are reports of a Chinese military base in Tajikistan and perhaps some security presence in the north of Afghanistan. China is also increasingly engaged in military drills with Central Asia states." Beijing's arms transfers through donations and sales

9

to the regional countries, such as Kazakhstan, Kyrgyzstan, Turkmenistan, Uzbekistan and Tajikistan, were modest until 2014. Since that year, China has ramped up arms transfers to the region, according to a Wilson Centre report this year. China built its Tajik military outpost in 2016, with facilities in the country's mountainous Gorno-Badakhshan province near the Afghan border. In addition to Russia, China has cooperated with Pakistan and Iran, countries that border Central Asia, and have economic, security or political interests in that region. "Beijing is clearly the dominant power in Central Asia, with India likely to lose some of the influence it used to enjoy over Kabul as a result of the substantial aid it provided before the U.S. withdrawal," said Alexander Cooley, director of the Harriman Institute at Columbia University".

Government of Tajikistan never communicated with the Taliban government due to their threatening attitude towards neighbouring states. Tajikistan views the seizure of Kabul by the Taliban as illegitimate and demanded an inclusive government in Afghanistan because it understands that Afghanistan is home to all nationalities. Journalist and writer, Bruce Pinnier, (Taliban Threats to Uzbekistan, Tajikistan Underline Tension between Militant Group and Central Asian Neighbors, Radio Free Europe, 13 Jan 2022) has noted consternation and concern of Tajikistan: "At a Collective Security Treaty Organization (CSTO) summit on January 10, Tajik President Emomali Rahmon said: "According to the Tajik intelligence services, the number of camps and training centers for terrorists bordering the southern borders of the CSTO in the north-eastern provinces of Afghanistan totals more than 40, and their numerical strength is more than 6,000 militants." Rahmon also told the leaders of Russia, Belarus, Armenia, Kazakhstan, and the head of Kyrgyzstan's cabinet of ministers taking part in the summit that "You and I know very well that since the second half of August 2021, thousands of members of [Islamic State], Al-Qaeda, [Jamaat] Ansarullah, Hizb ut-Tahrir, and other terrorist groups have been released from prisons in Afghanistan." Ansarullah is composed mainly of Tajik citizens who have been fighting alongside the Taliban for years. The Taliban reportedly deployed some of the Ansarullah fighters to guard the border with Tajikistan, prompting Dushanbe to further strengthen its forces along the Afghan border".

Central Asia has now become the hub of terrorism, extremism and smugglers who want to destabilize the region. In Tajikistan, deteriorating law and order causes torment. On 11 January, 2022, Ariana News reported deployment of Islamic Emirate of Afghanistan suicide squads along with

Tajikistan border. Tajik President Emomali Rahmon warned during a virtual Collective Security Treaty Organization (CSTO) summit that over 6,000 militants had grouped at over 40 camps near the country's Southern border. "In general, according to the intelligence services of Tajikistan, the number of camps and training centres for terrorists bordering the southern borders of the CSTO in the north-eastern provinces of Afghanistan totals over 40, and their numerical strength reaches more than 6,000 militants," warned President Rahmon during an emergency summit of the organization on the situation in Kazakhstan. The AN reported. However, Russia's TASS news agency reported President Rahmon's warning that the situation on the Tajik-Afghan border was becoming more complicated by the day. President of Tajikistan stressed that the increased activity of international terrorist groups in Afghanistan directly affects the CSTO collective security zone. "You and I know very well that since the second half of August 2021, thousands of members of ISIS (Daesh), al-Qaeda, Ansarullah, Hizb ut-Tahrir were released from prisons in Afghanistan." Moreover, writers and analysts, Paolo Sorbello and Franco Galdini, (What's All the Fuss about Terrorism in Central Asia? Reports from Central Asia about a future doomed to violent Islamic extremism in the region are thin on evidence. Diplomat, 16 August, 2017) have noted the rise of extremism in Kazakhstan:

"In August, two Foreign Policy (FP) articles charged that violent Islamic extremism is on the rise in Kazakhstan and Kyrgyzstan. The first dispatch focused on the Aktobe attack, when more than two dozen men robbed a gun shop and engaged in a series of shootouts with the Kazakh police and National Guard, leaving 25 dead, including 18 attackers, and spreading panic across the country. No sooner had the shock from the attack subsided than, a month later, a lone gunman killed nine in Almaty, Kazakhstan's largest city. A second report from the city of Osh, in southern Kyrgyzstan, argued that a combination of "ethnic strife, corruption, and poverty [could] derail the government's efforts to come to grips with a rise in extremist activity since the start of the Syrian civil war." According to FP, whereas the threat in Kazakhstan is home-grown, in Kyrgyzstan, it mostly emanates from the links between the local population and the raging conflicts in Iraq and Syria, where people, mostly from the country's Uzbek minority, have travelled to fight. Still, it is striking that while the dispatches correctly refer to the local socio-political dynamics of poverty, marginalisation and state violence, violent Islamic extremism is treated as the main focus, starting from the sensationalism of the quote used as a title for the Kazakhstan-focused piece: "Our future will be violent extremism." In other words, the authorities' claims that violent extremism is a major problem and is indeed growing are taken at face value, as is the link between violence and an ill-defined non-traditional (radical, Salafi) Islam. Instead, a series of unrelated attacks became enough evidence to confirm the credibility of the threat in Kazakhstan, despite the many doubts surrounding the official version of events. Why, for instance, didn't the Kazakh gunmen attack soft civilian targets? How can one reconcile the radical Islam allegation with reports that the Almaty shooter spent the night before the attack with a prostitute? Why was information contradicting the radicalization narrative – for example, that Kazakhstan's Interior Ministry called the Almaty gunman a "petty criminal" and the country's Prison Service denied he was "radicalized" while in detention – withheld?"

Musa Khan Jalalzai

London

Chapter 1

Resisting Radical Rebels: Variations in Islamist Rebel Governance and the Occurrence of Civil Resistance

Matthew Bamber and Isak Svensson

Abstract

During the Syrian civil war, different types of Salafi-Jihadi rebel groups controlled territory and established governance over civilians. Their governing strategies have been markedly diverse. In this study, we explore how this governance variation can help to explain the occurrence of civil resistance. We suggest that different types of rebel governance structures provide political opportunities for civilians to mobilize against those rebel groups through public demonstrations. In particular, we argue that it is middle-ranged opportunity structures of rebel governance that strongest incentivizes civil resistance by giving enough space for civilian mobilization but fewer alternative channels of expressing discontent. This argument is explored through an analysis of the variation between the three main Salafi-Jihadi rebel groups in Syria—IS, HTS and Ahrar al-Sham. We show how differences in the groups' four rebel governance dimensions—rebel collaboration, civilian inclusion, alliance structure, and repression—impact the political opportunities for civilians to mobilize against these groups. We find that HTS, the group that is in the middle range across these four governance dimensions, provided greater opportunities for civilian protests. This study uses a new dataset of civilian resistance events in Syria as well as interviews with civilians governed by these groups.

Keywords: Rebel governance civil resistance Syria Jihadism Islamic state HTS.

Introduction

Research on terrorist groups and non-state actors using political violence has increasingly recognized that many groups also tend to engage in rebel governance beyond engaging in warfare.[1] This is particularly the case for groups, termed terrorist state-building groups by Revkin (2018),[2] and who fight over radical Islamist goals and have increasingly engaged in various attempts of rebel governance in which they have established different manifestations of "jihadist statelets."[3] While there is a growing debate on the strategies of rebel governance employed by non-state armed groups in general,[4] and jihadist groups in particular,[5] we still know relatively little on the effect it has on the civilians' capabilities and incentives to challenge jihadist groups in power.

During the Syrian civil war, very different types of Salafi-Jihadi rebel groups have been in control of various parts of the territory and there sought to establish governance structures. The civilian population under their control have responded differently to the jihadist governance attempts. In particular, civil resistance—through active, manifest but nonviolent acts of discontent and disobedience—against jihadists was more common against some groups than others. In this study, we set out to explore this variation in the occurrence of civil resistance against Salafi-Jihadi groups. For example, when *Hay'at Tahrir al-Sham (HTS)* entered the town of Saraqib in July 2017 they were met with approximately 75 civilians staging demonstrations in an attempt to block their advance,[6] whilst in contrast, when the *Islamic State (IS)* advanced across northern Syria seizing 6 towns near to Aleppo, they were met with no such resistance.[7]

Our entry point for this discussion is that civilians and rebel groups are in a strategic, interdependent relationship with each other. Rebel groups seek to establish territorial control and receive the consent of the people under its domination, by the use of force or through other means. Civilians, on the other hand, can withdraw their consent and chose to resist rebel groups. While there are many different response strategies that civilians can employ, including obedience, taking up arms, and taking refuge, we are here interested in a particular type of civil action: taking up nonviolent but active opposition, that is, civil resistance. In the study of political violence, there is a growing scholarly attention being paid to studying the conditions for civil resistance.[8]

The rebel governance literature, on the one hand, and the civil resistance literature, on the other, has been largely studied in isolation from each other. While an emerging literature has tried to bridge these two fields in order to understand the strategic and interactive relationship between civilians and rebel-groups,[9] we still lack knowledge as to how the governing strategies of jihadist groups impact on the prospects for civil resistance. Comparative analysis of different types of jihadist groups has been lacking (a recent exception is Svensson and Finnbogason 2021[10] which is discussed more below), in particular in terms of the different conditions that they create for civil–rebel relationships and how this shapes the possibilities for civil resistance. In this study, we develop a political opportunity argument: different types of Islamist governance structures provide different political opportunity structures that enables civilians to mobilize against those rebel groups through public protests and demonstrations. In particular, we argue that it is middle-ranged opportunity structures of rebel governance that strongest incentivizes civil resistance, by giving enough space for civilian mobilization but fewer alternative channels of expressing discontent.

Our interest here lies in trying to understand how different forms of 'proto-states' governance establishments by Salafi-Jihadist groups in the context of the Syrian civil war impacted the response by civilians. Through a systematic comparison of the governance strategy of three main Salafi-Jihadi groups operating in the Syrian civil war, Islamic State (IS), HTS and *Ahrar al-Sham*, we demonstrate how differences in four central governance dimensions—groups' rebel collaboration, civilian inclusion, alliance structure, and repression—impacted the political opportunities for civilians to mobilize against these groups. We find that HTS, the rebel group that is in the middle range across these four governance dimensions, provided greater opportunity for civilian protests, in comparison to both IS and Ahrar al-Sham that were on opposite ends in terms of their governance structures.

Syria provides an analytically used context to study subnational variations in Islamist governance and its impact on rebel-civilian relationships. Since the inception of the 2011 civil war, Syria has been a breeding ground for different types of military-based non-state governance structures. Beyond the governance structures established by the Kurdish Syrian Democratic Forces, the Free Syrian Army, and Syrian local councils, Syria has also seen a plethora of Islamist factions and rebel groups. In this paper, we focus on comparing IS, HTS and Ahrar al-Sham that either emerged or developed in the Syrian Salafi-Jihadi milieu. Although these three groups are broadly defined as Salafi-Jihadi, the ideological differences, as well as practical considerations between the groups have resulted in different types of governance structures.

This study makes a number of contributions. Firstly, we make a novel contribution and link between the rebel governance and civil resistance literature by finding that the middle-ranged inclusionary governance structures of rebel groups have the strongest impact in terms of affecting the frequency of protests against them. Empirically, we contribute by presenting new sub-national data from the Syrian civil war, drawing from a recently collected dataset as well as in-depth interviews in Syria, Lebanon and Turkey. In this study, we also show that the political opportunity framework has broader applications and can provide insights into both the rebel governance and civil resistance fields. Our study is also part of a larger line of research seeking to understand how civil agency manifests itself in the context of violent settings and wars.[11] In Syria, civilians living under different types of rebel institutions have been suffering as victims, but as we demonstrate here, they have not only been victims. Civilians have also actively resisted the Islamist rebel rulers and their governance systems and have strategically tailored their responses to the contexts under which they have lived.

Theoretical Framework

This study is situated in the ongoing debate in the rebel governance literature regarding the different political governance institutions that rebel groups form when taking over territory.[12] An aspect of the rebel governance literature that remains understudied is the impact of a rebel group's religious ideology on its governance strategy, particularly in relation to Salafi-Jihadi rebel groups.[13] Although the specific tenets of Salafi-Jihadism do not have a commonly accepted definition[14] all three Salafi-Jihadi groups in this study believed that *jihad* (religiously sanctioned warfare) is an individual obligation for all Muslims and reject existing political systems and the international order.[15]

Amongst the most prominent attempts to define governance by Salafi-Jihadi groups is Lia (2015), who describes proto-states created by Salafi-Jihadi groups as having four characteristics, those being "intensely ideological, internationalist, territorially expansive, and irredentist."[16] However, this one fits all approach to Salafi-Jihadi groups has been criticized by authors including Schwab (2018),[17] and Stenerson (2018)[18] who state that this does not reflect the broad range of governance established by Salafi-Jihadi groups. Instead, Stenerson (2018)[19] devised two scales to show the range in Salafi-Jihadi groups governance: '*takfirism*,' the relationship to society in which the group operate, and 'pan-Islamism,' defining what the group fight for either the local nation or the international Muslim community (*Ummah*). Schwab (2020)[20] uses Stenerson's scale to argue that HTS would be considered integrationist and fighting for the Syrian nation, in comparison to IS's separation stance that fights for the *Ummah*.

In this study, we are interested in comparing those rebel groups with Salafi-Jihadist ideologies as they are manifested in their governance structures. Jihadism is a transnational social movement that was ideologically developed in Middle East but gains its traction through the anti-Soviet campaign in Afghanistan, although to describe the trajectory of the jihadist movement is beyond the scope of this study.[21] Political Islam is a broad term for a set of ideological movements, sharing the idea that Islam and Islamic law should have primacy as the basis for state governance. Political Islam is therefore an ideology of governance, although different groups and movements have very different perspectives on how such governance should be designed, constructed and implemented. Salafi-Jihadist groups can thus be seen as a sub-set of the broader ideological movement of Islamism, but that it is distinct and cannot be equated with the same.[22]

Recent comparative studies of the governance established by Salafi-Jihadi groups in Syria suggest that this variation in governance is the norm and that the governance strategy of Salafi-Jihadi groups can differ along several criteria. Furlan (2020)[23] developed a typology of rebel governance that she applied to several Salafi-Jihadi groups which included variation in their treatment of civilians, other rebel groups and governance goals. Moreover, the governing strategy of Salafi-Jihadi groups do not necessarily remain static; both Berti (2020)[24] and Drevon and Haenni (2020)[25] use detailed case studies of HTS in Syria to show that competition between Salafi-Jihadi groups, resources scarcity and the need to survive altered the governing strategy of HTS in Syria.

An element that is missing in this discussion is the explicit role of Salafi-Jihadi governance strategy on the impact of civil resistance. Although the topic of civilian inclusion in the case of IS has been studied extensively[26] and the broader rebel governance literature has focused extensively on the varied role that civilians play when interacting with rebel groups[27] few works have focused on the role of governing strategy's impact on civilian resistance. While Masullo (2020)[28] shows how ideational factors shape the civilian responses to armed groups, we focus on the opportunity structures of rebel governance strategies and argue that different types of rebel governance structures provide different possibilities for civilians to mobilize through protests.

The literature on civil resistance is built on the premise that civilians have it in their hands to withdraw support from leaders and regimes, a support which is ultimately necessary for maintaining power over time.[29] Whereas most of the research in the civil resistance literature has revolved around how civilians challenge leaders of states[30] including studies on why resistance groups take up violent strategies,[31] or how violent flank effect impact the trajectories of civil resistance campaigns.[32] There is also a growing literature on civil resistance strategies against rebel groups.[33] This literature has also demonstrated that rebel groups, which have taken control of a territory and its population need civilian support, and that civilians can use many different ways of countering or managing the rebel-groups' attempts to assert control over them. So far, this line of literature has not examined the context of jihadist groups, although this is now starting to change.

Building on insights from the social movement literature, the civil resistance literature has focused on the role of grievances, resource mobilization and political opportunity in creating conditions for civil resistance.[34] While these explanations may carry different weights, they speak to the fact that people who are unsatisfied with the status quo, need to have a sense of urgency to motivate them to act (*grievances*). At the same time, the opposition needs to have possibilities in terms of strength and resources to mobilize resistance (*resource mobilization*), as well as acting under some structural possibilities in terms of (temporal) openings or weaknesses on the challenged regime's side (*political opportunity*). Thus, while we see these as three compatible, rather than rival, explanations to the occurrence and outcome of civil resistance, we develop here the political opportunity argument.

Political opportunity theory suggests that would-be challengers of a regime in power carefully consider the political and social context in which they live and estimate their chances of success before launching mobilization efforts.[35] Tarrow (1998)[36] defines political opportunities as "dimensions of the political environment that provide incentives for collective action by affecting people's expectations for success or failure." Thus, the main drivers behind the occurrence of civil resistance are factors outside the control of a movement or civil society actor. What these dimensions are precisely, is somewhat debated,[37] but they relate to internal characteristics of the regime, in particular the degree of unity or divisions amongst the challenges elites, the political access for the opposition, the alliance structures of the regime, and the regime's capability and motivation for repression.

Political opportunity theory is commonly framed in terms of changes over time and explanatory factors are seen as dynamic: it is openings over time, through temporally limited weaknesses of the challenged regime that can provide windows of opportunity that movements or activists can capitalize on. While changes over time are definitely important, so are the differences between different opportunity structures. Here, we focus on the comparison between cases. We expect that middle-ranged rebel governance structures will combine insufficient repressiveness with a lack of enough foreign support through external alliance structures to be able to deter civil resistance. At the same time, such structures will have insufficiently developed civil-rebel institutional relationships and channels to create alternatives to mass mobilization and civil resistance. Here, we will build on insights from the study of the effect of political structures on civil war and political violence, and see this as a local-level representation of a larger, already established finding of political structures in the cross-country analysis of political systems: the inverted-U shaped relationship between risk of violent manifestation of social conflict and degree of democracy, where the middle-ranged semi-democratic countries have been at the greatest risk of political violence.[38]

Bridging these two literatures, we focus on the opportunity structures of rebel governance strategies and argue that different types of rebel governance structures provide different possibilities for civilians to mobilize through protests. We adapt the four dimensions in Schock's framework (1999)[39]—elite unity/divisions, political access, alliance structures and repression—to the context we study here: rebel-civilian relationships. In terms of elite unity and divisions, when there are domestic rebel coalitions and collaboration, then we would expect the space for civil resistance to be generally higher—the plurality of the rebel rulers would allow for more room of dissenting voices to be heard. In terms of political access, when there is civilian inclusion we would expect higher tolerance for protests and demonstrations. The alliance structure of the rebel groups is an important dimension of their governance strategies—in terms of reliance on external alliances—and can affect the opportunity structures for civil resistance—if the rebels appeal to a broader, international constituency it should be more attuned to the grievances of the local communities under its reach.

Whilst the higher the degree of repression in a governing strategy—and with repression we do not mean violence against their external enemies (such as the state, its military forces and even against civilians living under the control of a challenged state), but rather the attempts to assert control through violent and coercive means over the civilian population under its control—civilians would have less opportunity to resist through protests. While we see these as four different and distinct dimensions of rebel governance, they are not necessarily independent of each other, because rebel coalitions, civilian inclusion, alliance structures and repression are dimensions that may interact and shape each other. This is something we return to in the discussion at the end of the article.

Variation in resistance across different groups

This study draws on data on local-level demonstrations and protests against Salafi-Jihadist armed rebel actors in the context of the Syrian civil war. The data is gathered by screening English and Arab-speaking social media platforms and coding open civil resistance against jihadist groups. The procedure for the collection of the data and a comprehensive analysis of the data is done elsewhere in Svensson et al (2022).[40] Whereas the full dataset includes all jihadist armed groups, we here limit focus to only the three main Salafi-Jihadist groups.

Civil resistance in the form of demonstrations and protests was not distributed equally across the territories of the three jihadist armed groups studied here. As we can see, there were marked differences in terms of the occurrence of protests. Thus, in terms of occurrence of resistance, there is a falling scale across the three groups, with HTS standing out and experiencing significantly more civilian protests than both Ahrar al-Sham and IS. Protests did occur against IS, but were relatively rare, with only 31 protest events being recorded within the time period. One such example occurred in 2014, where a group of students, their relatives, and their teachers demonstrated in an IS held-neighborhood in Deir az Zur demanding that their schools be re-opened so that they could continue their studies.[41] In comparison, Ahrar al-Sham experienced twice as many protests, with 61 recorded in total. One notable example occurred in 2017, when approximately 250 demonstrators protested in Kafr Nobol, Idlib governorate, demanding that Ahrar al-Sham leaves the town.[42] In contrast, HTS experienced far more protests than either IS or Ahrar al-Sham, with a total of 357 recorded. Among these, the protest movements in Maarat al-Numan against HTS, is the most well-known and comprehensive campaign of all the protests against jihadist groups.[43] Beginning as a reaction to HTS's treatment of the locally rooted rebel group, the 13th Division, the protests continued over an extensive time period and constituted a total of 78 events.

The type of civilian demands that were raised against all three groups varied. In some cases, civilians demanded the unification of rebel groups or the ceasing of hostilities. For example, in 2017, following intense hostilities between HTS and Ahrar al-Sham, the city of Saraqab's people demonstrated, calling for a ceasefire between the two groups to avoid civilian casualties.[44] A large number of the protests were aimed at challenging the governance of the jihadist rebel groups. For example, in 2018, protesters in Saraqab occupied the city's main power plant and effectively managed to prevent HTS from dismantling it.[45] In July 2018, in As-Suwayda, dozens of civilians rallied outside the IS governorate building for a sit-in to demand the release of several women and children, following the execution of one of them the day before.[46] At other times, the protesters adopted maximalist demands, protesting against the group's presence itself, rather than its specific actions or policies. In 2014, in the town of Quriyeh, in Deir az Zur province, a local Islamist militia posted a video denying reports that its members had pledged loyalty to IS whilst local residents staged a demonstration demanding that IS be expelled from the province.[47] In Jarablus in 2018, following the killing of civilian, local residents demonstrated against the presence of Ahrar al-Sham, demanding their exit whilst chanting slogans, including "Jarablus is free, free, the factions go out."[48] In this study, however, we do not focus on the variation in protest demands, and in line with other studies on civil resistance, we study the occurrence of civil resistance as the dependent variable.[49] All public protests and demonstration are thus counted and treated the same irrespective of their demands.

The frequency of protests is one indicator of civil resistance, but this measurement does not take into consideration that the number of people protesting may vary at different occasions. Thus, it may be valuable to also examine the size of protests. Previous research has pointed to the role of mass-participation as a particularly important dynamic in nonviolent campaigns.[50] In order to gauge the extent of variation in not only the frequency of protests but their magnitude, we distinguish the protests in terms of size (number of people participating), where size is known. Their action shows that it there is a marked difference between HTS and the other two groups, consistent with the observation made above. HTS is particularly overrepresented when it comes to major- and medium-sized protests, compared to Ahrar al-Sham and IS.

It is important to note the difference in the size of territorial control over time between the three groups. The figures on protests should be interpreted in light of how much territory (and over how many people) the groups controlled. IS at its peak in January 2015 controlled over 90,000 km² of territory across Iraq and Syria,[51] and although the same level of territorial analysis has not been conducted on HTS and Ahrar al-Sham, we can reliably say both of their governance projects were far smaller as they were only concentrated in north-western Syria.

In addition, when comparing protest data, we assume that Syrian civilians residing in the territory of all three groups have a similar *proclivity to protest*. This assumption is based on the fact that the territory controlled by the three groups spans a relatively small width of just 400 km between Idlib and Deir az-Zur. This territory is ethnically relatively homogenous, dominated by Sunni Arabs (with small enclaves of Kurdish and Alawi minorities), with similar levels of urbanity and education levels amongst residents.[52] Further, this territory has been contested by multiple armed groups and the Syrian regime and each area has witnessed a high number of protests during the civil war.[53]

We further acknowledge that the repressive nature of IS may not only hinder civil resistance but also information of any such behaviour to be circulated more widely. The IS established stringent communication laws in Syria, amongst which the group banned mobile phones, Wi-Fi, and travel at varying times between 2013 and 2016. Punishable by death in many cases, it is likely that some civilians would have been reluctant to defy regulations, and consequently, civil resistance may have been under-reported in IS held territories. In contrast, those living under HTS were not subject to such strict regulations. We recognize this potential bias, which would under-report some of the resistance against IS compared to other groups. Still, relying on social media platforms is likely to be a more inclusive way of generating information than by, for example, just relying on international media. It is important to underline that case studies and interview-based studies on the situation under IS suggest that public protests and demonstrations were very rare. It should also be noted that while we study public protest here, we do not mean to say that this is the exhaustive range of civil resistance strategies. Civilians may respond, particularly in high-risk situations, with the withdrawal of support, rather than through demonstrations. Civilians can also engage in low-level resistance in and through their ordinary lives (everyday resistance) by not fully abiding with the social rules and legal laws created by the jihadist groups. Dissent also manifests itself in other ways. For example, the use of satire and humour has been an important practice.

Explaining the impact of different governing strategies

Across the course of the Syrian civil war, dozens of Salafi-Jihadist groups were created, fragmented, disappeared and were subsumed.[54] Three of the most prominent and territorial successful groups to emerge from the Syrian Salafi-Jihadi milieu were IS, HTS and Ahrar al-Sham. All three groups subscribe to a Salafi-Jihadi ideology and each held a common goal to gain and govern territory in their respective territorial domains. In spite of these similarities, each group held differing governing strategies that qualitatively varied along several criteria: rebel group collaboration, civilian inclusion, repression and political goals. This section draws on fieldwork interviews conducted with civilians that lived in HTS—controlled territories and with two groups of IS affiliated persons: civilian IS employees working in IS's federal and provincial governing institutions; and ordinary civilians who lived in IS-held territory in Iraq and Syria without any employment relationship to IS. The interviews took place during multiple trips to Iraq, Lebanon and Turkey over five months between 2018 and 2019. The interviews were conducted in Arabic or English and interviewees were located via a snowball sampling. The civilians who had lived in HTS and IS-controlled territory were initially located through NGOs and CSOs that currently run interventions and programs in post-IS and HTS areas or with refugees and IDPs from IS and HTS-controlled territory. Further details on the ethical and methodological challenges of this fieldwork have been discussed in Bamber (2020).[55]

Islamic State

IS has a two-decade long history of governance success and decline in Iraq and Syria; IS has engaged in three governance cycles in 2004, 2008 and 2014 which have each ended in territorial failure. Although with each cycle, IS has managed to govern greater amounts of territory more effectively, for a longer period of time. IS's governance goals, however, have changed over time; IS transformed from the local AQ province in Iraq, fixated on attacking the 'near enemy' and creating an Islamic state in Iraq, to establishing a transnational Islamic caliphate under Caliph Abu Bakr al-Baghdadi, headquartered in a new state stretching across Iraq and Syria. IS's most infamous governance episode occurred between 2014 and 2019 when IS at its 2015 peak possessed control of 90,000 square km of territory, generated $80- $100 million per month of revenue and possessed a standing army of approximately 60,000–90,000 fighters.[56] This ended in failure, however, with IS territorially defeated and it has resorted to insurgency tactics in its traditional strongholds of northern Iraq and eastern Syria.[57]

Rebel collaboration

Although IS initially collaborated with other Salafi-Jihadist groups during the early years of its formation in Iraq, IS is distinguished by its lack of governance collaboration with other rebel groups.[58] In areas under its control, IS refused to govern with other rebel groups, with IS in Syria concentrating on targeting rival rebel groups than the Syrian regime. This is typified in IS's governance approach in Raqqa province; in February 2013, Raqqa was under the control of various rebel groups and IS had control of a small part in the center. IS targeted the leaders of other groups in an assassination campaign, and once other groups banded together to attack a Syrian army base, IS exploited the weakness of their defenses in Raqqa and took over their territory.[59] IS deliberately targeted other rebel groups throughout its history and actively worked on destabilizing rival Salafi-Jihadi governance projects by both clandestinely recruiting members and openly declaring HTS to be illegitimate and part of IS. As a soldier of IS, who previously worked for HTS stated, "*I was approached by IS when I was with HTS. They offered us double the amount of money to stay with HTS secretly and to recruit new members, before IS took over an area.*"[60] When taking over areas previously governed by other rebel groups, IS mostly either killed, expelled the members or forced them to pledge allegiance and work for IS. As a former fighter for the FSA described: "*IS decided quickly that we all had to become members. I refused as I did not agree with the ideology, we were not fighting al-Assad .....IS tried to make an example out of me for refusing and arrested me twice.*"[61]

Civilian Inclusion

The IS had little to no civilian inclusion in its governance strategy. In those areas with a potentially strong competitive civilian governing apparatus— such as local councils in Syria, civil society organisations or Sunni tribes in Iraq or Syria—IS either dismantled eliminated or co-opted them.[62] In some areas, IS did create Tribal Engagement Offices that purportedly engaged with tribes and IS also used mass pledges of allegiance from tribal elders in its propaganda and messaging in an attempt to legitimatize its rule.[63] However, the actual impact of the tribes on IS's governing structures appears to be negligible; their influence appeared to have been tied to local disputes.

There appears to be remarkably little variation in IS's approach to civilian inclusion in spite of the large amount of territory IS controlled between 2014 and 2019. In the early stages of its territorial takeover in a province, IS simply took over previous institutions with little interference, however this swiftly changed after several months of IS's rule in an area.[64] As one teacher from al-Mayadin described: *"IS at first left us alone. But after several months though they established the Diwan [of Education] and everything changed."*[65] Although it has been documented that IS theoretically had courts in which civilians could lodge grievances against IS members, it is unknown the extent to which they were used by civilians or the number of courts actually established by IS.[66] Moreover, if civilians wanted to attain higher positions of responsibility in IS's governing institutions, better salaries or benefits, they had to become a member of IS and pledge allegiance to the caliph. IS used this forced membership strategy throughout its governing institutions; ensuring that civilians would not be included in any positions of responsibility. As an electrician from Deir az Zur province stated: *"If we became members then we had to do a shorter ideological course and they offered us more money ....a normal electrician got 90 USD if working in an office .... However, a colleague who pledged allegiance received 600 USD and became the deputy director of the office"*[67] whilst a doctor's daughter described how *"IS tried to get my father to join them ....they offered him a $1000 per month and preferential treatment. My father refused, but my uncle said yes to IS straight away and he became head of the Medical Office."*[68]

Alliance structure

Although historically rooted in the Iraqi Sunni insurgent movement, IS's alliance structure went beyond the nation-state; it aims to create and expand its extra-territorial Islamic caliphate across the world (Bunzel 2015). The IS's caliphate completely rejects the modern nation-state system, aiming to reestablish the methodology (*manhaj*) of the Prophet Muhammed and his four successor Caliphs. The global perspective, in which the front in Syria is seen as one outpost of a transnational alliance, is a perspective that permeated IS governance actions in diverse ways: leading to its split from Al Qaeda, its destruction of Iraqi-Syrian border posts under its control, removal of all references to 'Iraq,' 'Syria' and 'nation' from its school curriculum and receiving 81 pledges of allegiance from other Salafi-Jihadi groups around the world to establish external 'provinces' of its caliphate.[69] IS's transnational outlook was recognized by civilians living across IS territory, especially in relation to the local focus of Ahrar al-Sham and HTS. A civilian who worked for IS in its Raqqa tax office said *"IS didn't care about the revolution, they only came to Syria to expand the caliphate—they fought against groups that were trying to defeat Assad.*"[70] whilst a former HTS fighter, who attended an IS re-education ideology camp in Deir az Zur said *"they taught us that the only way to be Muslim is to live under a true Caliph; states are a deviation from Islam."*[71]

Repression

IS's governance strategy involved violent repression of opposition to its rule. Part of this strategy relates to IS's conception of blasphemy. Any decision made by a leader of IS became a *fatwa* due to their authority in IS's governing hierarchy; as a fatwa is the desire and implementation of God's will, then to question a decision of an IS leader, is to effectively question the will of God. Abdul, a lawyer who lived under IS in Aleppo and Deir az Zur, remarked: *"any contestation of IS's decisions became blasphemous and IS violently punished any person who opposed them."*[72] Although some civilians were dealt with more leniently if IS needed their skills, influence or capital,[73] IS violently repressed most persons who attempt to contest its governance. Revkin (2019, 2020)[74] has detailed the highly repressive legal system established by IS governing institutions and interviewees frequently gave examples of the violent repression they suffered under IS: *"I was stopped by a woman IS member for wearing the wrong clothes and showing some skin. They hit me on the street and both my husband and brother were lashed 20 time for allowing me to leave the house showing skin."*[75]

Hay'at Tahrir al-Sham

HTS is a Salafi-Jihadist group who have a history of shifting goals, divergent alliances and fragmentation, which eventually resulted in it emerging as the sole most powerful rebel group in Syria from 2017 onwards.[76] HTS emerged publicly in January 2012 as Jabhat al-Nusra, the officially sanctioned branch of AQ in Syria, that originally began as a cell of fighters sent to Syria by the IS leader, Abu Bakr al-Baghdadi. HTS publicly split from AQ in 2016 and governed territory in formal alliances with other rebel groups until 2017. HTS then successfully implemented a hegemonic governance approach when it formed a single monolithic Syrian Salvation Government (SSG), after defeating rival rebel groups and subsuming or coming to an agreement with other competitive governing actors.[77] As Al-Tamimi (2020) sums up: "by early 2019, HTS had secured its hegemony over the northwest [of Syria], which continues today."[78]

Rebel collaboration

HTS has had a complex relationship with other rebel groups; HTS at the beginning of its rule more openly collaborated and governed with other rebel groups, before shifting towards a hegemonic governing approach in its remaining territory.[79] At the end of 2012, HTS established the Aleppo Sharia Committee, with three other rebel groups, whose ambition was to "emulate the state, with offices regulating all spheres of life."[80] HTS continued this collaboration throughout its various name changes that cumulated in the Executive Administration of Jaysh al-Fateh, an alliance of six rebel groups dominated by HTS and Ahrar al-Sham, founded in March 2015 which "tested the ability of these factions to have common institutions and to provide a joint model of administration" in Idlib governorate.[81] True governing collaboration failed however as HTS and Ahrar al-Sham, "competed in governance and service provision"[82] and "maintained their own areas of control and influence in much of the northwest rather than creating a joint Jaysh al-Fatah administration throughout the entire province."[83] This uneasy alliance ended, however, when HTS began to pursue a logic factional hegemony, at both the military and the administrative levels.[84] HTS defeated Ahrar al-Sham in a series of clashes until it remained the sole rebel Jihadi rebel group in Idlib, and HTS formalized its rule under one central unified administration.[85] Although HTS still continue to collaborate with non-Jihadist factions in its territory,[86] the group maintained its dominance over Jihadist factions in the sphere of its control, refusing to collaborate with other rebel groups as it has done previously.

Civilian inclusion

HTS's approach to civilian inclusion in its governance caused a huge rift in the Jaysh al-Fatah governing alliance, of which Ahrar al-Sham and HTS were the most powerful members. HTS didn't want independent civilian members to join the governing structures al-Fatah created, instead preferring to put forward civilians affiliated to HTS. As a person from Iblib stated: *"HTS see themselves as rulers of the area they are based in, and they govern civilian affairs through a civil administration in quotation marks. They want a civilian body but one that is weak and completely under their control."*[87] Throughout its history, HTS has cooperated with civilian Syrian local councils,[88] although HTS has frequently tried to influence these councils by placing its affiliates in them. Although following its creation of the hegemonic SSG, commentators have argued about HTS's approach to civilian inclusion; for Schwab (2018),[89] HTS severely limited the role of civilian local councils and preferred to directly rule them, whilst for others, the SSG provides opportunities for the inclusion of educated, civilian elites as HTS are no longer worried about military factionalism.[90] Undoubtedly, however, HTS allowed civilians to raise complaints about the group's membership through formalized dispute mechanisms, a clear difference compared to IS. As several persons living in HTS- controlled areas stated, *"we could always turn to councils to complain against HTS and raise issues and complaints. They would listen and responded if it was justified,"*[91] whilst another interviewee stated *"HTS wanted to show that civilians were involved. They made it easy for us to speak to them, reach them, as we knew who they were and could speak to them as brothers."*[92]

Alliance structure

HTS has successfully portrayed itself as having a sole Syrian focus, especially in relation to the explicitly transnational caliphate ambitions of IS. HTS from the beginning had a focus on Syria, with the explicitly stated aim of overthrowing the Assad regime and integrating itself within the broader Syrian revolution movement. However, HTS's floated multiple times the ambition of establishing an Islamic Emirate in its territory[93] and the group's links to AQ led to skepticism over the actual intended goals of HTS in relation to the Syrian revolution.[94] HTS attempted to overcome these concerns by embarking on a process of "Syrianization"[95] by changing its alliance structure by severing its ties with AQ, and "emphasizing its 'Syria' focus, ... to placate concerns regarding the transnational goals of its al-Qaida organizational loyalties and heritage."[96] Indeed, several civilians that lived in areas under control of both IS and HTS highlighted the Syrian nature of HTS, as a key point of difference compared to IS: *"we know who HTS are, its members are from our area, our families and they are fighting together for the revolution"*[97] whilst *"IS only cared about itself; HTS scarified for the revolution, they only want the revolution to succeed."*[98]

Repression

There is some debate about the extent to which HTS's governance strategy permits repression of protests and demonstrations against its rule. Haid (2017)[99] quotes multiple civilian interviewees who believe that "HTS does not attack or disperse demonstrations" because HTS does not have the strength or willingness to fight directly against local communities as "they know it would be a lost battle."[100] However, Human Rights Watch (2019) documented that HTS has arbitrarily arrested and tortured civilians from Aleppo, Idlib and Hama "because of their peaceful work documenting abuses or protesting the group's rule."[101] HTS detained 184 persons in the space of three months which led Human Rights Watch to state that "HTS's crackdown on perceived opposition to their rule mirrors some of the same oppressive tactics used by the Syrian government."[102] Indeed, HTS's approach towards repression of civilians has caused schisms with other rebel groups. Heller (2016)[103] quotes an Idlib activist stating that HTS kidnapped six activists at a protest, after Ahrar al-Sham refused to give HTS permission to break up ongoing protests in Idlib in March 2016. As a result, Ahrar al-Sham took the step of publicly condemned HTS for its repression of demonstrations when both were part of the Jaysh al-Fatah alliance in March 2016.[104]

Ahrar al-Sham

Ahrar al-Sham was established in January 2012 through a merger of Salafi-Jihadi armed groups in North-western Syria. Over the following two years, Ahrar al-Sham transitioned from a group whose "stated aim was to establish a Syrian Islamic society that would adhere to Sharia law" and rejected secularism, democracy and its parliaments, to a group that signed a Revolutionary Charter that aspired to build a state of justice, law and freedom, with references to establishing an Islamic state removed.[105] Although for some commentators, "Ahrar is clearly still rooted in Islamist militancy,"[106] the success of this transformation managed to keep Ahrar al-Sham off the terrorist designation list and kept the support from its principal foreign backers Turkey, Qatar and Saudi-Arabia.

Until January 2017, Ahrar al-Sham were widely considered to be "one of the strongest Salafist factions in Syria"[107] and displayed "significant governance capacities and ambitions,"[108] with between an estimated 10–20,000 fighters.[109] Ahrar al-Sham previously governed territory in parts of Aleppo, Raqqa and Deir az Zur governorates, although its stronghold was in Idlib governorate, where it shared territory in an uneasy alliance with HTS. Clashes between the former allies during 2017–2018 resulted in the territorial and materially decimation of Ahrar al-Sham in Syria.[110]

Rebel collaboration

Ahrar al-Sham are most distinguished from other Salafi-Jihadi groups by its collaborative governing approach. As Jonsson (2016) notes "in an insurgency that has been exceptionally factionalised and characterised by incessant internecine fighting, Ahrar al-Sham has been comparatively adept at collaborating effectively with others."[111] From its earliest start,

Ahrar al-Sham has managed to collaborate with and subsume smaller Jihadi groups that aligned with its ideology at the time. Ahrar al-Sham formed three prominent rebel coalition organisations during the civil war; the Syrian Islamic Front in 2014, Islamic Front in 2014 and Jaysh al-Fatah in 2015.

Ahrar al-Sham's governance in Idlib was built on an uneasy alliance with HTS; the two largest members of the Jaysh al-Fatah governing coalition. The two groups split territorial control throughout Idlib, developing separate governing institutions that frequently both competed and collaborated with each other.[112] Although splits occurred over the hardline Jihadi rule that some groups wished to impose on Idlib, Ahrar al-Sham appeared to be successful collaborating positively in its alliances.[113] This came to an end when HTS broke its alliance with Ahrar al-Sham when it strived for military, political and security governance hegemony over Idlib governorate and defeated Ahrar al-Sham and its aligned groups in a series of clashes in 2017.[114] Ahrar al-Sham's collaborative approach to governance with other rebel groups therefore ended in its territorial defeat.

Civilian inclusion

Ahrar al-Sham's governance strategy included a relatively large role for civilians and relied on indirectly ruling though local councils that were filled by civilian technocrats. This culminated in Ahrar al-Sham's establishment of the Services Administration Commission (SAC) that relied on civilians to fill the key roles, albeit under the general protection of Ahrar al-Sham 's military arms.[115] This institutional arrangement appears to meet Ahrar al-Sham's publicly stated aim to let civilians run their own cities, with some commentators stating that Ahrar al-Sham's "behavior in the areas it controls seems to reflect a higher degree of tolerance for people being involved in their own governance as well as a higher degree of cooperation with the local population."[116] Indeed, Ahrar al-Sham's governance approach to civilians is shown in its judicial institutions in Idlib that resolved arguments between Ahrar al-Sham members and civilians that "guaranteed a higher level of accountability and security for the local population."[117]

Alliance structure

Ahrar al-Sham is a group that defines itself as local Syrian movement, composed of Syrian members with no links or alliances to transnational Salafi-Jihadi groups, its "political and military aims are also limited to Syria alone."[118] Ahrar al-Sham has undergone an overhaul of its alliance structure; in the early days when it was part of the Syrian Islamic Front and Islamic Front, Ahrar al-Sham's aim was to establish an Islamic state, with Sharia law as the sole authority and non-Muslims excluded from both society and governance.[119] With the signing of a Revolutionary Charter in 2014, Ahrar al-Sham's alliance structure changed. Many Ahrar al-Sham leaders rejected Salafi-Jihadism[120] and broke alliances with these previous Islamist group allies, as Ahrar al-Sham swore in the Charter to focus on establishing a Syrian society with respect for all minorities. Objectives that were incompatible within its previous alliance structure. Ahrar al-Sham have abided by its new alliance structure, despite the fact it caused many Ahrar al-Sham members to form a splinter group (Jaysh al-Ahrar), who ended up joining HTS.

Repression

Ahrar al-Sham's governance strategy appears to involve very low levels, if any, of repression of protests and demonstration against its rule. Rather Ahrar al-Sham has actively sought to distance itself from the repression inflicted by other Salafi-Jihadi groups. Most notably, in March 2016 when Ahrar al-Sham condemned HTS for its repression actions against civilian protests in Idlib.[121] Indeed, Ahrar al-Sham leaders reportedly even joined these protests to complain directly against HTS's repressive actions.[122]

Comparative analysis: how political opportunity structures affect the occurrence of civil resistance against jihadist governance

We will now draw the comparative analysis of the three groups together, by examining how rebel collaboration, civilian inclusion, repression and the goals influenced the political opportunity structure for Syrian dissenting voices under the jihadist groups' control.

From the comparision, it is clear that the rebel group in the middle range of their governance dimensions faced greater public civil resistance, shown through the frequency and size of protests. HTS, who governed far more in the middle ranges compared to Ahrar al-Sham and IS, who are at opposite ends of extremity, appear to provide greater political opportunity for civilians to mobilize against them.

Firstly, there were clear differences in terms of rebel collaboration between the three jihadist groups; IS fought against other rebel groups and was exclusive in its aspiration of control, whereas Ahrar al-Sham sought to be build stronger rebel-coalitions and collaboration, whilst HTS was somewhere in between. Both Ahrar al-Sham and HTS frequently collaborated with other rebel groups and local councils in its territory control, although this decreased over time for HTS. Ahrar al-Sham's highly collaborative approach to other rebel groups possibly reduced the need for civilians to engage in public protests as they had other means of lodging protests and complaints. Whilst for HTS, the partially collaborative approach gave civilians both the need and opportunity to protest publicly.

There was also a clear link in terms of political opportunity structures from civilian inclusion (or exclusion) towards propensity for engagement in civil resistance. In both Ahrar al-Sham and HTS's models of governance, civilians were given the opportunity to get involved, and some form of political access, that provided opportunity for civilians to mobilize on specific issues of protests. Ahrar al-Sham however governed with more civilian inclusion than HTS. This potentially provided more opportunity for civilians to work with Ahrar al-Sham on specific issues, diminishing the need to protest publicly outside of Ahrar al-Sham's governing institutions. IS by contrast entirely excluded civilians from its governance, and forced civilians working in its governing institutions to become members, which reduced the political opportunities for civilians to resist.

We know from previous research on civil resistance, that repression can sometimes quell uprisings and protests, and in other circumstances, serve as a trigger of further, increased mobilization.[123] Repression varied across the three groups; IS had by far the most heavily repressive governing strategy, although Ahrar al-Sham and HTS had a significant conflict over the latter's repressive approach in its shared Idlib territory. In IS areas, its suffocating governing repression led to less opportunity for civilians to protest, in comparison to the more lenient HTS and Ahrar al-Sham. Still, the level of repression was not linear alongside the occurrence of civil resistance: Ahrar al-Sham was more lenient than HTS but fewer demonstrations arose against them, compared to the more repressive HTS. The alliance structure of the groups differed: from IS's perspective, the Syrian context was a local manifestation of a global struggle and it relied on its international allies in the form of foreign fighters and supporters, both politically and practically. The constituency was not only, or mainly, the local base, but a more global outreach. Ahrar al-Sham was clearly more domestically and locally oriented: it was a Salafi-Jihadist group but focused on Syria. HTS partly disengaged from its international alliance and re-focused on the Syrian context as the conflict evolved. The need to be attentive to local audiences made HTS more receptive to protests movements and more likely that they should then listen to local voices: the chances of being successful by mobilizing protests thus affected the civilian opposition.

Alternative explanations

We will here take up some alternative possible explanations for why the occurrence of civil resistance varied across different Salafi-Jihadist groups in Syria. The first one is the issue of endogeneity. Could popular civilian resistance shape the governing strategies of the three Salafi-Jihadi groups, rather than the other way around (as we suggest in this study)? Our research design—comparing across groups rather than over time—cannot rule out this concern completely. However, 92 percent of the total protest events occurred from 2016 onwards, at which point each rebel group governing structures were already well established. This suggests that it is indeed governing structures influencing civilian public resistance, rather than the other way around. Still, the degree and type of how the different dimensions of governance are implemented can vary over time, and can potentially influence the propensity for civil resistance. With the current research design, we cannot establish this for certain, and we therefore call on future research to disentangle the relationship between governance and repression in more depth and detail. In particular by using causal process tracing and other ways to more credibly establish the causal pathways.

Extensive ("full") civilian resistance to rebel governance could, according to previous research, be expected in areas where civilians perceive their pre-existing customary institutions to be legitimate and functional.[124] Moreover, more closely tied networks between local elites and the population will predispose civilians to be more likely to resist rebel governance attempts.[125] Still, customary institutions and local elites, in particular, the tribal networks in Syria, do not appear to vary significantly in effectiveness and legitimacy between the areas of the three rebel groups' control prior to their establishment of the jihadist governance.[126] A further potential alternative explanation is the impact of *religious and ethnic mobilization* on the likelihood of protests; rebel groups who align with the religion and ethnicity of their civilian constituency might be likely to face resistance and protests as their interests align with those of the rebel group.[127] This explanation, however, does not appear relevant across these three cases. Ahrar al-Sham and HTS controlled primarily homogenous Sunni Arab territory, compared to the more diverse territory of IS that included a significant Kurdish and Christian population.[128]

A further mooted explanation is that rebel groups, whose governance structures developed in *contested territory*, would potentially lead to more opportunities for civil resistance as they would have to be more responsive to civilian demands due to rebel competition.[129] While this may account for why IS experienced less civil resistance in comparison with the other two jihadist groups, given IS's relatively exclusive and uncontested governance, this does not explain the variation in frequency of civil resistance between HTS and Ahrar al-Sharm. Both HTS and Ahrar al-Sham governed in competition within the same territory. Overall, this explanation does therefore not appear to have value in explaining the variation in frequency of protests. A potential alternative explanation is the role of *protest history*, meaning that certain areas are more likely to engage in protests because they have a history of networks, activists and civil society groups who could more easily facilitate protests. Although this cannot be ruled out, all the territory controlled by these groups have a strong history of protests throughout the civil war; Halterman et al. (2019)[130] show that each governorate had at least 20 protest events in the first year of the Syrian civil war. Further, under each jihadist group, protests did take place. Although some of these protests were multiple events, whilst others were singular, there is an assumed baseline that residents in each group's territory had the capacity to organize protests.

As for the civilians' *level of grievances*, we expect that they may have varied between the different rebel territories, however there are no systematic polls or surveys that can give a comprehensive picture of the level of grievances or popularity of governing structures. We do note, however that level of grievances do not co-vary with the occurrence of civilian protests. It could be expected that IS's governance structures were the most intrusive and, therefore less popular, as they were often perceived by local residents as alien or too harsh to the local population. In contrast, HTS went to great length to make its structures of governance more popular with its local communities. The anticipated varying level of grievances, therefore, does not co-vary with the occurrence of civil resistance.

Another explanation is the *modernization* explanation, which views the capacity for uprising as closely associated with the development of an area's economy, including its level of urbanization. However, there were few significant comparative economic differences integral to the group's territory. Moreover, while IS, HTS and Ahrar al-Sham governed both significant urban and rural demographic areas (Raqqa/Deir az Zur; Idlib/Aleppo and Idlib governorates respectively) IS, due to the size of its territory, was in fact in control of more urban areas.[131] Thus, a modernization (or urbanization) explanation would not be able to account for the sub-national variation we have identified in this study. As stated above, we see the political opportunity argument developed here, as complementing resource mobilization—as well as grievances explanations—which are from our perspective, are both necessary (but not sufficient) explanations to account for the variation across the three main jihadist groups in Syria. That is, we see that opposition activists and movements to jihadist governance in Syria take up civil resistance because they are motivated to do so, but also because they have both the resources to mobilize and see the structural possibilities for doing so.

Conclusion

This study has shown that the governing strategies of Salafi-Jihadi groups in Syria have an impact on both the frequency and size of protests by civilians against them. Different types of Islamist governance structures provide different political opportunity structures that enable civilians to mobilize against those rebel groups through public protests and demonstrations. In particular, we argue that it is middle-ranged opportunity structures of rebel governance, like HTS, that strongest incentivizes civil resistance, by giving enough space for civilian mobilization but fewer alternative channels of expressing discontent. This study had untaken a systematic comparison of their governing structures and shown their variation across four governing dimensions. The study helps to shed light on role of civil agency in violent contexts. As we have shown here, even in the midst of a civil war, civilians have self-organized protests and acts of disobedience against jihadist rebel-groups. This testifies to the role of civilians as an important set of actors to take into account when studying rebel governance, even when focusing on Salafi-Jihadi rebel groups. We have also demonstrated that there is a significant sub-national variation in the occurrence of civil resistance across the jihadist rebel-groups: HTS stood out from the other two jihadist groups in terms of being the most actively challenged rebel governance group.

The analysis of IS, HTS, and Ahrar al-Sham show how the four dimensions of rebel governance strategies—building on Schock's political opportunity framework—that are interrelated. The external alliance structure of IS cannot be properly understood, without taking into account the lack of civilian inclusion and rebel collaboration. Conversely, when a group relies on external alliances, the need to pay attention to domestic actors and constituencies will decrease. It is important to note that the four dimensions also carried different explanatory power in terms of occurrence of civil resistance. The use of repression is the strongest factor deterring civil resistance. Although the lack of civil inclusion, rebel collaboration and external alliance structures all played a role, it is difficult to ascertain exactly which of these dimensions provided the largest opportunity for resistance. Together, however, these four dimensions of governing strategies indicate the institutional space and structural political opportunity available for civilians to resist.

We should also acknowledge that the Salafi-Jihadi rebel group governance structures in Syria evolved over time. HTS shifted from an internationalist to a more nationalist agenda, disengaging from transnational jihadist networks. Whilst the repressive nature of IS was initially not fully implemented throughout its territory, but rather developed over time.[132] The implication is that the political opportunities for civilians to publicly protest can vary in line with these governing dimensions. While beyond the scope of this study, further studies and data collection on the temporal nature of protests and governance structures could shed light on this interesting aspect on the relationship between rebel governance and protests. Furthermore, this paper has shown the potential for the use of the political opportunity framework to be applied to civil resistance against rebel-governance structures in general, and civil resistance against jihadist groups in particular. We demonstrate that the framework has plausibility beyond opposition groups challenging established states, which was the context in which the theory was originally crafted. Doing so, we have reconceptualized the four opportunity factors into the context of rebel-civilian relationships. This may provide a new way of studying how space for civilians to express discontent can shape the trajectory of conflict between rebels and civilians.

This study has been written within the framework of the research project Resolving Jihadist Conflicts? Battles without Bullets. An earlier version of this paper was presented at the Political Islam in the Middle East and North Africa workshop at the Swedish Institute of International Affairs. Data for this study draws from the larger dataset collected for the book Svensson et al 2022, and this data has been coded by Nanar Hawach complemented with coding by Dino Krause. We appreciate excellent research assistance also by Alanna Smart. Disclosure statement. No potential conflict of interest was reported by the author(s). Additional information, Funding. The authors gratefully acknowledge financial support for this study from Riksbankens Jubileumsfond through grant [NHS14-1701:1], by Marianne och Marcus Wallenbergs Stiftelse through grant [MMW 2013.0025] and the Swiss National Science Foundation through grant [178426]. Notes on contributors. Matthew Bamber is a PhD candidate in International Relations at the Graduate Institute of International and Development Studies, Geneva and a Visiting Fellow at the Department of Peace and Conflict Research, Uppsala University. Isak Svensson is a Professor at the Department of Peace and Conflict Research, Uppsala University and the principal investigator of the international research project 'Resolving Jihadist Conflicts? Religion, Civil War, and Prospects for Peace.' Print ISSN: 0954-6553 Online ISSN: 1556-1836. 8 issues per year. Abstracted/indexed in: America: History & Life; CSA; Elsevier Scopus; Family Index Database; Historical Abstracts; IBR International Bibliography of Book Reviews; IBZ International Bibliography of Periodical Literature; International Bibliography of the Social Sciences (IBSS); International Political Science Abstracts; ISI: Current Contents - Social & Behavioral Sciences and Social Science Citation Index; Lancaster Index to Defence & International Security Literature; National Criminal Justice Reference Service Abstracts (NCJRS); OCLC; Periodical Abstracts (PerAbs); ProQuest; PsycINFO/Psychological Abstracts; Sage Criminal Justice Abstracts; The Lancaster Index; Thomson Reuters© Current Contents: Social & Behavioral Sciences; Thomson Reuters© Social Science Citation Index.

Taylor & Francis make every effort to ensure the accuracy of all the information (the "Content") contained in our publications. However, Taylor & Francis, our agents (including the editor, any member of the editorial team or editorial board, and any guest editors), and our licensors, make no representations or warranties whatsoever as to the accuracy, completeness, or suitability for any purpose of the Content. Any opinions and views expressed in this publication are the opinions and views of the authors, and are not the views of or endorsed by Taylor & Francis. The accuracy of the Content should not be relied upon and should be independently verified with primary sources of information.

Terrorism and Political Violence advances scholarship on a broad range of issues associated with terrorism and political violence, including subjects such as: the political meaning of terrorist activity, violence by rebels and by states, the links between political violence and organized crime, protest, rebellion, revolution, the influence of social networks, and the impact on human rights. The journal draws upon many disciplines and theoretical perspectives as well as comparative approaches to provide some of the most groundbreaking work in a field that has hitherto lacked rigour. Terrorism and Political Violence features symposia and edited volumes to cover an important topic in depth.

Resisting Radical Rebels: Variations in Islamist Rebel Governance and the Occurrence of Civil Resistance Matthew Bamber & Isak Svensson To cite this article: Matthew Bamber & Isak Svensson (2022): Resisting Radical Rebels: Variations in Islamist Rebel Governance and the Occurrence of Civil Resistance, Terrorism and Political Violence, DOI: 10.1080/09546553.2021.2019023 To link to this article: https://doi.org/10.1080/09546553.2021.2019023 © 2022 The Author(s). Published with license by Taylor & Francis Group, LLC. Published online: 15 Feb 2022. CONTACT Isak Svensson isak.svensson@pcr.uu.se Department of Peace and Conflict Research, Uppsala University, Box 514, Uppsala 751 05, Sweden TERRORISM AND POLITICAL VIOLENCE https://doi.org/10.1080/09546553.2021.2019023

Chapter 2

Rebel Governance, Rebel Legitimacy, and External Intervention: Assessing three Phases of Taliban Rule in Afghanistan

Niels Terpstra

Abstract

This article focuses on rebel governance and rebel legitimacy during the civil war. It investigates how external intervention in support of an incumbent government and withdrawal of external forces shape rebel legitimacy dynamics and rebels' opportunities to govern. It adopts a longitudinal perspective on Afghanistan's Taliban, analyzing three phases of the movement's existence. Moral forms of legitimacy resonated particularly during instances of external intervention, whereas pragmatic forms of legitimacy became more relevant after the withdrawal of external forces and during periods of the Taliban's opponents' ineffective government.

Introduction

In response to the 9/11 attacks on the United States in 2001, international coalition forces and their Afghan allies ousted the Taliban regime from power. Although the Taliban regime collapsed quickly, the movement re-grouped in Pakistan and re-appeared as an insurgency only a few years later. As of 2020, the Taliban controls large swaths of Afghanistan's territory. As in the 1990s, it has become increasingly involved in governance, expanding the reach of its judiciary and governors. Though the Taliban are known to rule by coercion and intimidation, the movement has also gained a level of legitimacy among segments of the civilian population at the expense of the Afghan state. However, how the Taliban legitimizes its rule and

39

how civilians respond to this require further empirical study. This article, therefore, focuses on how the Taliban has become involved in governance and how it has attempted to acquire legitimacy.

Several authors have investigated questions of rebel governance and legitimacy over the past decade, mainly from political science or anthropology perspective.[1] The recent academic literature on rebel governance aims for a better understanding of the interactions between rebels and civilians during the civil war.[2] It criticizes the 'failed state' paradigm and attempts to show that political and social order each exist in various ways during civil wars.[3] Related studies have tried to gain a better understanding of rebel legitimacy.[4] Rebels often draw from a variety of sources to legitimize their own existence and justify their rule.[5]

The dynamics of rebel governance and rebel legitimacy, however, do not exist in isolation from other powerful actors. The actions/responses of the state are relevant to the analysis of rebel legitimacy as well.[6] Powerful external actors may also influence the relations between armed groups and civilians.[7] Much research has been devoted to the effects of external support to rebel groups[8] and the attempts of rebel groups to acquire international legitimacy and/or recognition.[9] In this article I shift the perspective and demonstrate how powerful external actors that support the incumbent government shape (though less directly) the dynamics of rebel governance and rebel legitimacy. The presence of foreign enemy forces is an important source of legitimacy for rebel groups and has remained relatively under-studied in the literature on rebel governance. Rebel legitimacy is a function of present-day events but also of prior armed conflicts and societal tensions. As Schröder and Schmidt observe, 'the most important code of the legitimation of war is its historicity'[10]

In other words, the 'symbolic meaning of prior wars is re-enacted and reinterpreted in the present, and present violence generates symbolic value to be employed in future confrontations.[11] It is therefore necessary to study rebel governance and legitimacy from a longitudinal perspective. Whereas current sources of legitimacy, such as service provision and protection, are an important part of the analysis, the legitimizing effect of prior events and external interventions in particular, require further scrutiny. Omitting historical sources of legitimacy may lead to an incomplete understanding of rebel groups' legitimacy.

The Afghan Taliban has had a unique historical trajectory. Some members were part of the mujahideen[12] fighting against the Soviet regime; they then formed a separate insurgency (pre-1996), transitioned to a semi-recognized statehood (1996–2001), were ousted from power, and again started an insurgency against the new Afghan government and coalition forces (2001–2020). To understand where specific sources of legitimacy originate, it is necessary to consider the period prior to the US intervention in 2001 and even before the Taliban established itself as a separate movement in 1994. For example, many older generation Taliban commanders as well as many commanders and governors in the current Afghan government shared their experiences as mujahideen. This is still relevant today. Previous research regarding the historical trajectory of the Taliban takes different positions in terms of continuity and change.

As Ruttig notes, for example, 'the [Taliban's] organizational structure including the composition of its leadership, ideology, political aims and programme' has remained largely consistent from the 1990s until the 2010s.[13] Conversely, Strick van Linschoten and Kuehn warn against perceiving the Taliban's thinking and policies as static; rather, they insist they are evolving.[14] By applying the concepts of governance and legitimacy to the full timeframe of the Taliban, this article aims to show the specificities of both continuity and change. The findings are based on fieldwork data collected between 2013 and 2018 and insights from several previous studies.[15] This article makes empirical and conceptual contributions to the academic literature.

First, it reiterates that the Taliban has emphasized and de-emphasized specific religious, cultural, and political sources of legitimacy over the past decades. I argue that moral forms of legitimacy resonated particularly during instances of external intervention, while pragmatic forms of legitimacy became more relevant after the withdrawal of external forces and during instances of the Taliban's opponents' ineffective governance. Second, this article highlights the contrasting effects of external intervention on rebel governance and rebel legitimacy. External intervention in support of an incumbent government decreases the number of opportunities for rebel groups to govern while it increases the potential moral sources of rebel legitimacy. However, the departure of external forces gives rebels opportunities to govern, while it diminishes the resonance of some specific moral sources of legitimacy.

First, I discuss the theoretical background of rebel governance and rebel legitimacy. Then, I present my methodological considerations. Subsequently, I analyze the traces of governance and legitimacy in the pre-1996 insurgency phase, the phase of the Taliban's proclaimed Islamic

Emirate of Afghanistan (IEA) between 1996 and 2001, and the post-2001 insurgency phase. The last section presents the main findings and contributions.

Rebel governance and legitimacy during the civil war

Rebel governance

Rebel governance usually takes place under the conditions of civil war. Civil war can appropriately be defined as 'armed combat within the boundaries of a recognized sovereign entity between parties subject to a common authority at the outset of the hostilities.[16] Within the boundaries of that initial sovereign entity, several armed groups may operate, often competing with one another. This includes various types of rebel groups, militias, auxiliary forces, self-defence forces, para-militaries, warlords, and strongmen.[17] Hence, during a civil war, territorial control becomes fragmented and controlled by more than just state actors. Different warring parties fully or partially control territories, while other swaths of territories are contested with shifting frontlines.[18]

Crucially, however, the conditions of civil war do not necessarily result in 'ungoverned spaces.[19] sometimes, previous governance practices continue, and in other instances new governance practices emerge. As Kalyvas notes, insurgency can be understood as 'a process of competitive state-building.' [20] To gain a better understanding of the relationship between rebels and civilians during civil war, the concept of governance should not be understood as the prerogative of a formal government. I agree with Rosenau and colleagues (1992) and view governance as a more encompassing phenomenon. Governance embraces informal, non-governmental mechanisms of persons and organizations as well as formal institutions.[21] According to Kasfir; rebel governance is, at a minimum, 'the organization of civilians within the rebel-held territory for a public purpose.'[22]

As I define it, governance contains no prescriptive implications; it is comprised of the conduct of rebel-civilian relations regardless of morally good or bad behaviour or treatment by either side.[23] Previous studies show how armed groups are involved in various governance sectors, including security, justice, education, health care, taxation, and utility services.[24] In this article I focus on the Taliban's two main governance sectors: justice and security.[25] Changes regarding external involvement can create incentives for armed groups to become more prominently involved in governance.[26] After the withdrawal of external troops, power vacuums can emerge, which armed groups may exploit. In Sri Lanka, for example, the Liberation Tigers of Tamil Eelam (LTTE) suddenly controlled of much of the northern territories after the Indian Peace Keeping Forces (IPKF) withdrew in 1990. The Northern Jaffna peninsula came under full rebel control, and became the first locality that was de facto governed by the LTTE.[27] The vacuum that external political actors leave behind provides opportunities for rebels to govern.[28]

The dynamics of rebel legitimacy Rebel groups and civilians Rebels that are involved in governance cannot take their relationship with the civilian population for granted. The dynamics of legitimacy are in a permanent state of contestation.[29] Even rebel groups that rely mainly on coercion to implement their rule may pursue legitimation practices to increase civilian compliance. According to Suchman, legitimacy is a 'generalized perception or assumption that the actions of an entity are desirable, proper, or appropriate within some socially constructed system of norms, values, beliefs, and definitions.'[30] Despite the absence of juridical legitimacy or international recognition, rebel groups may hold a level of legitimacy among a particular constituency[31] While external legitimacy–i.e., how a rebel group is viewed and treated in the international arena–s an important element, particularly for secessionist movements,[32]

I largely confine my analysis to the relationship between rebels and civilians but take into account external actors that support the incumbent government as these influences the legitimation practices of the Taliban vis-à-vis civilians. For analytical purposes, I distinguish two forms of rebel legitimacy, but I acknowledge that these forms of legitimacy may empirically overlap and intertwine. These two forms of legitimacy are pragmatic and moral legitimacy. Pragmatic legitimacy is based on the provision of services, protection, or even a willingness to share power, while moral legitimacy is based on 'narratives of goodness, compatibility with existing norms and moral codes,' and, for example, 'explicitly referenced against religion or ethnicity.'[33] Pragmatic legitimacy includes the provision of basic services, sometimes referred to as 'delivery-based legitimation.'[34]

Pragmatic legitimacy can also be based on the rebel group's ability to provide protection or a relatively stable social and political order. Especially in countries racked by civil war, the capacity of an armed organization to offer protection and stability is important to civilian populations.[35] Moral forms of legitimacy refer to a broader set of social norms and moral codes in society. As Schlichte and Schneckener note, rebels' claims to legitimacy are often tied to encompassing ideologies or worldviews.[36] This includes, for instance, religious ideas of a political order. Moreover, rebels' claims to legitimacy are often rooted in 'communal myth-symbol complexes,' popular belief systems, traditions, and cultures.[37] Furthermore, moral claims to legitimacy are often made in reference to external threats and established enemy depictions.

By portraying the enemy as 'particularly brutal, inhuman and evil, the armed group aims not only to create solidarity but also to present itself and its violent actions as necessary, appropriate and comparatively less destructive.'[38] Crucially, without the recognition of followers, the legitimacy of a movement or its ideas does not exist.[39] Like the concept of power, rebel legitimacy is a relational notion, not a fixed attribute.[40]

Incumbent governments' responses

Although rebel groups stake their claim to legitimacy strategically, not all legitimation effects occur due to actions of the rebels alone.[41] Legitimacy is affected by contextual factors, such as the actions of opposing parties. In Sri Lanka, for example, the operations and actions of the Sri Lankan Armed Forces and the intervening IPKF also contributed to perceptions regarding the LTTE's legitimacy.[42] Corruption and misconduct within the Afghan government and the inability to protect its citizens legitimize the insurgency if the Taliban is relatively better capable of providing some rule of law and relative stability.[43] It is not a zero-sum game, but the incumbent government's actions also shape the dynamics of rebel legitimacy.

Powerful external actors

Powerful external actors affect the dynamics of rebel legitimacy too.[44] Some provide external support to rebel groups, such as military, moral, political, or material support.[45] In this article, however, I focus on powerful external actors that side with the incumbent government. The intervention of the Soviet Union and the intervention of the coalition forces have been important factors fostering armed resistance over time.[46]

Methodology

This article presents three case studies of rebel governance and legitimacy corresponding to three phases of Taliban rule. The first two phases are mainly based on document research. I relied on the vast amount of literature on the Taliban movement and the contemporary political history of Afghanistan. The third phase is mainly based on empirical evidence from fieldwork. Accordingly, this article combines a literature-based macro perspective with a more empirical micro perspective to connect past and present forms of Taliban rule. The findings are partly based on various fieldwork trips by the author to Afghanistan since 2013. I conducted fieldwork in Kunduz province and Kabul in 2013 and 2016 in collaboration with various Afghan research organizations.

In 2013, a total of 99 structured interviews were held with community members, militiamen, local elders, jirga/shura members, civil society representatives, Afghan Local Police (ALP) officers, and Afghan National Police (ANP) officers in Kunduz. On the German-led Provincial Reconstruction Team (PRT)[47] in Kunduz, I conducted indepth interviews with police trainers, military staff, diplomats, and NGO workers. During the fieldwork conducted in 2016, I interviewed various analysts, NGO workers, diplomats, military staff, and informants from Kunduz and Kabul. The latest set of interviews dates from late 2018. I cooperated with The Liaisons Office (TLO) in Kabul, and we developed a structured questionnaire with open ended questions in order to investigate the experiences of civilians under Taliban rule. Researchers from TLO who were originally from Kunduz province conducted 20 structured interviews with civilians who lived under the direct control and/or influence of the insurgency in Chahar Dara district, Kunduz province.

The themes covered during these interviews were the implementation of the Taliban's rule, modes of governance, governance interactions, service provision, and symbolism. Throughout 2018, local sources living under Taliban rule in Kunduz province were consulted to corroborate specific findings from interviews and open-source data. This sample of respondents is certainly not representative of Kunduz province or the population of Afghanistan. Nevertheless, the data provide unique insight into daily civilian life under Taliban rule. The data come with several limitations that should be kept in mind.[48] The triangulation of different sources has reduced but not eliminated these methodological concerns. The article proceeds with the analysis of the three selected phases of Taliban rule: early insurgency (pre-1996), semi-recognized statehood (1996–2001), and post-2001 insurgency (2001–2019).

From the fall of the Shah to the emergence of the Taliban insurgency (1973–1996)

Context of resistance: early Taliban 'fronts'

To understand the emergence of the Taliban, we need to study the 1970s and 1980s. In 1973, Mohammed Daoud Khan, supported by a fraction of

45

the military and leftist parties, seized power from his cousin (and long-term rival), King Zahir Shah, in a bloodless coup d'état.[49] Daoud ended the monarchy of the Shah and proclaimed a republic.[50] While attempting to sideline his leftist allies, Daoud also attempted to wipe out the Islamists that opposed him. Simultaneously, the opposition to Daoud, in the form of the Marxists and the Islamists, stepped up their recruiting efforts, seeking to weaken Daoud's power.[51] For years, Afghanistan had been courted by the United States and the Soviet Union in their Cold War rivalry, but by the 1970 s, the amount of Soviet advisors increased, and the Marxist People's Democratic Party of Afghanistan (PDPA) gained more support in urban areas.[52] Factions of the PDPA came to power in a coup d'état in April 1978, which was later referred to as the Saur Revolution.[53]

The newly established PDPA regime was not only interested in ruling the country but was also keen to transform Afghanistan by revolutionary policies of land reform, education reform, and changes in family law.[54] The revolutionary regime of the PDPA attempted to clear the country of religious elements and opposing forces, including traditional landowners, the old military establishment, and the Islamic clergy.[55] The regime rejected the country's traditional Islamic symbols of legitimacy by striking religious salutations from government speeches and decrees, and it changed the colour of Afghanistan's flag to red.[56] Overall, the regime legitimized its policies in Marxist terms. From the beginning, revolts against the PDPA involved religious motives and, occasionally, religious forms of organization.[57]

Prior to the 1979 Soviet invasion, the PDPA regime faced resistance since it was seen by many Afghans as 'godless' (kafer), but after the Soviet invasion, a nationalist element gained more prominence: the fight against an 'illegitimate foreign occupation'.[58] Hence, a crucial element in the mobilization of the broader public and its religious clergy was the arrival of Soviet troops in 1979–1980.[59] Overall, both Islamic resistance and nationalistic resistance were apparent in the 1970s and 1980s even before the Taliban existed as a separate movement. What became known as the Taliban movement emerged from religious networks that were part of the wider resistance in the 1980s.[60] The primary motivation of the mujahedeen groups and the first-generation Taliban among them can be described as political and based on religious infrastructure.

In the 1980s, the Taliban, led by their religious teachers, did not yet constitute a separate movement as we know it at the present time, but so-called 'Taliban fronts' already existed amongst the mujahideen.[61]

Early incarnations of these Taliban fronts were primarily mullahs leading their students[62]–taliban–as commanders.[63] These fronts consisted of madrassa-or mosque-centered networks. The Taliban fronts distinguished themselves from other mujahedeen groups by a more radically devoted form of religious jihad.[64] The ideologically heterogeneous resistance was re-interpreted as jihad after Pakistan officially and exclusively recognized seven Sunni Islamist resistance movements, known as the Peshawar Seven,[65] that exclusively received Western and Arab financial support.[66] The American Central Intelligence Agency (CIA) subcontracted its financial contributions through Pakistan's Inter-Services Intelligence (ISI), the country's main intelligence agency. The CIA's covert actions empowered the more radical factions of mujahideen, largely at the direction of the ISI.[67]

Traces of governance and legitimacy during the Taliban fronts

The religious clergy already operated so-called mujahideen courts during the Soviet–Afghan war. These pre-Taliban courts would settle disputes, and the mujahideen largely respected the court's judgements.[68] The courts were initially indistinguishable from the military clout of the commanders, but throughout the 1980s, courts were established as separate institutions at various locations in Afghanistan and run by clerics of different mujahideen groups.[69] What would become the Taliban leadership already yielded a certain status of legitimacy due to these religious courts. Mullahs set up structures providing conflict mitigation; they would pass judgements and issue edicts and fatwas that were mainly concerned with issues arising among the civilian population or between different mujahideen groups/factions.[70]

Therefore, a level of pragmatic legitimacy based on these groups' ability to settle disputes already existed. The Taliban fronts were different from other fronts in terms of composition and membership. While most of the other fronts were structured along tribal and kinship lines, the Taliban networks existed through their common educational backgrounds and their pursuit of religious studies.[71] Their experience as mujahideen during the Afghan–Soviet war instilled strong social ties among the religious students who had become fighters in the various Taliban fronts. Though not always in the same group, the Talibs had spent many years together, always in some form of close proximity or contact.[72] Even today, the Taliban frequently refer back to the 1980s jihad as part of their founding narrative.[73]

Soviet withdrawal and political fragmentation

The withdrawal of the Soviet Union in 1989 created a power vacuum. Political fragmentation and continued violence characterized the 1989–1994 period. Afghanistan descended into a brutal civil war between rivalling mujahideen groups and other strongmen.[74] The war against the Soviet Union had already lasted for ten years, and its impact on Afghan society was severe. An estimated one to two million Afghans were killed during the war, and land mines and indiscriminate bombing injured hundreds of thousands more.[75] Hence, a whole generation grew up as refugees or as fighters.[76] With the Soviet Union gone, much of the territory was open to armed opportunists and radical preachers.[77] Local armed groups continued to fight over land, water sources, and mountain passes at different localities.[78]

The various mujahideen groups became either players in the battle for Kabul or localized armed actors.[79] The multitude of commanders increasingly tolerated their fighters to loot and rape the civilian population, partly due to their inability to pay salaries and as an incentive to keep them fighting.[80] The key individuals that would eventually establish the Taliban as a separate movement in 1994 were relatively passive between 1989 and 1994.[81] Those who would come to form the senior leadership after 1994 used to be village mullahs or worked in religious education and therefore returned to their home villages or original madrassas.[82] Some mujahideen, however, reconvened in 1993 and 1994 to discuss the chaotic situation in Kandahar.

As Mullah Abdul Salam Zaeef – a key Taliban figure–interpreted the situation in early 1994, 'all over Afghanistan people faced the same situation; the entire province of Kandahar was crawling with rogue commanders and bandits lingering along the roads and cities.'[83] Allegedly, several mujahideen who operated in the earlier Taliban fronts approached Mullah Omar in 1994 with the request to respond collectively to the dire situation in Kandahar and other areas.[84] The founding meeting of what became the Taliban movement as we know it today took place in autumn 1994.[85] The initially fragmented political landscape of the civil war slowly transformed from 1994 onward due to the battlefield successes of the Taliban. By 5 November 1994, Taliban fighters had taken over Kandahar city. Initially, the Taliban's actions were reactive and not based on long-term goals.[86]

The movement, however, gained momentum and expanded from Kandahar province to Zabul, Helmand, and Uruzgan. It captured Herat in September 1995 and Jalalabad and Kabul in September 1996. The Taliban continued to target 'warlords who were deemed responsible for much of the destruction, instability, and chaos that plagued the country since the outbreak of the civil war.[87] An anti-Taliban front formed too late and was far from monolithic as its members kept subverting one another.[88] These rivalries rendered the opposition relatively ineffective even after Kabul fell to the Taliban.[89]

Traces of governance and legitimacy after the Soviet Union's withdrawal

The decline of legitimacy among the Taliban's opponents –including other mujahideen factions – during the early 1990s and the chaotic situation that followed set the stage for the Taliban's early success. The inability of various mujahideen factions to cooperate effectively weakened their legitimacy. The Taliban gradually expanded the reach of its Taliban courts nationwide from 1994 onward. In addition to the military advances, the movement presented itself as an organization with a strict religious ideology and the ability to reestablish law and order after years of disunity among various mujahideen and the exhausting civil wars.[90] Though the movement was certainly unable to live up to all its promises, it created a level of order in the areas it controlled. The civilian population had grown tired of the continuing wars between military commanders, and no credible end was in sight.[91] This context made the promises of the Taliban resonate, and large segments of the civilian population initially welcomed the Taliban's efforts to restore law and order.[92]

Phase one findings

During the presence of the Soviet forces, moral forms of legitimacy were most important, but pragmatic forms of legitimacy were also relevant. The early Taliban fronts derived their moral legitimacy from religious networks and sources. They claimed to be involved in a religiously 'justified' battle against 'foreign occupation.' Furthermore, some of the mujahideen courts already provided the Taliban fronts with a measure of pragmatic legitimacy. In the years after the Soviet withdrawal and the political fragmentation that followed, pragmatic forms of legitimacy became increasingly important, especially the Taliban's ability to provide law and order. These years laid the foundations for the IEA, as discussed below.

The Islamic Emirate of Afghanistan (1996–2001)

The Taliban captures Kabul, proclamation of the IEA

The second phase of Taliban rule followed the capture of Kabul in September 1996 and the proclamation of the IEA. Militarily, various commanders of Junbesh (Dostum), Jamiat-e Islami (i.e., Masoud, Rabbani, Atta Noor, and Ismail Khan), and Hezb-i Islami (Hekmatyar) continued to challenge the Taliban or had brief alliances with it but with limited success.[93] Overall, the Taliban was militarily successful and able to increase its control over Afghan territory significantly over these five years until the US-led intervention of 2001.

Governance during the IEA

The increased territorial control put the Taliban in a position to become more involved in governance.[94] During the IEA, the Taliban formed a two-track governance system, including a political–military leadership council based in Kandahar called the Supreme Council and an executive Council of Ministers in Kabul.[95] While the Supreme Council represented the Taliban as an insurgency, the Council of Ministers reflected the Taliban's efforts to transform into a state structure.[96] The Islamic clergy played a central role in the Taliban. In that sense, the Taliban's aspirations to govern marked a sharp break with long-standing Afghan political traditions. Despite the fact that religion had always played a significant role in Afghan politics, Muslim clerics had always functioned as servants of the state rather than its leaders.[97]

Given the role of the mullahs in the resistance against the Soviets, the clergy rose from 'social inferiority to a position of political power.'[98] That system of governance built on the unofficial power that mullahs already possessed: 'the power of the sermon.'[99] The position of mullahs strengthened when the Taliban regime turned them into the 'eyes and ears' in the villages and started to emphasize the collection of ushr and zakat, the religious taxes that traditionally made up the mullahs' income.[100] Although the Taliban has always claimed to implement sharia, there is an underlying ambiguity regarding its interpretation. As Otto notes, 'Like its counterpart "Islamic law" the term "sharia" is surrounded with confusion between theory and practice, between theological and legal meanings, between internal and external perspectives, and between past and present manifestations.'[101] There is not one static and uncontested sharia. There have been different interpretations throughout time, in various countries, and from various positions –e.g., lawmakers, judges, religious scholars, religious leaders, and academics.[102]

In fact, all Afghan constitutions except the Constitution of 1980 already endorsed the supremacy of sharia in Afghanistan, but the Taliban's interpretation of sharia was different from that of previous regimes.[103] During the IEA, the Taliban established its religious police, deployed by the Taliban's so-called Department for the Promotion of Virtue and the Prevention of Vice.[104] This department 'was given unlimited authority for the enforcement of all decrees issued by the Taliban Government.'[105] Its enforcement had a strong effect on public life, particularly for women. As Rashid notes, 'An announcement on Radio Kabul on 28 September 1996 stated that "thieves will have their hands and feet amputated, adulterers will be stoned to death and those drinking alcohol will be lashed." TV, video, satellite dishes, music, and games, including chess and football, were pronounced un-Islamic.'[106] Particularly women were discriminated against and severely constrained by the IEA regime. The regime essentially controlled every aspect of women's behaviour both in the private and public sphere.[107] As explained by Yassari and Saboory, women were:

> Forbidden to take employment, to appear in public without a male relative, to participate in government or public debate, and to receive secondary or higher education. As a result, women were deprived of the means to support themselves and their children. Only female doctors and nurses were allowed – under strict observation of the religious police – to work in hospitals or private clinics. These edicts were . . . enforced through summary and arbitrary punishment of women by the religious police.[108]

According to Edwards, the Taliban 'forced women in territory under their control to wear the burqa, the traditional Afghan head-to-toe veil that has a small patch of gauze over the eyes. They have declared that Saudi-style veils, which do not cover the eyes, are not allowed.'[109] The Taliban excluded women from all public places and enforced a strict code imposing the veiling and seclusion of women, and it banned all forms of entertainment.[110] The IEA's implementation of the law stood in stark contrast with that of the communist regime and with the norms and values of large segments of the population. As Yassari and Saboory explain:

> A decree issued in 1997 by Mullah Omar, the founder of the Taliban movement, declared that all the laws against the principles of Hanafi Islamic jurisprudence were not applicable. The Taliban announced via

the radio that after the seizure of Kabul, they would abolish all the laws and regulations of the communist regime and reintroduce the system of law that was in place during Zahir Shah's reign (1964-- 1973), with the exception of the provisions related to the king and the monarchy.[111]

During the IEA, the Taliban enforced a religious regime with a severe and coercive interpretation of sharia. [112] This included a violent display of public punishments, coercing the population to follow the rules that, among others, prohibited music, shaving beards, and flying kites and ordered the exclusion of women from public life.[113] Viewing themselves as custodians of Islamic justice, the Taliban courts were an important institution to materialize the Taliban's vision.[114] Its implementation of sharia through the mullahs had not been so prominent in the past because the Afghan state had assumed some of these functions.[115] Now that the Taliban had captured state institutions, it implemented its rules more widely and comprehensively.

Legitimacy during the IEA Pragmatic forms of legitimacy

While the Taliban was initially lauded for bringing a measure of security to the regions it captured, its social and religious policies were widely unpopular among the general public.[116] Its social and religious policies were met with resistance, particularly in the bigger cities.[117] Particularly in cities like Kabul and Mazar-e Sharif, the Taliban's conservative style of living contrasted with the modern lifestyle of much of the urban population and was confronted with pushback. For example, Wormer notes:

> *The commanders of the Taliban forces in Mazar-e Sharif did not stick to the agreement to share power with Malek Pahlawan and immediately introduced their interpretation of sharia law in the city instead. The Taliban soldiers closed the city's school as well as the university and tried to completely disarm all North Alliance militias, including Malek's. When some Wahdat units[118] resisted, an uprising against the Taliban broke out in one of the Hazara quarters and quickly seized the entire city. On 29 May, 1,000 to 1,500 Taliban soldiers were killed and nearly 3,000 captured.[119] To give another example, on 17 October 1996, over one hundred women in Herat protested against the closure of bath houses.[120] The women were beaten and arrested by the religious Taliban police, and men were warned to keep their women inside their houses.[121.]*

Moral forms of legitimacy

In April 1996, only a few months before the Taliban was able to capture Kabul, approximately 1,500 Islamic scholars from across Afghanistan gathered to meet. During this gathering, the Taliban's leader, Mullah Omar, was proclaimed the Amir ul-Mu-mineen ('Commander of the Faithful').[122] The proclamation aimed to project the universal nature of the movement that transcended tribal and ethnic divisions.[123] In its commissioned national anthem, the Taliban made no strong ethnic or Pashtun allusions; instead, it chose 'to refer to Islamic or other national symbols.'[124] The claimed legitimacy of the movement and its leadership was derived from Islam and was presented as standing in the tradition of previous caliphates.[125] The religious and political institutions merged into one person and one institution.

As Strick van Linschoten explains, 'some of the most symbolic and powerful/potent moments and statements from during the Taliban's rule come when the distinction was blurred; Mullah Mohammad Omar's assumption of the title amir ul-mu'mineen is perhaps the best example of this – a mosque was the site of what was directly a merger between religious and political spheres of activity.'[126] However, based on religious claims and sources, the Taliban's rule was not necessarily perceived as legitimate by the general public. Coercion strongly underpinned the Taliban's Emirate, which makes it questionable whether the extreme interpretations of religious sources attracted approval from the population.[127] Ibrahimi elaborates in that regard:

> *Although Afghanistan is an Islamic country and Islam has functioned as a source of legitimacy and jurisprudence for centuries, the Taliban's interpretation of Islam and its coercive approach to enforcing it was not broadly welcomed in the country. Except for individuals who joined the Taliban, the rest of the Afghan population, even the rural religious communities, did not tend to freely follow the Taliban's Islamism.*[128]

Moreover, in terms of legitimacy, the remaining perception of favouritism towards ethnic Pashtuns was a problem for the Taliban. The Taliban's ideology potentially allowed the movement to overcome ethnic, political, and regional barriers, but in practice, it failed to expand its core leadership beyond its parochial Pashtun base throughout the years.[129] As Ibrahimi explains:

> *. . . despite the Taliban's claim of being ethnically tolerant, there is numerous empirical data and evidence that indicate the IEA's ethnic-*

based behaviour. The IEA was entirely dominated by Pashtuns with other ethnic groups being excluded from the IEA's political and leadership arenas. For example, non-Pashtuns were largely excluded from the IEA's both governing councils, the Supreme Council and the Council of Ministers. Of the six original members of the Supreme Council, five were Pashtuns and only one ... was a Tajik from Badakhshan. Likewise, out of 17 members of the Council of Ministers in 1998, only two were non-Pashtuns.[130]

In a similar vein, Edwards's study indicates that the Taliban specifically encountered resistance from non-Pashtun communities. Most non-Pashtun groups showed 'little willingness to relinquish their hard-earned autonomy.'[131] Moreover, the ... *determination of the Taliban to impose their morality throughout the country ... further alienated groups with different and often considerably more liberal traditions (for example, with regard to female veiling and the right of individuals to worship as often and with whom they please) than those of the conservative and conformist Taliban.*[132]

A final problem regarding legitimacy during the IEA was the lack of a clear external enemy. What had 'glued' together some fighters of the mujahideen during the Soviet–Afghan war, for example, was a common enemy in the image of the Soviet Union and the Afghan government.[133] For the Taliban regime, the common enemy had become less obvious. As Barfield points out, 'In the absence of an external enemy, the Taliban found it difficult to gain legitimacy internally when so many Afghans saw its regime as too dominated by Pakistan and al Qaeda Arabs.'[134] Particularly from 1998 onward, the Taliban became more heavily reliant upon foreigners, such as Pakistani recruits from madrassas and international jihadis (e.g., Arabs, Uzbeks, and Chechens).[135]

Phase two findings

Although the Taliban proved to be militarily superior to its opponents during the 1990s, the movement faced several challenges once it was put to the test of governing the country. The Taliban was initially hailed for restoring order and security. Locally, this gave them a measure of pragmatic legitimacy. However, as the Taliban expanded its reach throughout the country, it became clear that its social and religious policies encountered fierce resistance, particularly in larger cities and within non-Pashtun communities. Moreover, an essential form of moral legitimacy disappeared during this phase due to the lack of a clear external enemy.

A return to ruling as insurgents (2001–2019)

Below, I discuss the third phase: the post-2001 insurgency. This analysis combines a macro perspective with a micro perspective of Chahar Dara district in Kunduz province. US-led intervention, the Taliban reverts to insurgency mode After the US and its allies ousted the Taliban regime from power in 2001, the Taliban leadership went into hiding, watching the events in Afghanistan unfold. The Taliban initially contemplated an inclusion in the new political system, but that seemed impossible given the US 'no talks with terrorists' policy.[136] Instead, the Taliban reverted to a strategy of insurgency. As early as April 2002, Taliban messaging re-appeared in Afghanistan in the form of night letters and leaflets, in which the movement called upon the population to resist the new Afghan government and its international allies.[137]

By mid-2003, the Taliban leadership had regrouped in Quetta, Pakistan. This is where the Rhabbari shura, also known as the Quetta shura, was established.[138] Based on a regional command structure, the initial council members were responsible for specific regions in Afghanistan.[139] During the resurgence phase of 2003 until 2005–2006, the Taliban re-emerged in most areas of Afghanistan.[140] In the first years, the structure transitioned from a state-like structure with ministries, a sub-national administration, and a security apparatus back to an insurgent or guerilla movement without a 'liberated zone' in which to establish a parallel government. Gradually, however, as its territory expanded, the Taliban became more involved in governance again.[141]

Governance during the post-2001 Taliban insurgency

With fluctuations over time, the movement controlled more territory and reestablished a parallel administration with provincial and district governors, judges, police, and intelligence commanders and a system of taxation.[142] Through its shadow judiciary and governors, the Taliban increasingly filled political spaces and regulated daily life in insurgent-controlled and contested territories.[143] The key development in governance has been the re-establishment and expansion of the Taliban's shadow judiciary.[144] By 2003, some of the Taliban courts had already re-emerged, though these were initially mainly reactive bodies that held sessions for specific events and issues.[145] If we consider Kunduz province, for instance, the Taliban judiciary was one of the main mechanisms that resolved judicial cases by 2018, but the exact figures are unknown.[146] Due to increased territorial control in Kunduz province, the Taliban judiciary expanded its reach.[147] A respondent from Chahar Dara confirmed that the 'Taliban has courts and judges, who resolve disputes based on Islamic Sharia and rules,'[148] and another respondent noted:

The Taliban might have one or two or more permanent judges, but it is also true that the Taliban uses a lot of mullahs of the mosque to resolve disputes. For example, there was a problem between families, then one day the imam of the mosque mediated and resolved the dispute. People knew that imam of the mosque had support from the Taliban. If anyone had had a problem with the decision, the imam could easily enforce it anyway due to the force of Taliban.[149]

In a recent study by the Afghanistan Analyst Network (AAN) in Dasht-e Archi district of Kunduz province, most respondents agreed that 'the Taliban "outgovern" the Afghan administration particularly in the justice sector in addressing disputes among local people.'[150] This is not because the Taliban judiciary system is perfectly organized but because the government justice system is essentially paralyzed, operating remotely from Kunduz city.[151] Locals tend to take their cases to Taliban courts because cases are generally 'adjudicated faster, without corruption and with satisfactory outcomes.'[152] The Taliban continues to implement its interpretation of sharia. According to one of the respondents, the Taliban 'make people pray on time in order to stay in accordance to Sharia.

[The Taliban] impose the veil, Chadari [burqa], on women in order to avoid bi Hejabi [unveiling]. Another example of their imposition is the prevention of people from playing music in their marriage parties. They even prevent the use of dollar currency.'[153] Another respondent noted that the Taliban 'prohibits youths to have smartphones. If anyone gets caught with a smartphone, the Taliban would severely punish that person.'[154] Another respondent mentioned that the Taliban representative in his village 'behaves respectfully with people and tries his best to resolve disputes. However, he hates government employees and always preaches that government employees are working for foreign infidels.

When Taliban members commit wrongdoing, he usually ignores the issue.'[155] Legitimacy during the post-2001 Taliban insurgency Pragmatic forms of legitimacy Continuing its efforts from the IEA, the obvious area for the Taliban to rebuild its political legitimacy after 2001 was its judiciary.[156] It has used the judiciary to legitimize itself, condemning the corruption in the Afghan state and providing an alternative. Weigand indicates that the ability to resolve disputes is one of the main sources of legitimacy for the Taliban.[157] According to Weigand, 'What matters much more [to the people] is the perception of the Taliban as being less corrupt than the state.'[158] Similarly, a respondent in my study explained, 'We do not have any issue with any group; the government and the Taliban do not differ much for us. We want a governing body that can keep people secure, and it should be in accordance with Islam. Otherwise, we have no problem with them; we just want peace.[159] A Pashtun farmer from Chahar Dara noted, 'People like that there is no robbery . . . in this Taliban-controlled area.'[160] Similar to other insurgent courts, the Taliban courts act as a measure of legitimacy and reach as well as an instrument used to extend and entrench that legitimacy.[161]

Moral forms of legitimacy

The Taliban has incorporated the international troop presence into its nationalistic narrative. Nationalism has been a key element of the Taliban's communications, beyond a purely Pashtun-centric message.[162] The purpose of that narrative has been to unite 'all Afghans' against foreign occupation. The narrative often includes references to the past, such as the hardships during resistance against the Soviets, the British, Genghis Khan, and Alexander the Great.[163] This nationalistic source of legitimacy gained more prominence in the post-2001 timeframe. The Taliban's interpretation of the post-2001 situation became a religious fight that continued against another 'foreign invader' with a 'puppet' Afghan regime.[164] The current framing corresponds to that during the Afghan–Soviet war: Non-religious outsiders occupy 'our' land in cooperation with an 'ingenuine' Afghan regime. The message conveyed is that the current coalition forces are the same as the Soviet army in 1980s.[165]

As in the earlier timeframes, the Taliban's policy has been to re-establish an Islamic system based on its interpretation of sharia. As Johnson notes, 'The Taliban continue to use Islamic piety, based loosely on the strict dogmatic Deobandi interpretation of Islam, to construct a jihadist image that evokes righteousness and greater justification to their violent anti-government military campaign.[166] The Taliban's perspective continues to be that all Muslims have a duty to protect their religion if it is threatened.[167] A 23-year-old farmer in Chahar Dara echoed the Taliban's interpretations and his own perceived religious duty: 'We are Muslims and follow the holy Quran. Islam mandates us to stop the current corrupt government and withstand foreigners who intend to destroy our country and distance us from Islam.[168] Others do not share the Taliban's religious interpretations and note, for example, that 'the Taliban have provided wrong interpretations of Jihad to locals, and they have brainwashed people through politicizing Islam and portraying a violent understanding of Jihad.'[169]

In a similar vein, a 43-year-old Pashtun school teacher from Chahar Dara stated, 'We are all Muslims, and we know what Islam is, the principles have been taught to us . . . The Islam that Taliban represents is not the true one; they are extremists, while Islam in every aspect of life always encourages people to choose moderation. This is the reason people do not always follow the rules that are enforced by the Taliban.'[170] According to a 28- year-old Uzbek from Chahar Dara, 'People have different opinions regarding the truth or falsehood of Taliban rules. Many believe the rules to be in compliance with Islam since they are uneducated and have insufficient religious knowledge. Meanwhile, the majority thinks that the current state is corrupt and non-Islamic, a sufficient reason that provokes many to fight against it.'[171] Regarding the rightfulness of the Taliban's interpretation of sharia and Islam in general, the expressions of the respondents oppose one another. A common religious symbol employed by the Taliban is its white flag with black text. As one of the respondents noted, 'The only thing about Taliban that is common everywhere is their flag.'[172] Usually the flag is inscribed with the shahadah, the Islamic profession of faith, but sometimes it reads 'Islamic Emirate of Afghanistan.' Since 2001, the Taliban has focused more on this outlook. As Osman notes,

> *The Taliban appear to have woken up to the importance of organisational symbols and their political meaning. Compared to how little they cared about their image during the 1990s and the initial years of the insurgency, the Taliban now project an increasing consciousness of their "brand." This is seen in both their media and the actions of fighters and officials on the ground.*[173]

Furthermore, the Taliban uses shabnameh, the so-called night letters.[174] As Johnson explains, night letters 'have been a traditional and common instrument of Afghan religious figures, jihadists and rebels to encourage people, especially (but not exclusively) rural populations to oppose both state authority and regulations.'[175] Common symbolism the Taliban uses in these night letters and other correspondence include stamps of the Islamic Emirate of Afghanistan.[176] The stamps indicate the formal nature of the documents issued by Taliban representatives, such as local imams. As a respondent pointed out, 'the Taliban have a particular stamp that they use to validate their letters.[177] similarly, a 28- year-old Uzbek respondent noted, 'Local imams also have stamps. Once, I went before a governor to address a problem. He asked me for a letter from the mosque imam confirming that I was a resident of Chahar Dara. When I referred to the imam, he issued the letter and stamped it, confirming me as a resident of the district. The stamp is credible in all commissions and Taliban-related offices.[178]

A 35-year-old Pashtun farmer noted, 'The Taliban uses its own paperwork, such as summoning letters.'[179] Johnson emphasizes in his study on Taliban night letters that it is nearly impossible to evaluate how the Taliban's night-letter campaign has contributed to support for the Taliban, but he indicates that 'Taliban narratives have clearly resonated' and 'where their messages have not resonated with the populace, the Taliban has compensated by waging an effective intimidation campaign.'[180] In the post-2001 timeframe, the Taliban has learned from earlier strategic misjudgments and tends to be more inclusive towards non-Pashtun communities. Particularly in the North, the Taliban has included different ethnicities. In Badakhshan, for instance, the Taliban started to recruit and install non-Pashtuns in key provincial positions and as fighters.[181]

This is remarkable since Badakhshan was a stronghold of long-term Taliban rival Ahmad Shah Masoud and a province that was not conquered during the IEA regime before 2001. As Ali notes, 'From 2008, and in sharp contrast to behaviour exhibited during the Taliban regime (1994–2001), the Taliban leadership council offered most local posts to this new generation of local Taliban, instead of merely using Badakhshani recruits from Pakistani madrassas as foot-soldiers.'[182] The Taliban has often been characterized as a Pashtun movement, but currently it is more accurately a movement with many Pashtun members.[183] Finally, in several of the interviews, the practice of bacha bazi[184] was mentioned. There is no clear legal definition of bacha bazi, but it generally refers to 'local powerful individuals keeping one or more boys, typically between 10 to 18 of age, for use as bodyguards, servants, dancers, and for sexual exploitation or other forms of harassment.'[185] Bacha bazi involves men in positions of power who exploit, enslave, and abuse young boys sexually or for entertainment.[186] Not every police chief is involved in bacha bazi, but it is a common practice.[187]

Bacha bazi seems most prevalent in northern Afghanistan, where it is associated with local militias and state security commanders.[188] Human Rights Watch reported that perpetrators of the sexual abuse of boys are rarely prosecuted, which can be partly explained by taboos regarding the issue, but is primarily 'because the perpetrators are often members of powerful militias or have the protection of state security forces.'[189] Based on the perceptions of the respondents, the Taliban positions itself as an organization that effectively counters bacha bazi and other 'forbidden practices.' A Pashtun farmer from Chahar Dara noted, 'People like that there is no robbery, that there is no gambling in this Taliban-controlled area.

There is no bacha bazi. People's sons are not taken by force for bacha bazi because some government commanders take underage boys by force to their checkpoints where they sexually abuse them.'[190] Similarly, another farmer from Chahar Dara noted, 'bacha bazi is a very bad thing; it is not allowed by the Taliban. People love and support the Taliban for stopping bacha bazi. In the same way, people hate the government for being involved in bacha bazi, because we know that almost each commander of the police has one or more boys who they use for dancing and for sex.'[191] Already during the 1990 s the Taliban opposed the practice of bacha bazi as one of its claims to a legitimate authority, and it continues to do so.[192] The Taliban deliberately refers to the actions of the Afghan security forces and pro-government militias as a source of its own legitimacy and uses them to justify its own policies.

Phase three findings

The beginning of the 21st century revealed new possibilities for the Taliban movement in terms of moral legitimacy and pragmatic legitimacy. With the international troop presence, the Taliban has faced an external enemy that is more clearly identifiable. The aspirations for the Islamic Emirate of Afghanistan–the name the Taliban continues to employ–have gradually revived against the backdrop of the US-led intervention. Moral legitimacy has become more important, as evident in the narratives about foreign occupation and religion being under threat by external forces. Pragmatic legitimacy continues to be relevant given the Taliban's ability to resolve disputes. The Taliban judiciary thereby exploits instances of corruption and incompetence of the Afghan state.

Conclusions

This article has made empirical and conceptual contributions. Empirically, it has shown that both pragmatic and moral forms of legitimacy have been relevant throughout these three phases of Taliban rule. In terms of pragmatism, the Taliban's ability to create a relatively safe and stable environment and to adjudicate disputes has been a legitimating factor for the movement. As Roy noted, if an actor in the context of the Afghan state appears as a relatively honest broker between local factions, clans, tribes, and ethnic groups, even if some are more favoured than others, it can be a major source of legitimacy[193] This finding also underpins Weigand's observation that 'the people's immediate concern is having any rule of law – regardless of its ideological sources.'[194] Moral sources of legitimacy, however, have certainly not been irrelevant.

The Taliban's narrative of a 'justified' struggle in the name of Islam and against external interference has provided them with a level of legitimacy as well, particularly in reference to external forces. Overall, the moral forms of legitimacy were more prominent during the presence of external forces, while pragmatic forms became more prominent following their withdrawal and during periods of the Taliban's opponents' ineffective governance. Complementary to the existing literature, this article has demonstrated the value of a longitudinal perspective on rebel governance and legitimacy. The post-2001 Taliban insurgency was not new to governing; it used prior networks, claims, and experiences. Several claims to legitimacy and policies continued albeit with small adjustments based contextual changes. Understanding rebel governance and legitimacy, therefore, also requires researchers to consider the contemporary history of armed conflict.

As Schroder and Schmidt previously noted, the 'symbolic meaning of prior wars is re-enacted and reinterpreted in the present.'[195] During the Soviet timeframe, the pre-Taliban fronts mobilized based on a perceived legitimate struggle against an external enemy that invaded Afghanistan. In the post-2001 timeframe, the foreign enemy image re-appeared in the form of the international coalition forces. Together with the corruption and ineffective governance by the state, the narrative of a nationalistic and 'necessary' armed resistance has been revived. Finally, this article has contributed to the existing literature by investigating how external intervention in support of the incumbent government affects the rebels' opportunities to govern and the dynamics of rebel legitimacy. It expands upon other studies that have either focused on external support for rebel groups or the strategies rebel groups employ to gain international legitimacy and/or recognition.

External intervention has contrasting effects on rebel governance and specific forms of moral legitimacy. On the one hand, external intervention decreases the number of opportunities of rebel groups to govern; on the other hand, external intervention increases the potential resonance of moral forms of rebel legitimacy. The departure of external forces also has contrasting effects on governance and moral forms of legitimacy. Withdrawal can create more opportunities for rebel governance as it opens political space while simultaneously undermining specific earlier forms of moral legitimacy when the rebels had a clearly identifiable external enemy.

Acknowledgments

Many thanks go to the Netherlands Organisation for Scientific Research (NWO) and the Hofvijverkring in The Hague for their financial contributions to this research project. I am indebted to The Liaison Office (TLO) in Kabul for its hospitality and invaluable contributions to this project. Finally, many thanks to (in alphabetical order) Rahmatullah Amiri, Sebastian van Baalen, Chris van der Borgh, Jolle Demmers, Toon Dirkx, Georg Frerks, Nelson Kasfir, Bart Klem, Jessica Maves-Braithwaite, and Nora Stel for their feedback, inspiration, and support at various stages of this research. Disclosure statement: No potential conflict of interest was reported by the author(s). Funding: This work was supported by the Netherlands Organisation for Scientific Research (NWO) [322-52-012]; and the Hofvijverkring, the Hague. Notes on contributor: Niels Terpstra is a PhD candidate and lecturer at the Centre for Conflict Studies, Utrecht University. His research interest centre around the nature of governance as carried out by non-state (armed) actors during violent conflict and policies of peace and state building during third-party interventions. His regional focus is on South Asia, particularly Afghanistan and Sri Lanka. ORCID: Niels Terpstra is the best analysts and research scholar on Rebel governance in Afghanistan.http://orcid.org/0000-0003-2707-5259. Small Wars & Insurgencies ISSN: 0959-2318 (Print) 1743-9558 (Online) Journal. From Rebel to Quasi-State: Governance, Diplomacy and Legitimacy in the Midst of Afghanistan's Wars (1979–2001) Romain Malejacq To cite this article: Romain Malejacq (2017) From Rebel to Quasi-State: Governance, Diplomacy and Legitimacy in the Midst of Afghanistan's Wars (1979–2001), Small Wars & Insurgencies, 28:4-5, 867-886, DOI: 10.1080/09592318.2017.1322332 To link to this article: https://doi.org/10. 1080/09592318.2017.1322332 © 2017 The Author(s). Published by Informa UK Limited, trading as Taylor & Francis Group Published online: 26 Jul 2017. Small Wars & Insurgencies, 2017 VOL. 28, NOS. 4–5, 867–886 https://doi.org/10.1080/0 9592318.2017.1322332. © 2017 The Author(s). Published by Informa UK Limited, trading as Taylor & Francis Group.
 Small Wars & Insurgencies provides an international and interdisciplinary forum for the academic and scholarly discussion of the historical, political, social, economic and psychological aspects of insurgency, counter-insurgency, limited war and irregular warfare. Peer-reviewed and long-established, Small Wars & Insurgencies invites papers concerned with, but not limited to, the following areas: insurgencies and guerrilla conflicts past and present, counterinsurgencies including national doctrines, terrorist movements and ideologies, irregular warfare and the debates on its historiography, peacekeeping and "humanitarian intervention". Essential reading, Small Wars & Insurgencies facilitates the discussion of historians, political scientists and students of International Relations and Security Studies on theoretical and practical issues related to the past, present and future of this critical

area of both international and domestic politics. The journal is historically focused and is keen to see contributions from scholars using primary and archival sources, as well as interviews. It also welcomes contributions investigating media, literary and cinema representations of insurgencies, counter-insurgencies and irregular warfare. Most issues include an authoritative review section, and the journal's policy is to have 2–3 special issues each year devoted to specific themes and issues, often edited by guest editors. Taylor & Francis make every effort to ensure the accuracy of all the information (the "Content") contained in our publications. However, Taylor & Francis, our agents, and our licensors make no representations or warranties whatsoever as to the accuracy, completeness, or suitability for any purpose of the Content. Any opinions and views expressed in this publication are the opinions and views of the authors, and are not the views of or endorsed by Taylor & Francis. The accuracy of the Content should not be relied upon and should be independently verified with primary sources of information. Taylor & Francis shall not be liable for any losses, actions, claims, proceedings, demands, costs, expenses, damages, and other liabilities whatsoever or howsoever caused arising directly or indirectly in connection with, in relation to, or arising out of the use of the Content.

Chapter 3

Afghanistan's Taliban: Legitimate Jihadists or Coercive Extremists?

Florian Weigand

Abstract

The military intervention in Afghanistan in 2001 was portrayed as a fight to oust the extremist Taliban. But the Taliban have long been regaining influence, with the military victory of the Afghan government and its foreign allies now seeming less likely than ever. In light of these developments, this article investigates what the affected people – rather than the foreign interveners – think about the Taliban, and whether they perceive them as coercive or legitimate. Building on a conceptual understanding of legitimacy that has been adjusted to the dynamics of conflict-torn spaces, the article suggests that people judge the Taliban on the basis of how their day-to-day behaviour is perceived. While the Taliban are a coercive threat in urban centres and other areas where they launch attacks, they nonetheless manage to construct legitimacy in some of the places which they control or can access easily. A major source of their legitimacy in these areas is the way in which they provide services – such as conflict resolution – which some people consider to be faster and fairer than the state's practices.

Introduction

The Taliban are usually depicted as ideological fighters – religious extremists who want to introduce harsh rules in Afghanistan, including the prohibition of music and the suppression of women. Their mode of governance stands in stark contrast to Western ideals, with the fall of the Taliban government in 2001 being portrayed as a victory against terrorism and human rights abuses. However, the influence of the Taliban and other armed opposition groups is steadily growing again throughout Afghanistan. They describe themselves as 'jihadists' that fight against the government and its foreign supporters. According to a report for the United States (US) Congress, not even 60 percent of the country's districts were under Afghan government control or influence in 2017 (SIGAR 2017, 87). At the same time the US is welcoming direct peace talks with the Taliban (Tolo News, February 24, 2016). This development raises the question as to what the affected people – rather than the foreign interveners – think about the Taliban.

In response, this article sets out to investigate the reasons why people in Afghanistan view the Taliban as legitimate or illegitimate. Such an analysis can help to move away from peacebuilding and statebuilding efforts, which rest on ideological assumptions of what ought to be built, to policies grounded in an understanding of what the affected people think. The article also helps to deal with the difficulty of conceptualizing legitimacy in conflict-torn spaces. To enable an analysis of legitimacy, a framework is developed herein that builds on the traditional understanding of authority and legitimacy, but which considers the characteristics of contexts with a low degree of monopolization of force. Three analytical ideal types are proposed that can help to explain obedience to social control: coercion, which achieves obedience through force and threats; instrumental legitimacy, which 'buys' obedience by responding to needs; and the traditional more substantive understanding of legitimacy, which is underpinned by shared values and a belief in rightfulness. This framework is applied to an empirical analysis of the local perceptions of authority in Afghanistan. Insights into these perceptions were gained through an extensive number of interviews, conducted in different parts of Afghanistan in 2014 and 2015.[1]

This paper draws on those interviews that were collected in the eastern province Nangarhar. It uses selected interviews to illustrate the findings of the wider analysis of perceptions in the province. At the time of these interviews, some districts of Nangarhar were under government rule and others were opposition-controlled. The interviews present a snapshot of the situation – and its perception – at a certain time, but more importantly they indicate that people judge the Taliban on the basis of what they actually do, and consider them to be legitimate or illegitimate depending on their day-to-day behaviour. In the government-controlled areas, the behaviour of the Taliban is perceived to be threatening and illegitimate by many, if not most. The main concern of people in these areas is not religious extremism but the attacks the Taliban launch and the instability they cause.

But in territories under Taliban control– as well as in some territories that are government-controlled which the Taliban can access –some people consider the Taliban to be legitimate. The findings suggest that this legitimacy is often not underpinned by 'big' ideological concerns, whether traditional or religious, but by the perception of being treated better by the Taliban than by the government. For instance, the Taliban successfully construct legitimacy by providing conflict resolution in a way that is perceived to be accessible, fast and fair. In the massively corrupt and volatile political order of Afghanistan, people appear to be longing mainly to be treated with respect and as equals, caring less about which code of law is actually applied. In some cases, the Taliban seem to be responding to these local demands better than the government.

Authority and legitimacy in conflict-torn spaces

The literature on legitimacy usually deals with political orders that are characterized by a high degree of monopolization of force. In such static settings, researchers can conceptually distinguish the institutionalized 'state' from the 'people' who bestow legitimacy. In this way, one can drill into the rational–legal source of legitimacy and investigate, for instance, how different policies affect a state's legitimacy. However, in a conflict-torn space there is, by definition, a contestation of at least two authorities, if not more. This conflict does not take place within the institutionalized structures of the state but outside of them. Usually, the state is part of the conflict, fighting with armed opposition groups, whether they are called rebels, militias, insurgents or terrorists.

In such a dynamic setting, the analysis of legitimacy becomes more complex due to the multiple referent objects, multiple audiences and multiple potential sources of legitimacy (von Billerbeck and Gippert 2017; Weigand 2015). The empirical analysis of a complex concept like legitimacy in such a dynamic setting requires a well-defined framework. It is suggested that in order to conceptualize the political order of conflict-torn spaces– the context in which legitimacy 'happens'–the static understanding of the Weberian ideal-typical state should be left behind. Adopting such blinkers narrows the focus down to the degree of monopolization of force in a defined territory. As a consequence, conflict-torn spaces are easily dismissed as 'failed' or 'fragile' states, a category based more on the absence rather than the existence of characteristics, and hence devoid of much analytical leverage. In order to focus on what is rather than what is not, herein the political order is considered to be dynamic and in a constant process of transformation.

In line with scholars such as Migdal and Schlichte (2005), political order is viewed in the present study as a constantly changing arena of competition involving multiple authorities. As Agnew points out, 'political authority is not restricted to states and ... is thereby not necessarily exclusively territorial' (2005, 441). Hence, choosing authority as the unit of analysis allows more flexibility in dealing with the globalized world order (see Kaldor 2009). Nonetheless, for this view on political order Weber's work is still considered to be fundamental. The understanding of authority which informs the present study is influenced by the German term Herrschaft, suggesting an analysis of governance beyond government. Weber defines the term as 'the chance of a specific (or: of all) command(s) being obeyed by a specifiable group of people' (1980, 122). Building on Weber, the expression authority is used to describe social control both as a relationship of command and obedience[2] and, accordingly, the (commanding) actor or entity to whose social control a group of people obeys.

The question driving this research is why people accept or even support an authority and obey. Conceptually speaking there are two options: either people want to obey or they have to obey. The voluntary obedience is based on legitimacy, whereas involuntary obedience is based on coercion. If authority rests on coercion then people are threatened or forced to obey in a violent or non-violent way.[3] The definition of legitimacy as voluntary obedience to social control is in line with traditional empirical definitions of legitimacy (e.g. Levi et al. 2009)–however, its referent object is not necessarily the state or government, but can be any authority. Further developing the conceptual understanding of legitimacy, it is suggested that a distinction should be made between two different kinds of theoretical reasons for voluntary obedience, which reflect two fundamentally different ways of looking at legitimacy.

For this purpose, the rational assessment of usefulness of authority is termed instrumental legitimacy, describing the extent to which an authority responds to needs. People may voluntarily obey authority simply because it is beneficial, or else because they have no alternative. But instrumental legitimacy is of a short-term nature, and only lasts as long as people benefit, or hope to do so in future. Instrumental definitions of legitimacy are implicit in policy literature through suggestions aiming at enhancing legitimacy through service delivery or improved performance. Substantive legitimacy, meanwhile is a more abstract normative judgement –a belief in rightfulness which is underpinned by shared values. Substantive definitions of legitimacy are dominant in the social science literature and go beyond the simple assessment of advantages and disadvantages, as they are centred on beliefs.

If a person believes that an entity has the right to exercise social control, he or she may also accept personal disadvantages. Hence, according to Weber, belief in the legitimacy of an authority [Legitimitätsglauben] is necessary to achieve long-term voluntary obedience (1980, 122). The most complex of these ideal types is substantive legitimacy. While coercion rests on force and threats, and instrumental legitimacy rests on the provision of goods and services, there are various sources of substantive legitimacy which can be categorized in different ways. Weber famously distinguishes between rational-legal, charismatic and traditional legitimacy, underpinning the belief in the right to exercise social control (2009, 78–79). Most of the contemporary literature on sources of legitimacy focuses more specifically on legitimacy within rational-legal systems that require a high degree of monopolization of force.

For instance, Scharpf (1997) describes input and output legitimacy as two dimensions of a democratic system, where output goes beyond simple service delivery and is linked to the input of the people through representative institutions that ensure accountability. And the psychology literature, looking particularly at democratic policing, suggests considering the procedures of how police officers interact with the public (e.g. Tyler 2004, 2006; Jackson et al. 2013; Mazerolle et al. 2013). Empirical research can help improve the understanding of the extent to which these concepts can also be used to explain voluntary obedience in a conflict-torn space with a low degree of monopolization of force.[4]

In a nutshell, this article proposes three analytical ideal types which explain why people may obey social control. Coercion forces people to obey. If authority rests on the traditional understanding of legitimacy, or what is called herein substantive legitimacy, people obey because they believe in the rightfulness of authority. This belief may, among other potential sources, result from traditions or rational–legal structures. Instrumental legitimacy, underpinned by usefulness, fills the conceptual gap between these two explanations for obedience. This is obviously a purely conceptual exercise. The categories are interconnected, and in almost every empirical case different sources of authority will play a role. The analytical distinction does not necessarily contradict any conclusion on the relationship between the concepts.

While normative definitions set the criteria with which to assess authority and legitimacy, these empirical concepts rest on Weber's general approach of making research as independent as possible from the researcher's own views and values (Beetham 1991). Hence, the framework allows researchers to work more inductively and investigate the perceptions of different groups of people to explain why they obey social control. The framework can be applied to analyse the sources of authority and legitimacy, independent of the political system in which the authorities operate and the degree of monopolization of force involved. On this basis, this framework is used to analyse the perceptions of people who are affected by the Taliban in Afghanistan and then draw conclusions about the basis of their authority and legitimacy. This, in turn, can also help to create a better theoretical understanding of the mechanisms that explain obedience to authority, especially with regard to sources of substantive legitimacy in conflict-torn spaces.

The Taliban in Afghanistan

The Taliban's history and claim of legitimacy

The 'armed opposition' or 'insurgency' groups in Afghanistan today are commonly associated with the label 'Taliban'. Indeed, after successfully turning an insurgency into a government in 1996 and being toppled again in 2001, the Taliban have returned to insurgency strategies to subvert the current government and its foreign allies. However, armed opposition today is a complex phenomenon, consisting of various groups and factions that change alliances fairly readily. The history of the Taliban is closely linked to the 'jihad' against the Soviet occupation of Afghanistan and the subsequent civil war.[5]

In response to the occupation, multiple Mujaheddin groups in the country took up arms to fight the Soviets, often with the support of Western countries that were channelling money and weapons through the Pakistani intelligence agency, the Inter-Services Intelligence (ISI) (Coll 2004). After the Soviet withdrawal from Afghanistan in 1989 and the fall of the pro-Soviet Najibullah government that held Kabul until 1992, the Mujaheddin groups turned against each other. Afghanistan quickly disintegrated into multiple regions controlled by different strongmen, fighting each other with changing alliances. At that time, the southern province of Kandahar was also divided. As foreign funding dried out in the province, competing commanders began to mistreat the population and extract money; the highways were littered with checkpoints of various groups who put chains across the road and demanded tolls (Strick van Linschoten and Kuehn 2012, 113–117; Rashid 2001, 22).

A number of Mujaheddin–many of whom had stopped fighting since the fall of the Najibullah government and returned to study at madrassas [religious schools] in Quetta and Kandahar – became increasingly concerned and disillusioned (Rashid 2001). In response, they formed a group around their leader Mullah Omar to 'restore peace, disarm the population, enforce Sharia law and defend the integrity and Islamic character of Afghanistan' (Rashid 2001, 22). They 'distanced themselves from the party politics of the Mujaheddin and signalled that they were a movement for cleansing society rather than a party trying to grab power' (23), calling themselves 'Taliban'– the 'students' or those 'seeking knowledge'.

However, this narrative of the history of the Taliban is disputed. Barfield (2010, 257) points to an alternative story of Pakistan shifting its support away from the strongman Hekmatyar and instead helping to form the Taliban to fight the new government in Kabul. In any case, the Taliban were successful in gaining local legitimacy quickly, as they portrayed themselves as a 'Robin Hood' taking a stand against Kandahari warlords (Rashid 2001, 25). Their popularity grew steadily, with more and more people joining the Taliban. By late 1994, the Taliban had taken control of Kandahar, and on 26 September 1996, they took Kabul (Barfield 2010, 258–260; Strick van Linschoten and Kuehn 2012, 144). While the Taliban expanded their influence further to the north, they introduced a new political order for the territory they controlled. They called this territory the Islamic Emirate of Afghanistan, which was governed by Mullah Omar, who had been proclaimed Amir Ul Mumineen [Commander of the Faithful], and a small shura [council] of selected people.

While they claimed to be implementing Islam, their way of de facto governing included many elements of the Pashtun's cultural code, the Pashtunwali. Building on this mix of values and ideas they enforced strict rules, including the prohibition of music and the exclusion of women from public life, which stood in sharp contrast to the lifestyle of the population in urban places like Kabul and Mazar-e Sharif (Barfield 2010, 261–263). They taxed the people, asking everyone to pay zakat–a form of income tax – and making farmers pay ushr [Islamic tithe], 10 percent of their produce (Nojumi 2002, 155). Meanwhile, a number of strongmen and their militias tried to defend the north of the country against the Taliban, banding together as the United Islamic Front for the Salvation of Afghanistan, which is also known as the Northern Alliance.

When the US and the United Kingdom (UK) launched so-called Operation Enduring Freedom in October 2001, their air support enabled the Northern Alliance to quickly advance and capture Kabul in November of the same year. The Taliban first retreated to Kandahar before going underground, with some of their commanders moving to Pakistan. They were excluded from the negotiations on the future of Afghanistan in Bonn in December 2001, in which–apart from the international community – mainly strongmen of the Northern Alliance participated. These negotiations resulted in the establishment of the International Security Assistance Force (ISAF).

While the Taliban were no longer of much relevance for the international community, they reorganized in the Afghan–Pakistani border area and began fighting again as an insurgency. Today the Taliban, who still call themselves the 'Islamic Emirate', claim legitimacy by portraying themselves as 'jihadists', fighting against the 'occupying' US forces and the 'infidel' government forces.[6] This rhetoric underpins most of the Taliban's public statements on their websites al-emarah and shahamat,[7] which are used to justify attacks and announce the beginning of the annual 'fighting season' in spring (D'Souza 2016, 24). For instance, in April 2016 the Taliban declared:

The Islamic Emirate's armed Jihad against the American invasion has completed fourteen years and is now in its fifteenth year. Jihad against the aggressive and usurping infidel army is a holy obligation upon our necks and our only recourse for reestablishing an Islamic system and regaining our independence (Shahamat English, April 12, 2016).[8]

Indeed, despite the ongoing international support, it is estimated that, in 2017, only 59.7 percent of Afghanistan's districts were under the control or influence of the Afghan government, with the insurgents controlling 11.1 percent and the remaining 29.2 percent of the districts being contested (SIGAR 2017, 88).[9] The fighting over the major city of Kunduz in the north of Afghanistan in 2015/16 illustrates that there is a chance of insurgency control continuing to expand, even into urban areas. However, while the numbers look impressive, the Taliban are also considered to be responsible for a large amount of civilian casualties (UNAMA 2017). Furthermore, the Taliban today are a fragmented movement, as illustrated by the complexity of the insurgency in Loya Pakita:

It is composed of four different strands. There are two networks led by the Haqqani and the Mansur families respectively. Besides them, there are Taliban groups acting independently from these two networks, led directly by the Taliban Rahbari or Ali Shura (Leadership or Supreme Council) or by individual influential commanders in Quetta. (Ruttig 2009, 59)

But the exact relationship between the various groups remains unclear. Ruttig concludes: 'The Haqqani and Mansur networks are clearly part of the Taliban universe ... but their modus operandi is that of semi-independent warlords who have joined the rather heterogeneous insurgency movement for reasons of expediency' (2009, 88).[10] Probably the best-known institution of the Taliban is the Quetta Shura. Mullah Omar used to be its head, with Mohammad Mansur as his deputy. In addition, there is the socalled Peshawar Shura, which has allegedly gained importance since Pakistan's ISI started shifting funds away from the Quetta Shura after it began opening up for negotiations and trying to open an office in Qatar (Martin 2014, 208). The fragmentation of the Taliban appears to have continued since Mullah Omar was revealed to have died in 2013. In July 2015, Mohammad Mansur was announced as Mullah Omar's successor (Giustozzi and Mangal 2015). However, members of the Rahbari Shura publicly complained about this decision, with one group led by Mohammad Rasoul – who fought the Soviets together with Mullah Omar – openly declaring war.

Meanwhile, the head of the Haqqani Network, Jalaludin Haqqani, was appointed as a deputy of Mansur (Osman 2015). Mansur was subsequently killed in a US drone strike in Pakistan in May 2016 and replaced by Mawlawi Haibatullah Akhundzada. However, according to Farrell and Semple (2017), Akhundzada is considered to be a weak leader by many within the Taliban, contributing to an ongoing fragmentation of Afghanistan's armed opposition. This fragmentation on the macro level is complemented by similar processes on the micro level. For instance, Smith describes the dynamics of the insurgency in Kandahar, explaining that 'there is no evidence that the formal structure of the insurgency has any real importance' (2009, 193). He points out that the Taliban in Kandahar are a much more dynamic and fluid 'entity', consisting of different units (see also Jackson and Giustozzi 2012).[11]

The Taliban's public legitimacy While the Taliban portray themselves and claim legitimacy on the basis of being 'jihadists' and wanting to 're-establish an Islamic system', it remains unclear how their legitimacy is perceived by Afghans. The importance of gaining a better understanding of what underpins legitimacy in the Afghan context has been widely acknowledged. Scholars working on peacebuilding, state-building, development and the international intervention in Afghanistan have emphasized that a major reason for failure is one of legitimacy (e.g. Goodhand and Sedra 2013; Kühn 2008; Roy 2004). While the international approach in Afghanistan focused on gaining legitimacy in the intervener's countries, local perceptions of what is legitimate – or not – were often ignored (Rubin 2006, 184–185) or misconstrued (Coleman 2017).

Building on this realization, most of the literature on legitimacy in Afghanistan looks at the state and the government. More quantitative, survey-based studies focus almost exclusively on service delivery, indicating an instrumental understanding of legitimacy. For instance, Sabarre et al. (2013, 17) conclude that 'perceptions of security are key indicators of legitimacy scores'. Scholars with a more substantive understanding of legitimacy often claim that local customs are crucial; pointing at what Weber would call traditional legitimacy. For example, Libel emphasizes the importance of the Pashtunwali over religion for the Pashtuns in the south and east of Afghanistan:

> *Pushtuns have tended to accept any government and its civic laws as long as the government is controlled by Pushtuns and follows the basics of the Pashtunwali, and as long as its governmental laws and decisions are sanctioned by Pushtun jirgas. (Liebl 2007, 507)*

The notion that legitimacy in Afghanistan is linked to traditions has also been adopted in the policy world. A USAID study claims: 'Legitimacy begins with empowering the local level with traditional decision-making processes and from there, slowly establishing links with the Weberian rational-legal institutions of the state can ensure accountability' (Melton 2015, 4). Conversely, other scholars point out that there are more general requirements which the state needs to fulfil to be considered legitimate. Barfield and Nojumi argue that historically, the government delegated authority to non-state actors, acting as mediators for grievances on the local level; according to their analysis, '[t]his system was highly functional and grounded in local perceptions of fairness and trust.

It crossed ethnic, linguistic and tribal boundaries with ease because it was in the interest of all parties to cooperate' (2010, 42). Similarly, Roy argues that the 'Afghan identity is based on a common political culture' (2004, 173). He suggests three criteria that the state in Afghanistan needs to fulfil to be considered legitimate: building on the concept of Afghanistan being an independent Muslim territory, acting as a mediating broker between competing groups and providing basic services. The Taliban's legitimacy post 2001 on the other hand has not been investigated much. Perception data indicates that public support for armed opposition groups in Afghanistan has been decreasing since 2009. According to the Asia Foundation (2016, 7), only 16.7 percent of the people in areas their researchers can access have sympathy for armed opposition groups today.

But this does not explain why people support the Taliban or consider them to be legitimate. Some of the sources of legitimacy that are discussed in the context of the Afghan state may also matter for the Taliban–in particular, 'tradition' in the form of the Pashtunwali could still play a key role. Liebl (2007) suggests that the people's expectations in the Pashtun areas of Afghanistan regarding governance rest on the Pashtunwali. At the same time, the Pashtunwali influences how the Taliban govern, matching local expectations. But service delivery may also provide the Taliban with some legitimacy. Giustozzi (2012) offers some helpful additional insights.

On the basis of interviews with members of the Taliban, he concludes that the provision of justice is central. When the Taliban manage to establish a local monopoly of force, Giustozzi argues, they can construct legitimacy by providing justice: 'by and large, the Taliban seem to have greatly benefited from their ability to mediate disputes among communities. It could be argued that such ability is a major source of legitimacy for the Taliban' (2012, 73). Building on these ideas, this paper further contextualizes the perception data and compares the Taliban's claims to legitimacy with the reasons why people perceive them to be legitimate – or not.

Local perceptions of the Taliban

To gain a better understanding of the Taliban's authority and sources of legitimacy, the ways in which they are perceived by members of the public are examined. To do justice to the 'fluid' nature of the Taliban, with characteristics varying spatially and changing over time, the analysis focuses on Afghanistan's Eastern province Nangarhar in 2014/15. This geographical focus complements the existing literature on the Taliban that concentrates mainly on the south of Afghanistan. Travelling from Kabul, it only is a three-hour ride by car to the city of Jalalabad, the capital of Nangarhar Province. The road follows Kabul River and twists down 1300 metres through the mountains. In the mountains, one can see patches of new asphalt on the road frequently, serving as reminders of the fuel trucks that have caught fire after being shot at from the mountains. Surobi District, which is one of the eastern districts of Kabul Province, is well known for frequent attacks on the Afghan National Security Forces (ANSF).

Leaving the mountains of Kabul Province behind, the road reaches the plains of eastern Afghanistan, first Laghman Province–where many people take a break for a photo with an old Soviet tank lying next to the road – and finally Jalalabad in Nangarhar Province. The terrain is much flatter and the temperature is much higher here than in Kabul. In this part of the country it hardly ever rains, and the heat is often unbearable in summer, but because of the pleasant temperatures in winter, Jalalabad was a popular seasonal home for many Afghan kings over the centuries. Today, with about 200,000 inhabitants, Jalalabad is one of the biggest cities in Afghanistan. From here, it is barely 80 km to the Pakistani border.

Indeed, the main currency used in this part of Afghanistan is the Pakistani rupee. Like most other parts of Afghanistan, the predominantly Pashtun province of Nangarhar was controlled by the Taliban from 1996 to 2001. Today governance in Nangarhar is dominated by a number of strongmen, who compete for influence (Jackson 2014). In the period during which the interviews were conducted, the Taliban had gained full control of many parts of the province again. However, the provincial capital Jalalabad remained under government control, with some districts close to the city being 'grey' areas, technically controlled by the government but also influenced by the Taliban. But even though the visible presence of the Taliban in Jalalabad was low, there was an atmosphere of fear, driven by suicide attacks, kidnappings and robberies. The interviews were conducted in the format of natural conversation, triggered by the use of open-ended questions.

As legitimacy is an abstract social phenomenon, which may be understood differently by different people, it was not used during the interviews. Instead, the discussion was on the Taliban more generally, using two thematic examples of exercising social control to investigate perceptions that can be related to legitimacy: security provision and conflict resolution. Of particular interest for the purposes of this research are the interviewees' explanations of strong positive or negative views regarding the Taliban, the reasons why they thought that the Taliban or other authorities should be responsible for security provision and conflict resolution, and their views as to who should govern Afghanistan in the future. Interviewees were selected in such a way that they covered a wide range of characteristics with regard to age, sex, income, social position and district of residence.

The research does not, however, build on a 'representative sample' in a positivist sense; being about the mechanisms of legitimacy, it does not aim at drawing general conclusions on the extent of the Taliban's legitimacy in Nangarhar, let alone Afghanistan. The details of the interviews this article draws on are given in the Appendix.[12] The selection of interviewees also depended heavily on pragmatic considerations, particularly access–hence, certain groups of people, particularly women and people living in areas controlled by the Taliban, are underrepresented. In addition, certain ideologies or views might be underrepresented, for instance because people who are critical of foreigners may be less likely to participate in a research project. It also turns out that the number of people interviewed who supported the Taliban is much lower compared to those who perceived the Taliban as a threat. As a consequence, it was necessary to work with a comparatively small number of interviews to understand what legitimizes the Taliban, while there are many more interviews which shed light on what delegitimizes them. However, understanding what delegitimizes the Taliban also helps to draw conclusions on the sources of legitimacy.

Jalalabad – the Taliban as a security threat

Even though the Afghan state was in control of Jalalabad at the time of this research, the Taliban frequently arose as a topic of conversation in the interviews, as both a historical and a contemporary phenomenon. Looking back to the time when the Taliban were in power, most interviewees had very positive memories and stated their satisfaction, particularly in terms of security. Comparing the past with the present, the mechanic Rahmanullah stated: 'I think the security situation is worse than 15 years ago. During the Taliban regime there were no kidnappings or other crimes in our province' (N31). Similarly, Khyber, a middle-aged man who was unemployed at the time of the interview, concluded:

During the Taliban regime there were no robberies, kidnappings or suicide attacks. During the first term of Karzai, the situation was good too. But now it has changed completely. The number of suicide attacks and kidnappings has increased, and there is a high level of corruption in the public administration. (N30).

Views like those of Rahmanullah and Khyber were widely shared, and not limited to Jalalabad. Also, in the more rural districts of Nangarhar, people often had good memories of the time when the Taliban were in power (e.g. N34, N35, N36). Nonetheless, some people, less frequently, also acknowledged that not everything was good during the Taliban's regime. For instance, the farmer Taher explained that under the Taliban the security situation was better but that his economic situation was worse (N28). Today the phenomenon of the 'Taliban' is considered to be more complex.

There are a number of armed 'opposition' groups with different interests and alliances, sometimes linked to strongmen or to the government, sometimes claiming to be 'Taliban' and sometimes only being labelled as 'Taliban' by others. The armed groups that are mentioned most frequently in the interviews are Hekmatyar's Hezb-e Islami[13] and the forces controlled by the Quetta Taliban Shura, also referred to as the Islamic Emirate, as well as the militias of the various strongmen. A local civil society activist explained the structure of the armed groups in Nangarhar as follows:

There are two main opposition groups here. It's the Islamic Party [Hezb-e Islami] and the Taliban. The Islamic Party usually only attacks foreigners, not the ANA [Afghan National Army] or the ANP [Afghan National Police]. The Taliban attack foreign and government forces. The Taliban also collect ushr and zakat, which the Islamic Party isn't doing. The Taliban are much stronger and consist of different factions. The government is linked to these groups as it has some of its people within the Taliban. In addition, strongmen – which often are part of the government too – hire militias to achieve their personal interests. Every strongman, every political party and every group has its own armed force. Most people just call all of these armed groups Taliban. (N18)

In 2015, a new opposition actor suddenly entered the ring, the so-called Islamic State Khorasan (IS-K), which people in Afghanistan widely referred to as Daesh. While in late 2014 not a single interviewee mentioned IS-K, in 2015 almost every interviewee was concerned about its growing influence in the province. At the time of the interviews, reports on the Islamic State in Afghanistan had been limited to Nangarhar. But soon after the Taliban declared 'jihad' against the group (Khaama Press, April 20, 2015; Osman 2016).[14]

Most of the people interviewed in Jalalabad had strong negative views on the Taliban as being responsible for multiple attacks that had killed a large number of civilians in the city. The positive memories from the past rarely translated to the present perception. For example, the university student Gulagha proclaimed: 'Taliban means "the ones who seek knowledge". But now it is nothing more than the name of an illegally armed group, which is destroying the country with bombs and suicide attacks' (N10). Similarly Rohullah, also a student, stated: 'Taliban for me means murderers. Especially city people hate them' (N08). Very negative perceptions were particularly prominent in the second round of interviews in the spring of 2015, reinforced by an attack on Kabul Bank in Jalalabad killing and injuring dozens of people around the time of the interviews. But Rohullah, like many of the interviewees, also blamed the Taliban for crime in the city.

Kidnappings by unknown groups were a regular occurrence during this period, and many people attributed them to the Taliban even though they appeared to be carried out only for income generation via ransom. Rohullah summarized: 'Jalalabad is not secure at the moment. On a daily basis we witness bombings and the crime rate is going up' (N08). Although people in Jalalabad blamed the Taliban for all kinds of criminal activities, they still perceived them as a political actor (e.g. N27, N29) – albeit one that is not necessarily fighting for ideological reasons, but as a tool of foreign intervention driven mainly by Pakistan to consciously cause insecurity in Afghanistan: 'In case the Taliban managed to stop the infiltration of their organization through foreigners they might be accepted. But our nasty neighbour Pakistan causes insecurity through the Taliban' (N07). Some people in Jalalabad had also experienced recent personal encounters with the Taliban. Based on these encounters, people in Jalalabad did not necessarily perceive the Taliban to be an armed group linked only to Pakistan, but also saw connections to the Afghan state. For instance, the civil society activist told me:

> My son was kidnapped and I was asked to provide them [the kidnappers] with 10 AK47s. … When I was walking out of the police station after filing my case, I got a call from the Taliban telling me that the police couldn't help me. About six months ago, I was attacked in front of a police station. And after filing my case they arrested a number of police officers. They called me to recognize their faces, but I was too afraid to do so. In fact, the police commanders cooperate closely with the illegally armed groups. Whenever these people notice that their interests are in danger they will take advantage of their links with the insurgents and call on them for help. (N18).

While the civil society activist was particularly open about his experiences, other interviewees also complained about the links they see between the police and the Taliban (e.g. N08). As far as the people interviewed in Jalalabad were concerned, the Taliban did not have much authority, as the people did not obey them – either voluntarily or because of coercion. They saw the Taliban mainly as a threat from the outside and a driver of insecurity, an agent of Pakistan that is responsible for numerous attacks. But people also blamed the Taliban for other crimes, often perceiving them as partners rather than opponents of criminal government authorities. Even though many interviewees had positive memories of the Taliban regime, these memories did not translate into an overall positive perception of the Taliban, as their perceptions rested only on the present activities of the

Taliban. The violent behaviour had delegitimized the Taliban in the eyes of the people, while the Taliban's attacks in Jalalabad also illustrated that the Afghan state was incapable of providing security for its citizens – even in major urban areas.[15] Hence, people had become dissatisfied with the Afghan state, making the attacks a successful delegitimization strategy for the Taliban.

Behsod and Surkh Rod – the Taliban as a sporadic phenomenon

In the other parts of Nangarhar province in which research was conducted – the districts of Surkh Rod and Behsod–people shared an overwhelmingly negative perception of the Taliban. In Behsod, which is a more rural district that is in close proximity to Jalalabad, almost all the interviewees saw the Taliban as the main source of insecurity. However, while some were concerned that 'security [was] getting worse day by day' (N34; see also N36, N40, N47, N51), most people were confident about the security situation (e.g. N35, N38, N39, N45, N48, N49). To explain this variation, many people pointed out that the Taliban were not active in all parts of the mainly government-controlled district. However, the Taliban did infrequently show up in some areas. For instance, the farmer Haiatullah reported: 'There are no Taliban in our village.

But they sometimes show up in Samarkhel village close by' (N44). In contrast to Jalalabad, the experience of insecurity in these areas was based less on attacks and more on the Taliban's attempts to extract money. Like other interviewees, the non-governmental organization (NGO) employee Subhanullah reported: 'Every now and then the Taliban come from Khogyani and Chaparhar districts and ask us for tithes. And when they come we feel insecure' (N40). But despite the limited presence of the Taliban in the district and their negative perception, they managed to recruit successfully in Beshod. An interviewee explained: 'Many people from our district go and join the Taliban because of poverty and unemployment' (N50). Only one of the interviewees in Behsod had an openly positive perception of the Taliban. The village elder Wais explained that he liked the Taliban because they were helping to solve conflicts on the community level:

> *Here in our village two brothers had a conflict on land rights. They went to the government to solve the conflict but nothing happened for a month. Then one brother went to the Taliban instead. They solved the conflict very quickly. And the result was acceptable for both brothers. (N34)*

As he was unsatisfied with the government's conflict resolution procedure and the growing insecurity, he expressed hope that in the future the Taliban would be the only provider of security and conflict resolution. He also explained that the Taliban offered 'mobile courts', making access much easier than the government. In the case of a conflict, people could request that they come by motorbike to help. Despite his preference for the Taliban over the government, Wais criticized, like everybody else, the interference of neighbouring countries:

'I don't like Iran and Pakistan because they cause insecurity in our country' (N34). But in contrast to most of the other interviewees, he did not see a connection between the neighbouring countries and the Taliban. Furthermore, he did not consider himself to be a Talib, and carefully distinguished between 'the Taliban' and 'the people in the village' in the interview. He complained that foreign and government forces sometimes accuse people from his village of being members of the Taliban: 'A month ago international forces and ANA soldiers came and accused our Mullah [of being] a Talib. They looted his house and burned his motorcycle even though he is innocent' (N34). According to Wais this reinforced the perception in his village that the government was a threat while only the Taliban could provide security.

The third area of Nangarhar in which this research was conducted is the district of Surkh Rod. Surkh Rod, like Behsod, is rural but still close to the urban Jalalabad – and like in Behsod, the interviewees there had mixed perceptions of the security situation, but widely agreed that the Taliban were the main threat (e.g. N01, N02, N03, N04, N05, N21, N23). However, according to the teacher Nader, the Taliban were only present and a concern in the Kakrak area of Surkh Rod at the time of the interviews (N16). Like in the other districts, the label 'Taliban' was used to describe all kinds of armed groups. For instance, Mohammad, a member of a local council reported: 'In general, security is enforced and there is no threat from insurgents. But there are criminal activities. ...

The Taliban use weapons to kidnap, rob, ambush and threaten people' (N05). The head of a civil society organization further explained that many people and groups describe themselves as Taliban: 'A great number of people are only fighting for their personal interests. But they do so using the Taliban label' (N02). As in Behsod, many people were reported as joining 'the Taliban' – although it remains unclear which group exactly – due to the pressures of poverty induced by unemployment (e.g. N16). Many interviewees concluded that the violence in the country was not a consequence of opposing ideologies, but instead only a matter of economic interests. In Surkh Rod and Beshod, it was the state authorities who dominated the political order – and, like in Jalalabad, many people perceived the Taliban as a threat.

In those parts of Behsod that were accessed frequently by the Taliban, this perception did not only rest on attacks and criminality in general, but, more specifically, also on the experience of the Taliban demanding obedience to their rules and attempting to extract money from people. Here the Taliban were an actual authority for people, albeit one founded on coercion rather than legitimacy. However, despite their negative reputation in both districts, some people decided to join the Taliban in order to make a living. And not everybody saw the Taliban as a threat, as the case of Wais indicates. While his support for the Taliban was an exception, he – like the other interviewees – formed his opinion on the basis of his perception of the behaviour of the state in comparison to the Taliban on a day-to-day basis.

His support for the Taliban was based on the perception of the Afghan state not only being incapable of providing security and conflict resolution, but even behaving in a threatening way, while he felt that the converse was the case with the Taliban. He, therefore voluntarily chose the Taliban for conflict resolution, indicating an authority resting not only on force but also on legitimacy. The Taliban's legitimacy in this case was based on very rational considerations: the experience of procedures he considered to be fast and fair. None of the interviewees explained support or rejection of the Taliban with more ideological considerations, such as a preference for a certain code of law (e.g. state law or Islamic law) or a preference for a certain defined procedure of how an authority should be gaining power (e.g. democracy or theocracy). Indeed, the interviews illustrate that pragmatic decision-making seems to play a key role, with people joining the Taliban to escape poverty and unemployment.

Khogyani and Sherzad – the Taliban as a provider of fast and fair conflict resolution

A number of interviewees in Jalalabad, Behsod and Surkh Rod turned out to be from other more distant districts, such as Khogyani, Chaparhard and Sherzad. Their 372 F. WEIGAND views offer valuable additional insights, as these districts were often described as the Taliban's 'bases' for driving insecurity in Nangarhar in the other interviews, but were difficult to access due to safety considerations. And indeed, many of these districts appeared to be at least partly controlled by armed opposition groups at the time of the interviews. The shopkeeper Obid (N13) and the engineer Khalid (N14) together described the situation in Khogyani District in the autumn of 2014. According to them, the security situation had become worse since 2010: 'Five years ago at least the main roads were safe. Today not even these roads are safe any more, as the number of bombings and kidnappings has increased dramatically' (N13 and N14). They assumed that the reason for this was the collaboration between government forces and other armed groups: 'The security is both enforced and sabotaged by the government, as the government cooperates with insurgency groups' (N13 and N14). And, according to them, the political landscape of insurgency groups was complex:

There are ... the Islamic Political Party [Hezb-e Islami], the Islamic Emirate, Mahaz, a new group called Karwan Fidaye as well as ordinary criminals. Karwan Fidaye is particularly active in Khogyani. Once they get you, escaping from them is very challenging. The members of this group cover their faces with black masks and people say that most of them are from Punjab in Pakistan. This group fights both the Taliban and the government. (N13 and N14).

According to the two interviewees, all of these groups would make attempts to extract money:

In rural areas they come several times per year and ask landowners to pay tithes. In cities they target rich people, by calling them or sending them threatening letters, asking for money. Two people who introduced themselves as members of the Mahaz Party called me recently, threatened me and asked for money. (N13 and N14).

But the interviewees also felt threatened by the government:

My father in law spent US$90,000–100,000 on building a house in the Ahmad Khail area of Khogyani. Now the head of the Afghan Local Police, Malik N. has taken the house. He refuses to leave the house, and doesn't even pay rent. The Taliban started to attack him and as a result the house got partly destroyed. A suicide bomber even blew him up inside the house. (N13 and N14).

They were not able to solve the conflict in the formal system:

When we wanted to complain about our house being stolen at the district police department, they didn't even let us inside because the head of the district police is also the head of the village and a friend of Malik N. (N13 and N14)

Given these circumstances, these two interviewees saw Taliban courts as the only feasible alternative:

'The next time I am involved in a conflict I will go to the Taliban first. They solve conflicts quickly. The government isn't solving my problems, it's making them bigger' (N13 and N14). Another interviewee, Wasiullah, a young man from Sherzad District, was even more convinced by the Taliban:

Sherzad district is completely controlled by the Taliban ... I think it is much better in Sherzad than in Jalalabad. Because in Jalalabad there are two governments in one city, in Sherzad it is only the Taliban. And all people in Sherzad are happy with the Taliban. (N33)

According to Wasiullah, the reason for this was not only the good security but also the fast and non-corrupt conflict resolution:

When a person has a problem, he goes to the Taliban. The Taliban then refer the conflict to their Hoquqe Department and courts. Their conflict resolution procedure is much simpler than the formal justice mechanisms. The decisions are made on the basis of Islamic law, and they are fast. They sometimes ask for a small bribe to cover the expenses of their motorcycle. But apart from that there are no costs for the involved parties. (N33)

When asked about the use of force by the Taliban, Wasiullah responded: 'Yes, they use force if necessary. But they are not corrupt. So people prefer the Taliban's conflict resolution' (N33). He expressed his hope that the Taliban would be governing the country again soon. It can be easily doubted whether, as Wasiullah claims, all of the people in Sherzad were happy with the Taliban – but it has to be acknowledged that some people in Sherzad District apparently did prefer the Taliban to other authorities, and that the Taliban have legitimacy because they do some things better than the government. And again, it is their day-to-day behaviour–the perceived speed and comparatively lower level of corruption –that was a major source of their legitimacy. The interviews with people from Khogyani District further support this narrative. The interviewees complained about the various insurgency groups collecting tithes. Nonetheless, they preferred the Taliban courts to the government ones for conflict resolution. This preference rested on their personal negative experiences of theft and unfair treatment by people associated with the government, combined with the perception of comparatively fast and fair procedures at the Taliban courts.

Conclusions

Given the complexity of the situation in Afghanistan as outlined throughout this article, it is difficult to define who the Taliban actually are, and how to categorize and distinguish them from other armed groups. Furthermore, a very prominent perception is that some of the armed 'opposition' groups are closely linked to criminal government authorities. Nonetheless, all of the people interviewed did have strong views on 'the' Taliban. These views were predominantly negative, which corresponds with survey data (Asia Foundation 2016). However, broader conclusions on the extent of the Taliban's legitimacy should not be made on the basis of this research, as the sample size is very small and is not aimed at being representative.

Whom people consider to be a legitimate authority can vary from village to village, from person to person and, over time. Still, the reasoning that underpins these different perceptions is very similar, indicating that the mechanisms that legitimize or delegitimize authorities are of a more general nature and remain relevant regardless of how the situation in Afghanistan develops. Overall, people appear to assess the Taliban pragmatically, predominantly based on the day-to-day experience of their behaviour rather than on their history or ideology. Further empirical research is necessary for a more complete picture which more closely examines Taliban-controlled areas, considers other provinces in Afghanistan and investigates the views of a larger number of people – including the self-perception of Talibs. However, two conflicting images of the Taliban emerged from Nangarhar.

While people in most parts of the government-controlled territories looked at them through the lens of 'insecurity', some people in the Taliban-controlled territories viewed the Taliban more favourably, focusing on their effective role in 'conflict resolution'. These views are closely aligned with the two different roles the Taliban play in Afghanistan, governing some parts or offering services that are associated with governing authorities while fighting in others. On the one hand, in the government-controlled areas, most of the interviewees perceived the Taliban as a coercive authority or simply as a threat to their security, group acting in the interest of Pakistan. This view stands in stark contrast to the picture of the Taliban as 'jihadists', which they use to claim legitimacy.

However, it is not religious extremism per se that people were concerned about; the negative public perception rested on attacks and other criminal activities in the city for which the Taliban were blamed. While some had positive memories of the Taliban regime, these thoughts did not translate into a positive perception today. In sum, it appears that the Taliban were not even trying to construct legitimacy, but were focusing on undermining the legitimacy of the state by illustrating that it could not protect its citizens. Nevertheless, in spite of the widespread rejection of the Taliban, some people from these areas decided to join the group in order to make a living. This choice to not only accept but become active with the Taliban can be read as legitimacy. However, this legitimacy appears to be purely instrumental, based not on beliefs but instead arising out of economic need. On the other hand, some residents from Taliban-controlled areas and territories that were technically government-controlled but accessible to the Taliban had more positive opinions.

These people described the Taliban as their preferred authority, or viewed their relationship with them as a voluntary one–which likewise indicates legitimacy. But again, it was not the Taliban's 'jihad' that people focused on; in terms of the Taliban's role in security provision, their legitimacy appears to have been instrumental. People viewed the Taliban as the best security provider for very pragmatic reasons, not because of values and beliefs. For instance, they considered armed opposition groups to be threatening but thought that the state was even worse, or they simply preferred having a monopoly of force over ongoing violent competition. But the Taliban's role in security provision was marginal for most, which instead focused on their positive role in conflict resolution, confirming Giustozzi's (2012) conviction that justice plays a key role in the Taliban's legitimacy.

Supplementing Giustozzi's theory, these findings indicate that the Taliban apply this strategy not only in territories in which they have a local monopoly of force, but also in some accessible territories that are government-controlled–thereby attracting people for conflict resolution and building legitimacy. This is noteworthy, since in the absence of a local monopoly of force, the Taliban's ability to enforce decisions is limited and requires more popular acceptance. Some people choose the Taliban because they think that the group responds better than the state to their need for fast and cheap conflict resolution, and accessibility plays an important role as well: for some, the Taliban courts are closer than the state ones, and in some instances, its 'mobile courts' even come to the village.

As such assessments are based on usefulness and personal advantage, they again illustrate that the legitimacy of the Taliban is very instrumental. This prevalence of instrumental legitimacy shows that many people simply think that the Taliban are the best available choice, or at least the lesser evil. Importantly, this makes their authority vulnerable. Supporters may easily be convinced to follow competing authorities, such as the state, if they were accessible and offered services of a similar speed and standard. However, there is also a substantive dimension to the Taliban's legitimacy in this context, as the interviewees also preferred the Taliban because of the fairness and predictability of their conflict resolution procedures. The repeated description of the Taliban as not being corrupt, or at least being less corrupt than the state, indicates that people do not only choose the Taliban for conflict resolution because they assume that they will have the best chances of winning their case or securing the best outcome, but also because the procedures correspond with a shared belief of what is right.

This shows that the perceived fairness of procedures – a source of legitimacy emphasized by scholars like Tyler (2004, 2006) in the context of political orders with a high degree of monopolization of force, as well as by Barfield and Nojumi (2010) in the context of Afghanistan's history – can play a central role in the construction of legitimacy in conflict-torn spaces today. More ethnographic research is necessary to explore the values that underpin the notions of 'corruption' and 'fairness' in Afghanistan – but the present research indicates that these values, most notably equality, are very general ones that are not necessarily linked to Islam, to the Pashtunwali or to other culturally-specific ideals. People seem to care less what kind of law is applied – whether it is state law, Islamic law or 'traditional' law – than about how the law is applied.

This finding illustrates that the Taliban's second claimed source of legitimacy – the 're-establishment of an Islamic system' – does not matter much for the people. What matters much more is the perception of the Taliban as being less corrupt than the state. Put differently, the people's immediate concern is having any rule of law – regardless of its ideological sources – to counter the perceived high level of corruption and arbitrariness. It is only when the procedures are clearly defined and implemented accordingly that there is a certain degree of predictability for people; and only when people have the feeling that everybody is treated the same way, regardless of money or influence, are the procedures of an authority considered to be fair. By living up to these very basic expectations and making people feel like equal subjects to their authority, not perfectly but better than the state, the Taliban – even if only perceived as the lesser of two evils – have already constructed some substantive legitimacy. This means that if the Afghan state is to win the fight against the Taliban, it is not sufficient to defeat them on the battlefield; the state also has to construct legitimacy more successfully than the Taliban – and, without having to compromise on human rights or democratic values, it can do so by taking some cues from its enemy.

Acknowledgments

My sincere thanks go to Jörg Friedrichs, Birte J. Gippert, Ashley Jackson, Mary Kaldor, Rachel Morrow, Abe Simons, Graeme Smith, Shalaka Thakur, Sam Vincent, Sarah von Billerbeck, Mirwais Wardak, Anna Wolkenhauer, two anonymous reviewers, and the JISB editorial team, as well as other friends and colleagues for their critical comments, valuable suggestions and background information. I would also like to thank the participants of the workshop on 'Governance and Development' at the University of Cape Town in April 2017 and of the 'International Studies Association's 58th Annual Convention' in Baltimore, Maryland in February 2017 for their comments on an earlier draft of this paper. Finally, I would like to express my deepest gratitude to Maiwand Rahimi and the people at PTRO, and to all who agreed to be interviewed for this project. Of course, I alone am responsible for any errors. Disclosure statement. No potential conflict of interest was reported by the author. Funding: Florian Weigand is an experienced research scholar. His analysis of Taliban way of operation in Afghanistan is a great lesson for the new generation of the county. This work was supported by the UK Economic and Social Research Council [grant number ES/ J500070/1]. Notes on contributor Florian Weigand is a Ph.D. candidate in the Civil Society and Human Security Research Unit, Department of International Development, London School of Economics and Political Science, UK. f.weigand@lse. ac.uk. Journal of Intervention and Statebuilding ISSN: 1750-2977 (Print) 1750-2985 (Online) Journal. Afghanistan's Taliban–Legitimate Jihadists or Coercive Extremists? Florian Weigand. To cite this article: Florian Weigand (2017) Afghanistan's Taliban – Legitimate Jihadists or Coercive Extremists?, Journal of Intervention and Statebuilding, 11:3, 359-381, DOI: 10.1080/17502977.2017.1353755 To link to this article: https://doi.org/10.1080/17502977.2017.1353755
The Journal of Intervention and Statebuilding is a cross-disciplinary journal devoted to critical analysis of international intervention, focussing on interactions and practices that shape, influence and transform states and societies. In 21st century political practice, states and other actors increasingly strive to transplant what they see as normatively progressive political orders to other contexts. Accordingly, JISB focuses on the complex interconnections and mutually shaping interactions between donor and recipient communities within military, economic, social, or other interventional contexts, and welcomes perspectives on political life of and beyond European state-building processes. The journal brings together academics and practitioners from cross-

Chapter 4

Culture, Education and Conflict: The Relevance of Critical Conservation Pedagogies for Post-conflict Afghanistan

Richard Mulholland

Abstract

There has been considerable focus on the widespread destruction of cultural heritage in Afghanistan since the destruction of the Bamiyan Buddhas by the Taliban in 2001 and much concern over the future of heritage in the region on the return of a Taliban regime in 2021, yet comparatively little has been written on the fate of Afghanistan's national collection of paintings, manuscripts, and works on paper. Through a quasi-experimental study and using a combination of evaluation methodologies, this paper discusses whether the overall impact achieved in conservation capacity-building and training schemes in conflict zones justify the cost and risk of operating in such regions. Using an international collaborative conservation training course carried out in 2020 at the Afghan National Gallery in Kabul as a case study, it discusses the appropriateness and effectiveness of the signature pedagogies in conservation when working in a conflict scenario, and highlights the limitations present in conservation training programmes in post-conflict scenarios and the need for sustainability of such programmes. The results of the study found that common constructivist-focused, Eurocentric conservation pedagogies may not be effective for training museum professionals in regions where this approach is unfamiliar.

Keywords: Afghanistan conflict pedagogy heritage conservation

Introduction

Destruction of cultural heritage has a long history of being used as a means by which to assert control, as a bargaining tool, or as political propaganda (Viejo-Rose 2007; Stone 2015; Brosché et al. 2017). However, cultural heritage and its wilful destruction have been placed in sharp focus in recent years due to the widespread media coverage of the destruction and looting of important cultural heritage sites in Mosul and Palmyra in Iraq in 2014 by Daesh/ISIS (Hassan 2015), and the sixth and seventh century Bamiyan Buddhas by the Taliban in Afghanistan in 2001 (Grissmann 2006; Harrison 2010; Leslie 2014). The unprecedented media coverage of the destructive acts of extremist groups in recent years has been both advantageous and disadvantageous in bringing attention to the lack of provision for securing significant cultural heritage sites and collections in regions of active conflict.

The impact of such media coverage is often a strong outpouring of support and condemnation from the public, which fosters a number of international conservation initiatives. While, arguably, this has created the perception that risk to cultural heritage in conflict zones is confined to dramatic, intentional acts of destruction and looting and less so on the impact of political instability, lack of literacy and education, and the effect of untrammelled urban development on heritage sites (Guzman et al. 2018; Gerstenblith 2009), robust international condemnation has enabled high impact conservation initiatives that have been designed to predict and protect heritage at risk in the future. A significant part of this has been the training of local conservators by museum professionals and educators from Europe and the USA. Despite overwhelmingly positive outcomes, the sustainability and long-term impact of these interventions is difficult to evaluate and the development and implementation of effective and appropriate pedagogical approaches for the provision of conservation and collections care education in active and post- conflict zones is under-researched.

Background

Afghanistan has a rich and troubled history. Despite immense progress in infrastructure, culture, and civil society though international development initiatives since 2001, the future of the region remains uncertain after the chaotic exit of international forces and the swift takeover of the country by a resurgent Taliban in 2021. Elimination of poverty and hunger, the provision of security, and the establishment of effective and stable governance were, and remain, primary concerns (Fitzgerald and Gould 2009; Yamin 2013). At the time of writing, the withdrawal of US and international troops from Afghanistan, the lack of effective governance and economic control, and the freezing of assets has led directly to an imminent humanitarian crisis. Increasingly frequent insurgent attacks, concerns for the position of women and girls in a post-withdrawal society, and widespread discrimination against non-Pashtun ethnic groups and Afghans who previously worked with foreign bodies all represent an ongoing concern for the future stability of the region (Akseer and Rieger 2019).

Invaded by Soviet Russia in 1979, Afghanistan became a proxy battleground for the primary actors of the Cold War. The Mujahadeen, supplied in arms and support by the US, helped bring about the end of the 10-year Soviet occupation of Afghanistan, yet left the region destabilised politically and economically. The vacuum that was left ushered in a destructive civil war, quickly followed by the short but brutal reign of the Taliban and the imposition of an extreme and restrictive form of Sharia Law across the country. During more than forty years of conflict, an estimated one million Afghans were killed, and half the population was displaced, largely fleeing to Pakistan or Iran. In 2020, refugees from Afghanistan represented the third largest refugee group in the world by country of origin (below Venezuela and the Syrian Arab Republic), and this has been a sobering trend since the 1980s (UNHCR Refugee Data 2020). Despite large international investment and a recovering economy between 2001 and 2021, Afghanistan is still considered a country of low human development, ranked 168 out of 189 world countries on the Human Development Index by the UNHCR (UNHCR 2020).[1]

Heritage destruction in Kabul

Long before the destruction at Bamiyan, the country's cultural heritage was profoundly affected by civil war. By some estimates, by the time of the invasion of the US-led coalition in 2001, in the region of 70 percent of the national museum's collection was lost, looted, or destroyed and countless historic sites were damaged (Dupree 2006). The Afghan National Gallery (ANG) and National Museum were both damaged and looted throughout 1993–1996, during the period of Mujahedeen inter fighting in Kabul, where both buildings were on the front lines of the conflict.[2] Jolyon Leslie, a founder member of the Society for the Protection of Afghan Cultural Heritage (SPACH), was witness to the destruction in Kabul in the 1990s and observed the looting of the National Museum first-hand and warned of the promises given to protect heritage by those in command: 'Between each of our visits, Mujahedeen fighters returned to loot, despite assurances from commanders who controlled the area that they would intervene to prevent this. The objects that we saw for sale on the roadside on the way back to the city after such visits, brought home to us that our appeals had fallen on deaf ears' (Leslie 2014).

At the time, many paintings in the national collection were saved by being removed from their frames, rolled up, and hidden by staff. Others were removed to the National Palace, Ministry of Foreign Affairs, and elsewhere. A catalogue of the collection prior to the destruction, (if it existed at all) did not survive, and so the extent of the loss is difficult to gauge. Losses at the National Museum, which was shelled during the conflict, were much larger, much worse, and more significant. Much of the core collection, however, was removed and stored in central Kabul. It survives today thanks to quick thinking staff. An important collection of early Qur'ans, manuscripts, and miniature paintings were removed and stored at the National Archives, where they remain today. Like the National Gallery, it is difficult to gauge how much of the National Museum collection has been lost through neglect, theft, or destruction. Inventory catalogues that survived the collapse of the building were destroyed, and paper records, furniture, and carved wooden sculptures were burnt. Militias looted what remained of the collection to sell on the black market and although international efforts to return stolen artifacts have had some success, much of the collection remains missing (Grissmann 2006).

Further deliberate destruction at the ANG and the National Museum occurred in 2001, where figurative sculptures, paintings, and film considered to be idolatrous were amongst objects destroyed by local Taliban commanders in Kabul.[3] Again, many objects survived thanks to the quick thinking and bravery of curators and archivists. Staff hid objects from the National Museum (Smith 2008), and much of the collection of the Afghan National Film Institute survived when staff hid original Afghan films behind a false wall, substituting them with low-quality copies of Indian and American films, which were promptly burned (Nasr 2019). At the ANG, figurative easel paintings were removed from frames and stretchers and hidden in attics and sometimes beneath the gallery carpets. In perhaps the most remarkable act of bravery, local doctor and artist, Mohammad Yousef Asefi, spent weeks in the stores of the ANG, painstakingly painting over human figures and other perceived offensive elements in paintings, using reversible gouache paint, and saving 122 paintings from the bonfire and the knife (Asefi 2019). Not all objects could be hidden, and the gallery's large collection of print, drawing, and watercolour portraits, which had remained on display or in storage, were almost all torn to pieces.[4]

The overarching motivations that lie behind cultural heritage destruction during conflict are complex, and while some authors have attempted to explore motives or provide systematic typologies of destruction (Brosché et al. 2017; Viejo-Rose 2007), the subject remains under-researched. In the context of Afghanistan, however, the destruction of the Bamiyan Buddhas and the actions of Daesh/ISIS in Iraq and Syria in 2014 fostered a general discourse in the international media that it was the cultural ideology of the Taliban that was entirely responsible for widespread heritage destruction in the region. Yet as pointed out above, much of the worst destruction, looting, and deliberate neglect of heritage sites and objects occurred before the Taliban first came to power. Indeed, prior to the imposition of a more radical policy on heritage in 2001, the Taliban initially assisted in the protection of Afghan heritage sites and collections (Harrison 2010). UN operatives in Kabul were in frequent contact with the Taliban authorities between 1996 and 2000 on policies for protecting cultural property and on the issue of the Bamiyan Buddhas.

Prior to 2001, the Buddhas were under the protection of the regime, viewed by Taliban leaders as having no idolatrous status, since the site was not a place of religious worship and Buddhism was no longer practiced in the country. With the support of the Taliban Minister of Culture, the UN, working together with SPACH, negotiated the secure storage and protection of the National Museum collections and much of the national collection of paintings (Grissmann 2006; Jolyon Leslie. Personal communication, 2020). It may be prudent to point out that since 2001, it has been politically expedient to underemphasise the wilful destruction and neglect of cultural heritage that occurred in the ten years prior to Bamiyan, in favour of focusing the narrative on the actions of the Taliban (and correlating these with those of Daesh/ISIS) as a way to promote soft diplomacy and to secure foreign funding for preservation and reconstruction projects. Nonetheless, it is fair to say that events between 1992, when Soviet forces left the country, and 2001 when the Taliban was overthrown by NATO forces, can be considered a monumental disaster for the country's cultural heritage.

Soft diplomacy and limitations for conservation interventions

Cultural heritage is seen as an important contributor to soft diplomacy in relations between developed countries and active and post-conflict zones, and the visibility of cultural diplomacy is regarded as having a key role in public diplomacy for the enhancement of international relations (Harrison 2010; Luke and Kersel 2013). However, there is a challenge in accurately assessing the long-term impact of such diplomacies, and several authors have pointed out the problematic nature of conceptualising a shared global heritage to promote diplomatic relations (Harrison 2010; Klimaszewski, Bader, and Nyce 2012; Kersel and Luke 2015). It is notable, for example, that the protection of cultural heritage was cited as a key outcome to promote both the invasion of Iraq in 2000 and of Afghanistan in 2001. Indeed, the United Nations Security Council Resolution S/Red/1333, which imposed a number of far-reaching sanctions on the Taliban and Al Qaeda in 2000 explicitly cites ' ... respect for Afghanistan's cultural and historical heritage' as an affirmation of the resolution (United Nations Security Council 2000). The negative effect of such sanctions on the provision of much-needed humanitarian aid have been widely reported (Ahmad 2001; Khabir 2001; Martin and Enderby Smith 2021).

Klimaszewski and colleagues have also noted that while heritage protection projects may aim to have wide impact and diplomatic efficacy, the central idea of a global shared heritage is predicated on assumptions made by those in power and may not always have the desired impact. Local community views are multi-faceted, and conservators and other heritage professionals engaged in post-conflict projects may not always have an informed and nuanced view of the forces that construct and divide a community (Klimaszewski, et al. 2012). Community engagement as a critical component of heritage conservation projects is widespread today in a way it was not in the past, but at the same time ethnic, social, economic, and other concerns are often unique to a particular demographic. Generic policies about how and what heritage should be preserved are not necessarily appropriate for all. To paraphrase Klimaszewski and colleagues – in Afghanistan, an ethnic Pashtun and an ethnic Tajik may have radically different perceptions of history and culture.

As noted, the impact of heritage projects is difficult to predict and assess. It is possible at the same time to engage community stakeholders in conservation and preservation decisions and acknowledge that there are multiple histories and voices that dictate how the past is seen and interpreted, while simultaneously and implicitly projecting the idea that 'the West knows best' (Kersel and Luke, 2015). This is especially true where projects are designed with well-intentioned and well-defined outcomes but are directed by one partner – typically the one providing the funds. At best this creates an imbalance where the developing country/conflict zone receives minor monetary and strategic advantage, but where the economically larger partner receives diplomatic power and influence (Klimaszewski, et al. 2012). At worst, misjudged cultural diplomacies may lead unintentionally to catastrophic consequences. International pressure and the promotion of the concept of shared global heritage were undoubtedly a key modifier in the Taliban's decision to reverse previous promises and carry out the wilful destruction of heritage in 2001 (Harrison 2010).

A key limitation for conservation interventions in Afghanistan is that Afghans in general have little or no concept of this global shared heritage. Heritage is rarely considered to be of national importance, particularly when stacked against the more present, much larger concerns over security, food, poverty, education, and health. Although the recent re-opening of the National Museum is a positive step forward, heritage in the post-withdrawal era can only be seen by the majority of Afghans as a luxury and of minimal importance in the present climate[5] (Becatoros 2021). Even prior to the catastrophic withdrawal of international forces in 2021, an incorruptible police force, humanitarian aid, a stable economy, and the installation of basic, modern infrastructure and facilities were a very real preoccupation for the population. In post-conflict recovery, as Stanley-Price rightly points out, it is difficult to quantify the immediate benefits of spending significant amounts of money on heritage preservation projects when compared with the building of a hospital or creating a reliable, consistent electricity supply (Stanley-Price 2005). Furthermore, cultural heritage education that might help to provide a national sense of cultural ownership is practically non-existent, even in the more educated urban regions. Cultural heritage was not included in any meaningful way in the general school curriculum, schools did not visit heritage sites, and few adults visited the National Museum, National Archives, or National Gallery. The connection between identity and heritage in Afghanistan is also complex. Cultural identity in the region is connected more to political, ethnic, and tribal affiliation rather than to a sense of national pride derived from a universally-owned heritage (Dupree 2006; Caesar and Rodriguez García 2006). The Ministry of Information and Culture, while supportive of heritage initiatives in general, was, and is, critically understaffed and underbudgeted.

Without education to place objects of other cultures in context with their own, many Afghans do not see cultural objects as art, and the idea that cultural heritage can be part of a solution to solve decades of conflict and distrust is difficult to understand. This is an important consideration, as education for the Afghan public is essential to foster understanding of conservation and what it can mean for what remains of the rich cultural heritage of the region. The National Museum in Kabul has been regarded as a powerful symbol of Afghanistan's recovery, but it is uncontroversial to state that the majority of Afghans know little about the collection. As Leslie points out, the *Afghanistan: Hidden Treasures from the National Museum* exhibition that was toured internationally in 2014, and displayed in high profile museums in New York, London, and many other cities, has led to a situation where people in the US, Europe, and UK are much more familiar with items in Afghanistan's national collection than are the people of the region (Leslie 2014). Isakhan and Meskell have similarly argued that UNESCO's mission to revive the spirit of Mosul in Iraq and reconstruct the old city after the destruction wrought by Daesh/ISIS in 2014 relied on 'problematic assumptions about how the local population value and engage with their heritage, how they interpret its destruction and the value they place on its reconstruction' (Isakhan and Meskell 2018).

Corruption is also acknowledged as a major issue for international heritage projects in Afghanistan, at present ranked at 165 out of the 180 most corrupt countries in the world (Corruption Perception Index 2020). A total of 83.7 percent of participants in a 2019 Asia Foundation survey believed corruption is a significant problem for the region, and a quarter of Afghan citizens stated that they experienced corruption or bribery in 2020 (Akseer and Rieger 2019). Prior to the 2021 withdrawal, the World Bank's Worldwide Governance Indicator for 2017 showed that Afghanistan is among the world's 10 worst performers in terms of government effectiveness, regulatory quality, rule of law, and control of corruption (Bak 2019). In 2019, bribery was considered to be endemic and considered a normal part of applying for jobs, interacting with government bodies, and for admission to schools and universities (Akseer and Rieger 2019). Despite an encouraging move by the present administration toward modernisation, it remains to be seen how the resurgent Taliban, even if recognised as a legitimate government, will tackle such persistent problems.[6]

The number of NGOs working in Afghanistan increased greatly in the years after the 2001 fall of the Taliban, and more recently these have included several that focus specifically on cultural heritage.[7] However, many Afghans are somewhat sceptical about the role of both national and international NGOs (Mitchell 2017). While overall impact has been strong, there is a great deal of scepticism about international educational programmes in

Afghanistan, specifically focused on where international aid money is spent. Michell notes that by 2010, Kabul was swamped with a number of short training courses provided by various donors and organisations – many of which were criticised for being superficial, supply-driven, and uncoordinated. Additionally, this kind of training was rarely independently evaluated, and typically conducted without a baseline, making it difficult to assess its impact (Mitchell 2017). Cultural heritage projects, particularly for historic sites and monuments, have largely had positive outcomes, but there remain examples of short-sightedness. The Afghan National Archives, for example, received a large and valuable supply of conservation materials from the UK in 2007, yet were not given instruction in what these were, or how they should be used with the collection, and the materials have remained unopened since they were delivered (Anonymous 2020). Viejo-Rose has observed that while NGOs and foreign governments are often called upon to reconstruct, restore, and recalibrate cultural heritage in post-conflict regions, it is rare that local communities are consulted, and these interventions can often 'adopt a paternalistic role, with echoes of colonialism' (Viejo-Rose 2007). Barakat echoes this view and notes that there is inherent risk that 'imported and externally imposed models ignore the two most basic needs for humans in the aftermath of conflict: to reaffirm a sense of identity and regain control over one's life' (Barakat 2005). While intentions are good and local scepticism may be unfounded, short-term conservation interventions can nonetheless be met with some suspicion in the region.

Conservation training in Afghanistan

Over the last 20 years, a large number of NGO, international government, and foundation-driven capacity-building and educational projects have taken place in developing countries and post-conflict zones to train local conservators. Notable interventions in Iraq (Pearlstein and Johnson 2020), Myanmar (Henderson et al. 2021), India (Seymour et al. 2019; Haldane et al. 2012), Afghanistan (Cassar and Nagaoka 2007; Stein 2017; Boak 2019) and the Central Asian republics (Stein 2019) have yielded strongly positive impacts.[8] In Afghanistan, organisations such as the Afghan Cultural Heritage Consulting Organisation (ACHCO), and the Society for the Preservation of Afghan Cultural Heritage (SPACH) have a long history of implementing heritage projects for both collections and archaeological sites which have incorporated training of local Afghans. Early Buddhist wall paintings in the network of caves behind the niches in Bamiyan where the Buddhas once stood, continue to be the subject of a significant conservation and educational campaign (Maeda 2006), and the formation of the Turquoise Mountain School in Kabul in 2006 may be viewed as a model of how the training of local Afghans in traditional artisan crafts such as stone carving and manuscript painting can have a significant and sustainable impact on cultural heritage in the region, while providing income for local communities.[9]

Some authors, however, have cautioned against the privileging of elite, expert, and Eurocentric knowledge over local sources, particularly on the preservation of monumental heritage (Barakat 2005; Stanley-Price 2005; Nankivell 2016). In an Inverse Document Frequency (IDF) study of media coverage of heritage destruction in Iraq and Syria, Nankivell found that Western experts and institutions were quoted or referred to nearly 2.5 times more than Iraqi or Syrian experts or institutions, and that where they were cited, the truthfulness and validity of statements by locals and government officials were questioned or required confirmation from another source (Nankivell 2016). Perhaps more importantly, others highlight the danger of equivocating the loss of heritage with the loss of people and living culture, and the reinforcement of more dominant, Western discourses in heritage (Chulov 2015; Hassan 2015; Fredheim and Khalaf 2016). While educating conservators with little or no background in the subject may require the teaching of the foundational principles of modern conservation, the pedagogical approaches typically used in Eurocentric conservation courses may be difficult and unfamiliar to those unused to these forms of learning.

Conservation education in Afghanistan. HUNAR: A Case Study

Heritage Unveiled: National Art Restoration (HUNAR) was one of three heritage conservation projects funded by the British Council's Cultural Protection Fund and implemented by a partnership between the Foundation for Culture and Civil Society (FCCS) and Sayed & Nadia Consultancy at the Afghan National Gallery, part of the Ministry of Culture and Information of the Afghan Government. A 2018 field study in Kabul by the project team surveyed the damaged collection at the ANG and identified 50 easel paintings and works of art on paper in need of urgent conservation. These were fully conserved during the second phase in 2019, which also brought conservation materials from the UK to build and equip modular paintings and works on paper conservation studios in Kabul.

A key objective for the HUNAR programme in 2020–2021 was to address the lack of skills and knowledge in heritage management and conservation in Afghanistan. This included the design and implementation of a simple collections management database at the ANG, the translation of key conservation sources on paper and easel paintings conservation into Dari and Pashto, and an intensive training course for participants from the National Gallery, National Museum, National Archives, Kabul University, the Art Institute, and four provincial galleries. The training took the form of a short, ten-day course on the theory and practice of collections management, conservation, artists' materials and techniques, and preventive conservation to be carried out *in situ* in Kabul in 2020. However, the advent of the COVID-19 pandemic and a worsening security situation in Kabul meant that travel to the region was not possible, and the training was moved online. The course was provided via recorded lectures with live translation, followed by a live online 'Q&A' session with all participants. A small group of high-scoring trained participants were then selected to travel to regional galleries at Kandahar, Herat, Balkh, and Nangarhar to train local staff in condition reporting and basic collections management.

Social and gender inclusion was promoted strongly throughout the project. As with most sectors in Afghanistan, there are structural inequalities that make accessing decision-making and leadership roles in the heritage sector difficult. In most provinces there are no female employees in the sector. HUNAR was the first project of its kind to carry out a formal gender and social inclusion assessment for the heritage sector in the region. In Afghanistan, a clear international sustainable development goal is to promote the empowerment of young women (Wimpelmann 2017), and the inclusion of heritage in the international development agenda represented a significant opportunity to re-appraise the role of women in contemporary Afghanistan, especially since women are over-represented in higher education art and design courses, the traditional entry route into heritage roles (Hashimi 2021). The Ministry of Culture employees 2023 people, of which 14 percent are female. However, the vast majority work in the capital. The ratio is almost non-existent in the provinces, where in general there is also very low education attainment for women. While female heritage workers report little workplace gender discrimination (salary scales are the same for both men and women), widespread corruption means that overtime and favouritism are widespread. Ethnically, the majority of workers in heritage positions are Tajiks (63 percent), followed by Pashtun (26 percent), Hazara (7 percent), Uzbeks (2 percent), and others (3 percent). This, at least, is consistent with proportional distribution of ethnic groups around the country (Afghan Ethnic Groups 2011). In the conservation training component of the HUNAR project, the participant balance was 60/40 male/female in Kabul and 82/18 in the provincial galleries (Hashimi 2021).

A needs assessment was carried out via simple gap analysis and an anonymous needs survey completed by all participants prior to the project. Given the low baseline, gap analysis between present knowledge and skill in the region and that of an ideal target situation (for example, in a conservation department in a UK museum) was of limited use. Unsurprisingly, in the needs analysis survey, 100 percent of respondents cited the need for training and capacity building in the region as a priority, along with the restoration of conflict-damaged paintings and the need for quality conservation materials. Overall impact for the training was assessed by a peer-reviewed impact evaluation report carried out in 2021 by S&N Consultancy. The impact evaluation took place following an established quasi-experimental design, where both a comparison and control group both received training, but with different durations and methods. Quasi-experimental designs offer an opportunity to gather causal evidence where a randomised control trial (RCT) is impossible or impractical to implement. In this context, data from a comparison group that is as similar as possible to the intervention group is captured via a counterfactual scenario (what the outcome would have been had the project/intervention not been implemented). While controlled trials remain the 'gold standard' for impact studies, several authors have outlined the distinct advantages of quasi-experimental studies over RCTs, particularly where rapid impact evaluation is required (White and Sabarwal 2014; Campbell et al. 2017).

For HUNAR, comparative data on participants' performance before and after training was calculated using a scenario-based counterfactual in order to provide a rapid, meaningful impact assessment. Programme stakeholders were asked to assign a number to different parts of the project, and these were compared to assess the total impact of the project. The data from the non-equivalent control group was drawn from the participants from the four regional galleries after they were trained by the highest scorers from the original treatment group. Criteria for measuring pre- and post-assessment. (Hashimi 2021). To establish the overall net impact, project stakeholders were asked to assess both the effect of the programme and the effect of a scenario-based counterfactual alternative (an ideal programme). The impact evaluation was based on probability that the project would have the desired outcome. Overall, general conclusions showed that there was an increase efficiency in ANG staff work practices of 86 percent, particularly through practical workshops, exposure to previously unknown international standards in conservation and preservation, and through the use of a written resource library in local languages (Hashimi 2021).

To assess the overall impact of the conservation training programme, participants were asked to complete a short test before the training in order to demonstrate their baseline knowledge, and then again after the training. Overall, the progression from the pre-course test to the post-course test showed incremental but significant gains. Participants from the pre-treatment group (nine participants from the Afghan National Gallery), who had experienced some training under the previous field study had a broader range of improvement (ranging between 9 percent improvement at the lowest and 65 percent at the highest). Participants from the HUNAR treatment group (18 participants from other heritage and higher education institutions) demonstrated significantly stronger improvements of between of 30 and 85 percent. The control group, which was comprised of participants from regional galleries who were trained over a shorter duration by Afghan trainers from the treatment group, and who did not participate in group activities also made strong gains (20–45 percent) indicating that the training of trainers had a successful outcome. In general, male participants performed better than female, and younger participants performed considerably better overall than their older counterparts.

Outcomes were positive and indicated that the training methodology was effective. Younger participants were observed to be considerably more engaged in both the theory and practice of collections care and conservation, indicating a strong interest for the subject. However, a clear theme that emerged was that engagement with the theoretical lectures and group discussion and exercises was less favourable. Additionally, for many participants, there was a strong bias toward a desire to learn aesthetic restoration techniques over (the much more needed) basic preventive conservation and collections care. A clear limitation was in the translation of both documents and spoken lectures with technical terms and concepts that were often challenging to translate into local languages. Many technical terms associated with preservation and conservation in English do not have an equivalent in Dari and Pashto, and staff from different heritage institutions often used different terms for the same concepts. To support this, key theoretical conservation texts were translated into both languages for participants. However, the assessment of written test results and condition reporting exercises strongly indicated that these were not consulted by participants. Participant feedback highlighted access to international expertise in conservation as an important factor in the training, as there is a lack of expertise in heritage and collections care in general. However, with this in mind, learning was generally expected to be passive, and reflective practice and critical or enquiry-based approaches were less successful.

Overall, the results demonstrated that while short-term courses and workshops certainly made significant gains in addressing the knowledge gap in heritage conservation in Afghanistan, lack of engagement with theoretical aspects, reflection, and decision-making in a group context still requires some work to achieve. It may be that the culture of education in the region favours a more behaviourist, authority-based approach, or simply that these structures of learning require more time to enact the required culture change. It is likely that a move from short-term training and workshops to a longer-term educational structure for cultural heritage staff would be more sustainable. This, of course, requires culture shift in the approach to learning in the region, and not inconsiderable investment, but also perhaps a more cautious and adaptable approach from international educators. It seems likely that where possible, attention should be focused less on sending international experts to the region, which requires significant cost in terms of travel and security and remains fairly low impact given the small number of participants able to attend, and more towards the development of longer term training. A strategic focus on the root cause – the lack of general education in art history, heritage science, collections management, museology, and preventive conservation – is also required. Similarly, the complete lack of conservation literature in Dari and Pashto, and the large cost of translation is a notable issue that remains to be addressed. The creation of a resource library on preventive conservation and a simple digital database for documenting the collections at the ANG is a significant improvement, but whether this can be expanded to cover collections in institutions across Afghanistan remains to be seen, as cross-institutional cooperation is also lacking even amongst the small number of institutions in Kabul. Working on a local curriculum for elementary conservation and collections care at an Afghan university is an endeavour that would significantly facilitate sustainability in heritage conservation in the region. However, whatever the format of training provided, observations made during the HUNAR project, and noted above, also suggest that the direct application of the signature pedagogies typically used in international postgraduate conservation programmes may not always be directly applicable to learners in Afghanistan and similar regions (Shulman 2005).

Toward an effective conservation pedagogy for conflict zones

In general, the signature pedagogies in conservation are fairly traditional, and in many ways, have not changed much from the apprenticeship-style training that was the norm for many years. Because of this studio apprenticeship heritage, conservation students can sometimes feel that the subject is a practical/scientific one with a theoretical framework loosely attached. Theory, ethics, problem-solving, and decision-making are all key skills in conservation practice (Henderson and Parkes 2021.) Yet the integration of theory and practice can sometimes be a challenge for students (Di Pietro, Buder, and Künzel 2021). Initially the HUNAR approach to training followed recognisable and fairly standard constructivist pedagogies utilising reflective practice, discussion, and collaborative problem-solving, with a conscious and intentional distancing from notions of imposing the authority of the expert toward a more interactive, student-focused learning experience.

However, this approach, while somewhat effective, failed to consider that students from more traditional cultural backgrounds often expect to be taught in a formal behaviourist manner. Avoiding careless over-generalisation, the teaching team observed that in most cases, students did not expect to engage in group discussion, or question key principles provided by the teacher. Furthermore, participants often expected to be provided with a single solution to a given problem and requested a 'manual of conservation' that would tell them how to conserve an object from beginning to end. Students also found it challenging to engage with conservation and preservation theory. In a post-training survey in 2019, theory was often viewed as mundane and dull and with little relevance to practice (Mulholland 2019). Participants tended to privilege practical aesthetic restoration techniques over theoretical concepts. A bias toward practical training is perhaps expected for most conservation learners, but deeper cultural feelings were likely also a factor in this case. The strong preference for learning restoration of paintings over basic storage, display, and disaster management principles for example, was reflective not only of the students' educational background (most are fine art graduates), but also perhaps linked to the fact that the full aesthetic restoration of paintings thought to have been destroyed may be seen as political and social victory over fundamentalism and tyranny.

In his study of constructivist learning theory, Hein notes that our epistemological views dictate our pedagogical views (Hein 1991). In other words, our own understanding of learning the theory and practice of conservation tends to influence how what we believe will be effective for all learners. There is an increasing body of literature on how international students learn in Eurocentric contexts, particularly when students from more traditional societies study in a 'Western' pedagogical context. Overall, students from more traditional and conservative cultures often expect to memorise information and feed it back in the same way. O'Creevy and van Mourik found in a recent study on the experience of Japanese students in UK HE institutions that the idea of the university entrance exam in Japan, in which the answers are largely learned by rote, often led to the presumption that assessment would follow this pattern in UK HE institutions, sometimes with less than favourable results (O' Creevy and van Mourik 2016) Although the correlation is far from exact, Afghan students, in this limited study, appeared to find this form of learning to be more familiar.

Realistically, of course this is not true of all international students and all 'non-Western' societies, but both the literature and empirical observation suggest that this may be a contributing factor in many students' learning regardless of culture. In conservation, the subject traditionally has a number of rules and practices of learning – an existing academic scaffolding – and to be a competent and confident practitioner requires a tacit understanding of reflective decision making and creative problem-solving (Schon 1991). This is not always immediately understandable for students unfamiliar with the context. Inexperienced learners in conservation in general, as noted above, often request a key text on a single issue – something to inform them of the right answer to a problem. This is correlated particularly well in a well-researched study by Ramsden et al. on learning in the medical sciences. The authors noted that inexperienced medical students tended to use a more descriptive approach in their problem solving, using elementary and surface links between symptoms and diagnoses. More mature learners, on the other hand, were used to a more critical approach with more complex, causal chains of reasoning and were able to relate previous case studies and knowledge to the problem more effectively (Ramsden, Whelan, and Cooper 1988).

Another important issue for capacity-building in conflict zones is the ability to work optimally in digitally enhanced environments where teaching in person may be impractical. A key impact of the COVID-19 pandemic throughout 2020–2021 was the pressure testing of online pedagogies, on which much has already been written (see for example Morin 2020). Some authors note however, that the impact of digital creative pedagogies may or may not result in a new and improved set of creative and competent capacities (McWilliam 2007). Applied to the enhancement of conservation capacity in regions of conflict, online/remote technologies may simply be derivative and at risk of reproducing existing social dynamics. While the overall picture of the impact of COVID-19 on conservation education is not yet clear, recent work on remote learning in the advent of the pandemic in the medical sciences has highlighted the pedagogical opportunities for creative teaching for practical/vocational subjects, and this certainly has some correlation with conservation education (Morin 2020).

Head has written critically about the pedagogy of discomfort, outlining that how we teach in the context of conflict and war might also reveal innate structures of power (Head 2020). However, more traditional approaches to transmitting information may be a foundational requirement before constructivist approaches can be introduced. Though it is well outside the remit of this paper to interrogate critical pedagogical theories, there may well be aspects of this approach that are relevant in reflecting upon the Eurocentric approaches typical in conservation interventions within conflict zone scenarios. In the 1970s the formal lecture began to be criticised, notably by Paolo Freire, as an outdated means of simply 'banking education', wherein information is passively 'deposited' in student/participant by an authority/expert on the subject and not reflected upon, questioned, or criticised (Freire 1970). Foundational work on constructivist approaches to education has led to a much more critical and reflective pedagogy in higher education in Eurocentric/'Western' societies. Yet, in practice, the formal and theoretical lecture can allow foundational knowledge of a subject to be provided within a short space of time.

Often students in higher education (and by extension adult learners) in more traditional cultures find the freedom to participate in more reflective discussions around a topic to be daunting, particularly where it may be less practiced culturally. In a 2018 study of lecturers to undergraduate in the UK, Clark found that although most lecturers identified as constructivist teachers and critical pedagogues, many found that it was difficult to engage undergraduate (and some postgraduate) students in reflective and critical thought if they had not been exposed to this kind of learning before (Clark 2018). This may be a critical lesson in our approach to teaching heritage conservation in cultures with which we are unfamiliar. In Clark's study, one participant observed that students may in fact find themselves at a disadvantage if they are suddenly exposed to a more democratic and critical educational setting. Today, the constructivist, flipped classroom approach is employed in many, if not most, postgraduate conservation courses, where critical reflection on decision-making is an integral part of learning to be a competent conservator (Henderson and Parkes 2021). The approach may well be beneficial in challenging the authority of the expert, but the power balance between teacher and student in more traditional cultures is complex, may be more deeply rooted, and not be simple (or desirable) to overcome in a short course or workshop.

It is important to point out that this phenomenon is not only observed in more traditional or conservative cultures. Di Pietro et al. have noted that in the context of conservation in the Bern undergraduate programme in Switzerland there was a weakness in graduates' ability to apply their knowledge in new and unfamiliar scenarios (Di Pietro, et al. 2021). The authors carried out an employee evaluation survey in which a key finding was that many Swiss cultural heritage employers found a disconnect between the education of the conservation students and the application of their knowledge in new contexts. The HUNAR project highlighted a similar disconnect, and many Afghan students struggled when faced with applying what they had learned to unfamiliar problems in the context of their day-to-day work. While a great deal of domain-specific knowledge could be absorbed from the HUNAR lecture course, the reflection and critical thinking required to be a competent collections care or conservation practitioner was a considerably more challenging skill to acquire.

The postgraduate conservation student today is generally expected to be self-directed and a self-determinate learner in order to become a capable and competent practitioner. In practice, this follows both *andragogical* and *heutagogical* approaches to learning. Andragogy, defined in the 1970s by Knowles and others, privileges learning process above learning content as the most effective approach for adult learners. It emphasises self-directed learning, where learners are actively involved in identifying their needs and planning how these needs are met. Instruction is task-oriented and based on enquiry or problem-solving (Knowles 1975). The approach allows learners to develop the capacity for self-direction and utilise the input of their own personal experience, beliefs, and cultures. Above all, students need to know *why* they are learning something and have this firmly planted in a practical context. A more recent iteration of this is *heutagogy*, which emphasises self-determined learning – a more holistic approach toward developing capability in addition to competency (Bhoryrub et al. 2010; Archino 2020). Teacher control over learning and structure lessens with both andragogy and heutagogy. However, both require significantly more maturity and autonomy from the learner, which can be difficult to achieve if the learner lacks confidence or familiarity from their own learning background.

In this model of self-determined learning, Cairns has shown that students must learn both competencies and capabilities (Cairns 1996). Competencies are understood as a proven ability in acquiring knowledge and skills within a subject domain – arguably easy to acquire and demonstrate in conservation, where the teacher typically demonstrates, while the student observes, imitates, and practices, while at the same time considering how theoretical frameworks are applied to a particular problem. Capabilities, on the other hand, are characterised by learner confidence in their own competencies and an ability to take action to formulate and solve problems in both familiar and unfamiliar settings. When learners are *competent*, they demonstrate a range of knowledge and skills that can be repeated. When they are *capable*, according to heutagogical theorists at least, their competence is extended, and they are able to adapt to new situations (Gardner et al. 2008). The dual focus better addresses the needs of learners in complex and changing cultural environments and facilitates adaptation of theory to practice in decision-making and problem-solving.

This has particular relevance to the experience of teaching adult learners with little or no previous knowledge of cultural heritage, preservation, or conservation. There is a commonality in students' need to find a 'textbook' answer to a single problem, and not to engage in a sophisticated way with theoretical frameworks to enhance their capabilities in applying their knowledge to real and more unfamiliar problems. In the absence of elementary knowledge in art history, cultural theory, conservation theory and museology, it is perhaps unsurprising that Afghan students felt that a lecture series on preventive conservation was not immediately applicable to their own experience as heritage professionals. Where the use of case studies, reflection, and self-evaluation are useful in modern conservation education, for students that lack the elementary structural knowledge that underpins conservation, these strategies may be unfamiliar and, in some cases, inappropriate in many circumstances.

Returning to the participants in the HUNAR study, implementation of small-group learning, while demonstrably successful for postgraduate conservation students in the UK, was less successful in the context of Afghanistan. An example of effective constructivist learning in the Conservation of Fine Art masters degree course at Northumbria University, UK is where students are asked to work in small groups on a single problematic case study or question, then present their discussion/ research back to the class, with the lecturer acting as chair/mediator for the discussion. In this way, all participants are given the opportunity to learn individually, while simultaneously working as a group and communicating their theoretical learning to the class. Implementing a similar situation for participants in Afghanistan only works where there is a presumption that participants have the experience of group discussion and working with peers. Though very competent learners, we observed that participants in Kabul often did not have the experience or capacity to work in small groups and to apply their learning to a complex case study. Following the andro-heutagogical model, learners were initially asked to carry out a certain amount of self-directed learning and apply this to a hypothetical case study, for example on disaster recovery, or on the organisation of an exhibition. The exercise is intended to develop capability and competency in various areas related to collections care/management in an unfamiliar setting. Lacking a direct model for the unfamiliar scenario from the relevant lecture or a specific answer to the problem caused some confusion and resulted in a general inability to adapt new learning to solve the problem.

Henderson and Parkes have recently demonstrated that conservators have a strong theoretical and tacit understanding of social values and an understanding not only of their duty to society to protect, but also of the meanings and values embodied in a cultural object, site, or cultural practice. They stress a values-based competency framework that is goal-oriented, rather than a more process-driven pedagogy. This may well have particular relevance for conservation education in complex scenarios, given that both time and equipment are often limited. As the authors state, 'the intuitive, fluid, decision-making that embodies real expertise take hundreds of hours of repeated experiences and reflection to achieve' (Henderson and Parkes 2021). This is rarely achievable either practically (in the short intensive training sessions typical of conservation interventions in active and post-conflict zones), or culturally (in terms of the implementing the andro and heutagogical approaches described above) in the context of more traditional cultures. It may be that we should 'transform students from passive docile learners into critical co-investigators in dialogue with the teacher' (Freire 1970). However, this may be significantly more difficult to achieve in some cultures than others.

Conclusion

It is important to state that there is no common narrative for cultural heritage and the peoples that it represents. This limited study has demonstrated that although international conservation interventions in post-conflict zones can have significant impact, it is often challenging to create a sustainable impact where cost and security issues generally mean that training takes place over an intensive, but short, period of time. The HUNAR case study presented here by no means describes all conflict-zone interventions. However, it is a useful example that has relevance for future interventions, and it serves as a useful reflection upon the variable ways in which diverse students learn across cultures. For Afghanistan, the only solution is to create long-term institutional change in the country, which is not a simple task. The project team continues to work with international partners and the Afghan Ministry of Information and Culture on developing a full-time conservation programme at Kabul University. While Afghanistan is in an increasingly precarious position at the present time, and hopes dim by the week, and with the risk to its people and its cultural heritage again highlighted by the international community, international development remains crucial. Yet, it is paramount to remain critical and self-reflective about the impact international interventions can have, maintain a cautious approach, and above all understand how we might maximise our efforts to highlight the vital importance of cultural heritage in the region and throughout all world conflict zones.

Culture, Education and Conflict: The Relevance of Critical Conservation Pedagogies for Post-conflict Afghanistan. Richard Mulholland. Received 3 August 2021. Accepted 31 December 2021. KEYWORDS. Afghanistan, conflict, pedagogy, heritage, conservation. Richard Mulholland *richard.mulholland@northumbria. ac.uk Department of Arts, Northumbria University, Burt Hall 201, City Campus, Newcastle upon Tyne NE18ST, United Kingdom. © 2022 The Author(s). Published by Informa UK Limited, trading as Taylor & Francis Group. This is an Open Access article distributed under the terms of the Creative Commons Attribution License (http://creativecommons.org/licenses/by/4.0/), which permits unrestricted use, distribution, and reproduction in any medium, provided the original work is properly cited. Acknowledgements: The author is extremely grateful to the British Council-Cultural Protection Fund, who funded the project, and who continue to make significant impact for cultural heritage in conflict zones throughout the world. Particular thanks are due to Daniel Head, Project Grant Manager at the BC-CPF for his help and guidance throughout. Much gratitude is due to Ms Nadia Hashimi, project manager of HUNAR and CEO of S&N Consultancy, who worked tirelessly to ensure the project was a success. Thanks are also due to the Ministry of Culture and Information, former Islamic Republic of Afghanistan; to Mr Timor Shah Hakimyar (Director at FCCS, Kabul) and his staff; and particularly to Ms Elsa Guerreiro, Director of International Fine Art Conservation Studios (IFACS) Bristol, who brought* the project to the author's attention and coordinated the conservation component with great patience and expertise. Also, thanks to conservators Michael Correia and Fred Stubbs, who were invaluable to the work in Kabul. Mr Jolyon Leslie, founder member of SPACH and ACHCO, and Dr Gill Stein (Oriental Institute, University of Chicago) provided incredibly useful insights into present and past conservation interventions in Afghanistan. Above all, this paper is dedicated with deep appreciation and respect to colleagues at the National Gallery, National Museum, National Archives, and heritage institutions throughout Afghanistan who were enthusiastic participants throughout the project, and who remain in the country to protect and preserve its cultural heritage in the face of severe limitations and not inconsiderable danger. No potential conflict of interest was reported by the author. Ethics approval. This non-interventional study employed participant survey and assessment data. All participants were provided with an information sheet and signed an informed consent form. Participants were informed that they may withdraw their contributed information at any point. All personal data is anonymised. All participant data is held on secure servers at the University of Northumbria and at S&N Consultancy. This article has been republished with minor changes. These changes do not impact the academic content of the article. Additional information. Funding. This project was funded with a Project Grant by the British Council's Cultural Protection Fund (grant number IMP-516-19), in partnership with the Department for Digital, Culture, Media and Sport, UK. Studies in Conservation is the premier international peer-reviewed journal for the conservation of historic and artistic works. The intended readership includes the conservation professional in the broadest sense of the term: practising conservators of all types of object, conservation, heritage and museum scientists, collection or conservation managers, teachers and students of conservation, and academic researchers in the subject areas of arts, archaeology, the built heritage, materials history, art technological research and material culture. Studies in Conservation publishes original work on a range of subjects including, but not limited to, examination methods for works of art, new research in the analysis of artistic materials, mechanisms of deterioration, advances in conservation practice, novel methods of treatment, conservation issues in display and storage, preventive conservation, issues of collection care, conservation history and ethics, and the history of materials and technological processes. Scientific content is not necessary, and the editors encourage the submission of practical articles, review papers, position papers on best practice and the philosophy and ethics of collecting and preservation, to help maintain the traditional balance of the journal. Whatever the subject matter, accounts of routine procedures are not accepted, except where these lead to results that are sufficiently novel and/or significant to be of general interest. The International Institute for Conservation of Historic and Artistic Works and our publisher Taylor & Francis make every effort to ensure the accuracy of all the information (the «Content») contained in our publications. However, The International Institute for Conservation of Historic and Artistic Works and our publisher Taylor & Francis, our agents (including the editor, any member of the editorial team or editorial board, and any guest editors), and our licensors make no representations or warranties whatsoever as to the accuracy, completeness, or suitability for any purpose of the

Chapter 5

The Taliban, ISIS-K, Al Qaeda, the Haqqani Network, their Atrocities, Torture and the Degradation of Afghan Nation

Terrorist organisations suchlike ISIS, and the Taliban through Facebook, YouTube and Twitter invite young people to join their networks by using various marketing techniques. These terror groups are marketers as well as consumers to a degree; their recruiters 'market' boys and use them as human bombs against civil society and military infrastructure. They supply suicide bombers across Asia and the Middle East in a cheap rate. Religious and political vendettas are being settled by using suicide bombers against rival groups or families. This generation of fear and panic is controlled by extremist elements and non-state actors. Fear and terror marketing systems are updated every year and new destruction techniques are introduced. The way the Afghan Taliban design their strategies for training and brainwashing suicide bombers is not quite different from the suicide techniques of the ISIS-K. They market fear and terror according to their demand. If we deeply consider the terrorism marketing techniques of both the Afghan Taliban and the IS-K, we will clearly observe approximation in their way of killing.

The concept of suicide attacks, or dying in order to kill in the name of religion become supreme ideal of Taliban and IS-K groups that have been carrying out suicide attacks against the innocent civilians of Afghanistan and Pakistan. After the US invasion of Afghanistan, Taliban resorted to suicide terrorism to force the United States and its NATO allies to withdraw their forces from the country and restore Emirate Islami of Taliban. Taliban and the IS-K became dominant forces in suicide terrorism to internationalise and justify it. Modern suicide terrorism emerged in Afghanistan after 9/11, but it was introduced in different shapes. Over the past two decades, the tactic of suicide terrorism in Afghanistan and Pakistan were modified and justified by religious clerics. According to expert, Assaf Moghadam (Suicide Terrorism, Occupation, and the Globalization of Martyrdom: A Critique of Dying to Win, published in 2006), "the growing interest in suicide terrorism in recent years has generated a steep rise in the number of books that address a topic that is inherently fascinating—a mode of operations that requires the death of its perpetrator to ensure its success". In Dying, in order to kill Strategic Logic of Suicide Terrorism is possible to assemble statistical data about terrorist incidents. Experts and analysts, Yoram Schweitzer and Sari Goldstein Ferber, in their research paper (Al-Qaeda and the Internationalization of Suicide Terrorism. Jaffee Center for Strategic Studies, Tel Aviv University. Memorandum No. 78 November 2005) have highlighted some aspects of Istishhad or suicide terrorism:

"The concept of istishhad as a means of warfare is part of an overall philosophy that sees active jihad against the perceived enemies of Islam as a central ideological pillar and organizational ideal. According to al-Qaeda's worldview, one's willingness to sacrifice his or her life for Allah and 'in the path of Allah' (fi sabil allah) is an expression of the Muslim fighter's advantage over the opponent. In al-Qaeda, the sacrifice of life is of supreme value, the symbolic importance of which is equal to if not greater than its tactical importance. The organization adopted suicide as the supreme embodiment of global jihad and raised Islamic martyrdom (al-shehada) to the status of a principle of faith. Al-Qaeda leaders cultivated the spirit of the organization, constructing its ethos around a commitment to self-sacrifice and the implementation of this idea through suicide attacks. Readiness for self-sacrifice was one of the most important characteristics to imbue in veteran members and new recruits. The principal aim of a jihad warrior: sacrifice of life in the name of Allah, is presented in terms of enjoyment: "We are asking you to undertake the pleasure of looking at your face and we long to meet you, not in a time of distress…take us to you." The idealization of istishhad, repeated regularly in official organizational statements, is contained in its motto: "we love death more than our opponents' love life. This motto encapsulates the lack of fear among al-Qaeda fighters of losing temporary life in this world, since it is exchanged for an eternal life of purity in heaven".[1]

Taliban and the IS-K emerged as terrorist organizations with their dynamic structures. The ISIS reshaped jihadist landscape with its bloody strategy more than that of the Taliban. In Afghanistan, US and NATO forces ousted the Taliban and in a way paved the road for establishment of the IS-K terrorist group. In 2006, when NATO deployed its forces across the south, insurgents shifted to asymmetric tactics. On 19 October 2021, Taliban's acting Interior Minister hosted a ceremony in Kabul to honour suicide bombers responsible for the killings of innocent Afghans, and deployed suicide brigades to take on Pakistani forces on Durand Line. He praised the families of 1,500 suicide bombers in Afghanistan and fixed monthly salary for them. In October 2021, ISIS suicide bombers attacked the Fatemiyyeh Brigade's mosque in Kandahar, killing at least 33 people and injuring 74 others. Another attack in 2022, in which an IS-K suicide bomber hit a mosque in Kunduz, killing at least 100 people. However, BBC in its news story (Iraq bombing: IS says it was behind deadly suicide attacks in Baghdad, published on 22 January 2021) reported attacks of IS-K in Afghanistan. Suicide tactics of ISIS and IS-K in Iraq and Afghanistan are identical but recent development in using Armoured Suicide Vehicles (ASV) in Iraq made a huge difference. Expert, Ellen Tveteraas (Under the Hood–Learning and Innovation in the Islamic State's Suicide Vehicle Industry, Studies in Conflict & Terrorism, 2022) has documented operations of the ISIS armoured Suicide Vehicles in Iraq that emerged around Baghdad in October 2014:

"The first reports of up-armoured suicide vehicles in Iraq emerged around Baghdad in October 2014, with the Islamic State employing Humvees left behind by the Iraqi army following the fall of Mosul in June that same year. Because they were a limited resource and had utility in other aspects of battle, these cars proved impractical to use for suicide bombings in high numbers. Combining the benefits of the Humvee with the requirement for mass production, the group gradually developed a reproducible and bulletproof design based on civilian vehicles. Personnel would cover all or parts of cars with thick iron plates, slanting it in front to increase the effective thickness of the metal and heightening the odds of small arms and heavy munitions ricocheting off. They also added metal grids to increase the distance between exploding munitions and the car. In rural operations, the group would paint the armour beige to blend in with desert terrain and make the discovery by reconnaissance units more difficult. In urban operation the armour would be painted in more radiant colours to mimic civilian vehicles. The added armour initially caught the Iraqi military off-guard, and to effectively stop some of these new contraptions they had to procure Kornet missiles at around $250 000 apiece. Suicide operatives were the purview of the special skills bureau, with prospective bombers organized in a section called the Martyrdom Operatives Battalion (Katibat al-Istishadiin). Members of the suicide battalion would normally arrive at the area of operation shortly before the execution of an attack and spend the preparation period in isolation with clerics to build the mental fortitude required to execute this type of mission. The battalion had no shortage of volunteers and, following the group's acquisition of territory, its size far outgrew the tactical demand for suicide operations."[2]

After the American Army took to one's heels at midnight, Afghanistan faced numerous political, economic and health care challenges. Causes of the failure of Central Intelligence Agency (CIA) and NATO's intelligence machine to stabilize Afghanistan, or defeat Taliban were multitudinous. First, Afghan Army officers and commanders sold their weapons and check posts to Taliban to address their financial hardship because they were denied their salaries in war zones. Second, they started transporting terrorists in Army vehicles and helped the Islamic State in carrying out suicide attacks against civilians and government installations. Third, they protected foreign intelligence networks, plundered military funds and resources due to their personal and anti-state attitude. Fourth, the Afghan Army and the National Directorate of Security (NDS) intelligence agency were on the payroll of CIA and NATO member states to implement their agendas. Fifth, Generals of Afghan National Army (ANA), directors of foreign office and national security office maintained secret accounts abroad to easily receive funds from foreign intelligence agencies. Some of them were involved in money laundering, and some were tasked to humiliate Afghans in print and electronic media. Sixth, the issue of landmines was also not addressed properly by the US and NATO member states which prompted the death of thousand civilians. Seventh, the Afghan army was personally involved in planting landmines in Pashtun provinces to intercept the Taliban incursions. On 15 March, 2021, Daily Siasat reported the killing of more than 120 Afghans by landmines every month. Directorate of Mine Action Coordination of Afghanistan (DMAC) said in a statement: "An average of 120 people, including children were being killed or maimed by unexploded ordnance and landmines, every month". Expert and analyst, Michael A. Peters in his research paper (Declinism' and discourses of decline-the end of the war in Afghanistan and the limits of American power, Educational Philosophy and Theory) has documented the real failure of US Army in Afghanistan and the abrupt announcement of the Biden administration to leave Afghanistan surprised everyone and caused a rift with NATO allies who wanted to stay in Afghanistan:

"The ignominious end of the Afghan War after twenty long years, often referred to as the 'forever war', was brought to an abrupt end by Joe Biden in such haste that it surprised everyone and caused a rift with NATO allies who wanted to stay a presence in Afghanistan. Whatever spin can be placed on the end of US involvement, the withdrawal was messy and unplanned, air lifting US troops and well over 120,000 Afghan US supporters from Kabul airport. Many more Afghans who were part of the US war effort remain trapped in the country. Even with American support, the Afghan army was routed in a week and the Afghan government also collapsed. The embattled president Ashraf Ghani fled the country reportedly with a 'helicopter full of cash'. His swift departure left the best possible opening for the Taliban, who are talking of forming an 'open, inclusive Islamic government' and have established an interim government yet without the representation of women. President Biden first went on record as saying that nation-building was never part of the original mission yet the official justification for the Americans being in Afghanistan after the killing of Bin Laden had evaporated. Mission-creep set in with the downscaling US forces from 20,000 a couple of years ago to less than 2,000 in the final years".[3]

With the establishment of Taliban government in Afghanistan in 2021, mentally and physically tortured civilians experienced every mischance and stroke of bad luck. The proxy militia inflicted deep pain and torment on minorities by attacking mosques and religious places, and protecting Pakistani and Central Asian terrorist organizations. Women were tortured, humiliated and incarcerated, girls were deprived from education and their schools were shamelessly closed. After taking control of Ghazni province on 21 August 2021, they used inhuman and illegal strategies and policies that resulted in huge barriers to women's health and girls' education. Afghan women experienced collapsed human rights and risk of basic rights, and were treated like goats and dogs. Human Rights Watch (HRW) and SJSU interviewed women in Ghazni province and documented their spiralling prices for food, transportation, and schoolbooks. The poorer and hungry parents sold their girls and sons for a piece of bread. Taliban kidnapped women, sexually abused and tortured transgender then killed them. Some women felt heightened risk because of gender, ethnicity and religious sect. Human Rights Watch in its recent report (Afghanistan: Taliban Deprive Women of Livelihoods, Identity: Severe Restrictions, Harassment, Fear in Ghazni Province-18 January, 2022), noted intimidation of villagers by Taliban fighters: "Taliban authorities have also used intimidation to extract money, food, and services. 'When the Taliban visit a village, they force the households to feed them and collect food items from people,' a woman from a village said. 'The Taliban and their fighters call us in the middle of the night to cure and give special treatment to their patients and families,' a health worker said. They enter the hospital with their guns, it's difficult for the doctors and nurses to manage."[4] HRW noted.

Following the US and NATO withdrawal from Afghanistan, more than 3,000 Hazara Muslims were tortured and forcibly evicted from their homes by Taliban terrorist militia. As mentioned earlier, Taliban and the IS-K terrorist organizations have been killing Hazara Muslims in all provinces of Afghanistan since 1990s, destroying their houses and kidnaping their women and girls for sexual exploitation. After the 9/11 terrorist attacks in the United States, the Hazara Muslims experienced further harassment and intimidation. Successive Afghan governments failed to protect their agricultural land, houses and children. In her recent research paper, analyst and expert, Kate Clark (Afghanistan's conflict in 2021 (2): Republic collapse and Taliban victory in the long-view of history. Afghanistan Analysts Network, published in 30 December, 2021) documented civilian's pain, killings, and destruction after the US withdrawal from Afghanistan:

"The high number of civilians killed and injured in the conflict in 2021 was striking because the war in Afghanistan was then being fought mainly between Afghans. After the US-Taliban February 2020 agreement, which bound the two parties not to attack each other, but allowed the Taliban to attack the Afghan National Security Forces (ANSF), the US largely removed itself from the battlefield. This spared the Taliban their most dangerous enemy, while denying the Afghan National Security Forces US support except in extremes. It translated into the US taking a much reduced and sporadic part in the war after February 2020. According to the US's own published statistics, the number of 'weapons' dropped by the US Air Force in 2020 was 1,631 (almost half of the yearly total came in the two months before the Doha agreement was signed), compared to 7,362 in 2018 and 7,423 in 2019, and 801 in 2021 (first eight months only). In the chart below, it can be seen that the number of air munitions fell after February 2020 and rose somewhat in autumn 2020 as the US used airstrikes, for example, to drive back Taliban offensives in the south (see a call by Amnesty International for safe passage for civilians out of Lashkargah in October and Washington Post reporting on Kandahar in November). The number of munitions that the US Air Force dropped again after Biden's decision to withdraw, rising only in August 2021 as the US Air Force made last-ditch efforts to shore up the ANSF..... The campaign of targeted killings, which were often unclaimed but largely believed to be carried out by the Taliban, that had begun in late 2020, did not let up, but represented the third most likely way for civilians to be injured or killed: UNAMA said the campaign targeted an "ever-widening breadth of types of civilians... human rights defenders, media workers, religious elders, civilian government workers, and humanitarian workers." The campaign also targeted members of the ANSF. According to one security source in Kabul, twice as many ANSF were targeted and killed or injured as civilians."[5]

The Taliban militia killed more than 5000 members of former Afghan security forces. The HRW accused leadership of "condoning" the "deliberate" killings. Taliban were held responsible for a bloody campaign of murder and torture against journalists and rights activists. Taliban with the assistance of Pakistani ISI located addresses of Afghan soldiers and government officials who helped the US and NATO in the illegal war against Afghanistan. HRW in its report (Afghanistan: Taliban Kill, 'Disappear' Ex-Officials: Raids Target Former Police, Intelligence Officers, published on November 30, 2021) noted, "Taliban forces in Afghanistan have summarily executed or forcibly disappeared more than 100 former police and intelligence officers in just four provinces since taking over the country on August 15, 2021. The 25-page report, "'No Forgiveness for People Like You,' Executions and Enforced Disappearances in Afghanistan under the Taliban," documents the killing or disappearance of 47 former members of the Afghan National Security Forces (ANSF) – military personnel, police, intelligence service members, and militia – who had surrendered to or were apprehended by Taliban forces between August 15 and October 31." [6]

The IS-K group was also in contact with Lashkar-e-Jhangvi (LeJ) and Lashkar-e-Taiba (LeT) in Jalalabad to target the Taliban forces, but failed to gain control of Jalalabad province. On December 11, 2014, former Interior Minister of Pakistan, Rehman Malik told a local news channel that IS-K had established recruitment centres in Gujranwala and Bahawalpur districts of Punjab province. The wall-chalking campaign and leaflets prompted fears about the terrorist group making inroads in the country. According to the leaked government circular in Balochistan and Khyber Pakhtunkhwa provinces, ISIS recruited more than 10,000 to 15,000 fighters in 2015 for the next sectarian war in Pakistan. In Kabul, on 08 December, 2014, Reuters reported a 25-year-old student from Kabul University vowed to join the mujahideen of IS-K. "When hundreds of foreigners, both men and women, leave their comfortable lives and embrace Daesh, then why not us?" he asked. The influx of terrorist groups like the Islamic State of Khorasan in Jalalabad province challenged the writ of the Taliban local administration. Former Afghan President Ghani also warned that 30 terrorist groups were operating across the country posed serious threat to the national security of Afghanistan. The UN experts also believed that more than 45,000 terrorists were fighting against the Afghan National army and between 20 to 25 percent were foreigners. Pakistan military establishment secured peace agreements with certain Taliban factions by legitimising the Talibanization of the region. Experts and analysts, Qasim Jan, Yi Xie, Muhammad Habib Qazi, Zahid Javid Choudhary and Baha ul Haq in their research paper (Examining the role of Pakistan's national curriculum textbook discourses on normalising the Taliban's violence in the USA's Post 9/11 war on terror in South Waziristan, Pakistan. British Journal of Religious Education, 2022) have documented talibanization process of Waziristan:

"After 9/11, South Waziristan attracted global attention as an epicentre of terrorism. In the wake of the US invasion of Afghanistan, the Taliban and al-Qaida escaped from Afghanistan through the North-western border to the tribal areas including South Waziristan, Pakistan. Pakistan, as the US ally, launched several military operations against these religious militants, mainly the Taliban, in this hideout. However, Pakistan's military establishment has been accused of playing a 'secret double game', named 'tournament of shadows', clandestinely supporting militants including the Taliban as their 'strategic asset'. At a later stage, the Pakistani establishment secured peace agreements with certain Taliban factions, legitimising the Talibanization of the region. The legitimisation of the Talibanization, in this context, refers to the state of Pakistan's approval of the Taliban's styled Sharia law in South Waziristan. Its practices included public flogging, hand amputation, beheading and stoning to death, proportionate to minor/major offences of the accused/guilty. Besides eroding the writ of the state (Pakistan), these peace agreements resulted in the creation of new binary i.e. 'Good Taliban' who pointed their guns on Afghanistan and fulfilled the objectives of Pakistan's security establishment, while those who didn't fall in line were called 'Bad Taliban'. The peace deal helped the Taliban and their affiliates in finding safe heavens in South Waziristan. Their commanders visited schools and colleges and delivered speeches about the glorification of Jihad and sacrifices for the cause of Allah/Muslim God. Hence, the Talibanization of the border region of tribal areas seems to be linked to Pakistan's strategic interests in Afghanistan and the South Asian region".[7]

Terrorism, violence and civil war in Afghanistan prompted catastrophe, displacement and financial destruction. With the establishment of the IS-K terrorist group in 2015, and its war against Taliban and the Afghan government further added to the pain of civilian population. The IS-K killed women, children and kidnapped young girls, looted houses and beheaded senior citizens in all provinces of Afghanistan. Both Pakistan and former Afghan government facilitated and financially supported Daesh and transported their terrorist fighters to their destination. The IS-K carried out dozens of terrorist attacks in Pakistan and Afghanistan with the help of ANA. The group has trained its fighters to carryout biological and nuclear terrorist attacks. Expert and analysts, Eric Schmitt (in "ISIS Branch Poses Biggest Immediate Terrorist Threat to Evacuation in Kabul", published on 03 November, 2021, The New York Times) has highlighted rivalries between Taliban and the IS-K terrorist group in Afghanistan:

"The rivalry between the Taliban and its partners and ISIS-K will continue after the last American troops leave, analysts say. And the fragile cooperation between American and Taliban commanders is already fraying, and the two could easily revert to their adversarial stances. The American military is treating the Taliban's red line about Aug. 31 seriously. The recent evacuations have been possible because of Taliban cooperation—in allowing most people to reach the airport unscathed, and in working against the threat of ISIS attacks, commanders say. After Aug. 31, military officials say, there is a real concern that at best, the cooperation with the Taliban will end. At worst, that could lead to attacks on U.S. forces, foreign citizens and Afghan allies, either by Taliban elements or by their turning a blind eye to Islamic State threats. Mr. Biden has pledged to prevent Afghanistan from again becoming a sanctuary for Al Qaeda and other terrorist groups that want to attack the American homeland. Military commanders say that will be a difficult task, with no troops and few spies on the ground, and armed Reaper drones thousands of miles away at bases in the Persian Gulf. In the February 2020 agreement with the Trump administration, the Taliban vowed not to allow Al Qaeda to use Afghan territory to attack the United States. But analysts fear that is not happening and that Al Qaeda remains the longer-term terrorism threat."[8]

In 2015, the IS-K was established to fight and tackle Pakistan based extremist groups who were trying to hijack the US war according to their agenda. Pakistanis from Southern Punjab rushed to join the terrorist infrastructure to sustain their poor families. In 2020, according to former Interior Minister of Pakistan, Rahman Malik, more than 80,000 poor madrasa students from Southern Punjab had joined the IS-K and participated in the civil war in Syria, Iraq and Afghanistan. These revelations generated panic in both Pakistan and Afghanistan that these fighters will further add to the pain of the Pakistan military establishment in the near future. The IS-K's intent is clear, and the Wilayat Khorasan is the ISIS most viable and lethal regional affiliate based on an expansionist military strategy. This is designed to enable the group's encirclement of Jalalabad city and is foundational to its expanded operational reach. Despite their Wahhabi backgrounds, the IS-K and Taliban groups follow a common agenda to destabilise Central Asia. The relationship between the Taliban and ISIS in Afghanistan is friendly. Taliban and ISIS are parts of a broader Deobandi and Wahhabi movements in Afghanistan who want to create misunderstanding between Islam and the west. Clayton Sharb, Danika Newlee and the CSIS iDeas Lab in their joint work (Islamic State Khorasan (IS-K), Center for Strategic and International Studies, 2018) have highlighted the IS-K global agenda and its intentions in Kashmir and Pakistan:

"IS-K carries out its global strategy in different operating environments by curating it to local conditions. Consider, for example, the divided region of Kashmir. It sits at the top of the Indian subcontinent and serves as a flashpoint for conflict between historically feuding nuclear powers, Pakistan and India. With nationalistic leaders dominating politics in both Islamabad and New Delhi, perpetual unrest in the disputed territories, and precedent of state-sponsored terrorism, Kashmir is fertile ground for future IS-K subversion. In Afghanistan and Pakistan, IS-K's strategy seeks to delegitimize the governments and degrade public trust in democratic processes, sowing instability in nation-states, which the group views as illegitimate. Recently, in the lead up to 2018 parliamentary elections in Afghanistan, IS-K warned citizens in Nangarhar province, "We caution the Muslims in the province from approaching election centres, and we recommend that they stay away from them so as to safeguard their blood, as these are legitimate targets for us." IS-K claimed multiple attacks on "elections centres" and security forces during the Afghan parliamentary elections, following through on their warning to "sabotage the polytheistic process and disrupt it."[9]

The IS-K is the strangest non-state actor in Afghanistan that poses a serious security threat to Taliban and Pakistan. The IS-K has deep roots in South Asia, with its branches in Pakistan, India, and some Southeast Asian states. Well-organized and well-established organization with over 250,000 trained fighters that can anytime challenge the authority of the failed state in Afghanistan. There are countless books and journals in markets and libraries that highlight the infrastructure of the IS-K with different perspectives and view its operational mechanism and suicide technique with different glasses. My glasses are not as different from them as I have written books on the suicide operation of the ISIS and IS-K, and contributed article to the newspapers and journals. The IS-K threat to the existence of Taliban is intensified by the day as the group consecutively targeted government installations and public places. Expert and analyst, Mohammed Mokhtar Qandi in his paper (Challenges to Taliban Rule and Potential Impacts for the Region: Internal and external factors are weakening the Taliban, making the group's long term stability increasingly unlikely, Fikra Forum, The Washington Institute for Near East Policy, 09 February 2022) has noted the intensifying threat of ISIS and IS-K in Afghanistan, and asserted that the ISIS seeks to be an alternative to the Taliban movement:

"ISIS views the Taliban movement as a major strategic foe in South Asia. From the outset, members of Khorasan Province began questioning the Taliban's legitimacy in jihadi circles, which helped ISIS win new followers who splintered from the movement. Furthermore, ISIS may be attractive to those seeking revenge on the movement. In some cases, ISIS has attracted former Afghan intelligence members as well as younger middle-class youth who may become increasingly disaffected with the Taliban. There is also the dispute between the Taliban and the Salafist current inside Afghanistan that is not affiliated with Khorasan Province. The Taliban's harassment of these Salafists may push them to join the ranks of ISIS, or at least provide a haven for its members. Since the Taliban came to power by force, their lack of legitimacy can quickly lead to a decline in their popular support vis-à-vis ISIS, especially if they fail to meet the needs of the people and improve the economic situation. Despite the power that the Islamic State demonstrated in Khorasan, it is unlikely that the movement will be able to plan or launch attacks on distant targets. However, if ISIS-Khorasan succeeds in controlling more territories in Afghanistan and recruiting elements who resent Taliban, it will be tantamount to reviving the organization in the Middle East. On the one hand, the organization will intensify its propaganda and its claims that it is the sole carrier of the banner of jihad and hence, must be supported in establishing the Islamic caliphate as a global project. This will provide the organization with many opportunities to set up training camps for its elements and export them to the Middle East where they previously experienced a harsh defeat".[10]

Transnational extremist groups suchlike IS-K, Lashkar-e-Taiba, al Qaeda, and Taliban are relying on domestic extremist organizations that control thoughts and minds of citizens. The yesteryear analysis explored survival of groups in alliances. We can find these trends in Afghanistan where Taliban have entered into alliance with different Pakistani and Arab terrorist groups. Although ISIS also collaborated with different Afghan, Pakistani and Central Asian organizations, but it follows American agenda and wants to export jihad and suicide terrorism to Central Asia. In areas under its control, the IS-K terrorist group manage its own strategies of governance. The terrorist group killed hundreds in Afghanistan to justify its presence. In Afghanistan, if other groups leave the area under their control, the IS-K will either kill its members or force them to pledge allegiance and work with IS-K. Experts and analysts, Amira Jadoon, Abdul Sayed and Andrew Mines in their research paper ("The Islamic State Threat in Taliban Afghanistan: Tracing the Resurgence of Islamic State Khorasan", The Combating Terrorism Center at West Point, January 2022, Volum 15, Issue-1) have noted military confrontations between Taliban and the Islamic State of Khorasan:

"Since its inception, ISK has viewed the Afghan Taliban as its main strategic rival in the region.100 In a quest to outbid and outcompete its rival, ISK has not only attacked Afghan Taliban targets regularly since 2015, but also recruited heavily from the organization's ranks and leadership, which ISK has categorized into three general groups: first, the 'sincere Taliban jihadis' who defected to join ISK; second, those who kept a neutral stance toward ISK; and third, the ones who are the puppets of regional governments and motivated by personal interests. ISK has made delegitimizing the Afghan Taliban's purity as a jihadi movement one of its main messaging priorities. This is reflected in ISK's media campaigns for the last several years, which consistently highlight idolatrous Afghan Taliban-supported or tacitly approved religious and cultural practices, as well as relationships with foreign states that ISK views as heretical. Undermining the Afghan Taliban's legitimacy as a jihadi movement is a key pillar to ISK's organizational identity that is unlikely to change. Since the former took power, ISK's strategy has evolved not only to challenge the Afghan Taliban's legitimacy as the predominant jihadi force in the region (given their negotiations with the United States, and links to Pakistan, China, and Iran), but also their competency as a governing actor. ISK's two-pronged attack on the Afghan Taliban's legitimacy is likely to persist as long as the Taliban remain in power."[11]

On 19 April 2022, Radio Free Europe/Radio Liberty reported Uzbek Presidential Spokesman Sherzod Asadov denial of the IS-K claim that it had fired missiles towards Uzbekistan, and called on Uzbek citizens to disregard what he called provocations. According to the Defense Ministry and Uzbekistan's border guard troops, there were no active military developments along the Uzbek-Afghan border, the situation was stable, Asadov said in a statement placed on Telegram. Moreover, Salam Times reported the IS-K claim that a rocket attack against Uzbekistan from neighbouring Afghanistan was fired and it was the first such bombardment of the Central Asian nation by the group. "The group fired 10 Katyusha rockets at Uzbek forces stationed in the border city of Termez in southern Uzbekistan, IS-K said, adding that the attack followed an audio message from an IS-K spokesperson. On April 17, IS-K called on all fighters around the world to carry out "big and painful" attacks targeting officials and soldiers". Salam Times noted.[12] These rocket attacks generated fear in Central Asia amid prevailing political and economic uncertainty in Afghanistan and raised concerns that the group was expanding its recruitment campaign in the country and posed a serious threat to the region. The "ISIS is seizing the current power vacuum in Afghanistan as an opportunity to rapidly increase the number of its militants across the country, said Mohammad Naim Ghayur, a military analyst in Herat. The increasing number of attacks carried out by ISIS in recent months indicated that this terrorist group had not only solidified its footprint but also had built its capacity to challenge Afghanistan's security," Salam Times noted. Expert and analyst, Roshni Kapur in his paper (The Persistent ISKP Threat to Afghanistan: On China's Doorstep. Middle East Institute, January 6, 2022), has noted recent attacks of the IS-K in Afghanistan:

Two separate bombs were detonated in Dasht-e-Barchi in Kabul on December 10, killing two and injuring three others. Although no group has claimed responsibility for the attack, the Islamic State of Khorasan Province (ISKP) is likely behind the latest bout of violence. IS-K's fingerprints have been on other attacks. One of the worst, which killed over 180 people and injured hundreds, took place outside the Kabul airport in August 2021 during the final days of evacuations….The Taliban and ISKP will try to project themselves as the authentic representative of Islam and use that as a recruitment and expansion strategy. Nevertheless, experts have said that rivalry between the two is likely to be confined to a protracted guerrilla-style conflict with direct battles and clashes instead of descending into a civil war. While the Taliban has given amnesty to former security members, the same concessions have not been extended to ISKP. The Taliban is likely to carry out raids against ISKP hideouts, similar to the operation in Nangarhar and detainment of 80 ISKP fighters, as the latter seeks to pose a formidable challenge to the Taliban's rule. ISKP is also likely to regroup, change its modus operandi, become more resilient, and recruit more hardliner fighters to enhance its position in Afghanistan and the surrounding region. Although the US launched a drone strike against ISKP in late August 2021, it has not implemented a long-term counter-terrorism strategy against ISKP. The intelligence-gathering and surveillance systems used by the US and its allies have been dismantled. The chief of US Central Command, Gen. Frank McKenzie, also confessed that Washington is providing only limited security assistance to the Taliban to counter the threat from ISKP. Regional countries may step into the security void to prevent the threat of ISKP spilling into their territories".[13]

Concerns of India are genuine that the Taliban and the IS-K terrorist groups can anytime transport their fighters with sophisticated weapon into Kashmir and Punjab. In March 2022, Indian Army seized US made weapons in Kashmir. Now, there were speculations that if the Taliban guaranteed security, South and Central Asian states would recognize the Taliban government. Beijing is also at the spike due the Taliban attitude towards neighbouring states. China is in hot water that if the East Turkestan Islamic Movement (ETIM) collaborated with the IS-K terrorist group they might possibility orchestrate terrorist attacks in Xinjiang province. Editor of Terrorism Monitor, Jacob Zenn in his article (Islamic State in Khorasan Province's One-Off Attack in Uzbekistan, Volium XX, Issue 9, 06 May 2022) has highlighted issue of the IS-K missile attack and response of Uzbekistan:

"On April 18, 2022, the Islamic State (IS) released a short video of Islamic State in Khorasan Province (ISKP) fighters firing rockets from the outskirts of Mazar e Sharif, Afghanistan into Termiz, Uzbekistan.Uzbekistan denied that any ISKP attack took place on its soil. This was in lieu of the fact that IS provinces tend to be accurate about their claims, albeit inflating the severity and casualties of their attacks. According to the Uzbek presidency's spokesperson, the reports of the ISKP attack were not "reality" and there were no military operations on Uzbekistan's territory nor any instability along its borderlands.....A more plausible explanation came from the Taliban's deputy spokesperson, however, who asserted that ISKP did launch rockets toward Uzbekistan from Afghan territory, but the rockets failed to reach the Uzbekistan border. As is typical of Taliban foreign policy, the deputy spokesperson affirmed that Afghan soil would not be allowed to be used by any militant group to attack any external country. Video footage also emerged of the Taliban uncovering the ramshackle hideout that ISKP had used to fire the rockets, including the empty rocket launchers".[14]

Taliban are in deep water due the attitude of international community and domestic sectarian and terrorist organizations that have put their government at spike. Their recognition social problems are associated with their domestic policies, torture, humiliation, arrest and closure of girl's schools. Islamic State-Khorasan Province has retrieved military and financial strength and now challenge their authority and carrying out suicide attacks to target religious places. Expert and analyst, Amy Kazmin in her article (ISIS-K insurgency jeopardises Taliban's grip on Afghanistan: New rulers accused of betraying Islam by jihadis intent on creating ideologically pure caliphate, October, 26, 2021) has highlighted military and political rivalries between Taliban and the Islami State of Khorasan in Afghanistan:

"After the Taliban Two months after the Taliban seized power, violence, death and fear still stalk Afghanistan. US troops might have departed but the new Islamist rulers in Kabul are now threatened by an insurgency launched by Islamic State-Khorasan Province, an Isis-inspired jihadi movement that has deep ideological differences with the Taliban. Since the Taliban takeover in August, ISIS-K has mounted a series of suicide bomb attacks, including at the Kabul airport and at two Shia mosques, as well as assaults on Taliban convoys, which have killed hundreds. Analysts have warned of further violence as Isis-K tries to prevent the Taliban from consolidating their grip on Afghanistan. ISIS-K's more hard-line stance has proved attractive to disgruntled Taliban fighters. Dismayed at the new regime's reluctance to impose tougher restrictions on women and its diplomatic overtures to countries such as the US, China and Russia, former Taliban members have switched allegiance to ISIS-K. "The American war is over, but the Afghan wars are not," said Avinash Paliwal, deputy director of the SOAS South Asia Institute, and author of "My Enemy's Enemy", a book about Afghanistan. The Taliban's long time goal has been to establish an Islamic government in Afghanistan. But Isis-K, which has been active in Afghanistan since 2015, wants to establish an Islamic caliphate across Afghanistan, Pakistan and parts of India and Iran. Isis-K militants consider the Taliban, who have held talks with regional powers and the US in a quest for diplomatic recognition, as "filthy nationalists" who have betrayed the greater Islamic cause, according to an analyst. "Isis-K sees the Taliban as just another kind of political outfit- cutting a deal with the Americans- that is ideologically not pure," Paliwal said. "Their aim is to destabilise an already struggling regime."[15]

Taliban's controversial policies and their resentment towards minorities in Afghanistan divided communities on sectarian bases. As there is no state and legitimate government in the country, they arrest, torture and sexually abuse women with impunity. They have arrested dozens of intellectuals, doctors, former military officers, journalists and social media activists. Some were tortured to death and some were hanged publicly. Analyst and expert, Salman Rafi Sheikh in his article (Eight months on, Taliban's rule is far from stable: Resistance groups are mounting an increasingly potent challenge to the Taliban and may have Pakistan's clandestine support, Asia Times, May 2, 2022) has noted internal policies of Taliban of divided and rule. He also painted a picture of their violence and incompetency to stabilise Afghanistan and maintain friendly relations with neighbouring states:

"On April 29, a blast in Kabul in a mosque belonging to a Sunni minority group – the Zikris – killed at least 50 people. On Thursday, a bomb blast in a van carrying Shiite Muslims in the northern city of Mazar-e-Sharif killed at least nine people. The attack on the Shiite van came after Taliban leaders claimed to have captured an ISIS-K mastermind of the previous attack in Mazar-e-Sharif on a Shiite mosque that killed at least 31 people. These attacks challenge the Taliban leadership's claims to have eliminated opposed terror groups like ISIS-K, offered full protection to minorities and claimed groups like ISIS-K do not pose a serious threat. While their claims have by now clearly been proven wrong, there is little denying that the continuing success of ISIS-K is directly tied to the Taliban regime for several reasons. First, some hardliner groups within the Taliban – including the Haqqanis, who control the Ministry of Interior responsible for tackling such threats and whose ties with the ISIS-K go back to their joint attacks on the US-NATO-Afghan forces – are reluctant to take effective tough action against the terror group. It was the same internal division with ISIS-K that led the Taliban, despite their apparent ideological rivalry with the group, to release several hundred ISIS-K fighters after their August takeover, allowing the organization to increase its numbers to 4,000, according to a February 2022 estimate by the UN, from 2,000 previously. This has allowed the ISIS-K to operate freely inside Afghanistan, giving it the leeway to establish cells in almost all of Afghanistan's provinces".[16]

Chapter 6

Suicide Brigades, IS-K Military Strength and Taliban's Misrule in Afghanistan

In January 2022, Taliban announced to put in place a Suicide-Brigade. Before this development, the Taliban acting Interior Minister, Sirajuddin Haqqani and acting Defence Minister Mullah Muhammad Yaqoob hosted a ceremony in Kabul to honour Afghan and Pakistani Suicide Bombers responsible for the killings of thousands of Afghan and Pakistani citizens. Sirajuddin Haqqani, is representing the Haqqani Network-affiliated with the Taliban and al Qaeda. The group has been behind some of the deadliest attacks in the country two-decade-long war, including a truck bomb explosion in Kabul in 2017 that killed more than 150 people. Unlike the wider Taliban, the Haqqani Network has been designated a Foreign Terrorist Organisation by the US. It also maintains close ties to al Qaeda. Haqqani who carries a US bounty of $10m met with the US Chief of counter-terrorism in February 2022 in Kabul to discuss the exponentially growing tension in Afghanistan. Haqqani has been killing Afghan civilians since 2003, and the group's fighters were trained by the Pakistan Army to serve the interests of US and NATO forces in Afghanistan. They used Improvised Explosive Device in suicide attacks, and destroyed critical national infrastructure in the country. The group was based in North Waziristan, Pakistan in yesteryears, while now is part of Taliban government. Adopting strategy of suicide bombing was not an easy task for Haqqanis, but with the support of Pakistan Army, the group recruited thousands of its fighters for suicide terrorism.

Some scholars have asserted that suicide attacks were legitimate and HALAL in Islam, while conversely, majority of Barelvis, Deobandis and Liberal scholars understand that suicide terrorism is strictly prohibited in Islam that cause deaths and catastrophe. Suicide terrorism in Pakistan and Afghanistan have been neglected by Middle Eastern scholars due to their limited information about the military tactics of terrorist groups.

Expert and analyst, Atal Ahmadzai in his paper (Dying to Live: The "Love to Death" Narrative Driving the Taliban's Suicide Bombings) highlighted the Istishhadi narrative of Taliban: "The Taliban in Afghanistan have embraced suicide bombings since 2003. Within a short period of time, the group developed an infamous industry of manufacturing 'human bombs.' They soon became the leading terrorist organization in the world, claiming responsibility for the greatest number of suicide bombings. Two narratives assist the Taliban in supplying their bombing campaigns with large numbers of bombers. First, an Istish-haadi narrative, which is based on authoritative reasoning derived from sacred texts. In addition, the group has resorted to logical fallacy/circular reasoning in producing the desired narrative. This narrative serves as the conceptual foundation for providing moral-legal legitimacy to suicide bombings. However, legitimization does not mean the practicality of these terminal missions, especially in a social and cultural milieu that is dismissive of suicide killing in warfare. To overcome this challenge, the group constructed yet another narrative; "love to death." It is based on an irrational and dystopian interpretation of the mundane existence. It promotes an alternative comprehension of reality that is beyond the premises of time and space, one which does not bear any relation to rationality. Two aspects of these narratives are prominent. First, martyrdom is the central tenet of the Taliban's suicide bombing industry. However, their understanding of martyrdom induced by suicide bombings is different. The decision to choose subjects for these bombings does not reside with the bombers, but rather is bestowed upon them by the divine."[1]

With the establishment of Islamic State (ISIS) in Syria and Iraq, and its secret networks and propaganda campaign in Pakistan and Afghanistan, the international community focused on the proliferation and smuggling of chemical and biological weapons in the region. Recent debate in Europe-based think tanks suggests that, as the group retrieved nuclear and biological material from the Mosul University in Iraq, it can possibly make nuclear explosive devices with less than eight kilograms of plutonium. The debate about bioterrorism and biodefense is not entirely new in the military circles of South Asia; the involvement of ISIS in using biological weapons against the Kurdish Army in Kobane is a lesson for Pakistan and Afghanistan to deeply concentrate on the proliferation of these weapons in the region. A document from Pakistan's Internal Security Policy (2014-2018) categorically stated that the country's security faced the threat of nuclear terrorism. The threat, according to the document's contents, is in addition to the possibility of chemical and biological terrorism. As the fatal war against terrorism has entered a crucial phase, another powerful extremist militant group (IS-K) has emerged with a strong and well-trained army in Afghanistan and parts of Pakistan to establish an Islamic state. The massacre of 100 innocent civilians, including an Afghan national army soldier in the Ajristan district of Ghazni province by IS-K forces, and the brutal killings of children in the Army School in Peshawar have raised serious questions about the future of security and stability in South Asia. The Tehreek-e-Taliban Pakistan (TTP) claimed responsibility and called it a revenge attack for the Pakistan Army's Operation Zarb-e-Azb in North Waziristan and erstwhile FATA regions. Research Scholars Amira Jadoon, Andrew Mines and Abdul Sayed, in their research paper (The evolving Taliban-ISK rivalry, published on 07 September 2021, The Interpreter), have reviewed the IS-K attacks on Kabul airport:

"The attack on evacuation efforts at the Kabul airport by the Islamic State-Khorasan Province (ISK, ISKP, or ISIS-K) triggered much speculation about the Afghan Taliban's ability to constrain terrorism in the country. But it also served as a reminder of the intense rivalry between the Taliban and ISK; while the attack's lethality shocked many, the two organisations have engaged in intense clashes as militant organisations since ISK's emergence in 2015. However, as the Afghan Taliban now transition into a legitimate political entity, the nature of their clashes is likely to change as ISK will tackle the Afghan Taliban as more of a state actor–whose credibility can be undermined domestically and internationally. In order to understand this new phase of the Taliban-ISK rivalry, it's important to look forward, but also to frame the recent attack by ISK within the context of the original clash between the two groups' ideologies and agendas; there are important lessons from the past that can help us assess how the two groups may compete for dominance in Afghanistan, and the associated security implications".[2]

The Looting and ransacking of Afghanistan's natural resources by NATO and the United States, and their criminal militias; suchlike the ISIS and Taliban terrorist groups, caused misunderstanding between the Afghans and International Coalition that they all were involved in looting of mineral resources of their country. The IS-K controls a large amount of territory in Afghanistan, and that includes parts of the country's rich mineral wealth, especially talc, chromite and marble. According to the Global Witness research report, several insurgents' groups, militias, Taliban and the ISIS are deeply involved in the plunder of these resources: "The Islamic State in Afghanistan (ISKP) controls major mining sites in eastern Afghanistan and has a strategic interest in the country's rich mineral resources, new

130

Global Witness research shows–a powerful example of the wider threat posed by armed groups and corrupt actors in Afghan mining. The Islamic State in Afghanistan (ISKP) controls large talc, marble and chromite mines in the Islamic State stronghold of Achin district in the Nangarhar province of eastern Afghanistan–the same area where in April 2017 the US military dropped the 'Mother of All Bombs' against ISKP-held caves. Nangarhar was the deadliest Afghan province for US troops in 2017. An estimated 380,000 tons of talc was imported into the United States in 2017. On average around 35 percent of US imports are from Pakistan, according to the US Geological Survey. From our research we also estimated that around 80 percent of Pakistan's 2016 exports of talc actually originated in Afghanistan. Of those exports, 42 percent went to the US, and another 36 percent went to EU countries, especially the Netherlands and Italy".[3]

However, in 2016, Global Witness report (War in the treasury of the people: Afghanistan, lapis lazuli and the battle for mineral wealth) noted the importance of mining, especially of lapis lazuli, for the Taliban in Afghanistan. The report warned that armed groups including the Taliban were earning tens of millions of dollars per year from Afghanistan's lapis mines, the world's main source of the brilliant blue lapis lazuli stone, which is used in jewellery around the world. Moreover, experts and analysts, William A. Byrd and Javed Noorani, in their report (Industrial-Scale Looting of Afghanistan's Mineral Resources, 2017, the United States Institute of Peace) warned that international community and different sectarian, militant and terrorist organization of Pakistan and Afghanistan are looting mineral resources of Afghanistan on an industrial scale: "Based on the evidence from fieldwork and case studies, a different explanation is far more compelling. The post-2001 Afghan government from the time of its formation has been politically penetrated by networks of power holders—actors with their own access to the means of organized armed violence—whose members are involved in, or at least benefiting from, ongoing mineral exploitation. These networks, which had formed and developed during the resistance against the interests of different power holders and funding their political and security expenditures; reductions in one kind of rent may well push the political system to increase rents in other spheres of activity. The high profits that can be relatively easily obtained from mineral looting constitute a strong pull factor attracting interest groups into the mining business. These profits have become progressively more accessible as experience is gained, markets are identified and exploited (for example, lapis in China, and talc in Europe), transport channels open, and business linkages are developed. Such dynamics can result in snowballing of extraction over time, as has occurred in the case of lapis, talc, and apparently chromite, among others".[4]

The presence of the ISIS terrorist group in South East Asian states suchlike Philippines and Indonesia, has generated fear and intimidation. The Philippines has so far controlled ISIS but its recruitment process hasn't halted. In Malaysia, the Eastern Sabah Security Command (ESSCOM) eliminated individuals attempting to create a safe haven in Sabah for Abu Sayyaf members fleeing from the AFP. In Indonesia, national counter terrorism force hasn't achieved their gaol, but trying to dismantle sleeping cells. However, more than 2,000 nationals of South Asian states have joined the ISIS terrorist group in Iraq, Syria and Afghanistan. Citizens of some states have joined Al Nusra terrorist group. These recruitments heighten concerns about the potential threat posed by returnees who may seek to relocate to the region with the fall of ISIL's so-called caliphate. The IS-K was founded in 2015 by the US army to counter Taliban in Afghanistan. Immediately after its establishment, the IS-K launched attacks against Shia communities, state and private institutions, and government targets in major cities across Afghanistan and Pakistan. The IS-K targeted minorities suchlike Hazara and Sikhs, journalists, aid workers, security personnel and government infrastructure.

BBC reported (11 October 2021) establishment of the Khorasan-K, and its successful attacks in Iraq, Syria and Afghanistan: "Islamic State Khorasan Province - is the regional affiliate of the Islamic State group. It is the most extreme and violent of all the jihadist militant groups in Afghanistan. IS-K was set up in January 2015 at the height of IS's power in Iraq and Syria, before its self-declared caliphate was defeated and dismantled by a US-led coalition. It recruits both Afghan and Pakistani jihadists, especially defecting members of the Afghan Taliban who don't see their own organisation as extreme enough. "Khorasan" refers to a historical region covering parts of modern-day Afghanistan and Pakistan." The power structures, social institutions and local authorities of the Central Asian states are unable to work with radical Islamic groups. The prospect of nuclear terrorism in Central Asia and possibly in Russia, is crystal clear. The risk of a complete nuclear device falling into the hands of terrorists will cause consternation in the region. Nuclear terrorism remains a constant threat to global peace".[5]

Despite initial scepticism about the group's existence from analysts and government officials alike, IS-K is responsible for attacks against civilians in Afghanistan and Pakistan. Wilayat Khorasan, or ISIS-K, intends to secure Afghanistan to legitimize the Islamic State's caliphate across the 'Khorasan Province' including portions of Central Asia, China, Iran, the Indian Subcontinent, and Southeast Asia. In 2014, a Pakistani terrorist Hafiz Saeed Khan became the first leader of the ISIS-K terrorist group, Hafiz Saeed Khan was commander of TTP in Pakistan. He brought Sheikh Maqbool and other individuals to the Khorasan leadership. Expert and analyst, Niels Terpstra (2020) Rebel governance, rebel legitimacy, and external intervention: assessing three phases of Taliban rule in Afghanistan, Small Wars & Insurgencies,31:6, published on 25 May 2020) in her research paper has documented dynamics of Taliban, Mujahideen and rebel governance and legitimacy:

"The dynamics of rebel governance and rebel legitimacy, however, do not exist in isolation from other powerful actors. The actions/responses of the state are relevant to the analysis of rebel legitimacy as well. Powerful external actors may also influence the relations between armed groups and civilians. Much research has been devoted to the effects of external support to rebel groups and the attempts of rebel groups to acquire international legitimacy and/or recognition. In this article, I shift the perspective and demonstrate how powerful external actors that support the incumbent government shape (though less directly) the dynamics of rebel governance and rebel legitimacy. The presence of foreign enemy forces is an important source of legitimacy for rebel groups and has remained relatively under-studied in the literature on rebel governance. Rebel legitimacy is a function of present-day events but also of prior armed conflicts and societal tensions. As Schröder and Schmidt observe, 'the most important code of the legitimation of war is its historicity. 'In other words, the 'symbolic meaning of prior wars is re-enacted and reinterpreted in the present, and present violence generates symbolic value to be employed in future confrontations.' It is, therefore necessary to study rebel governance and legitimacy from a longitudinal perspective. Whereas current sources of legitimacy, such as service provision and protection, are an important part of the analysis, the legitimizing effect of prior events, and external interventions in particular, require further scrutiny. Omitting historical sources of legitimacy may lead to an incomplete understanding of rebel groups' legitimacy."[6]

The perception that Taliban are ideological fighter is wrong, the reason for that they are acting like terrorist organizations, carrying out suicide attacks against civilians and destroy everything they don't like. They have committed war crimes, beheaded innocent Muslims, kidnapped women and children and used them for sexual exploitation. They are proxies of Pakistan's military establishment, barking for the American Army and ISI equally. They have established suicide brigades, and threatened Afghanistan's neighbours. They have looted natural resources and established units of the Pakistan Army in several provinces of the country. Later on, Pakistan Air Force targeted Afghan civilians in Panjshir, Khost and Kunar provinces. The Taliban's relationship with al Qaeda and the IS-K further generated fear and consternation. As Afghanistan remained a top destination for foreign terrorist groups, Taliban entered into alliances with different groups. Expert and research scholar, Asfandyar Mir in his recent paper (The IS-K Resurgence, published on 08 October 2021), noted hostilities between Taliban and the IS-K group, and the enmity between the two groups:

"ISIS-K sees the Taliban as an irreconcilable enemy that needs to be militarily defeated. The enmity between the two groups has been aggravated by sustained military hostilities, but the main cause remains their sectarian difference. ISIS-K subscribes to the Jihadi-Salafism ideology—and plays up the 'purity' of its anti-idolatry credentials. The Taliban, on the other hand, subscribe to an alternative Sunni Islamic sectarian school, the Hanafi madhhab, which ISIS-K regards as deficient. The two groups also differ over the role of nationalism. ISIS-K fiercely rejects it, which runs counter to the Afghan Taliban's aims of ruling over Afghanistan. One recurring question is if the Taliban have used ISIS-K as a cover for violence, especially in the lead up to their August takeover. The former Afghan government, for instance, would argue that ISIS-K and the Afghan Taliban—specifically its sub-group the Haqqani Network—were collaborating on violent attacks in cities, but the U.S. government didn't support this assessment. On August 31, President Joe Biden observed that ISIS-K and the Taliban are "sworn enemies." The United Nations has also cast doubt on any major strategic alignment between ISIS-K and the Taliban but suggests the possibility of localized collaboration between elements of the two groups. Some analysts believe that ISIS-K's co-optation with Taliban defectors—specifically from the Haqqani Network—contributes to this conflation".[7]

The growing military and political influence of IS-K in Afghanistan, means that the Taliban government and its allies have failed to bring stability to Afghanistan. Ethnic violence has created a hostile environment across the country. The Hazaras are being subjected to violence and torture. Afghans who returned from Pakistan face violence and harassment and are struggling to survive in their own country, but regional Taliban warlords are not willing to allow them to return to their hometowns. There are more than three million internally displaced Afghans who also face the wrath of Taliban warlords and private militia commanders. At present, IS-K is trying to extend its tentacles to all parts of the Afghan state. The Taliban also do not have armed drones, which are needed for use against al Qaeda and IS-K targets. ISIS in 2014 declared a caliphate in Iraq and in 2015, IS-K was established in Afghanistan. The Asia Pacific Group on Money Laundering and Global Centre on Cooperative Security in its report (Financing and Facilitation of Foreign Terrorist Fighters and Returnees in Southeast Asia," Asia Pacific Group on Money Laundering and Global Centre on Cooperative Security, published in November 2021) has documented some aspects of Foreign Terrorist Finance and operational mechanism of terrorist groups across the globe:

"There is a long-standing desire of some groups in the Southeast Asia region to establish Islamic rule, which may be part of why ISIL targeted Southeast Asia for recruitment. A Bahasa-language video titled Joining the Ranks urged Southeast Asians to travel to Syria, and ISIL's propaganda and social media support networks influenced numerous regional groups and thousands of individuals to pledge support, most notably at a wave of public rallies in 2014. That same year, ISIL established the Katibah Nusantara, a military unit within ISIL for Malay-speaking individuals. The unit sought to address communication challenges between ISIL and its Southeast Asian FTF recruits, many of whom were not fluent in Arabic or English. Katibah Nusantara recruited, united, trained, and mobilized FTF recruits from Southeast Asia. The unit was first led by Indonesian national Bahrum Syah, who traveled to Syria at the age of 29. Bahrum Syah's leadership later faced competition from other prominent Indonesians, including Abu Jandal (also known as Salim Mubarok) and Bahrun Naim. According to some accounts, Katibah Nusantara had as many as 200 members, though other estimates are much lower, closer to 30–40.....Bahrum Syah worked with M. Fachry, together with the support of Omar Bakri Muhammad, to establish the Forum of Islamic Law Activists (FAKSI) in 2013, which became the "engine" of the pro-ISIL network in Indonesia".[8]

Afghan society had to collect its shattered pieces during the last four decades of war without the presence of a legitimate and functioning state, but internal migration, power games and foreign interference washed away its dreams. Civil War has destroyed the state, its institutions, and devastated the economy. The mujahideen in the 1990s did not discriminate between innocents and criminals in the course of fighting in Kabul. From 1992 to 1994, they killed over 60,000 men, women and children in Kabul alone. The rise of the Taliban in 1994 kept the war ignited and they started their business with a new strategy of killing, abduction and humiliation of the innocent citizens of the country. The criminal structure that fuelled the civil war is still in place. Jihadist groups in Afghanistan have played major role in Civil War. Their competition was known due to their mutual differences and power game. Afghan government and its international partners underestimated the power of the IS-K due to its foreign origin and the ISIS perceived lack of local connections. Experts and analysts, Niamatullah Ibrahimi and Shahram Akbarzadeh in their research paper (Intra-Jihadist Conflict and Cooperation: Islamic State–Khorasan Province and the Taliban in Afghanistan, Studies in Conflict & Terrorism) have noted the intra-jihadists conflict and cooperation:

"To the extent that a nationalist/transnationalist distinction holds, the Taliban and ISIS occupy the two different ends of the spectrum in the global jihadist movement. While ISIS is generally recognized for its ambition of dismantling borders and recruiting from across the world, the Taliban is often noted for their nationally focused strategy in Afghanistan. Specifically, IS-K was established to revive the historical region of Khorasan, which besides Afghanistan included parts of Iran, Pakistan, and Central Asia. ISIS and the Taliban are also two of the richest jihadist organizations. Although IS-K remains comparatively small in Afghanistan, ISIS quickly became a dominant actor in the global jihadist industry, accumulating an unprecedented share of material and symbolic resources. In 2016, with an annual budget of US$2 billion, ISIS was the richest jihadist group in the world. With an estimated $800 million annual budget, according to Forbes Magazine, the Taliban ranked one of the richest terrorist organizations in the world. Consequently, the IS-K represented an important shift in Afghanistan's jihadi industry by bringing two of the most resourceful jihadist organizations with two different strategies into a single theatre of conflict. In this section, we will discuss some of the key commonalities and differences of the two groups as members of the jihadist movement industry, before examining how those differences influences their relationship in Afghanistan."[9]

Private mercenaries and foreign funded militias once more reshaped the culture of Civil War in Afghanistan in a modern form, and contributed significantly to the Taliban disputed leadership and misgovernment. They received financial and military support from domestic and international stakeholders to consolidate the form of armed governance, and the collapsed infrastructure of the Afghan State. The past 42 years of conflict and transformation of social fabric have configured the political landscape of Afghanistan, and significantly empowered local war criminals. The collapse of the Afghan state in 1992 and 2021, left a huge political and military vacuum permeated by Mujahidin militias, Taliban, the ISIS and US militias. Afghan politicians and warlords also gained financial and political advantage from the building-up of these inexplicable militias while Interior and Defence Ministries sought to take them under their control. The Taliban return to power brought further destruction and poverty to the country, where Afghan citizens are selling their daughters for food. The US, Europe and Iran that could not defend the values of democracy are now finding themselves in a tight spot as their influence and rules-based world order continues to be questioned by the revisionist trio of China, Russia and Iran.

The fall of Afghanistan to the Taliban generated a news terror threat in South and Central Asia. The Taliban's close relationship with several Pakistani terror groups and its inability to govern the whole country may turn Afghanistan into a nest of terror militias. In Afghanistan, close cooperation between Daesh and some disgruntled Taliban groups added to the pain of the Taliban Government. The Khorasan terrorist group, which emerged with a strong military power in 2015, is in control of important districts in Jalalabad province. The group's military tactics include beheading, public prosecution, kidnapping, and torture, looting and raping, and also forcing families from their homes. Due to the weakness of Taliban and local administration, the IS-K expanded its networks to all districts of Jalalabad. In Kunar, Nuristan and Jalalabad provinces, more than 13 terrorist groups were operating with their strong networks. Some of the groups including Quetta Shura, Tora Bora Jihadi group, Gul Buddin Hekmatyar group, Salafi group, Fidayee Karwan, Sia Pushan groups (identified as black-clad and masked terrorists) were in clandestine collaboration with the Khorasan group, TTP, and Lashkar-e-Islam group. In Mohmand Agency, Jamaat Al Ahrar and TTP were operating in collaboration with ISKP. Expert and analysts, Sushant Sareen in his paper (The ISKP is Nothing but an Exaggerated Threat, Special Report. Of Observer Research Foundation: Afghanistan and the New Global (Dis)Order: Great Game and Uncertain Neighbours, published on December 2021) has documented suicide terrorism of the Islamic State-K in Afghanistan that targeted mosques and religious places of Hazara Muslims:

"After the horrific suicide bombing at the Kabul airport in August 2021, the international spotlight and scrutiny shifted from the Taliban and its close ally al-Qaeda to the shadowy terror group Islamic State Khorasan Province (ISKP). Suddenly, the real problem in Afghanistan was not the capture of that country by the Taliban, but the presence of the ISKP. The Taliban and Pakistan are being presented as the good guys who everyone should help and fund to fight against the ISKP, which is the real threat to global security. With US President Joe Biden calling the ISKP "an archenemy of the Taliban," it seems like a slam dunk for the new narrative that is being manufactured of 'good Taliban' vs 'bad ISKP'.The US military seems to have developed so much faith, trust, and confidence in the Taliban that they even share extremely sensitive information with them. There is now talk of intelligence sharing with the Taliban to target ISKP. Even as the ISKP is being built up as some kind of ISIS on steroids to justify possible cooperation, coordination and even collaboration with the Taliban regime, no one is asking some simple questions: just how dangerous is the ISKP really? Does it have a global or even regional footprint outside the Afghanistan-Pakistan (AfPak) region or is it a local terror group with a very tenuous international affiliation? Is it only using the label of an international terror brand to build its profile? What are its strength and capabilities to carry out big terror attacks outside of AfPak region and destabilise other countries? The data just does not bear out the hype surrounding ISKP".[10]

The full body of Islamic State machine is strong as its radio stations, photographic reports, and bulletins are being circulated in different languages. The Internet is also the source of propaganda of the IS-K groups where experts of the group disseminate controversial information through videos and articles. Moreover, the group challenged the presence of US and NATO forces in Afghanistan. Some members of the Afghan parliament severely criticised the United States and its NATO allies for their support to the Islamic State. They also raised the question of foreign financial support to the terrorist group, and asked the Unity Government to positively respond to the brutalities and atrocities of the IS-K commanders. However, Daesh also spread its evil tentacles to the North to control provinces bordering Russia and China. The group wanted to infiltrate into Chinese Muslim province and parts of Central Asia and challenge the authority of local governments there. The civilian deaths in Afghanistan became a routine as innocent women and girls were kidnapped, raped and tortured in the group's secret prisons in Kunar and Jalalabad provinces. The Islamic State fighters were being facilitated by the corrupt commanders of the Afghan army. They were sheltered, armed and transported by them to their destination. Editor Iain Overton and researchers, Aman Bezreh, Chris Hitchcock, Jacob Berntson, Jen Wilton, Jennifer Dathan, Khalil Dewan,

Leyla Slama, Michael Hart, Shaza Alsalmoni, Sophie Akram and Tim Hulse in their paper (Understanding the Rising Cult of Suicide Bomber. Action on Armed Violence (AOAV) have highlighted some aspects of suicide terrorism in Tunisia and the Arab world:

"Jihadi organisations have been very effective in targeting grievances created by lack of economic opportunities in Tunisia, and have according to the people AOAV has spoken with in areas like Ettadhamen managed to recruit youth by offering them a way out of poverty. Besides the salaries that some organisations pay, joining a jihadi group might also function as revenge against the state which has failed to provide opportunities for its citizens. Moreover, given the traditional antagonism between the Tunisian state and conservative strands of Islam, joining a radical Salafist serves as act of ultimate rebellion. Last but not least, groups like IS also offer recruits a standing in which they enjoy status and a sense of fulfilment, which is the direct opposite of what many young unemployed Tunisians feel. Much of these sentiments and perceptions are found in the case of Houssam Abdelli, who was 28 years old when he detonated himself on the bus in Tunis in 2015. Abdelli was from a poor family, and neighbours and friends that AOAV spoke with said that he was worried about their financial well-being. From Ettadhamen, Abdelli worked as a street seller, selling plants and clothes. According to his friends, he had tried to find a better job, but had had no success. He reportedly drank alcohol and smoked hashish several times per week".[11]

Chapter 7

The Haqqani Terrorist Network, Lashkar-e-Taiba, Taliban and the Islamic State of Khorasan's Plundering of Mineral Resources in Afghanistan and their expedition Towards Central Asia

They are rolling again with punches to Afghanistan, with blood stained faces, lethal technology, nuclear technology, and strategies of destruction. They want to terminate more Afghan women and children, destroy more houses, more bridges and more buildings, but this time Afghan will never support their war crimes, and will never support their military operations. The Ukraine War has lidded and covered transmogrifies faces and blood stained hands of US and NATO war mongers who killed thousands in Afghanistan. The US House of Republicans went on the offensive against President Joe Biden, attacking his handling of the situation in Afghanistan. Mr. Michael McCaul said President Biden had blood on his hands". Former President Donald Trump and Republican lawmakers' slammed Joe Biden after the Kabul blasts. "Joe Biden's hands are drenched with blood after the botched withdrawal from Afghanistan". Lawmaker said. Now these war criminals want to return on the pretext that Afghanistan has become nest of terrorism. What do they want from a poor country? They want to use Afghanistan against Russia and China, or Pakistan. Their intentions are not clear. Writer David Markichok (Asia Times, 22 April 2021) warned that as London left the door open for NATO allies to return to Afghanistan in the event any "threat" re-emerges to the free world. Analyst and expert, Ashok K. Behuria in (Fighting the Taliban: Pakistan at war with itself, published in 2007, in Australian Journal of International Affairs, 61:4, 529-543) has noted Former Pakistani Army Chief General Musharaf's concerns about shift of centre of gravity of terrorism from al Qaeda to Taliban:

"General Pervez Musharraf, President of Pakistan, admitted on 15 September 2006 that the "centre of gravity of terrorism" had shifted from Al Qaeda to the Taliban and that the Taliban was a "more dangerous element because it has roots in the people" unlike Al Qaeda and was "more organised". He regarded the Taliban as an "obscurantist social concept" and argued that the real danger lay in the emerging strength of the Taliban and in the possibility of converting their resistance "into a national war by the [Pashtuns] against ... all foreign forces'. The resurgence of the Taliban was the pet theme of analysts and observers who tracked developments in Afghanistan since 2004-2005. In Kabul in August 2007, Musharraf expressed his concern about "a particularly dark form" of terrorism confronting the region and said that people of Pakistan and Afghanistan faced "a great danger in the shape of fringe groups, a small minority that preaches hate, violence and backwardness".....The case of pro-Taliban militants laying siege on the Red Mosque at the heart of the Pakistani capital, in February 2007, until they were flushed out through military action, along with the rising incidence of suicide attacks against security forces in the tribal areas of Pakistan and the spread of the influence of the Taliban beyond the tribal areas in recent years, suggest that the Taliban phenomenon will affect Pakistan for a prolonged period and warrants a deeper analysis of the malaise that is affecting the Pakistani state at the moment".[1]

The Taliban and Haqqani terrorist organizations failed to stabilise Afghanistan. They imposed restrictions on women and journalist, on politicians to hide their crimes of sexual exploitation, murder of innocent Afghans including former army and police officers and soldiers. They are molesting transgender, gays, women and young girls and torture them in secret torture cells. Taliban and Haqqani terrorist group nothing know how to govern Afghanistan and how to reinvent state institutions. They are recruiting young generation for suicide mission and intimidating Tajikistan, Iran and Uzbekistan by firing missiles across the borders and deploying suicide brigades along with their borders. They train terrorist organizations of Central Asia, Pakistan and the Arab world, adorn them with sophisticated arms and suicide jackets. Haqqani has a long history in Afghan politics and militancy stretching back to 1970s and was a major recipient of foreign funding during the Soviet jihad; during this period, Haqqani was regarded as a valuable asset by the CIA. On 16 May 2022, online media outlet journalist Jawad Etimad told ToloNews that Taliban arrested him while covering a blast in PD5 of Kabul city. Mr. Etimad said he spent two days in a cell of Islamic Emirate. "They prevented me from making footage. They beat me with kicks and punches. And then they arrested me," he said. Journalists voiced criticisms that the Islamic Emirate's forces prevent them from covering the security incidents in Kabul. "When a security incident happens in an area we go there to cover the incident. Unfortunately, we are not being allowed cover the incident," said Farogh Faizy, a journalist. "The media has the right to make footage. Whenever there are restrictions on access to information, it is a violation of the law", said Masroor Lutfi, head of the Afghanistan National Journalists Union.

Pakistan once more wants to wash hands with the blood of Afghan citizens by allowing US and NATO to establish military bases in the country. They have trained strong armies of the IS-K and Taliban who will further their hegemonic agendas in Central Asia, Pakistan and China. They will make Central Asia and Afghanistan the nether regions and may possibly use weapons of mass destruction. They de novo and over again need the £3-trillion mineral resources to stabilize their economies, but this time, things will shape differently. Russia and China will interfere, and India will be supporting and Pakistan will play as a proxy. Russian Today reported that the UK intention to entre Afghanistan if realised threatening situation coming from the country again, UK under Secretary for the Armed Forces James Heappey told MPs. "If some part of the Afghan territory turns into "an ungoverned space" providing safe haven to international terrorists and threatening "the UK homeland or to the interests of our allies," London would not hesitate to act "unilaterally and multilaterally through NATO," a former Afghan Army officer said. Expert and analyst, Cosmin Timofte in his paper (Unlikely Friends: What role would the USA play in the fight between ISIS K and the Taliban? The Institute of New Europe's Work, published on 29 November 2021) has reviewed the UK withdrawn from Afghanistan after 20 years of fighting, which then paved the way for the Taliban to return to power. The US and NATO will arm both Taliban the ISIS to keep ignite the fire in order to easily plunder mineral resources of Afghanistan. They will bomb positions of Taliban in order to push them to the brink and make the country vanquish at the hands of the IS-K terrorist group. Recent engagement between Pakistan and the United States is crystal clear that they want to take the war inside China, or Russia:

The United States has withdrawn from Afghanistan after 20 years of fighting, which then paved the way for the Taliban to return to power at a speed that exceeded many estimations; reaching Kabul in around 10 days since the retreat started. The evacuation was made on the basis of the peace deal the US and the organisation forged under Trump. During the evacuation, the Taliban were declared as and "by Biden's Administration, which is a positive signal for the relationship the two parties may have. However, the emerging chaos from the evacuation and the change in government has prompted the Islamic State Khorasan Province (to s trike with the intent of establishing and empowering themselves and destabilising the new Taliban rule. This is most accurately acknowledged when one considers the timing of the Kabul airport attack, which killed over 100 people during the evacuation. With the Taliban striking back against IS-K, who is perhaps their biggest contester in the region at the moment, the United States is put in a position where it must consider its post war role in Afghanistan. It is a not question of whether the US might intervene, but in what measure it will. Chairman of the US Joint Chief of Staff General Milley said "it's possible" for the US to work with the Taliban against ISKP. If cooperation between the US and the Taliban is possible, then one must take a look into how will it materialise. It is not simply a question of eradicating a common enemy, but also the first glimpse over the new relationship between the two will have in the future".[2] Expert and commentator, Hassan Abu Haniyeh in his commentary (Daesh's Organisational Structure, published on 03 December 2014) has documented organisational infrastructure of the Islamic State in Iraq and Syria:

"On the eve of the US invasion and subsequent 2003 occupation of Iraq, Zarqawi worked hard to rebuild his jihadi network from a solid foundation that had already been established in the Afghanistan's Herat province. He began by building an inner circle of his most loyal followers. The most prominent among them were Abu Hamza al-Muhajir, an Egyptian national who took over the group after Zarqawi's demise; Abu Anas al-Shami, a Jordanian who became the group's first spiritual advisor; Nidhal Mohammed Arabiat, another Jordanian from the city of Salt, who was considered the group's top bombmaker and thought to be responsible for most of the group's car bombs; Mustafa Ramadan Darwish (also known as Abu Mohammed al-Libnani), a Lebanese national; Abu Omar al-Kurdi; Thamer al-Atrouz al-Rishawi, a former Iraqi military officer; Abdullah al-Jabouri (also known as Abu Azzam,) also an Iraqi; Abu Nasser al-Libi; and Abu Osama al-Tunisi. All of them were killed in 2003 except Abu Azzam, who was killed in 2005. Among the Jordanians most trusted by Zarqawi were Mowaffaq Odwan, Jamal al-Otaibi, Salahuddin al-Otaibi, Mohammed al-Safadi, Moath al-Msoor, Shehadah al-Kilani, Mohammed Qutaishat, Munther Shihah, Munther al-Tamuni, and Omar al-Otaibi. To rebuild his network, Zarqawi employed the ideology, ideas and jurisprudence he had learned at the hands of his mentor, Abu Abdullah al-Muhajir, who had a profound impact on Zarqawi's fighting doctrine and approach to jurisprudence. Zarqawi's network grew and developed quickly, but never had a specific name and did not adhere to a clearly defined structure".[3]

The United States illegitimate invasion of Iraq was with the motive to destroy the country and plunder its oil and mineral resources. That invasion generated several suicide terrorist organizations that killed thousands of women and children with impunity. Iraqi Muslims were beheaded, tortured, sexually abused and killed by these terrorist groups who received funds and weapons from the US Army. Since 2003, these terrorist groups carried out 900 suicide attacks against Iraqi civilians, killed over 10,000 women and children. They used female suicide bombers because they were easily crossing police and army checkpoints. The bomber women were motivated to attack US forces. According to the Action on Armed Violence report, dated 01 January 2017, actual knowledge about the education level of these bombers were difficult to find but one thing is clear that they were educated and brainwashed. There was also no real correlation between education and suicide bombers in Iraq and Syria. In areas where communal support for suicide bombing exists it can also help to motivate individual bombers. Most Salafi-Jihadi propaganda includes continuous, general references to the importance and nobility of martyrdom and martyrs, which likely translates to increased social status.

Suicide bombers in Syria and Afghanistan died in Vehicle-Borne operations. In Iraq, they proved to be ideal for launching against advancing ISF units from concealed garages. On 21 January 2021, VoA reported Islamic State suicide bombers attacks in a market in Iraq's capital killing at least 32 people and wounding 110 others. Expert and analyst Ellen Tveteraas "Department of Politics and International Relations, University of Oxford, Oxfordshire, United Kingdom" has highlighted operational mechanism of the ISIS terrorist group in Iraq, and performance of Martyrdom Operatives Battalion (Katibat al-Istishadiin), and its associates in her paper (Under the Hood–Learning and Innovation in the Islamic State's Suicide Vehicle Industry. Studies in Conflict & Terrorism, published on 13 February, 2022). She also noted that suicide operatives were the purview of the special skills bureau:

"Suicide operatives were the purview of the special skills bureau, with prospective bombers organized in a section called the Martyrdom Operatives Battalion (Katibat al-Istishadiin). Members of the suicide battalion would normally arrive at the area of operation shortly before the execution of an attack and spend the preparation period in isolation with clerics to build the mental fortitude required to execute this type of mission. The battalion had no shortage of volunteers and, following the group's acquisition of territory, its size far outgrew the tactical demand for suicide operations. The Islamic State was not the first group to find itself in this situation. Around 2006, an ISI document shows that it too had more suicide bombers than the group was able to deploy. However, while ISI was unable to utilize aspiring bombers for logistical reasons, the Islamic State was arguably unwilling to waste them. Winter's analysis of suicide attack use in 2015-16, suggests that the group appeared reluctant to use bombers in campaigns where it did not feel it could win. While this changed during the Battle of Mosul in 2016–2017, it corresponded with the impression of several interviewees, one of whom remarked, "The Islamic State does not use suicide bombers unnecessarily, they are cheap, but they are also indispensable. "While the Islamic State kept using inconspicuous suicide vehicles in clandestine operations, it also designed a new type with an emphasis on repelling, rather than avoiding, incoming fire. This expanded the tactical functions of suicide vehicles. In addition to their utility in guerrilla assaults and as symbolic acts of terrorism, they could now be integrated into battlefield operations to weaken enemy defence positions in advance of ground-troop assaults, in some ways paralleling the use of traditional artillery. This capability became particularly pertinent following the fall of Mosul in June 2014, when the Islamic State obtained enough arms to equip nearly 50,000 soldiers from Iraqi military stocks and sought to further expand the state."[4]

Writer Pepe Escobar in his article (Who profits from Kabul suicide bombing? ISIS-Khorasan aims to prove to Afghans and to the outside world that the Taliban cannot secure the capital, published on 30 August, 2021) documented links between the Haqqani terrorist group and the IS-K of Khorasan. However, he also noted that the suicide bomber who carried out the Kabul airport attack was identified Abdul Rahman Logari and his attack was organised by an IS-K sleeper cell: "Founded in 2015 by emigré jihadists dispatched to southwest Pakistan, IS-K is a dodgy beast. Its current head is one Shahab al-Mujahir, who was a mid-level commander of the Haqqani network headquartered in North Waziristan in the Pakistani tribal areas, itself a collection of disparate mujahideen and would-be jihadis under the family umbrella. Washington branded the Haqqani network as a terrorist organization way back in 2010, and treats several members as global terrorists, including Sirajuddin Haqqani, the head of the family after the death of the founder Jalaluddin Haqqani. Up to now, Sirajuddin was the Taliban deputy leader for the eastern provinces–on the same level with

Mullah Baradar, the head of the political office in Doha, who was actually released from Guantanamo in 2014. Crucially, Sirajuddin's uncle, Khalil Haqqani, formerly in charge of the network's foreign financing, is now in charge of Kabul security and working as a diplomat 24/7. The previous ISIS-K leaders were snuffed out by US airstrikes in 2015 and 2016. ISIS-K started to become a real destabilizing force in 2020 when the regrouped band attacked Kabul University, a Doctor without Borders maternity ward, the Presidential palace and the airport. NATO intelligence picked up by a UN report attributes a maximum of 2,200 jihadists to ISIS-K, split into small cells."[5]

The IS-K is militarily strongest terrorist organization in Afghanistan that not only challenged the Taliban government, but Central Asian states as well. Having established centres across Afghanistan and some Central Asian state to recruit thousands of fighters and adorn them with modern technology and weapons, the IS-K needs a strong military infrastructure to commence its military campaign. In Syria and Iraq, the ISIS killed thousands civilians and generated a strong revenue by transporting oil and narcotics drugs across Africa and Europe. In yesteryears, in Afghanistan, IS-K controlled rich mineral wealth, especially talc, chromite and marble. In 2017, Global Witness reported displacement of more than 60,000 people by fighting between IS-K and the Taliban for control of other mineral-rich districts close to Achin. A Taliban official explicitly linked the ferocity of the battle to the struggle over the mines. The IS-K's interest in Afghanistan's minerals should be an urgent wake-up call not just for the fight against extremist armed groups, but for the wider reform that the sector has been lacking so far. In each case, the Islamic State opportunistically sought to establish itself in an area primed for insurgency by both poor governance and a population susceptible to religious extremism. Global Witness noted. Expert and analyst, Michael Rubin in his commentary (Biden ignores Afghanistan at America's peril, The National Interest, 28 April, 2022) has raised the question of President Niden abandonment of Afghanistan and recent wave of terrorism:

"Recent mosque bombings are ominous because they suggest terror is about to get much worse. In the past, the Afghanistan fighting season began in April when winter snows melted enough to allow movement. The White House and Pentagon appear to have misinterpreted the relative calm which followed the U.S. withdrawal as a sign that the Taliban could consolidate control and, if provided enough aid, govern. In reality, the calm was illusionary. While Uzbekistan denies that there was a cross-border rocket attack into Termez on April 11, 2022, locals confirm the strike and say a diplomatic convenience motivates the denials. Also naive was the notion that the Taliban's desire for legitimacy would give the international community leverage. Two weeks ago, the Russian government quietly handed the Afghanistan embassy in Moscow over to a Taliban diplomat. Videos circulating on Telegram and Signal showing the Taliban flag now draped inside the building, with diplomats loyal to the former government unceremoniously booted from the embassy by the Russian government. The Russian move shows the gullibility of those who believed international opprobrium would be enough to ensure the Taliban respected women's rights. An even greater error—the blame for which transcends administrations—was the belief that the United States could co-opt the Taliban as an ally in the fight against even worse terror groups".[6]

The establishment of the ISIS networks in Tajikistan and Uzbekistan raised several questions including the failure of Tajik law enforcement agencies to intercept infiltration of ISIS fighters into the country. The Islamic State is now recruiting young people into its ranks, and supports them financially. In view of this development, Tajikistan introduced new legislation in 2015 allowing authorities to pardon citizens who voluntarily return home and express regret that they joined militant groups abroad, but, notwithstanding this legislation, people of all walks of life are joining Daesh consecutively. On 06 November 2019, BBC reported terror attack of the ISIS fighters on Checkpost of Tajik border with Uzbekistan, and killed 17 people. Analyst Damon Mehl in his paper (Damon Mehl, CTC Sentinel, November 2018, Volume-11, Issue-10), noted some aspects of the development of ISIS networks in Tajikistan:

"Jamaat Ansarullah, an Afghanistan-based Tajikistani terrorist group, was formed in 2010 with likely fewer than 100 members and has since received support from the Islamic Movement of Uzbekistan (IMU), the Taliban, and al-Qaeda. The group's stated mission is to bring an 'Islamic' government to Tajikistan. Beginning with its foundation, Jamaat Ansarullah sporadically published videos and disseminated messages through its website, which has been inactive since 2016. The group's leader Amriddin Tabarov was killed in Afghanistan in December 2015 and Tabarov's son-in-law Mavlavif Salmon was appointed as the new leader by the end of 2016. In 2014, Jamaat Ansarullah sent some of its members to fight in Syria with Jabhat al-Nusra, an al-Qaeda-aligned group now known as Hayat Tahrir al-Sham. At a point in 2014 or 2015, some Jamaat Ansarullah members ended up fighting alongside the Islamic State. The Islamic State subsequently began financially supporting Ansarullah, according to Afghanistan expert Antonio Giustozzi, citing a Jamaat Ansarullah commander. This support reportedly caused fissures between Jamaat Ansarullah and al-Qaeda, and by 2015, Ansarullah received 50 percent of its financial backing from the Islamic State. In October 2014, a Jamaat Ansarullah member going by the name Mansur stated on the group's website that Jamaat Ansarullah considered the Islamic State a jihadi organization, but had paused its decision on whether to accept the Islamic State's claim of being the caliphate".[7]

The Chechen fighters have also established networks across the Russian Federation and want to retrieve sophisticated weapons and weapons of mass destruction. The group in Afghanistan receives military training to strengthen its army for the future war against Russia. Pakistan have also trained Chechen commanders years ago, while during their jihad against Russia, some reports confirmed the participation of over 1000 Pakistani jihadists and retired military officers in fighting alongside their fighters. Analyst and researcher, Christian Bleuer (Chechens in Afghanistan: A Battlefield Myth That Will Not Die, published on 27 June 2016) noted the presence of Chechen leadership in Afghanistan: "Extremist members of Chechnya's rebel movement adhere to ideas tied to jihad and the creation of an Islamist state. Afghan and foreign officials say as many as 7,000 Chechens and other foreign fighters could be operating in the country, loosely allied with the Taliban and other militant groups. Local reporting by Pajhwok News, sourced to the Logar governor's spokesman, was slightly different, naming the targets as "Taliban Commanders Mullah Saber, Mullah Sabawon and Mullah Bashir," but also noting the presence of Chechens–in this case, three Chechen women who were allegedly killed. Khaama Press also reported the incident, noting that "[f]oreign insurgents fighting the Afghan forces is not new as scores of militants from Chechnya and other countries are routinely reported killed during the fight with the Afghan forces," with the caveat that "[t]he anti-government armed militant groups have not commented regarding the report so far."[8]

The 2021 Kabul bombing killed 103 people, while at least 1,300 persons were injured, Afghan Health Ministry noted. Writer and expert, Pepe Escobar (Who profits from the Kabul suicide bombing? ISIS-Khorasan aims to prove to Afghans and to the outside world that the Taliban cannot secure the capital. Asia Times, published on 27 August 2021) noted in his article that "responsibility for the bombing came via a statement on the Telegram channel of Amaq Media, the official Islamic State (ISIS) news agency. This means it came from centralized ISIS command, even as the perpetrators were members of ISIS-Khorasan". Expert and analyst, Michael W. S. Ryan in his research paper (ISIS: The Terrorist Group That Would Be a State, published in U.S. Naval War College) has described historical journey of the ISIS in Iraq and Syria. He also noted that the "ISIS developed its strategic approach within the modern jihadist tradition, which al Qaeda violently introduced to the United States with a series of escalating attacks, culminating in the attacks of September 11, 2001". Michael W. S. Ryan has argued that the 'ISIS used a strategic plan for establishing an Islamic Emirate, as presented in broad strokes by another al Qaeda strategist with the pseudonym Abu Bakr Naji and learned from U.S. operations, especially from the use of Sunni tribes during the successful "surge" in Iraq, which came close to destroying al Qaeda in Iraq.[9]

After the Taliban takeover, smuggling of narcotics drug, money extortion, and illegal extraction of minerals resources exacerbated. Taliban profited from minerals in Jalalabad, Badakhshan and Helmand provinces. Global Witness noted how local elites had to control extraction and employ people mainly from their own families, paying a set amount to the Taliban, which the source estimated at ($1,900-$4,770) a month. Taliban also collect taxes of ushr and zakat. They took a third of the value of the output this way. The Taliban searched for international recognition, as well as assistance to avoid a humanitarian and economic disaster in Afghanistan. However, no country officially recognised the Emirate, and the UN referred to the Taliban as the 'de facto' authorities. With its extensive territorial control and reach all over the country, the Taliban has taxed cultivation, processing, and smuggling of drugs; and units and members of the Taliban have been intensely involved in all these elements. The Taliban basically now controls one of the largest reserves of natural resources that the world very much needs. These comprise materials such as copper, iron, gold, and lithium. This gives the Taliban considerable leverage when dealing with external interests and possibly gives them political capital with which to negotiate. The Taliban derived income from mining directly under their control and are measured to stem further incomes from at least some of the mining areas controlled by the warlords."[10]

The IS-K was in control of Achin from late 2014 to 2018, but Taliban couldn't tolerate and declared war against the group, but the US Army airstrikes caused further widespread destruction in the area. The Taliban defeated Daesh in Achin. Now the US government wants to send its army back to Afghanistan to control all mineral sites in order to support its economy. The Biden government wants to stabilize its economy be containerising more than $1 trillion mineral resources of Afghanistan. Moreover, in its press release (06 June 2016) Global Witness warned that Afghanistan's famous lapis mines are source of funding for the Taliban and armed groups. A new investigation reveals how Afghanistan's 6,500 year old lapis mines were driving corruption, conflict and extremism in the country. Global Witness found that the Taliban and other armed groups were earning up to 20 million dollars per year from Afghanistan's lapis mines, the world's main source of the brilliant blue lapis lazuli stone, which was used in jewellery around the world. As a result, the Afghan lapis lazuli stone should now be classified as a conflict mineral. Global Witness warned. The Global Witness' investigation also warned that the "Badakhshan mines were a strategic priority for the so-called Islamic State. Unless the Afghan government acts rapidly to regain control, the battle for the lapis mines was set to intensify and further destabilise the country, as well as fund extremism".[11]

Writer Asad Mirza (For quick revenue, Afghan mining wealth is the best option for Taliban: A decade back some US geologists had calculated the mineral reserves in Afghanistan to be in excess of $1 trillion, published on 14 March 2022) has noted that Afghan mining wealth was the best option for Taliban and the current Taliban administration, its Mining Ministry was apparently engaged in a lot of activities. However, Mirza argued that countering the deeds of the past Taliban administration, which blasted the two Bamiyan statues in 2001, this time Dilawar tried to assure by saying that these antiquities would be protected but how it hasn't been decided: "His preference would be to move the whole city to somewhere nearby and reconstruct it. Many prize artefacts have been shifted to the Kabul Museum. Mes Aynak flourished between the first and seventh centuries. Reportedly there are Buddhist monasteries, stupas, graveyards and wall paintings beneath the mountain. Its eastern flank is covered with antique structures that formed the city".[12] Global Witness interviewed a wide range of relevant sources, including a number from Khogyani and Sherzad and individuals with direct knowledge of the trade. According to Global Witness report, "the most direct of these sources was the Taliban official cited above, who described the revenues from the mines as critical to the group's survival in the district. He put the total daily income just from the major mining area of Ghunday at Rs 500,000 to Rs 1.2m ($4,760-$11,430)". Expert and writer, Nik Martin (Afghanistan: Taliban to reap $1 trillion mineral wealth, published on 18 August 2021) has documented Taliban revenue and financial benefits from illegal extraction of mines in Afghanistan. He also noted that Pakistan was also set to benefit from Afghanistan's minerals wealth because Islamabad supported the Taliban:

"The Taliban have been handed a huge financial and geopolitical edge in relations with the world's biggest powers as the militant group seizes control of Afghanistan for a second time. In 2010, a report by US military experts and geologists estimated that Afghanistan, one of the world's poorest countries, was sitting on nearly $1 trillion (€850 billion) in mineral wealth, thanks to huge iron, copper, lithium, cobalt and rare-earth deposits. In the subsequent decade, most of those resources remained untouched due to ongoing violence in the country. Meanwhile, the value of many of those minerals has skyrocketed, sparked by the global transition to green energy. A follow-up report by the Afghan government in 2017 estimated that Kabul's new mineral wealth may be as high as $3 trillion, including fossil fuels. Lithium, which is used in batteries for electric cars, smartphones and laptops, is facing unprecedented demand, with annual growth of 20 percent compared to just 5-6 percent a few years ago. The Pentagon memo called Afghanistan the Saudi Arabia of lithium and projected that the country's lithium deposits could equal Bolivia's-one of the world largest. Copper, too, is benefiting from the post-COVID global economic recovery-up 43 percent over the past year. More than a quarter of Afghanistan's future mineral wealth could be realized by expanding copper mining activities".[13]

The looting and ransacking of Afghanistan's natural resources by Taliban and criminal militias; such as the IS-K terrorist group, caused misunderstanding between the Afghans and International Coalition that they all were involved in looting of mineral resources of their country. The IS-K controls large amount of territory in Afghanistan, and that includes parts of the country's rich mineral wealth, especially talc, chromite and marble. According to the Global Witness research report, several insurgents' groups, militias, Taliban and the ISIS are deeply involved in the plunder of these resources. These are the aspects discussed in the book by prominent authors. Now the IS-K has retrieved huge amount of money from illegal mines and smuggling of narcotics drug, and Taliban also receive billions from drug trafficking and illegal mining. Expert and analyst, Tim McDonnell in his article (The Taliban now controls one of the world's biggest lithium deposits: Illegal mining of lapis lazuli, a gem, is a major source of revenue for the Taliban, 28 December, 2021) argued that in 2010, an internal US Department of Defense memo called Afghanistan the Saudi Arabia of lithium:

"Global demand for lithium is projected to skyrocket 40-fold above 2020 levels by 2040, according to the International Energy Agency, along with rare earth elements, copper, cobalt, and other minerals in which

Afghanistan is naturally rich. These minerals are concentrated in a small number of pockets around the globe, so the clean energy transition has the potential to yield a substantial payday for Afghanistan. In the past, Afghan government officials have dangled the prospect of lucrative mining contracts in front of their US counterparts as an enticement to prolong the American military presence in the country. With the Taliban in charge, that option is likely off the table........The Taliban can't simply flick a switch and dive into the global lithium trade, Schoonover said. Years of conflict have left the country's physical infrastructure—roads, power plants, railways— in tatters. And at the moment Taliban militants are reportedly struggling even to maintain the provision of basic public services and utilities in the cities they have captured, let alone carry out economic policies that can attract international investors. Competing factions within the Taliban would make it very difficult for any company to negotiate mining deals, and China is unlikely to extend to the group the scale of infrastructure loans that would be required to bring any sizable mining operations online, said Nick Crawford, a development economics researcher at the International Institute for Strategic Studies think tank."[14]

Both Sherzad and Khogyani districts of Jalalabad province were entirely under the control of Taliban. In Badakhshan for example, the payments to the Taliban were linked to wider abuses around mining by a local militia. The story of financial source of Taliban and the IS-K terrorist group is complicated but evidences showcase that the three terrorist groups have been looting and plundering mineral resources of Afghanistan since 2015, they have also established a competent international trade networks for selling their plundered precious stones, gold and talc. While they generate money then purchase sophisticated weapons, modern surveillance system and invite young fighter from Pakistan based extremist and terrorist groups in order to strengthen their military positions. The Taliban and Islamic State also received millions of dollars from Europe, the United States, Pakistan and Qatari regime. They also received huge financial assistance from Iran and Saudi Arabia. The US and NATO have betrayed their Afghan proxies, spies and slaves by leaving them maroon and vulnerable in Afghanistan for Taliban to kill them one by one with impunity. After they left, they were dragged from their homes and taken to unknown places and killed shamelessly. Some were killed extra-judicially by terrorirists of Haqqani Network and Taliban in front of their relatives, sons and daughters, but champions of human rights never realised their pain and screech. They supported Taliban and the Islamic State financially and militarily, and trained their fighters in their bases.

They purveyed military intelligence and instructed their Afghan spies to transport their suicide bomber to their destinations. Afghan police and the army played a bigger role in protecting the IS-K and Taliban suicide bombers in their bases and houses. The rise of ISIS in Afghanistan posed serious security concerns according to a September 2016, Russian Foreign Ministry's Director of the Second Asian Department in Afghanistan, Kabulov claimed that about 2,500 ISIS combatants were in Afghanistan and the organization was preparing to expand from Afghanistan into other Central Asian countries and Russia, giving Moscow reasons to worry. Nuclear terrorism in Central Asia and Russia has risen important questions about the US and NATO policy towards Russia that without using biological and nuclear weapons against the country, its dream of supreme power will vanish. Authors Christopher McIntosh and Ian Storey (20 November 2019) in their well-written analysis have elucidated the real motive of US and NATO hegemonic design:

"While terrorist organizations vary widely in their internal organization and structure, almost all are highly sensitive to benefits and costs, both external and internal. By examining these, it will become clear that terrorists might have more to lose than gain by proceeding directly to an attack. Doing so might alienate their supporters, cause dissent among the ranks, and give away a bargaining chip without getting anything in return. While there is any number of far more likely scenarios for nuclear terrorism broadly understood, we focus only on groups with a working nuclear device, not a radiological dispersal device or the ability to attack a nuclear reactor. The threat posed by an operational device is fundamentally different, not least because possession would radically change the nature of the organisation as a strategic, warfighting group. A large body of work in terrorism studies teaches us that terrorist groups do behave strategically.[15]

Scholar and Lecturer Department of Social Sciences, Lahore Garrison University Pakistan, Dr. Yunis Khushi in his research paper (A Critical Analysis of Factors and Implications of ISIS Recruitments and Concept of Jihad-Bil-Nikah, published on 26 June 2017), noted important aspects of the ISIS training bases, and activities of women brigade of the Daesh-including Jihad-Bil-Nikah:

"The recruitment for ISIS has been going on in Pakistan for the past more than 3 years, but the Foreign and the Interior Ministries of Pakistan have been constantly denying the presence and activities of ISIS in Pakistan. Law Enforcement agencies have very recently arrested many people from Lahore, Islamabad, Karachi and Sialkot who were associated with ISIS networks. Men have been recruited as jihadis or mujahids and women as jihadi wives to provide sexual needs of fighters who are fighting in Syria, Iraq and Afghanistan. Many women, impressed and convinced through brainwashing with the concept of Jihad-Bil-Nikah, got a divorce from their Pakistani husbands and went to marry a Mujahid of ISIS for a certain period, came back gave birth to the child of Mujahid, and remarried their former husband. Some decide to continue that marriage for the rest of their lives. All of this is being done to obtain worldly wealth and later eternal life in Heaven because ISIS is paying something around 50,000 to 60,000 Pakistani currency per month to every warrior, which is a hefty amount for an unemployed youth suffering in unemployment, poverty and inflation in Pakistan, which is ruled by corrupt ruling elite for the past 68 years and masses only got poverty for being true Muslims and patriot Pakistanis. Most secret and law-enforcement agencies have behaved like silent bystanders to the activities of ISIS in the country. Is this an unofficial channel of providing soldiers to provide the Saudi demands for fighters to fight on behalf of Saudi armies in Yemen and Syria?"[15]

These trained terrorists managing attacks on civilian and government installations in Central Asia. Tajikistan's long, porous border with Afghanistan is a source of security concerns the reason for that transnational threats such as violent extremism and narcotics trafficking have intensified. Tajik nationals are present in Afghanistan and sometimes cross the border for terrorist attacks. Tajikistan has experienced several violent incidents attributed to IS-K, including prison riots in 2018 and 2019 and a 2019 attack on a border post. Taliban, the IS-K and Pakistan bases terrorist organizations are trying to expand their networks to Central Asia and Africa. Muslim were forced by the US army and CIA to join al Qaeda and ISIS terrorist groups and the ISIS sought the allegiance of the aggrieved communities. The US strike in Jalalabad killed 36 innocent people. The blast destroyed three underground tunnels as well as weapons and ammunition. However, ISIS denied that any of its fighters were killed or injured, according to a statement in Arabic distributed by the terror group's media wing, Amaq News Agency. "This was the right weapon against the right target," Gen. John Nicholson, commander for US forces in Afghanistan, told a press conference. Expert and writer Rushni Kapur in her paper (The Persistent ISKP Threat to Afghanistan: On China's Doorstep, Middle East Institute, published on January 6, 2022) has documented atrocities of the Islamic State of Khorasan in Afghanistan:

"Two separate bombs were detonated in Dasht-e-Barchi in Kabul on December 10, killing two and injuring three others. Although no group has claimed responsibility for the attack, the Islamic State of Khorasan Province (ISKP) is likely behind the latest bout of violence. ISKP's fingerprints have been on other attacks. One of the worst, which killed over 180 people and injured hundreds, took place outside the Kabul airport in August 2021 during the final days of evacuations. The increasing number of attacks demonstrates the growing threat posed by the ISKP. ISKP has been emboldened by the withdrawal of foreign forces whose previous counterterrorism measures had constrained their activities in Afghanistan. The group is leveraging the power vacuum and lack of political stability to increase their foothold and mount a challenge to the Taliban's rule, monopoly on violence, and efforts to gain international recognition. Moreover, ISKP is trying to absorb disillusioned Taliban fighters and other smaller militant groups into its fold. Although the Taliban has given assurances that Afghanistan will not be used as a launchpad for incursions into neighbouring countries, the growing number of attacks claimed by or attributed to ISKP raise concerns about whether the former has a firm hold on the country. Despite capturing ISKP-held districts in the past, countering the group is proving to be harder this time for the Taliban as they transition from a guerrilla-style insurgency to a government. Beijing's overriding security concerns are spill over effects from the Taliban's takeover of Kabul to other militant groups, the absorption of East Turkestan Islamic Movement (ETIM) fighters into ISKP fold, and possibility of orchestrating attacks in Xinjiang province".[16]

The Islamic State has been more influential during the past decade in Afghanistan and captured several districts where Taliban were unable to penetrate. All jihadist groups, including the ISIS Philippines, the ISIS in Indonesia, Thailand and Bangladesh have direct and indirect presence in Afghanistan. In 2017, ISIS was able to overrun the city of Marawi. ISIS-Philippines. Both the al-Qaeda and ISIS core groups and their franchises have the capacity to use terrorist tactics ranging from improvised explosive devices, vehicle borne improvised explosive devices, suicide bombings, drone attacks, and mortar launchings. An ISIS franchise in Sri Lanka, the National Tawheed Jamaah, was the perpetrator of the 2018 Easter Day attacks that killed more than 300 people in seven separate targets.[17] Assistant Professor and Research Faculty with Terrorism, Transnational Crime and Corruption Center (TraCCC) and the Schar School of Policy and Government at George Mason University, Mahmut Cengiz, in his paper (ISIS or al-Qaeda: Which Looms as the Greater Threat to Global

Security? Small War Journal, published on 01 October, 2022) has noted some aspects of the ISIS presence and operational mechanism in Libya and Egypt:

"The ISIS-Libya emerged in Derna, a port city in eastern Libya, in 2014 when a group of 300 former Libyan members of the Battar Brigade returned to their country after fighting in Syria and allied with the Ansar al-Sharia terrorist group. ISIS-Tunisia emerged in 2015 when the group was involved in attacks in Sousse, Tunisia, including the targeting of the Bardo Museum. ISIS-Tunisia has maintained its capacity to carry out attacks in the country, where the group executed two suicide attacks in 2019. In Egypt, which also hosts many jihadist terrorist groups, most of the attacks by these groups have occurred in the northern Sinai area. ISIS-Sinai was to blame for 320 terrorist attacks between 2013 and 2017. This ISIS franchise originated from the Sunni Salafist Ansar Bayt al-Maqdis terrorist group that declared war against the Egyptian government immediately after the ouster of President Mohamed Morsi in a July 2013 military coup. The origin of the ISIS-Somalia franchise dates to 2012 when al-Shabaab assigned Abdul Qadir Mumin to operate in its remote outpost in Puntland in northeastern Somalia. ISIS-Democratic Republic of Congo (ISIS-DRC) emerged in 2017 in the Democratic Republic of Congo when militants from a new brand of the rebel group Allied Democratic Forces (ADF). Known as the City of Monotheism and Monotheists, the group leaned toward ISIS. The ADF is an Islamist group that has fought against the governments of the DRC and Uganda for several years. The US Department of State designated ISIS-DRC as a foreign terrorist organization in 2021 along with the ISIS branch in Mozambique (ISIS-Mozambique)".[18]

Chapter 8

Arbitrary Power and a Loss of Fundamental Freedoms: A look at UNAMA's first major human rights report since the Taliban takeover

AAN Research Scholar Kate Clark

UNAMA has published its first major report on human rights in Afghanistan since the Taliban came to power on 15 August 2021. It covers many issues, including detentions, torture and extrajudicial killings, the rights of women and girls and civilian casualties. One recurring theme is the arbitrary way the new administration often works and the unpredictability of its laws, punishments and procedures. Also underlined in the report, says AAN's Kate Clark, is the critical importance of 'fundamental freedoms', the right to peaceful protest and dissent, the existence of a free media and lively human rights organisations, in helping curb the arbitrary power of the state. These, the report documents, have been increasingly under

UNAMA's new report, Human Rights in Afghanistan – 15 August 2021 to 15 June 2022, is comprehensive and authoritative, detailing violations of a wide range of human rights and freedoms by what UNAMA refers to throughout as the 'de facto' authorities. It also traces institutional and other changes that have made it harder and more dangerous for Afghans to seek redress, complain, document abuses, or even know the new administration's rules.

This AAN report traces some of the areas highlighted by UNAMA's Human Rights Service (UNAMA HRS). They include new ways the state is violating Afghans' rights, for example, Taliban restrictions on women and girls' access to education, work and travel – although these echo the first Taliban Emirate's even more extreme curbs. There are also some very old and familiar violations, revenge attacks on members of the former regime, for example, or the methods of torture used by the Taliban's General Directorate of Intelligence (GDI). Anyone versed in the history of state torture in Afghanistan will recognise the use of kicking, punching and slapping, beatings with cables and pipes and the use of mobile electric shock devices on security detainees. (See AAN's dossier of reports on detentions and torture here.)

This AAN report also looks at what has facilitated these violations of Afghans' rights: the clamping down on human rights defenders and the media, the suppression of free speech and peaceful protest and changes in state institutions, which all help to make the deployment of arbitrary and unaccountable state power so much easier. As always, for far greater detail, including accounts of individual incidents, and the Taliban's response to UNAMA's findings, the 58-page report is worth reading in full. There are also whole sections in the UNAMA report that this report has not covered, including civilian casualties up to the Taliban's seizure of power and since (a subject AAN hopes to return to), conditions in Afghanistan's prisons and the Taliban's use of excessive force at checkpoints.

Extrajudicial killings, arbitrary detention, torture, enforced disappearances, cruel, inhuman and degrading punishments

UNAMA's monitoring has indicated a "clear pattern with regards to the targeting of specific groups by the *de facto* authorities." These include former members of the Afghan National Security Forces (ANSF), former government officials, individuals accused of affiliation with the armed opposition groups, the National Resistance Front (NRF) and the Islamic State in Khorasan Province (ISKP), journalists and civil society, human rights and women's rights activists and those the Taliban authorities accuse of 'moral crimes'. UNAMA says the Taliban's general amnesty for former government officials and especially former members of the ANSF has been violated:

Between 15 August 2021 and 15 June 2022, UNAMA HRS recorded 160 extrajudicial killings (including 10 women), 178 arbitrary arrests and detentions, 23 instances of incommunicado detention and 56 instances of torture and ill-treatment of former [ANSF] and government officials carried out by the de facto authorities. These incidents occurred in almost all parts of the country and have affected a range of individuals with differing levels of affiliation to the former government: from senior officials to drivers, bodyguards and relatives of former government and [ANSF] members.

In the first two months of the new administration, UNAMA says, there were reports of groups of individuals being killed, for example, 17 people in Kandahar city between 14 and 15 August, and 14 members of the ANSF who had surrendered in Khedir district of Daikundi province on 31 August. From October 2021 onwards, UNAMA says, it is individuals, rather than groups, have been targeted, often with a person taken out of their house and summarily shot. The list of examples includes two former female Afghan National Police Officers who were reportedly arrested in Kabul and whose bodies were found on 13 November by the side of a road in Gardez, capital of Paktia province. UNAMA has also tracked the arbitrary detentions and torture, not only of former ANSF and government officials themselves but also their relatives.

Since the Taliban capture of power, UNAMA has also documented the new administration targeting Afghans they accuse of being members or supporters of the National Resistance Front. UNAMA has recorded 18 extrajudicial killings, 54 instances of torture and ill-treatment, 113 arbitrary arrests and detentions and 23 cases of incommunicado detention of people accused of being linked to the NRF, mostly in Panjshir and Baghlan provinces. On 31 May, in the Khenj district of Panjshir, for example, "*de facto* security forces reportedly arrested 22 civilians accused of supporting the NRF. Three were reportedly released following mediation by community elders, while the remaining 19 were transferred to Dashtak prison and then to an unknown location." Afghans with alleged links to ISKP have been the focus of some particularly gruesome abuses. UNAMA says it has documented 59 extrajudicial killings, 22 arbitrary arrests and detentions and seven incidents of torture and ill-treatment by the authorities of individuals accused of ISKP affiliation since 15 August, mainly in Nangrahar province and especially in Chaparhar district and Jalalabad city. Extrajudicial killings in the region, it says, reached a peak in October and November 2021.

The incidents followed a similar pattern – bodies, often dismembered and/or beheaded were found, sometimes hanging from trees. Often the victim had been arrested by de facto authorities one or two days prior to the discovery of their body. In some instances, the circumstances around the killing – including the perpetrator – remains unknown, with bodies being found accompanied by notes stating that the individual was killed because they were an ISIL-KP member.

One of the examples UNAMA gives is the discovery of the body of a tribal elder on 15 November in Chaparhar district.

He had been arrested by the de facto authorities from a mosque the day prior, and was allegedly targeted for suspected [ISKP] affiliation. His body was dismembered, beheaded and his eyes had been gouged out. He reportedly also had bullet wounds.

UNAMA has also looked at the punishments given to those accused of violating moral or religious codes and has documented 217 instances of cruel, inhuman and degrading punishments since 15 August 2021. They range from shopkeepers in Lashkargah city in Helmand being slapped and kicked in April because they had not gone to pray in the mosque to a man in Tirin Kot, Uruzgan province, convicted of adultery and sentenced to public flogging on 21 February by representatives from the Departments for the Propagation of Virtue and Prevention of Vice, of Information and Culture, and of Justice, judges and the provincial governor. In Badakhshan, a woman who had accused her brother-in-law of sexual assault on 10 October was herself arrested by the provincial chief of police; both she and her alleged perpetrator were sentenced to lashing and were then ordered to marry. On 14 February, in the same province, in Nusay district, a woman and man were publicly stoned to death, accused of having an extramarital relationship, having reportedly been sentenced by the district governor.

The UNAMA report singles out the Taliban intelligence agency, the GDI, for violations, saying it has recorded instances of killings – both in the form of extrajudicial killings and as a result of severe torture – of detainees. On 19 December, for example, in Meskinabad village in Dasht-e Archi district, Kunduz, "a former Afghan Local Police officer was arrested by *de facto* GDI outside his house. On 22 December, *de facto* GDI summoned his relatives for a meeting where they handed over the man's dead body." Arrests and detentions by the GDI, the report says, often appear to be arbitrary, with individuals reportedly not informed of the specific charges against them, family members not informed of their whereabouts or denied visits, not granted access to defence lawyers and only seen by a doctor after having been tortured or ill-treated. In some instances, it says, detentions were based on an individual's role as a media worker or civil society activist.

Curbs on dissent, protest and reporting

Importantly, the UNAMA report also traces a gradual clamping down on the right to protest and other 'foundational freedoms'. It points to the campaign of largely unclaimed targeted killings of human rights defenders, journalists and media workers in late 2020 and early 2021, which had already created a climate of fear by the time the Taliban came to power. Many journalists, human rights defenders and activists then sought to flee

Afghanistan, fearing a crackdown by the new administration and indeed, since their takeover in August 2021, says UNAMA, the new authorities have:

Increasingly limited the exercise of human rights such as freedom of peaceful assembly and freedom of opinion and expression, cracking down on dissent and restricting civic space in the country. The arbitrary arrests and detention of journalists, human rights defenders, protesters have had a chilling effect on freedom of the media and civic activism. The absence of due process in the arrests and detention carried out by the de facto GDI puts individuals outside the scope of judicial supervision and increases the risk of extended pre-trial detention periods. The increasingly intrusive role and activities of the de facto [Ministry for the Promotion of Virtue and Prevention of Vice] have compounded such concerns.

UNAMA documents the Taliban's increasing crackdown on peaceful protest, including pursuing activists with house searches, arbitrary arrests and incommunicado detention, all especially problematic for women. Meanwhile, the "once rich Afghan media landscape" has also been under attack, with arbitrary arrests (122 cases, one concerning a woman), incommunicado detention (12, all men), torture and ill-treatment (58 cases, one concerning a woman) and threats or intimidation (33 cases, three concerning women) documented. The report said interlocutors "have increasingly highlighted the role of the *de facto* GDI in exerting pressure on media entities and journalists through threats, arbitrary arrests, incommunicado detentions."

As for civil society actors and human rights defenders, the UNAMA report says, they have "stopped their operations in most provinces, fearful of repercussions and restrictions imposed by *de facto* authorities," while journalists have "increasingly resorted to self-censorship to cope with the new media environment." All in all, says UNAMA, the human rights situation "has been compounded by the measures taken by the *de facto* authorities to stifle debate, curb dissent and limit the fundamental rights and freedoms of Afghans.

Facilitating abuse

By curbing both protests and dissent and the documentation and reporting of violations, the Emirate has made it easier for further violations to be perpetrated. The Emirate has also facilitated abuses by its officials in other ways. One theme running through the UNAMA report is the arbitrary nature of the new administration, of how rules are decided and enforced and violations punished by Taliban officials and agencies. One example is the role of the newly re-established Ministry for the Promotion of Virtue and Prevention of Vice (commonly referred to as the vice and virtue ministry), whose mandate, the UNAMA report says, "seems to include a mix of policy setting, advice, monitoring, complaints management, and enforcement authority on a range of issues connected with the *de facto* authorities' interpretation of what is needed to ensure the propagation of virtue and prevention of vice." (See AAN's recent report on the thinking behind the new ministry here.) Over the first ten months of the Taliban administration, UNAMA says it has noted increased instructions from the ministry whether prohibitions, for example, on music, displays of images of women, and the use of cosmetics, or ordering, for example, face-coverings for women, *mahrams* (close male relative) to chaperone women in public and public prayers for men, or advice "on a seemingly open-ended set of other issues (including but not limited to the length of hair and beards; restrictions on women's practicing sports, driving, access to public bathing establishments)."

Many of these instructions, says UNAMA, involve the "curtailment of fundamental human rights such as freedom of movement, freedom of expression and right to privacy." Their legal nature is also uncertain, and often they are "simply announced by a spokesperson in a media interview or via Twitter, leave the system open for interpretation and abuse." There has also been wide variation in what provincial departments of the ministry have instructed citizens locally to do or not to do. Moreover, the scope of the instructions, UNAMA says, "seems to be purposefully vague, which poses concerns in terms of compliance with the principle of legality, and the element of specificity."

UNAMA has documented cases where ministry personnel have punished people for violating *advice* or when they had not actually broken rules. For example, in January 2022, in Taloqan, capital of Takhar province, city, vice and virtue officials "verbally abused a group of three women who were shopping in the bazar with their young children because they were out of the house without a *mahram*" while in April, in Lashkargah in Helmand province, officials verbally abused a group of women who were shopping in the bazaar without *mahrams* and beat male shopkeepers for allowing the women to be in their stores unaccompanied; the police subsequently arrested 12 shopkeepers. Yet, the official rule for women is that a mahram is only required for journeys of more than 78 kilometres, while the instruction for women not to leave the house unless necessary is advisory only.

The vice and virtue ministry is also the avenue where citizens are supposed to be able to make complaints through a telephone hotline and a three-stage adjudication or referral decision-making process. UNAMA does not report on how well this is working, but does say that the Taliban's abolishment of the Afghanistan Independent Human Rights Commission (AIHRC), an A-status national human rights institution under the Paris Principles, on 4 May 2022 "leaves a void that will be difficult to fill. Notwithstanding the establishment of some avenues for citizens to submit complaints to various *de facto* governmental entities, the absence of an independent national human rights institution will inevitably affect human rights accountability in Afghanistan."

Violations of the rights of women and girls

"Despite prior assurances during negotiations in Doha and at a 17 August 2021 press conference in Kabul," writes UNAMA, "that assured women of their rights 'within the framework of Sharia law'" and that there will be "no violence (…) and no discrimination against women," women and girls have seen the progressive restriction of their human rights and freedoms. These, it says, stem from the Taliban's "conservative theo-political position on the role of women." Most fundamentally, there are no women in the Taliban's cabinet or indeed any decision-making forums at national or sub-national levels, denying them the opportunity even to be consulted on matters that affect them and their families. Restrictions, either de facto or as official orders or 'advice', specifically on the lives of women and girls include: the ongoing closure of girls' schools beyond sixth grade; forcing women to have mahrams outside the home, including only allowing women to leave the country if they are with a mahram; orders for women to cover their faces outside and only leave the home if necessary; gender segregation of parks, gardens, and picnic venues in Kabul and; bans on employment by the government except in key roles, for example, health, education and some policing. Widows, the report says, and other women heading households are particularly affected by many of these orders, given that many are predicated on women having male 'guardians' to support and represent them.

Afghanistan's often poor record on violence against women has worsened, with "the dissolution of dedicated mechanisms established to deal with cases of violence against women and girls." Even where the Taliban have promoted some rights for women, for example, Mullah Hibatullah Akhundzada's 3 December 2021 decree on women which upheld their women not to be forced into marriage and for widows to enjoy their inheritance rights, UNAMA said it had recorded instances where the authorities – including judges, provincial governors and others – had broken this ruling. For example, on 15 February, in the Tarin Kot district of Uruzgan province, a woman and her brother were summoned to court regarding her rejection of an offer of marriage, reported UNAMA.

The judges of the de facto Primary Court tried to force the woman to accept, and when she refused they beat her and her brother severely. They were forced to flee their home, fearing further retribution, and her other brother who stayed behind was subsequently detained by the de facto authorities in an attempt to get the woman to accept the proposal.

In another example, from 27 April, a 15-year-old girl told UNAMA she had been sold to an older man by her father, whom she did not want to marry and from whom she had run away with another man whom she married. After her father filed a complaint, the police locked her up, ordered her to divorce her husband and marry the man of her father's choosing. She remains in detention, with her case reportedly before the court. For any woman or girl facing domestic violence or sexual assault, the restrictions on their basic rights and freedoms – to work, go to school, travel, and leave the country – and their absence now from decision-making and as judges and lawyers in courts, all make it easier for violent perpetrators to abuse their victims unhindered. It also makes it less likely for victims to get redress. And for women as a whole Taliban restrictions on their rights and freedoms, says UNAMA, "has effectively marginalized and rendered Afghan women voiceless and unseen."

Conclusion

UNAMA Human Rights Service is now the only extant, on-the-ground, nationwide body documenting human rights violations and trying to hold the new administration to account. It is also one of the few bodies that continues to engage with the Taliban at central, provincial and district levels, bringing, as it says, credible reports of human rights violations to the attention of relevant ministries and departments and raising awareness of human rights standards, instruments and mechanisms.[1] UNAMA says it has appreciated "the willingness of the de facto authorities to engage on various issues, including reports of human rights violations." It has provided a critical public service in producing and publishing this report. The report ends with an almost philosophical defence of human rights and how respect for them is integral to Afghanistan's future: *Ten months after the Taliban takeover, Afghanistan still faces uncertainty over its political, security and socio-economic future. The economic, financial and humanitarian crisis, exacerbated by the sanctions and suspension of non-humanitarian aid flows, continues to negatively affect Afghans' human rights, including to an adequate standard of living.*

Afghan women and men legitimately expect from the de facto authorities an inclusive governing vision that fosters peace, social cohesion and economic development. It is imperative that such a vision is based on fundamental human rights, as without them people's participation in public affairs is limited, security is ephemeral, and development is not sustainable. Human rights are not only about complaints being heard, but also about different voices being able to be expressed without fear and being valued as enriching social life. Unless specifically stated otherwise, all material on this site was created, authored and/or prepared by AAN. AAN's material is licensed under a Creative Commons Attribution-NonCommercial-NoDerivatives 4.0 International (CC BY-NC-ND 4.0), unless stated otherwise. This means you are free to copy, distribute and transmit the work, provided that it is: (1) properly attributed to AAN, with a link to the original webpage; (2) used for non-commercial purposes only; (3) not changed in any way. In all other cases, you should contact AAN for prior permission at info@afghan-analysts.org The AAN logo is the trademark of the Afghanistan Analysts Network and cannot be used without prior written permission. AAN's Executive Board is responsible for the overall research agenda, management and fund-raising. The Executive Board members also serve as senior analysts. The AAN Executive Board. Kate Clark, Co-Director and Senior Analyst @KateClark66. Kate Clark has worked at AAN since 2010. She was Country Director (2014-16) and has been a co-director since 2017. Kate's interest in Afghanistan began in 1991 when she went to Peshawar in Pakistan on holiday and spent time with Afghan refugees there. In 1999, she was posted to Kabul as the BBC correspondent – at the time the only western journalist based in the country. She reported on drought and war, but also on football and tourism, travelling widely on both sides of the frontline. Kate was expelled by the Taliban in early 2001, but returned to cover the 2001 war, contributing to award-winning coverage. After 2002, Kate was based in London, but returned to make radio and television documentaries about the insurgency, weapons smuggling, opium and war crimes. At AAN, Kate focuses on the war, including civilian casualties, the Afghan Local Police and 'campaign forces' and detention and torture. She has also written on Afghanistan's plants, birds and the environment. Kate has an MA in Middle Eastern Politics from Exeter University in Britain and previously worked in the BBC Arabic Service. She has also lived, studied and worked in the Middle East. Contacts: For general enquiries, please write to us at: info@afghanistan-analysts.org. Members of the AAN Executive Board can be reached at: Thomas Ruttig: thomas@ afghanistan-analysts.org. Kate Clark: kate@afghanistan-analysts.org. Jelena Bjelica: jelena@afghanistan-analysts.org. AAN's Admin and Finance team can be reached at: admin@afghanistan-analysts.org

Chapter 9

Dying to Live: The "Love to Death" Narrative Driving the Taliban's Suicide Bombings

Atal Ahmadzai

Abstract

Embracing the tactic of suicide bombings first in 2003, the Taliban in Afghanistan quickly emerged as the leading terrorist group in the world that has claimed responsibility for such bombings. Over a period of more than ten years, the group has indiscriminately carried out hundreds of suicide bombings across the country. How has the Taliban managed to operationalize one of the most notorious bombing tactics against all the existing social and cultural odds of Afghan society? To answer this question, this study, by applying qualitative thematic analysis, examined the contents of the Taliban's written and audio-visual materials on suicide bombings. Two dominant narratives, namely "Istish-haadi" [seeking martyrdom] and "love to death," that are at the core of the Taliban's produced literature on suicide bombings, have supplied the group with dispensable human bombs. These bombers, the study concludes, are "dying to live".

Keywords: Afghanistan, human bombs, martyrdom, political violence, suicide bombings, Taliban bombers, Taliban terrorism.

Introduction

Although the history of suicide missions can be traced back to ancient times, suicide bombings are a modern form of political violence.[1, 2] These bombings were pioneered in Lebanon in the early 1980s.[3] They soon spread to other armed conflicts around the world, including Sri Lanka, Turkey, and Chechnya.[4] However, it was only in the post-9/11 world that the incidence of suicide bombings increased exponentially, making suicide bombings the outstanding characteristic of contemporary global terrorism. With the initiation of the War on Terror, suicide bombings have systematically transformed from a unique form of political violence to a full-blown warfare tactic for terrorist groups. These groups, which include the Taliban in Afghanistan, have embraced these bombing tactics to advance their agendas by inflicting unexpected violence and thereby affecting the political climate.[5]

While terrorist groups easily find and marshal hundreds of individuals to willingly walk or drive toward an enemy risking death, the phenomenon of suicide bombings has remained an enigma. To unwrap this enigma, scholars have studied different terrorist groups that resorted to the use of this tactic. An overwhelming majority of these studies are focused on suicide bombings in the Middle East, mainly in Palestine, Lebanon, and Iraq.[6] However, one group that, somehow, did not attract that much attention, is the Taliban with their suicide bombings in Afghanistan. Only a limited number of studies have looked at the Taliban's human bombs. Semple studied the case of the Taliban's suicide bombings from the perspective of the group's ideological orientation and organizational structure.[7] Williams provides a general commentary on different aspects of the Taliban suicide bombings.[8] The United Nations Assistance Mission to Afghanistan (UNAMA) describes Taliban's suicide bombings mainly through the lens of civilian casualties.[9] By utilizing different quantitative approaches, Rome argues that the Taliban's suicide bombers are incompetent and for that reason do not constitute the group's main strength.[10] Edwards' ethnographic approach to suicide bombings in Afghanistan asserts that these bombings have a sacrificial orientation.[11]

The present study explores the motivations that lead Taliban bombers to blow themselves up to kill and destroy. The study examines whether Taliban suicide bombers are "dying to win," "dying to kill," "dying to expiate," or, paradoxically, "dying to live."[12] The article proceeds in four sections. Initially, it briefly describes the methodology used for this study. Subsequently, the article explores the particularities of the Taliban's suicide bombings. Within this section, the author sheds light on how the Taliban's suicide bombings differ from suicide bombings in the Middle East. In the third section, the author explores the narratives that are at the core of the Taliban's suicide bombings. Lastly, before ending with a concluding note, the article briefly discusses its findings in the light of the relevant literature.

Methodology

The Taliban [from the Arabic 'Talib'='student', used by adding -'an' as plural in Pashtu] have published and disseminated materials to justify and promote their suicide bombings. This qualitative explorative study aims to analyse the contents of the group's specific materials on its suicide bombers which are scarce. This is unlike the situation in Palestine or in Iraq with the ubiquity of suicide bombers' farewell letters or their detailed biographies.[13, 14] To cope with such scarcity, this study mined any type of relevant materials that the Taliban have published, including written (manifestos, books, articles, and poems), verbal (sermons/preaching, ballads) and visual (preoperational proclamation and warfare promotional clips) sources.

Data Mining and Cleaning

Government and Internet media counter-terrorism measures have made Jihadi electronic prints notoriously unstable.[15] To overcome this challenge in the data mining process, the study conducted a web-based search of the Taliban's official and affiliated websites as well as a general web search. In total, 19 of the Taliban's official and affiliated websites and tens of non-affiliated websites were explored. In addition, this study also used YouTube and Facebook, primarily to mine relevant audio-visual materials of the group.

Given the ephemeral and migratory nature of the Taliban's electronic print, it took this study three years (from March 2016 to April 2019) to periodically explore, identify, and scrap the Taliban's official and affiliated websites and social media accounts. In addition, the instability of the group's media outlets made it difficult to identify a specific coverage time period for the search. To overcome this problem, the author of this article decided to arrange the search and scraping processes periodically/in waves. Over the course of three years, a total of six waves of websites identification, searching, and scraping episodes were conducted. In total, most scraped materials were published or republished between 2012 and 2019 by different outlets. The searches were conducted in Pashtu, Dari (Farsi), Urdu, Arabic, and English. Key search words and phrases were translated from one language to another during the data mining process. Subsequently, for redundancy, the key terms and words were conjugated with other terms and phrases that have recursive usage for suicide bombings in mainstream and social media outlets.

In total, thousands of pieces of materials containing the key search words and phrases were mined. Most of these materials were reproduced and republished in multiple sources. For that reason, the first step of data cleaning was to address multiplicity by identifying and discarding duplicate materials. The second phase of data cleaning focused on identifying materials that were produced by the Taliban and their affiliated sources. For that purpose, 'medium of dissemination' was used as the key identification marker. Only materials that were published and disseminated by the Taliban's official and affiliated websites were included in the corpus. The organization's logo was used as the identification marker for visual materials.

The Corpus

In total, 50 items, including two books, 16 articles/commentaries, 2 of the Taliban's codes of conduct, 21 suicide bombers' proclamation clips, and nine audio sermon/preaching clips were identified as the corpus of this study.[16] In the last 10 years, at least, much has been written in Pashtu, Dari/Farsi, Arabic, and even Urdu languages about the suicide bombings of the Taliban. However, this body of literature is not or cannot be directly related to the group. This study rigorously collected, carefully screened, and robustly processed a portion of the literature that can be verifiably related to the Taliban. As a result, this study considers the corpus as the universe of the Taliban's publications on their suicide bombings. This corpus represents the period between 2012 and 2019. A reporting bias relevant to the contents of the corpus must be acknowledged. This study assumes that the Taliban may have more recorded preoperational proclamation clips of their suicide bombers than those that the group has released. During data processing, it became evident that the group is highly selective in releasing clips, using only those suicide bombers who have targeted military installations or personnel. Most bombers who have targeted populated and urban areas remained unreported.

Such a reporting bias resulted in the inclusion of a limited number of preoperational clips in the corpus, which may have quantitative effects on the analyses of the study. However, given the thematic similarities among the preoperational clips in the corpus, this study assumes that the qualitative impacts of the reporting bias on the analyses of this study are minimal, if any at all. Subsequently, the study classified the contents of the corpus into two folders. First, the "Taliban Official" folder included materials reflecting the Taliban's official standing on suicide bombings, including the books, articles/ commentaries, preaching clips, and military operational promos. Second, the "Suicide Bombers" folder contained materials related to the suicide bombers—the preoperational proclamation videos.

Analyzing the Data

By applying a qualitative thematic analysis method, this study seeks to comprehend the motives behind the bounded system of the Taliban's suicide bombings. Operationally, thematic analysis identifies patterns and trends within a set of qualitative data.[17] As such, the method is intended to explore the underlying themes and narratives in the Taliban's suicide bombings literature. Practically, pertaining to the contents of extremist media, thematic analysis gives more significance to the language used in the construction of the given ideas and narratives.[18] This distinctive ability of the method allows the study to analyze the use and types of language that the Taliban and their suicide bombers use in their written and spoken materials. This specific method has been used by Macnair & Frank (2017), Khosravi et al. (2016), and Goerzig & Al-Hashimi (2015) to study the contents of extremist/Jihadi media.[19-21] Initially, the audio and video clips were transcribed. To avoid losing meaning, none of the pieces in the corpus were translated. Subsequently, four categories, namely Justification, Occupation/Invasion, Criticism, and Miscellaneous, were identified in the transcripts of the "Taliban Official" folder.

Similarly, four categories, namely Life, Occupation/Invasion, Afterlife, and Miscellaneous, were identified in the transcripts of the "Suicide Bombers" folder. After identifying the categories with colour schemes, coding was applied to each coloured text. Subsequently, each section of the coded text was extracted from the documents and compiled in a new document named after the specific category. Four new documents, namely Justification, Invasion, Criticizing, and Miscellaneous with a suffix of "Taliban Official," were created from the transcript in the "Taliban Official" folder. The same number of documents, namely Life, Invasion, Afterlife, and Miscellaneous with a suffix of "Taliban Bomber," were created from the transcripts in the "Suicide Bombers" folder. By size, the heaviest (worded) document within the "Taliban Official" folder was "Justification," followed by "Criticizing," "Miscellaneous," and "Invasion." Similarly, in the "Taliban Bomber" folder, the heavy-worded document was "Afterlife," followed by "Life," "Miscellaneous," and "Invasion."

In the next stage, different themes were identified within each of the Category Documents. The "Miscellaneous" and "Invasion" categories did not show any specific themes and the contents were widely scattered around different issues and topics, including but not limited to the "hardship the Prophet suffered," "the suffering of Muslims," "message to family," "the movement of Taliban," and the "sacrifice of Taliban." In the last phase of the analysis, the author examined each thematic area for the existence of underlying reasoning and narratives. The study focused on identifying the type, nature, and ubiquity of the reasons used in the identified themes. In each theme, a given reasoning or narrative was identified and highlighted. At the end, authoritative/religious reasoning exclusively based on sacred scripts (the Quran and Hadith) and stories, largely imaginative, emerged as the two main underlying reasons used in the different thematic areas.

Characteristics of the Taliban's Suicide Bombings

The birth of the Taliban's post-9/11 insurgency is in parallel with their embrace of suicide bombings.[22] In 2003, the group introduced this tactic in Afghanistan by carrying out its first attack in the capital Kabul.[23, 24] Before this, no evidence exists to suggest the use of this tactic by any domestic actor at any time in the prolonged warfare history of the country. Similarly, this study did not trace any evidence indicative of the Taliban resorting to suicide bombings prior to 2003. In addition to consulting other sources, the present study systematically reviewed the online repository of the Taliban Source Project (TSP) but found no evidence suggesting that the group has mentioned, discussed, or even promoted suicide bombings, in an array of terminology, between the period of 1994 and 2003.[25] Subsequently, the group quickly created an infrastructure to train suicide bombers; plan and execute attacks and generate high-quality propaganda materials.[26] Based on the Robert Pape's CPOST data that was accessed in April of 2016, in more than a dozen years (2003–2015), the Taliban emerged as the leading terrorist organization in the world that has claimed responsibility for the most suicide bombings.[27] Out of the total 5,430 suicide bombings that 104 terrorist groups have carried out across the globe since 1981, the Taliban claimed 774 (14.25 percent of the total) of them; only second to the 2,520 unclaimed bombings in the Annex).[28] Similarly, analysis of the Global Terrorism Database (GTD) data (1970–2018) reveals that second to Iraq, Afghanistan has the highest number of suicide bombings, with 1,339 or 19.1 percent of the total 7,011 carried out since 1970.[29] This positioned Afghanistan as having the second-highest number among the 49 countries where the most suicide attacks were carried out.[30]

From a strategic perspective, the introduction and the rapid expansion of suicide bombings within the Afghan theatre of operation is critical. Some scholars considered this transfer from the Middle East an alarming and dramatic strategic shift in global terrorism.[31,32] However, paradoxical to this strategic significance, the case of the Taliban's suicide bombings has not attracted the required scholarly attention. This case has largely remained in the shadow of the most-studied cases of suicide bombings in the Middle East. At both policy and strategic levels, any comprehension of the Taliban's suicide bombings based on over-generalized conclusions of suicide bombings in the Middle East is problematical and in the end misleading. Such an approach may have helped in a preliminary exploration of the Taliban's "human bombs," but it cannot amount to an in-depth and robust understanding of this rapidly expanding case of extreme political violence. The dynamics of the two cases—suicide bombings in the Middle East and those in Afghanistan—are different and so are nature and circumstances surrounding suicide terrorism in these two distinctive theatres of operation. The cultural, historical, and strategic attributes and contexts of the two geographic regions need to be taken into consideration. These distinctive characteristics indicate a stark contrast between the dynamics of these two cases.

Differentiating the Taliban's Suicide Bombings from Those in the Middle East

First and foremost, the existence of a customary value system in Afghanistan facilitates a social and cultural context that is different from that in the Middle East. The Pashtunwali code of conduct, in addition to other aspects of life, has shaped the warfare conduct and ethos of Afghans. (For more on Pashtunwali, see: Barfield 2010[33] and Habibi 1962.[34] Unlike in the Middle East, where strategic implications of suicide terrorism overshadowed its normative and legal aspects, in Afghanistan these bombings are scrutinized based on the traditional code. The Taliban, inspired by their fundamentalist religious orientation, disregard the traditional warfare ethos. As a result, they have based their conduct of warfare on extremist religious thoughts and interpretations. This fundamentalism, including the use of suicide bombings, is largely imported from the Middle East.[35-37] For example, one of the warfare norms of Pashtunwali that defies the conduct of committing suicide in warfare is "Tura", Literally meaning 'sword,' this notion in warfare demands bravery by fighting face-to-face, not even under the cover of the night.[38] Inflicting indiscriminate violence by trickery tactics in the battlefield [the two defining characteristics of suicide bombings] is considered as cowardice.[39] More specifically, in Pashtunwali, bravery is not defined by dying in war. Metaphorically, it is the nature and place of the

172

wound—the one that indicates face-to-face engagement—that defines a warrior's bravery.[40, 41]

Secondly, dying in warfare or for any given cause, per se, is not a virtue of warriorship in Pashtunwali. In the Middle East, this may have been a value within some cultural groups (see Ergil 2000.[42]). Here is where a fine, yet critical distinction, between simply dying for a cause and fighting for a cause to the extent of death must be made. In dying for a cause, the virtue is in dying. In fighting to death for a cause, however, the virtue is the cause that needs to be defended to the extreme limit. Pashtunwali promotes defending specific causes and values including, but not limited to, individual and collective dignity and honour to the extent of death. This distinction has made the practice of embracing death without a fight—characteristic of suicide bombings—unpopular within Afghan traditional warfare ethos. Traditional Afghans will indeed fight to the death, perceiving this as an honourable deed; however, their warrior ethos does not normally include killing themselves deliberately.[43]These cultural values have facilitated a critical and hostile public mindset toward suicide bombings. On the other hand, in the Middle East, at least in some theatres of operation such as Palestine and Iraq, the existence of public support toward suicide bombings is well documented (See[44-50]). The overall social aversion against suicide bombings in Afghanistan can be illustrated by the fact that when the Taliban first resorted to suicide tactics, many Afghans refused to accept that the performers of these attacks were Afghans.[51]

This shows that the Taliban has operationalized their suicide bombings in a strategic milieu with strong social and cultural aversions toward killing oneself in war. For these reasons, the Afghan resistance groups fighting against the Soviets in the 1980s avoided the use of suicide bombings. Although thousands of Arab fighters from the Middle East and North Africa with Salafi Jihadist ideology and familiar with suicide terrorism joined the Afghan Mujahedeen to fight against the Soviets, these foreign fighters were not allowed to diverge from the local cultural/traditional warfare ethos. However, post 9/11, the Taliban's new warfare ethos based on a fundamentalist interpretation of Islamic law, put into question some traditional values and conducts.[52] In order to operationalize their suicide bombings in a social and cultural context that is hostile to using suicide missions in warfare, the Taliban had to rely on more psychological and ideological interventions and arrangements. Based on the mentioned differences, inferring comprehensions about the Taliban's suicide bombings from the conclusions drawn from suicide bombings in the Middle East is not conclusive, but rather based on overstretched and stylized facts. To understand the Taliban's suicide bombings, the phenomenon must be studied and treated as an independent case, surrounded by distinctive social and cultural circumstances including the Afghan cultural resentment to suicide bombings.

Taliban's Written and Spoken Materials on Suicide Bombings

The Taliban's approach to cope with the social resentment toward suicide bombings is systematic. In addition to disseminating materials, they have included relevant guidelines on suicide bombings in their official code of conduct—the Layeha (For the translated Layeha, see; Clark 2011[53]). In general, the group has disseminated written, verbal, and visual materials. The written texts are mostly conceptual contents, including three books that are rich in religious script and are intended to provide moral-legal legitimacy[54-56]The conceptual materials heavily rely on complex religious reasoning, which suggest that they are not likely intended for public consumption, but rather for religiously informed debates. The Taliban's initial written work on suicide bombings originated from Arab Jihadi sources. In 2004, soon after adopting suicide bombings as one of the insurgency's main warfare tactics, the Taliban translated and disseminated Yusuf Al-ayeri's book on martyrdom-seeking operations. In this booklet, Al-ayeri, the founder of Al-Qaeda in the Arab Peninsula, inferred the claimed legitimacy of suicide bombings from Islamic sources. In addition to other sources, his work is dependent on the writings of Ibn Taymiyyah. This medieval-era controversial Islamic theologian wrote extensively on the legal and moral aspects of Jihad-related issues, including its obligatory rather than optional status, killing oneself, civilian casualties, and executing traitors (see; Ibn Taymiyyah (1995)[57]).

Contrary to the written materials, the audio recordings of sermons of the group's ideologues, preachers, and sympathizers are simple in language and are emotionally enhanced and value-laden. These speeches use both religious and mundane/strategic reasoning and are largely intended for public consumption. The visual contents that include the group's operational promos and the suicide bombers' preoperational proclamations are the only sources that directly depict suicide bombers talking about these operations. Compared to the frequency of their suicide bombings, the Taliban seldom releases the proclamation clips of their suicide bombers. In addition, the group does not practice writing farewell letters or producing detailed biographies of the bombers. This is different in Palestine, where writing farewell letters among the suicide bombers is common.[58] This may have two reasons. First, to avoid public scrutiny. Tactically, the group does not take ownership and claim responsibility of suicide bombings that target public places with massive civilian casualties. Secondly, due to the strong social and cultural hostility/aversion toward suicide bombings, the group safeguards the bombers' relatives and family from possible social resentment by not releasing most of their suicide bombers' proclamations.

The Underlining Narratives

This study has uncovered the existence of two dominating narratives that the Taliban have used to promote their suicide bombings. The first is an explicit narrative of "Istish-haadi"[59] while the second is an implicit "love to death" narrative.

1. The Istish-haadi [Seeking Martyrdom] Narrative

Since its establishment as a religious militant group in 1994, the raison d'être of the Taliban's political ideology has been to establish the rule of the divine. It is practically and theoretically not feasible to distinguish what is political for the group and what is religious. They have consistently justified their ideology/political thoughts and warfare ethos and conducts based on the interpretations and narratives they derive from scripture—the Quran and the Hadiths. This also goes for the Taliban's arguments with regard to suicide bombings—these are exclusively based on religious doctrines. To assert the moral-legal legitimacy of suicide bombings, the Taliban has exclusively based its reasoning on the notion of martyrdom/ Shahada in Islam. From the notion of Shahada, they inferred the narrative of martyrdom-seeking or Istish-haad. This narrative is frequent in their materials. In fact, the group officially named their suicide bombings as "Istish-haadi" [martyrdom-seeking] attacks. At the core of this narrative is the debate on Intehar and Istish-haad.

The Intehar and Istish-haad Debate

The Taliban's written literature on suicide bombings revolves around the two notions of "Intehar" and "Istish-haad." Intehar is an Arabic term that is widely used for "suicide." It also is a well-known and broadly used term in Pashtu and Dari (Farsi); the two main languages in Afghanistan. On the other hand, Istish-haad also an Arabic word, means "seeking martyrdom." This is not a commonly used term but is widely known among religious scholars. The teaching on suicide in mainstream Islamic jurisprudence is clear: there is a broad-based consensus within all branches and sects of Islamic jurisprudence regarding the legal status of committing suicide, it is forbidden. [60]In their writings, the Taliban do not contest this. Quite the reverse, the group explicitly denounces suicide as a sinful conduct that is religiously outlawed and prohibited.[61] However, the debate does not end there. To provide a full explanation on the issue, the Taliban explored: What constitutes suicide (Intehar)? Are suicide bombings suicide? To answer these questions and to differentiate between "Intehar" and "Istish-haad," the Taliban apply a hermeneutic approach by deriving different meanings from religious texts, differentiating their suicide bombings from killing oneself. The group argues that the fundamental reason for the prohibition of suicide in Islam is not the act of killing oneself per se, but the cause(s) behind the killing.

The debate revolves around the mundane and the sacred. If killing oneself is a result of existential problems, including material or emotional attachments or despair, then the act is considered "Intehar," which is a vice.[62] They argue that as humans owe their life/existence to the divine, individual human beings do not own it and thereby, they do not have any right to either end or waste it for materialistic and mundane reasons.[63] Materialistic association with life is considered a deviation and killing oneself is forbidden because it indicates a materialistic and emotional association to life.[64] For the Taliban, it is not the inherent value of life that led to the prohibition of suicide, but rather the deviation from the celestial purpose of life. However, if the reasons for killing oneself relate to nonexistential and divine circumstances—engaging in jihad—then giving up on life is considered Istish-haad.[65] Based on such reasoning, the Taliban oppose referring to their suicide bombings as "suicide attacks" and instead call them Istish-haadi [martyrdom-seeking] attacks. Citing global Jihadist sources, the Taliban argue that giving up on life for religious purposes constitutes a deep-rooted tradition in Islam, and that the legitimacy of Istish-haad is attested by the sacred texts. They denounce mainstream Islamic authorities and scholars who have condemned and edicted suicide bombings as religiously outlawed.[66-68] The Taliban claims that as the legitimacy of Istish-haad is explicitly proven in sacred texts, its legal status is therefore beyond opinion, consensus, and reasoning.[69-72]

Sources of Legitimacy

Taliban resort to two sources to claim the legitimacy of their suicide bombings. First, by authoritative reasoning based on the [interpretations of] scripture. Secondly, by applying a circular reasoning that revolves around Jihad, Martyrdom, and Istish-haad. Authoritative Reasoning: The Taliban's standing on the moral and legal legitimacy of suicide bombings is assertive. They claim that such legitimacy is well-grounded in the sacred texts, therefore there is no room for further reasoning. They frequently cite the following Hadith with a decontextualized interpretation as a source of legality. The Hadith reads (translation): The Prophet said, "By Him in Whose Hands my life is! Were it not for some men amongst the believers who dislike to be left behind me and whom I cannot provide with means of conveyance, I would certainly never remain behind any Sariya' (army-unit) setting out in Allah's cause. By Him in Whose Hands my life is! I would love to be martyred in Allah's Cause and then get resurrected and then get martyred, and then get resurrected again and then get martyred and then get resurrected again and then get martyred (Sahih al-Bukhari Book 56, Hadith 15).

In addition, the Taliban also cite the following very similar Hadith to support the claim that seeking martyrdom is religiously recommended as an ultimate goal. It reads (in translation): Allah's Messenger said, "By Him in Whose Hand my life is, I would love to fight in Allah's cause and then get martyred and then resurrected (come to life) and then get martyred and then resurrected (come to life) and then get martyred, and then resurrected (come to life) and then get martyred and then resurrected (come to life)." Abu Huraira used to repeat those words three times and I testify to it with Allah's Oath (Sahih al-Bukhari (Book 94, Hadith 1).The Taliban has borrowed numerous similar Hadiths from global Jihadists and Salafi sources that claim legitimacy of suicide bombings based on holy scripture. Unlike mainstream Islamic jurisprudence that provides highly contextualized interpretations and meanings of the sacred texts, the Jihadist sources, and for that reason, the Taliban, take recourse to literal and decontextualized meanings. Circular Reasoning: The group also infers the legitimacy of suicide bombings by applying a circular reasoning, which links jihad, martyrdom, and suicide bombings in a complicated and confusion-inducing logic. The fallacy includes justifying the effectiveness of suicide bombings in terms of inflicting violence on the adversaries.[73]Subsequently, they construct the jihad-martyrdom-suicide bombing nexus.

The argument starts with insisting the necessity and obligation of Jihad due to the helpless circumstance of Muslims in different parts of the world. The argument continues by promoting martyrdom as the desired and divinely recommended outcome of Jihad and a divinely recommended conduct.[74] Subsequently, the argument focuses on proving suicide bombings to be the only conduct with certain and unescapable probability of inducing martyrdom.[75] By referring to the uncertainty of becoming martyred during conventional warfare engagements, Taliban preachers encourage their fighters to adopt suicide tactics as the most practical path for realizing the sense of urgency of martyrdom. Only the martyred are the ones who succeeded. Survival in the battle is a vice.... We don't know if we will die cursed or blessed. Only embracing the Istish-haad is the salvation...and you all should promote [it] among your families and offspring.[76]

Istish-haad is Not Sacrifice

The Taliban's interpretation of suicide bombings goes beyond the notion of sacrifice. Two factors, the ownership of life and the source of the decision of giving up on life, differentiate their conceptualization of suicide bombings from that of sacrificial conduct. The Istish-haadi narrative is based on the ontological assertion that the soul and body of human beings, and for that reason of suicide bombers, is owned by the divine.[77] Thus, suicide bombers do not own their lives nor souls. This invalidates the notion of sacrifice, as ownership of the sacrificial gift is principally and practically the prerequisite in offering the sacrifice. As life does not belong to the bombers, they cannot sacrifice what is not theirs. The second element that differentiates the Taliban's suicide bombings from sacrifice is the decision to carry out the act. While sacrifice is often voluntary, the Taliban asserts that choosing the subject for a suicide bombing is not the decision of the bomber, but of the divine. Therefore, the decision can neither be contested nor denied as the attack is not the killing of oneself, but rather the obligation to carry out a decision made otherworldly. This argument constructs a special and chosen identity for the bomber. The Taliban argues that to be chosen for giving up life for the rule of the divine is a privilege that not everyone is entitled to, but only those who are chosen.[78]

To support this claim, the Taliban's sources narrate a verse from the Quran, which reads that God makes martyrs among you (Cf. chapter 3, verse 140 in the Quran).[79] Consequently, the Taliban infers that carrying out suicide bombings is a practice of trading off the earthly life for the one hereafter. However, humans do not have the will to make this choice. It is the exclusive right of the divine to choose subjects for such a transaction. This divine selection, in addition to shaping a chosen identity for the bombers, constructs a sense of inevitable obligation. The suicide bombers, who are already overwhelmed by their chosen status, become indebted to follow up with the decision. The status that is promised to suicide bombers in response to the trade-off is not immortality, but satisfied eternity. Within Islamic teaching, the immortality in the hereafter is universal for everyone.

However, trading off life by committing suicide leads to a state of satisfied eternity.[80-82].

2. The 'Love to Death' Narrative

Analyzing the Taliban's material on suicide bombings also reveals the existence of a "love to death" narrative. An extreme version of this narrative is characterized by a disdain for life and a love for death. Messages that discourage the love of life and glorify death are plentiful and explicit in the Taliban's materials, especially in their preoperational proclamations. In the following excerpt from a clip, the bombers fervently speak of their experience as a journey toward the ultimate reality—from the illusive life to a satisfied eternity. While discouraging any attachment with the earthly being, the bombers passionately talk about the hereafter:

"... to my [family], when you hear about my martyrdom do not express sorrow but jubilation, as I am returning [the life] back without wasting and investing it in this vice [world]...."[83]

They explicitly appeal to giving up on loving life through embracing death, as any attraction toward, or attachment with, earthly life is a divergence and deviation from the ultimate reality:

"How can serving yourself, country, home, kids... justify your [earthly] existence in hereafter? ... it is not late; come on! Follow this path [suicide]...."[84]

In addition, the willingness to detach from life and embrace death is promoted as the exclusive strength of Muslims' youth's force:

"The true lovers are those who celebrate the message of their death as good news, their pride, and their triumph...They [suicide bombers] know what to love...." [85]

However, the Taliban does not consider the "love to death," narrative as nihilistic, but rather portrays it as a path toward the ultimate reality. Their bombers predominantly and ardently talk about an alternative realm that is beyond the dimensions of time and space. They preach that the worldly existence is not real but rather an illusion and a wearisome ordeal; and that embracing death is the journey toward the true existence. They sound convinced that what they are chosen for—suicide bombing—will end such an ordeal:

"...so, be careful! Shall not be deceived by the colours of the life; shall not be shackled by the love of materials, offspring, and loved ones. All these are contemptuous. Hence! Move towards the battle fields and run towards those paradises that are as expanded as skies and...."[86]

These bombers seem ecstatic. They speak of an alternative state, induced by the fact that they will soon transition to an ultimate reality, one that will allow them not to feel the pain and hardship of existence.[87] Such an alternative understanding of life and existence is a recurring theme in the clips of suicide bombers:

"My brothers! There won't be any worries, all the pains and problems of this life will go forgotten... my appeal to all believers! Who want to get satisfaction and peace, come and join us, you will get the eternal peace."[88]

In their proclamations, Taliban suicide bombers convey their message with a pleasant and satisfied demeanour. In addition, the visual effects used to enhance the clips made the images of the bombers more radiant. The explicit speech and the clear outlook of the bombers implicitly exudes a state of satisfaction and peace. The bombers express satisfaction in being the chosen one for trading off the illusive state of existence on earth with the real, satisfied, and eternal one. The intention is to convey the message that the opportunity of Istish-haad that is bestowed upon these bombers induces such satisfaction and peace.

Discussion

The Taliban's conceptual work on suicide bombings is not original. On the contrary, they recycle the radical Islamists and Salafi literature of the Middle East. These sources have inferred the claimed moral and legal legitimacy of suicide bombings from controversial Islamic literature whose history goes as far back as the medieval times, in particular the controversial 13th-century Islamic theologian Taqi-u-Din Ibn Taymiyyah, who has remained a major point of reference within the global Jihadist literature, and for that reason, also in the Taliban's writings on suicide bombings. In the 18th century, Ibn Abdul Wahab of the Najd, the founder of the Salafi/ Wahabi school of thought, has built upon the work of Ibn Taymiyyah.[89,90] This challenges Edwards' assertion that Abdullah Azam, the ideologue of the Arab fighters during the Afghan Jihad in the 1980s, was the one who provided a scriptural basis for the promotion of martyrdom and killing oneself and civilians in Jihad.[91] Azam simply tried to contextualize the existing controversial literature to the realities of the late 20th century. Although Arab fighters have promoted and encouraged martyrdom operations, the question that remains unanswered is why suicide bombings could not hold their ground during the Afghan Jihad against the Soviets in the 1980s.

While the Jihadist and Islamists were using suicide bombings in Lebanon and later in Palestine in the 1980s, their peers in Afghanistan simply did not. Why? Edwards could not provide an explicit answer to this question. However, the differences in the ideological and cultural orientations of the Arab fighters and the Afghan Mujahideen should have prevented the former in operationalizing their tactic of suicide bombings on the Afghan front. Ideologically, the disconnect between the Arab fighters and the Afghan Mujahideen was obvious.[92] Largely being followers of Hanafi jurisprudence, the Afghan Mujahideen, including their mainstream Sunni scholars of the original Deobandi school of thought, were not accommodating the radical doctrines of Ibn Taymiyyah and Abdul Wahab that Azam was preaching. In addition to the doctrinal disconnect, culturally, the warfare ethos of the Afghans stood in stark contrast with that of the Arab fighters. This may have caused the absence of suicide tactics during the Jihad era. Johnson argues that the absence of suicide missions in Afghanistan before the Taliban was due to the cultural aversion of Afghans to suicide.[93]

However, with the radicalization and proliferation of Pakistani Madrasas, the ideological orientation of the Deobandi school of thought in Pakistan has shifted. The process that was initiated in the late 1970s by the Pakistani dictator General Zia with financial support from the Saudis and the United States was aimed at broader strategic goals.[94] This ultimately caused the emergence of a new generation of Pakistani and Afghan Deobandi Ulema (religious scholars), including the Taliban, whose ideological orientation is guided by radical Islamist doctrines. The contents of the Taliban's literature on suicide bombings, including the constructed narratives—'love to death' and Istish-haadi—and their underlying reasoning, confirm the group's radical ideological shift. Gopal and van Linschoten (2017) argue that over the past two decades, the Taliban's ideology has transformed from 'traditionalist' Islam to a form of political Islam espoused in the Arab world.[95] Similarly, Giustozzi (2007) asserts that the neo-Taliban's post-2002 ideological orientation transformed from their original rigid ultraorthodox Deobandi way of thinking toward a more internationalist Islamist ideology.[96] More specifically, Brahimi (2010) argues that the adoption of suicide bombings by the Taliban is a radical ideological evolution from conservative Deobandi Islam toward fundamentalism/Islamism.[97]

While the Taliban has recently publicly rejected any affiliation with the global and regional Jihadist groups such as Al-Qaeda and ISIS, the group's decision to resort to suicide violence and its underlying logic is inspired by the theological reasoning promoted by the extremist Jihadi groups with a global outlook. The group's reasoning, logic, and epistemological orientation has converged with the reasoning advanced and promoted by groups ranging from the Muslim Brotherhood to Al-Qaeda.[98] Particular to suicide bombings, the group not only has become more radicalized in promoting indiscriminate violence, but also resorted to promote irrationality among its potential suicide bombers. A deeper scrutiny of the group's suicide bombings' corpus points to the existence of an irrational and dystopian understanding of reality and existence. This narrative promotes "love to death" and is prominent in the Taliban's suicide bombers' speeches. However, it is not an individual orientation. The foundation is provided by the group's "Istish-haadi" narrative, which is drawn from a decontextualized and reinterpreted comprehension of the notion of martyrdom in Islam. The group has constructed these narratives to serve two strategic purposes. First, to morally and legally legitimize the violence of suicide bombings. For their individual recruits, these narratives provide a moral cover for the violence they inflict.[99]

This is a rational tactic for tackling the strong cultural aversion of Afghan society to suicide bombings, which is largely shaped by the traditional warfare ethos of the Pashtunwali code of conduct. The social resentment to suicide bombings was so strong that initially the Taliban had to rely on non-Afghan human bombs (usually Arabs or Pakistanis).[100, 101] As such, there was a need for the Taliban to dilute this aversion and operationalize suicide bombings by constructing appropriate authoritative/religious reasoning. Thus, they adopted a scriptural Istish-haadi narrative that links suicide terrorism with the notion of martyrdom. Secondly, against the backdrop of the strong local cultural ethos, it was not practical for the Taliban to operationalize their suicide campaigns solely relying on the notion of martyrdom. Therefore, to sustain and perpetuate their campaigns, they constructed an irrational narrative of "love to death." While both of these objectives are part of a rational strategy, the group has resorted to promote an irrational and dystopian way of thinking among its potential suicide bombers. Taliban's "love to death" is suicidal and irrational. In their preoperational speeches, the bombers reveal both suicidal tendencies and an irrational and twisted explanation of life. They hold earthly existence to be illusive and the hereafter to be real. Hence for them, embracing death is the journey from an illusive status toward an ultimate reality. The bombers' denial of the reality of the material world defies Edwards' assertion of suicide offerings (sacrifice) as a means to materialize the sacred and mundane worlds.[102] In this regard, the main discrepancy between Edwards' sacrificial assertion and the Taliban's narratives lies in the conceptualization of the ends and the means.

For Edwards, the logic of suicide as a sacrificial act is to establish and materialize pathways between the sacred and the profane worlds through the mediation and destruction of the victim [the bomber and those killed].[103] However, for the suicide bombers and the Taliban, martyrdom-seeking is an instrument that facilitates the journey from the illusive material world toward a real, sacred existence. By studying the case of the Pakistani Taliban, Sheikh argues that through suicide bombings, the actor is prioritizing an otherworldly mission over worldly goods.[104] Hence, while Edwards' ethnographic scrutiny of the Taliban's suicide bombings is based on the overarching assumption of rationality, the Taliban's materials point to a dystopian and irrational understanding of existence. Both narratives mentioned here are heavily shaped by specific interpretations of religious texts. Semple argues that the religious case presented in the profiles of the Taliban's suicide bombers is unsophisticated and largely non-textual. He rightly observed that all Taliban suicide bombers invoke religion, but not in a sophisticated manner.[105] This is true when it comes to the speeches of the bombers.

The Taliban's ideologues and preachers, however, heavily rely on, and cite, sacred text. Some of the proclamation clips were edited with audio effects that narrate verses from the Quran. In addition, the group's written materials are highly sacred text–based and contain complex religious reasoning. In general, religious text is an inseparable aspect of the Taliban's narratives on suicide bombings. This is unlike some of the generalized secular and grievance-based assertions for suicide bombings, including those of Pape 2003[106] Talal 2007[107] and Egril 2000.[108] On the contrary, the Taliban's use of religion is similar to Bloom's argument. Bloom identified similarities between contemporary suicide terrorism with the medieval Shi'a Muslim Assassins in terms of indoctrinating their followers to the level of irrationality and the use of religious rhetoric to justify the infliction of violence.[109] Both the irrational orientation of the bombers and the use of religious rhetoric explicitly exists in the Taliban's narratives on suicide bombings. To eliminate any possible doubt about the religious legitimacy of suicide bombings, the Taliban avoids resorting to secular reasoning. For example, they do not refer to their Istish-haadi attacks as heroic martyrdom, which may reflect an earthly/secular goal. This is unlike what Hafez found about Iraqi jihadist suicide bombers. Hafez argues that in order to avoid overwhelming their audience by complicated ideological and political discourses, Iraqi jihadists use simplistic narratives of glory and heroic martyrdom.[110]

The Taliban does the complete opposite. In addition to the use of complex authoritative/religious reasoning, they resort to logical fallacy and circular reasoning to induce confusion among their listeners/followers. Given the fact that the Taliban has continuously faced strong societal resistance, this may have played a role in the Taliban resorting to the use of complicated authoritative reasoning and logical fallacy. Since the traditional Pashtoonwali code of warfare does not include references to support the newly adopted warfare tactic of suicide bombings, this may have led the Taliban to resort to circular logic and complex religious reasoning. Culturally, the traditional Afghan warfare ethos does not promote embracing death as a value. This both shapes and defines the existence of a deeply rooted social mindset on heroism in warfare; that is to fight face-to-face until the end. This is another reason that the Taliban avoids using the notion of 'heroism' in their narratives. Rather, the Taliban exclusively based their argumentation on fundamentalist interpretations of religious texts.

This interpretation consists of a dystopian understanding of life and reality and has shaped the Taliban's 'love to death' narrative. The fluidity and highly contextualized nature of religious texts can easily be misinterpreted for constructing erroneous authoritative narratives. Soufan argues that by using scripture, lore, and codes of conduct, organizations like Al-Qaeda often develop their own countercultures which are usually going beyond accepted social and religious norms.[111] This is certainly true for the Taliban's suicide bombings. Taking advantage of the multiple ways of scriptural interpretation, they have constructed narratives that promote an irrational socialization and a misleading understanding of life and reality. Such alternative understandings/countercultures have generally been overlooked by those scholars who largely dissect suicide bombings under the overarching presumption of rationality. For example, Talal claims that killing oneself is not uncommon in peace and preparing to die is not uncommon in war.[112]

This assertion confuses two completely opposing orientations to life: the glorification of death, and the love of life. Killing one in peace is not the same as willing to die in war by carrying out suicide attacks. Killing one in peace due to despair and overwhelming existential problems/pains does not constitute the 'love to death' orientation of the performer of the act. Quite the reverse, it conveys the message of hopelessness and an inability to celebrate life. It is the extreme form of rejection of not having a life without despair or pains. Here, the end is not dying, but rather ending the pains and despair that overburden life and living. Similarly, altruistic missions and the willingness to kill or be killed on the battlefield is aimed at the ultimate envisioned goal of life and freedom, for oneself and/or for other group members. Here once again, the end is not dying but rather standing up for life and its given associated values to the end. The Taliban's narratives on suicide bombings neither suggest heroic martyrdom nor do altruistic missions, as conceptualized by Durkheim and Johnson.[113-115] The Taliban's narratives express a strong bond and love, not with life, but with death. Life and existence for the Taliban's aspiring suicide bombers is illusive, deceptive, and leading to vice. Conversely, embracing death is understood as transcending from this illusive life into a real, eternal, and highly satisfactory state of being. Such orientations may be viewed as what Strenski, Semple, and Fierke refer to as martyrdom.[116-119]

However, the Taliban's understanding of martyrdom induced by suicide is different. They place a distinction between martyrdom induced during regular warfare engagements and the "martyrdom-seeking" operations (suicide bombings). While the notion of martyrdom has a highly contextualized interpretation within mainstream Islamic jurisprudence, the "Istish-haadi" conceptualization is its most radical and fundamentalist interpretation. The Taliban differentiate Istish-haadi attacks with martyrdom in regular warfare engagements by constructing a chosen identity of the suicide bombers. They argue that suicide bombers, unlike regular fighters, are divinely chosen. The purpose of this distinction goes far beyond seeking any political or moral justifications. Rather, it serves as an instrument of recognition and obligation. The bombers, in addition to their special identity/recognition, also have the inevitable obligation to carry out the divine-given mission. Strategically, this closes any potential avenues of retreat by the bombers.

In the case of Iraq, Hafez revealed the elevation of the Iraqi suicide bombers' identity to that of an extraordinary moral being as a result of their ultimate sacrifice.[120] Similarly, the Taliban acknowledge the bombers' special identity, but the reason for this is not due to sacrifice. It is due to the divine selection of the bombers. As such, the bombers are willing to accept the divine decision by embracing death. Hence, contrary to what

185

has been asserted by scholars like Hafez[121] and Msellemu[122], the motivation to embrace death is not merely seeking otherworldly reward systems of eternity, promises of paradise, or immortality in highly pleasurable circumstances. On the contrary, a complex system of divine recognition, worldly obligation, and otherworldly satisfaction is driving the Taliban's bombers to embrace death.

Conclusions

The Taliban in Afghanistan have embraced suicide bombings since 2003. Within a short period of time, the group developed an infamous industry of manufacturing "human bombs." They soon became the leading terrorist organization in the world, claiming responsibility for the greatest number of suicide bombings. Two narratives assist the Taliban in supplying their bombing campaigns with large numbers of bombers. First, an Istish-haadi narrative, which is based on authoritative reasoning derived from sacred texts. In addition, the group has resorted to logical fallacy/circular reasoning in producing the desired narrative. This narrative serves as the conceptual foundation for providing moral-legal legitimacy to suicide bombings. However, legitimization does not mean the practicality of these terminal missions, especially in a social and cultural milieu that is dismissive of suicide killing in warfare. To overcome this challenge, the group constructed yet another narrative; "love to death." It is based on an irrational and dystopian interpretation of the mundane existence. It promotes an alternative comprehension of reality that is beyond the premises of time and space, one which does not bear any relation to rationality. Two aspects of these narratives are prominent. First, martyrdom is the central tenet of the Taliban's suicide bombing industry. However, their understanding of martyrdom induced by suicide bombings is different. The decision to choose subjects for these bombings does not reside with the bombers, but rather is bestowed upon them by the divine. This renders the decision to embrace death indisputable and binding for the bombers.

In addition, such selection renders their actions as solely following through with divine orders rather than committing suicide. The second noteworthy aspect of the Taliban's narratives is their specific conceptualization of life. They consider death by suicide bombing as a transformation from an illusive and transient earthly existence toward a real and satisfied eternity. This is a crucial element as it promotes the idea of 'love to death' whereby death is regarded not as demise, but a passage toward a satisfied eternity. The Taliban resorted to the construction and use of these narratives as a strategic lifeline for their insurgency. Without "human bombs" at their disposal, the insurgency might well have faded away. Resorting to suicide bombings for the Taliban became a rational tactic in order to ensure the continuation and longevity of their insurgency. However, they pay a high price for this as the meaning of life and reality that the Taliban has constructed in their narratives is irrational, dystopian, and suicidal. For the Taliban's bombers, the decision to embrace the certainty of death with little or no hesitation is beyond any logical and rational justification. These bombers are seeking life by willingly and joyfully embracing death. Scholars have advanced different theses regarding the motives of suicide bombers, including a desire to win, to kill, to expiate, and as a reaction to injustice. However, the message that the Taliban's suicide bombers explicitly send out regarding their willingness to embrace death is outside the realm of rationality. The absurd message is that they are dying to live.

About the Author: Atal Ahmadzai is a postdoctoral research associate at the School of Government and Public Policy at the University of Arizona, where he is investigating the governance systems of the Taliban. He holds a Ph.D. in Global Affairs/IR from Rutgers-University. As a practitioner and researcher in development studies, Dr. Ahmadzai has firsthand knowledge and field experience in conflict-ridden areas, including Afghanistan. *The Terrorism Research Initiative (TRI) seeks to support the international community of terrorism researchers and analysts by facilitating coordination and engaging in cooperative projects. The globally-circulated online journal Perspectives on Terrorism has 9,400 regular subscribers and is viewed by many more occasional website visitors annually. The Terrorism Research Initiative is the parent organisation of Perspectives on Terrorism (PoT). It has three directors: Robert Wesley, Alex P. Schmid and Edwin Bakker. It was formed in 2007 and now includes a broad association of individual scholars and representatives of institutions. TRI seeks to provide the academic community as well as counterterrorism analysts and practitioners with science-based tools to contribute to the enhancement of human security by collaborative research. TRI is working to build a truly inclusive international research community and seeks to empower it by creating synergies that can extend the impact of each participant's research. One of its initiatives involves the establishment of national and (sub-) regional networks of post-graduate researchers working on their doctoral theses on terrorism, counterterrorism and related subjects. To stimulate high-quality research, TRI also issues an annual award for the best Ph.D. thesis in the field of terrorism and counterterrorism studies. The Terrorism Research Initiative is headquartered in Vienna, Austria. Its main academic affiliation is, however, with the Institute of Security and Global Affairs (ISGA) of Leiden University's The Hague Campus in the Netherlands. Two of its three directors are (or, until recently, were) associated with ISGA. Robert Wesley, the president of TRI and one of its three directors, is located in Vienna, where he is CEO of KIVU Technologies. Perspectives on Terrorism is a peer-reviewed online journal published by Prof. em. Alex P. Schmid and Prof. James J.F. Forest and their Editorial Team. Each issue of the journal contains typically a mix of articles, research notes, bibliographic resources and reviews from experienced, seasoned researchers as well as from more recent newcomers to the field – including post-graduate students finishing their PhD theses. Subscription is free and registration to receive an e-mail of each bi-monthly issue of the journal can be done here. Alex P. Schmid (Editor-in-Chief) can be reached at: apschmid@gmail.com. James J.F. Forest (Co-Editor) can be reached at james_forest@uml.edu*

Chapter 10

Tablighi Jamaat and its Role in the Global Jihad

South Asia Democratic Forum

Abstract

This SADF Policy Brief deals with Tablighi Jamaat (TJ), a transnational Islamic missionary movement. Despite declaring itself as officially apolitical and non-violent, TJ is cited by German and other European intelligence reports that underline (manifold) threats originating from the movement. An increasing number of assessments emphasise TJ's function as a catalyst, gateway, springboard, or antechamber for an extreme and militant interpretation of Islam – indoctrinating Muslims into Jihadists. Experts point out that TJ 'has appeared on the fringes of several terrorism investigations, leading some to state that its apolitical stance simply masks a "fertile ground for breeding terrorism". In spite of this, up until this point, the majority of critical evaluations by international intelligence have not reached public discourse or political decision-making processes in the states where TJ holds a significant presence. Especially in Europe and the US, TJ remains largely unknown outside Muslim communities – and when known, actions and motives are misread. This lack of knowledge regarding the dissemination of an Islamic supremacist agenda facilitates TJ's function as a driving force for Islamic extremism and as a major recruiting agency for the cause of Global Jihad - the movement bluntly threatens societies based on liberal and democratic norms. TJ has a relatively clandestine character, but reports point to TJ being extremely effective at spreading Islamic fundamentalism. In sum, TJ is seen as an essential component of a phenomenon which the French political- sociologist Bernard Rougier (2020) calls an 'Islamist Ecosystem'. We believe this concept is most useful to understand the role that TJ plays in the Global Jihad.

Keywords: Tablighi Jamaat, Religious Ideology, Transnational Organisation, Islamic Movement, Islamist Ecosystem, Islamic Fundamentalism, Global Jihad, Terrorism, Intelligence, Radicalisation, War of Ideas, Tablighisation.

Introduction

Not much is known about TJ. The group's founder, Maulana Muhammad Ilyas (1885–1944), was not in favour of writing about the movement and made it a principle to keep away from the press (and other media) as well as avoid detailed publications elaborating on the movement's membership and activities. It was one of Ilyas' convictions that 'action and practice were the best method to effectively change minds' (Putra, 2013, p.19). The movement presents itself as officially apolitical, preferring 'word-of-mouth instruction to public, written or online communiqués; [thus] TJ has heretofore flown largely under the analytical radar' (AFPC, 2012, p.1). This stands in sharp contrast with other pan-Islamic groups (for example, the Muslim Brotherhood or Hizb ut-Tahrir). Academic and mainstream literature describes TJ as an 'Islamic missionary movement', 'Islamic revivalist organization' or 'transnational Islamic pietist movement' (Horstmann, 2007, p.107), 'transnational Islamic reform movement' (Siddiqi, 2018, p.1), among other terms. TJ originated in India in the 1920s as a reaction to what was perceived as the depraved state of Islam in the South Asian region (Pieri, 2012, p.103), and Ilyas largely directed the principles guiding the organisation's 'formal structure'. Since its formation, and to this day, TJ adopts the form of an 'informal organization and keeps an introvert institutional profile' (Putra, 2013, p.22). Importantly, the movement did not build up any formal bureaucracy or employs paid staff. TJ consists of small groups (jamaats) of perhaps eight or ten people who are expected to finance themselves.[1]

Officially, TJ (as an organisation) does not ask for donations and depends in financial terms upon the resources of its senior members' (Putra, 2013, p.22). 'Double-memberships' with other religious organisations are not unusual for Tablighi. Jamaats are based on regular meetings and (preaching) journeys. Tablighi educational and missionary endeavours are organised in four ways: one day a week, one three-day period a month, one forty-day period a year, and one four-month tour (ideally abroad) at least once in a lifetime. One of the core activities of local jamaats involves going out door-to-door on converting missions (Putra, 2013, p.22). It is important to note that belonging to – or being a member of – TJ does not involve any formal registration process.[2]

Ilyas also formulated a set of principles[3] to guide preachers as well as instructions to carry out the organisation's core mission: to revive and revitalise Islam among its adherents, dilute the influence of other religions, and renew the purity and spirit of Islam as conceived by Prophet Muhammad and his companions. Riyaz Timol states that TJ's 'distinct style of activism' seeks to reinvigorate basic Islamic piety among Muslim communities through the persistent creation and dispatch of its jamaats composed of 'itinerant lay preachers to sympathetic mosques around the world' (Timol, 2019, p.20). TJ sees 'Muslims as being under threat of becoming corrupted by the modern world' (Freedman, 2006, p.32), as such, the movement's core raison d'être is da'wa, or Islamic proselytization, (Timol, 2019, p.20) 'making Muslims into true Muslims'. The group's apolitical and peaceful nature is much stressed. Alexander R. Alexiev states that 'from its inception, radical Deobandi attitudes permeated Tablighi philosophy. The movement rejected modernity as antithetical to Islam, excluded women was hostile to Shiites and syncretic Muslims, and preached that Islam must subsume all other religions' (Alexiev, 2011, p.83).

Over the years, as TJ grew in size and influence, its traditional structure was strengthened by additional resources and leaders and, in fact, gained the framework necessary for the creation of a global network. Subsequently, the movement has expanded from local to national, and further into a transnational movement. It is reported that TJ operates in at least 165 countries (Putra, 2013, p.17) – some estimations suggest that TJ is active in around 200 countries – with significant influence, not only in several majority Muslim, but in 'non-Muslim' majority countries in the West (Putra, 2013, p.17). At present the organisation's activities are coordinated via centres and headquarters known as 'Markaz' (Salam, 2020b). The organisation's international headquarter is located at the Bangla Wali Masjid Nizamuddin Markaz, in New Delhi, India. TJ's European headquarter is located at the Dewsbury mosque, UK (Alexiev, 2011, p.45). Like the jamaats, the Markaz are organized based on voluntary work and its members are self-financed (Putra, 2013, p.22).

The group holds national headquarters in several countries where they are active. In some countries, there is a formal shura with an Amir, while in others TJ units are run without a formal Amir. All local and state workers are asked to appoint an arbitrator or Amir-e-mashwara for their regular mashwara – consultation on various programmes from the mosque level to district, state and even in some cases national-level work. This arbitrator is selected by the local group for a limited period and the position is rotative

(Pieri, 2015). Today, TJ's annual congregations (three days gathering, known as Ijtima) in Bangladesh (Tongi, near Dhaka), Pakistan (Raiwind) and India (Bopal), attract the largest number of Muslims outside the annual Islamic pilgrimage Hajj in Mecca (Reetz, 2004, p.298; Pieri, 2012, p.103). With tens of millions of followers,[4]TJ is today the largest Islamic globally operating movement (Sikand, 2003, p.42). In this context, it seems perhaps obvious that TJ aims to recruit as many followers as possible. This is important because of TJ's recruitment process and the secrecy surrounding the internal structure ('closed door meetings'[5]).

The Sunday Telegraph states that 'no limit was placed on the potential pool of [TJ] converts, and so, implicitly, the ultimate objective was the Tablighisation of the world'. Moreover, it is argued that 'the group, for all the mystique that surrounds it, has been diligent, and, today, with a growing presence in the West, it is viewed by anxious critics as a Trojan horse of Islamic fundamentalism'. Furthermore, the Tablighi possess a 'scant regard for the logic of loyalties of national territory' (Putra, 2013, p.17). This can of course become a challenge for the integration of Tablighi in host countries. Policy Analysts and Islamic scholars are fiercely divided in their assessments of TJ. On one side some scholars denounce any a-priori ties between TJ and terrorism and stress that Tablighis implicated in terrorist activities 'represent a miniscule percentage' of the movement (Hedges, 2008, p.6). On the other side, a growing number of experts state that there is clear evidence that TJ as an organisation is linked to global Jihadism. Despite this debate about the real nature of TJ and its massive expansion, 'this movement hardly gets governments suspicion' in Western countries (Putra, 2013, p.19).

The Concept of 'Islamist Ecosystem'

TJ can be seen as a component of a phenomenon which the French political-sociologist Bernard Rougier (2020) calls an 'Islamist Ecosystem'. His example involves a network established in French suburbs which links schools, mosques, sports halls, shops, and even prisons. 'The components of this ecosystem'–foremost the Muslim Brotherhood, Salafist groups, and TJ, among others – are "competing" to control social spaces (neighbourhoods, associations, etc.); however, "they join forces against a common enemy, secularism, which they hate above all else". All these movements have been "working" within the neighbourhoods for a long time – through "religious entrepreneurs", preachers engaged in a real territorial conquest' (French Sénat, 2020a, p.33). TJ conducts 'initial preaching that paved the way by bringing young people back to Islam before they, now interested in the things of faith, turned to a more learned version of Islam' (Rougier, 2020). As such, TJ contributes to 'the expansion of ecosystem resources which in turn feeds the jihadist dynamic, providing its fighters with the ideological and material bases legitimising the fight against global society (Rougier, 2020). Preachers and recruiters from TJ are 'deployed there to detect weak spirits capable of forming the first line of the Holy War'.

Tablighi are sometimes seen as oscillating on an ideological continuum between moderate and radical positions, between TJ as organisation and militant Jihadist groups (Ragazzi, 2014, p.13, referring to CEIS and Change Institute). 'This ecosystem does not advocate armed struggle on French soil [as well as in other countries with a TJ presence] but maintains a logic of rupture with global society and its institutions. This rupture is then exploited by the theological and political argument of the jihadists' (Rougier, 2020). In other words, joining TJ could turn out 'to be the first step on the road to extremism'. Farhan Zahid describes TJ as 'system driver and integral element of Islamist Violent Non-State Actors internal dynamics'. Furthermore, he identifies TJ as 'one of the agents responsible for Islamist activities' which acts in many cases as 'a nursery for indoctrinating Islamist terrorists'.

Tablighi Jamaat in the focus of the international intelligence community

German Intelligence

In its 2019 Report on the Protection of the Constitution (Verfass ungsschutzbericht, BMI, 2020b, BMI, 2020a), the Federal Interior Ministry of Germany (Bundesministerium des Innern, für Bau und Heimat, BMI) points to that, even though the country has not witnessed any major terrorist attack since August 2017, 'the threat posed by Islamist terrorism remains at high levels' (BMI, 2020b, p.27). For the last few years, the country's domestic intelligence agency–Bundesamt für Verfassungsschutz (BfV, Federal Bureau for the Protection of the Constitution[6]) and its counterparts at the state level (State Bureaus for the Protection of the Constitution,[7] Landesamt für Verfassungsschutz/LfV) – under the BMI –, have been publishing these reports. Focusing on Germany's internal security situation, these reports assess external threats, indigenous left and right-wing groups, and the threat potential by Islamist extremists and terrorists (organisations and individuals) in the country, among several other issues.

Already at the occasion of the presentation of the 2004 Annual Report (BMI, 2005), the then German Federal Minister of Interior, Otto Schily, warned that Islamic terrorism poses the greatest global threat to Germany.[8] TJ was first mentioned in the 2004 report (Mukhopadhyay, 2005, p.332). It was classified as one of the foreign Islamist organisations active in Germany (BMI, 2020a). Among other concerns regarding TJ, the report specifically mentions a considerable increase in its support base[9] (BMI, 2005, pp.190-191) contributing to the overall rise in reported membership levels of foreign Islamist organisations in the country. The latest BMI 2019 report (2020a, pp.181, 224; 2020b, p.26) – compiled by the BfV –, as well as reports by several agencies at the state level (for example, BSTMI, 2020, pp.39-40; NMIS, 2020, pp.230, 232) continue to recognize TJ as part of the potential threat by 'Islamist extremism/Islamist terrorism'. German intelligence agencies hold that several factors justify monitoring TJ as a potential threat in the context of 'Islamist extremism/Islamist terrorism'.

When assessing TJ's threat potential, the '2019 Report on the Protection of the Constitution' states that 'the rejection of secular principles and the demarcation from non-Muslims' through TJ, 'can lead to the formation of closed parallel societies and at least passively promote individual radicalisation processes' (BMI, 2020a, p.224). These phenomena had already been mentioned by the BfV in 2011, which stated that 'the successful proselytizing efforts of TJ often lead to a visible change in the social behaviour of the recruits. The rejection of Western values can have a socio-political disintegration effect in non-Muslim countries and contribute to the emergence of parallel societies. This can promote individual radicalisation processes and thus create the conditions for a further slide into a terrorist environment'[10] (BMI, 2012, p.308). Overarching visions of TJ draw additional attention by German intelligence agencies: namely its long-term goals to establish an Islamist regime (NMIS, 2020, p.230) and make Sharia law universal.[11] From the TJ's perspective, this requires a comprehensive Islamization of their host countries' societies. The purpose of all TJ activities is to achieve 'the transformation of the society shaped by Western values into an Islamic form of society' (BMI, 2006, p.194). Here, both the BfV and the LfVs are concerned that the notion of an Islamic societal transition could also 'extend to jihadist ideas' (MIKNW, 2013, p.128). The Nordrhein-Westfalen State Office for the Protection of the Constitution (LfVNW) states that TJ must be classified as an 'extremist movement' (MIKNW, 2013, p.128).[12]

More specifically, German intelligence sees a threat potential in 'the pursuit of an exemplary practice of faith in the sense that TJ includes a largely verbatim and rigid interpretation of the Koran and its legislation, so that the fulfilment of religious regulations is given priority in principle over a way of life based on state law[13] (NMIS, 2020, p.231). Thus, TJ's ideology – especially propagating Sharia law as the basis of its social model, contradicts essential democratic principles, in particular that of the separation of state and religion' (BMI, 2012, p.309; NMIS, 2020, p.231). Here an area of concern for the LfVNW is that 'TJ calls for the application of all sharia law provisions' (MIKNW, 2010, p.109). 'This includes the application of the provisions of classical Islamic procedural law, classical Islamic law of marriage and divorce, and the so-called "Hadd" penalties (e.g., the flogging of offenders), which are not only incompatible but directed against the liberal democratic basic order (freiheitliche demokratische Grundordnung) of Germany' (MIKNW, 2010, p.109; BSTMI, 2020, p.39). Furthermore, the image of women represented by TJ, largely expressed in the social exclusion of women (NMIS, 2020, p.230; BSTMI, 2020, p.39)[14]cannot be reconciled with Germany's constitutional principles.

TJ presents itself as apolitical and non-violent (unlike other Islamist groupings such as Salafist circles) but the assessment of the organisation by security authorities is different (NMIS, 2020, p.231; IBW, 2012, p.67). In this context, it is interesting to mention that violent clashes between different factions of TJ occurred in the past, undermining the movement's narrative of promoting non-violence. Most remarkable were the events in the aftermath of TJ's leadership decision to establish a 'governing body' (Shura[15]) in 2015 (BMI, 2020a, p.2004). During the following years, particularly in 2018, strong reactions among the Tablighi led to serious clashes between opponents and supporters of the innovation in several countries, foremost in Bangladesh–but also in European states, such as the UK[16] (BMI, 2020a, p.224). The Baden-Württemberg State Office for the Protection of the Constitution (LfVBW) stressed that 'various investigative procedures and trials in recent years have clearly shown that the one-sided interpretation of Islamic sources –with the aim of aligning the behaviour of an individual Muslim strictly according to Islamic standards –can, in individual cases, lead to an intensive transfer of ideology'[17] (IBW, 2012, p.67). As indicated above, the vast scope for interpretation of the movement's ideology makes the emergence of a jihadist orientation within TJ possible (IBW, 2012, p.67; MIKNW, 2013, p.128).

195

It is noteworthy, that 'in the literature of TJ a pronounced glorification of the militant jihad can be found. Therefore, although it is true that there is no explicit call for militant jihad, jihad is described as the 'outstanding duty of faith of every Muslim' (MIKNW, 2010, p.109). Thus, some Islamist terrorists had life-changing experiences through their membership and exposure to TJ (MIKNW, 2010, p.109). TJ became a focus of the German judiciary as well; in fact, the movement's hostility towards the country's constitution has already been the subject of several court decisions. For example, the Administrative Court (Verwaltungsgericht/VG) of Bayreuth (State of Bavaria/Bayern) concluded in one of its decisions[18] that TJ supported international terrorism. For the judges involved it was clear that several persons belonging to TJ had committed terrorist attacks in different countries – or were linked to TJ in their terrorist attacks. At the very least, this grouping is used to facilitate individual terrorists' journeys or as a point of contact (NMIS, 2007, p.28). The Administrative Court (VG) Ansbach (State of Bavaria/Bayern) issued two resolutions (9 and 18 May 2005), stating that TJ supports terrorism. In addition, it was stated that TJ endangered the liberal democratic basic order and the security of Germany. As early as 24 November 2005, the VG Bayreuth had established that the suspicion of TJ's support of terrorism was objectively justified (NMIS, 2007, p.28). In its judgment of 2 March 2005,[19] the VG Hannover followed the previous decision of VG Bayreuth. It classified TJ as an organisation whose objective is directed against the liberal democratic basic order of the Federal Republic of Germany (NMIS, 2007, p.28).

The Thüringen State Office for the Protection of the Constitution (LfVT) came to a similar conclusion and stated that 'although TJ itself does not actively support Islamist terrorism, it does seem to serve as a recruitment base for violent Islamist groups and jihadist networks'[20] (TI, 2012, p.142; BMI, 2012, p.308). The BfV described TJ not only as a recruitment pool but also as a 'catalyst for Jihadist recruitment efforts' (BMI, 2012, p.308). More concretely, TJ is seen as cultivating such a conservative understanding of Islam among its followers that several organisations and networks just must add a 'Jihadist component' to recruit the Tablighi (BMI, 2012, p.308). In addition, there are indications that 'the largely common ideological base of TJ with Jihadists and other militant groups enables the latter to make use of the global TJ infrastructure' (HHBI, 2012, p.51; TI, 2012, p.142). Here, the Nordrhein-Westfalen State Office for the Protection of the Constitution (LfVNW) goes a step further by arguing that 'recent cases suggest that TJ, on the one hand, endorses Islamist and jihadist ideas in its ranks, and that on the other hand, its global networks are being used by Islamist terrorists – and that TJ tolerates this'[21-22] (MIKNW, 2013, p.128).

It appears that there is a growing awareness within Germany's intelligence community regarding potential causal links between TJ's missionary activities, particularly religious trainings and instruction courses, and the radicalisation of individual followers. The BfV warned already in 2005 that 'trainings by TJ can constitute for individual young Muslims an entry into Islamism and – subsequently – also into Islamist-terrorist groups'[23] (BMI, 2006, p.194). The federal agency emphasizes the significance of study tours abroad [namely those to Pakistan] offered by TJ. It is stated that 'successfully proselytised people are often provided several months of training events in Pakistani Qur'anic schools [madrasas]. Such intensive training courses can indoctrinate participants and make them receptive to Islamist ideas'[24](BMI 2006, p.226). 'In individual cases, trainees then found their way to "Mujahideen" training camps in Afghanistan'[25](BMI 2006, p.226).

Finally, it must be mentioned that the targets of TJ's missionary activities in Germany are mostly young people from social and weaker segments of society, or those who feel a lack of belonging[26] (BMI, 2006, p.194). Furthermore, in the sermons it became clear that TJ in Germany has not only 'fallen-from-faith Muslims' as a target group, but also different believers' (BSTMI, 2007, p.53). The fact that TJ also wants to appeal to German decision-makers such as mayors and parliamentarians demands special attention (BSTMI, 2007, p.53). The LfVBW identifies the potential threat that 'this can lead to a re-Islamisation, especially among young Muslims who have been discriminated against or feel disadvantaged. This revival then leads to rejection and demarcation from the surrounding society, whether it is supposedly Islamic or non-Islamic'[27](IBW, 2012, p.67).

French Intelligence

The French intelligence agency Direction Générale de la Sécurité Intérieure (DGSI, General Directorate for Internal Security) in its '2018 Rapport. Etat des lieux de la pénétration de l'islam fondamentaliste en France' (2018 Report–state of the situation regarding the lodging of Islamic fundamentalism in France) describes TJ[28]as one of the four most active Islamist movements in the country – besides the Frères Musulmans (Muslim Brotherhood), Salafistes (Salafists), and the Mouvement Turc ('Turkish Movement') – constituting 'the ultimate risk' in the form of 'an advent of a counter-society on national territory' (DGSI, 2018, p.3).

Furthermore, the DGSI states that TJ experienced a strong development in the 1970s – playing a major role in the re-Islamization of working-class Muslims in suburban areas (banlieues;[29]DGSI, 2018, pp.4, 109). Here, the French intelligence service sees a major threat. For even though it classifies TJ as apolitical, the movement 'constitutes a reservoir of individuals in total break with society' (DGSI, 2018, p.4). The DGSI is particularly vigilant regarding TJ's growing influence within the educational system. More specific concerns regard the indoctrination of the teenager and parents by TJ supervisors, the influence of [TJ] imams on children education, and the immense difficulties faced by non-Muslim families (foremost Jewish ones) to get their children enrolled in public educational institutions where the majority of children are Muslims (DGSI, 2018, pp.62-63). This partly reflects the threat potential of antisemitism among Tablighi identified by German intelligence agencies.[30]

Another major concern of the DGSI, is that through to the strong cohesion among active Tablighi – reinforced through religious practises, teaching missions, and omnipresent prayers among others –, the social ties of adherents outside the Tablighi community disappear quickly (DGSI, 2018, p.108). Indeed, many Tablighi are experiencing a 'turn-over' within the movement. Here the DGSI states that 'in general, after observing an important rigorism in his practice of Islam, the individual ends up moving away from the movement. The weakness of the religious discourse served in the organisation (based on some literalist precepts) and the lack of prospects offered by the preaching activity have the effect of causing individuals to leave to other Islamist 'offers', especially Salafists' (DGSI, 2018, p.108).

This assessment by the French intelligence is further substantiated by reports on behalf of the Commission[31]of Inquiry[32]'on the organization and means of state services to deal with the evolving terrorist threat following the fall of the Islamic State' by the French Senate. In a 2018 report (French Sénat, 2018, p.34) it is stated that TJ – described as a sectarian movement – can also be considered as fundamentalist because of its literalist reading of the Qur'an and its orthopraxy, and this despite its links to a Sufi tradition which Salafists fight (sometimes through arms). Islamic fundamentalisms [and their respective representatives–organisations as well as individuals] have complex, often conflicting relationships for the control over territories, communities or places of worship (French Sénat, 2018, p.68). In his official rhetoric, TJ stresses its differences with Salafism (which is seen as a school of ignorance). TJ seems to view itself as a bulwark in the fight against

Salafism: 'But many young people discover Islam via TJ before joining the Salafist movement, or even radical organisations' (French Sénat, 2018, p.68).

In a bipartite report (French Sénat, 2020a; 2020b) by the same Senate Commission of Inquiry, it is declared – referring to expert Bernard Rougier –, that even if there is no organisation or agreement between the different foreign Islamist groups in France, they form an 'Islamist ecosystem' (French Sénat, 2020a, p.33). The reports further highlight that despite TJ's claim of being apolitical, it 'advocates a logic of rupture with French society' (French Sénat, 2020a, p.35) and 'often sets the stage for Salafism' (Bernard Rougier quoted in French Sénat, 2020a, p.35). It is interesting to mention that the second part of the report, identifies a kind of hybridisation (French Sénat, 2020b, p.42), obviously referring to the above-mentioned 'Islamist Ecosystem'. More concretely, it is stated that some terrorists are initially trained by TJ and then transited through the Muslim Brotherhood and Salafist movements (French Sénat, 2020b, p.42). It is also claimed that TJ is constantly used as a gate of entry for the before-mentioned Islamist organisations (French Sénat, 2020b, p.42). When TJ is present in a mosque, there is a particularly good chance that, a few months or years later, the Salafists have taken their place. It's almost mechanical (French Sénat, 2020b, p.72).

Even though different Islamist groups compete in the control of the version of Islam (understood as ideology) prevalent in a neighbourhood, territory or prison, they are bound together when it comes to defining themselves in relation to – and in opposition with – French society. A strong common ground involves all these competing and converging components of Islamism, which undeniably share the same hatred of secularism (French Sénat, 2020b, p.71). TJ in this context 'advocates in a non-violent way a progressive logic of breaking with the institutions of global society' (French Sénat, 2020b, p.71). Observers believe that the TJ acts as a 'foundation for radical Islamic terrorism'. According to one estimate, 'perhaps 80 percent of Islamist extremists have come from Tablighi ranks, prompting French intelligence officers to call TJ the "antechamber of fundamentalism"' (Alexiev, 2011, p.84; 2005). The French expert on Islam Gilles Kepel stresses that theoretically TJ is opposed to violent action, whether political or jihadist. However, to this Policy Brief's interpretation, the religious radicalization they propose sometimes serves as a foreplay, or even as a gateway to terrorism. Kepel refers – as does the German intelligence, to the involvement of Tablighis in terrorist attacks.[33]

A noted French scholar, Marc Gaborieau, closely examined TJ activities in France and other European countries. He believes that TJ's philosophy and transnational goals include the 'planned conquest of the world' from the outset (Gaborieau, 1999, p.21). He further sees TJ as a militant movement, since the Tablighis are able 'to organise people quasi militarily' (Gaborieau, 1999, p.21). The author also rejects the movement's pacifist claim and notes that Tablighi have never condemned violence (Vilela, A. J., et. Al., 2006, p.50). Thus, experts see TJ as 'a way to join more radical movements' in France, as well as in other countries in Europe and Asia (Vilela, A. J., ET. Al., 2006, p.50). Notably, Gaborieau refers to Felice Dasetto, who describes TJ as a 'Total Institution' comparing Tablighi with 'sects'. Dasetto adapts Erving Goffman's (1961) concept of 'Total Institution' to TJ context.

A 'Total Institution' is 'a place of residence and work where many like-situated individuals, cut off from the wider society for an appreciable period of time, together lead an enclosed, formally administered round of life' encompassing most day-to-day activities (Goffman, 1961, p.xiii). Furthermore, Gaborieau deemed the group's strategy – especially regarding politics –, difficult to understand. Still, it seems clear to him that TJ is not entirely apolitical since its aim is the Islamisation of society. The French scholar argues that TJ possesses 'a far-sighted conception of politics' which goes 'beyond the narrow borders of nation-states'. According to Gaborieau, the Tablighi strategy is to first build individuals and institutions 'which over time may exert a more lasting Tablighi political influence' (Gaborieau, 1999, p.21). For him, this sets TJ apart from other Islamist organisations which have only a short-sighted conception of politics (Gaborieau, 1999, p.21).

Perspectives of other European Intelligence Forces

The observations and assessments by Germany's intelligence agencies are supported by other members and experts of the European intelligence community. Regarding Muslim radicalism in Europe, the General Intelligence and Security Service of the Netherlands (AVID) identifies a new phase in the development of Islamic radicalism related to the presence of not only the Muslim Brotherhood (MB) and the Hizb ut-Tahrir (HT) but also TJ (AVID, 2007, p.42). The MB, the HT and TJ are described as radical da'wah[34] movements encouraging the rise of Islamic neo-radicalism (AVID, 2007, pp.27, 48). They employ different strategies and tactics, disagree on certain ideological and theological interpretations; however, their objectives greatly converge (AVID, 2007, pp.27, 48). In another report, AVID stresses that Tablighi are a variant of radical Islam and 'manifest themselves in non-violent, radical-Islamic puritan groups' which overtly propagate isolationism, advocating 'exclusivism[35] and parallelism' (AVID, 2004, p.38).

In Portugal, too, TJ became a focus of the country's intelligence services, foremost for the Serviço de Informações de Segurança (SIS, Intelligence and Security Service). According to Maria do Céu Pinto, since 2001, the country's intelligence and law enforcing agencies have identified links 'between individuals residing in Portugal and radical Islamic operatives within the ideological network of Al Qaeda, as well as logistical and support activities for terrorism, namely of a criminal nature' (Pinto, 2012, p.115). According to SIS sources, aside detecting organisation's structures and monitoring individuals (especially their travels abroad), TJ's funding has constituted one of the most important points of SIS surveillance (Vilela, A. J., et. Al., 2006, p.49-50; Marques, T., & Vilela, A. J., 2006, p.52). This funding constitutes a major cause for concern among observers of TJ. This for several reasons: firstly, there are contradictions between TJ leadership's official rhetoric as regards the funding of missionary tours and gathering abroad of its adherents.

On the one hand, as mentioned above, TJ claims that members are responsible for covering expenditures themselves. Conversely, however, it is reported that TJ offers financial support for such travel activities. For example, Marc Gaborieau – referring to investigations by the French police – points out that TJ funded trips to India and Pakistan for unemployed young Muslims. This defers from TJ's principle of self-financing (khuruj), supposedly an inherent characteristic of Tablighi. Furthermore, the movement appears to hold enormous financial resources. This is relevant since 'the envoi of missionaries all over the world is expensive to the institution' (Marques, T., & Vilela, A. J., 2006, p.52). Secondly, TJ is apparently 'averse to financial and banking records' (Marques, T., & Vilela, A. J., 2006, p.52). Thus, TJ does not use formal banking channels so as to avoid any scrutiny of its funds. It seems to rely instead on the informal Hawala money transfer system based on transactions in cash.[36]

Lastly, funding sources remain anonymous and there is no accessible data regarding the numbers or profiles of those who visit (and donate to) TJ offices and centres. According to Francesca Marino, TJ is being investigated by Italian intelligence and law enforcing agencies. Italian authorities suspect that a 'cultural centre' of the movement as well as individuals are involved in collecting and/or transferring money to fund Jihadist activities abroad. During its investigation, the police detected an 'illegal funding network'–with ties to Pakistani sources – not only running associations and activities in Italy, but also maintaining links to TJ. Drawing on interviews with members of the country's intelligence community as well as the press, Pinto states 'that in some Wahabi and conservative mosques the religious discourse has become stricter and more intolerant' and that there is the possibility that TJ 'developed more extremist tendencies, at least on the fringes' (2012, p.199).

Noivo, who also refers to Portuguese intelligence, states that TJ uses 'Portugal as a platform for spreading its pan-Islamic message to Portuguese-speaking countries in Africa and Latin America, particularly Brazil, and that there are indications that 'the movement's message has been the catalyst for the radicalisation of some of its members' (Noivo, 2010, pp.4-5). Furthermore, as is the case in other European countries, Noivo stresses that in Portugal too there is the threat perception that due to its action and self-exclusion from social and political participation, TJ constitutes an interpretation of Islam 'that perpetuates 'otherness', thus possibly jeopardising integration and, consequently, social harmony' (Noivo, 2010, p.5). Based on publicly available information collected by the Nachrichtendienst des Bundes (NDB), Switzerland's intelligence agency, and the Swiss Federal Office of Police, the Centre for Security Studies (CSS, ETH Zürich) describes TJ (besides the HT) 'in regard to Islamist inspired violent radicalization' as 'most commonly been considered a gateway organization' (Vidino, 2013, p.27).

Views from Russia and Central Asia

The Center for Information and Analysis COBA,[37] emphasises that already over a decade ago, Russia (as well as other several Central Asian nations) banned TJ for constituting an extremist group.[38] It is reported that the ban of TJ is based on a recommendation by the Collective Security Treaty Organisation (CSTO[39]). The recommendation was adopted by Russia and other Central Asian states –all except Kyrgyzstan. TJ was included in the Russian Federal List of Extremist Organizations. After an appeal in May 2009, the Russian Supreme Court ruled (and thus confirmed) that TJ was to be considered an extremist organisation and banned its activity.

According to the Prosecutor General's statement, the court had resolved that the activities of TJ's structural divisions 'threaten interethnic and inter-religious stability in Russian society and the territorial integrity of the Russian Federation'. Russian prosecutors argued that 'the said religious association's purposes include the establishment of global supremacy through disseminating a radical form of Islam and the foundation of a unified Islamic state called the Global Caliphate on the basis of regions with traditionally Muslim populations'. According to Russian political analyst E.N. Yegorov, 'in the long run, the influence of this movement on the religious-political situation should not be underestimated'.[40]The researcher further states that TJ 'defiantly refuses to participate in politics, but there are reasons to believe that the strategic goals of its activities are connected precisely with politics and power'. There is a notion that Tablighi do 'not call for a change in the social system or creating caliphate'. Then again, according to Kyrgyz expert K. Murzakhalilov, TJ does impose demands and transmit these into the social and political processes in host countries around the world.

Besides domestic concerns, the Russian news agency Interfax highlighted that 'the law enforcement agencies of some Central Asian states consider the Tablighi Jamaat as a potential threat to their national security'. In Tajikistan, 'Tablighi Jamaat's activities were banned by a court too'. In Kazakhstan in 2012, law enforcement agencies broke off the activities of over 200 TJ missionaries operating illegally as an unregistered organisation. Subsequently, the Kazakh Prosecutor-General's Office declared on February 26, 2013, that TJ 'had been designated as extremist and all its activities in Kazakhstan were now considered illegal'. In both Tajikistan and Kazakhstan numerous Tablighi were arrested and given lengthy jail sentences for running afoul of national laws against miscreant versions of Islam and for advocating extremism (AFPC, 2012, p.6-7). It is interesting to note that as is the case in France and other European countries, also here TJ influence in education causes concerns to authorities and regional experts. According to Tologon Keldibayev, educational grassroots activities by Tablighi preachers are hardly noticed, if at all

Finally, it is also interesting to mention that concerns by European intelligence agencies and other observers are reflected in US intelligence sources. Susan Sachs reports that the FBI is much worried with TJ's influence in the country. Since 9/11, Tablighi have 'increasingly attracted the interest of federal investigators'. According to US law enforcement officials, TJ serves as 'springboard into militancy'. More concretely, despite its fundamentalist character, TJ appears to potential adherents (and authorities) as 'a natural entree, a way of gathering people together with a common interest in Islam' and not as a militant or terrorist outfit. However, the US intelligence is aware that TJ activities are exploited by international terrorist organisations such as Al Qaeda. In 2003, Michael J. Heimbach,

Deputy Chief of the FBI's International Terrorism Section, stated: 'We have a significant presence of Tablighi Jamaat in the United States, and we have found that Al Qaeda used them for recruiting, now and in the past' (Freedman, 2006, p.41). Here, like in most other countries with an active TJ presence, a major concern among authorities regards TJ's susceptibility to infiltration and manipulation. Prosecutors are convinced that extremists using TJ structures, particularly its gatherings, as an 'assessment tool to evaluate individuals with particular zealousness and interest in going beyond what's offered' by TJ itself. In brief, like their European colleagues, US intelligence agencies concluded that TJ serves as a recruiting ground for terrorists. Law enforcement officials and moderate Muslim scholars state that what worries them most about the Tablighi Jamaat is its disengagement from society.

Tablighi Jamaat and international terrorism – A symbiotic relation

International counter-terrorism officials who monitor TJ state that in several cases terrorists have emerged from the movement or had at least peripheral links with TJ (Freedman, 2006, p.47). Mukhopadhyay points out that there are numerous examples of individuals – including westerners – who joined the armed Jihad in Syria, Iraq, Afghanistan, and other places (2005, p.336) and were involved in terror attacks in their home countries after being influenced by TJ preaching. A French intelligence official states that TJ serves 'definitely as fertile ground for breeding terrorism'). According to Fred Burton and Scott Stewart, TJ provides a meeting platform, an unsupervised facilitation centre, which can offer refuge and even a hiring place to terrorists. There are also indications that TJ serves not only as recruitment ground but effectively as operational headquarters for terrorist cells. An example concerns the March 2004 train bombings in Madrid (Neumann & Rogers, 2007, pp.38-39) – it is reported that three leading members of TJ network carried out this terror attack (Neumann & Rogers, 2007, pp.52-53).

There are numerous other cases in which TJ played a role in leading followers to violent extremism. For example, some of the individuals allegedly involved in the plot to blow up several airlines en route on transatlantic flights in August 2006, had links to TJ (Neumann & Rogers, 2007, pp.53). Other terrorist plots and attacks to which members of TJ have been connected strengthen the argument that TJ is 'increasingly active as a recruitment agency for terrorist cadres' (Alexiev, 2011, p.86). They include the following: according to Freedman, federal prosecutors in the US have suggested in October 2002 that TJ was identified as a springboard by at least one of the defendants of a terrorist group known as the 'Portland Seven' (2006, p.48). This last Jihadist cell was allegedly trying to fight with the Taliban and Al Qaeda against American forces; it also conspired to bomb a synagogue and was charged with providing material support to Al Qaeda (Freedman, 2006, p.48). Another example concerns the so-called 'Lackawanna Six' case in September 2002 in which those involved were coordinating a secret trip by one member to join a terror training camp in Afghanistan. This group had a clear link to TJ and was using one of TJ's training courses in Pakistan as an excuse and cover for their activities. 'American Taliban' John Walker Lindh was found as a traitor for his role in aiding the Taliban in Afghanistan.

Before joining the Afghan Taliban, he joined a group of Tablighi missionaries on a proselytizing tour to Pakistan. The Tablighis also helped Lindh to enrol in a Madrasa so as to handle some of the administrative and logistic hurdles (Freedman, 2006, pp.47-48). Other indicted terrorists include Mohammed Siddique Khan and Shehzad Tanweer (two of the suicide bombers from the July 7, 2005, London transit attacks that killed 52 civilians), the 'shoe bomber' Richard Reid, the 'dirty bomber' Jose Padilla, and Lyman Harris, who sought to bomb the Brooklyn Bridge. These were all members of TJ at one time or another (Alexiev, 2011, p.86).TJ's name also came up in the July 2007 attempted bombings in London and Glasgow, Scotland. Furthermore, the fourteen men[41]arrested in Barcelona in January 2008 for allegedly plotting to attack the Barcelona transit system had links with TJ as well[42](Alexiev, 2011, p.86). The two perpetrators of the San Bernadino massacre in December 2015 not only pledged loyalty to the IS but had also worshipped at the local TJ mosque. Furthermore, it is reported that among over 50 Indians who have gone to fight for IS in Iraq and Syria, about a third had links to TJ (AFPC, 2012, p.7).

Concluding Remarks: TJ as engine of an Islamist Ecosystem

There have been several instances of violent Islamists who started their path with TJ. TJ's activities (particularly at the grassroots level) and the subsequent role it plays within the Islamist Ecosystem, ensures that Jihadist organisations do not have to export Jihadism and Islamism from Pakistan and other South Asian countries to Europe and North America, since the work on the field is already accomplished. Actually, it can be stated that this Islamist Ecosystem works in two directions. One direction can be said to evolve from 'outside' TJ –through the infiltration of TJ gatherings and activities followed by manipulation and recruitment of Tablighi.

Another operates from 'inside' TJ – by preaching an ultra-conservative interpretation of Islam-, Tablighi provides not only an intellectual platform but also a course of action which may result in acts of terrorism. Both dynamics are mutually reinforcing. The problem of TJ's ambiguity creates an enabling environment in which individuals may find jihadism appealing and ultimately become terrorists (AFPC, 2012, p.7). This ambiguity can also be described as an attempt to keep a neutral position between different camps. As Freedman rightly points out, 'Tablighis do not collaborate with other religious groups with whom they disagree; neither do they fight them. They do not support Islam's jihad obligation neither do they oppose it. They do not support violent terrorism; neither do they criticize it when it occurs' (2006, p.32). This 'neutrality' gives Tablighi flexibility to deny the responsibility regarding terrorist cases conducted by its (former) members.

Furthermore, it helps to cultivate their image of being apolitical and peaceful, blurring the line regarding as to which degree TJ supports Jihad and the implementation of Shari'a law. At the same time, this supports Tablighi efforts to portray themselves to their host governments as a moderate force able to counterbalance radicalisation among Muslim communities. This can also lead to severe consequences, foremost grievances and frustrations among Tablighi. According to a former Tablighi, these ambiguous positions of TJ 'can galvanize identity crises, making individuals more susceptible to extremism and bring them into contact with more radical actors' (Mubin Shaikh[43]quoted in AFPC, 2012, p.7). Such an interaction between radicalised elements and an organisation like TJ, 'which has no political dimension but a sectarian functioning, can be influential in provoking attitudes and sentiments of frustration in which the more active means and ideologies of the militants may become of more interest' (The CEIS and Change Institute quoted in Ragazzi, 2014, p.13). Such experiences can create a situation in which TJ might start 'serving as a front for terrorists and terrorist groups–either intentionally or unintentionally' (Freedman, 2006, p.32). Consequently, as an essential part of the Islamist Ecosystem, TJ functions as an engine that supports Jihadist aims to 'produce terrorism' directly on the soil of target countries. Indeed, to some experts, the 'neutrality' of Tablighi 'enough to make them culpable'.

It is crucial for the understanding of the TJ as a pillar within the Islamist Ecosystem to be aware that it does not stay within national parameters, but that it indeed has an international dimension as well. There are clear indications that Pakistan takes on a central role in TJ symbiosis with other Jihadist organisations and movements. As outlined above, the 'TJ also serves as a de facto conduit for Islamist extremists' and for groups such as the Taliban, Harkat-ul-Mujahideen, Al Qaeda, and IS to recruit new fighters. Significantly, 'Tablighi recruits do intersect with the world of militant Jihadism when they travel to Pakistan to receive their initial training'. By offering Tablighis major facilities for their educational training and preaching tours, TJ structures provide the key hub for connecting militant Jihadists and Tablighis. In other words, TJ's facilities in Pakistan offer locations where Jihadist spotters can look for potential new recruits. This process can be best summarised in the words of Alexiev, who states: 'While there is no concrete evidence of direct recruitment for terrorist purposes by Tablighi members, there is no doubt that at least some people that first discover radical Islam through this organisation, eventually gravitate to extremist and terrorist activities. One way in which this is accomplished is by sending 'promising recruits' to the Tablighi headquarters in Raiwind, Pakistan, for four months of additional religious training. While there, recruits are approached by Pakistani jihadist organizations and end up in the terrorist training camps' (Alexiev, 2011, p.84). According to Burton and Stewart, 'this link provides a medium through which Tablighis who are disgruntled with the group's apolitical program could break orbit and join militant organizations'.

In sum, the fact that TJ became a focus of the international intelligence community highlights a growing awareness regarding the need to monitor not only apparent militant organisations, but also self-described non-violent apolitical religious movements. Since 9/11 European authorities started to recognise that radical Islamic groups are finding renewed targets for their anti-West, anti-US, anti-Semitic, pro-Jihadi rhetoric – which not only challenges European society and legal order but also serves to transform radicalised Islamists into Jihadists and international terrorists. TJ exemplifies this symbiotic relation. The Tablighis' (followers of TJ) rigid understanding of Islam and the movement's related goals and activities not only enhance the challenges of indoctrination and counter-integration but also create a favourable environment for the emergence of Islamist terrorism. More concretely, TJ's ideology stands in clear contrast to the liberal democratic order (freiheitliche demokratische Grundordnung) of Germany as well as the constitutional principles of other European states. This is relevant because TJ belongs to those Islamist organisations 'that endeavour to achieve their anti-constitutional aims using legal means' (BMI, 2020b, p.31). The preaching and teaching by TJ go far beyond the rejection of Western value systems: they makes Tablighi and their adherents 'susceptible to Islamist positioning' (Mukhopadhyay, 2005, p.336) and serves as a gateway for the creation of 'Jihadist milieus'. As such, one can state that we are witnessing Tablighi and Jihadists working in tandem within the symbiotic network of an Islamic Ecosystem, enhancing the threat of international terrorism and Jihadism.

Recommendations

Due to the secrecy surrounding TJ – the lack of formal membership combined with a low level of institutionalisation, and the lack of centralized (administrative) control –the movement is difficult to monitor. It is reported that European security agencies are yet to hold the necessary scope of action (authority) to adequately investigate TJ. Intelligence forces and other law enforcing agencies were not able to fully articulate the role TJ as an organisation plays in support of Jihadism. Supervision of TJ (centres and individuals) must be intensified, including financial transactions. More focus is needed regarding not only suspect surveillance of (potential) militant Islamists, but also of individuals who are promoting radicalisation. The case of TJ clearly demonstrates that Islamist indoctrination often leads to acts of terrorism. It also appears that during the last 15 years, reports by European intelligence agencies either were not fully considered by much of the political leadership, or were otherwise not translated in concrete policies. We must send a strong and consistent message that the propagation of an ideology based on the supremacy of one religion, gender inequality, anti-Semitism, and other forms of religious intolerance (which pave the way for radicalisation and the eulogy of violence) will not be tolerated in liberal democracies. This also includes a 'zero tolerance' policy towards the promotion of rigid faith practices which undermine the integration of societies and lead to an alienation from democratic norms and values.

Due to its large size, it is apparent that not all Tablighi are (potential) terrorists, and that TJ is not per se a Jihadist group. Nevertheless, we need to change the notion among (several) political decision makers and experts to deny a-priori links between TJ and the Global Jihad. It is often seen as extremely effective to differentiate among Islamist groups based on their attitudes towards violence (and politics). However, the case of TJ shows the distinction between militant from non-militant organisations is of limited use. Both usually have the same overall goals: making ultra-orthodox Islam universal, implementing Shari'a law and establishing a (worldwide) caliphate. In this sense, the decision regarding whether to use violence only marks tactical differences between TJ and militant Jihadist groups. The result is the same: the unfolding of a 'war of ideas' against the notion of a society based on liberal democratic norms and value systems.

European governments need to understand the movement's global network, particularly the dynamics by Tablighi within the Islamist Ecosystem. It is apparent that TJ activities, foremost recruitment and mobilisation processes, fundraising, and training are being exploited by global Jihadists – with or without the consent of TJ leadership. Regardless, preaching an ultra-conservative interpretation of Islam always creates an enabling environment for the support of international terrorism. More specifically, TJ teachings promote the legitimacy of (militant) Jihad and do not leave room for a liberal, moderate interpretation of Islam. As such, the notion that TJ is 'helpful in facilitating grassroots counter-radicalisation programmes by providing the necessary religious arguments' (Neumann & Rogers, 2007, p.94) against global Jihadism must be severely questioned.

Dear Mr Jalalzai: Thank you very much for your kind words. We are indeed very proud of our research on fanaticism and Jihad in particular. All our work can be reproduced, as long as its authorship and first publication reference are clearly and properly indicated. Best wishes for your editorial work. Best regards. Paulo Casaca. The South Asia Democratic Forum (SADF) is a Brussels-based think tank devoted to South Asia and its relationship with the European Union (EU) in the context of a global, changing world. SADF was an initiative based on the vision of both our Community forefathers and our contemporaneous, such as Jacques Delors: a world with democratic (national and supranational) institutions where all nations, peoples, traditions, and beliefs are respected without backward hierarchies or any kind of prejudice. The EU itself has strived for half a century to develop into such a democratic body and aims to contribute significantly to freedom, peace, democracy, and development both in Europe and elsewhere in the world. Proud of our history and its achievements, yet duly conscious of the many drawbacks, we view democracy as a common heritage of human development and civilisation around the world, be it the traditionally acknowledged Greek archipelago, the under-studied Indus Valley or the even lesser known cultures around the world, all of which valued human freedom and dignity. It is our belief that international or even globalised institutional cooperation constitute today a crucial means for humanity to overcome its common challenges and build a better future for our descendants. Our aim is to connect these different networks and to provide an alternative source of analysis on South Asian affairs for European policy makers. To this end, SADF organises high-level contacts, stimulates studies and evaluations, designs and disseminates research methods and concepts, combines networks and supports; it brings together people, private and public institutions, that can contribute to Europe-South Asia related cooperation and understanding. Action: Other than our annual conferences that aim at highlighting what we perceive as the most important opportunities and challenges faced by the region, SADF produces in-house research and policy advice, and promotes promising external research dedicated to enduring peace, regional cooperation, democracy building, and integrated development in the South Asian region through its external publications. In the series 'Contemporary South Asian Studies' directed and animated by SADF, we published and intend to continue to publish major works on the opportunities and challenges faced by the region. SADF cooperates with like-minded civil society think tanks and other organisations and aims at offering public guidance for the conduct of democracies.

The goal of the Democracy Research Programme (DRP) is to contribute, to the understanding of political and socio-economic trajectories in contemporary South Asia. As such, the DRP recognizes the overlap of the processes of nation-building, state-building, economic modernisation, civil society development and democratisation. The specific topics of this research programme are generated on the basis of SADF's mission and goals, covering all key facets of democratisation. Subsequently, the DRP focuses on the monitoring and analysis of the quality of democracy and the causal factors determining the processes of democratic transition and consolidation as well as (potential) backslashes. Within these benchmarks, the DRP centres its work on investigating how democratisation is shaped and affected by domestic and international actors and institutions. The guiding principle of the DRP is to contribute to the creation and transfer of knowledge, providing policy-oriented research findings and subsequent policy-advice, and to strengthen SADF capacities to serve as the premier institution for South Asia competence in Europe. By working towards a better understanding of democratic mechanisms, SADF's overall goal is to advocate the strengthening of democratic institutions and the entrenchment of democratic values in South Asia at all levels of government and society at large. Regional Cooperation Research Programme: The goal of the Regional Cooperation Research Programme (RCRP) is to contribute to the understanding of regional cooperation paths in South Asia, recognising that sustainable development processes are fostered by institutional and economic cooperation between people, communities, cities, regions and nations. The research topics cover the different aspects of regional cooperation, including economic, environmental, technological and institutional aspects. Complementary to the understanding of regional cooperation paths in South Asia, the RCRP monitors the situation of the different aspects of regional cooperation in South Asia in order to be able to connect the knowledge gained in the research effort with the pressing challenges of the present. Within these benchmarks, the RCRP focuses its work on investigating how regional cooperation in South Asia evolves and how people, communities, stakeholders, governments and institutions influence it. The guidelines of the RCRP include contributing to the creation and transfer of knowledge, providing policy recommendations on emerging issues based on research findings, and strengthening SADF capacities to serve South Asia regional cooperation and sustainable development. Company number: BE 0831.084.518, RPM Bruxelles, Avenue des Arts 19, 1210 Brussels, Belgium

Chapter 11

Central Asian Extremists, the Kazakhstan Turmoil and the Danger of Nuclear and Biological Terrorism

The United States manages 3,750 nuclear warheads, while press release from the State Department confirmed 2,000 warheads to be dismantled. President Biden announced that under the AUKUS agreement, Australia would retrieve nuclear powered submarine while President Putin exhibited his disagreement on the deteriorating regime of arms control but reduced the number of warheads deployed on Russia's ballistic missiles to meet the New START limit. Nuclear weapons experts and analysts, Hans M. Kristensen and Matt Korda (2021) have noted that 'Russia's nuclear modernization program was motivated in part by Moscow's strong desire to maintain overall parity with the United States'. On 28 July, the United States and Russia restarted bilateral Strategic Stability Dialogue. The Biden administration upheaved prospect of restricting military manoeuvres and missile deployments in Eastern Europe insomuch as Russia corresponds at the fore of dialogue on its military deployment in Ukraine, but hostile attitude of the Biden administration further caused scepticism when the country's leadership unnecessarily demonstrated superiority and military strength. In January 2022, People's Republic of China, France, Russia, the United Kingdom and the United States in a joint statement declared the avoidance of nuclear war.

The statement of nuclear powers confirmed their commitment to work with all state to create a security environment more conducive. "We intend to continue seeking bilateral and multilateral diplomatic approaches to avoid military confrontations, strengthen stability and predictability, increase mutual understanding and confidence, and prevent an arms race that would benefit none and endanger all. We are resolved to pursue constructive dialogue with mutual respect and acknowledgment of each other's security interests and concerns". The statement noted. The US assertion that Moscow might create environment of a false flag operation in Eastern Ukraine as a pretext for invading all or part of the country was repudiated by Russian military. "Russia is laying the groundwork to have the option of fabricating a pretext for invasion, including through sabotage activities and information operations, by accusing Ukraine of preparing an imminent attack against Russian forces, according to an email of state department sent to the country's bureaucrats and technocrats. In November 2021, President Biden and Chinese President held their first face-to-face conversation on managing great power competition and averting a new Cold War but both sides failed to produce a diplomatic breakthrough.

On January 15, 2022, in his interview with Newsweek, Russia's Ambassador to the United States Anatoly Antonov warned that 'NATO's eastward expansion is one of the major threats to Russia's national security, as the flight time to cities in the country's European part is becoming shorter, Russia's Ambassador to the United States Anatoly Antonov said in an interview with Newsweek. The continuing advance of the North Atlantic bloc to the east is one of the main threats to Russia's national security. As the bloc approaches our border proper, the flight time of NATO air and missile weapons to Moscow, St. Petersburg and other cities in the European part of the country is reduced," Antonov said. "How would the US Government react if Washington, New York or Los Angeles were 'under the bombsight'?"."NATO is constantly building up its offensive potential, demonstrating military force along the perimeter of the Russian territory. "NATO's efforts aimed at the military development of the former Soviet republics are unacceptable to us. This is fraught with the deployment of missile systems and other destabilizing weapons that directly threaten our country. As a result, the risks of escalation and direct military clashes in the region and beyond will increase manifold. Everything has its limits. We are, in fact, on the edge of precipice," the ambassador told Newsweek.

China, Russia and the United States are locked in an intensifying competition to export their respective fifth-generation fighter jets. The Biden administration has been in deep trouble since the test of Russia's anti-satellite missiles, and its contemptible defeat in Afghanistan, and issued warning of Russian hybrid war in Europe, but the US forces continue to destabilise Middle East and Central Asia. Contrariwise, the EU member states are well aware of their security and friendship with Russia by extending hand of cooperation. In this bigger strategic game, Russians and Americans have the same reason for modernising their nuclear forces. In yesteryears, President Vladimir Putin developed modern weapons and restored the real Russian place in the international community. Since Russia seized Crimea in 2014, the country has begun to build basing sites for their advanced systems, including the Iskanders missile, but nuclear experts warned that if Russia deploys nuclear weapons there, it would spark complex problems. Analyst Scott Ritter (RT News, 28 April, 2020) highlighted the START agreement and complication of US and Russia's inventions of modern technologies and weapons, which could exacerbate the process of nuclear war preparations:

"Both the US and Russia are engaged in the early stages of developing new strategic nuclear weapons to replace older systems. These weapons, which will cost trillions of dollars to develop and deploy, are with few exceptions still many years away from entering into service. A five-year extension of New START would provide both nations time to reach an agreement which responsibly addresses the need for strategic nuclear force modernization while continuing the past practice of seeking additional cuts in their respective nuclear arsenals........China's intransigence runs counter to the official US position, most recently articulated in a State Department report sent to Congress regarding Russian compliance with the New START Treaty. While the report finds that Russia is complying with its treaty obligations, the treaty does not cover enough Russian strategic systems, including several that have been previously announced by President Putin, and leaves China to operate with no restrictions in terms of the size and scope of its strategic nuclear arsenal".[1]

Perhaps, China is also preparing to build new missile technology, expand anti-satellite capabilities and increase nuclear material production. The question is how China can use nuclear weapons as the country maintains policy of peaceful coexistence? In 2019, its Defence White Paper noted the country stickled to the policy of no first use of nuclear weapons at any time, and under any circumstances, but recent hostile nuclear environment has forced the country to deploy a nuclear triad of strategic land, sea, and air-launched nuclear systems to defend its territorial integrity and national security. Despite the progress made by international conventions, biological and chemical weapons are still a precarious threat in Europe and Central Asia.

According to Russia's new military doctrine, the possibility of limited uses of nuclear weapons at the tactical and operational levels and of chemical and biological weapons is possible. As the United States has established biological weapons laboratories in Central Asia and used these weapons against civilian population of Afghanistan, Russian military leadership has taken these developments seriously. Russia is training its chemical and biological army on a modern streak. New CBRN defence vehicles and equipment can be used in the fight against coronavirus. Its forces have also undertaken more CBRN training to the future war effectively. The danger from these weapons is so consternating, and the dirty bomb material and its fatalities diverted attention of terrorist groups to biological weapons. Smuggling of nuclear weapons is a serious challenge in Europe and Central Asia, while smuggling of these weapons in Africa has threatened security of the region.

For more than two decades, the threat of nuclear and biological weapons in Central Asia has been at the forefront of international security agenda. Nuclear experts have often warned that terrorists and extremist organizations operating in Central Asia can anytime use dirty bomb and nuclear explosive. These groups must be prevented from gaining access to weapons of mass-destruction and from perpetrating atrocious acts of bioterrorism. Russia and some Central Asian States have applied professional measures to protect their nuclear weapons sites but nuclear proliferation still poses a grave threat to the national security of all states. Military experts and policymakers have also expressed deep concerns that if the Islamic Movement of Uzbekistan, Chechen extremist groups, Katibat Imam Bukhari and the IS-Khorasan, operating in the region gain access to nuclear explosives, it might cause huge destruction and fatalities. There are several extremist and terrorist groups operating in Tajikistan where they are recruiting members of local religious groups, and civilians from all walks of life to prepare them for the fight against Russia. Analyst Leonid Gusev (01 February 2020) his recent paper noted activities of extremist groups in Tajikistan:

"As in the other countries of the region, the main recruiting platform used by ISIS (a terrorist organization banned in Russia) in Tajikistan is the Internet. There are some 3 million Internet users in Tajikistan, 80 per cent of them accessing extremist content through social media either deliberately or accidentally. During their meeting in May 2018, President of Tajikistan Emomali Rahmon and President of Belarus Alexander Lukashenko expressed their commitment to strengthening cooperation in the fight against terrorism, extremism, drug trafficking and the illegal arms trade. In October 2019, Tajikistan hosted a joint military exercise of the Collective Security Treaty Organization (CSTO) member states, "Indestructible Brotherhood 2019." One of the components of that exercise, according to Commander of the Central Military District of the Russian Federation,

Colonel-General Alexander Lapin, consisted of antiterrorist operations. Tajikistan is a tension hotspot in Central Asia in terms of religious extremism and terrorism. A particular source of danger is neighbouring Afghanistan, where about 60 per cent of the lands along the frontier are engulfed in clashes between government forces and the Taliban and other radical Islamist groups. At the same time, there is almost no security along the Afghan-Tajik border, including the issue of drug trafficking. The local Tajik forces supporting border guards are scant, especially since the Kulob Regiment was relocated from the 201st Russian military base to Dushanbe. Yet the government has so far managed to control the situation."[2]

Recent events in Kazakhstan and Tajikistan have raised the prospect of extremist and jihadist groups using biological, radiological and chemical weapons against military installations and critical national infrastructure in both states. Russia is vulnerable to such attacks by these terrorist groups who received military training from the US army in Afghanistan and Pakistan. The greatest threat to the national security of Russia stems from the business of nuclear smuggling of state sponsored terror groups operating in Central Asia. Increasingly sophisticated chemical and biological weapons are accessible to these organizations and ISIS and their allies, which is a matter of great concern. These groups can use more sophisticated conventional weapons as well as chemical and biological agents in near future as the US Special Force is already in control of Pakistan's nuclear and biological weapons. They can disperse chemical, biological and radiological material as well as industrial agents via water or land to target schools, colleges, civilian and military personnel. They were trained by US and NATO forces, and tested these weapons in Afghanistan. These groups also received training of dangerous weapons in different military units of Pakistan army.

As international media focuses on the looming threat of chemical and biological terrorism in Central Asia, the ISIS is seeking access to nuclear weapons. The crisis is going to get worse as the exponential network of ISIS and its popularity in Afghanistan caused deep security challenges. This group could use chemical and biological weapons once it strengthens its bases in Central Asia and Russia. The possibility of a nuclear technology transfer by an irresponsible state like Pakistan and Iran to the ISIS command is still reverberating in international press. In an interview with a local television channel, the late Dr. Abdul Qadir Khan categorically said that Pakistan's nuclear smuggling activities did take place from 1992 to 1998 while both Nawaz Sharif and Benazir Bhutto were in power.

Recent debates in print and electronic media about the possible use of Chlorine Bombs or biological weapons in Central Asia have caused deep concerns in government and military circles that radicalized jihadists returning from Syria and Iraq may possibly use these weapons with the cooperation of local supporters and some states. Yet, experts have warned that the acquisition of nuclear weapons by the Islamic State (ISIS) poses a greater threat to the national security of regional states. The gravest danger arises from access of extremist and terror groups to the state-owned nuclear, biological and chemical weapons. The growing use of Chlorine Bombs is a matter of great concern. The first such incident occurred when the ISIS commanders gained access to the Iraqi nuclear weapons site in Mosul University.

However, recent cases of nuclear proliferation and attacks on nuclear installations across the globe have further exacerbated the concern about the threat of nuclear attacks in Caucasus regions, Russia and Tajikistan. The threat of chemical and biological jihad has raised serious questions about the security of Central Asian states nuclear and biological weapons. Experts have warned that the Central Asia, Pakistan and Afghanistan based jihadists, and the Taliban pose a great security threat. Improvised explosive devices and chemical and biological weapons are easily available in Asian and European markets and can be transported to the region through human traffickers. The influx of trained terrorists and extremist groups from several Asian, African and European states has raised concerns that those who sought asylum through fake documents in Russia could pose a threat to the country. In a press conference in Australia, President Obama declared that if his government discovered that ISIS had come to possess a nuclear weapon, he would get it out of their hands. The fear of such attacks still exists in Central Asia because thousands of European nationals joined ISIS's military campaign in Syria and Iraq.

In 2013, chemical attacks in the outskirts of Damascus posed a direct threat to all Arab states, and forced the UN Security Council to adopt a resolution on chemical weapons in Syria. The international operation of transporting the components of these weapons out of Syria was completed in the first half of 2014. In 2015, the ISIS tried to gain access to these weapons and used chlorine bombs in Iraq and Syria. On 06 January, 2015, cases of ISIS using chemical weapons in Iraq and Syria emerged. These chemical attacks illustrated that ISIS and the Syrian opposition chosen to use chemical weapons preferentially in Iraq and Syria. In Russia and Central Asia, ISIS is seeking these weapons to use them against the armed forces of the region.

216

In one of its issues magazines (Dabiq), claimed that Islamic State sought to buy nuclear weapons from Pakistan but experts viewed this claim as baseless.

Before the rise of ISIS, the Islamic Movement of Uzbekistan (IMU) was the main Central Asian extremist organisation in the field. Its base of operations is in Afghanistan and Pakistan. Central Asian fighters linked to ISIS headquarters in Syria also participated in acts of terrorism in other countries. The ISIS has previously restrained itself from getting involved in attacks in Central Asia as the group's leadership emphasised that attacking this region was not the highest priority. In July 2018, five Tajik men killed four foreign cyclists in a car-ramming attack, accompanied by an on-foot gun and knife assault in the Khatlon province of Tajikistan. The presence of Daesh in Iraq and Afghanistan, and participation of Central Asian jihadists in it prompted consternation in the region. In Syria, the radical Islamic militants from Central Asia established terrorist organisations of their own. These terrorists have Salafi-Wahhabi inclinations and are among the backers of al-Qaeda, al-Nusra Front, and Daesh group. In his Diplomat analysis (20 September 2016), Uran Botobekov, documented videos and extrajudicial killing in Iraq and Syria:

"Recently, Central Asians saw on YouTube a terrible video of a teenager, Babur Israilov from Jalal-Abad in southern Kyrgyzstan, on his way to becoming a suicide bomber. In the video, Babur cries before being sent to his death in an armoured car laden with explosives in Fua, Syria. One of the fighters gathered around encourages him, saying in Uzbek that Satan intervenes at crucial moments to confuse a Muslim's mind, so he should think only of Allah. Further in the video sentimental Arabic music plays, the armoured personnel carrier moves, and, at the fatal moment, the bomb explodes[3]. According to Radio Free Europe/Radio Liberty, Babur Israilov was a member of an extremist group of Uzbeks–Imam Bukhari Jamaat–which fights alongside Jabhat al-Nusra in Syria. Just like the father of the British boy JoJo, resident of Suzak district in the Jalal-Abad region of Kyrgyzstan Tahir Rahitov saw his son Babur via video. According to Tahir, his wife died in 1995 and the boy was raised by his grandmother. In November 2013 Babur left for Russia in search of work. In March 2014 he arrived in Syria via Turkey, joined Imam Bukhari Jamaat, and fought alongside Jabhat al-Nusra against the government of Bashar al-Assad".[4]

On 06 November 2019, Masked Daesh militants attacked a check post on the Tajik-Uzbek border overnight, triggering a gun battle that killed 15 militants, a guard and a policeman.[4] There was no immediate announcement from the militant group, which claimed responsibility for a series of assaults in Tajikistan. Five of the gunmen were captured after the attack on the Tajik side of the border, 50 km (30 miles) southwest of the capital Dushanbe, Tajikistan's National Security Committee noted. The investigation into the 03 April 2017 terrorist attack on the St. Petersburg metro station focused on a man of Central Asian origin with possible ties to Syrian rebel groups. The attack raises concerns about the threat posed both by Daesh and extremists within Russia's sizable Central Asian community. Investigators identified Akhbarzhon Dzhalilov as the prime suspect in the attack on the St. Petersburg metro that left 14 people dead and 49 injured. Dzhalilov is an ethnic Uzbek from the Southern Kyrgyzstani city of Osh who obtained Russian citizenship in 2011. Eight more people, mostly from Kyrgyzstan, were detained in St Petersburg and Moscow on suspicion of assisting Dzhalilov.[5]While Tajikistan remains vulnerable to jihadist extremism due to its proximity to jihadist hotbeds, pre-existing networks and difficult socio-economic conditions, it appears that the central radicalization issue is the diaspora abroad, led by Tajiks living in Russia.

Since the beginning of 2017, a string of jihadist terrorist attacks involved Central Asian citizens, mainly of Uzbek and Kirgiz origin. Russia's Federal Security Service (FSB) detained Abrar Azimov from Central Asia. He was accused as one of the organizers of the attack, and the one who had trained Jalilov. However, Azimov refused to admit his guilt in court during the hearing. By the end of April, the FSB arrested 12 people of Central Asian descent in the Kaliningrad region suspected of involvement with the Jihad-Jamaat Mujahedin extremist group. The alleged leader of the cell was placed by Uzbekistan on a wanted list for extremist crimes.

The rise of ISIS in Afghanistan posed serious security concerns according to a September 2016 statement of Zamir Kabulov, the Russian Foreign Ministry's Director of the Second Asian Department in Afghanistan. Mr. Kabulov claimed that about 2,500 ISIS combatants were in Afghanistan and the organization was preparing to expand from Afghanistan into other Central Asian countries and Russia, giving Moscow reasons to worry. Nuclear terrorism in Central Asia and Russia has risen important questions about the US and NATO policy towards Russia that without using biological and nuclear weapons against the country, its dream of supreme power will vanish. Authors Christopher McIntosh and Ian Storey (20 November 2019) in their well-written analysis have elucidated the real motive of US and NATO hegemonic design:

"While terrorist organizations vary widely in their internal organization and structure, almost all are highly sensitive to benefits and costs, both external and internal. By examining these, it will become clear that terrorists might have more to lose than gain by proceeding directly to an attack. Doing so might alienate their supporters, cause dissent among the ranks, and give away a bargaining chip without getting anything in return. While there is any number of far more likely scenarios for nuclear terrorism broadly understood, we focus only on groups with a working nuclear device, not a radiological dispersal device or the ability to attack a nuclear reactor. The threat posed by an operational device is fundamentally different, not least because possession would radically change the nature of the organisation as a strategic, warfighting group. A large body of work in terrorism studies teaches us that terrorist groups do behave strategically. Communications within Al Qaeda, Princeton Near Eastern Studies expert Michael Doran has written, have shown that the group behaves "almost exclusively according to the principle of realpolitik," and is "virtually compelled[" to do so by the "central doctrines of Islamic extremism" itself. While it may not appear so based on terrorists' tactics, most groups have all the hallmarks of strategic decision-making, command and control, and sensitivity to costs. This is all the truer for the hypothetical that concerns us: Only a large, well-organized, and heavily funded group would be able to attain operational nuclear capability. Regardless of what one thinks about the debates regarding terrorist organizations and their ability to acquire these weapons—either by theft or gift—acquisition and maintenance is going to be resource-intensive and difficult".[6]

If terrorist groups such as ISIS or Lashkar-e-Tayba and Tablighi Jamaat determine to go nuclear, what will be the security preparations in Central Asia to intercept these groups? These and other Pakistan based groups can attempt to manufacture fissile material needed to fuel a nuclear weapon—either highly enriched uranium or plutonium, and then use it. Moreover, there are possibilities that Pakistan, Afghanistan and Central Asia based extremist and jihadist groups can purchase fissile material in black market or steal it from a military or civilian facility and then use that material to construct an improvised nuclear device. Yet today, with Russia rising again as a military power, the grim logic of nuclear statecraft is returning. In his nuclear risk analysis, Simon Saradzhyan (Russia Matters, Simon Saradzhyan, (August 06, 2019) argued that there is possibility of nuclear war between Russia and the United States:

"Is the risk of a nuclear war between the U.S. and Russia now higher than at the height of the Cold War? Yes, it is, according to an article former U.S. Energy Secretary Ernie Moniz and former U.S. Sen. Sam Nunn have penned for Foreign Affairs. "Not since the 1962 Cuban Missile Crisis has the risk of a U.S.-Russian confrontation involving the use of nuclear weapons been as high as it is today," the co-chairs of the Nuclear Threat Initiative warn in their commentary published in August. 6, 2019. To back their claim, the two American statesmen describe an imaginary scenario in which Russian air defense systems shoot down a NATO aircraft that has accidentally veered into Russian airspace during a wargame in Russia's Kaliningrad exclave in 2020".[7]All but, 15 years ago, Graham Allison (September/October 2004) noted the possibility of nuclear terrorism in Russia by Chechen terrorists. Chechen have had a long-standing interest in acquiring nuclear weapons and material to use in their campaign against Russia. He is of the opinion that Chechen had access to nuclear materials, and their experts were able to make nuclear explosive devices:

"To date, the only confirmed case of attempted nuclear terrorism occurred in Russia on November 23, 1995, when Chechen separatists put a crude bomb containing 70 pounds of a mixture of cesium-137 and dynamite in Moscow's Ismailovsky Park. The rebels decided not to detonate this "dirty bomb," but instead informed a national television station to its location. This demonstration of the Chechen insurgents' capability to commit ruthless terror underscored their long-standing interest in all things nuclear. As early as 1992, Chechnya's first rebel president, Dzhokhar Dudayev, began planning for nuclear terrorism, including a specific initiative to hijack a Russian nuclear submarine from the Pacific Fleet in the Far East. The plan called for seven Slavic-looking Chechens to seize a submarine from the naval base near Vladivostok, attach explosive devices to the nuclear reactor section and to one of the nuclear-tipped missiles on board, and then demand withdrawal of Russian troops from Chechnya. After the plot was discovered, Russian authorities disparaged it, and yet it is ominous to note that the former chief of staff of the Chechen rebel army, Islam Khasukhanov, had once served as second-in-command of a Pacific Fleet nuclear submarine".[8]

The Islamic State (ISIS) and Central Asian terrorist groups seek biological and nuclear weapons to use against security forces in Russia and Central Asia. The modus operandi of ISIS or ISIS inspired individuals are diverse and show no moral restraints–as recent attacks in Brussels and Berlin demonstrated. The use of biological and chemical weapons by terrorists has prompted huge fatalities in Iraq and Syria. However, preventing dangerous materials from falling into the hands of ISIS, Pakistani terrorist groups, and Central Asia extremists is a complex challenge. Since 2013, there has been extensive use of chemical weapons in armed conflicts in Syria by US backed terrorist groups. The deadliest attacks were carried out with chemical agents by the ISIS terrorist group in Syria that needed significant knowledge and the specialized resources. In October 2017, Columb Strack in his paper revealed that the ISIS is the first terrorist group that developed chemical weapons:

"The Islamic State is the first non-state actor to have developed a banned chemical warfare agent and combined it with a projectile delivery system. However, it appears to have been forced to abandon its chemical weapons production after the loss of Mosul in June 2017. The absence of chemical attacks outside of Mosul after the city became cut-off from the rest of the 'caliphate' earlier this year indicates that the group has not established alternative production facilities. But U.S. intelligence believes that a new chemical weapons cell has been set up in the Euphrates River Valley. In late July 2015, the Islamic State fired several mortar bombs at Kurdish People's Protection Units (YPG) positions near the city of Hasakah in northeastern Syria. A statement released by the YPG after the attack described how the explosions had released "a yellow gas with a strong smell of onions," and that "the ground immediately around the impact sites was stained with an olive-green liquid that turned to a golden yellow after exposure to sunshine".[9]

The possible use of nuclear and biological weapons by the ISIS, Central Asia extremist groups, Chechens, Taliban and Pakistani sectarian terrorists in Central Asia and Russia would be a greater security challenge for the region and Russia that fights the ISIS in Syria. Pakistan has established its own extremist networks in Chechnya and Central Asia once more to lead the US fight against Russia in the region. The country's army has been training and financing ISIS, Chinese extremist groups and Mujahedeen from Central Asia in various districts since 2001. Connor Dilleen (Asia Times-30 May 2019) in his recent article noted activities of Central Asia terrorists' groups in Afghanistan:

"During a recent visit to Tajikistan, Russian Federal Security Service Director Alexander Bortnikov claimed that around 5,000 militants based in Afghanistan from a group known as Islamic State Khorasan, or IS-K, had been redeployed to the north of the country, near its border with the former Soviet states of Central Asia. Bortnikov's statement has been treated with some skepticism, with Moscow accused of exaggerating the threat posed by IS-K to advance its own objectives in the region. But his comments make it timely to revisit the question of whether IS may emerge as a genuine threat not just to Afghanistan but also to the broader Central Asian region. To date, the states of Central Asia—Kyrgyzstan, Uzbekistan, Tajikistan, Turkmenistan and Kazakhstan—have been relatively free of terrorist incidents involving Islamist groups. Between 2008 and mid-2018, 19 attacks categorized as terrorism occurred across the region, resulting in around 140 fatalities. Most of these attacks targeted law enforcement agencies, and regional governments have claimed that they disrupted another 61 attacks during 2016 alone. IS was involved in several of these events. In July 2018, a group claiming allegiance to IS killed four foreign tourists outside of the Tajik capital of Dushanbe, and in November, Tajik authorities claimed that they had detained 12 suspects with alleged ties to IS who were planning an attack against a Russian military base and school".[10]

However, the return of these groups from Pakistan, Afghanistan and Syria will cause national security challenges. In Sialkot District of Punjab province in Pakistan, the army trains and supports an ISIS women brigade for future war. Dr. Younis Khshi in his research paper has noted activities of these women in Pakistan where many women have impressed and convinced through brainwashing with the concept of Jihad-Bil-Nikah, got divorce from their Pakistani husbands and went to marry a Mujahid of ISIS for a certain period, came back gave birth to the child of Mujahid, and remarried their former husband. Some decide to continue that marriage for the rest of their lives. All of this is being done to obtain worldly wealth and later eternal life in Heaven because ISIS is paying something around RS/50,000 to 60,000 per month to every warrior.

However, Mr. Uran Botobekov (The Diplomat, January 10, 2017) has also reported the presence of Central Asian women in Syria and Iraq: "Based on 2014 and 2015 data, there were around 1,000 women from Central Asia in Iraq and Syria's combat zones. According to Indira Dzholdubaeva, prosecutor-general of the Kyrgyz Republic, there are over 120 Kyrgyz women in Syria and Iraq. Chairman of the National Security Committee (KNB) of Kazakhstan, Nurtay Abykaev, has said there were 150 Kazakh women in ISIS ranks in Syria. The authorities of Uzbekistan, meanwhile, have said that up to 500 Uzbek women are in Syria, Iraq, and Afghanistan with various groups. The Ministry of the Interior of Tajikistan claims that over 200 Tajik women have gone to the war zones in Syria together with their husbands. However, the website of the Ministry of the Interior has published the names and photos of only five Tajik women who are wanted due to their membership in ISIS".[11]Moreover, analyst and expert of current affairs, Nick Mucerino (November 5, 2018) has noted the threat to Russia from Islamic State returnees from Syria, Iraq, Pakistan and Afghanistan:

"The threat posed by Russian speaking fighters who travelled to fight under the Islamic State in Syria presents a complicated problem for both Russia and its allies to address. Just like its Western counterparts, Russia is worried that these returnees will mount deadly attacks on the country's soil. The danger presented by Russian speaking foreign fighters loyal to the Islamic State is not lost on the Kremlin. Since its emergence during Syria's civil war in 2013, Russians and Russian speaking nationals from the former Soviet Union have been a prominent presence among the terror group's fighters. In February 2017, President Vladimir Putin, citing security service figures, stated that approximately 4,000 Russian citizens and 5,000 from Central Asia followed ISIS' appeals for aid. Many took part in helping to establish its 'caliphate', or the proto-state it carved out of the lands ISIS seized from Iraq and Syria. This figure is the largest in Europe and even outnumbers the citizens from Arab states including Saudi Arabia and Tunisia, who travelled to join the Group. The large presence of Russian speakers is further reflected in the fact that it is the second most common language among ISIS fighters and several of its top commanders belong to the former USSR. Independent security experts have estimated that about 400 of those fighters have already returned to Russia after fighting in Syria".[12]

The US-Taliban deal encouraged extremist groups from Central Asia and China that now with the support of Pakistan and Taliban; they will exacerbate operational activities in Central Asia and Russia. They receive training in dangerous weapons and nuclear explosives in Pakistan and Afghanistan. A women military brigade (Dr. Yunis Khushi-June 26, 2017) of the ISIS and Taliban receives training of dangerous weapons under the supervision of Pakistan's army in Sialkot district of Punjab province. In his (The Diplomat, 08 April 2020) article, Uran Botobekov noted the zeal and felicitations of these groups:

"Al-Qaeda-backed Central Asian Salafi-Jihadi groups were highly encouraged by the US-Taliban agreement which was signed in February 2020, aiming to bring peace to Afghanistan. Some Uzbek groups such as Katibat Imam al-Bukhari (KIB), Katibat Tawhid wal Jihad (KTJ), the Islamic Jihad Union (IJU), and Tajik militants of Jamaat Ansarullah (JA), and Uighur fighters of Turkestan Islamic Party (TIP) from China's Xinjiang region, have already expressed their clear opinion about this particular deal through their respective Telegram accounts. Some of the groups congratulated the agreement, while others dedicated emotional eulogies to the Taliban. The KIB, which is formed primarily from Uzbek, Tajik and Kyrgyz militants from Central Asia's Ferghana Valley, was one of the first organisations to congratulate the Taliban, denouncing it as "the great victory of the Islamic Ummah". On February 29, 2020, Abu Yusuf Muhajir, the leader of KIB's Syrian wing, in his congratulatory letter said: "The US and NATO forces, who imagine themselves to be the rulers of the entire world and the divine judges of human destinies, and claim divinity on earth have stunned the world with their humiliation, disgrace, and failure of the crusade." The KIB leader proceeds by saying that "the Americans were forced to sign an agreement with the Islamic Emirate of Afghanistan, which they considered a helpless crowd and below their dignity, but they [the Taliban] survived all difficulties with the support of Allah and gained strength."[13]

Nuclear terrorism remains a constant threat to global peace. Access of terrorist organizations to nuclear material is a bigger threat to civilian population. Terrorist groups can gain access to highly enriched uranium or plutonium, because they have the potential to create and detonate an improvised nuclear device. Since the ISIS has already retrieved nuclear materials from Mosul city of Iraq, we can assert that terrorist groups like ISIS and Katibat Imam Bukhari, and Chechen extremist groups can make access to biological and nuclear weapons with the help of local experts. Nuclear facilities also often store large amounts of radioactive material, spent fuel, and other nuclear waste products that terrorists could use in a dirty bomb. Without access to such fissile materials, extremist and radicalized groups can turn their attention toward building a simple radiological device. The most difficult part of making a nuclear bomb is acquiring the nuclear material, but some Muslim and non-Muslim state might facilitate the ISIS, Lashkar-e-Toiba, Chechen extremist groups and Afghanistan and Pakistan based groups to attack nuclear installations in Russia and Central Asia.

Information on how to manipulate nuclear material to produce an explosive device—an improvised nuclear device, which would produce a nuclear explosion and a mushroom cloud, or a radiation-dispersal device, which would spread dangerous radioactive material over a substantial area—is now available widely. Daesh (ISIS) seized control of the Iraqi city of Mosul in 2014. Pakistan has also been heavily dependent on outside supply for many key direct- and dual-use goods for its nuclear programs. It maintains smuggling networks and entities willing to break supplier country laws to obtain these goods. Many of these illegal imports have been detected and stopped. These illegal procurements have led to investigations and prosecutions in the supplier states, leading to revelations of important details about Pakistan's complex to make nuclear explosive materials and nuclear weapons. According to some reports that weapons-grade and weapons-usable nuclear materials have been stolen by terrorist groups from some states. Once a crude weapon is in a country, terrorists would transport it in a vehicle to city and then detonate it in a crowded area.

The ISIS magazine (Dabiq-May 2015) published article of British journalist John Cantlie, in which he warned that the ISIS terrorist group had gained capabilities to launch major terrorist attack: "Let me throw a hypothetical operation onto the table. The Islamic State has billions of dollars in the bank, so they call on their wilayah in Pakistan to purchase a nuclear device through weapons dealers with links to corrupt officials in the region. The weapon is then transported overland until it makes it to Libya, where the mujahidin move it south to Nigeria. Drug shipments from Columbia bound for Europe pass through West Africa, so moving other types of contraband from East to West is just as possible. The nuke and accompanying mujahidin arrive on the shorelines of South America and are transported through the porous borders of Central America before arriving in Mexico and up to the border with the United States. From there it's just a quick hop through a smuggling tunnel and hey presto, they're mingling with another 12 million "illegal" aliens in America with a nuclear bomb in the trunk of their car".[14]

On 25 March 2016, Daily Telegraph reported militants plan to attack the Brussels nuclear plant: "In the wake of claims the Brussels attackers had planned to set off a radioactive 'dirty bomb', Yukiya Amano, the Director General of the International Atomic Energy Agency said: "Terrorism is spreading and the possibility of using nuclear material cannot be excluded. The material can be found in small quantities in universities, hospitals and other facilities. "Dirty bombs will be enough to (drive) any big city in the world into panic. And the psychological, economic and political implications would be enormous," said Mr Amano. One security expert suggested that the terrorists could have been plotting to kidnap the nuclear researcher they had been filming with a view to coercing the scientist into helping them make a 'dirty bomb'. The Newspaper reported. State sponsorship of nuclear terrorism in Central Asia is matter of great concern as some states support terrorist groups such as the ISIS, Taliban, Katibat Imam Bukhari, Chechen groups, and Lashkar-e-Toiba, and provide dangerous weapons. These states can sponsor terrorist groups to launch nuclear attack inside Russia or Central Asia.[15]

Citizens of five central states have joined the ISIS networks to take the war into the region and inflict fatalities on the civilian population. Russia is a strong country in case of law enforcement and intelligence infrastructure, but newly established commando units of ISIS have gained a professional approach to traditional guerrilla war. As far as foreign fighters and ISIS are concerned, prior to the start of Syria's civil war in 2011, Central Asia had periodically seen trickles of citizens leaving to fight in Syria and Iraq. In domestic stability, states of Central Asia are better than Pakistan, Afghanistan and some states of the Gulf region, but the fear of chemical and biological war has vanished. The threat of returned fighters moving underground and engaging in terrorist attacks is greater if there is no process to reintegrate and absorb them into a reasonably open society.

It is known that the Katibat-i-Imam Bukhari group (KIB) has established two branches. The group's main fighting force of more than 500 militants is led by leader Abu Yusuf Muhojir. The chechen fighters are also looking for material of dirty bomb and nuclear weapons to use it against Central Asian and Russian army, but didn't retrieve so for. They are in contact with some states in South Asia and Middle East to receive fund from these regions, and purchase readymade dirty bomb. Afghan and foreign officials say as many as 7,000 Chechens and other foreign fighters could be operating in the country, loosely allied with the Taliban and other militant groups. According to recent reports, 6,000 militants from Central Asia and the Caucasus have already been enlisted in ISIS ranks. The largest radical group in Uzbekistan, Imam Bukhari Jamaat, has joined ISIS in Syria. Experts say there are over one thousand Uzbek and Tajik militants still fighting under the banner of ISIS.

There are speculations that some Russian technocrats and politicians are stressing the need for the establishing a jihadi group like the ISIS to further the interests of Russia in Central Asia and Middle East and fight against the NATO and American forces in Afghanistan. Russia is now third among top countries from which ISIS receives its recruits. The majority of them come from the North Caucasus, but also increasingly from Central Asia. The most prominent North Caucasians among the ISIS ranks have been the Chechens. Shortly before Russia's Syria intervention, the Russian government claimed that between 2,000 and 5,000 militants had joined

ISIS; weeks after the entry of Russia into the conflict, however, that figure jumped to 7,000 out of a total of approximately 30,000 foreign fighters active within the ranks of the Islamic State.

If we look at the expertise of these groups, and their multifaceted military training, on their return to the region, they might possibly target biological and chemical laboratories and nuclear installations in Central Asia and Russia. There are states that will provide weapons and training to make the region a hell. Newsweek's Daily Beast blog provided another version of an overspill, already apparently happening in 2010. They quoted a "Taliban sub-commander in the northern Afghan province of Kunduz": ... jihadist allies from Central Asia have started heading home ... encouraged by relentless American drone attacks against the fighters' back bases in Pakistan's tribal areas ... they're expanding their range across the unguarded northern Afghan border into Tajikistan to create new Taliban sanctuaries there, assist Islamist rebels in the region, and potentially imperil the Americans' northern supply lines ... [beginning] in late winter 2009.... In Kunduz they joined up with fighters from the Islamic Movement of Uzbekistan (IMU).[16]

In his recent research paper, Leonid Gusev, an expert of Institute of International Studies, Moscow State Institute of International Relations of the Ministry of Foreign Affairs of the Russian Federation (MGIMO) has noted some consternating cooperative measures and planning's of the extremist groups of Central Asia: "Central Asian countries experience diverse intersecting influences: they feel changes in the situation in the Caucasus, in the Xinjiang autonomous territory of China, in Afghanistan and the Middle East. Militants from various terrorist groups in the region cooperate, many of them fighting in Syria and Iraq. But the biggest threat to Central Asia's security is the situation in Afghanistan, where the Taliban provide organisational and logistics support to the Islamic Movement of Uzbekistan (IMU). Despite sustaining a significant blow, with its main groups squeezed out of the region, it still maintains a presence in the form of underground groups that could become active at any time, joining forces with the radical Tajik opposition and Uyghur separatists. Cells of the Islamic State (ISIS) (a terrorist organisation banned in Russia) also operate in the region......... Tajikistan is a tension hotspot in Central Asia in terms of religious extremism and terrorism. A particular source of danger is neighbouring Afghanistan, where about 60 per cent of the lands along the frontier are engulfed in clashes between government forces and the Taliban and other radical Islamist groups. At the same time, there is almost no security along the Afghan-Tajik border, including the issue of drug trafficking".[17]

Nuclear trafficking in South Asia and Europe was a key concern while the nuclear blacke marketing networks were uncovered in Libya to Syria, Malaysia and Afghanistan. Recent media reports identified Moldovan criminal groups that attempted to smuggle radioactive materials to Daesh (also known as the Islamic State of Iraq and Syria, or ISIS) in 2015. Cases of nuclear smuggling in Central Asia were made in recent cases. Muhammad Wajeeh, a Research Associate at Department of Development Studies, COMSATS Institute of Information Technology, Abbottabad Pakistan in his research paper (Nuclear Terrorism: A Potential Threat to World's Peace and Security- JSSA Vol II, No. 2) has reviewed a consterning threat of nuclear terrorism in South and Central Asia:

"ISIS is believed to have about 90 pounds of low-grade uranium (which was seized from Mosul University in Iraq were the invasion of the city in 2014) that can be used in the Dirty Bomb's to create serious panic among the public. In 2015 and 2016, ISIS became the leading high profile jihadist group in Iraq and Syria. Moreover, ISIS carried out attacks in Paris on November 13, 2015, killing 130 civilians and injuring more than 100 people. The ISIS carried out a series of three coordinated suicide. Bombings in Belgium: one at Maalbeek Metro Staon, Brussels and two at Brussels Airport in Zaventem, killing about 32 civilians and injuring 300 people. During the attacks, a G4S guard working on the Belgian nuclear research center was also murdered and it le the world believing that the ISIS has a potential plot to attack the nuclear facility either to steal the radioactive material for dirty bomb or to release the radioactive material and waste into the atmosphere. These attacks also raised the issue of nuclear security, a discovery made by the Belgian authorities that the ISIS has kept an eye on the local nuclear scientists and their families. Moreover, two Belgian nuclear power plant workers at Deol having knowledge of the nuclear sites joined ISIS and could provide assistance to exploit them for terrorist purposes. On March 30, al-Furat, the media wing of ISIS, threatened attacks on Germany and Britain on the eve of Washington Nuclear Security Summit 2016".[18]

Chapter 12

The Islamic State, the Taliban, and Afghanistan's White Talc Mountains

The Global Witness Research Report

Summary

In April 2017, the largest non-nuclear weapon in the United States arsenal, the 'Mother of All Bombs', crashed into a hillside in the district of Achin in Eastern Afghanistan, targeting a network of tunnels held by the Afghan affiliate of the Islamic State (known as Islamic State – Khorasan Province, or ISKP). But on satellite photos, craters of another sort stand out, starting just a few hundred meters from the impact area: the marks of extensive mining for minerals at sites along the length of the valley.

ISKP controls a limited amount of territory in Afghanistan, but that includes parts of the country's rich mineral wealth, especially talc, chromite and marble. There are conflicting indications about how much they have exploited the mines so far: the available satellite imagery does not appear to show vehicles in the main ISKP-controlled area around Achin's Momand valley, and several sources denied mining had taken place since ISKP seized it in mid-2015. At the same time, multiple other credible sources reported that they have indeed benefitted at least to some extent from extraction and from taxing the minerals trade, and that they had done so with a tighter grip than the Taliban.

Whatever the reality, the danger is clear. Natural resources have long had a place in ISKP strategy in other countries, and that seems to be echoed in Afghanistan. In late 2017 more than 60,000 people were displaced by fighting between ISKP and the Taliban for control of other mineral-rich districts close to Achin: a Taliban official explicitly linked the ferocity of the battle to the struggle over the mines. An Afghan police source said ISKP had attempted to build a road to smuggle minerals south over the border to Pakistan. As early as 2015, an Afghan ISKP commander described control of mines in one mineral-rich province as a key priority, saying: "at any price, we will take the mines."

But the threat from ISKP is just one dramatic illustration of the much wider danger of conflict and corruption around Afghanistan's resources. In Nangarhar, our research documented the Taliban's grip on the talc trade, which generates millions for them from just a few districts. Satellite imagery shows extensive activity, including use of heavy machinery, at sites reported to be under Taliban influence, and trucks carrying minerals are routinely taxed. The onward trade is reportedly dominated by politically-connected strongmen, and widespread corruption costs the government millions in revenue. Beyond Nangarhar, mining has been a key revenue source for insurgents, strongmen and illegal militias – and a key driver of instability – across the whole country.

And while talc may be the least glamorous of conflict minerals, ultimately much of its value comes from America and Europe. Our research indicated that almost all Afghan talc generates revenue for the Taliban, and almost all is exported to Pakistan. The majority of Pakistani exports in turn actually originate in Afghanistan: and the largest single market for them is the United States, with European countries not far behind. Consumers in those countries are almost certainly unwittingly helping to fund the insurgency.

There are no easy responses to this challenge. But there are basic measures which are realistic and could help, and which the government and its allies have yet to implement so far. Part of this is direct pressure. Minerals like talc and marble need trucks to transport and are relatively easy to interdict. Much more could also be done to increase controls on the trade in Pakistan, and further up the supply chain. A greater emphasis on security in mining areas is another fundamental step, although clearly a difficult and risky one: it is hard to deal with illegal mining if armed groups hold the mines.

Those measures would help to target the Islamic State and Taliban directly, but returning the mines to government control will be of limited benefit if abusive extraction simply continues under other masters. And durably displacing abusive extraction is difficult without filling the resulting vacuum, with a cleaner extractive sector that benefits all Afghans. That is the ultimate endgame in any case: the aim is not to close down the trade but to make it legitimate. In other words, the Islamic State's interest in

Afghanistan's minerals should be an urgent wake-up call not just for the fight against extremist armed groups, but for the wider reform that the sector has been lacking so far.

And there are eminently realistic measures to implement that reform, based on the three core principles of transparency, community benefit and monitoring, and stronger oversight. They include amending the law to make contract publication a condition of validity, creating a single transparent account to be used for all payments as a condition for their receipt, and using the network of Community Development Councils to deliver a percentage of mining revenues to local communities. If ordinary traders and local communities can profit from legal mining, it will give them a reason to push back (to the extent they are able) against the takeover of resources by armed groups or corrupt strongmen, and reduce the political pressure on the government to turn a blind eye to abuses.

For its part, the Afghan government is relying on mining to help fund its budget and grow the economy, and has specifically identified talc as a priority for development. But without stronger action, it is hard to see those hopes being realistic. To be fair, the government says it recognises the problem, and it deserves real credit for publishing mining contracts and making some strong commitments on more systematic reforms. But progress in actually implementing those reforms has been much more limited, with critical measures like revenue transparency and community benefit often more of an ideal than a reality, and amendments to the mining law still under discussion. A 2015 ban on the talc trade showed that the government could impose effective restrictions on illegal mining, but was dropped within months under pressure from traders. And as a whole, the international response has also been inadequate (with some exceptions): the key concern of the Trump administration, for example, seems to be to press the Afghan government to give US companies a greater stake in Afghan resources.

The scale of the challenge is significant – especially for the Afghan government, which faces many other problems, not least a large-scale insurgency. None of our recommendations offers a silver bullet. But even if the government and its partners cannot tackle illegal mining everywhere, they could start by making limited, key areas (like the Nangarhar mines) a particular focus for security and a showcase for reforms, and put in place the higher-level changes which are within their control. Without action, as Nangarhar so powerfully demonstrates, the reasonable expectation is that Afghanistan's resources will do much more harm than good. That is a threat which must not be ignored.

1. Restrict illegal mining by armed groups in Nangarhar

a. Block the transit of talc, chromite, marble and other minerals from areas of Nangarhar under the influence of illegal armed groups, while moving as quickly as possible to create the conditions for 'clean' extraction, even if this is initially in a limited area.

b. Make it a higher priority within security strategy to protect key resource-rich areas and associated transit routes, including mining sites in Nangarhar. Prioritise political means where possible.

c. Ensure any enforcement or security actions are tied to wider measures like those outlined below, and to negotiations with local communities and protections for livelihoods –so long as this does not undermine efforts to exclude armed groups and strongmen from the trade.

2. Give local communities reasons to support legal mining

a. Create effective mechanisms for a community share in legal revenues, community monitoring of mining, and community or artisanal ownership of mines. Ensure local communities can control what projects their revenues are used for, under appropriate safeguards including transparency and community monitoring. As a first option, consider distributing the funds as supplements to the budgets of Community Development Councils.

b. Within Nangarhar, make community benefit from or ownership of mines a central element of wider efforts to reduce insurgent influence in the area.

3. Reform laws and oversight to make illegal mining harder and legal mining more attractive

Put in place basic transparency and oversight reforms to make abusive mining more difficult and create space for legal extraction that benefits the country and local communities. In particular:

a. within the next six months, amend the mining law and regulations in order to:

1. Make the publication of contracts a condition of their validity.

2. Require the publication of production and payment data.

3. Require the creation of a single transparent subaccount of the Treasury Single Account, to be used for all extractive sector payments as a condition of their receipt, and published at least quarterly The published statement must include clear identification of the relevant individual project for each payment, and information on the basis on which it was made, such as amount and grade of production.

4. Create a public register of beneficial ownership, and require companies to register and update their entries as a condition of bidding for or holding government contracts.

a. Strengthen the oversight capacity and practices of the Ministry of Mines, specifically information and contract management, cadastre, community relations, and inspection functions. Develop management capacity and mechanisms for artisanal and small-scale mining.

b. Reform contracting processes to strengthen transparency and ensure companies are treated fairly. Move towards a license rather than contract model for extractive concessions. At a minimum, mandate the use of model contracts incorporating the strongest available protections against corruption and conflict, developed in conjunction with civil society, local communities, and mining companies.

4. Use satellite imagery to monitor key mining sites

a. systematically monitors key mining sites using satellite imagery, including both optical and radar data. Make all images at commercially available resolutions automatically available to the public to allow transparent and broad-based monitoring of the sites, and share higher resolutions with established and reputable CSOs.

5. Control supply chains

a. Work with trade partners and consumer countries to put in place strong controls over supply chains from conflict affected areas, including a requirement for due diligence by both Afghan companies and those from major importing countries.

Key actors

The Islamic State in Afghanistan is a relatively loose set of armed groups which have declared allegiance to the wider Islamic State extremist movement centred in Syria and Iraq. It grew mainly from fighters loyal to the 'Pakistani Taliban' (Tehreek e Taliban e Pakistan, TTP). Others have defected from the Afghan Taliban, and the two groups remain in violent competition.[1]

The Taliban came to prominence in 1994, during the civil war that followed the end of the Soviet occupation of Afghanistan.[2] While they lost almost all of their territory after the US-led invasion in 2001, they are now estimated to control 41 of Afghanistan's 407 districts and contest an additional 118.[3] Before 2015, the Taliban was present in areas of Nangarhar that now form the heartland of the Islamic State in Afghanistan, and they are still a major force in the province.[4] The Government of the Islamic Republic of Afghanistan and its allies are fighting both the Taliban and the Islamic State, but US forces in particular have focused attention on ISKP out of proportion to the small size of the group.[5] This includes a major offensive in April 2017, Operation Hamza.[6]

1. Support Afghan efforts to strengthen resource governance

a. Provide full material and political support for government reforms of extractive sector governance, notably the mining-related measures discussed in the National Anti-Corruption action plan and the reform of the Ministry of Mines. Explicitly prioritise strengthening of oversight, governance and conflict prevention.

b. Provide or fund the acquisition of high-resolution satellite imagery for monitoring of key extractive sites by the Afghan government as set out above, and direct your own intelligence resources to exposing and understanding links between resources, armed groups and corrupt actors.

c. All importing countries for Afghan minerals, oil and gas should commit to requiring that companies carry out risk assessment and due diligence on their supply chains, at a minimum to the standard set out in the OECD Due Diligence Guidance for Responsible Supply Chains of Minerals from Conflict Affected High Risk Areas.

2. Make stronger resource governance a priority for your engagement with Afghanistan

a. Integrate the most important extractive governance reforms into core benchmarks for mutual accountability between the Afghan government and its partners. Agree a single common set of more detailed benchmarks for donor support to the Ministry of Mines in particular.

b. Hold the Afghan government to its existing commitments to strengthen natural resource governance, and raise the need for urgent reforms through political engagement at the highest level.

c. Avoid creating any pressure for new natural resource contracts in areas that are at elevated risk from conflict or armed groups, or before basic protections (like the measures set out above) have become effective. Focus your engagement in Afghanistan on achieving these conditions as rapidly as possible.

Introduction

The involvement of armed groups in mining obviously has implications for the future of Afghanistan, and illustrates wider dangers around the abusive exploitation of the country's natural resources. Yet little systematic research on the subject exits. This report aims to fill that gap, at least in part. Our findings are based both on commercially-available satellite imagery, and interviews with a range of sources with credible knowledge of the local situation. Owing to security concerns around the report, especially for individuals in Afghanistan, we felt it necessary to go to exceptional lengths to ensure anonymity, and have included substantially fewer details than we normally would about the nature and background of the sources. We are confident in the credibility of our information, and are willing to discuss our research methodology with responsible third parties.

The report briefly covers the background of the Islamic State in Afghanistan (for more detailed accounts, see the sources cited in the endnotes).[7] It then documents the extent of ISKP's control over resources and the evidence around how far they have been able to exploit them. This is closely linked to a discussion of their broader strategic interest in natural resources, drawing on evidence from their competition with the Taliban in other parts of the province, and briefly looking at the rest of Afghanistan. This is followed by our findings on Taliban involvement in mining in Nangarhar— highlighting the wider risk of armed groups profiting from mining. We also document the supply chains which ultimately fuel armed groups in Afghanistan, before finally discussing policy responses: there are a number of realistic options, even if it there is no silver bullet.

Throughout the report the name 'Islamic State–Khorasan Province' or ISKP, is used to distinguish the Afghan affiliate of the Islamic State from the main body of the Islamic State in Iraq and Syria, which we will refer to as ISIS.[8] "Islamic State" is used when referring to the movement as a whole (although we fully acknowledge that the term is rejected in many quarters

235

as a usurpation of the name of Islam).[9] Some Afghan sources referred to the Islamic State using the Arabic term 'Daesh', a somewhat pejorative abbreviation of the name where they did, that term has been retained.

Locations mentioned in the text can be found on the relevant maps. Some place names could not be located with the maps available: this may partly reflect the fact that mining sites are often located away from settlements, which provide the great majority of names on the available lists.[10]

Most prices cited in Nangarhar were expressed in Pakistani Rupees (colloquially known as kaldars), as the currency is widely used in the border areas.[11] For conversions in the report, a rate of 105 Pakistani Rupees (Rs) to one US dollar ($) was used, which closely approximates the rate between August 2015 and December 2017.[12] For Afghanis, a rate of 68 Afghanis (Afs) to one US dollar was used, which roughly corresponds to the rate from December 2015 to November 2017.[13] Weights are expressed in kilograms and metric tons.

Global Witness gratefully acknowledges the considerable assistance provided by Sarmap SA in obtaining, processing and analysing satellite imagery. Sarmap's contribution was particularly critical to enable us to access Synthetic Aperture Radar imagery and conduct analysis of optical imagery. We are also grateful to Digital Globe for its invaluable assistance in accessing wider satellite imagery. Finally, and most importantly, this report could not have been written without the support and work of many others. We deeply regret that we cannot list them, but very gratefully acknowledge their contribution.

Unglamorous conflict minerals–talc, chromate and marble

Our sources described mining of three key minerals in the areas under ISKP influence: talc, chromite, and marble. Other minerals like tourmaline may also be mined, but they are relatively insignificant.[14] Talc (hydrated magnesium silicate–$Mg_3Si_4O_{10}(OH)_2$) is the softest mineral known to man.[15] The name is of Persian origin, possibly reflecting the long history of talc mining in Afghanistan and the region.[16] Usually processed into a fine white powder, it easily absorbs moisture and oils, and can serve as a lubricant. Perhaps best known for its use in talcum powder or baby powder, it also has important applications in ceramics, paint, paper, plastics, rubber, insecticides, and other products.[17] Global output was around 8.1m tons in 2017.[18]

Afghanistan possesses talc of very high quality, with exceptionally high-grade deposits in the Khogyani/ Sherzad area, and only slightly less pure material in Achin.[19] Resources in Achin total an estimated 1.25m tons, distributed in narrow, irregular beds of one to 15 metres in width, and generally less than 240 m in length.[20] Artisanal mining has taken place there since the 1920s.[21] Chromite (iron chromium oxide – $FeCr_2O4$) is a heavy, dark mineral, globally important as the only economic ore of chromium, which is widely used as an essential element in the production of stainless steel and other steel alloys.[22] Global production was about 31m tons in 2017.[23]

Marble (metamorphosed calcium carbonate – $CaCO3$) produced in Afghanistan is also renowned for its quality, with significant deposits of high-grade onyx marble.[24] Its uses range from flooring and tiles to decorative objects. There are reports of substantial smuggling, especially from Helmand province, where marble is the second largest source of revenue for the Taliban after narcotics.[25]

1-The Islamic State in Afghanistan: a complex threat

The movement calling itself the Islamic State[26] established its first nascent presence in Afghanistan only in 2014, and officially launched in early 2015.[27] Since then, they have expanded to become a threat in several provinces, but have also faced resistance from both the Taliban and government forces which has frustrated or reversed their growth. Nonetheless, they retain the ability to strike – and bases from which they aim to expand their insurgency across the country.

An important affiliate

In January 2015, the leadership of the Islamic State of Iraq and Al-Shams (ISIS) declared the creation of the Khorasan wilayat or governorate– "Khorasan" being a historical term for a region encompassing Afghanistan, Pakistan and parts of other countries.[28] The group's creation was important for the Islamic State. It marked the first official ISIS affiliate outside of the Arab world, [29] had an important religious dimension,[30] and allowed ISIS to challenge their rival Al Qaeda on the territory where they have their primary base, in the Afghanistan-Pakistan border regions.[31] Indeed, ISKP's initial attacks were against the Taliban, Al Qaeda's ally and protector.[32]

ISKP quickly grew into a significant force after it was established. Government offensives in Pakistan's tribal areas helped push militants, including foreign fighters, into Afghanistan, swelling the ranks of the movement,[33] which quickly became active in a dozen provinces around the country (including a number of northern provinces beyond their original Pashtun power base).[34] In July 2015, the Islamic Movement of Uzbekistan (IMU), a significant foreign-led militant group based in Badakhshan province in northern Afghanistan, also pledged bay'at [allegiance] to ISIS.[35] In Nangarhar, the fractured nature in many areas of both tribal society, and of the pre-2015 insurgency, made particularly fertile ground for an ISKP coup.[36]

Most estimates put the overall strength of ISKP at 1,000 to 3,000 fighters, with numbers in Nangarhar specifically put at 750-2,000.[37.] The core leadership from the start has been former members of the Pakistani Taliban group Tehreek-e-Taliban (TTP).[38] Afghan and international security forces in fact claim that 70-80 per cent of ISKP fighters are Pakistanis, but this may be an overstatement, given the impact of Afghans defecting to ISKP from the Taliban; a late 2016 USIP report found these made up the majority of mid-level commanders.[39] Even so, the Pakistani influence in the group could have significant implications for its ability to expand.[40] There is also a notable (and reportedly growing) international contingent (although the numbers of foreign fighters in Afghanistan are notoriously prone to exaggeration).[41]

Franchises like ISKP receive at least a nominal level of management from the senior Islamic State leadership,[42] and for its part ISKP also asserts that its Afghan operations support the larger, Levant-centred IS fight.[43] However, the extent of more practical links between the two organisations are still subject to debate. There is a good deal of opportunistic re-branding by armed groups, with operational ties both among them and to IS leaders much less clear.[44] Indeed, some groups, especially those in Ghor and Jowzjan, may essentially be criminal networks that have taken the ISKP name.[45]

Nonetheless, one senior Afghan ISKP commander asserted that he had visited the ISIS senior leadership in Iraq and received seed funding from them, and that ISKP commanders shaped their strategy in line with guidance from ISIS.[46]There are other reports of small cash transfers (see below),[47] and General John Nicholson, the commander of international forces in Afghanistan, stated in early 2017 that ISIS was exercising "operational guidance" over ISKP.[48] Overall, there does seem to be some tie, even if there is no routine command-and-control.

A well-resourced insurgency

The growth of ISKP has been helped by the allure of the Islamic State brand, but also by the resources they could offer (although the exact extent and source of their funding is very difficult to establish).[49] This may be changing now, with some observers reporting the movement is facing financial difficulties, but others indicated that their resources still appear considerable. The UN Sanctions Committee reported in January 2017 that "ISIL is struggling financially in Afghanistan, where it has resorted to extortion of the local population and has had to stop paying its fighters at times."[50] Their May 2017 report, however, cited official sources reporting that ISKP "continues to appear to be well equipped and funded, with interlocutors reporting that it pays its fighters between $200 and $500 per month."[51] Some of this funding – about $100,000 a month–was reportedly being transferred from the core ISIS group in Iraq and Syria, despite the substantial declines in their income.[52] Whether this has changed with loss of almost all ISIS territorial control by late 2017 remains to be seen.

ISKP 's substantial propaganda work[53] and continued ability to launch operations certainly suggest that they have an independent source of funds.[54] Their fighters also appear to be paid relatively well, with several other sources supporting the UN's findings, including Global Witness interviewees from two provinces.[55] They have reportedly been burning poppy fields rather than financing themselves from narcotics – another reason to think they would be particularly interested in minerals.[56] Taxes on locals (the ushr and zakat of Islamic tradition),[57] as well as cruder extortion or theft from individuals are thought to be a key income source,[58] as are donations from sympathisers.[59] As we shall see, natural resources are another source of funds, even if their precise contribution is unclear.

Stalled but dangerous

Since 2015, ISKP has carried out a number of high-profile operations, including a string of attacks in the cities of Jalalabad and Kabul (although they may not have carried out all the operations that have been attributed to them).[60] Their methods have often been brutal even by the standards of the Afghan conflict,[61] which has alienated at least some potential supporters, and could be another factor limiting their growth.[62] They are also exceptional in the way they have explicitly targeted the Hazara ethnic minority, who are largely Shia Muslims, in an apparent attempt to foment sectarian conflict–a deeply worrying development.[63]

239

However, ISKP's initial growth quickly created a sharp backlash, as the movement found itself the enemy of all–the Taliban, the Afghan government, and international forces. By the end of 2015, the group had been rolled back from several provinces.[64] In February 2017, General Nicholson estimated that operations since early 2016 had reduced the number of ISKP members by half, and their territory by two-thirds.[65] A series of ISKP leaders have also been killed.[66]

Yet as of late 2017, the movement was thought to have significantly rebuilt its numbers, with no sign of a let up in their recruiting.[67] There are fears these are being boosted by fighters displaced from lost Islamic State territories in Syria and Iraq,[68] and even that the safe haven of Afghanistan may be being used to plot attacks in the Unites States.[69] Groups claiming loyalty to ISKP are active in a clutch of provinces[70]–notably Logar, Kunar, and Nangarhar in eastern Afghanistan, but also more distant territories like Jawzjan in the north.[71] These are all mineral rich areas, even if it is not clear how far that has driven the pattern compared to other factors.[72]

Nangarhar is the heartland of the remaining ISKP presence. The movement had a "comfortable position" in eight districts of the province by mid-2015,[73] after brutal clashes with the Taliban.[74] While they quickly lost many of these gains, the movement remained strong in Kot, Deh Bala, and Achin, especially their stronghold in the Momand valley.[75] This position lasted more or less intact until March 2017, when the government and its international allies launched a sustained campaign, including 'Operation Hamza', which dislodged ISKP from Kot district and put them under serious pressure in Achin.[76] (This may be why Nangarhar was the deadliest province for US troops in 2017.)[77] Nonetheless, they were still able to hold part of their territory, and even to relaunch renewed efforts in other parts of the province shortly afterwards.[78]

ISKP have faced major setbacks after their impressive initial expansion. Their brutality and lack of local roots, and the strong opposition they face, mean that the threat they pose to the country as a whole is limited at present. But they have shown resilience, retain a powerful brand and significant resources, and are still able to mount terrorist operations, as the attacks in Kabul show. Even as the Islamic State deals with the loss of its territory in Iraq and Syria, the danger of renewed expansion of the movement's affiliate in Afghanistan should not be discounted.

2-The threat on the ground: ISKP's hold on the mines of Nangarhar

Even in their reduced state, ISKP control a rich swathe of mineral resources. Although there is mixed evidence on the extent to which they have been able to exploit them, there are some grounds for the Afghan governments concern that: "The mines of Afghanistan can be a good economic source for [the Islamic State]."[79]

Riches in their Hands: The resources ISKP controls in Achin

Achin district of Nangarhar is where the ISKP first emerged in Afghanistan, and is the heartland of their current presence.[80] They are under substantial military pressure from US and Afghan forces– including the use in April 2017 of the American military's largest nonnuclear bomb, the Massive Ordinance Air-Blast (MOAB) device, popularly called the 'Mother of All Bombs'.[81] Nonetheless, the movement has so far proved resilient despite its setbacks.

In late 2016 a source described how ISKP was particularly present around the mining areas: "Before, Daesh (…) were only in the hills (…), where the mines were. Now they have come to the villages – it is a sign that they are stronger."[82] The source said sites under ISKP control included Nargesai and Ai Tang in Achin, and Sangorai just over the border in Kot, which they said produced talc (shawkanai in Pashto) and chromite (sangina).[83](Locations of the corresponding place-names are shown on our map, although the mining areas may not be immediately adjacent to them).

According to the source, all these areas held both talc and chromite, and might each have more than a dozen individual mines. They said other minerals were also occasionally mined, including transparent and green precious or semi-precious stones (the first of these could be possibly quartz, while the other seems likely to be tourmaline, although it was referred to as emerald).[84] Another informed source confirmed that there were ISKP-controlled sites at Nargesai, Ai Tang, and Sangorai, with between 5 and 20 individual mines at each site.[85] This source said all three sites produced both talc and chromite, adding that tourmaline could also be found at Ai Tang.[86] "Everywhere that has the mines, [ISKP] now has a lot of focus that they take [them]," the source noted in mid-2016. "The local people (…) say that today (…) they have got more mines. (...) They take them from the people, from the Taliban, from whoever has them."[87]

A third informed source had knowledge of four different sites in the area where he said ISKP was mining.[88] They said Nargesai had talc, but also white marble and what he called lapis lazuli (there appear to be no confirmed reports of lapis being found in the area, and it is possible this is nephrite or some similar coloured marble).[89] The source noted that there was a place where talc was stockpiled in Nargesai, something which may be visible on the satellite imagery. As of late 2016 the source was also aware of other sites at Shne Kanda in Achin district, and Lagharjo and Yanak in Kot; and said the first two of these held marble, while Yanak had both marble and chromite.[90] All the sites had been held by the Taliban before ISKP took them over in late 2015: "There was a little fighting between Daesh and the Taliban–the Taliban gave up to the mines to the people [when they fled] and the people gave them to Daesh."[91]

Despite all the military pressure, ISKP's hold on these mining areas appears to be enduring, and may be expanding.[92] "It is propaganda that they are getting weak," one source said in mid-2017: "they are getting stronger day by day." [93]Local elders issued a similar warning in late 2017.94 In mid-2017 the movement claimed to have captured the district of Chaparhar from the Taliban,[95] and they at least temporarily captured the strategic Tora Bora area (in Pachir Wa Agam district, less than 30km from Achin) – an area that includes a valuable marble mine.[96] In early 2018, two traders mentioned that ISKP held Tora Bora at least for the moment, though one said the mine "is not very active."[97]

At the end of 2017, major ISKP/Taliban clashes were reported in Khogyani, likely partly around the control of mines (see below). In early 2018 two traders independently reported that the Waziro Tangai area of the district was under ISKP control, and that the mines there were active, although a third said their control (and presumably any income) was limited to just a more distant part of the valley.[98] If it spreads, it could allow the movement to significantly increase its revenues.

There is doubt over the significance of the MOAB bomb in particular. The insecurity and lack of access on the ground makes it difficult to confirm claims of significant ISKP casualties, and one detailed analysis found much less damage than initially reported.99 One informed source Global Witness spoke to was sceptical that the MOAB had done much harm.[100] Indeed, one local rumour was that the crater conveniently left by the bomb was being used for mining.[101] While that is almost certainly false (or at least distorted), it is telling that satellite imagery shows the existence of mines just a few hundred metres from the bomb site.[102]

A more intense exploitation

Several of our sources indicated that ISKP's exploitation of the mines was a step change above the normal practice of the Taliban both in terms of investment in machinery and expertise, and of the degree of security and control the exercise over the sites. That would be another sign of the importance of extractives to the movement – although it should be noted that the satellite data raises questions about how significant recent mining activity has actually been.

One informed source described how the level of extraction increased at the mines in Achin as the hold of ISKP strengthened. "The people of the village work with them – the number of workers has become a lot," he said in late 2016. "Before it was from 20-40 people [at one mine, in different shifts], now it is from 50-100."[103] He said a munshi [secretary or administrator] kept the books at the mines. In mid-2017 he reported that activity had further increased, and that ISKP had opened an office in Suriya Bazaar, near Sayed Akhmadkhel village in Kot, where they would pay and recruit workers, and deal with traders.[104]

The source reported that heavy tracked machinery was used at some mines, with extraction mainly carried out with large pneumatic jackhammers mounted on excavators, and wheeled excavators used to load the trucks.[105] This equipment would be brought over from other mines when demand was high. While machinery had been used before ISKP took over the mines, "they brought more."[106] A different source similarly said that after ISKP took over another site they knew of, ISKP brought in more machinery and intensified exploitation: "now the number [of machines] has increased. (…) Extraction has gone up."[107] The source said most of the mine sites had an excavator and a loader. In mid-2016 a third source said that the rent for an excavator would be $5,000 a month, with driver.[108]

The reports of machinery being used at the mines may be linked to the confiscation of vehicles that were already at the site. One source reported that ISKP took "the private excavators by force."[109] A researcher told Global Witness that the Bilal Musazai company, which has a contract for talc mines in the Momand valley, lost "around 100" vehicles when the Islamic State took over.[110] Even if that number was exaggerated, this may explain the reports of ISKP bringing in machines. That could in turn imply that the extraction was only as mechanised as before, not more.

ISKP had also brought in foreign engineers to help extraction, one source claimed:[111] he said locals believed they came from Pakistan, Arabia, and possibly even Western countries (although the basis for their belief was accents and appearance rather than anything more definite, and sightings of 'Chechens' and other foreigners are notoriously unreliable).[112] The engineers were not constantly on the site but visited on rare occasions "to show people where to mine."[113] A second source similarly claimed that more skilled professionals–the machinery drivers for example–were brought in from outside, while a third also noted the presence of "foreigners" as well as Pakistanis.[114] (Several sources actually reported that foreigners were working as ordinary labourers, which may be significant, as the lack of local labour was one reason a number of observers said that ISKP could not be extracting significant amounts.

A tighter grip

The sources also reported that ISKP imposed substantially tighter security around the mines they controlled, with phones banned, and workers searched and monitored. In late 2016 one source reported that workers were only allowed in the mining areas when it was time for their shift: "They work in a very disciplined and strict way."[115] The source said security was even higher around one other mining site, not far from Ai Tang, where they claimed ISKP were extracting stones with a 'colour like emeralds'.[116] Whether this is indeed emeralds, or just tourmaline, it is a much more precious stone by weight. "Local people are not allowed in there at all. The workers are foreigners, they do the mining themselves and take it away themselves (…) even [having] a mobile phone [in that place] is a crime."

A different source told Global Witness that when the Taliban controlled the mines, they would take a share of the mine revenues, as well as taxes in the form of ushr and zakat–but the actual exploitation was done by local entrepreneurs. "The mine was in the hands of the people–of the maleks [local elites]," the source said.[117] When ISKP took over, they changed the system, to directly exploit the mines themselves.[118] Locals were still employed as labourers, but they were "their people," linked in some way to the Islamic State. Work was much more closely controlled, the source claimed, and again, locals were not allowed to be in the area when they were not on their shift.[119] But the source also said that unlike other sites, at the Yanak marble mines "now the local shura is extracting, but the Islamic State has half share" – with a local businessman providing machinery in exchange for a share of the stone.[120]

A third informed source similarly reported that in the past "the big people rented the mine."[121] Now that ISKP had taken over the mines, they said in mid-2016, "the Maliks [local powerbrokers] and commanders are finished. (…) These people are so upset that they cry."[122] But the source claimed ordinary people had benefited from the change. Under the Taliban, the local businessmen who exploited the mines paid labourers a flat rate of Rs2,500 (about $24) for a ton of production – however many people were involved. Now people were happy, as the ISKP would pay a $400 monthly salary "whether you work a lot or little."

Contradictory evidence

A number of indirect sources support the testimony set out above.[123] Matt DuPée, an author and Afghan expert with the US Department of Defence, told Global Witness that sources from Achin had reported that ISKP was controlling mines and profiting from the talc trade as of late 2017, and he had also heard that ISKP was extracting minerals directly.[124]Separately, Borhan Osman of the Afghanistan Analysts Network reported that a credible source in Nangarhar had mentioned ISKP taxing talc trucks in mid to late 2015, and that local elders said the movement was exploiting 3-4 mines.[125] A June 2017 USIP report also noted that ISKP reportedly had taken control of talc mines in Achin and was "directly extracting and selling it to traders."[126] Finally, in April 2017 the governor of Nangarhar warned that "Nangarhar's regions which have forests and mines are insecure. Taliban and Daesh militants are mining illegally and destroying forests in those areas. This is an income source for their war which has to be rooted out."[127]

However, a number of other sources cast doubt on this narrative. In mid-2017 a purported ISKP source denied that the movement was making money from minerals, saying that "no one can touch the mines in (...) districts which are under the control of the Islamic State."[128] The journalist Franz Marty also reported a conversation with a former ISKP commander (albeit a low-ranking individual who appeared unaware of the location of the mines), who said the movement's leaders had ordered a stop to all economic and social activities (not only mining, but also schooling and other services) in order "to put their whole focus on their armed struggle."[129]

Of course, such individuals might have an inventive to conceal any activity. But Marty also cited a former miner from the area who said Daesh closed the mines.[130] A senior trader Global Witness interviewed in mid-2017 also said that ISKP "are not allowing us to work in the Achin mines."[131] And an elder with strong links to the area said "Daesh does not extract" the mines (though he claimed they were profiting from illegal logging): "Daesh never stopped people from mining (...) but since this area was insecure and people left the area, so the mining stopped."[132]

The researcher David Mansfield found that mining briefly continued in the immediate aftermath of the ISKP takeover in May 2015, but had been essentially dormant since the exodus of locals caused by the Taliban counteroffensive in July.[133] Finally, a senior Afghan police officer with recent experience in the province said that the Islamic State had not allowed extraction (he thought to avoid security risks, and possibly to deny the government the benefit of the trade) and that in any case access to the ISKP-controlled areas was too dangerous and too restricted by the government for mining to be possible: "Since Daesh came not one kilo was extracted."[134]

On the question of the lack of workforce, it is worth noting that some of the sources reported the presence not just of technicians but of ordinary workers from Pakistan: "they have their own labourers," one said in late 2016.[135] ISKP "gives a good salary but people do not want to work there – they are afraid. (…) very few [locals] work there. This is I think why they brought people from outside."[136] In mid-2017 the same source reported that: "now they have changed, so they are inviting [local] people (…) before it was their own people from Momand and Pakistan (…) it was people who had relations with them. Now it is not – they are using locals as well" (although they said the majority were still from outside – including "people from Sindh" in Pakistan).[137] A second source said that "locals that are now with Daesh" worked the mines, as well as foreigners,[138] while a third said that: "Both locals and themselves [ISKP] do labouring."[139] In theory, this could provide at least a partial explanation of how the mines could have been operational even with most locals having fled.

Smuggling Routes

One question around any possible ISKP extraction is how the stone would travel out of the area. There appears to be no passable route for trucks south over the Spinghar Mountains to Pakistan, although there are certainly smaller paths through which weapons and other less bulky goods are regularly smuggled.[140] A leading talc trader in the province said ISKP "cannot take it through the mountains, they have to transport it through main roads, so they cannot mine for themselves."[141] Again, the former senior police officer said traffic from ISKP controlled areas would be restricted by government check posts on the roads.[142] This seems plausible given the limited number of exit routes, the relative ease of interdicting large talc trucks, and the clear strategic urgency of blocking a trade which could help fund the Islamic State.

But there is some evidence that material may be finding a way out nonetheless. In early 2018, a credible firsthand source described one trader buying chromite from Ai Tang and taking it out of the area on a small truck through "a smuggler road."[143] This involved quite small quantities (around 4 tons a load), and it is not clear how many trucks travelled that route, but it could be enough to represent significant extraction. While the source did not reveal who he bought the chromite from, Ai Tang was mentioned by several other sources as within the ISKP area of influence.

Two of our other key sources similarly referred to talc leaving the area by smuggling routes – although the extent of their first-hand knowledge was unclear. "There are hundreds of roads," one said–possibly even including the long route west through Paktia province Kurram Agency, one of Pakistan's Federally Administered Tribal Areas.[144] Another reported that "it goes on the official road through Torkham," before adding that the "smuggler road (…) is through Kot" – presumably meaning the initial part of the exit route before the main Jalalabad-Torkham highway.[145] Overall, while the route south seems out of the question, it is at least possible that there could be a route west of the main mining area, exiting through Kot rather than Achin district.

Global Witness investigates and campaigns to change the system by exposing the economic networks behind conflict, corruption and environmental destruction. Global Witness is a company limited by guarantee and incorporated in England (No.2871809) Global Witness Lloyds Chambers, 1 Portsoken St, London E1 8BT, United Kingdom. Global Witness. 1100 17th Street NW, Suite 501, Washington, DC 20036, USA ISBN 978-1-911606-18-5. Our goal is a more sustainable, just and equal planet. We want forests and biodiversity to thrive, fossil fuels to stay in the ground and corporations to prioritise the interests of people and the planet. We want justice for those disproportionately affected by the climate crisis: people in the global south, indigenous communities and communities of colour, women and younger generations. We want corporations to respect the planet and human rights, governments to protect and listen to their citizens, and the online world to be free from misinformation and hate. When founded in 1993, we were pioneers in seeing the link between natural resources, conflict and corruption. For over 25 years, we have investigated and exposed environmental and human rights abuses in the oil, gas, mining, and timber sectors, and tracked ill-gotten money and influence through the global financial and political system. Today, we continue to focus on abusive actors, misuse of power and financial flows, but have turned our focus on some of the most urgent issues facing humanity: the climate emergency and attacks on civic space. We work to hold companies and governments to account for their destruction of the environment, their disregard for the planet and their failure to protect human rights via campaigns to: curb the flow of finance enabling destruction of climate-critical tropical forests challenge industry efforts to present fossil gas as climate-friendly end corporate complicity in environmental and human rights abuses protect land and environmental defenders standing up to climate-wrecking industries tackle the spread of division, hate and disinformation on digital platforms end corporate corruption and ensure companies in the natural resource sector can no longer operate above the law over 25 years of creating change. Soldiers escorting illegally-logged luxury timber, Phnom Aural Global Witness investigations are known for their meticulous attention to detail and we use an ever-evolving variety of techniques including undercover filming and scraping and analysing open source and leaked data sets. For instance, in 2020 we conducted our most ambitious data-driven investigation to date, uncovering the illegal deforestation linked to Brazil's biggest beef companies. Our communications, events and partnerships bring issues to the attention of audiences around the world and onto the political agenda. Meanwhile, through our advocacy we successfully shape and secure laws, sanctions and changes in business practice to ensure transition to a just and sustainable future. Global Witness Foundation. Suite 13A-410 Palo Alto, CA 94301. 855 El Camino Real. The Foundation supports research and investigations into the causes and effects of the exploitation of natural resources by public and private entities throughout the world, specifically where such exploitation is used to fund conflict, human rights abuses and corruption. These objectives are fulfilled by donating funds to Global Witness. Therefore if you would like to send a USD donation please send directly to the Global Witness Foundation. All USD donations made to the Global Witness Foundation will be tax-deductible to the full extent allowed by law. Global Witness Foundation will provide acknowledgement of the donation for the donor's tax records. For all other purposes, please contact the Global Witness office in Washington, D.C. directly. General Enquiries: Phone: +44 (0)20 7947 0309. Email: mail@globalwitness.org. Media Enquiries: Phone: + 44 (0)7912 517 127. Email: media@globalwitness. org. Fundraising Enquiries: Phone: +44 (0)20 7947 0309 (option one). Email: development@globalwitness.org. Office addresses: London, Global Witness Green House, 244-254 Cambridge Heath Road, London E2 9DA. Phone: +44 (0)20 7947 0309

Chapter 13

Salafism, Wahhabism, and the Definition of Sunni Islam

Rob J. Williams

According to Pew, 85-90 percent of Muslims worldwide are Sunni. Despite such a vast population figure, there is no definitive answer to what makes a Muslim Sunni. This question has become especially complicated over the past two centuries with the rise of various Sunni reform movements across the Muslim world. This essay seeks to develop a working definition of Sunni Islam that existed prior to 1800 and then show how reform movements since 1800 have diverged from that definition. For the purposes of this essay, a traditional Sunni Muslim is a Muslim who adheres to one of the four Sunni *maddhabs*, or schools of law.[1] A reformist Sunni, on the other hand, does not follow any of the four *maddhabs* and instead relies on different authorities and interpretations of scripture when it comes to leading their religious life.[2] Two of the most prominent reform groups are the "Salafis" and the "Wahhabis", terms that also lack strong definitions, have a nebulous association and are often seen as the face of Sunni Islam worldwide.

I argue that, despite the prevalence of Salafism and Wahhabism in contemporary times, the Salafis and the Wahhabis are not one and the same. Wahhabi and Salafi groups took advantage of favorable historical circumstances to rise out of obscurity to become the powerful forces in contemporary Islam that they are today. This paper synthesizes history, law, and political science together in order to create a focused picture of why Sunni identity is confused in the modern day. One common thread among Salafis, Wahhabis, and other disparate Sunni groups, however, is that they all were forced to react to the sudden saliency of modernity, as defined by

Western, Enlightenment ideals. The seeds of contemporary division were sown in differing reactions to modernity. Discussions and debates between different Sunni groups are now a pressing issue in contemporary Islam.

"Traditional" Sunni Islam

Before I delve any further into the essay, the meaning of the term "traditional Sunni Islam" and a "traditional Sunni Muslim" must be defined. Jonathan Brown uses the term "late Sunni Traditionalist" to describe a Sunni Muslim who adheres to one of the four Sunni *maddhabs*, or schools of law. The four Sunni schools are the Hanafi, Maliki, Shafi'i, and Hanbali schools. Each has their own unique way of interpreting Islamic law, as well as a rich tradition of legal work that stretches back to the time of the Prophet Muhammad himself.[3] The Hanafi School arose first historically in the eighth century CE. It is named after Abu Hanifa, who was the first figure in this lineage of Islamic jurisprudence.[4] Abu Hanifa focused his interpretations of Islamic law on analogical reasoning, or *qiyas*, as opposed to the study of the traditions of Muhammad and his companions, or *hadith*.[5] Hanafism is united by its reliance on *qiyas* but it is also by no means monolithic. A split occurred in the tenth century based on geographic and jurisprudential lines. Scholars led by Abu Yusuf in the city of Balkh (modern Afghanistan) applied *qiyas* differently than scholars in Baghdad under Muhammad al-Shaybani.[6] Hanafism also became the most widespread maddhab because it was adopted by the Ottoman Empire, which extended its control over much of the Islamic world during a time frame from roughly 1400-1800.[7]

One key feature of Ottoman legal code was that it placed little emphasis on *hadith* in its application of Islamic law, which would become a major issue with the various reform movements that arose after 1800.[8] The Maliki school developed next, arising in Medina in the Hijaz region of modern Saudi Arabia.[9] This school is named for Malik ibn Anas, who studied under Abu Hanifa.[10] Scholar Alfonso Carmona writes that the teachings of the Maliki school fall into two categories: the transmission…of Medinan legal traditions and the explanation of [Malik's] own *ra'y*, a term translatable as judicial reasoning".[11] Thus, this school focuses on the practices of the first community of Muslims and Malik's own reasoning to determine how they should live as Muslims. Like the Hanafis, the Malikis do not place much emphasis on *hadith* in their jurisprudence.[12] They do so because the *hadith* sometimes have unreliable *isnads*, or chains of narrators. This allows for people to sometimes "put words into the Prophet Muhammad's mouth".[13] This potential unreliability is why both the Hanafi and Maliki schools focused on other forms of jurisprudence besides *hadith*.

Maliki jurisprudence, tracing its scholarly lineage back to Abu Hanifa, was able to exist alongside Hanafism and especially flourished in the Maghreb region of North Africa (modern Morocco, Algeria, and Tunisia).[14] The Shafi'i *maddhab* adopts a hybrid approach that synthesizes elements from the Hanafis and the Malikis.[15] This school is named for its' principal scholar, Muhammad ibn Idris Ash-Shafi'i, more commonly known as al-Shafi'i.[16] He was born in the same year that Abu Hanifa died and studied under Malik ibn Anas. He began his career as a Maliki jurist, but studies in Iraq led him to adopt some Hanafi principles as well.[17] One of the most distinguished Shafi'I contributions to Islamic law was *usul al-fiqh*, or a focus the sources of Islamic law.[18] *Usul al-fiqh* provides sources of Islamic law, gives a method for interpreting those sources, and then provides a system for distinguishing scholars from Islamic lay people.[19] Another example of the Shafi'I hybrid approach comes from how they determine *ijma*, or consensus, about jurisprudential issues. For the Malikis, *ijma* comes from the practices of the people of Medina.[20] But a Shafi'I can find *ijma* anywhere in the Islamic world, which would include *qiyas* (which is favored by the Hanafis).[21] Another important feature that distinguishes the Shafi'i school from its Maliki and Hanafi counterparts is that for a Shafi'i, "only the Qur'an can explain the Qur'an".[22] This means that only work from the Qur'an can override something written in the Qur'an. *Hadith*, *qiyas*, *ijma*, and any other source of jurisprudence is subordinate to the Qur'an. The Shafi'i hybrid approach also allowed it to co-exist alongside the Hanafi and Maliki *maddhab*s, becoming especially prevalent in Egypt, as well as Yemen, Lebanon, Syria, and Palestine.[23]

The Hanbali school differs greatly from the three *maddhab*s previously discussed because the Hanbalis place a strong emphasis on hadith as a source of jurisprudence.[24] Abu 'Abd Allah Ahmad b. Muhammad ibn Hanbal is the scholar credited with starting this school.[25] According to scholar Abdul Hakim Al-Matroudi, Ibn Hanbal ""granted precedence to sound *hadith* over practice [*amal*] *ra'y* [analogy in any form], and *ijma* [consensus]".[26] Thus, all non-revealed sources of law were de-emphasized.[27] Ibn Hanbal sought to use analogy only as a last resort, using unverified *hadith* or *hadith* with weak *isnads* if there was no definitive evidence to disprove them.[28] Ibn Tayymiyah, a jurist who became popular among the Wahhabis, was also a leading proponent of the Hanbali *maddhab*. His ideas, however, were not shared by the contemporary ruling elite in Damascus and he was jailed and eventually exiled to Egypt.[29] Thus, the Hanbalis were not as popular as other schools were in the Levant. Ibn Tayymiyah's reformist mindset earned the local ruler's enmity and thus Hanbalis faced a less receptive atmosphere in the Levant. The Hanbali School did, however, take hold in Arabia and the Persian Gulf region, which would serve as the epicenter of one important Islamic reform movement: Wahhabism.[30]

"Modernity" and Crisis

From the eighth century CE until the nineteenth century CE, the four schools of Islamic jurisprudence were the main sources for Muslims to determine how they should live their lives. But during the nineteenth century, the arrival of "modernity" fundamentally altered this worldview and shook it to its core. Scholar Johnathan Brown attributes this shake-up to the arrival of colonialism and Western ideas, with subsequent reform Islamic movements emerging out of Islamic interactions with European people and ideas. Brown divides these movements into four categories: the Late Sunni Traditionalists, Modernist Salafism, Traditionalist Salafism, and Islamic Modernism.[31]The Late Sunni Traditionalists are embodied by the four *maddhabs* that were explained in the previous section, while the other three categories are reform groups with some similarities and overlap but also a considerable degree of difference."

Brown describes the arrival of the West and its ideas, known as "Modernity", as a fundamental struggle for Muslims because they had not experienced nor adapted any form of Modernity until they encountered the modern West. Muslims saw themselves as the chosen people of God, but they still found themselves crushed under the boot of the West.[32] European technology greatly aided their conquest of the Muslim world. Scholar Marilyn Waldman writes that the British had taken over India by 1818, and over the next hundred years extended their control over much of the rest of the Muslim world, especially with the establishment of British and French mandates after World War I.[33] Even the Ottoman Empire was forced to adapt to modernity. The Tanzimat, a reform period stretching from 1839-1878, gave all Ottoman subjects equality under the law and limited the power of the sultan, ideas which were in *vogue* in Europe at the same time period.[34] Perhaps the most notorious example of European technological supremacy is the Battle of Omdurman in 1898. British forces used machine guns to mow down thousands of Sudanese Muslims resisting British conquest as part of the Mahdist movement that opposed British expansion into the Sudan out of Egypt.[35]

Once European authority had been established, the colonizers gradually moved to replace Islamic law with European style law. The motive for doing so was primarily to ensure that European power rested on more than brute military strength. Implementing European-style law also allowed for colonizers to extend economic control over Muslim nations as well.[36] This process began in British India in 1772 at the behest of the British East India Company. A process known as the Hastings Plan created a multi-tiered legal system with British administrators at the highest level, British administrators who conferred with local Muslims judges at the second level, and solely Muslim judges at the bottom level. Inherent in the Hastings Plan design is the notion that Muslim laws could be subsumed by British legal codes, which always took precedence over local customs. This process was formed by the Orientalist notion that Muslim (and Hindu) law was essentially "a mass of individual opinions" and has no systematic nature, which required a European legal system to establish some semblance of order.[37]

The establishment of European "order" essentially stripped Muslim judges of their ability to interpret Islamic law and instead forced them to adhere to European (more specifically in this case British) notions of law. In the 1780s and 1790s, British administrators essentially removed all influence of Islamic law when it came to enforcing laws related to homicide, on the grounds that Islamic law granted "extra-judicial privileges" to the victim's next of kin.[38] Hallaq writes that by 1861, there was essentially no trace of Islamic law left in British India, with Muslim judges being forced to look to higher courts in British India and in Great Britain itself for guidance about interpreting laws, instead of the Quran.[39] This matters because it muddied the idea of what it meant to be Sunni. Although Sunnis comprise the majority of Muslims, not all Muslims are

Sunni. Thus, when looking at British administration in India, issues pertinent to Sunni Muslims are not automatically applicable to their Shi'i counterparts, making this question one of Sunni identity, as opposed to Muslim identity as a whole. In British India, there were not only four different *maddhabs*, but also European administrators' cherry-picking different areas of Islamic jurisprudence to suit their own ends. This meant that nineteenth century Muslims were confronted with a bewildering and often contradictory set of principles about how to live their lives. However, this "muddying" of Islamic law was not exclusive to India. The Ottoman Empire also experienced profound changes in its legal system after it made contact with Europeans. As early as the 1720s, the Ottoman Empire had adopted legal codes that prescribed non-*sharia* punishments. Fariba Zarinebaf analyzed Ottoman court records during this time and found that one-third of crimes associated with theft (i.e. larceny, burglary, and property theft) were punished with forcible conscription as oarsmen in Ottoman galleys.[40] This may come as a surprise to those with a shallow depth of knowledge about Islam and Islamic law, given that *sura* 5:38 of the Qur'an ostensibly prescribes the theft for punishment as amputation of the hand or finger. However, after looking at how the Ottomans actually administered justice, it is clear that such punishments were rarely used.[41]

Corporal punishment, as prescribed by *sharia*, occurred only in times of social upheaval; legal codes were usually highly discretionary.[42] Forced service in galleys was used to punish crimes ranging from owning a tavern to homicide to sex crimes to "selling light bread."[43] Rather than amputate limbs, Ottoman judges made criminals oarsmen in galleys or banished them to islands in the Mediterranean. Prisons were occasionally used to house convicts as well, but it was not very popular.[44] Prisons became more popular as a discretionary punishment towards the end of the nineteenth century as galleys were replaced by different types of ships.[45] As compared to European punishments at the same time, Ottoman punishments were often less severe. I will return again to property crime as an example. While Ottoman judges in Istanbul were sending thieves off to the galleys, England's Parliament passed a law that made theft of linen from textile factories punishable by death. Thus, corporal and capital punishment was codified in European laws, while the Ottomans used capital punishment only against bandits and rebels.[46] This matters because Ottoman law is closest example that we have to how law was practiced in the pre-modern Muslim state at the time of the Prophet.

Any sources prior to the Ottomans are too sparse to provide definitive information about pre-modern Islamic legal practices. Fundamental differences in how Islamic law and Western law operate exacerbated the crisis of muddied ideas of Islamic law. European law operates in a positivist manner. This means that the source of law ultimately comes from an individual who imposes that law on others under threat of punishment.[47] Thus, according to positivist law, someone obeys the law because a central authority of some kind told them to, and they will be punished if they do not. According to Wael Hallaq, a modern (see Western) state does not have an obligation to make its citizens morally good. On the contrary, it seeks to rule over a Hobbesian human race that is bent on controlling both the natural world and other humans.[48] Positivist law, above all else, focuses on keeping order and does not seek to have any moral impact on the lives of those who follow it. Islamic law operates under a completely different principle. There are three types of authority in Islam: *amr*, *hujja*, and *taqlid*.[49] Amr is the ability to command, and comes only from God himself.

It can also be delegated by God to an *amir*, or a person who holds such power; the Prophet Muhammad would be an example of an *amir*.[50] *Hujja* roughly translate to the word "authority" and comes from four sources: the Qur'an, the Sunna (sayings attributed to Muhammad, including *hadith*), analogical reasoning, and consensus.[51] Finally, *taqlid* is the authority of judges and men learned in the ways of Islamic jurisprudence, who are called *mujtahid*.[52] Amr supersedes *hujja*, and *hujja* supersedes *taqlid*.[53] The Qur'an provides Muslims with a set of natural laws that are based on morality, according to the principle of *haqq*, which Hallaq describes as "divine truth and justice".[54] Thus, for Muslims, obeying the law is not merely a secular matter. Islamic law is not the code of a mortal man; it is God's own prescription for living a morally good life. Unlike a Western state, an Islamic state enforcing true Islamic law does so in the attempt to make sure that its citizens live morally good lives. Punishment for violating Islamic law thus comes from God, not a human ruler.[55] Thus, Islamic law is not codified and has no uniform or universal standards. A European, who only knows positivist law and its universal potency, would see Islamic law as "arbitrary".

But from the perspective of a practitioner of pre-Modern Islamic law, all of the *maddhabs* and the judges are informed by the Qur'an and seek what is the best moral verdict in a case. Ottoman legal codes were clearly reflective of this trend; avoidance of amputation and emphasis on forced conscription or banishment meant that Ottoman legal punishment was meant to be corrective instead of punitive.[56] This also makes the gradual "phasing out" of Islamic law under European rule all the more devastating for Muslims. Muslims lost more than just a legal code: their entire moral compasses had to be subordinated to European ideas, which placed Muslims judges in situations where they would be forced to rule against their moral convictions because European powers mandated that European law be followed. Here we return to Brown's groupings of Sunni Muslims. The "late Sunni traditionalists" placed an even greater emphasis on the *maddhabs* and their related legal scholarship in response to the arrival of Western-style "modernity", thus maintaining the status quo when it came to the interpretation of Islamic law.[57] Many Muslims continued to follow their chosen *maddhab*.

Modernist Salafism

Modernist Salafism is the third major Islamic reform movement with its roots in the colonial era. It sets itself apart from Ottoman legal practices in that Modernist Salafism, and Salafism as a whole, bypasses the centuries of legal scholarship that emerged after the time of the Prophet. The term "Salafism" comes from the Arabic word *salaf*, or the first generations of Muslims. A Salafi, in a broad sense, is anyone who believes that the earliest generations of Muslims embody Islam in its purest form.[58] Modernist Salafis believed in the same core principles as Late Sunni Traditionalists, but took a markedly different approach to reform than the Late Sunni Traditionalists. Led by scholars like Muhammad Abduh' and Rashid Rida, Modernist Salafis believed that many *hadith* were unreliable.[59] However, instead of discarding the *hadith* in its entirety, Modernist Salafis like Abduh' and Rida wanted to reexamine the *hadith*.[60] Muhammad Abduh' believed that *mutawatir hadith* needed to be obeyed. A *mutawatir hadith* is one that can be traced back to the Prophet Muhammad via multiple *isnads* (*sahih*).[61]

Since *hadith* of this variety are doubtlessly the word of Muhammad, and by extension God, they can be considered valid. However, most *hadith* are non-*mutawatir*, and thus Abduh' believed that they required some form of reexamination. Because of their dubious authenticity, Abduh' also believed that no Muslim should be compelled to believe non-*mutawatir hadith* (also known as *ahad*) or called an apostate for refusing to follow them.[62] This would also allow for Muslims to both adhere to core Islamic beliefs while also embracing European customs and modes of thought. Abduh' also rejected much of the body of traditional Muslim scholarship after the salaf and sought to discern his own interpretations instead.[63] Rashid Rida was Abduh's senior student and successor to his thought. Rida believed the same things as listed previously about the *hadith* that Abduh' did, but also added to Abduh's ideas. Rida thought that *hadith* containing *isra'iliyyat* should not be accepted because modern (see Rida's contemporary) scholars had the advantage of comparing such *hadith* to actual Jewish scripture, a luxury that earlier scholars lacked.[64] Rida further clarified Abduh's point about *ahad hadith* by stating that because so many of the *ahad hadith* contradict or fail to support one another, they cannot be believed as the sole basis of faith. Rida's example was a *hadith* which stated the after the sun sets, it prostrates itself before God. Since this contradicted modern science, but was an *ahad hadith*, it does not need to be believed.[65] In other words, making *ahad hadith* "optional" allowed for Modernist Salafis like Abduh' and Rida to ensure that Islamic beliefs and European modernism were not mutually exclusive and thus embrace both modernity and Islam to a limited extent. Modernist Salafis responded to colonialism by changing or rejecting parts of Islamic practice that ran counter to the ideals of Modernity.

Traditionalist Salafism

Traditionalist Salafis are similar to Modernist Salafis in that they both looked to the earliest generations of Muslims for guidance about how to live their lives. However, Traditionalist Salafis differed greatly from their Modernist Salafis in that they focus on *hadith* exclusively as their way of returning to the ways of the *salaf*.[66] Muhammad ibn 'Abd al-Wahhab, the ideological father of Wahhabism, is one iteration of a Traditionalist Salafi reformer.[67] Traditionalist Salafis discard *hadith* entirely if they have been proven to be weak by scholarly analysis. This idea is best embodied by the claims of reformer Muhammad Nasir al-Din al-Albani.[68] An important feature of Traditionalist Salafism is its absolute trust in *mutawatir hadith* and other *hadith* that have not been proven unreliable.[69] Thus, belief in proven (or simply not yet *un*proven) *hadith* is a requirement for a Muslim to be considered a true Muslim. This is important because it applies to both *mutawatir* and *ahad hadith*.[70] Thus, Traditionalist Salafism takes a much stricter view of a Muslim's obligation to obey *hadith*. This also means that evaluation of *hadith* needs to happen constantly, and that the words of previous generations of scholars regarding a *hadith's* authenticity or reliability do not need to be blindly accepted.[71] This narrow view of what constitutes proper sources of faith for Muslims may also create Salaficentric ideas of what it means to be Muslims. Traditionalist Salafis are often at odds with Late Sunni Traditionalists. Traditionalist Salafi bypassing of centuries of Muslim legal scholarship leads Late Sunni Traditionalists to level accusations of arrogance against Traditionalist Salafis.[72] In terms of responding to modernity, Traditionalist Salafis choose not to adopt any European ideas at all and instead place more stock in their own faith and religious texts.

Wahhabism

Wahhabism, as briefly touched upon in the previous section, is a Traditionalist Salafi reform movement. It overlaps with Salafism in that both choose to disregard anything that is not *salaf*, which includes centuries of Islamic scholarship and adherence to any of the *maddhabs*.[73] Both Wahhabis and Traditionalist Salafis also reject Sufism in its entirety because they deem it an aberration.[74] It constitutes *bid'a* ("innovation"), or any custom created after the third century of Muslim scholarship.[75] Wahhabis themselves actually prefer to be called "Ahl al-Tawhid", or "asserters of divine unity".[76] *Tawhid* is a concept loosely translated as "oneness", especially belief in the oneness of God. Any monotheistic religion has its own equivalent of *tawhid*, or an interpretation as to what the idea of "one deity" might mean. Since Wahhabis prefer to classify themselves by this term, they view themselves as strong believers in the oneness of God. For Wahhabis, *tawhid* has three distinct parts. The first is *tawhid al-rububiyya*, which states that God alone holds the title of lord (*rabb* in Arabic).[77] The second is *tawhid al-asma wa 'l-sifat*, which scholar Hamid Algar describes as "a simple affirmation of God's name without interpretation".[78]

The third part of *tawhid* is *tawhid al-'ibada*, or the worship of God exclusively. Algar states that this is the most important part of tawhid, because anyone who fails to do this is not a true Muslim.[79] One extremely important implication of these beliefs is that Wahhabis, like Traditionalist Salafis, are at odds with Late Sunni Traditionalists because the two groups reject the entire foundation of Late Sunni Traditionalism; namely, the four Sunni *maddhabs*. Another important connection between Traditionalist Salafis and Wahhabis comes in the form of Rashid Rida[80]: he was one of the first non-Saudi scholars to throw his support behind the Saudi State, which adhered to Wahhabi beliefs.[81] However, despite Wahhabi connections with Traditionalist Salafism, the two are not synonymous. Nor are they interchangeable. Wahhabism sharply diverges from Traditionalist Salafism, and all the other Islamic reform movements in this essay, in the way it treats other Muslims and non-Muslims. A Late Sunni Traditionalist may quarrel with his Modernist and Traditionalist Salafi peers, and they may quarrel with him. However, none of those three groups regards the other's approach to Islam as false or heretical. They may disagree, but they do not try to force their views on other Muslims. Instead, they focus on attempting to persuade people to take their view with argument.[82]

This is not so with Wahhabis. If you disagree with the Wahhabi view of what it means to be Muslim (see the three portions of *tawhid*), it is more than a religious argument. Muhammad ibn 'Abd al-Wahhab himself referred to jurists who opposed his ideas as "the spawn of Satan".[83] Failing to follow a literal reading of Wahhabi monotheism means that, in the eyes of a strict Wahhabi, you are a heretic or an apostate.[84] This is a problem because an apostate forfeits their life and property by committing apostasy, which means that their deaths and seizure of their property at the hands of "true believers" is justified.[85] Wahhabis also have an extremely broad view of what constitutes apostasy and heresy. Any form of innovation, or *bid'a*, was considered apostasy.[86] Wahhabis considered rationalist thought as a construct imposed by the Greeks, Sufism as a Persian ancillary to "pure Islam", and that veneration of grave sites came from Turkey and not the Prophet Muhummad's original entourage.[87] Wahhabis view anything and everything that did not come from the first three generations of Muslims (the *salaf*) as *bid'a* and thus apostasy.

This fixation on the ways of the *salaf* also lends Wahhabism an ethnocentric character: it holds the Bedouin lifestyle (which was nomadic and very different from the lives of non-Bedouin Muslims) of the *salaf* as superior to all other forms of living.[88] Wahhabis believe that Muslims were humiliated by colonial conquests because Muslims had strayed away from the lifestyle that God wanted them to take. Wahhabis could regain God's favor and thus beat back Europeans if they returned to the lifestyle of the *salaf* that God intended.[89] Finally, there is no middle ground for a Muslim: they are either an apostate or they are not.[90] Being classified as an apostate was a damning absolution. It is worth noting that Wahhabi intolerance has managed to manifest itself militarily at various points in Saudi history. An example is the wholesale slaughter of the city of Karbala in modern Iraq in the early nineteenth century by Saudi Wahhabi forces, as well as the desecration of numerous religious sites. It was a center of Shi'ite worship and thus "apostasy", which made genocide and plunder acceptable[91] A similar massacre happened in Ta'if in the Hijaz region of Saudi Arabia in 1803, where all books that were not the Qur'an and *hadith* burned on top of the slaughter of inhabitants.[92] Furthermore, when Saudi-Wahhabi forces captured Mecca, they demolished various domes and mausoleums over the graves of the Prophet Muhammad's family and Companions because worship at such shrines constituted *bid'a*.[93]

But in spite of Wahhabism's intolerant and even pro-Arab ideas, it has managed to become popular in contemporary times among Muslims across the world. How can this be? The answer lies in the history of Saudi Arabia as a state. Both Wahhabism and the modern Saudi States had their origin in the Najd region of Saudi Arabia, which is essentially the interior of the modern Saudi state.[94] Scholar David Commins describes Najd as a "remote backwater of Arabia where the tradition of scholastic learning was shallow". Much of the population was illiterate and mainly worked as nomads herding animals or as subsistence farmers in small towns. Only the ulama, or religious scholars, were educated.[95] Hamid Algar likewise describes Najd as "intellectually marginal".[96] This also meant that none of Islam's great empires, i.e. the Ottomans, had ruled Najd.[97] Thus, Najdi intellectual tradition, which grew to become Wahhabism, was free to develop on its own, free of outside influences but also preventing the spread of its tradition beyond the confines of Arabia. All of this changed with the ascendancy of the Sa'ud family. Muhammad ibn 'Abd al-Wahhab[98] briefly studied in the Hijaz and largely bounced around Najd, failing to find a permanent home as a member of the ulama due to his extreme ideas.[99] Al-Wahhab was even chastised and expelled from the town of Huraymila by his father. This came after al-Wahhab's zealous exportation of his ideas in the local community of al-Uyayna got his entire family kicked out of the town (of al-Uyayna).[100] Al-Wahhab later married into a prominent family of al- Uyayna, but was also expelled due to his destruction of the tomb of Zayd ibn al-Khattab, one of Muhammad's companions, as well as for stoning to death a woman accused of adultery.[101]

However, this proved very convenient because al-Wahhab next landed in al-Dir'iyya, where the Sa'ud family was planning to take over Najd. The Sa'ud family under Muhammad ibn Sa'ud offered al-Wahhab protection in exchange for his sanction of their expansion across Najd.[102] In this way, Saudi expansion across Najd meant that not only would it expand Muhammad ibn Sa'ud's secular control, it was also a *jihad* against people who failed to share al-Wahhab's vision of Islam.[103] However, the Ottomans and Egyptians managed to keep the Wahhabi-Saudi alliance under control for much of the eighteenth and nineteenth centuries.[104] The modern state of Saudi Arabia needed the help of a colonial power in order to take shape. The British first made contact with the Saudi-Wahhabis in 1865 and gave them money and weapons in an attempt to help destabilize the Ottoman Empire.[105] The culmination of the British and Saudi-Wahhabi alliance came during World War I, when the head of the Saudi family, Ibn Sa'ud, was knighted in 1915.

His troops also received extensive training and financial backing from the British.[106] Ibn Sa'ud turned his British-trained troops into an elite shock force called the Ikhwan and used them to wipe out his main rival for control of the Arabian peninsula, Sharif Husayn of Mecca.[107] Once political control of Arabia was consolidated under Saudi rule, the Saudi state ensured that Wahhabi beliefs became the only accepted norm, at the cost of 40,000 public executions and 350,000 amputations.[108] However, when the Saudis tried to expand into Iraq, the British used the Royal Air Force to stop Saudi expansion and thus prevent Saudi control and Wahhabi ideas from spreading beyond Arabia. Oil proved to be the decisive factor in allowing for the expansion of both Saudi political influence and Wahhabi ideas abroad.[109] Saudi oil money built schools and mosques in other Muslims nations that were taught by Wahhabi preachers or supporters, which is what has allowed their ideas to gain traction abroad[110], in spite of Wahhabism's original, puritanical tendencies. Wahhabis also promote their beliefs abroad via organizations like the Muslim World League and student organizations like the Muslim Student Organization of North America.[111]

The Saudi state also played a pivotal role in supporting other like-minded Traditionalist Salafi groups. One of the most important of these Salafi groups is the Muslim Brotherhood, founded in Egypt in 1928.[112] The early Muslim Brotherhood shared Wahhabi resistance to Modernity's influence over Muslims and championed Islam as not only "the true religion" but also an effective way to run secular affairs.[113] However, this also meant that also took on a distinctly nationalistic character.[114] The Muslims Brotherhood not only opposed the British government in Egypt, but also the Nasser regime that took power in the 1950s. This helped turn the Brotherhood down a more confrontational path, with Sayyid Qutb stating that contemporary modern society existed in a state of *jahiliyya*, or religious barbarism, a view consistent with Wahhabism.[115] As Nasser became popular as a pan-Arab nationalist figure, the Muslim Brotherhood and Wahhabi-Saudi state established a close relationship, with the Muslim Brotherhood acting as a Wahhabi proxy that combatted non-religious Arab nationalism.[116]

During the 1960s, King Faysal spread Wahhabi influence even further by establishing the World Muslim League to promote Muslim (see Wahhabi) values and ways of living, which spread its influence throughout the Middle East and West Africa through the establishment of mosques and schools built with Saudi oil money.[117] This now bring us to the present and pressing dilemma of so-called "Islamic radicalism". By now, it is evident that Wahhabism can be intolerant and has spread rapidly over the last two hundred years and especially in the twentieth century. However, this spread has not come with a universal notion of what Wahhabi practice and monotheism looks like. As a result, the disparate groups that the Wahhabis patronize have differing ideas of what it means to be a true Sunni Muslim. The Soviet invasion of Afghanistan in the 1980s showed how far Wahhabi ideas had spread in Muslim nations worldwide. The *jihad* against the Soviets in Afghanistan incubated many groups that shared puritanical Wahhabi views. One of the most important was the MAK, or Maktab al-Khidmat. This group was founded by Abdullah Azzam, a respected cleric who studied at prestigious religious schools like al-Azhar in Cairo and Damascus University.

Its purpose was to bring Arabs to fight in Afghanistan, as part of their duty, as both individuals and as members of Muslim society, to defend Islam from outside attack.[118] The group was financed by a wealthy young Saudi named Osama bin Laden, who used his financial leverage to gain more control over MAK and take power away from Azzam. With the blessing of the Saudi (see Wahhabi) grand *mufti*, or judge, bin Laden built training camps to educate MAK fighters on both warfare and Islam (of the Wahhabi variety). Bin Laden also helped facilitate communication between various MAK fighters after the Soviets withdrew from Afghanistan in 1989.[119] This had two main benefits for bin Laden and groups who share Wahhabi beliefs. The first was that the MAK fighters now had a clear vision of what "pure" Islam, molded into shape by teachers who were Wahhabis or supported Wahhabi beliefs. The second was that the fighters now had the training and the means to coordinate their efforts to bring about pure Islam elsewhere in the Muslim world, which became the main goal of al-Qai'da after bin Laden formed it in 1988.[120]

Eli Alschech's analysis of "Salafi-jihadis" in Jordan provides a compelling case study of different Wahhabi-influenced groups that fall under the "Salafi-jihadi" umbrella, al-Qai'da included. Alshech defines a Salafi-jihadi as a rejection of traditional Salafism that embraces violence as both an inevitable and acceptable means of defending Islam against from both the West and the ruling elite of Muslims nations.[121] The end goal of Salafi-jihadis is to "purge Muslim society of immorality and non-Islamic practices", after which only a pure form of Islam remains.[122] Like Wahhabis and Traditionalist Salafis, Salafi-jihadis view pure Islam as the first three hundred years of Muslim scholarship and nothing else.[123] However, unlike the Wahhabis in the Arabian Peninsula, Salafi-jihadis are hostile toward the ruling elite of any Muslim nation. In Jordan, Salafi-jihadism began to take shape in the 1990s under two men: Abu Muhammad al-Maqdisi and Abu Mu'sab al-Zarqawi. During the early 1990s, al-Maqdisi was the more respected scholar of the two.[124] Originally, the Salafi-jihadi movement in Jordan was more focused on a refusal to participate in Jordanian society, which they viewed as un-Islamic.[125]

Declarations of *takfir* (declaring other Muslims to be apostates) were few and far between. However, all of that changed when al-Zarqawi went to Afghanistan in the late 1990s. Al-Zarqawi studied different Salafi thinkers like Sayyid Qutb, and adopted Qutb's views. This meant that any Muslim who lives in an area controlled by apostates (Western or non-Western) is an apostate simply by virtue of their ruler's apostasy.[126] This applies to any form of non-Islamic governance: democracy, communism, and even ba'athism (Arab nationalism along the lines of Nasser).[127] Another important idea that al- Zarqawi adopted was that making war on apostates in Muslim-majority lands was a more important struggle than making war on the West. War should be waged in the West only after pure Islamic rule returns to Muslim-majority lands.[128] al-Maqdisi strongly disagreed and wrote that Salafi-jihadis should take the "utmost care" to avoid hurting Muslims, despite the fact that these Muslims may be sinners.[129] al-Maqdisi wanted to focus Salafi-jihadi efforts on fighting the West, and that attacking Muslims was an illegitimate *jihad*.[130]al-Zarqawi also placed an emphasis on piety as a measure of being a true Muslim, as opposed to al-Maqdisi's emphasis on scholarship. For al-Zarqawi, a person who lacks "uncompromising zeal" is not properly religious and thus an apostate. This attracted many recruits to al-Zarqawi's camp.[131] The split between was also accentuated by the return of Jordanian participants in the Afghan-Soviet War in the 1980s, who favoured views along the lines of al-Zarqawi's.[132] After al-Zarqawi was given command of al-Qaida in Iraq in 2003, his camp splintered off from al-Maqdisi's Jordanian Salafi-jihadis. Alschech gives them the label "Neo-Takfiris" due to their revival of Sayyid Qutb's thought and emphasis on *takfir*.[133]

Conclusion

It is clear that Islamic reform movements since 1800 cover an entire spectrum of beliefs, and respond to modernity, as introduced by Europeans, in a similarly broad manner of beliefs. As Lumbard points out, the most popular reform movements (i.e. Modernist and Traditionalist Salafis, as well as the Wahhabis) tend to either completely embrace European ideas at the expense of European ideas or utterly reject them.[134] The intolerant and ethnocentric nature of certain reformist factions also make it extremely difficult to reconcile any reform movements with the "status quo" as embodied by the Sunni Traditionalists. Thus, Sunni Muslims, who make up 85-90 percent of all Muslims, do not have any concrete, mutually agreed upon idea of what it means to be a Sunni Muslim. Not only does this divide Muslims themselves, it also make it extremely difficult, if not impossible, to explain what a Muslim is to other people in the world. So, this also means that Western scholars, when studying Islam, also fail to grasp what it means to be Muslim. The fundamental problem is that instead of trying to work out an answer to that question themselves, the West arrogantly reverts to Orientalist assumptions and stereotypes about what it means to be Muslim.

Despite of the ever-changing and even nebulous nature of Sunni Islam, the West make its own monolithic image of Islam and deems the Western conception of Islam as the true nature of Islam. This happens in spite of the fact that the West has largely created the issue of identity among Sunni Muslims due to their imposition of European governmental and legal structures on Muslim peoples and nations that operated in a fundamentally different way than such structures did in the West. The single most important impact of the various Islamic reform movements of the nineteenth century is the Salafi-Wahhabi leveling of Islamic religious authority. Without the *maddhabs* to provide some semblance of structure to interpret Islamic texts and practices, a menagerie of different views proliferate. This allows for groups like ISIS, the successor group to al-Zarqawi's al-Qaida in Iraq, to claim that they can create a "caliphate" that rules with a positivist interpretation of Islamic law.

However, Wael Hallaq showed that Islamic law has a moralistic fiber and is thus incompatible with a Western notion of a state. When a group like ISIS, or even the Wahhabi marriage to the Saudi state, attempts to set religious doctrine, Islam ends up being twisted to suit their own narrow doctrinal views. Late Sunni Traditionalists, through their respect and active contribution to well over a millennium of Islamic scholarship, are able to respond to maintain their faith in the face of Modernity without resorting to violence. The authority of the *maddhabs* and connected legal scholarship provides the necessary continuity. The West assumes that Salafism, Wahhabism, and terrorism are all the same, while failing to see the truth: Western ideas created an atmosphere that made Muslims feel compelled to reform.

That atmosphere produced a bewildering variety of different movements that all look similar at first glance but in reality are quite different. Marshall Hodgson points out that around 1800, Western nations and institutions were just beginning to take a dominant position on the world stage. They seemed to have forgotten that Islamic nations and institutions had been more advanced than European ones for hundreds of years prior to 1800.[135] However, the West treats them all Muslims as the same and thus utterly fails to understand Muslims at all and reverts to Islamophobic and Orientalist conceptions of Islam as compensation. But the question of identity in Sunni Islam still remains. The idea of innovation once again comes to the fore. Wahhabi and some Salafi groups condemn anything outside the practice of the *salaf* as *bid'a*, or innovation. Innovation was also a key part of Western thought at the advent of Modernity. Authority came not from tradition but rather from individual discovery[136], a trend reflected by the scholarship of Muhammad Abduh.[137] The problem with this view is that tradition, i.e. of the different *maddhabs*, becomes *bid'a*, or innovation, in the eyes of Wahhabi and some Salafi groups. The legal tradition of the *maddhabs* spans more than a millennium and answers important questions that the *salaf* did not. But when this body of scholarship is rejected by Salafi and Wahhabi groups, something needs to fill the gap. Salafis and Wahhabis inadvertently fill this gap with Western/Modernist ideas, which completely changes the type of Islam that they practice. Thus, a contemporary Sunni Muslim is ultimately someone who respects the authority of not only their own chosen Islamic tradition, but Islamic tradition in general.

Chapter 14

Understanding PKK, Kurdish Hezbollah and ISIS Recruitment in Southeastern Turkey

Kerem Övet, James Hewitt and Tahir Abbas

Abstract

This paper provides an explanation for how the PKK, Kurdish Hezbollah, and ISIS, representing distinct ethno-nationalist, Islamist and ideologically motivated political movements, radicalize and recruit supporters in the regions of Eastern and Southeastern Turkey. In doing so, this paper contributes to ongoing theoretical debates about radicalization and recruitment. This study reveals how various regionally specific structural factors encourage radicalization and recruitment into violent politico-ideological movements. In particular, state oppression of ethnic minorities, economic inequalities, geography, and local demographics. While existing literature on radicalization focuses on push factors (structural) combined with pull factors (ideology), this research demonstrates that structural factors in Eastern and Southeastern Turkey are both push and pull factors in processes of radicalization.

Ideologically distinct radical groups, including the Kurdistan Worker's Party (*Partiya Karkerên Kurdistan*, PKK), Kurdish Hezbollah, and Islamic State of Iraq and Syria (ISIS), arguably recruit from the same populations in Eastern and Southeastern Anatolia. These regions contain the highest rates of participation in the PKK[1] and Kurdish Hezbollah[2] while hosting ISIS cells in Adıyaman, Gaziantep, and Adana.[3] These regions, possessing long and permeable land borders with Syria, Iraq, and Iran, and being extensively affected by large-scale refugee flows, have distinct geopolitical importance for understanding an array of radicalization practices.[4] To comprehend

266

why such diverse radical groups successfully recruit in these particular regions, this study addresses the question: what factors make Eastern and Southeastern Anatolia a fertile recruitment ground for the PKK, Kurdish Hezbollah, and ISIS? Considering how multiple, ideologically diverse groups recruit in this socio-politically and demographically unique context will contribute to furthering theoretical explanations of radicalization and recruitment.

In this explanatory research, we analyze the interplay of various push and pull factors that drive people to join the main radical organizations in these regions. Six in-depth interviews were conducted with individuals with long-standing personal connections or insight into radical organizations in Turkey. These interviews were contextualized with secondary sources that draw upon interviews with group members from the PKK and Kurdish Hezbollah. The findings of this study highlight state oppression, economic struggle, displacement and migration, and particular geographic aspects as influential factors in radicalization that are specific to the Eastern and Southeastern Anatolian regions. We propose a new conceptualization, *structural radicalization*, to draw attention to the locally specific, structural factors that impact individual lived experiences and which are instrumental in radicalization in the two regions. Structural radicalization is distinct from many popular theoretical approaches to radicalization that focus on an individual's radicalization process without an in-depth consideration of the socio-political and systemic context in which a radical group or ideology may appeal to members of an affected population. In this regard, this study challenges and develops commonly held conceptions of radicalization processes.

Besides its theoretical contribution, this research is important for several reasons. First, there are significant restrictions on researching the Eastern and Southeastern regions of Turkey. Apart from the physical dangers in the field, in recent years hundreds of academics have been convicted of "spreading terrorist propaganda" by critiquing military practices in the regions.[5] This has given rise to a lacuna in the literature on radicalization in Turkey. Second, problems of (in)security in Turkey are usually attributed to the PKK and often researched with this bias. As a result, relatively little objective or systematic research is being conducted on radicalization in the Kurdish-majority areas of Turkey. Western academia is also partly responsible for this deficiency in knowledge: while considerable research has been carried out on radicalization in or concerning Western countries, studies of radicalization in Muslim-majority countries are limited. This research directly contributes to filling this gap.

In what follows, we first provide background for the case study. Second, we present the theoretical grounding for the analysis, anchoring the research in debates from the fields of terrorism and civil- and ethnic-conflict studies. Following this, we describe the methodology used in this study, which is qualitative, interpretative, and evaluative. Fourth, we present the findings of the interviews conducted concerning radicalization in Eastern and Southeastern Turkey, under four sub-headings determined by the themes generated from the data: the history of oppression, economics and demographics, internal displacement and migration, and geography. In conclusion, we argue that structural, macro-level factors—such as relative economic deprivation and forced migration stemming from systemic inequalities and military repression, compounded by unique geographic factors—combine to create fertile ground for recruitment to radical organizations at the local level. In these conditions, diverse ideologies compete to recruit from those groups whose loyalty to the state has been eroded.

In line with Mark Sedgwick's recommendations, we do not use the terms "radical" or "radicalization" in any absolute sense.[6]Rather, we specify our continuum and position "radical" in relative opposition to "moderate", wherein "moderate" relates to mainstream, state-sanctioned Turkish norms and values that are underpinned by the rule of Turkish law. As such, our analysis and conceptualization of structural radicalization depict the process of structural and systematic factors unique to the region that compel individuals to think and act in ways that are contradictory to predominant Turkish norms, values, and laws.

Eastern & Southeastern Turkey: An Overview

The Socio-Political Context

Around 64 percent of Southeastern Anatolia, 79 percent of Mideastern Anatolia and 32 percent of Northeastern Anatolia are ethnically Kurdish and Kurdish-Zazas.[7] Apart from the Turks and Arabs, which constitute the largest minority groups in Southeastern Anatolia, there are also a small number of Assyrian and Armenian communities in the region.[8] Additionally, by 2016, Turkey hosted more than 2.7 million Syrian refugees due to the civil war.[9] The Kurdish-majority Eastern and Southeastern regions have the lowest GDP per capita of Turkey, as well as the highest unemployment rates in the country, both in general and among the youth population specifically.[10] Furthermore, studies indicate that Kurds are disproportionately affected by economic crises, are more likely to suffer unemployment, and may face discrimination in the labor market.[11]

The Eastern and Southeastern regions have been dominated by two mass political orientations—Kurdish nationalism and Sunni Islamism— witnessing large swings in electoral support between the pro-Islamic conservative Justice and Development Party (*Adalet ve Kalkınma Partisi*, AKP) and the secular Kurdish-nationalist People's Democratic Party (*Halkların Demokratik Partisi*, HDP). These two parties present different understandings of the "Kurdish Issue". AKP leader President Erdoğan, unlike his predecessors, accepts the existence of Kurdish identity, but positions ethnic identities as subordinate to the uniting supra-identity of Islam, presenting the Kurdish movement as anti-Islamic.[12] The HDP represented ethnic Kurdish nationalism up to 2015; since then, they have shifted the narrative away from ethnicity to focus on citizenship rights for all marginalized and oppressed groups.[13] The end of the Peace Process between the state and the PKK in 2015 and the AKP's lack of support for Kurds fighting ISIS in Syria caused a surge in support for the HDP among Kurds in the first of the 2015 general elections.[14] This prompted the AKP to suppress the HDP and left-wing and Kurdish NGOs, politically and militarily, to appeal to Turkish-nationalist and Islamist voters, resulting in hundreds being imprisoned and thousands being killed in the years since.[15]

A History of Political Violence in Anatolia

The PKK has formed the primary threat to Turkish military security in the Eastern and Southeastern regions since its founding in the 1970s. New conflicts began in the 1980s with the rise of Kurdish Hezbollah. More recently, ISIS emerged and used the Southeast as a passage to Syria, forming cells, and recruiting from the local population.[16] These three organizations are ideologically disparate and each one faces unique challenges in recruiting from the population. Since his imprisonment in 1999, PKK leader Öcalan has shifted the ideological narrative away from that of a vanguard-driven independence movement to democratic confederalism and autonomy; however, in practice, this clashes with the group's long-standing Leninist-Stalinist tendencies.[17] The secular PKK has traditionally struggled to appeal to the predominantly Sunni Muslim Kurds of Anatolia.[18] As such, for pragmatic purposes, the organization has taken a less hostile stance toward Islam in recent years.[19] Turkey's conflict with the PKK is estimated to have cost 40,000 lives and displaced perhaps one million people.[20] Nearly 5,000 deaths have been recorded since the peace process broke down in July 2015, including members of Turkish security forces, PKK militants, and civilians.[21]

Kurdish Hezbollah, founded in Batman, Southeastern Anatolia, cemented itself as the predominant violent Islamist movement in Turkey in the 1980s and 1990s.[22] Inspired by the Iranian Revolution—although Kurdish Hezbollah is a Sunni Islamist group and unrelated to the Lebanese Hezbollah—they sought to initiate an Islamic revolution. They recruited from mosques, primarily focusing on Diyarbakır, where they had an influence over almost all the mosques by the mid-1990s.[23] Hezbollah used violence to predominate other movements and recruited young, often poorly educated people from other Islamist groups.[24] In the late 1980s, along with the establishment of the village guard system, the state supported Hezbollah as a way of mobilizing Kurds against the PKK.[25] Violent clashes followed, dividing Kurdish communities and even families between the opposing organizations.[26] The period between 1991 and 1995 saw the peak of violence between the PKK and Hezbollah, before the latter transitioned away from violence in the 2000s and founded a legal political party, Hüda-Par.[27]

ISIS is a more recent and extreme Jihadi-Salafi organization, with the aim of establishing a caliphate harking back to a seventh-century ideal.[28] Research into ISIS has revealed that the organization managed to build extensive networks in Eastern and Southeastern Turkey.[29] The Southeastern cities of Adıyaman, Diyarbakır, Bingöl, and Muş became recruitment grounds for ISIS, and Adana and Gaziantep were chosen by the organization as assembly grounds.[30] Moreover, the Suruç, Diyarbakır, and Ankara bombings perpetrated by ISIS in Turkey, which resulted in 149 deaths and thousands wounded, were organized in Adıyaman.[31] Additionally, 2015-2016 saw four bombing attacks in Gaziantep in which 66 people lost their lives and hundreds were wounded; all were perpetrated by local branches of ISIS.[32]

Conflicts in Syria and Iraq have had a significant impact on Southeastern Turkey. As of June 2017, more than 53,000 names were on a Turkish list of individuals suspected of attempting to join the conflicts across the border.[33] Opposing ISIS in Syria, the Kurdish People's Protection Units (*Yekîneyên Parastina Gel*, YPG) is an offshoot of the PKK, sharing resources, intelligence, manpower, and ideology.[34] It is estimated that more than 8,500 people joined the YPG from Turkey.[35] Moreover, the Ankara and Bursa attacks carried out by the PKK in 2016 against Turkish civilians have shown an operational connection to Kurdish-majority cantons in northern Syria, where the perpetrators reportedly received military training in YPG camps.[36]

Structural Radicalization in Turkey

This paper proposes a new conceptual focus in the debates on radicalization and non-state political violence, for which we have coined the term *structural radicalization*. Our theoretical approach considers locally specific factors as instrumental in radicalization processes. It emphasizes the importance of aspects of an individual's or community's lived experience that predispose them to join to radical movements. The findings highlight issues that are structural and specific to the Eastern and Southeastern Anatolia regions of Turkey, which contribute to recruitment for the PKK, ISIS, and Kurdish Hezbollah. These are factors, such as state oppression, that in turn produce economic hardships, forced displacement and migration, and cultural suppression, compounded by regional geographic particularities. This research is grounded in, and further develops, theoretical debates from the fields of terrorism and radicalization studies, as well as ethnic conflict and civil war studies.

There is a long-standing debate on how political violence is connected to exclusionary policies and state repression. Piazza's quantitative research found that economic discrimination against minorities significantly increases the likelihood of domestic terrorist attacks,[37] although no significant association was found with religious or linguistic discrimination.[38] Furthermore, Piazza found that state repression, in general, is a stimulating factor for domestic terrorism; however, he also analyzed the impact of various types of repression and found that repression of participation—particularly electoral participation and expression of labor rights—increases domestic terrorism, as do minority discrimination and physical and religious repression.[39] Correspondingly, Matesan's study found that restrictive and exclusionary policies lead Middle Eastern Islamist groups to adopt more violent rhetoric, with the likelihood of violent action increasing when a group feels its physical integrity is imperiled due to state violence or repression.[40]

Karreth et al. found that when civilians are systematically targeted during counter-insurgency campaigns, human rights conditions post-conflict are substantially worse than pre-conflict levels. The systematic targeting of civilians and ensuing poor human rights *leads to* (or *precipitates*) the "dynamic of radicalization and revenge" on behalf of (former) opposition

271

groups: government brutality against civilians produces a more extreme opposition movement, increasing recruitment motivated by revenge and support for armed groups and rebel leaders.[41] Their study supports previous research that highlights how repression drives radicalization and recruitment to terrorist groups by alienating and victimizing members of marginalized groups.[42]

Buhaug et al. measured the association between ethno-nationalist civil war and characteristics of large ethnic groups excluded from power. They not only confirmed that the probability of conflict increases with the exclusion of powerful minority groups, but also found that groups that are located far from the capital and settled in rough terrain are more likely to be involved in ethnic conflict.[43] A large-scale quantitative study by Cederman et al. found that when ethnic groups are excluded from state power, the probability of armed conflict increases.[44] Another study by Cederman et al. analyzed the relationship between transborder ethnic kin (TEK) groups and civil war and concluded that the relative size of a TEK group impacts the likelihood of violence in a curvilinear way—i.e. intermediate-sized ethnic groups, relative to the size of the group holding state power, are most likely to engage in violence. While state control may have a conflict dampening effect for large TEK groups, excluded transborder stateless communities, such as the Kurds, contain greater potential for conflict.[45]

The cross-border nature of Kurdish communities and their geographic context affects operational possibilities for radical groups in the border regions, influencing both recruitment and group sustainability. Eccarius-Kelly highlights that smuggling across the borders with Turkey's neighbors is commonplace and is considered a profession for segments of the population. Turkey's geographic position provides an ideal opportunity for the PKK to significantly bolster its finances through involvement in the illicit drug trade too, although this may damage their image and legitimacy among Kurdish communities.[46] Smuggling activities are dangerous, however, as the Roboski incident in 2011 highlighted; the attack on a group of Kurdish smugglers by the Turkish air force worsened Turkish-Kurdish relations during a peace process that had been gaining momentum at the time.[47]

The discussion thus far has considered the relationships between exclusion from political and economic power, state repression, and political violence. However, radicalization stemming from the macro-structural level must also relate to the individual and their motivations for participation in a violent struggle. State repression can produce (re)constructions of identity narratives that challenge the authority and legitimacy of the state. Such identity constructions, often comprising victimhood narratives that reinforce a process of othering, may suggest a vulnerability to recruitment by radical organizations. Kruglanski et al. explore these themes in their "significance quest" model of radicalization, acknowledging the potential for a "socially based significance loss," observing that "often, experience of significance loss relates to one's social identity that is disrespected by others."[48] This may cause an individual to pursue significance gain through participation in a violent organization.[49] This study builds upon the literature discussed above, furthering our knowledge of the interplay between systemic and structural factors and individual lived experiences in radicalization processes.

Research Design and Methodology

The primary aim of this paper is to explain the fundamental reasons for Eastern and Southeastern Anatolia being a fertile recruitment ground for radical and violent movements by examining various structural factors that can lead to radicalization, thereby advancing theoretical explanations of radicalization and recruitment. By taking a macro-level, region-specific perspective, grounded in the literature discussed above, we expected socio-political, spatial, geographic, economic, and, more broadly, systemic factors to be root causes of radicalization, increasing the likelihood of ideological influences pulling individuals toward specific movements. We predict the demographic and economic factors that are unique to the region to be important elements in this picture of structural radicalization. To test this hypothesis, the research focuses on three major terrorist organizations in the region: the PKK, Kurdish Hezbollah, and ISIS. Other organizations will be excluded from the process due to their limited size and influence, various organizational fragmentations, and difficulties in comparison.

The ideological diversity between these three groups that are all able to recruit from the same population is suggestive of a macro-structural primary cause of radicalization. While quantitative approaches highlight a relationship between political violence and factors relating to economic deprivation, demographics, repression, and distinct geographic features, qualitative analysis is needed to provide a deeper understanding of these dynamics in our localized case study. Therefore, this qualitative research is primarily built on six in-depth semi-structured expert interviews conducted in November and December 2019. The interviewees were selected based on their long-standing personal or professional experience relating to political violence in the Eastern and Southeastern regions of

Turkey. The individuals were also specifically chosen to provide a balanced sample, representing different sides of the political divide and a mixture of prior involvement with the Turkish state (e.g. military) or non-state armed actors (e.g. PKK). A balanced sample improves the validity of the findings, especially considering the sensitive and politicized nature of the subject matter. The interviewees were initially contacted either via intermediate contacts in Turkey or via direct contact through social media, plus one which snowballed from another interview. All of these interviews were face-to-face interviews conducted in Istanbul during late 2019 besides one, which was conducted through Skype due to the interviewee's location at the time. All but one were willing to be recorded and translations from Turkish to English were undertaken by one of the authors. Pseudonyms are used throughout: the focus of this paper is sensitive for Turkish national security discourse and the exposure of the real names of our interviewees may pose a threat to their lives and freedom. Thus, even though the interviewees were willing and prepared to use their real names, we use pseudonyms due to ethical and security reasons.

The first interviewee was Cevdet, who previously directed a commando regiment and Special Forces team in the Eastern and the Southeastern Anatolia regions. After his military service, he became a security studies scholar and adviser, producing several books and other publications. The second interview was conducted with Ali, a journalist with expertise on Kurdish Hezbollah, having researched the group since the 1990s and publishing several books on the "Kurdish issue" and Islamic organizations in Turkey. The third interviewee was Tarık, a professor at one of Turkey's top universities, who researched the "Kurdish issue" between the years 2013 and 2015 but could not reveal the results of his research due to political pressures after the end of the Peace Process between the PKK and Turkish State. He shared the results of his research during the interview. The fourth interview was with Sarp, a journalist and author who has conducted extensive research on ISIS networks in Turkey and has spoken with dozens of ISIS militants and their families. The fifth interview was conducted with Zehra, a former leftist guerrilla fighter from the 1968 generation in Turkey. She is now a writer and a documentary film director in the Eastern and Southeastern Anatolia regions. The final interview was with Baran, an ex-PKK member who was imprisoned for 10 years and later became a writer, exposing the PKK's use of child soldiers and intra-organizational killings.

This study also includes references to a meeting organized to share the results of a research project aimed at finding the reasons for "the radicalization among the Kurdish youth" by the Rawest Research Company based in Diyarbakır, and its top-level employee, Ferhat. Books that contain interviews with (former) group members and local people with direct experience are utilized as valuable secondary sources, such as *Kurdish Hizbullah in Turkey: Islamism, violence and the state* by Mehmet Kurt,[50] *ISIS Networks* by Doğu Eroğlu,[51] *ISIS in Turkey* by İsmail Saymaz,[52] *Looking Behind the Mountain* by Bejan Matur,[53] *It is Not as You Know* by Canan Rojin Akın and Funda Danışman,[54] and *Mehmed's Book* by Nadire Mater.[55] These sources provide valuable contextualization for the findings from our interviews.

One limitation of this research is the relative lack of available primary data relating to ISIS in Turkey and Kurdish Hezbollah. The interviews conducted with Ali and Sarp, and the books written by Saymaz, Eroğlu, and Kurt, highlighted above, constitute the primary building blocks of research on ISIS in Turkey and Kurdish Hezbollah, but there is a relative lack of empirical data about these organizations in academic literature with which to contextualize our findings. Despite gathering data from a balanced sample of interviewees to address validity concerns relating to political bias, as researchers from Turkey and the U.K., we acknowledge the potential risk of unintended bias when interpreting and analyzing the data. Moreover, the region-specific focus limits the generalizability of these findings; in fact, it is the structural, demographic, economic, and geographic uniqueness of the locality that, we argue, make it such a fertile recruitment ground for extremist organizations. However, with many shared structural and systemic dynamics felt across the borders in Iraq and Syria, it will hopefully open a path for further studies, especially on radicalization among ideologically disparate organizations operating in a shared locality and population. More generally, this macro-level, yet qualitative and region-specific, case study approach contributes to the body of knowledge upon which radicalization theory can be tested and refined. In the section that follows, we analyze our findings in light of existing theoretical literature and shed light on the interplay between context-specific push and pull factors.

Findings and Analysis

A range of themes relating to radicalization in Eastern and Southeastern Anatolia emerged from the interviews conducted for this research. These themes can each be understood as elements of a relationship between the push and pull factors of radicalization: pushing an individual away from state-sanctioned Turkish identity, political expression, and rule of law toward radical groups that sanction the use of violence for political and ideological ends. The discussion of our findings, contextualized with references to secondary sources, is structured around the following themes, each describing a dimension of radicalization. First, a history of oppression by the Turkish state encourages marginalization and alienation of Kurds in Eastern and Southeastern Anatolia from Turkish society, reinforcing distinctive identification narratives that can be manipulated by radical groups to recruit. Second, relative economic deprivation pushes individuals toward groups that offer solutions to these inequalities, whether in the form of material gain or a sense of self-worth. Third, displacement and internal migration, often outcomes of state oppression, create a rupture in people's lives, dislocating them from social and familial ties; alienated in a new habitat, the desire for new social networks and purpose make individuals vulnerable to recruitment and radicalization. Fourth, the mountainous terrain and geographic remoteness create factors that affect the likelihood of radicalization: in particular, the proximity to Iraq, Syria, and Iran enables the trans-national movement of people and physical resources, but also nonmaterial elements such as identifications, politics, and ideologies.

History of Oppression

Military Abuses

The following quotation from Professor Tarık encapsulates much of the discussion that follows. Touching on themes of violence, torture, resistance, and the mountainous habitat in which rebel groups operate, it underlines the importance of understanding the context in which radicalization occurs:

It doesn't matter if it is Islamist or Communist... If a culture of protest was formed... I mean going to the mountains, using force, resisting... And if some people have been killed, tortured or jailed for that... The new generation find themselves inside this culture and socialize themselves within this culture. I mean none of the Turks grow up in an environment where the main plan for people is taking a weapon and going to the mountains! You can never find this socialization in İzmir or Aydın, but you can find it in Diyarbakır. The important thing is the environment that you are born in, what you see when you first open your eyes, in which street you socialize, what your family tells you as their memories... As I understand it, since Sheikh Said, the problem of the Kurds is the environment they socialize in.

Radicalization does not happen in a vacuum. The argument that many Kurds in Eastern and Southeastern Anatolia are born and socialized into a cultural environment of resistance against the state is implicitly assumed by our interviewees and the findings explored throughout the rest of this section. Since the 1980 coup and the Turkish operations against the PKK that followed, executions, torture, forced displacements, arbitrary arrests, and murders of Kurdish journalists, activists and politicians became common in the Eastern and the Southeastern Anatolia regions.[56] Although, according to former leftist guerilla fighter Zehra, military abuses predated the 1980 coup: "Even when I was in the Kurdish villages back in the 1970s, the Turkish army was a monster for these people." Military abuses marginalized Kurdish communities. For instance, a PKK member cited by Matur highlights military atrocities as a factor that pushed her toward the PKK:

I was 13 when my village was burned down by the army. The soldiers came at 5:00 am and took all of us out of the village. They stripped all the men naked and started to torture them. My uncle's son had a Qur'an in his hand. The soldiers even took that and threw it onto the fire.[57]

Our interviewee's observation about the impact of the social and cultural environment in which people experience early socialization resonates with the ethnographic research of Neyzi and Darıcı. Their findings underline how childhood experiences of abuses by the military, particularly those affecting the child's parents, continue to have an influence in adulthood.[58] Neyzi and Darıcı refer to the notion of *bedel*: a sense of obligation to repay a historical debt to the sacrifices of the Kurdish community of the 1980s and 1990s. This narrative provides the basis for how the individuals build their morality and produces expectations of reciprocation through political actions.[59] Accounts of abuses by the Turkish military are common, and are consistent with evidence that when civilians are targeted in counter-insurgency campaigns, human rights worsen post-conflict.[60] Such abuses may foment "a dynamic of radicalization and revenge,"[61] particularly when use of torture is overt.[62] Kurdish resentment toward the Turkish state and the AKP has worsened since the end of the Peace Process and the crackdown on the HDP in 2015. As Ferhat of the Rawest Research Company informed one of the authors: "the Kurds are losing their belief in democratic representation", warning that "this might further increase the radicalization in the region."

Secular Reforms

Communities in Eastern and Southeastern Turkey were impacted by Kemalist reforms to religion. One interviewee, Ali, emphasizes how secular reforms failed to penetrate these regions, creating social antagonisms that contributed to Kurdish Hezbollah's increased influence:

Due to several factors, one of them being geography, Turkish modernization could not enter this region. At least, it couldn't succeed. Despite the bans applied by the state, madrassas, lodges, and even the most religious sects have somehow been preserved and continued their existence. Diyanet [the Directorate of Religious Affairs] has become incapable of even in controlling the mosques. Kurdish Hezbollah, since the 1980s, has grown in these mosques.

Over time, these religious distinctions between the Southeastern regions and the rest of Turkey reinforced differences in identity and enabled narratives of religious oppression to act as push factors away from the Turkish state. Islamist groups—such as Hezbollah and, later, ISIS—utilized these narratives to recruit from the regions. For instance, the statement below is from the "39. Koğuş," one of Kurdish Hezbollah's propaganda books:

Since the beginning of this system, it is a structure constructed against Islam. They killed our scholars, mullahs, and sheikhs. This system banned the Qur'an, turned our mosques into military posts and horse shelters. They are the ones who slaughtered Sheikh Said and his friends. Again, they are the ones who banned everything related to Islam. Today, we are here to show that they couldn't succeed. Today, we are here to defend Islam![63]

Kemalist reforms impacted Southeastern regions differently from the more secular West of the country, reinforcing secular-religious identity distinctions. The limited reach of state authority also allowed radical groups to develop in these circumstances. Identity distinctions fomented by repression sow the seeds of radicalization by creating perceptions of alienation and victimization that push people away from state-sanctioned norms. Issues stemming from systematic oppression set the context for the discussion that follows, and marginalization of communities in these regions is often interconnected with other factors emphasized by our interviewees.

Economics and Demographics

The Eastern and Southeastern regions of Anatolia have the lowest GDP per capita and the highest unemployment rate in Turkey, both in the general population and among young people.[64] Several of our interviewees emphasized economic factors that are specific to these regions as causes of radicalization. These primarily relate to the relative economic deprivation compared to other areas of the country, partly stemming from the failure of the state to develop the regions since the Republic's foundation, but socioeconomic class and demographics were also highlighted as relevant factors that exacerbate economic issues and provide opportunities for radical groups to recruit.

Relative Economic Inequality

Cevdet, security studies scholar and ex-Special Forces commander, highlights state failure to provide modernization and economic opportunity, largely due to geography, as a push factor for radicalization:

Neither the Republic nor the Ottoman Empire could have brought modernization to these lands. In urban centers, education and culture have been shaped by local Islamic sects. In the villages, we cannot even mention education. They have never seen a proper service from the state, but have been abandoned by the state. The only means of existence for these people was cross-border smuggling to Iraq, Iran, and Syria, and this has also been prohibited by the Turkish state. There is no place in Hakkari or Şırnak where you can earn money from agriculture; it's all mountains. These people literally have nothing left. In a place such as this, of course a person can radicalize.

Cevdet's argument stresses not only how mountainous terrain impacted socioeconomic development in Turkey but also that the proximity to neighbouring states with porous borders offers opportunities too. Biner highlights that when faced with high unemployment and poverty, cross-border activities become a key aspect of the informal economy in the area.[65] Cevdet's point suggests that the crossover of economic and geographic factors provides both push and pull factors for engagement with illicit behaviours. Fundamentally, economic deprivation compels individuals to seek alternative sources of income. Ali explains how the financial pull of ISIS recruitment appeals in such circumstances:

For some people, it wasn't "terror" that they were participating in. They believed that they would have a new life under the Islamic State, and some of them had it. There are many people from Eastern and Southeastern Anatolia who migrated to Syria or Iraq during the reign of the Islamic State but never participated in clashes. Instead, they became officers at border control, worked as editors in ISIS news agencies, or opened a bakery that cooked food for the fighters. This opportunity that ISIS created, and the money it provided, of course, pulled people. And when you think how close everything was, participation wasn't an issue for the people living in that region.

Ali's point is similarly made by a source cited by Eroğlu (2018), a documentary photographer and researcher from Gaziantep, Southeastern Anatolia:

If money can be made, a person from Gaziantep gets into that business without hesitation, including becoming an Islamist. If you go to villages between Jarabulus and Elbeyli you can find many people voting for HDP but carrying goods for ISIS. This is a commercial relationship; it is not important what you carry, you just do your job and get your money. It might be cigarettes, it might be tea, it might be weapons or drugs… it doesn't matter. Border trade is always like that.[66]

Again, economic opportunity is stressed as a pull factor for joining ISIS, particularly due to convenience for those in the border regions. Another interviewee, Sarp, argues that economic causes are at the root of radicalization:

If you asked an ISIS fighter about his reasons for going to Syria, he would talk about the general cleavage among the society between the religious and the secular. After that, he would probably continue with anti-Western sentiments and, in the end, he would explain everything with the struggle of the Ummah. However, if you get to the deeper thoughts of that person, he would then start to tell you rational things, mainly economic reasons that he may not have understood while joining the organization.

Sarp here argues that religious and ideological narratives may be superficial and, instead, structural economic factors are a root cause of ISIS recruitment. These findings relate to previous studies that emphasize the economic struggles of those in the Eastern and Southeastern regions, highlighting that Kurdish communities are disproportionately hit by economic crises, labour market discrimination, and worsening unemployment and under-employment.[67] Furthermore, our findings underline the relationship between those economic factors and recruitment to radical groups in those regions.

Socioeconomic Status

Some of our interviewees stressed that socioeconomic class is an influential factor in terrorist recruitment. For instance, Tarık highlights the relevance of this factor to PKK recruitment:

Of course, there are examples of people that joined the PKK from college or top universities, but these boys and girls are a small minority among thousands of militants. These people are not the mass target of the PKK. This problem, in the end, is a class issue. If you were a Kurd mixed with the middle or upper class in Turkey, you would not join PKK. At the most you may become a Kurdish nationalist, but that's it, you would not become a terrorist.

Another interviewee, Zehra, also emphasizes this class dimension. She argues that the PKK and HDP, both potential routes for pro-Kurdish political activism, are distinguished by economic class and perceptions of opportunity:

Why would the family of Ahmet Türk [a wealthy senior HDP politician] join the PKK? Is this the same with a child from the suburbs of Şırnak or Cizre? Can Ahmet Türk be the same as these people? This is also a matter of class. Many important people among the tribes became politicians. In other words, these are not the striking power of the PKK. The PKK mainly consists of children from the suburbs because these people have nothing to lose. So, they see their liberation inside the organization.

The arguments about socioeconomic class raised by Tarık and Zehra stress an important point: ideology, in this case Kurdish nationalism, may encourage political activism, but the individual's economic class and social status influence whether that finds expression via the political system or militancy. These findings support Özeren et al.'s study that analyzed records of 2,312 PKK members and found that 78 percent were unemployed before joining, and 71 percent had no employed family member.[68]

These findings highlight a relationship between socioeconomic factors and radicalization, supporting Piazza's research on the relationship between socioeconomic discrimination against minorities and terrorism.[69] People left with limited employment opportunities and insufficient state support in Eastern and Southeastern Turkey tend to become key recruitment targets. Economic circumstance, class, and the possibilities of the transborder black market economy are both push and pull factors in determining associations with radical groups in these regions.

Sociodemographics

The Southeastern Anatolia region has a fertility rate, population growth rate, average household size, and infant mortality rate all above the national average.[70] Five cities in the Eastern and Southeastern regions of Anatolia have the highest infant mortality rates, and they have the highest average number of children per household.[71] In addition, these regions contain the ten highest fertility rate cities in Turkey.[72] Our interviewees emphasized these demographic factors as worsening the economic struggles of those in the region. In particular, the large family size was claimed to impact youth poverty and lack of opportunity, making many vulnerable to recruitment by groups that offer socioeconomic support and status. Baran, an ex-PKK member who has recently published a book on PKK child soldiers, highlights how these issues influence PKK recruitment:

A lot of militants inside the PKK are children. I am talking about at least 20,000 children since the 1980s. Their parents were responsible for them. As a family, you cannot blame this solely on the convincing power of the organization. Especially during the 1990s, the PKK requested one child from every Kurdish family to join the PKK under what they call "compulsory military service," and some of the families even gave their children voluntarily because they were having trouble looking after them. But you should also understand the families: they have eight, maybe nine children and an armed militant comes and wants your child, who cares? I mean, in this context, it would also not matter if it was the PKK or another organization.

Ali likewise suggests family size as a causal factor for the recruitment of children by Hezbollah in the region:

Although Hezbollah may be considered more of an urban organization than the PKK, the overall demographics of the group members are not different. This is because most of the children who have joined Hezbollah were from migrant families who came from the countryside. They had more children than the urbanized people. Most of these children that I talked to told me that they were in search of shelter before participating in the activities of Hezbollah. Probably, the organization gave them the family bliss that they were searching for.

Baran and Ali's observations emphasize how economic and demographic problems combine and can lead to children being cast out, unable to be supported by their families, vulnerable to the lure of a new familial support network provided by a group that offers subsistence and shelter.

Ali's statement also resonates with Kurt's argument that Hezbollah has been successful in cultivating a sense of group belonging while "instilling the notion of *the pursuit of a high ideal* among the less well-educated, socioeconomically disadvantaged and dispossessed youth."[73]

Cevdet also emphasizes the effects of family size, but instead considera the child's perspective and perceptions of status:

One of the main reasons why people join the PKK is because of their families. They have seven to eight children and then they can't look after them. They don't care if they go to school, they don't care what they eat, and they don't even care if they are alive. But the PKK does. For these children, the PKK becomes a "new home," a "new shelter." The organization gives them the chance of being a "national hero," a chance to be a micro-celebrity for a child who can never be an important person otherwise, even for his family. And most importantly, the PKK gives them a weapon. Think of a child who can never play with toys and a child who has never been spoiled in his life... For that child, the feeling of carrying that gun is the same as becoming the king of the world!

This supports Kruglanski et al.'s "significance quest" model of radicalization.[74] An undervalued child in a large but poor family, with little possibility of prosperity, may feel insignificant and lack foreseeable opportunities to improve their status. If an organization offers the chance to become a "national hero" or "micro-celebrity," in addition to financial support, shelter, and a social network, then this is a significant pull factor. Thus, economic and demographic factors combine to both push and pull toward radicalization. When combined with a perceived significance loss at the communal level—identified with the individual's religious or ethnic group—joining an organization such as the PKK, Hezbollah or ISIS provides not only a path for significance for the individual but also a group identity. The pull of this significance quest is therefore twofold and relates individualistic motivations to group victimization narratives.

Internal Displacement and Migration

The conflict with the PKK in the 1990s led to the Turkish military displacing approximately 3,500,000 people, predominantly Kurds, by forcibly evacuating almost 3,500 villages and hamlets, although these figures vary considerably depending on the source.[75] This led to an influx of migration to the cities of Southeastern Anatolia. Diyarbakır, for instance, saw its population increase from 381,000 to over 800,000.[76] The displacements removed communal and kinship networks, exacerbating unemployment and poverty.[77] Displacement and migration emerged as common themes from our interviewees, underlining how these dynamics were exploited by radical organizations.

Tarık highlights how those who were "reterritorialized" from the villages to the cities of the regions may become reliant on a radical group as a replacement for their lost socioeconomic networks:

If you want to talk about the radicalization in the Eastern and the Southeastern Anatolia regions of Turkey you should talk about the story of people who were reterritorialized. The terrorist organizations appear to be a path for the people who couldn't join the "main formula of happiness" in Turkey. You can call this the "Turkish Dream." Only the mainstream Kurds join this formula: the ones living in centers, or the ones who are integrated after immigration. But the others... I mean the ones who are taken from their lands and put into a city without anything, these people lose all of their socioeconomic networks. For those people, the only thing they can lean on is an organization. It doesn't matter if it is the PKK or ISIS. The organization and the things it gives, only that matters... If a person's inclination to become a radical is at level three when he is in his village, then it is at level fifteen when he migrates to a city.

The reference to the "Turkish Dream" and how, for many Kurds, this is an unobtainable ambition, relates again to Kruglanski et al.'s "significance quest" model of radicalization.[78] If the "main formula of happiness" is not possible due to "reterritorialization" and being uprooted from their socioeconomic networks, individuals may gain a sense of self-worth by joining a radical organization. Ali highlighted the same point, emphasizing that the internally displaced are a recruitment target for radical groups in the region, regardless of ideology: "How do you think that ISIS and the PKK, or the PKK and Hezbollah, recruit people from the same families? You know, there are many families whose two sons went to different organizations that are fighting against each other. This is not a coincidence. This is because they recruit from the same mass: from the ghettos, among the poor people who have just arrived in cities and who are searching for an identity or searching for a place to get rid of their loneliness. This is the same in Diyarbakır, in Adıyaman, in Muş, in Gaziantep, and Şırnak. Not only in Istanbul or in Ankara. Many people have migrated to the big cities in the region due to village evacuations and due to economic conditions in the countryside. These are the main targets of organizations.

Like Tarık, Ali's reference to people searching for identity and seeking to alleviate their loneliness stresses how displacement and migration can create a rupture in people's lives that radical organizations exploit. Recruiters take advantage of those struggling with social dislocation, furthermore identifying that an individual may be more easily recruited if they already have a social tie to the organization, which leads them to target these kinship ties. Sarp expands on this point concerning ISIS: I can tell you that ISIS recruiters were targeting families as such because they knew if they can indoctrinate one of the siblings, the others may also join. As you know, the kinship ties among Kurds are really strong and ISIS built its primary recruitment method on these kinship ties.

Cevdet suggests that this process of displacement and migration leads to a clash in the cities between urban and rural cultures. He describes how the Kurds that have been displaced from their villages struggle to recreate the village's collective values and bonds, that is, the "traditional superstructure." He states that "[...] when they come to the city, they cannot find these values and this superstructure collapses. And, although they try to become a part of the city, they cannot. They stay in between being urban and rural." Cevdet argues that this creates distinct segments among the population in the cities that the displaced move to. He says he witnessed this dynamic during his military service in Cizre and Şırnak, arguing that it directly relates to radicalization and recruitment among these populations: There are two kinds of people living there: the core population of the city in the center called "Öz Cizreliler" who had been living in the city for centuries, and the peasants who came to the periphery of the city after village evacuations. The ones in the center humiliate these newcomers. Imagine that you are a peasant who had lost everything and came to the city in search of a new start, and you feel that you have nothing in common with the people around you. And, you have no one. After this point, your process would be accidental terrorism. Because not only would you have a sense of Kurdish ethnonationalism but you would also be a conservative coming from the countryside... It would be just be a toss-up which organization radicalize you first.

Cevdet's observations stress the impact of social dislocation and the resulting culture clashes and alienation between different parts of the city's population. Cevdet also states that such individuals may hold multiple beliefs (ethno-nationalism and religious conservatism) that while not inherently contradictory, render them susceptible to the pull of groups with a range of different ideologies. To summarize, the preceding discussion highlights

285

how systemic issues cause locally-experienced tensions, creating a context in which elements of the population are vulnerable to radicalization. Displacement and migration—often stemming from military aggression in the countryside—fracture collective bonds and challenge one's culture and identity, creating insecurities for radical organizations to exploit.

The Impact of Geography

The geography of the Eastern and Southeastern regions was stressed by several interviewees as an issue that affects radicalization and organizational recruitment. The mountainous environment made it more difficult for the state to economically develop and culturally influence the region. In addition, the proximity to neighboring states provides an opportunity for the trans-national movement of people and materials, plus the exchange of ideas, self-identifications, and ideologies across state boundaries. Some of these factors have been touched upon already, but given how prominent the geographic point was among our interviewees, it deserves further elaboration.

Ali describes the influence of geographic isolation and the physical and cultural vicinity to neighboring states: The mountainous terrain of the region has caused several difficulties for the central authority. I mean, think about an imam sent to a village that has been isolated from the rest of the society for centuries. How can he tell them that the religion they have believed for years is not true? But also, don't forget the importance of the location [...] for a Kurd living in that region, Syria, Iraq, and Iran mean a lot. It is not only because they are close to these countries but because there are relatives of the Kurds living in those countries. They feel close to them in heart and mind, and can easily be affected by events across the border. For instance, the appearance of Kurdish Hezbollah in the region in the 1980s is primarily based on the Iranian Revolution. Kurds have been exposed to its effects much more than the other people. For the ones who had problems with Turkish modernization and Western values, the Iranian Revolution showed an alternative way.

This quote draws attention to how remoteness from Ankara and Istanbul influences Kurds within the region, as the mountainous border region connects them to alternative political and ideological influences. Similarly, Cevdet emphasizes the impact of geographic isolation and argued that geographic conditions created a distinct "mountain culture" that acts as a source of radicalization:

The reason why people are more inclined to radicalize in the Eastern and Southeastern Anatolia regions is that they are not civic people. They have a mountain culture. Think about the geographic conditions and the climate. I lived there for years. Snow falls in November, becomes three meters in December, and stays until April. These people live for months in isolation without any physical connection to any part of the country. They cannot send their children to school, and if they get sick, they cannot reach a doctor.

While he describes a "mountain culture" as a cause of radicalization, he highlights extrinsic factors, such as isolation from public services, as fundamental issues. Our interviewees present support for Buhaug et al., who have highlighted the increased likelihood of ethnic conflict when large ethnic groups are excluded from power and located far from the capital and in a location with rough terrain.[79] Studies on the impact and advantages of proximity to state borders,[80] and those concerning the relationship between transnationalism of excluded ethnic kin groups and violence,[81] also find some support in our findings.

Discussion and Conclusions

The aim of this study was to deliver a comprehensive picture of the causes of radicalization in the Eastern and Southeastern regions of Turkey. It has demonstrated how regionally specific factors enable ideologically disparate terrorist groups to recruit and radicalize from the same population. Highlighting structural and systemic dynamics as influential in radicalization among the PKK, Kurdish Hezbollah, and ISIS, representing both ethno-nationalist and Islamist ideologies, it emphasizes these contextual factors as significant determinants of radicalization. The findings highlight structural issues stemming from state oppression and inequalities, compounded by geographic, economic, and demographic factors, as driving forces for radicalization in Turkey. The factors highlighted in this study compose our proposed typology of push and pull factors in structural radicalization, distilled below. Unlike previous literature on radicalization, which describes structural factors as pushing toward radicalization while ideology pulls, this paper demonstrates how structural factors in the Eastern and Southeastern regions of Turkey both push and pull.

Long-term oppression sets the context of early socialization for Kurds in Eastern and Southeastern Turkey has a causal link with many other factors that can pull an individual down the path of radicalization. Suppression marginalizes communities and reinforces divergent identity narratives, whether they be Islamist or ethno-nationalist. Decades of suppression of Kurdish identity, political exclusion, human rights violations, forced migrations, and economic abandonment by the state fueled widespread grievances, pushing people toward the PKK, Kurdish Hezbollah, or ISIS. These findings support prior research identifying the relationship between state repression and political violence.[82] At the micro and meso levels of analysis, studies that underline the role of personal and group grievances in radicalization practices also find support;[83] as do those that highlight overt abuses by state forces as a cause of backlash from among the population.[84]

The lack of economic development in these regions has caused relative deprivation and lack of economic opportunities, fomenting grievances against the state but also creating perceptions of discrimination and lack of status. Economic inequality has been compounded by restrictions to Kurdish political representation, especially since the failed peace process. These economic factors increase the attraction of radical organizations that may provide both financial opportunity and a response to inequalities. Our findings, therefore, support studies highlighting the relevance of socioeconomic and political exclusion of particular groups to political violence.[85]

Demographics, particularly large family size, was highlighted as an important factor that worsens economic issues and generates opportunities for recruitment to radical organizations. Displacement and forced internal migration create ruptures in people's lives and can make them susceptible to radicalization and recruitment, partly for financial reasons but also due to dislocation from previously held familial and kinship ties. Recruiters prey on immigrants to the cities, whose loneliness and insecurity are compensated by the organization, which offers them self-worth and purpose. This pull factor relates to Kruglanski et al's. "Significance Quest" model of radicalization.[86] The impact of domestic migration is interconnected with repression and economic factors and deserves further study and recognition in theories of radicalization processes.

Our findings highlighting geographic remoteness and mountainous terrain as factors influencing radicalization complement Buhaug et al.'s analysis of the likelihood of ethnic conflict relating to distance and roughness of the terrain.[87] The geographic features of Eastern and Southeastern Turkey limit state access, economic development, and provision of services, pushing people in the area to seek opportunities with non-state organizations. Meanwhile, the proximity to state borders also produces opportunities for local communities. Alternative means of economic opportunity via the cross-border black market, aided by kinship ties that transcend state lines, present pull factors toward cooperation or association with terrorist groups that operate there, regardless of ideology.

Our conceptualization of structural radicalization emphasizes the overlapping impact of various systematic, demographic, geographic, and economic factors that are unique to the Eastern and Southeastern regions of Turkey as the basis for radicalization. Although generalizability is a limitation of this study, the research develops a theoretical understanding of radicalization by highlighting how an interplay of structural factors can create both push and pull factors that influence radicalization and recruitment to ideologically diverse groups operating in the same locality. Further research into the relationship between these groups, and how specific structural factors influence radicalization, is needed to improve our understanding of these dynamics. In particular, we suggest that the impact of displacement on radicalization is a theme that deserves greater attention.

screening and refereeing by two anonymous referees. Publication Office: Taylor & Francis, Inc., 530 Walnut Street, Suite 850, Philadelphia, PA 19106. Readership: Political scientists, social scientists, psychologists, political analysts, members of the military, and academic researchers as well as members of the interested public. Authors can choose to publish gold open access in this journal. Read the Instructions for Authors for information on how to submit your article. Print ISSN: 1057-610X Online ISSN: 1521-0731. 2 issues per year. Abstracted/Indexed: America: History & Life; American Bibliography of Slavic and Eastern European Studies (ABSEES); CSA; EBSCOhost Online Research Databases; Elsevier Scopus; Expanded Academic ASAP (Gale Group); H.W. Wilson Indexes; Historical Abstracts; International Bibliography of the Social Sciences (IBSS); International Political Science Abstracts; ISI: Current Contents - Social & Behavioral Sciences and Social Science Citation Index; Lancaster Index to Defence & International Security Literature; National Criminal Justice Reference Service Abstracts (NCJRS); OCLC; PAIS International; Periodical Abstracts Research (PerAbs); ProQuest Research Library; PsycFirst; PsycINFO/ Psychological Abstracts; Research in Higher Education Abstracts; Sage Abstracts; SwetsWise All Titles; Thomson Reuters© Current Contents: Social & Behavioral Sciences; Thomson Reuters© Social Science Citation Index; and Ulrichs Periodicals Directory. Taylor & Francis make every effort to ensure the accuracy of all the information (the "Content") contained in our publications. However, Taylor & Francis, our agents (including the editor, any member of the editorial team or editorial board, and any guest editors), and our licensors, make no representations or warranties whatsoever as to the accuracy, completeness, or suitability for any purpose of the Content. Any opinions and views expressed in this publication are the opinions and views of the authors, and are not the views of or endorsed by Taylor & Francis. The accuracy of the Content should not be relied upon and should be independently verified with primary sources of information. Taylor & Francis shall not be liable for any losses, actions, claims, proceedings, demands, costs, expenses, damages, and other liabilities whatsoever or howsoever caused arising directly or indirectly in connection with, in relation to, or arising out of the use of the Content.

Chapter 15

Nuclear, Chemical and Biological Terrorism in Central Asia and Russia: Al Qaeda, the ISIS Affiliated Groups and Security of Sensitive Biological Weapons Facilities

Edward Lemon, Vera Mironova and William Tobey

Foreword by Simon Saradzhyan

In the fall of 2016 Fletcher School professor Monica Duffy Toft and I were completing work on an issue brief[1] in which we argued that the Islamic State should be further rolled back and dismantled rather than allowed to remain in the hopes that it would somehow become a normal state. IS was already in retreat at the time, having lost much of the territories it had once controlled in Syria and Iraq. Watching this made me, like many other analysts of political violence, wonder what surviving foreign fighters—which, at the time, included an estimated 5,000-10,000 individuals from post-Soviet Eurasia—would do next if IS and other jihadist Salafi groups in the Levant disintegrated. To ascertain their next moves, one had to begin by discerning what made them leave their home countries and eventually go to IS in the first place, and whether/how their motivation may have evolved in the course of their stay with the group. As someone focusing on Eurasia, I was particularly worried about what nationals of the Central Asian states would decide to do next and what impact their decisions and actions would have as some of the regimes in these countries were considerably more fragile and, therefore, more vulnerable than, say, Vladimir Putin's government. Another reason behind my interest in the subject is that the threat by violent extremists hailing from Central Asia had not been, in my view, as thoroughly examined as that posed by jihadists in and from Russia's North Caucasus.

Specifically, I had three sets of questions in mind:

(1) What causes nationals of Central Asia to take up arms and participate in political violence and what might those of them who have gone to fight in Iraq/Syria decide to do next?;

(2) if they decide to return to post-Soviet Central Asia enmasse, can this region become a major source of violent extremism that transcends borders, and possibly continents, in the wake of IS's demise?; and

(3) is there a threat that chemical, biological, radiological or nuclear materials stored anywhere in Central Asia will be used by the returning nationals of Central Asia or others for purposes of WMD terrorism (considering that al-Qaeda has sought nuclear weapons and IS has used chemical weapons) and, if so, how serious is this threat? We asked three scholars to answer these questions.

Vera Mironova is best known for her research on individual level behaviour in conflict environments and her fieldwork involving extensive interviews with former and active fighters. Edward Lemon is known for his research examining the intersection of authoritarian governance, religion, security and migration in Eurasia, along with his fieldwork in the region. Finally, William Tobey offers unparalleled expertise and years of experience in the U.S. government's nuclear security and non-proliferation initiatives. Fortunately, they all agreed to delve into the issues, refining my initial questions in ways that made their answers even more illuminating than I had hoped for. The results of their tremendous efforts are presented here, skilfully fused into one narrative by Russia Matters editor Natasha Yefimova-Trilling with assistance from our project's editorial assistant and student associates, in what I think is an insightful paper on the threat of violent extremism within and emanating from Central Asia.

Executive Summary

In the summer of 2018, the scenic, impoverished Central Asian nation of Tajikistan appeared in international headlines when Islamic State terrorists claimed credit[2] for the killing of four Western cyclists who were run over by a car, then shot and stabbed to death. This was the first known terrorist attack on foreigners in Central Asia since a suicide bombing[3] of the Chinese Embassy in Kyrgyzstan in 2016, and it appears to have been inspired by IS propaganda, though we do not know how much the group was involved in planning the attack, if at all. The violence serves as a jarring reminder that Islamist radicals from the five Central Asian nations once under Moscow's control—Kazakhstan, Kyrgyzstan, Tajikistan, Turkmenistan and Uzbekistan—have become noteworthy players on the field of international terrorism. Thousands of radicals from formerly Soviet Central Asia have travelled to fight alongside IS in Syria and Iraq; hundreds more are in Afghanistan. Not counting the fighting in those three war-torn countries, nationals of Central Asia have been responsible for nearly 100 deaths in terrorist attacks outside their home region in the past five years. But many important aspects of the phenomenon need more in-depth study.

This research paper attempts to answer four basic sets of questions adapted from the ones mentioned in the foreword:

(1) Is Central Asia becoming a new source of violent extremism that transcends borders, and possibly continents? (2) If so, why? What causes nationals of Central Asia to take up arms and participate in political violence? (3) As IS has been all but defeated in Iraq and Syria, what will Central Asian extremists who have thrown in their lot with the terrorist group do next? And (4) Do jihadists from Central Asia aspire to acquire and use weapons of mass destruction? If so, how significant a threat do they pose and who would be its likeliest targets? None of the answers is as straightforward as we would like, and far more attention should be paid to the differences and similarities among the five Central Asian states. But key findings generated by our research include the following:

- The civil war in Syria and the rise of IS in the Middle East have spurred an increase in the number of Central Asians participating in extremist violence beyond their home region; however, comparatively speaking, the international threat should not be exaggerated: Although Central Asians make up about 1 percent of the world's population, they were responsible for 0.14 percent of the world's terrorist attacks in the past decade, based on data from the Global Terrorism Database.[4]

- While the causes of radicalization vary widely, field research by two of the authors, as well as other scholars, suggests that two significant factors are (a) real and/or perceived injustices or failures that lead to an extreme rejection of society and (b) affinity for "a culture of violence." These factors can overlap with a search for adventure and/or a sense of belonging and meaning. Contrary to popular belief, relative poverty, religiosity and lack of education do not seem to be strong predictors of radicalization.

- These authors' research also suggests that a significant number of Central Asian extremists who went to fight in the Middle East became radicalized abroad, primarily while working in Russia or Turkey.

- Other scholars' research suggests that recent terrorist attacks and plots with a jihadist agenda in peaceful countries have more often been the work of local residents without combat experience than by former combatants.

- The next steps of Central Asian jihadists in foreign combat zones are exceedingly difficult to predict. Those who manage to escape from Iraq and Syria will have three basic options: to continue their fight in a different conflict zone, Afghanistan being the most likely; to go back to Central Asia, which does not seem like an option many find appealing; and to settle in a third country, whether to live peacefully or to keep fighting.

- The evidence indicates that Afghanistan-based militant groups, most notably the Islamic State Khorasan Province (ISKP), are targeting Central Asian recruits. But the inflow of foreign fighters is less intense than to Syria and Iraq in 2014-2015.

- While lone attackers attempting to commit acts of violence— whether inspired by radical propaganda or other factors—will continue to be difficult to identify before they do damage, policymakers and law-enforcement authorities would be wise to cooperate across borders in tracking those Central Asian extremists who plug into networks of like-minded radicals and/or criminal groups.

- Much work needs to be done to provide better security for the radiological sources in use in Central Asia; however, the threat vectors for chemical, biological, radiological and nuclear weapons involving Central Asia appear not to pose an imminent danger either within the region or outside it.

Central Asia and International Terrorism Today

Nationals of the five Central Asian states once under Moscow's rule have been prominent in the global landscape of violent extremism in two ways in recent years: by taking part in combat on the side of jihadist groups like the Islamic State and by plotting and/or carrying out terrorist attacks in nonwar zones inside and outside their home region. Quantitatively, relative to the region's population, the available data suggest that Central Asia as a whole accounts for a disproportionately high percentage of foreign fighters in Syria and Iraq, but a disproportionately low number of terrorist attacks worldwide. This is a much generalized summary, to be sure, accounting neither for individual variation among the five countries nor for the non-quantifiable aspects of violent extremism, but it a starting point. It is also a basis to say with confidence that Central Asia has become a source of violent extremism that transcends borders and continents.

As far as foreign fighters are concerned, prior to the start of Syria's civil war in 2011 the former Soviet republics of Central Asia had periodically seen trickles of citizens leaving to fight for radical causes abroad, mostly in Afghanistan/Pakistan. But the expanding war in Syria and the rise of IS there and in Iraq in 2013, opened the doors for Central Asians to engage with extremist violence on a much larger scale than before. While coming up with accurate figures is next to impossible, a tally of the most recent estimates of how many fighters have gone to Syria and Iraq from ex-Soviet Central Asia ranges approximately from 2,000 to upwards of 4,000, totalling perhaps one-third to nearly one-half of the contingent from the former Soviet Union and 5-10 percent of "foreign terrorist fighters" worldwide, to borrow the European Commission's terminology.[5] Considering that the ex-Soviet Central Asian states account for less than one percent of the world's population,[6] this figure suggests a disproportionately high representation among the foreign-fighter contingent in the Middle East.

An equally confounding problem for counterterrorism analysts is the potential for violence among individuals from Central Asia residing outside their home region that have not fought in combat zones or undergone intensive military training. Between 2014 and 2017, according to our tally, men from Uzbekistan and Kyrgyzstan carried out five high-profile terrorist attacks in New York, Stockholm, Istanbul, St. Petersburg and Karachi, four of them just last year. While two of those cases (Pakistan and Turkey) involved assailants with significant military training, two of the other attacks (Sweden and Russia) were perpetrated by men who may have tried but failed to join IS, though evidence in the Russia case isspotty; and the fifth attacker, in the U.S., clearly had no combat experience or military training with extremist groups. Three of the attacks took place in countries with significant Central Asian Diasporas: Russia (3-7 million), the U.S. (about 250,000), Turkey (100,000-200,000) and Europe (under 100,000). Overall, in the past five years terrorist attacks carried out by perpetrators from Central Asia have killed more people outside the region than inside it over the past decade—96 versus 91, not counting attackers. (See tables below.)

That said, as noted above, citizens of Central Asia have been involved in relatively few of the world's recent terror attacks. Based on data from the EU Terrorism Situation and Trend reports[19] for 2014-2017, Central Asians perpetrated just one of the 65 attacks in the European Union,[20] one of the 77 attacks in Turkey, one of the 27 attacks in the United States and one of the 153 alleged attacks in Russia.[21] The more comprehensive Global Terrorism Database,[22] or GTD, based at the University of Maryland, includes at least two other fatal attacks in Russia reportedly committed by Central Asians, though available details on these are spotty. They include an attack on police in the city of Astrakhan (some perpetrators reportedly[23] born in Kazakhstan or were Russian-born ethnic Kazakhs), as well as the widely reported[24] beheading of a four-year-old by an Uzbek nanny whom investigators said could have been mentally ill. Worldwide, between 2008 and 2017, Central Asians were involved in 68 of the 48,546 terrorist attacks recorded in the GTD, excluding those that took place in Syria, Iraq and Afghanistan—or just 0.14 percent.

Aside from actual attacks, Central Asian nationals have been detained in numerous incidents on suspicion of plotting attacks or aiding those who might carry them out. As noted below, some of these cases may involve political manipulation or shoddy investigative work. In the U.S., which has a relatively robust legal system, as well as a practice of counterterrorism stings,[25]several terror-related cases have centred on suspects from Central Asia. For example, three Brooklyn men—one citizen of Kazakhstan and two of Uzbekistan—were arrested[26] in 2015 on charges of conspiring to give material support to IS; according to the State Department, [27] in 2015 an Uzbek refugee was sentenced to 25 years in prison by a U.S. court after planning bomb attacks for which he sought advice from the Islamic Movement of Uzbekistan, or IMU, ii and in late 2016 a Dutch-Turkish citizen was convicted in the U.S. for serving as an IMU fundraiser and facilitator; this June a refugee from Uzbekistan residing in Colorado was found guilty[28] of trying to aid the Islamic Jihad Union, a splinter group of the IMU.iii

These disturbing numbers have led some scholars to contend that the international terrorist threat emanating from Central Asia is "a reality that cannot be ignored,"[30] while media headlines have declared the region to be a "growing source of terrorism"[31] and "fertile ground" [32] for recruitment.

While radicalization clearly does occur in Central Asia, some research suggests that the primary recruiting ground for Central Asian fighters among jihadist groups may be in Russia among the millions of Central Asian migrants' therein; this, however, is not a consensus view. In Central Asia itself, recruitment has been particularly active in the agricultural south of Tajikistan (Khatlon province),[33] isolated mining and oil-drilling cities in the western Kazakh desert (Zhezkazgan, Aktobe, Atyrau) and in predominantly ethnic Uzbek communities in Kyrgyzstan's Ferghana Valley.[34]

The destructive potential of violent extremists from Central Asia may be amplified by their ability to cooperate with other groups, particularly from elsewhere in the former Soviet Union, though not only. Some Central Asians have risen to positions of authority within IS and other international terrorist organizations, expanding their networks and clout: Most notably, Col. Gulmurod Halimov, the U.S.-trained head of Tajikistan's paramilitary police, or OMON, rose to become the Islamic State's "minister of war" after spectacularly defecting to the group in May 2015. Also, in 2015, the IMU—which has long worked with al-Qaeda and the Taliban in Afghanistan and Pakistan, and claimed joint responsibility[35] with Tehrik-i-Taliban Pakistan for the 2014 airport attack in Karachi—declared its allegiance to the Islamic State. The extremist group Imam Bukhari Jamaat, labelled by the U.S. State Department as "the largest Uzbek fighting force in Syria," and possibly a second, much smaller Uzbek group, cooperated with al-Nusra Front and Ahrar al-Sham to overrun Idlib in July 2015.[36] These examples notwithstanding, it is also worth noting that wartime alliances are often unstable, as illustrated by the acrimonious split in 2013 within Jaish Muhajireenwal Ansar between fighters from the Caucasus and from Central Asia.[37]

As noted above, the number of fatalities resulting from terror attacks by Central Asian jihadists outside the region has exceeded the number within it, but that does not mean acts of domestic terrorism have been insignificant. It is interesting to note that, unlike the instances of extremist violence abroad, most of the 18 deadly attacks within Central Asia in 2009-2018 targeted government officials, including police, rather than civilians. This is clearly reflected in the fatality counts: 80 representatives of the state, 11 civilians and 50 attackers. Moreover, four of the five Central Asian countries have been shaken by other forms of political violence, claiming well over 1,500 lives between 2005 and 2012. (Insular Turkmenistan has had neither political violence nor terror attacks that we know of.)

Despite the abundance of media reports and other research available, many questions about Central Asians' developing role in international terrorism remain unanswered, and any quest for those answers will be complicated by several factors. One is the extent to which various actors—including authorities in all the countries concerned—have manipulated or exaggerated the terrorist threat and can continue to do so.[40] Indeed, Tajikistan's official position[41] on this summer's fatal attack on the cyclists has been that it was perpetrated by the country's main political opposition group,[42] banned in 2015, the Islamic Renaissance Party of Tajikistan; this claim persisted despite a video posted by the IS media outlet Amaq showing four of the attackers pledging allegiance to the Islamic State. In another example of muddied waters, after Kazakhstan's deadliest attack thus far, in Aktobe in June 2016, the authorities could not agree on a narrative, vaguely stating[43] that the attack had been "ordered from abroad" without providing evidence or details. Uzbekistan, according to the U.S. State Department,[44]"routinely uses security concerns related to terrorism as a pretext for detention of suspects, including of religious activists and political dissidents."

Another global problem with access to reliable information is that violent extremists who work alone or in small groups often undergo radicalization out of public view, making them particularly difficult to identify before they do damage. The United States has experienced this repeatedly, including the cases of the 2013 Boston Marathon bombers—ethnic Chechens who had spent part of their childhood in Kyrgyzstanvi—and the Uzbek immigrant who killed eight people[45] in New York with a rented truck in 2017. In light of these constraints, it is important to recognize the limits of what we can actually know about the transnational threat coming from Central Asia.[46]

Drivers of Radicalization

Each individual's exact pathway to terrorism is different and catchall explanations of recruitment fail to reflect the complex dynamics at play. It is possible, however, to make some general observations about why Central Asians join terrorist groups. Perhaps surprisingly, research has indicated that poverty, lack of education and high levels of religiosity do not necessarily correlate with susceptibility to recruitment; conversely, the evidence suggests that many recruits are better off financially and better educated than the average person in Central Asia,[47] and also not particularly religious prior to radicalization. Instead, leitmotifs in fighters' biographies include a culture of violence—whether through previous combat experience, petty crime or combat sports—and disillusionment or de-socialization stemming from unfulfilled aspirations, a sense of injustice, disengagement from social support networks, a diminished sense of self-worth or some combination of these factors.

Many of the cases of Central Asian fighters for whom we have sufficient evidence to draw conclusions about their radicalization mirror a phenomenon observed by French political scientist Olivier Roy in Europe among first-generation migrants and their descendants—namely, that a diminished sense of status, accomplishment, fulfilment and/or social connectedness leads individuals to reject society, and radical ideologies provide justification for an extreme but empowering form of that rejection. Thus, Roy argues that we are seeing "not the radicalization of Islam, but the Islamization of radicalism."[48] For Roy, "the typical radical is a young, second-generation immigrant or convert, very often involved in episodes of petty crime, with practically no religious education, but having a rapid and recent trajectory of conversion/reconversion."[49]

Studies among Kyrgyz, Uzbek and Tajik communities—including field research conducted by two of this paper's authors—indicate that, often, recruits to extremist militant causes have experienced real and/ or perceived personal injustices or failure as migrants, whether through discrimination, failed romantic relationships, thwarted career aspirations or other experiences of powerlessness.[50] Here, it is important to note that migration in and of itself does not cause radicalization: Central Asians have been migrating to Russia for more than 20 years, while joining terrorist organizations is a more recent phenomenon affecting a small fraction of migrants. Among that minority, however, their experience as migrants can be a significant catalyst for their radical rejection of society and embrace of political violence. An example from Edward Lemon's fieldwork in Moscow in 2015 is illustrative of this. In April of that year, young Tajik construction workers were living in converted shipping containers as they built a new overpass near Moscow's Spartak stadium for the 2018 soccer World Cup. They recounted how recruiters whom they believed to be from Chechnya had come around their encampment calling people to Islam. One young man, whom they called Nasim, was drawn to the group:

He arrived in Moscow back in 2013. He was a smart guy, spoke good Russian and wanted to find a good job. But he couldn't. So he ended up in construction. In 2014, he went home and married a girl from his village. But soon after he came back the marriage was not good. He became more angry and bitter. When the recruiters came, he found their promises attractive. He never prayed before or talked about religion, but now he talked about jihad. One day he disappeared. The next thing we heard he was in Syria. One Uzbek former fighter who joined Islamic State on his own initiative told a similar story of disillusionment in a long interview with another of this report's authors, Vera Mironova. In describing his journey from Moscow to Syria, Mohammed (not his real name) became visibly frustrated recalling the discrimination he experienced in Russia, where he came when he was 16. "People considered us second-rate," he said, noting as an example that he could not approach local girls because they would never consider him, or any other poor, uneducated migrant from Central Asia, as a possible partner. (In Syria Mohammed married a 16-year-old Kazakh girl who came there with her family.)

Like Nasim and Mohammed, many young Central Asians who have experienced personal failures and marginalization start to feel alienated and disillusioned with their lives—whether abroad, at home or in an adopted country where they have settled as immigrants. Terrorist groups, including IS, have capitalized on this potential for resentment in their messaging, specifically targeting vulnerable individuals and offering them the promise of a different life. Such groups offer recruits meaning, a collective identity and individual fulfilment. Islamic State, in its propaganda, also claimed the absence of any discrimination in its fledgling caliphate, pointing to the equality of all Muslims. The heroic image of jihadist projected by such organizations, the promise of a wage and welfare, the adventure and brotherhood of membership in a violent extremist group can be appealing to a small minority of disillusioned individuals.

As noted above, a sense of injustice or disillusionment strong enough to lead to radicalization can arise among non-migrant Central Asians as well, often nudged along by the region's repressive and corrupt governments. For example, a key recruiting ground in Kyrgyzstan, as mentioned before, has been the Uzbek community in the Ferghana Valley. This ethnic minority bore the brunt of interethnic violence in 2010, sometimes facilitated[51] by local officials and followed[52] by little government effort to investigate or hold perpetrators accountable. More broadly, the former Soviet republics of Central Asia have some of the worst corruption[53] and least reliable[54] systems of justice in the world. They have also tended to regulate religious practices with a heavy hand. All the Central Asian ex-fighters interviewed by Vera Mironova mentioned the severe restrictions on religious freedoms in their home countries and for some this was a factor in their decision to leave. Both Tajikistan and Uzbekistan, for example, have either explicit or de facto limitations on men's right to wear beards and women's right to wear hijabs. Some of the Uzbek interviewees also pointed out that they had been under surveillance by local law enforcement for their religious activities, so they felt like they had no option but to leave.

For most recruits from Central Asia, however, religion seems to play a limited role in their lives until they begin to be exposed (and receptive) to extremist content. They often discover or rediscover Islam with a neophyte's zeal, rapidly embracing a simplistic, good-versus-evil takfiri narrative that pits believers against non-believers. Evidence from the Tajik case reflects this. Most of them leave behind close-knit communities and an authoritarian system where the government has closely monitored and restricted religious practices for the past hundred years. They find themselves in migrant communities where religion in its different guises is discussed more openly. While most maintain close links to their relatives and communities at home, some become alienated in their new environment[55] and seek new sources of connection or meaning. Contrary to Islamophobia stereotypes, those with high levels of religious knowledge have often proved integral to counter-radicalization efforts.[56]

Our field research also indicates that there seems to be a link, in some cases, between recruitment to wage jihad in the Middle East and a prior connection to what the Russian scholar Vitaly Naumkin calls a "culture of violence," whether through crime, combat, violent sports or some combination of these. In one example, a Tajik named Anvar had served a short prison sentence for theft as a young man and then migrated in 2013 to Russia to work on a construction site in Moscow. He spent much of his free time at a gym, training in mixed martial arts. An IS recruiter operating out of the gym began grooming him, making him believe it was his duty as a Muslim to go to Syria; Anvar left to join IS in early 2014. Some of the most prominent fighters hailing from Central Asia were battle-hardened veterans, as described in more detail below. Many recruits had been petty criminals in their youth.[57] Tajik militant leader Nusrat Nazarov, for example, had been a drug dealer in Kulob.[58] Others have been active in combat sports.[59] Alan Chekranov, a Tajik fighter prominent on social media, was a three-time national champion in mixed martial arts.[60]Naumkin contends that terrorism offered these men an opportunity to express their masculinity and live out violent fantasies.[61]

It is also worth pointing out that many Central Asians are pulled into violent extremist groups through their social networks, recruited by people who know them.[62] Such networks work through both offline and online contact. After Nasim left for Syria in 2014, for example, he was joined by two other individuals from his village in southern Tajikistan. In some villages in Kazakhstan, Kyrgyzstan and Tajikistan entire extended families, numbering up to 40, have left for Syria and Iraq. Finally, it is worth noting that those who choose violent forms of radicalism may confront very different logistical challenges: Carrying out an unsophisticated terrorist attack—for example, mowing down people with a vehicle—takes less planning and involves fewer chances both to be interdicted and to have a change of heart than does joining a terrorist group in a foreign country, which requires obtaining travel documents, crossing multiple borders and paying for the journey.

What Might They Do Next?

In examining the question of Central Asian militants' next steps, most analysts of international security have focused on the extremists affected by the decline of ISIS and Jabhat Fateh al-Sham—formerly known as the al-Nusra Front, an al-Qaeda affiliate—in Syria and Iraq. We will do the same. What will happen to these men and their families if their host groups lose all their territory in the region? Surviving ex-fighters have three basic options other than detention by local authorities: join a violent group in another conflict zone, migrate to a peaceful country or return home, with the latter two options possible both for those who want to demilitarize and for those who want to keep the fight going. All of these scenarios require money and connections to leave the region, doing which has become increasingly difficult[63] over the past few years. After the IS stronghold of Raqqa fell in 2017, prices for smuggling non-Arab foreigners out of Syria rose to around $10,000 per adult, and about one-third that for a child, so not many people could afford it, especially those with families. Moreover, people from Central Asia often look different than other jihadists in the region, so it was harder for them—even compared to fighters from other parts of the former Soviet Union, like Russia—to pass unnoticed though government or Kurdish checkpoints.

Existing evidence suggests that a mass return to Central Asia remains unlikely, largely due to local authorities' heavy-handed policies.[64] Our tally from earlier this year, based on open sources, showed only about 300 returnees to all five countries combined, not including non-combatant family members.[65] Some analysts have even speculated that sending radicalized citizens to fight in Syria and Iraq may benefit the regimes in the region, helping them transfer the threat of Islamic terrorism out of their own countries.[66] In all of the Central Asian states, an influx of former fighters would certainly pose a huge challenge in terms of demobilization

302

and reintegration. Jailing ex-combatants enmassed could create new problems: In November 2018, IS reportedly claimed responsibility[67] for a prison riot in Tajikistan that left at least 23 dead.[68] While that claim has not been verified, Tajikistan's foreign minister said the unrest was provoked by members of extremist organizations.[69]

This leaves the other two options: new war zone or third country. As noted at the beginning of this report, the most likely conflict zone for migration would seem to be Afghanistan, while the peaceful countries that could serve as sanctuaries for ex-fighters include Ukraine, Turkey and potentially some European Union states.[70] According to various reports,[71] over 800 Central Asians have been killed in the Middle East. If the numbers of dead and returnees, given above, are accurate, this would leave between 850 and over 3,000 survivors, including an undisclosed number in prison.[72] In order to better predict where certain individuals could go next, it may be useful to consider why they went to the Middle East in the first place. In general, the migration of Central Asians to join IS and other radical violent groups in Syria and Iraq can be divided into three "waves" as described below. Readers should note, however, that this is very much a generalization. For example, at the time of the first wave, made up largely of veteran militants, there were also some early recruits who had been working or studying in Syria at the time that protests broke out in early 2011.

- The first wave, primarily in 2011-2012, mostly included people with combat experience in Tajikistan's civil war (1992-1997) and Afghanistan/Pakistan (Waziristan), with the Taliban and Taliban affiliated groups. These men went with the explicit goal of fighting. At that point, in the very beginning of the armed conflict, there were no major armed coalitions, only many separate groups, or jamaats, of foreign fighters largely segregated by language. With time, some of those groups merged with IS, while others continued fighting against Bashar al-Assad's forces as semi-independent formations, sometimes in an alliance with the al-Nusra Front. According to former IS fighters interviewed by Vera Mironova, these people were among the most professional and experienced foreign combatants in Syria. Many of them started, as did other Russian-speaking fighters, in the Jaish Muhajireenwa Ansar under the command of Omar (or Umar) al-Shishani, an ethnic Chechen from Georgia, and followed him to IS after he became a military commander for the jihadist group. Because of their experience, many assumed positions as trainers. For example, according to one interviewed ex-fighter, his military base had a Kazakh sniper instructor who had cut his teeth in Waziristan and several Uzbek experts in explosives and topography, which also had come via Waziristan.

- The second wave, roughly in 2012-2014, was made up largely of fighting-age males with no combat experience, coming mostly from Russia and Turkey where they had been working. While some were actively recruited, others travelled on their own initiative and sometimes had a hard time getting to the Syrian battlefield. For instance, Mohammed, the Uzbek who recalled feeling like a second-class citizen in Russia, said in an interview that he had been working and studying in Moscow when events in Syria caught his attention and, although he was not religious, he felt the need to go fight against Assad. It was easier said than done. First, he asked around at mosques, but was kicked out because people assumed he was a mole or provocateur working for the Russian security service. Then he searched on Russian-language social media and eventually found people already fighting in Syria. At first, they also did not believe him, but ultimately agreed to take him in if he flew to Turkey. He bought a ticket and soon joined Jaish Muhajireenwa Ansar, later moving to al-Nusra and then to IS. It's worth noting that not everyone wanted to fight for IS, which some fighters accused of excessive violence or misguided religious ideology. As of August 2018, within the anti-Assad rebel bloc, Central Asians were fighting with the Turkistan Islamic Party, Katibat al-Tawhid wal Jihad and Liwa Mujahedeen wal Ansar, among other groups. Although they are considered semi-independent, they often coordinate their military activities with al-Nusra, which publicly cut its ties to al-Qaeda in 2016 and changed its name to Jabhat Fateh al-Sham.

- The third wave of people, which trickled in with the first two but intensified significantly after the declaration of a caliphate in 2014,[73] included whole families, together with women and children, eager to start a new life in what they saw as a newly established country, a Promised Land for Muslims. Central Asia has long experienced wide scale out-migration, so the idea of moving to a different country was not new. Many of these people sold their apartments and cars back home and bought houses in IS-controlled territory. They took along schoolbooks to continue their children's education in their native language. They even took their diplomas and other educational certificates—further suggesting that their goal was a new life, not a suicide mission. Some of the men did not go through boot camp or own a weapon. In the Middle East they managed to live relatively normal lives, working as engineers or social workers, caring, for example, for the families of killed IS fighters. In short, for many this was a "one-way journey," whether seeking adventure, martyrdom or a new life.[74]

Based on Vera Mironova's research, Central Asian fighters who have managed to leave IS can be divided into two basic subgroups: those who had given up on the idea of a caliphate, or had grown disillusioned with the ideology of IS, and those from the IS leadership and intelligence service (Amnivii) who left with money and are considering regrouping in another geographic area. The former include a small, elusive group sometimes called the "excessive" takfirists, who consider IS insufficiently stringent in its pursuit of sharia-based rule. Many of these are currently living peacefully and working in civilian occupations in their countries of hiding; some are even actively working to discourage potential IS supporters. The second subgroup is a dangerous one. These ex-fighters are looking for countries with weak security where they could take control of territory, such as Afghanistan.

Among the world's existing conflict zones, it is indeed Afghanistan—with its geographical proximity and linguistic affinities with Central Asia—that appears to be a logical destination for ex-fighters and new recruits alike.[75] Three radical groups operating there have roots in post-Soviet Central Asia: the Tajik group Jamaat Ansurallah,viii which pledged allegiance to IS in 2017 after having once been affiliated with al-Qaeda, which, in turn, had been strong in Afghanistan prior to 9/11; Uzbekistan's IMU, often referred to by Afghan officials as Jundallah; and its splinter group, the Islamic Jihad Union, or IJU, which has a base[76] in Sar-e Pul, less than 100 miles from the border with Turkmenistan, albeit with an estimated 25 fighters. All these organizations, however, have been weakened by years of war, and it has been the Islamic State - Khorasan Province (ISKP) that has been most active in trying to recruit fighters from Central Asia.[77]

The group declared its existence as an affiliate of IS in January 2015.ix Like IS, it has developed a sophisticated media presence outmatching the Taliban's[78] and it has targeted Central Asian recruits directly: In March 2018, for example, the group released a video in which Uzbek fighters called on militants in Syria and Iraq to join it.[79] ISKP's messaging, like IS's, stresses the purity of its Salafi ideology and the obligation of believers to engage in jihad and romanticizes life as a fighter. ISKP propaganda also projects a transnational cause centred on apocalyptic narratives from the Prophet Muhammed about jihadis from Khorasan winning a decisive victory near the end of times.[80] ("Khorasan" is a Persian word referring to the territory of modern-day Afghanistan and parts of Central Asia.) For recruits from Central Asia, the ISKP's promises of expansion into the region may be more appealing than the Taliban's nationalist vision, which focuses strictly on Afghanistan and has ruled out northern expansion.

The ISKP's actual strength, in numbers and influence, remains contentious and hard to ascertain.[81] Over its nearly four years, the ISKP extended its presence beyond its initial base in Nangarhar province to establish control of two districts in Jowzjan in northern Afghanistan, only to be routed there by the Taliban in July 2018. Russian officials have consistently emphasized the group's might, with a top Russian military commander estimating in April 2018 that the ISKP has 10,000 fighters.[82] A U.S. military spokeswoman said[83] around the same time that the group was believed to have only about 2,000 fighters, and the general in charge of U.S. Central Command, Joseph Votel, said earlier that year that "Moscow has exaggerated the presence of the ISIS-K threat."[84] According to U.N. estimates, 3,500 to 4,000 militants are fighting with ISKP, with 750 of them originating in Central Asia.[85]

Afghan officials, meanwhile, have estimated that the ISKP has 3,000 foreign fighters alone.86 (In August 2017 a senior Afghan security official put the number[87] of foreigners fighting for both IS and the Taliban in his country at roughly 7,000, most of them from Pakistan, Uzbekistan and Tajikistan; this is much less than the estimates of foreign fighters in Syria and Iraq, which have run as 40,000.[88]) The ISKP has faced all matter of challenges: With its coercive approach to governance and unpopular policies, such as publicly banning poppy cultivation while benefitting[89] from the trade, the group has struggled to gain a foothold in Afghanistan. Three of its emirs have been killed[90] and, in November 2017, NATO claimed that U.S. forces had killed 1,600 of its militants.[91] Fighting with Taliban factions has also weakened the organization, despite occasional attempts at détente.[92] Veteran Afghanistan researcher Antonio Giustozzi concluded[93] in late 2017 that the ISKP, damaged by infighting, dependency on external funding and setbacks in the Middle East, "is past its peak in Afghanistan, if not in terms of military capabilities, certainly in terms of jihadist image."[94]

For now, the flow of foreign fighters to Afghanistan seems insignificant when compared with the peak of IS recruiting from Central Asia in 201415. Moreover, if IS's proto-caliphate in Syria and Iraq became attractive to some foreigners when it controlled significant territory and really had come to resemble a state, Afghanistan's radical groups do not seem to offer that: While the Taliban remains extremely powerful, it has full control of only

4 percent of the country's provinces, according to a BBC estimate[95] from January; around the same time, Afghan officials reportedly said[96] that rebels control 14.5 percent of the country's territory, while another 29 percent is contested by both sides. The ISKP controls far less territory[97] than that, mostly in eastern Afghanistan on the border with Pakistan, and the group has not managed to create the same state functions as IS did in its heyday in Syria/Iraq. That said, the damage it inflicts locally is substantial: According to an October 2018 U.N. report[98] on Afghanistan, the ISKP accounted for more than half the year-on-year increase in civilian casualties caused by "anti-government elements" in the first nine months of the year (and 25 percent of the absolute total of such casualties), while Nangarhar province, its home base, recorded the most civilian casualties for that time period, with 554 deaths and 940 injured.

There is no question that Central Asians are among the foreigners fighting in Afghanistan. In addition to the Uzbeks and Tajiks in the Taliban, many of the non-Afghans in today's ISKPx are militants from Pakistan and Uzbekistan who have fought in the region since the 1990s According to Giustozzi,[99] in the summer of 2017, the ISKP split into two factions, one of them led by an ethnic Uzbek former IMU commander known as Moawiya,[100] or sometimes referred to in press reports as Mawlavi Habib ul-Rahman; his men were mainly Central Asians—including members "of the Omar Ghazi Group (an offshoot of the IMU which fully joined IS) and Shamali Khilafat, a group made up of Afghan Tajiks and Uzbeks"—and his group claimed to have 3,800 members. There is also evidence that fighters from other Central Asian republics have joined the group, particularly from Tajikistan, which shares with Afghanistan both a border and closely related languages (Tajik and Dari).

In the summer of 2018, for instance, over 100 IS fighters from Moawiya's group[101] including[102] children, surrendered[103] to Afghan authorities after combat with the Taliban. The local governor said[104] there had been numerous foreign fighters in the group, Uzbeks and Tajiks among them, who had not surrendered and may have wound up with the Taliban. (A video[105] that reportedly circulated days later on pro-Taliban social media seemed to show 25 captured Central Asian fighters not only from Tajikistan and Uzbekistan, but a few from Kazakhstan and Kyrgyzstan as well.) Indeed, Tajik President Emomali Rahmon claimed in May 2018 that dozens of his citizens had joined the ISKP.[106] That same month Kabul extradited to Tajikistan three alleged IS sympathizers, who had crossed into

Afghanistan from Iran, a route of major concern to Afghan authorities.[107] (Linguistically, Tajik and Dari are closely related to Farsi.)

About 10 cases of Tajiks entering the country via Iran have been reported in the media since mid-2017—for example, that of 18-year-old Shodidjon Boyev, who had worked as a labor migrant in Russia before trying to travel to Syria via Turkey. Having failed to reach Syria, he reportedly[108]traveled to Iran before crossing into Afghanistan in December 2017 and ending up in an IS training camp. Ex-fighters could also settle in a stable third country. After leaving IS, many fighters end up in Turkey, which shares a border with Syria, but in 2016 Ankara started a crackdown on ex-IS fighters on its territory. (Egypt, Georgia and Malaysia have likewise gotten stricter than before.) In Turkey, some fleeing militants get detained for extradition to their homeland; others are offered the option of buying a ticket to a third country where a visa is not required.[109] Given that Ukraine has a visa-free regime with most post-Soviet states, and was once a place where fake identification papers were relatively cheap and easy to buy, it has become a transit zone for many Russian-speaking ex-fighters, but is unlikely to be their final destination. Many of the ex-fighters interviewed by Vera Mironova said they aimed to travel to former Soviet republics where they could find work and blend in more easily in their ethnic communities, but most hoped to settle ultimately in Western Europe, and some have already entered Europe illegally. It is difficult to predict where exactly these fighters will go because many of their decisions hinge on changes in government policies and illegal networks to buy documents, which they monitor closely. As noted above, these people could try to embark on a peaceful life, disillusioned with jihad, or they could plot attacks, whether of their own volition or following someone's orders.

Thus far, IS-related attacks and plots outside of Syria, Iraq and Afghanistan have more often been the work of local residents sympathizing with the group than of former foreign fighters.[110] Militants from Central Asia seem to follow this pattern to some extent—the stark exceptions being the 2014 Karachi attack, carried out by IMU militants, and the Istanbul attack of 2017: Abdulkadir Masharipov, who killed 39 revelers in a nightclub on Jan. 1, 2017, had trained in an al-Qaeda camp in Afghanistan in 2011 and confessed to carrying out the attack on orders from Islam Atabiyev, a Russian, Raqqa-based IS leader also known as Abu Jihad.[111] The Stockholm attack in April 2017 was something of a "hybrid": It was carried out by Rakhmat Akilov who had been deported back to Sweden from Turkey in 2015 after he was caught attempting to join IS.[112]

The charges against Akilov stated that he had been in contact with more than 30 Islamic State fighters in Iraq, Syria and Afghanistan prior to the attack; according to Akilov's testimony, he had been "prepared" by Abu Dovud, the nom de guerre of Tajikistan native Parviz Saidrakhmonov.[113] Claims to a connection with foreign fighters in the St. Petersburg case are more tenuous: The accused suicide bomber, Akbarzhon Jalilov, had migrated with his family to the city and lived there from 2011 to 2015. In November of that year he reportedly[114] moved to Turkey, where he lived until December 2016 when he was deported for overstaying his visa and moved back to St. Petersburg. Russia's state-owned-TASS news agency reported:[115]within days of the attack that law-enforcement officials suspected that he may have left Turkey for Syria and trained with IS.

One early, unverified claim[116] of responsibility came from a little known group claiming links to al-Qaeda; other media reports,[117]citing unnamed Russian and Kyrgyz security sources, said the suspected mastermind of the attack was, like Jalilov, an ethnic Uzbek from Kyrgyzstan, who commanded a group of Central Asian fighters in Syria and was suspected by Kyrgyz authorities of organizing the 2016 attack against the Chinese Embassy. Russian investigators have reportedly[118] accused Jalilov's alleged accomplices of receiving and then passing on money for the attack from "an active member of an international terrorist organization" in Turkey. Most Central Asian ex-fighters hoping to return to a peaceful life seem wary of heading back to their home countries. As noted above, our tally showed only about 300 returnees. The region's governments, like Russia's, [119] have often been heavy-handed with returning ex-fighters and have not been keen to develop re-integration policies for those who engaged in combat. The governments of Tajikistan and Kazakhstan, for example, have amended legislation to revoke the citizenship of those convicted of being members of terrorist organizations, giving the state the right to bar or deport them.

Tajikistan has introduced an amnesty program, but its success seems to be limited: While dozens of ex-fighters have been pardoned, [120] a provincial police chief said earlier this[121] year that, of 72 amnestied fighters, 34 had returned to IS. According to several former IS members now in hiding, comrades who were extradited to Russia, Turkmenistan and Uzbekistan have never been heard from again. The ex-fighters are particularly afraid of torture at the hands of authorities back home, which made many of their brothers-in-arms opt to stay in Syria and die there. So real was the fear of torture or "being disappeared" that one ex-fighter awaiting extradition from Turkey to Tajikistan slit his wrists before he could be returned, according to his cellmate in a deportation prison in Istanbul.

Central Asian Nuclear, Chemical and Biological Terrorism Threat Vectors

Central Asia could be relevant to the threat of chemical, biological, radiological or nuclear (CBRN) terrorism in several ways. First, because the region was the home of significant Soviet-era production and testing activities, it could be a source of material. Second, because many of the Islamic State's foreign fighters came from the region those who survive the conflicts in Syria and Iraq and return to it could potentially bring with them CBRN expertise and nihilist motivations gained from IS efforts. Third, because large and sensitive Russian facilities are located close to the region, and the borders are relatively porous, Central Asian countries could be used as a haven or trans-shipment point to exploit any thefts from Russian facilities; for example, the closed city of Ozersk, which contains one of Russia's largest nuclear weapons-related facilities with thousands of weapons' worth of fissile material, lies less than 175 miles from Russia's frontier with Kazakhstan—the world's longest contiguous land border.[122]

Central Asia as a Potential Source of CBRN Material

Kazakhstan, Kyrgyzstan, Tajikistan, Turkmenistan and Uzbekistan are all "states parties" to the Biological and Chemical Weapons Conventions and the Non-proliferation Treaty, which prohibit them from holding stocks of nuclear, chemical or biological weapons. There are, moreover, no current, public and credible claims that any of these countries are violating that treaty obligations.[123] Thus, the regional threat of diversion or theft of nuclear, chemical or biological weapons or materials from existing state programs is negligible. Central Asia was, however, the home of significant Soviet-era nuclear weapons activities. The Soviets mined and milled 10,000 tonnes of uranium in Tajikistan.[124] They set off over 450 nuclear detonations at Semipalatinsk, Kazakhstan.[125] About a tenth of those tests were of such low yields that the fissile material was left "readily recoverable" should terrorists have been sufficiently knowledgeable and motivated to take it.[126] The Soviet authorities also left behind in Kazakhstan 600 kilograms of 90-percent-enriched uranium, mostly in the form of metal chunks and oxide pellets—enough for about two dozen nuclear weapons—at the unsecured Ulba Metallurgy Plant,[127] and spent fuel containing 10 tonnes of highly enriched uranium and 3 tonnes of weapons-grade plutonium in a relatively unsecure facility at Aktau on the shores of the Caspian Sea.[128]

Central Asia was also beset by Soviet biological weapons activities. Vozrozhdeniye Island, a biological-weapons test site straddling present day Uzbekistan and Kazakhstan, is the world's largest dumping ground for anthrax agent. Soviet scientists and technicians moved hundreds of tonnes of the deadly brew there in 1988 to cover up the illicit Soviet biological-weapons program, from their production facility at Sverdlovsk.[129] Moreover, another one of at least six Soviet biological-weapons production plants operated at Stepnogorsk, Kazakhstan—the only one outside of Russia—and was capable of churning out about 300 tons of agent in 220 days.[130]

When the Soviet Union dissolved, this lethal mess fell to the fledgling Central Asian republics. Fortunately, their governments welcomed U.S. cooperative threat-reduction assistance[131] and signal non-proliferation successes followed—sometimes in cooperation with Russia, including in the return of fresh and spent highly enriched reactor fuel from Central Asian research reactors. Only a short distance ahead of metal scavengers active in the area, the U.S. and Kazakh governments completed work in 2012 to secure the highly enriched uranium and plutonium left from Soviet nuclear tests, under a project that spanned the Bush and Obama administrations.[132] Earlier, Project Sapphire removed 600 kilograms of highly enriched uranium from Ulba in 1994.[133] The U.S. National Nuclear Security Administration funded a massive effort to repackage and transport spent fuel from the BN-350 reactor at Aktau to a secure storage site in north-eastern Kazakhstan completed in 2010.

The United States also facilitated the dismantlement of the biological facilities at Stepnogorsk, remediation of the dumping ground on Vozrozhdeniye Island and deployment of physical protection and accounting measures in Kazakhstan and Uzbekistan.[134] This has largely negated the threat posed by biological facilities and materials abandoned by the Soviet Union. Thus, the legacy of nuclear and biological materials left by the Soviet Union and the implicit threat that they could fall into terrorist hands were effectively addressed by international cooperative efforts to consolidate, secure and dispose of the material. Radiological sources remain in Central Asia and, if stolen, could be used in unconventional attacks by terrorists. They have been less well addressed by cooperative threat-reduction efforts because they serve ongoing and important industrial and medical purposes. Approximately 1,000 Category 1-3 radiological sources are currently in use in Central Asia, with the overwhelming majority in Kazakhstan.[135] Generally located in hospitals, universities and industrial sites, these sources are often less well-protected than nuclear facilities.[136]

Returning Fighters as a Source of CBRN Threat

The fate of defeated Central Asian fighters from the Islamic State and other violent extremist groups will obviously play a critical role in their ability to spread an IS-related CBRN threat. From 2014 to 2017, the Islamic State produced and used chemical weapons in 37 separate attacks,[137] but there is only one recorded incident of an IS chemical-weapons capability being transferred outside of Iraq or Syria, and it was to Australia,[138] with no public evidence of participation by Central Asians. IS also surveilled the home of a Belgian nuclear official, although the purpose of that action remains obscure. In 2015, the IS publication Dabiq alluded to an interest in nuclear terrorism. The article with murky intent and provenance warned: "Let me throw a hypothetical operation onto the table. The Islamic State has billions of dollars in the bank, so they call on their wilāyah in Pakistan to purchase a nuclear device through weapons dealers with links to corrupt officials in the region. The weapon is then transported overland until it makes it to Libya, where the mujāhidīn move it south to Nigeria."[139]

No concrete plots or preparations by ISIS to obtain nuclear weapons or material, however, have been discovered and publicly disclosed. Moreover, even in 2015 when IS controlled far more people, resources and territory than they do today, David Albright and Sarah Burkhard concluded that "Daesh's public boasts and fantasies about its easy pathways to nuclear weapons should be dismissed."[140] In Mosul, Iraq, IS controlled facilities that housed two large Cobalt-60 radiological sources, but, possibly unaware of what they had, the militants left them unmolested.[141] Thus, there is no publicly available evidence that any fleeing Central Asian Islamic State fighters are linked to any IS CBRN efforts in Syria or Iraq, or that they have undertaken such activities after their departure from IS-held territory. While mindful of the need to avoid argumentum ad ignorantiam, it does not appear that the out-migration of Central Asian IS fighters from the Middle East poses a current CBRN terrorism threat vector.

Proximity of Sensitive Russian Facilities to Central Asia

Much of Russia's nuclear archipelago is strewn across the Urals, originally chosen by Stalin's secret police for the region's isolation and therefore security. These vast facilities house sufficient fissile material for thousands of nuclear weapons in hundreds of buildings.[142] The closed cities are no longer embedded in a totalitarian police state. They now face changing demographics and the emergence of ideologies that might undermine the security of the facilities. The Carnegie Moscow Center's researchers

Alexey Malashenko and Alexey Staroshin noted: "There have been significant changes in the composition and distribution of Russia's Muslim community during the era of President Vladimir Putin. In particular, as Islam expands in the Ural Federal District, religious and political life there is evolving. Much of this expansion is due to the arrival of Muslim migrants from Central Asia and the Caucasus, and some migrants bring with them religious radicalism—a challenge that requires a more effective official response."[143]

While the threat that stolen Russian materials could be transferred to Central Asia—or used elsewhere—for terrorist purposes are a plausible concern, no publicly available evidence reveals such a plot. Russia attracts millions of Central Asians as seasonal workers and manual laborers, many of them in Russia illegally. Because of their status, these workers are often exploited and abused by their employers, contributing to the possibility that their migrant experience fosters extremism.[144] While such workers are unlikely to have direct access to weapons-usable materials, they could form a network to be employed by insiders to smuggle pilfered material out of Russia for fabrication into a viable weapon or transhipment to another region. As noted above, the closed city of Ozersk lies within 170 miles of the Kazakh border. Theft from these facilities, albeit mostly non-nuclear, is a common occurrence.[145] Moreover; smuggling of arms and narcotics in the region is so prevalent that it threatens, according to one researcher, to "curtail Central Asia's development."[146] Authorities have interdicted trafficking of radiological sources from Russia into Kazakhstan, although the purpose of the smuggling is unclear.[147]

Net Assessment

When the Soviet Union dissolved, Central Asia was left with a large inventory of CBRN materials and facilities. Cooperative threat reduction efforts by the U.S. government and those of Central Asian states eliminated or greatly reduced the vulnerability of that material. Moreover, it is likely that any terrorist group that succeeded in obtaining CBRN weapons or materials would seek a target more lucrative than a Central Asian state. It is plausible that CBRN material stolen in Russia could be taken to Central Asia for transhipment or fabrication into a usable weapon. Much work needs to be done to provide alternatives to or better security for the radiological sources in use in Central Asia. The international spread of perhaps thousands of Central Asian IS fighters could pose a severe security threat. Their activities bear close scrutiny, particularly to ensure that they do not attempt to use knowledge that might have been gained in Iraq or Syria regarding CBRN attacks. Moreover, ongoing vigilance in securing sensitive facilities is critical, as complacency leads to vulnerability. Nonetheless, so far, from publicly available information, the CBRN threat vectors involving Central Asia appear not to pose an imminent peril either within the region or externally.

For Further Consideration

As we have noted throughout this paper, the threat of violent extremism emanating from Central Asia has raised many as yet unanswered questions. Research on the topic is complicated by the many overlapping, sometimes tangled lines of inquiry worth pursuing: Some violent actors are radicalized at home, others abroad; some choose to perpetrate violence in low-cost ways as lone actors, while others go to great lengths to travel to distant war zones; getting access to those who have participated in jihadist violence is not easy; official assessments of the threat are often warped by political considerations; the list of complicating factors goes on.

That said, it is worth restating some of our basic conclusions:

- The turmoil in Syria and the rise of IS allowed thousands of Central Asians to take part in extremist violence outside their countries of residence, and perhaps inspired violent actions by a small number of individuals who did not travel to the war zone; however, nationals of Central Asian countries have been behind only 0.14 percent of attacks recorded in the Global Terrorism Database over the past decade, while making up about 1 percent of the world's population.

- Research suggests that two significant causes of radicalization are (a) a rejection of society based on real and/or perceived injustices or failures and (b) experience with or attraction to "a culture of violence," whether through previous combat experience, violent sports or crime.

- A large number of Central Asians fighting in the Middle East seem to have been radicalized outside of Central Asia, while working as labour migrants in Russia or Turkey.

- It is extremely difficult to say what Central Asian jihadists' next moves might be. The three main options seem to be: move on to a different conflict zone, with Afghanistan as the likeliest destination; return to Central Asia, where local governments are not rolling out the

314

welcome mat; move to a third country, which requires money and/or connections, whether to abandon the fight or pursue it further.

- IS's Afghanistan branch is actively recruiting Central Asians but the flow of fighters is much lower than to the Middle East three or four years ago.

- Based on other researchers' work, recent terrorist attacks and plots in the West have more often been the work of local residents than itinerant former IS fighters.

- Tracking networked jihadists will require international cooperation among law-enforcers and other stakeholders.

- There does not seem to be an imminent danger of WMD attacks emanating from Central Asia, although better security is needed for radiological sources in use in the region.

The questions that still need to be answered are myriad. A good list of them can be found at the end of the December 2017 report "Russian-Speaking Foreign Fighters in Iraq and Syria:[148] Assessing the Threat from (and to) Russia and Central Asia" by the Center for Strategic and International Studies. A few that interest us in particular include the following:

1. We have a good understanding of how Central Asians have been recruited, but why are certain individuals more susceptible than others?

2. Here we have focused on the 0.005 percent of the region's population who have joined violent extremist groups, and on the relatively small number of attacks they have committed. But what factors have made 99.995 percent of the population not take this route and put up with hardships without resorting to violence?

3. On a practical level, will countries in Central Asia take back their citizens who are currently in prison in the greater Middle East? (Formally they refuse to do so; however, it is possible that some of these people may have been quietly let back into their countries of origin if considered "useful" by the authorities.)

4. Finally, what are the salient distinctions among the five Central Asian countries in the context of radicalization and international terrorism? Until we know more in answer to these and other questions it seems

like a fool's errand to make policy recommendations. Nonetheless, a few obvious suggestions do come to mind for officials and the various international and non-governmental organizations working in the relevant fields:

- Examine the decision-making processes of fighters who joined IS and other extremist groups as closely as possible. If they left their country, why? How did they choose their destination, militant group and/or targets? What made violence attractive? And so on. Interview them directly with the help of trained professionals to learn about the underlying problems that pushed them to jihad.

- Find ways to reduce the perceived injustices that can make individuals vulnerable to recruitment, such as corruption, abuse of power by law enforcement and other officials and discrimination against certain groups, e.g., ethnic Uzbeks in southern Kyrgyzstan. (Further strengthening community policing may be one step in this direction.)

- Provide better security for the radiological sources in use in Central Asia.

- Ensure that information about potential terrorist threats is not skewed by Central Asian governments to get more money for military equipment or counterterrorism measures or to justify heavy-handed practices.

- Since so many Central Asian jihadists are recruited as labor migrants, help develop sustainable modes of improving economic opportunities at home where they will continue to have social support networks while earning a living.

Russia Matters is a project launched in 2016 by Harvard Kennedy School's BelferCenter for Science and International Affairs and made possible with support from Carnegie Corporation of New York. The project's main aim is to improve the understanding of Russia and the U.S.-Russian relationship among America's policymakers and concerned public. Russia Matters likewise endeavours to build bridges between academe and the policymaking community. Russia Matters BelferCenter for Science and International Affairs Harvard Kennedy School 79 John F. Kennedy Street Cambridge, MA 02138. Edward Lemon is the DMGS-Kennan Institute Fellow at the Daniel Morgan Graduate School. Dr. Lemon was previously a Mellon Postdoctoral Teaching Fellow at the Harriman Institute at Columbia University. He gained his PhD in international studies from the University of Exeter in the United Kingdom in 2016. Vera Mironova is a visiting scholar in Harvard University's Economics

Department, and is also affiliated with the Davis Center. From 2015 to 2018, she was an International Security Fellow at the BelferCenter for Science and International Affairs. William Tobey is a senior fellow at Harvard's BelferCenter for Science and International Affairs and the director of Belfer's U.S.-Russia Initiative to Prevent Nuclear Terrorism. Russia Matters BelferCenter for Science and International Affairs Harvard Kennedy School 79 John F. Kennedy Street Cambridge, MA 02138. www.russiamatters.org. https://www.russiamatters.org/analysis/jihadists-ex-soviet-central-asia-where-are-they-why-did-they-radicalize-what-next.

Notes to Chapter

Chapter 1: Resisting Radical Rebels: Variations in Islamist Rebel Governance and the Occurrence of Civil Resistance. Matthew Bamber and Isak Svensson

1. Zachariah Mampilly, *Rebel Rulers: Insurgent Governance and Civilian Life during War* (Ithaca, NY: Cornell University Press, 2011).

2. Mara Redlich Revkin, *When Terrorists Govern: Protecting Civilians in Conflicts with State-Building Armed Groups* (Rochester, NY: Social Science Research Network, January 29, 2018). https://papers.ssrn.com/abstract=3047495 (accessed December 1, 2021).

3. Brynjar Lia, "Understanding Jihadi Proto-States," *Perspectives on Terrorism* 9, no. 4 (2015). http://www.terrorismanalysts.com/pt/index.php/pot/article/view/441 (accessed November 13, 2017).

4. Zachariah Mampilly and Megan A. Stewart, "A Typology of Rebel Political Institutional Arrangements," *Journal of Conflict Resolution* 65, no. 1 (2021): 15–45.

5. Jerome Drevon, "The Jihadi Social Movement (JSM): Between Factional Hegemonic Drive, National Realities, and Transnational Ambitions," *Perspectives on Terrorism* 11, no. 6 (2017): 55–62.

6. SMART News, "احتجاجات في سراقب بإدلب لمنع عنصر اقتتال أحرار الشام' وتحرير الشام' ودخول الأخيرة للمدينة (فيديو)," *SMART News Agency*, July 15, 2017. https://smartnews-agency.com/ar/wires/2017-07-15-احتجاجات-في-سراقب-بإدلب-لمنع-اقتتال-أحرار-الشام-و-تحرير-الشام. (accessed October 18, 2019).

7. Anne Barnard and Thomas Erdbrink, "ISIS Makes Gains in Syria Territory Bombed by Russia," *The New York Times*, October 9, 2015. https://www.nytimes.com/2015/10/10/world/middleeast/hussein-hamedani-iran-general-killed-in-syria.html (accessed December 2, 2021).

8. Erica Chenoweth and Jay Ulfelder, "Can Structural Conditions Explain the Onset of Nonviolent Uprisings?" *Journal of Conflict Resolution* 61, no. 2 (2017): 298–324; and Lasse Rørbæk, "Ethnic Exclusion and Civil Resistance Campaigns: Opting for Nonviolent or Violent Tactics?" *Terrorism and Political Violence* 31, no. 3 (2016): 1–19.

9. See, for example, Ana Arjona, *Rebelocracy: Social Order in the Colombian Civil War*, Cambridge Studies in Comparative Politics (New York, NY: Cambridge University Press, 2016); and Sebastian van Baalen, "Local Elites, Civil

Resistance, and the Responsiveness of Rebel Governance in Côte d'Ivoire," *Journal of Peace Research* 58, no. 5 (2021): 930–44.

10. Isak Svensson and Daniel Finnbogason, "Confronting the Caliphate? Explaining Civil Resistance in Jihadist Proto-States," *European Journal of International Relations*, 27, no. 2 (2021): 572–95.

11. See, for example, Maia Hallward, Juan Masullo, and Cécile Mouly, "Civil Resistance in Armed Conflict: Leveraging Nonviolent Action to Navigate War, Oppose Violence and Confront Oppression," *Journal of Peacebuilding & Development* 12, no. 3 (2017): 1–9; Oliver Kaplan, *Resisting War: How Communities Protect Themselves* (Cambridge: Cambridge University Press, 2017); Juan Masullo, "Civilian Contention in Civil War: How Ideational Factors Shape Community Responses to Armed Groups," *Comparative Political Studies* 54, no. 10 (2021): 1849–84; and Jana Krause, *Resilient Communities: Non-Violence and Civilian Agency in Communal War* (Cambridge: Cambridge University Press, 2018).

12. Mampilly and Stewart, "A Typology of Rebel Political Institutional Arrangements."

13. An exception to this is the study on taxation and ideology by Mara Redlich Revkin, "What Explains Taxation by Resource-Rich Rebels? Evidence from the Islamic State in Syria," *The Journal of Politics* 82, no. 2 (2020): 757–64.

14. See Thomas Hegghammer, "Jihadi-Salafis or Revolutionaries?," in *Global Salafism*, ed. Roel Meijer (New York: Oxford University Press, 2014): 245–66; and Shiraz Maher, *Salafi-Jihadism: The History of an Idea* (Oxford: Oxford University Press, 2016).

15. Anne Stenersen, "Jihadism after the 'Caliphate': Towards a New Typology," *British Journal of Middle Eastern Studies* 47, no. 5 (2018): 774–93.

16. See note 3, p. 39.

17. Regine Schwab, "Insurgent Courts in Civil Wars: The Three Pathways of (Trans) Formation in Today's Syria (2012–2017)," *Small Wars & Insurgencies* 29, no. 4 (2018): 801–26.

18. See note 15.

19. See note 15.

20. Regine Schwab, "Governance of Jabhat Al-Nusra" (presented at the Islamist Rebel Governance Workshop, Geneva: The Graduate Institute of International and Development Studies, 2020).

21. See Gilles Kepel, *Jihad: The Trail of Political Islam*, trans. by Anthony F. Roberts, Edition Unstated (Cambridge, MA: Belknap Press; An Imprint of Harvard University Press, 2003); and Fawaz A. Gerges, *The Far Enemy: Why Jihad Went Global* (New York: Cambridge University Press, 2009).

22. Maher, *Salafi-Jihadism*.

23. Marta Furlan, "Understanding Governance by Insurgent Non-State Actors: A Multi-Dimensional Typology," *Civil Wars* 22, no. 4 (2020): 478–511.

24. Benedetta Berti, "From Cooperation to Competition: Localization, Militarization and Rebel Co-Governance Arrangements in Syria," *Studies in Conflict & Terrorism* (2020): 1–19.

25. Jerome Drevon and Patrick Haenni, "The Consolidation of a (Post-Jihadi) Technocratic State-Let in Idlib," *Project on Middle East Political Science*, 2020. https://pomeps.org/the-consolidation-of-a-post-jihadi-technocratic-state-let-in-idlib (accessed December 1, 2021).

26. See Furlan, "Understanding Governance by Insurgent Non-State Actors"; Mara Redlich Revkin, *Relative Legitimacy and Displacement Decisions During Rebel Governance* (Rochester, NY: Social Science Research Network, October 14, 2019). https://papers.ssrn.com/abstract=3365503 (accessed February 17, 2020); Craig Whiteside and Anas Elallame, "Accidental Ethnographers: The Islamic State's Tribal Engagement Experiment," *Small Wars & Insurgencies* 31, no. 2 (2020): 219–40; and Mampilly and Stewart, "A Typology of Rebel Political Institutional Arrangements."

27. See Jeremy M. Weinstein, *Inside Rebellion: The Politics of Insurgent Violence* (Cambridge: Cambridge University Press, 2007); Lindsay L. Heger and Danielle F. Jung, "Negotiating with Rebels: The Effect of Rebel Service Provision on Conflict Negotiations," *Journal of Conflict Resolution* 61, no. 6 (2017): 1203–29; Ana Arjona, *Rebelocracy: Social Order in the Colombian Civil War*; and van Baalen, "Local Elites, Civil Resistance, and the Responsiveness of Rebel Governance."

28. Masullo, "Civilian Contention in Civil War."

29. See Gene Sharp, *The Politics of Nonviolent Action* (Boston, MA: P. Sargent Publisher, 1973); and Kurt Schock, *Unarmed Insurrections: People Power Movements in Nondemocracies*, 1st ed. (Minneapolis, MN: University Of Minnesota Press, 2004).

30. See Peter Ackerman and Chris Kruegler, *Strategic Nonviolent Conflict: The Dynamics of People Power in the Twentieth Century* (Westport, CT: Praeger, 1993); Erica Chenoweth and Maria J. Stephan, *Why Civil Resistance Works: The Strategic Logic of Nonviolent Conflict* (New York, NY: Columbia University Press, 2011); and Sharon Erickson Nepstad, *Nonviolent Revolutions: Civil Resistance in the Late 20th Century*, Oxford Studies in Culture and Politics (Oxford: Oxford University Press, 2011).

31. Benjamin Acosta, "Exclusionary Politics and Organized Resistance," *Terrorism and Political Violence* (2019): 1–23.

32. Margherita Belgioioso, Stefano Costalli, and Kristian Skrede Gleditsch, "Better the Devil You Know? How Fringe Terrorism Can Induce an Advantage for

Moderate Nonviolent Campaigns," *Terrorism and Political Violence* 33, no. 3 (2021): 596–615.

33. Ana Arjona, "Civilian Resistance to Rebel Governance" in *Rebel Governance in Civil War*, edited by Ana Arjona, Nelson Kasfir, and Zachariah Mampilly (Cambridge: Cambridge University Press, 2015), 21–46; and Hallward et al., "Civil Resistance in Armed Conflict."

34. Charles Butcher and Isak Svensson, "Manufacturing Dissent: Modernization and the Onset of Major Nonviolent Resistance Campaigns," *Journal of Conflict Resolution* 60, no. 2 (2016): 311–39; and Chenoweth and Ulfelder, "Can Structural Conditions Explain the Onset."

35. Doug McAdam, John D. McCarthy, and Mayer N. Zald, *Comparative Perspectives on Social Movements: Political Opportunities, Mobilizing Structures, and Cultural Framings* (Cambridge: Cambridge University Press, 1996); Sidney Tarrow, *Power in Movement: Social Movements and Contentious Politics*, Cambridge Studies in Comparative Politics, 2nd ed. (Cambridge: Cambridge University Press, 1998); and David S. Meyer, "Protest and Political Opportunities," *Annual Review of Sociology* 30, no. 1 (2004), 125–45.

36. Tarrow, *Power in Movement*, 76–77.

37. Kurt Schock, "People Power and Political Opportunities: Social Movement Mobilization and Outcomes in the Philippines and Burma," *Social Problems* 46, no. 3 (1999): 355–75.

38. See Håvard Hegre Tanja Ellingsen, Scott Gates and Nils Petter Gleditsch, "Toward a Democratic Civil Peace? Democracy, Political Change, and Civil War, 1816–1992," *The American Political Science Review* 95, no. 1 (2001): 33–48; and Edward N. Muller and Erich Weede, "Cross-National Variation in Political Violence: A Rational Action Approach," *The Journal of Conflict Resolution* 34, no. 4 (1990): 624–51.

39. See note 37.

40. Svensson, Isak, with Daniel Finnbogason, Dino Krause, Luís Martínez Lorenzo, and Nanar Hawach (2022). *Confronting the Caliphate: Civil Resistance in Jihadist Proto-States*, Oxford University Press.

41. Syrian Observatory Human Rights, "Islamic State Closes 2 Institutions in Deir Ezzor • The Syrian Observatory For Human Rights," *The Syrian Observatory Human Rights* (2014). https://www.syriahr.com/en/7252/ (accessed December 1, 2021).

42. SMART News, "احتجاجات في سراقب بادلب لمنع اقتحام داعش أحرار الشام' وخدو الأخيري للمدينة (فيديو)."

43. Sadek Abdul Rahman, "Maarrat Al-Nu'man: A Hundred Days of Confrontation with al-Nusra Front," *AlJumhuriya.Net*, 2016. https://www.aljumhuriya.net/en/content/maarrat-al-nu percentE2 percent80 percent99man-hundred-

days-confrontation-al-nusra-front (accessed December 1, 2021); and Umberto Bacchi, "Syria: Maarat al-Numan Civilians Protest against al-Qaeda's Nusra Front after Attack on US-Backed Rebel Group," *International Business Times UK*, 2016. https://www.ibtimes.co.uk/syria-maarat-al-numan-civilians-protest-against-al-qaedas-nusra-front-after-attack-us-backed-1549421 (accessed December 1, 2021).

44. Manhal Bareesh, "Saraqib's Local Elections Show How Democracy Can Break Through in Syria," *Syria From Within | Chatham House*, 2017. https://syria. chathamhouse.org/research/saraqibs-local-elections-show-how-democracy-can-break-through-in-syria (accessed December 1, 2021).

45. SMART News, "تحرير الشام" لقن احتجاجات في مدينة سراقب رفضا لقرار" محطة الكهرباء,' *SMART News Agency*, January 30, 2018. https://smartnews-agency.com/ar/wires/2018-01-30-احتجاجات-في-مدينة-سراقب-رفضا-لقرار-تحرير-الشام-لقن-محطة-الكهر.

46. SMART News, "إعتصام لليوم الثاني في السويداء للمطالبة بالمختطفين لدى تنظيم 'الدولة'," *SMART News Agency*, April 10, 2018b. https://smartnews-agency.com/ar/wires/2018-10-04-إعتصام-لليوم-الثاني-في-السويداء-للمطالبة-بالمختطفين-لدى-تنظيم.

47. Syrian Observatory Human Rights, "ISIS on Retreat in Deir Al-Zor after Surprise Attack • The Syrian Observatory For Human Rights," *The Syrian Observatory For Human Rights*, 2014. https://www.syriahr.com/en/4484/ (accessed December 1, 2021).

48. SMART News, "مظاهرة في مدينة جرابلس بحلب للمطالبة بخروج الفصائل," *SMART News Agency*, June 1, 2018. https://smartnews-agency.com/ar/photos/2018-06-01-مظاهرة-في-مدينة-جرابلس-بحلب-للمطالبة-بخروج-الفصائل-ووقف-463#0.

49. See, for example, Butcher and Svensson, "Manufacturing Dissent"; and Chenoweth and Ulfelder, "Can Structural Conditions Explain the Onset."

50. Chenoweth and Stephan, *Why Civil Resistance Works*.

51. IHS Markit, "Islamic State Territory Down 60 Percent and Revenue Down 80 Percent on Caliphate's Third Anniversary, IHS Markit Says," 2017. https://www.businesswire.com/news/home/20170629005484/en/Islamic-State-Territory-Down-60-Percent-and-Revenue-Down-80-Percent-on-Caliphate percentE2 percent80 percent99s-Third-Anniversary-IHS-Markit-Says (accessed October 15, 2020).

52. For detailed maps of urban/rural divide in Syria, see Fabrice Balanche, *Sectarianism in Syria's Civil War* (Washington Institute for Near East Policy, 2018). https://www.washingtoninstitute.org/uploads/Documents/pubs/SyriaAtlasCOMPLETE-3.pdf (accessed December 7, 2020).

53. Andrew Halterman, Jill Irvine, and Khaled Jabr, "Do the Answers You Get Depend on the News You Read? Protests and Violence in Syria," 2019. https://andrewhalterman.com/files/Halterman_Irvine_Jabr_v3.pdf.

54. Seth Jones, Charles Vallee, Clayton Sharb, Hannah Byrne, Danika Newlee and Nicholas Harrington, *The Evolution of the Salafi-Jihadist Threat* (Washington, DC: Center for Strategic and International Studies, November 2018).

55. Matthew Bamber, "Honeymoon, Peak and Degradation: Three Phases of Islamic State's Rebel Governance Effectiveness" (paper presented at Islamist Rebel Governance Workshop 2020, The Graduate Institute, Geneva).

56. Daveed Gartenstein-Ross, "How Many Fighters Does the Islamic State Really Have?" *War on the Rocks*, 2015. https://warontherocks.com/2015/02/how-many-fighters-does-the-islamic-state-really-have/ (accessed December 12, 2017).

57. Hassan Hassan, "Insurgents Again: The Islamic State's Calculated Reversion to Attrition in the Syria-Iraq Border Region and Beyond," *CTC Sentinel* 10, no. 11 (2017). https://ctc.usma.edu/insurgents-again-the-islamic-states-calculated-reversion-to-attrition-in-the-syria-iraq-border-region-and-beyond/ (accessed October 18, 2019).

58. See note 54.

59. Michael Weiss and Hassan Hassan, *ISIS: Inside the Army of Terror* (New York: Regan Arts, 2016).

60. Malik, 31, fighter, Hasakah province. Interview: May 2019, Turkey.

61. Karam, 42, janitor, al-Khayr province. Interview: May 2019, Turkey.

62. Rudayna Al-Baalbaky and Ahmad Mhidi, *Tribes and The Rule of the "Islamic State": The Case of the Sytian City of Deir Az-Zor* (Beriut: Issam Fares Institute for Public Policy and International Affairs, 2018).

63. Whiteside and Elallame, "Accidental Ethnographers."

64. Raquel Da Silva, Matthew Bamber, and Nicolas Lemay-Herbert, "Exploring the Strategic Narrative of Governance and Statebuilding by the Islamic State" (paper presented at European Conference on Political Research 2020).

65. Yara, 33, teacher, al-Khayr province. Interview: May 2019, Turkey.

66. Mara Redlich Revkin and Ariel I. Ahram, "Perspectives on the Rebel Social Contract: Exit, Voice, and Loyalty in the Islamic State in Iraq and Syria," *World Development*, 132 (2020): 104981.

67. Farouq, 36, electrician, al-Khayr province. Interview: May 2019, Turkey.

68. Ruba, 27, student, al-Khayr province. Interview: May 2019, Turkey.

69. Aaron Y. Zelin, "The Islamic State's Territorial Methodology," *The Washington Institute*, 2016. https://www.washingtoninstitute.org/policy-analysis/islamic-states-territorial-methodology (accessed December 2, 2021).

70. Abbas, 39, accountant, Raqqa province. Interview: November 2018, Lebanon.

71. Jabar, 19, fighter, Deir az Zur (al-Khayr) province. Interview: May 2019, Turkey.

72. Abdul, 41, lawyer, al-Khayr province. Interview: January 2019, Online.

73. See note 64.

74. Revkin, *When Terrorists Govern*; and Revkin, *Relative Legitimacy and Displacement Decisions*.

75. Nour, 43, housewife, Deir az Zur province. Interview: November 2018, Lebanon.

76. Schwab, "Governance of Jabhat Al-Nusra"; and Aymenn Jawad Al-Tamimi, *Idlib and Its Environs: Narrowing Prospects for a Rebel Holdout* (Washington, DC: The Washington Institute for Near East Policy, February 2020).

77. See note 25.

78. Al-Tamimi, *Idlib and Its Environs*, 4.

79. See note 25.

80. See note 20, p. 6.

81. See note 20.

82. Ibrahim Al-Assil, "Al-Qaeda Affiliate and Ahrar al-Sham Compete for Control in Idlib," *Middle East Institute*, 2017. https://www.mei.edu/publications/al-qaeda-affiliate-and-ahrar-al-sham-compete-control-idlib (accessed October 15, 2020).

83. See note 78.

84. Sam Heller, "Keeping the Lights On in Rebel Idlib," *The Century Foundation*, 2016. https://tcf.org/content/report/keeping-lights-rebel-idlib/ (accessed October 15, 2020).

85. See note 25.

86. See note 78.

87. Quoted in Schwab, "Governance of Jabhat Al-Nusra."

88. See note 25.

89. See note 17.

90. See note 25.

91. Interview with Abbas, 28, logistics worker, Idlib governorate. Interview: Turkey, May 2019.

92.   Interview with Bassam, 38, lawyer, Idlib governorate. Interview: Online, January 2019.

93. Charles Lister, *Profiling Jabhat Al-Nusra* (Washington, DC: Brookings Institution, July 2016).

94. Aymenn Jawad Al-Tamimi, *From Jabhat Al-Nusra to Hay'at Tahrir al-Sham: Evolution, Approach and Future* (Berlin: Konrad Adenauer Stiftung, 2016).

95. Sultan Al Kanj, "Reviewing the Turkey–HTS Relationship," *Chatham House*, 2019. https://syria.chathamhouse.org/research/reviewing-the-turkey-hts-relationship (accessed October 15, 2020).

96. See note 93, p. 23.

97. Interview with Abdalhadi, 36, unemployed, Deir al Zur and Idlib governorate. Interview: Turkey, May 2019.

98. Interview with Hafsah, 26, student, Aleppo and Idlib governorate. Interview: Turkey, April 2019.

99. Haid Haid, "Resisting Hayat Tahrir Al-Sham: Syrian Civil Society on the Frontlines," *Adopt Revolution*, 2017.

100. Interview quoted in Haid, "Resisting Hayat Tahrir Al-Sham."

101. Human Rights Watch, "Syria: Arrests, Torture by Armed Group," *Human Rights Watch*, 2019. https://www.hrw.org/news/2019/01/28/syria-arrests-torture-armed-group (accessed October 15, 2020).

102. *Ibid.*

103. See note 84.

104. See note 93.

105. Karin Göldner-Ebenthal and Ahmed Elsayed, *Salafi Jihadi Armed Groups and Conflict (de-) Escalation* (Berlin: Berghof Foundation, December 2019).

106. Aron Lund quoted in Michael Jonsson, *Biding Its Time: The Strategic Resilience of Ahrar al-Sham* (Stockholm: Swedish Defence Research Agency, December 2016), 2.

107. Haid Haid, "Resisting Hayat Tahrir Al-Sham."

108. See note 105, p. 9.

109. See note 93.

110. See note 25.

111. Jonsson, *Biding Its Time*, 3.

112. See note 84.

113. Sam Heller, "Ahrar Al-Sham's Revisionist Jihadism," *War on the Rocks*, 2015. https://warontherocks.com/2015/09/ahrar-al-shams-revisionist-jihadism/ (accessed October 15, 2020).

114. See note 25.

115. See note 84.

116. Robert S. Ford and Ali El Yassir, "Yes, Talk with Syria's Ahrar al-Sham," *Middle East Institute*, 2015. https://www.mei.edu/publications/yes-talk-syrias-ahrar-al-sham (accessed December 1, 2021).

117. See note 105, p. 9.

118. See note 111, p. 5.

119. See note 105.

120. See note 113.

121. Felix Legrand, "The Strategy of Jabhat Al-Nusra / Jabhat Fath Al-Sham in Regarding the Truces in Syria," *Noria Research*, 2016. https://noria-research.com/strategy-regarding-truces-in-syria/ (accessed December 2, 2021).

122. Ali Melhem, "Locals in Idlib Take on Al-Nusra Front," *The New Humanitarian*, 2016. https://deeply.thenewhumanitarian.org/syria/community/2016/03/19/locals-in-idlib-take-on-al-nusra-front (accessed October 15, 2020).

123. Brian Martin, "From Political Jiu-Jitsu to the Backfire Dynamic: How Repression Can Promote Mobilization," in *Civil Resistance: Comparative Perspectives on Nonviolent Struggle*, ed. Kurt Schock (Minneapolis, MN: University of Minnesota Press, 2015): 145–67.

124. Arjona, "Civilian Resistance to Rebel Governance."

125. van Baalen, "Local Elites, Civil Resistance, and the Responsiveness of Rebel Governance."

126. For a detailed discussion on tribes in Syria, see Haian Dukhan, *State and Tribes in Syria: Informal Alliances and Conflict Patterns*, 1st ed. (New York: Routledge, 2018).

127. See note 1.

128. See note 52.

129. Stathis N. Kalyvas, *The Logic of Violence in Civil War*, Cambridge Studies in Comparative Politics (Cambridge: Cambridge University Press, 2006), 13.

130. See note 44.

131. See note 52, p. 7.

132. See note 55.

Chapter 2: Rebel Governance, Rebel Legitimacy, and External Intervention: Assessing three phases of Taliban rule in Afghanistan. Niels Terpstra

1. Weinstein, Inside Rebellion; Mampilly, Rebel Rulers; Klem and Maunaguru,"Insurgent Rule"; and Hoffmann and Verweijen, "Rebel Rule."

2. Kasfir, "Rebel Governance."

3. Stel, "Governing the Gatherings," 20–30.

4. Schlichte and Schneckener, "Armed Groups and the Politics of Legitimacy"; Duyvesteyn, "Rebels & Legitimacy"; Schoon, "Building Legitimacy"; Terpstra and Frerks, "Rebel Governance and Legitimacy"; Worrall, "(Re-)Emergent Orders"; and Kasfir, "Foreword."

5. Terpstra and Frerks, "Rebel Governance and Legitimacy."

6. Schoon, "Building Legitimacy," 748.

7. Kasfir, Frerks, and Terpstra, "Introduction," 257.

8. O'Neill, From Revolution to Apocalypse, 142–48.

9. Huang, "Rebel Diplomacy in Civil War"; and Malejacq, "From Rebel to QuasiState."

10. Schröder and Schmidt, "Introduction," 9.

11. Ibid., 9.

12. In general terms, the mujahideen can be characterized as a 'force of religious nationalists: communities – particularly those from rural areas – were motivated to participate in the jihad by religious fatwas sanctioning jihad, but also to protect their land, their villages, traditions and customs' (Strick van Linschoten, 2016, p. 112).

13. Ruttig, "How Tribal Are the Taliban?" 23–24.

14. Strick van Linschoten and Kuehn, The Taliban Reader, 1.

15. Edwards, Before Taliban; Barfield, "Establishing Legitimacy in Afghanistan"; Barfield, Afghanistan; Ruttig, "How Tribal Are Taliban?"; Strick van Linschoten and Kuehn, An Enemy We Created; Strick van Linschoten and Kuehn, The Taliban Reader; Strick van Linschoten, "Mullah Wars"; Ibrahimi, "The Taliban's Islamic Emirate of Afghanistan (1996–2001)"; Weigand, "Afghanistan's Taliban";Jackson, "Life under the Taliban Shadow Government"; and Johnson, Taliban Narratives.

16. Kalyvas, The Logic of Violence in Civil War, 5.

17. Kasfir, Frerks, and Terpstra, "Introduction," 259.

18. Kalyvas, The Logic of Violence in Civil War, 210–20.

19. Duyvesteyn et al., "Reconsidering Rebel Governance"; Kasfir, Frerks, and Terpstra, "Introduction," 258; and Murtazashvili, "A Tired Cliché."

20. Kalyvas, Logic of Violence, 218.

21. Rosenau et al., Governance without Government, 4.

22. Kasfir, "Rebel Governance," 24.

23. Kasfir, "Dilemmas of Popular Support in Guerrilla War," 4.

24. Mampilly, Rebel Rulers; Arjona, Kasfir, and Mampilly, Rebel Governance in Civil War; Duyvesteyn et al., "Reconsidering Rebel Governance"; Arjona, Rebelocracy; and Kasfir, Frerks, and Terpstra, "Introduction."

25. For a discussion on the Taliban's current involvement in other governance sectors, such as education and health care, or its taxation practices, see Jackson (2018).

26. Kasfir, Frerks, and Terpstra, "Introduction," 274.

27. Terpstra and Frerks, "Governance Practices and Symbolism," 1013.

28. See note 26 above.

29. Mampilly, Rebel Rulers, 56.

30. Suchman, "Managing Legitimacy," 574.

31. Terpstra and Frerks, "Rebel Governance and Legitimacy," 285.

32. Terpstra and Frerks, "Governance Practices and Symbolism," 1035–36.

33. Worrall, "(Re-)Emergent Orders," 715.

34. Schlichte and Schneckener, "Armed Groups and the Politics of Legitimacy," 418.

35. Kalyvas, "Promises and Pitfalls of an Emerging Research Program"; and Terpstra, "Statebuilding, Legal Pluralism, and Irregular Warfare."

36. Schlichte and Schneckener, "Armed Groups and the Politics of Legitimacy," 417

37. Ibid., 417.

38. Ibid., 417–18.

39. Kasfir, "Foreword," xiii.

40. Weber, The Theory of Social and Economic Organization, 359; and Kasfir, "Foreword," xiii.

41. Terpstra and Frerks, "Rebel Governance and Legitimacy," 281.

42. Ibid., 281.

43. Weigand, "Afghanistan's Taliban," 376.

44. Huang, "Rebel Diplomacy in Civil War"; and Podder, "Understanding the Legitimacy of Armed Groups," 698–701.

45. See note 8 above.

46. Johnson, Taliban Narratives, 31–33.

47. The PRTs were invented by the United States. They generally consist of military compounds with military officers but also include diplomats and reconstruction experts who work together on reconstruction.

48. The security situation in Kunduz has been dire, particularly since the temporary fall of Kunduz city to the Taliban in September 2015. Common data collection challenges include the following: threats to the personal security of researchers and respondents, scarcity of data, lack of monitoring of field surveyors, high staff turnover within research organizations, unsteady access to certain districts at certain points in time, incorrect expectations of researchers and respondents regarding data collection, multiple layers of interpretation in the data collection process, and social desirability in the answers of respondents.

49. Malejacq, "From Rebel to Quasi-State," 871.

50. Barfield, Afghanistan, 211.

51. Ibid., 215.

52. Johnson, The Afghan Way of War, 206.

53. Ibid., 207.

54. Barfield, Afghanistan, 225.

55. Safi, "The Afghan Taliban's Relationship with Pakistan," 14; and Barfield, Afghanistan, 225.

56. Barfield, Afghanistan, 225.

57. Ruttig, "How Tribal Are the Taliban?" 10.

58. Ibid., 10.

59. Strick van Linschoten and Kuehn, An Enemy We Created, 18.

60. Ruttig, "How Tribal Are the Taliban?" 11; and Safi, "The Afghan Taliban's Relationship with Pakistan."

61. Ruttig, "How Tribal Are the Taliban?" 11; Safi, "The Afghan Taliban"s Relationship with Pakistan," 15; and Strick van Linschoten and Kuehn, An Enemy We Created, 43–50.

62. 'Talib' literally translates to 'student.' 'Taliban' or 'Taliban' is plural and translates to 'students.' Mullahs are religious leaders usually – at least at a very basic level – educated in Islamic traditions and Islamic law.

63. Strick van Linschoten and Kuehn, An Enemy We Created, 45.

64. Ibid., 45.

65. The Peshawar Seven included Hezb (Hekmatyar), Hezb (Hales), Jamiat (Rabbani), Harakat (Nabi Muhammadi), Ittehad (Sayyaf), Nejat (Mujaddedi), and Mahaz (Gailani) (Ruttig 2010, p. 11).

66. Ruttig, "How Tribal Are the Taliban?" 11.

67. Coll, Directorate S, 2.

68. Strick van Linschoten and Kuehn, An Enemy We Created, 46.

69. Giustozzi and Baczko, "The Politics of the Taliban's Shadow Judiciary, 2003–2013," 201; and Strick van Linschoten and Kuehn, An Enemy We Created, 47.

70. Strick van Linschoten, "Mullah Wars," 111.

71. Strick van Linschoten and Kuehn, An Enemy We Created, 46.

72. Ibid., 67.

73. Ibid., 43.

74. Johnson and Mason, "Understanding the Taliban and Insurgency in Afghanistan," 73.

75. Coll, Directorate S, 1.

76. Strick van Linschoten and Kuehn, An Enemy We Created, 66–67.

77. Coll, Directorate S; and Giustozzi, Empires of Mud.

78. Giustozzi, Empires of Mud, 50.

79. Staniland, Networks of Rebellion, 126–27.

80. Giustozzi, Empires of Mud, 83.

81. Strick van Linschoten, "Mullah Wars," 20.

82. Ibid., 20.

83. Zaeef, Strick van Linschoten, and Kuehn, My Life with the Taliban, 60–61.

84. Strick van Linschoten and Kuehn, An Enemy We Created, 114.

85. Zaeef, Strick van Linschoten, and Kuehn, My Life with the Taliban, 65. The Taliban movement garnered support of Pakistani authorities, but it was certainly not founded by Pakistan (Safi, 2018, p. 17). For example, alongside the inception of the movement in 1994, a Taliban office was opened in Quetta in Pakistan. One of the Taliban buildings there was used to 'recruit new fighters into the movement, another house was a place where injured Taliban were treated medically,' and a third building 'functioned as storage facility' (Safi, 2018, p. 18).

86. Strick van Linschoten and Kuehn, An Enemy We Created, 117.

87. Johnson and Mason, "Understanding the Taliban and Insurgency in Afghanistan," 74.

88. Giustozzi, Empires of Mud, 82.

89. Ibid., 82.

90. Giustozzi and Baczko, "The Politics of the Taliban's Shadow Judiciary," 203.

91. Giustozzi, Empires of Mud, 83.

92. Barfield, Afghanistan, 261.

93. Barfield, Afghanistan; Giustozzi, Empires of Mud; and Mukhopadhyay, Warlords, Strongman Governors, and the State in Afghanistan, 136.

94. Depending on the strictness of the definition, the Taliban ceases to be a rebel group or an insurgency once it capture the capital and the majority of Afghanistan's geographical territory. Nevertheless, for the sake of the longitudinal analysis in this article, I decided to expand the scope of the conditions and also consider the full timeframe of 1996–2001 a continuation of rebel governance and rebel legitimacy.

95. Ibrahimi, "The Taliban's Islamic Emirate of Afghanistan (1996–2001)," 947–48.

96. Ibid., 947–48.

97. Barfield, Afghanistan, 263.

98. Ruttig, "How Tribal Are the Taliban?" 12.

99. Ibid., 12.

100. Ibid., 12.

101. Otto, "Introduction," 23.

102. Ibid., 23–49.

103. Yassari and Saboory, "Sharia and National Law in Afghanistan," 312.

104. Edwards, Before Taliban, 302–3.

105. Yassari and Saboory, "Sharia and National Law in Afghanistan," 291.

106. Rashid, Taliban, 2000, 50.

107. Yassari and Saboory, "Sharia and National Law in Afghanistan," 292.

108. Ibid., 292.

109. Edwards, Before Taliban, 295–96.

110. Barfield, Afghanistan, 262.

111. Yassari and Saboory, "Sharia and National Law in Afghanistan," 292.

112. Ibrahimi, "The Taliban's Islamic Emirate of Afghanistan (1996–2001)," 955.

113. Rashid, Taliban, 2001, 303–4.

114. Strick van Linschoten, "Mullah Wars," 121.

115. Ibid., 121.

116. Barfield, "Problems in Establishing Legitimacy in Afghanistan," 288.

117. Barfield, Afghanistan, 261–63; and Weigand, "Afghanistan's Taliban," 363.

118. Hezb-e Wahdat is a political movement in Afghanistan. Like most Afghan political movements, it is rooted in the anti-Soviet resistance. Political Islamism is its ideology, but it is mostly supported by ethnic Hazaras, who follow a Shia interpretation of Islam.

119. Wörmer, "The Networks of Kunduz," 22.

120. Rashid, Taliban, 2001, 163.

121. Ibid., 163.

122. Barfield, Afghanistan; Strick van Linschoten and Kuehn, An Enemy We Created. There is debate regarding why exactly this occurred (Strick van Linschoten and Kuehn, 2014, pp. 130–34). It was an important moment for the Taliban movement itself and how it was seen by the outside world. Some interpreted it as a sign that Mullah Omar was the legitimate person to establish an Islamic government in Afghanistan. Some Talibs who were present at the meeting allegedly stated that it served to diffuse internal rivalries within the movement, while others mentioned the push for Pakistani influence (Strick van Linschoten and Kuehn, 2014, pp. 131–33).

123. Strick van Linschoten and Kuehn, An Enemy We Created, 133.

124. Strick van Linschoten, "Mullah Wars," 101.

125. Strick van Linschoten and Kuehn, An Enemy We Created, 133.

126. Strick van Linschoten, "Mullah Wars," 27.

127. Barfield, "Problems in Establishing Legitimacy in Afghanistan."

128. Ibrahimi, "The Taliban's Islamic Emirate of Afghanistan (1996–2001)," 956.

129. Barfield, Afghanistan, 263.

130. Ibrahimi, "The Taliban's Islamic Emirate of Afghanistan (1996–2001)," 955.

131. Edwards, Before Taliban, 301.

132. Ibid., 301.

133. Malejacq, "From Rebel to Quasi-State."

134. Barfield, Afghanistan, 263.

135. Ibid., 260.

136. Ruttig, "How Tribal Are the Taliban?" 19.

137. Strick van Linschoten and Kuehn, The Taliban Reader, 226.

138. Ibid., 227.

139. Ibid., 227.

140. Ruttig, "How Tribal Are the Taliban?" 19.

141. Jackson, "Life under the Taliban Shadow Government," 9.

142. Ruttig, "How Tribal Are the Taliban?" 21.

143. Giustozzi, "Hearts, Minds, and the Barrel of a Gun"; and Jackson, "Life under the Taliban Shadow Government."

144. Giustozzi and Baczko, "The Politics of the Taliban's Shadow Judiciary, 2003–2013," 199.

145. Strick van Linschoten and Kuehn, The Taliban Reader, 227.

146. IWA, "Corruption and Justice Delivery in Kunduz Province of Afghanistan," 14.

147. IWA, "Corruption and Justice Delivery in Kunduz Province of Afghanistan," 14–15; and Ali, "One Land, Two Rules."

148. Interview code: 2018–13.

149. Interview code: 2018–05.

150. Ali, "One Land, Two Rules," 11.

151. Ibid., 11.

152. Ibid., 11.

153. Interview code: 2018–16.

154. See note 148 above.

155. Interview code: 2018 – 19.

156. Giustozzi and Baczko, "The Politics of the Taliban's Shadow Judiciary," 19–20.

157. See note 43 above.

158. Ibid., 376.

159. Interview code 2018–16.

160. Interview code: 2018–03.

161. Ledwidge, Rebel Law, 72.

162. Johnson, Taliban Narratives, 31.

163. Ibid., 32–33.

164. Ibid., 32.

165. Ibid., 36.

166. Ibid., 22.

167. Ibid., 24.

168. Interview code: 2018 – 12.

169. Interview code: 2018 – 20.

170. Interview code 2018 – 09.

171. Interview code: 2018 – 13.

172. Interview code 2018 – 14.

173. Osman, "Rallying Around the White Flag," 1.

174. Johnson, "The Taliban Insurgency and an Analysis of Shabnamah"; and Johnson, Taliban Narratives.

175. Johnson, "The Taliban Insurgency and an Analysis of Shabnamah," 318.

176. Interview code: 2018–12; 2018–15.

177. Interview code: 2018 – 19.

178. Interview code: 2018 – 13.

179. Interview code 2018 – 01.

180. Johnson, "The Taliban Insurgency and an Analysis of Shabnamah (Night Letters)," 339.

181. Ali, "The Non-Pashtun Taliban of the North."

182. Ibid.

183. See Strick van Linschoten, "Mullah Wars" 99.

184. The literal translation of bacha bazi from Dari is 'boy play.'

185. SIGAR, "Child Sexual Assault in Afghanistan," 1.

186. Jones, "Ending Bacha Bazi," 66.

187. Reid and Muhammedally, "Just Don't Call It a Militia"; and SIGAR, "Child Sexual Assault in Afghanistan."

188. Reid and Muhammedally, "Just Don't Call It a Militia," 42.

189. Ibid.

190. See note 160 above.

191. Interview code: 2018–01.

192. See https://www.pbs.org/wgbh/frontline/film/dancingboys/ (Accessed 11 June 2019).

193. Roy, "Development and Political Legitimacy," 173.

194. See note 43 above.

195. See note 10 above.

Bibliography

Ali, Obaid. The Non-Pashtun Taliban of the North: A Case Study from Badakhshan, Afghanistan Analysts Network. Kabul: Afghanistan Analyst Network, 2017. https://www.afghanistan-analysts.org/the-non-pashtun-Taliban-of-the-north-a-case-study -from-badakhshan/.

Ali, Obaid. One Land, Two Rules (3): Delivering Public Services in Insurgency-Affected Dasht-e Archi District in Kunduz Province. Kabul: Afghanistan Analyst Network, 2019.https://www.afghanistan-analysts.org/one-land-two-rules-3-delivering-publicservices-in-insurgency-affected-dasht-e-archi-district-in-kunduz-province/.

Arjona, Ana. Rebelocracy: Social Order in the Colombian Civil War. New York: Cambridge University Press, 2016.

Arjona, Ana, Nelson Kasfir, and Zacharia Mampilly. Rebel Governance in Civil War. New York: Cambridge University Press, 2015.

Barfield, Thomas."Problems in Establishing Legitimacy in Afghanistan." Iranian Studies 37, no. 2, June (2004): 263–293. doi:10.1080/0021086042000268100.

Barfield, Thomas. Afghanistan: A Cultural and Political History. Princeton, NJ: Princeton University Press, 2010.

Coll, Steve. Directorate S: The C.I.A. And America''s Secret Wars in Afghanistan and Pakistan, 2001-2016. London: Allen Lane, 2018.

Duyvesteyn, Isabelle. "Rebels & Legitimacy; An Introduction." Small Wars & Insurgencies 28, no. 4–5 September 3 (2017): 669–685. doi:10.1080/09592318 .2017.1322337.

Duyvesteyn, Isabelle, Georg Frerks, Boukje Kistemaker, Nora Stel, and Niels Terpstra. "Reconsidering Rebel Governance." In African Frontiers: Insurgency, Governance and Peacebuilding in Postcolonial States, edited by J. I. Lahai and T. Lyons, 31–40. Farnham: Ashgate, 2015.

Edwards, David B. Before Taliban: Genealogies of the Afghan Jihad. Berkeley: University of California Press, 2002.

Giustozzi, Antonio. Empires of Mud: War and Warlords in Afghanistan. London: Hurst, 2009.

Giustozzi, Antonio. "Hearts, Minds, and the Barrel of a Gun: The Taliban''s Shadow Government." Prism: A Journal of the Center for Complex Operations 3, no. 2 (2012): 71–80.

Giustozzi, Antonio, and Adam Baczko. "The Politics of the Taliban''s Shadow Judiciary, 2003–2013." Central Asian Affairs 1, no. 2, September 12 (2014): 199–224. doi:10.1163/22142290-00102003.

Hoffmann, Kasper, and Judith Verweijen. "Rebel Rule: A Governmentality Perspective." African Affairs 118, no. 471 (2018). doi:10.1093/afraf/ady039.

Huang, Reyko. "Rebel Diplomacy in Civil War." International Security 40, no. 4 April (2016): 89–126. doi:10.1162/ISEC_a_00237.

Ibrahimi, S. Yaqub. "The Taliban''s Islamic Emirate of Afghanistan (1996–2001): 'Warmaking and State-Making" as an Insurgency Strategy." Small Wars & Insurgencies 28, no. 6 November 2 (2017): 947–972. doi:10.1080/09592318 .2017.1374598.

IWA. Corruption And Justice Delivery In Kunduz Province Of Afghanistan. Kabul: Integrity Watch Afghanistan (IWA), 2018.

Jackson, Ashley. Life under the Taliban Shadow Government. London: Overseas Development Institute (ODI), 2018.

Johnson, Robert. The Afghan Way of War: Culture and Pragmatism: A Critical History. London: Hurst, 2014.

Johnson, Thomas, and Chris Mason. "Understanding the Taliban and Insurgency in Afghanistan." Orbis: A Journal of World Affairs 51, no. 1 (2007): 71–89. doi:10.1016/j. orbis.2006.10.006.

Johnson, Thomas H. "The Taliban Insurgency and an Analysis of Shabnamah (Night Letters)." Small Wars & Insurgencies 18, no. 3 (September, 2007): 317–344. doi:10.1080/09592310701674176.

Johnson, Thomas H. Taliban Narratives: The Use and Power of Stories in the Afghanistan Conflict. London: Hurst, 2018.

Jones, Samuel V. "Ending Bacha Bazi: Boy Sex Slavery and the Responsibility to Protect Doctrine." Indiana International & Comparative Law Review 25, no. 1 (2015): 63–78.doi:10.18060/7909.0005.

Kalyvas, Stathis N. The Logic of Violence in Civil War. New York: Cambridge University Press, 2006.

Kalyvas, Stathis N. "Promises and Pitfalls of an Emerging Research Program: The Microdynamics of Civil War." In Order, Conflict, and Violence, edited by S. Kalyvas, I. Shapiro, and T. Masoud, 397–421. New York: Cambridge University Press, 2008.

Kasfir, Nelson. Dilemmas of Popular Support in Guerrilla War: The National Resistance Army in Uganda–1981-86, 1–46. Los Angeles: University of California, 2002. http://citeseerx.ist.psu.edu/viewdoc/download?doi=10.1.1.564.47 44&rep=rep1&type=pdf.

Kasfir, Nelson. "Rebel Governance - Constructing a Field of Inquiry: Definitions, Scope, Patterns, Order, Causes." In Rebel Governance in Civil War, edited by Ana Arjona,

Nelson Kasfir, and Zacharia Mampilly, 21–46. New York: Cambridge University Press, 2015.

Kasfir, Nelson. "Foreword: How Legitimacy Helps Explicate Rebel Governance." In Rebels and Legitimacy: Processes and Practices, edited by Isabelle Duyvesteyn, xii–xvii. New York: Routledge, 2019.

Kasfir, Nelson, Georg Frerks, and Niels Terpstra. "Introduction: Armed Groups and Multi-Layered Governance." Civil Wars 19, no. 3, July 3 (2017): 257–278. doi:10.1080/13698249.2017.1419611.

Klem, Bart, and Sidharthan Maunaguru. "Insurgent Rule as Sovereign Mimicry and Mutation: Governance, Kingship, and Violence in Civil Wars." Comparative Studies in Society and History 59, no. 3, July (2017): 629–656. doi:10.1017/S0010417517000196.

Ledwidge, Frank. Rebel Law: Insurgents, Courts and Justice in Modern Conflict. First published. London: Hurst, 2017.

Malejacq, Romain. "From Rebel to Quasi-State: Governance, Diplomacy and Legitimacy in the Midst of Afghanistan's Wars (1979–2001)." Small Wars & Insurgencies 28, no. 4–5 September 3 (2017): 867–886. doi:10.1080/09592318.2017.1322332.

Mampilly, Zachariah Cherian. Rebel Rulers: Insurgent Governance and Civilian Life during War. Ithaca, NY: Cornell University Press, 2011.

Mukhopadhyay, Dipali. Warlords, Strongman Governors, and the State in Afghanistan. New York: Cambridge University Press, 2014.

Murtazashvili, Jennifer. "A Tired Cliché: Why We Should Stop Worrying about Ungoverned Spaces and Embrace Self-Governance." Journal of International Affairs 71, no. 2 (2018): 11–29.

O'Neill, Bard. From Revolution to Apocalypse: Insurgency and Terrorism. Dulles, VA: Potomac Books, 2005.

Osman, Borhan. Rallying around the White Flag: Taliban Embrace an Assertive Identity Afghanistan Analysts Network. Kabul: Afghanistan Analysts Network, 2017. https://www.afghanistan-analysts.org/rallying-around-the-white-flag-Taliban-embrace-an -assertive-identity/.

Otto, Jan Michiel. "Introduction: Investigating the Role of Sharia in National Law." In Sharia Incorporated, edited by Jan Michiel Otto. Leiden: Leiden University Press, 17–50, 2010.

Podder, Sukanya. "Understanding the Legitimacy of Armed Groups: A Relational Perspective." Small Wars & Insurgencies 28, no. 4–5 September 3 (2017): 686–708.doi:10.1080/09592318.2017.1322333.

Rashid, Ahmed. Taliban: Militant Islam, Oil, and Fundamentalism in Central Asia. New Haven, CT: Yale University Press, 2000.

Rashid, Ahmed. Taliban, Translated by Tinke Davids. Amsterdam: Atlas, 2001. Reid, Rachel, and Sahr Muhammedally. 'Just Don"t Call It a Militia": Impunity, Militias, and the 'Afghan Local Police". New York: Human Rights Watch, 2011.

Rosenau, James N., and Ernst-Otto Czempiel, and others. Governance without Government: Order and Change in World Politics. Vol. 20 vols. New York: Cambridge University Press, 1992.

Roy, Olivier. "Development and Political Legitimacy: The Cases of Iraq and Afghanistan." Conflict, Security & Development 4, no. 2 (August, 2004): 167–179. doi:10.1080/1467880042000259095.

Ruttig, Thomas. How Tribal are the Taliban? Afghanistan's Largest Insurgent Movement between Its Tribal Roots and Islamist Ideology. Kabul: Afghanistan Analyst Network,June 2010. https://www.afghanistan-analysts.org/publication/other-publications /how-tribal-are-the-taliban.

Safi, Khalilullah. The Afghan Taliban"s Relationship with Pakistan. Translated by Joesp Mohr. LISD White Paper. Liechtenstein Institute on Self-Determination, 2018. https://dataspace.princeton.edu/jspui/bitstream/88435/dsp01q811kn387/1/WhitePaper_No.4 percent28Safi percent29.pdf

Schlichte, Klaus, and Ulrich Schneckener. "Armed Groups and the Politics of Legitimacy." Civil Wars 17, no. 4 (2016): 409–424. doi:10.1080/13698249.2015.1115573.

Schoon, Eric W. "Building Legitimacy: Interactional Dynamics and the Popular Evaluation of the Kurdistan Workers" Party (PKK) in Turkey." Small Wars &Insurgencies 28, no. 4–5 September 3 (2017): 734–754. doi:10.1080/09592318.2017.1323407.

Schröder, Ingo, and B. Schmidt. "Introduction: Violent Imaginaries and Violent Practices." In Anthropology of Violence and Conflict, edited by B. Schmidt and I.

Schröder, 1–24. New York: Routledge, 2001.

SIGAR. Child Sexual Assault in Afghanistan: Implementation of the Leahy Laws and Reports of Assault by Afghan Security Forces. Wahsington: Special Inspector General for Afghanistan Reconstruction (SIGAR), 2018. https://sigar.mil/pdf/inspections/SIGAR percent2017-47-IP.pdf.

Staniland, Paul. Networks of Rebellion: Explaining Insurgent Cohesion and Collapse.Ithaca, NY: Cornell University Press, 2014.

Stel, Nora. "Governing the Gatherings: The Interaction of Lebanese State Institutions and Palestinian Authorities in the Hybrid Political Order of South Lebanon"s Informal Palestinian Settlements." PhD diss. Utrecht University, 2017. http://dspace.library.uu.nl/handle/1874/348090.

Strick van Linschoten, Alex. "Mullah Wars: The Afghan Taliban between Village and State, 1979-2001." PhD diss. King"s College London, 2016.

Strick van Linschoten, Alex, and Felix Kuehn. An Enemy We Created: The Myth of the Taliban/Al Qaeda Merger in Afghanstian, 1970-2010. London: Hurst, 2014.

Strick van Linschoten, Alex, and Felix Kuehn. The Taliban Reader: War, Islam and Politics. London: Hurst, 2018.

Suchman, M. C. "Managing Legitimacy: Strategic and Institutional Approaches."Academy of Management Review 20, no. 3 July 1 (1995): 571–610. doi:10.5465/AMR.1995.9508080331.

Terpstra, Niels. "Statebuilding, Legal Pluralism, and Irregular Warfare: Assessing the Dutch Mission in Kunduz Province, Afghanistan." Peacebuilding (11 June 2019):1–21. doi:10.1080/21647259.2019.1620907.

Terpstra, Niels, and Georg Frerks. "Rebel Governance and Legitimacy: Understanding the Impact of Rebel Legitimation on Civilian Compliance with the

LTTE Rule." Civil Wars 19, no. 3 (2017): 279–307. doi:10.1080/13698249.20
17.1393265.

Terpstra, Niels, and Georg Frerks. "Governance Practices and Symbolism: Public
Authority and De Facto Sovereignty in 'Tigerland." Modern Asian Studies
52, no. 3 (2018): 1001–1042. doi:10.1017/S0026749X16000822.

Weber, Max. The Theory of Social and Economic Organization, Translated by
Talcott Parsons and A. Henderson. New York: Oxford University Press, 1947.

Weigand, Florian. "Afghanistan's Taliban – Legitimate Jihadists or Coercive
Extremists?" Journal of Intervention and Statebuilding 11, no. 3 July 3
(2017):359–381. doi:10.1080/17502977.2017.1353755.

Weinstein, Jeremy M. Inside Rebellion: The Politics of Insurgent Violence.
Cambridge:Cambridge University Press, 2006.

Wörmer, Nils. The Networks of Kunduz: A History of Conflict and Their Actors:
From 1992 to 2001. Kabul: Afghanistan Analyst Network, 2012.

Worrall, James. "(Re-)emergent Orders: Understanding the Negotiation(s) of Rebel Governance." Small Wars & Insurgencies 28, no. 4–5 September 3 (2017):
709–733.doi:10.1080/09592318.2017.1322336.

Yassari, Nadjma, and Mohammad Hamid Saboory. "Sharia and National Law in
Afghanistan." In Sharia Incorporated, edited by Jan Michiel Otto, 273–318.
Leiden: Leiden University Press, 2010.

Zaeef, Abd al-Salām, Alex Strick van Linschoten, and Felix Kuehn. My Life with
the Taliban. New York: Columbia University Press, 2010.

Chapter 3: Afghanistan's Taliban: Legitimate Jihadists or Coercive Extremists?
Florian Weigand

1. The material presented herein builds on a larger research project which
   involved fieldwork in Afghanistan from May 2014 to November 2015 (after
   several research visits between 2011 and 2013). In this time, more than 250
   interviews were conducted at the community level, with Afghan authorities as
   well as with international stakeholders in different provinces of the country.
   More than 60 of these interviews took place in Nangarhar Province.

2. Some scholars refer to 'compliance' instead of 'obedience'. Building on Weber,
   here the term 'obedience' [Gehorsam] is used to define 'authority' [Herrschaft].

3. For an exploration of the relationship between coercion and legitimacy, see
   Gippert (2017).

4. For a more extensive analysis of the limitations of the traditional understanding
   of legitimacy in a conflict-torn setting, see von Billerbeck and Gippert (2017).

5. For a detailed history of the Taliban, see e.g. Barfield (2010), Cramer and
   Goodhand (2002), Edwards (2002), Rashid (2001), and Strick van Linschoten
   and Kuehn (2012).

6. For a discussion of the Taliban's ideology, see Gopal and Strick van Linschoten (2017).

7. The website shahmat was offline at the time of publication.

8. For a discussion of the Taliban's views on a future state, see Osman and Gopal (2016).

9. In 2014/15, the period during which the interviews were conducted, the number of districts controlled or influenced by the Taliban was still considerably lower, but was growing steadily (see e.g. Smith 2014).

10. For a recent analysis of the relationship between the Taliban and the Haqqani Network, see Joscelyn and Roggio (2017).

11. Jackson and Giustozzi's (2012) work on humanitarian access to areas under Taliban influence further illustrates how policies of the Taliban leadership are not necessarily implemented on the local level. Therefore, 'rules are fluid and vary depending on who is in charge' (Jackson and Giustozzi 2012, iii).

12. For their protection, the names of all interviewees were replaced with pseudonyms.

13. Hezb-e Islami was one of the biggest Mujahedin groups during the Soviet occupation, established and led by Gulbudin Hekmatyar. From 2001 to 2016, and in the period during which the interviews were conducted in Afghanistan, Hezb-e Islami consisted of a political wing, a political party with numerous MPs in the Afghan parliament, and a military wing that was fighting the Afghan state as an insurgency group under the leadership of Hekmatyar. After signing a peace deal, Hekmatyar returned to Afghanistan in May 2017 (see Rasmussen 2017).

14. For a summary of the history of the Islamic State in Nangarhar, see Osman (2016).

15. For a discussion of 'spectacular violence' in Kabul, see Esser (2014).

References

Agnew, John. 2005. "Sovereignty Regimes: Territoriality and State Authority in Contemporary World Politics." Annals of the Association of American Geographers 95 (2): 437–461.

Asia Foundation. 2016. Afghanistan in 2016 – A Survey of the Afghan People. San Francisco, 2016.

Accessed 19 June 2017. http://asiafoundation.org/wp-content/up-loads/2016/12/2016_Survey-ofthe-Afghan-People_full-survey.Apr2017.pdf.

Barfield, Thomas J. 2010. Afghanistan. Oxford: Princeton University Press.

Barfield, Thomas J., and Neamatollah Nojumi. 2010. "Bringing More Effective Governance to Afghanistan: 10 Pathways to Stability." Middle East Policy XVII (4): 40–52.

Beetham, David. 1991. "Max Weber and the Legitimacy of the Modern State." Analyse & Kritik 13: 34–45.

Coleman, Katharina P. 2017. "The Legitimacy Audience Shapes the Coalition: Lessons From Afghanistan, 2001." Journal of Intervention and Statebuilding 11 (3): 339–358.

Coll, Steve. 2004. Ghost Wars. This Secret History of the CIA, Afghanistan and Bin Laden, From the Soviet Invasion to September 10, 2001. London: Penguin Books.

Cramer, Christopher, and Jonathan Goodhand. 2002. "Try Again, Fail Again, Fail Better? War, the State, and the "Post-Conflict" Challenge in Afghanistan." Development and Change 33 (5): 885–909.

D'Souza, Shanthie Mariet. 2016. "Taliban: The Rebels Who Aspire to be Rulers." Journal of Asian Security and International Affairs 3 (1): 20–40.

Edwards, David B. 2002. Before Taliban – Genealogies of the Afghan Jihad. Berkeley and Los Angeles: University of California Press.

Esser, Daniel. 2014. "Security Scales: Spectacular and Endemic Violence in Post-Invasion Kabul, Afghanistan." Environment & Urbanization 26 (2): 373–388.

Farrell, Theo, and Michael Semple. 2017. "Ready for Peace? The Afghan Taliban after a Decade of War." RUSI Briefing Paper, January 2017.

Gippert, Birte Julia. 2017. "Legitimacy and Coercion in Peacebuilding: A Balancing Act." Journal of Intervention and Statebuilding 11 (3): 321–338.

Giustozzi, Antonio. 2012. "Hearts, Minds, and the Barrel of a Gun – The Taliban's Shadow Government." Institute for National Strategic Studies Prism 3, no 2. Accessed February 2, 2016.https://www.ciaonet.org/attachments/20157/uploads.

Giustozzi, Antonio, and Silab Mangal. 2015. "The Taliban in Pieces." Foreign Affairs, August 3, 2015. Accessed February 2, 2016. https://www.foreignaffairs.com/articles/afghanistan/2015-08-03/taliban-pieces.

Goodhand, Jonathan, and Mark Sedra. 2013. "Rethinking Liberal Peacebuilding, Statebuilding and Transition in Afghanistan: an Introduction." Central Asian Survey 32 (3): 239–254.

Gopal, Anand and Alex Strick van Linschoten. 2017. "Ideology in the Afghan Taliban." Afghan Analysts Network. Accessed July 1, 2017. https://www.afghanistan-analysts.org/wp-content/uploads/2017/06/201705-AGopal-AS-vLinschoten-TB-Ideology.pdf.

Jackson, Ashley. 2014. "Politics and Governance in Afghanistan: the Case of Nangarhar Province." Secure Livelihoods Research Consortium Working Paper 16. Accessed February 2, 2016. http://www.areu.org.af/Uploads/EditionPdfs/Politics percent20and percent20Governance percent20in percent20Afghanistan percent20the percent20Case percent20of percent20Nangarhar percent20Province.pdf.

Jackson, Ashley, and Antonio Giustozzi. 2012. "Talking to the other side. Humanitarian engagement with the Taliban in Afghanistan." HPG Working Paper, December 2012. Accessed June 19, 2017.https://www.odi.org/sites/odi.org.uk/files/odi-assets/publications-opinion-files/7968.pdf.

Jackson, Jonathan, Aziz Z. Huq, Ben Bradford and Tom R. Tyler. 2013. "Monopolizing force? Police legitimacy and public attitudes towards the acceptability of violence." Psychology, public policy and law 19 (4): 479–497.

Joscelyn, Thomas, and Bill Roggio. 2017. "Taliban again affirms Haqqani Network is an integral part of group." The Long War Journal. June 2, 2017. Accessed June 19, 2017. http://www.longwarjournal.org/archives/2017/06/taliban-again-affirms-haqqani-network-is-an-integral-part-of-group.php.

Kaldor, Mary. 2009. "The Reconstruction of Political Authority in a Global era." In Persistent State Weakness in the Global Age, edited by Denisa Kostovicova and Vesna Bojicic-Dzelilovic,179–196. Surrey: Ashgate.

Khaama Press. 2015. "ISIS, Taliban announced Jihad against each other." April 20, 2015. Accessed February 2, 2016. http://www.khaama.com/isis-taliban-announced-jihad-against-each-other-3206.

Kühn, Florian P. 2008. "Aid, Opium, and the State of Rents in Afghanistan: Competition, Cooperation, or Cohabitation?" Journal of Intervention and Statebuilding 2 (3): 309–327.

Levi, Margaret, Audrey Sacks and Tom Tyler. 2009. "Conceptualizing Legitimacy, Measuring Legitimating Beliefs." American Behavioral Scientist 53 (3): 354–375.

Liebl, Vern. 2007. "Pushtuns, Tribalism, Leadership, Islam and Taliban: A Short View." Small Wars &Insurgencies 18 (3): 492–510.

Martin, Mike. 2014. An Intimate War: An Oral History of the Helmand Conflict, 1978-2012. Oxford and New York: Oxford University Press.

Melton, Kevin. 2015. Focusing on State Legitimacy: Succeeding in Kandahar and Beyond. USAID Study, 4 March 2015.

Mazerolle, Lorraine, Sarah Bennett, Jacqueline Davis, Elise Sargeant and Matthew Manning. 2013. "Legitimacy in Policing: A Systematic Review." Campbell Systematic Reviews, 2013: 1. The Campbell Collaboration. Accessed June 19, 2017. http://library.college.police.uk/docs/MazerolleLegitimacy-Review-2013.pdf.

Migdal, Joel S., and Klaus Schlichte. 2005. "Rethinking the State." In The Dynamics of States – The Formation and Crises of State Domination, edited by Klaus Schlichte, 1–40. Aldershot and Burlington: Ashgate.

Nojumi, Neamatollah. 2002. The Rise of the Taliban in Afghanistan – Mass Mobilization, Civil War, and the Future of the Region. New York, Hampshire: Palgrave.

Osman, Borhan. 2015. "Toward Fragmentation? Mapping the post-Omar Taliban." Afghan Analysts Network. November 24, 2015. Accessed November 28, 2015. https://www.afghanistan-analysts. org/toward-fragmentation-mapping-the-post-omar-Taliban/?format=pdf.

Osman, Borhan. 2016. "The Islamic State in "Khorasan': How it began and where it stands now in Nangarhar." Afghan Analysts Network. July 27, 2016. Accessed June 17, 2017. https://www.afghanistan-analysts.org/the-islamic-state-in-khorasan-how-it-began-and-where-it-stands-nowin-nangarhar/.

Osman, Borhan, and Ananad Gopal. 2016. "Taliban Views on a Future State." NYU Center on International Cooperation, July 2016. Accessed June 17, 2017. http://cic.nyu.edu/sites/default/files/taliban_future_state_final.pdf.

Rashid, Ahmed. 2001. Taliban – Islam, Oil, and the New Great Game in Central Asia. London and New York: I.B. Tauris.

Rasmussen, Sune E. 2017. "Fear and doubt as notorious 'butcher of Kabul' returns with talk of peace." The Guardian. May 4, 2017. Accessed June 17, 2017. https://www.theguardian.com/world/2017/may/04/afghan-warlord-gulbuddin-hekmatyar-returns-kabul-20-years-call-peace.

Roy, Oliver. 2004. "Development and Political Legitimacy: the Cases of Iraq and Afghanistan."Conflict, Security & Development 4 (2): 167–179.

Rubin, Barnett R. 2006. "Peace Building and State-Building in Afghanistan: Constructing Sovereignty for Whose Security?" Third World Quarterly 27 (1): 175–185.

Ruttig, Thomas. 2009. "Loya Paktia's Insurgency – (i) The Haqqani Network as an Autonomous Entity." In Decoding the New Taliban – Insights From the Afghan Field, edited by Antonio Giustozzi, 57–88. New York: Columbia University Press.

Sabarre, Nina, Sam Solomon and Timothy Van Blarcom. 2013. "Securing Legitimacy: Examining Indicators of State Legitimacy in Afghanistan." D3 Systems, May 2013. Accessed 19 June 2017.http://www.d3systems.com/wp-content/uploads/2013/11/Securing-Legitimacy_SabarreSolomon Van-Blarcom-v3.pdf.

Scharpf, Fritz W. 1997. "Economic integration, democracy and the welfare state". Journal of European Public Policy 1 (4): 18–36.

SIGAR (Special Investigator General for Afghanistan Reconstruction. 2017. "Quarterly Report to the United States Congress." Apr 30, 2017. Accessed June 19, 2017. https://www.sigar.mil/pdf/quarterlyreports/2017-04-30qr.pdf.

Smith, Graeme. 2009. "What Kandahar's Taliban Say." In Decoding the New Taliban – Insights From the Afghan Field, edited by Antonio Giustozzi, 191–210. New York: Columbia University Press.

Smith, Graeme. 2014. "Taliban "gaining ground" as Afghan audit drags on." DW interview. July 29, 2014. Accessed June 19, 2017. http://www.dw.com/en/taliban-gaining-ground-as-afghan-auditdrags-on/a-17820792.

Strick van Linschoten, Alex, and Felix Kuehn. 2012. An Enemy we Created – The Myth of the Taliban-Al Qaeda Merger in Afghanistan, 1970-2010. London: C. Hurst & Co, 2012.

Tyler, Tom R. 2004. "Enhancing Police Legitimacy." The ANNALS of the American Academy of Political and Social Science 593 (84): 84–99.

Tyler, Tom R. 2006. "Psychological Perspectives on Legitimacy and Legitimation." Annual Review of Psychology 57 (1): 375–400.

UNAMA (United Nations Assistance Mission in Afghanistan). 2017. Afghanistan: Protection of Civilians in Armed Conflict - Midyear Report 2017. Accessed July 19, 2017. https://unama.unmissions.org/sites/default/files/protection_of_civilians_in_armed_conflict_midyear_report_2017_july_2017.pdf.

University of Texas Libraries. 2012. "Afghanistan – Provinces and Districts." Accessed June 19, 2017.http://www.lib.utexas.edu/maps/middle_east_and_asia/txu-pclmaps-oclc-814380561-afghanistan_provinces_and_districts-2012-02.jpg.

Von Billerbeck, Sarah, and Birte Julia Gippert. 2017. "Legitimacy in Conflict: Concept, Challenges and Practice." Journal of Intervention and Statebuilding 11 (3): 273–285.

Weber, Max. 1980. Wirtschaft und Gesellschaft. Grundriss der Verstehenden Soziologie. Tübingen: J.C.B. Mohr (Siebeck).

Weber, Max. 2009. "Politics as a Vocation." In From Max Weber: Essays in Sociology – Edited, with an Introduction by H. H. Gerth and C. Wright Mills – With a New Preface by Bryan S. Turner, edited by Bryan S. Turner, 77–128. London: Routledge.

Weigand, Florian. 2015. "Investigating the Role of Legitimacy in the Political Order of Conflict-torn Spaces." Security in Transition Working Paper 04, 2015. Accessed June 19, 2017. http://www. securityintransition.org/wp-content/uploads/2015/04/Legitimacy-in-the-Political-Order-of-Conflicttorn-Spaces.pdf.

Chapter 4: Culture, Education and Conflict: The Relevance of Critical Conservation Pedagogies for Post-conflict Afghanistan. Richard Mulholland

1   The statistics on the Anglo-American and NATO conflict in Afghanistan are sobering. By the time of the 2001 defeat of the Taliban, the vast majority of Afghans still lived in villages with no electricity. According to the most recent

data from the Watson Institute Costs of War project at Brown University, between 2001 and 2022 the total number of deaths directly attributable to conflict in Afghanistan was estimated at 176,000. NATO forces lost 3484 troops, of which 2324 were from the US military. The US spent around 2.3 trillion dollars (Watson Institute 2021). Despite the staggering loss of life, quality of life did not dramatically increase over the period. In 2019, lack of employment opportunities (72 percent) and lack of educational opportunities (38.5 percent) were cited as the biggest issues facing young people. 72 percent of respondents stated they feared for their personal safety daily, a percentage that has steadily risen in the survey since 2012 and is undoubtedly higher after the withdrawal of international forces from the region. In 2019, the Taliban were still perceived as the most significant group threat, with only a slightly diminished perception of threat from Khorasan group/Daesh/ISIS (Akseer and Rieger 2019). This threat remains all too present in 2022, exacerbated by the prospect of an imminent refugee and humanitarian crisis. At the time of writing, the UNHCR has warned that nearly 55 percent of the population face extreme levels of hunger.

2   For a comprehensive overview of the troubled history of the Kabul National Museum from 1920 to 2006; see Grissmann 2006.

3   Although a small number of random acts of ideological heritage destruction had occurred since the Taliban seized power in 1996, in general it was not widespread until October 2001, when Taliban leader, Mullah Mohammed Omar, having previously issued a decree in 1999 demanding the protection of all cultural relics in Afghanistan and harsh punishment for illegal excavations and looting, reversed this decision, citing the Western privileging of funding the preservation of statues over humanitarian aid, and proclaimed that figurative representations of living beings should be destroyed (Grissmann 2006; Harrison 2010).

4   Since watercolours, prints, and drawings were considered of lesser value than oil paintings, and suspicion would be raised were Taliban inspectors to find the walls and storage rooms empty, staff made the difficult decision to sacrifice this collection to save more important works (Anon, ANG, personal communication October 2019).

5   At the time of writing, several months after the 2021 withdrawal of international forces, the resurgent Taliban regime in Kabul has opened the National Museum, restored the Ministry of Culture and Information, and has made promises to protect cultural heritage in the region. However, the ANG and other heritage institutions remain closed and female staff have not yet been permitted to return to work.

6   From 1996 to 2001, only three countries - Pakistan, The United Arab Emirates (UAE), and Saudi Arabia – formally recognised the Islamic Emirate of Afghanistan under the Taliban as a legitimate government. At the time of

writing, no government has formally recognised the 2021 Islamic Emirate under Taliban leadership.

7 Between 2000 and 2014, 891 NGOs were identified in Afghanistan, of which about 388 were Afghan, 268 were International, and 45 were undetermined. The majority of these NGOs were in education and health. In cultural heritage, the Afghan Cultural Heritage Consulting Organisation (ACHCO), Society for the Protection of Afghan Cultural Heritage (SPACH), and Foundation for Culture and Civil Society (FCCS) are notable exceptions.

8 The Oriental Institute at the University of Chicago has implemented a number of far-reaching training partnerships for the conservation of archaeological objects in Afghanistan and more recently for the 'C5' Central Asian republics (Kazakhstan, Kyrgyzstan, Tajikistan, Turkmenistan, and Uzbekistan). From 2018 to 2020, the Institute organised intensive workshops for conservators from the national museums from the five republics.

9 Founded in Afghanistan in 2006 by HRH Prince of Wales, Turquoise Mountain has restored over 150 historic buildings, trained over 15,000 artisans and generated over $17 million in sales of traditional craft items in Afghanistan, Myanmar, Saudi Arabia, and Jordan. See: https://www.turquoisemountain.org/afghanistan [Accessed 2 August 2021]

References

Afghan ethnic groups: A brief investigation. 2011. Civil-Military Fusion Center. Norfolk: NATO Allied Commands Operation. [Google Scholar]

Ahmad, K. 2001. "Aid Organisations Rebuke UN for Afghanistan Sanctions." The Lancet 357: 45. [Crossref], [PubMed], [Web of Science °], [Google Scholar]

Akseer, T., and J. Rieger. 2019. Afghanistan in 2019: A Survey of the Afghan People. The Asia Foundation. [accessed 29 July 2021]. https://asiafoundation.org/publication/afghanistan-in-2019-a-survey-of-the-afghan-people [Google Scholar]

Anonymous. 2020. Afghan National Archives, Kabul, Personal Communication. [Google Scholar]

Archino, Sarah. 2020. "Addressing Visual Literacy in the Survey: Balancing Trans-disciplinary Competencies and Course Content." Art History Pedagogy and Practice 5: 1. [Google Scholar]

Asefi, M. Y. 2019. Interview. By Richard Mulholland. 15 October 2019. [Google Scholar]

Bak, M. 2019. Corruption in Afghanistan and the role of development assistance. Bergen: U4 Anti-Corruption Resource Centre (U4 Helpdesk Answer 2019:7) [Google Scholar]

Barakat, S. 2005. "Post-war Reconstruction and the Recovery of Cultural Heritage: Critical Lessons from the Last Fifteen Years." In Cultural Heritage in Post

War Recovery, edited by N. Stanley-Price, 26–40. Papers from the ICCROM forum. Oct 4–6. Rome: ICCROM. [Google Scholar]

Becatoros, E. 2021. Afghan Museum Reopens with Taliban Security – and Visitors. Associated Press News, 6 December 2021. [Google Scholar]

Bhoryrub, J., J. Hurley, G. R. Neilson, M. Ramsay, and M. Smith. 2010. "Heutagogy: An Alternative Practice-Based Learning Approach." Nurse Education in Practice 10 (6): 322–326. [Crossref], [PubMed], [Google Scholar]

Boak, E. 2019. "From Conflict Archaeology to Archaeologies of Conflict: Remote Survey in Kandahar, Afghanistan." Journal of Conflict Archaeology 14 (2–3): 143–162. [Taylor & Francis Online], [Web of Science °], [Google Scholar]

Brosché, J., M. Legnér, J. Kreutz, and A. Ijla. 2017. "Heritage Under Attack: Motives for Targeting Cultural Property During Armed Conflict." International Journal of Heritage Studies 23 (3): 248–260. [Taylor & Francis Online], [Web of Science °], [Google Scholar]

Caesar, B., and A. R. Rodriguez García. 2006. "The Society for the Preservation of Afghanistan's Cultural Heritage: An Overview of Activities Since 1994." In Art and Archaeology of Afghanistan: Its Fall and Survival, edited by J. van Krieken-Pieters, 15–38. Leiden: Brill. [Google Scholar]

Cairns, L. 1996. "Capability: Going Beyond Competence." Capability 2: 80. [Google Scholar]

Campbell, D. T., J. C. Stanley, N. L. Gage, T. Bärnighausen, P. Tugwell, J. A. Røttingen, I. Shemilt, et al. 2017. "Experimental and Quasi-Experimental Designs for Research. Quasi-Experimental Study Designs Series - Paper 4: Uses and Value." Journal of Clinical Epidemiology 89: 21–29. [Crossref], [PubMed], [Web of Science °], [Google Scholar]

Cassar, B., and M. Nagaoka. 2007. Project Final Report: Project of Endangered Movable Assets (EMA) of the National Cultural Heritage - 24225110KAB. Documentation and Conservation of Collections in the National Museum of Afghanistan, Unpublished Report. UNESCO. March 15, 2007. [Google Scholar]

Chulov, M. 2015. "A Sledgehammer to Civilisation: Islamic State's War on Culture" The Guardian. 7 April 2015. [Accessed on 11 January 2022] http://www.theguardian.com/world/2015/apr/07/islamic-state-isis-crimes-againstculture-iraq-syria. [Google Scholar]

Clark, L. B. 2018. "Critical Pedagogy in the University: Can a Lecture be Critical Pedagogy?" Policy Futures in Education 16 (8): 985–999. [Crossref], [Web of Science °], [Google Scholar]

Corruption Perception Index. 2020. Transparency International. [accessed 29 July 2021]. https://www.transparency.org/en/cpi/2020/index. [Google Scholar]

Di Pietro, G., A. Buder, and M. Künzel. 2021. "Improving Transfer in the Education of Conservators- Restorers." In Transcending Boundaries: Integrated Approaches to Conservation, ICOM-CC 19th Triennial Conference Preprints, Beijing, 17–21 May 2021, edited by J. Bridgland. Paris: International Council of Museums. [Google Scholar]

Dupree, N. H. 2006. "Prehistoric Afghanistan: Status of Sites and Artefacts and Challenges of Preservation." In Art and Archaeology of Afghanistan: Its Fall and Survival, edited by J. van Krieken-Pieters, 79–94. Leiden: Brill. [Google Scholar]

Evaluation of UNHCR's Country Operation: Afghanistan. 2020. ITAD Ltd. The United Nations Refugee Agency. [Google Scholar]

Fitzgerald, P., and E. Gould. 2009. Invisible History: Afghanistan's Untold Story. San Francisco: City Lights. [Google Scholar]

Fredheim, L. H., and M. Khalaf. 2016. "The Significance of Values: Heritage Value Typologies Re-Examined." International Journal of Heritage Studies 22 (6): 466–481. [Taylor & Francis Online], [Web of Science °], [Google Scholar]

Freire, P. 1970. Pedagogy of the Oppressed. London: Continuum. [Google Scholar]

Gardner, A., S. Hase, G. Gardner, S. V. Dunn, and J. Carryer. 2008. "From Competence to Capability: A Study of Nurse Practitioners in Clinical Practice." Journal of Clinical Nursing 17 (2): 250–258. [PubMed], [Web of Science °], [Google Scholar]

Gerstenblith, P. 2009. "Archaeology in the Context of War: Legal Frameworks for Protecting Cultural Heritage During Armed Conflict." Archaeologies 5: 18–31. [Crossref], [Web of Science °], [Google Scholar]

Grissmann, C. 2006. "The Kabul Museum: Its Turbulent Years." In Art and Archaeology of Afghanistan: Its Fall and Survival, edited by J. van Krieken-Peters, 49–61. The Netherlands: Brill. [Google Scholar]

Guzman, P., Pereira Roders, A. R., and B. Colenbrander. 2018. "Impacts of Common Urban Development Factors on Cultural Conservation in World Heritage Cities: An Indicators-Based Analysis." Sustainability, 10: 853. https://doi.org/10.3390/su10030853 [Crossref], [Web of Science °], [Google Scholar]

Haldane, E., S. Glenn, S. Hunter, and L. Hillyer. 2012. "Raksha: Raising Awareness of Textile Conservation in India." In Post Prints, American Institute for Conservation of Historic & Artistic Works 40th Annual Meeting Albuquerque, New Mexico May 2012, Vol. 22, edited by A. Holden, S. Stevens, J. Carlson, G. Peterson, E. Scuetz, and R. Summerour, 19–31. [Google Scholar]

Harrison, R. 2010. "The Politics of Heritage." In Understanding the Politics of Heritage, edited by R. Harrison, 154–196. Manchester: Manchester University Press. [Google Scholar]

Hashimi, Nadia. 2021. Impact Evaluation Report: Heritage Unveiled: National Art Restoration Project, Unpublished Report. [Google Scholar]

Hassan, H. 2015. Religious Teaching that Drives Isis to Threaten the Ancient Ruins of Palmyra. The Guardian, 24 May. [Accessed on 29 July 2021]. http://www.theguardian.com/world/2015/may/24/palmyra-syria-isis-destruction-of-treasures-feared. [Google Scholar]

Head, N. 2020. "A Pedagogy of Discomfort? Experiential Learning and Conflict Analysis in Israel – Palestine." International Studies Perspectives 21: 78–96. [Crossref], [Web of Science ®], [Google Scholar]

Hein, G. 1991. Constructivist Learning Theory. The Museum and the Needs of People. Conference Papers. CECA: International Committee of Museum Educators. Jerusalem Israel, 15–22 October 1991. [Google Scholar]

Henderson, J., A. Dawson, U. Kyaw Shin Naung, and A. Crossman. 2021. "Preventive Conservation Training: A Partnership Between the UK and Myanmar." In Transcending Boundaries: Integrated Approaches to Conservation, ICOM-CC 19th Triennial Conference Preprints, Beijing, 17–21 May 2021, edited by J. Bridgland, 1–6. Paris: International Council of Museums. [Google Scholar]

Henderson, J., and P. Parkes. 2021. "Using Complexity to Deliver Standardised Educational Levels in Conservation." In Transcending Boundaries: Integrated Approaches to Conservation, ICOM-CC 19th Triennial Conference Preprints, Beijing, 17–21 May 2021, edited by J. Bridgland, 1–9. Paris: International Council of Museums. [Google Scholar]

Isakhan, B., and L. Meskell. 2018. "UNESCO's Project to 'Revive the Spirit of Mosul': Iraqi and Syrian Opinion on Heritage Reconstruction After the Islamic State." International Journal of Heritage Studies 25 (11): 1189–1204. [Taylor & Francis Online], [Web of Science ®], [Google Scholar]

Kersel, M. M., and C. Luke. 2015. "Civil Societies? Heritage Diplomacy and Neo-Imperialism." In Global Heritage: A Reader, edited by L. Meskell, 70–94. Chichester: John Wiley & Sons. [Google Scholar]

Khabir, A. 2001. "UN Sanctions Imposed Against Afghanistan While Thousands Flee." The Lancet 357: 207. [Crossref], [Web of Science ®], [Google Scholar]

Klimaszewski, C., G. E. Bader, and J. Nyce. 2012. "Studying Up (and Down) the Cultural Heritage Preservation Agenda: Observations from Romania." European Journal of Cultural Studies 15 (4): 479–495. [Crossref], [Web of Science ®], [Google Scholar]

Knowles, M. S. 1975. Self-Directed Learning. New York: Association Press. [Google Scholar]

Leslie, J. 2014. Cult, Culture and the Need for Public Education: Why the National Museum in Kabul has Little Meaning for Afghans. Afghanistan Analysts

Network. 21 November 2014 [Accessed 29 July 2021]. https://www.afghan-istan-analysts.org/cult-culture-and-the-need-for-public-education-why-the-national-museum-in-kabul-has-little-meaning-for-afghans/. [Google Scholar]

Luke, C., and M. M. Kersel. 2013. U.S. Cultural Diplomacy and Archaeology: Soft Power, Hard Heritage. New York: Routledge. [Crossref], [Google Scholar]

Maeda, K. 2006. "The Mural Paintings of the Buddhas of Bamiyan: Description and Conservation Operations." In Art and Archaeology of Afghanistan: Its Fall and Survival, edited by J. van Krieken-Peters, 127–145. Amsterdam: Brill. [Google Scholar]

Martin, G., and C. Enderby Smith. 2021. "UN Sanctions." In The Guide to Sanctions, edited by R. Barnes, P. Feldberg, N. Turner, A. Bradshaw, D. Mortlock, A. Thomas, and R. Alpert, 9–27. London: Global Investigations Review. [Google Scholar]

McWilliam, E. 2007. "Is Creativity Teachable? Conceptualising the Creativity/Pedagogy Relationship in Higher Education." In Proceedings of the 30th HERDSA Annual Conference, edited by G. Crisp, and M. Hicks, 1–8. Higher Education Research and Development Society of Australasia Inc. [Google Scholar]

Mitchell, D. F. 2017. "NGO Presence and Activity in Afghanistan, 2000–2014: A Provincial-Level Dataset. Stability." International Journal of Security and Development 6: 1. [Crossref], [Web of Science ®], [Google Scholar]

Morin, K. 2020. "Nursing Education After Covid-19: Same or Different?" Journal of Clinical Nursing 29 (17–18): 3117–3119. [Crossref], [PubMed], [Web of Science ®], [Google Scholar]

Mulholland, R. 2019. Post-training Survey of Participants, Afghan National Gallery, unpublished report. Kabul. [Google Scholar]

Nankivell, S. 2016. "Speaking of Sledgehammers: Analysing the Discourse of Heritage Destruction in the Media." Unpublished MPhil Dissertation. University of Cambridge. [Google Scholar]

O' Creevy, M., and C. van Mourik. 2016. "'I Understood the Words but I Didn't Know What They Meant': Japanese Online MBA Students' Experiences of British Assessment Practices." Open Learning 31 (2): 130–140. [Taylor & Francis Online], [Google Scholar]

Pearlstein, T., and J. S. Johnson. 2020. "Recording and Archiving Conservation Education Approaches in Iraq, 2008–2017." Journal of the American Institute for Conservation 59 (1): 53–64. [Taylor & Francis Online], [Web of Science ®], [Google Scholar]

Ramsden, P., G. Whelan, and D. Cooper. 1988. "Some Phenomena of Medical Students' Diagnostic Problem Solving." Medical Education 23 (1): 108–117. [Crossref], [Web of Science ®], [Google Scholar]

Schon, D. A. 1991. The Reflective Practitioner: How Professionals Think in Action. New York: Routledge. [Google Scholar]

Seymour, K., R. Hoppenbrouwers, L. Pilosi, and V. Daniel. 2019. "What Does an 18th Century Dutch Hindeloopen Period Room and a 21st Century Training Project Have in Common?: Answer the Indian Conservation Training Program." The Picture Restorer 55: 36–44. [Google Scholar]

Shulman, L. S. 2005. "Signature Pedagogies in the Professions." Daedalus 134 (3): 52–59. [Crossref], [Web of Science ®], [Google Scholar]

Smith, R. 2008. Silent Survivors of Afghanistan's 4,000 Tumultuous Years. Art Review. New York Times. May 23 2008. [Google Scholar]

Stanley-Price, N. 2005. "The Thread of Continuity: Cultural Heritage in Post-war Recovery." In Cultural Heritage in Post War Recovery, edited by N. Stanley-Price, 1–17. Papers from the ICCROM forum, Oct 4–6. Rome: ICCROM. [Google Scholar]

Stein, G. 2017. "The Oriental Institute Partnership with the National Museum of Afghanistan." In The Oriental Institute Annual Report 2016–2017, edited by C. Woods, 136–143. Chicago: University of Chicago. [Google Scholar]

Stein, G. 2019. "The Oriental Institute Partnership with the National Museum of Afghanistan." In Cultural Heritage Preservation work in Afghanistan and Central Asia 2018–2019, edited by C. Woods, 27–36. Chicago: University of Chicago. [Google Scholar]

Stone, P. G. 2015. "The Challenge of Protecting Heritage in Times of Armed Conflict." Museum International 67 (1–4): 40–54. [Taylor & Francis Online], [Web of Science ®], [Google Scholar]

The Forbidden Reel. 2019. dir. by Nasr, A. Canada: National Film Board of Canada/Loaded Pictures. [Google Scholar]

UNHCR Refugee Data. 2020. [accessed 29 July 2021]. https://www.unhcr.org/refugee-statistics/. [Google Scholar]

United Nations Security Council. 2000. Resolution 1333 (2000), 19th December 2000. [Google Scholar]

U.S. Costs to Date for the War in Afghanistan, in Billions FY2001-FY2022. Watson Institute for International & Public Affairs, Brown University [accessed 13 December 2021]. https://watson.brown.edu/costsofwar/ figures/2021/human-and-budgetary-costs-date-us-war-afghanistan-2001–2022. [Google Scholar]

Viejo-Rose, Dacia. 2007. "Conflict and the Deliberate Destruction of Cultural Heritage." In Conflicts and Tensions, edited by H. Anheier, and Y. R. Isar, 102–119. London: Sage. [Crossref], [Google Scholar]

White, H., and S. Sabarwal. 2014. Quasi-Experimental Design and Methods. Methodological Briefs no 8: Impact Evaluation. UNICEF. [Google Scholar]

Wimpelmann, T. 2017. The Pitfalls of Protection: Gender, Violence, and Power in Afghanistan. Oakland: University of California Press. [Crossref], [Google Scholar]

Yamin, S. 2013. "Global Governance: Rethinking the US Role in Afghanistan Post 2014." Journal of South Asian Development 8: 2. [Crossref], [Web of Science °], [Google Scholar]

Chapter 5: The Taliban, ISIS-K, Al Qaeda, the Haqqni Network, their Atrocities, Torture and the Degradation of Afghan Nation

1. Yoram Schweitzer and Sari Goldstein Ferber, in their research paper (Al-Qaeda and the Internationalization of Suicide Terrorism. Jaffee Center for Strategic Studies, Tel Aviv University. Memorandum No. 78 November 2005

2. Ellen Tveteraas (Under the Hood–Learning and Innovation in the Islamic State's Suicide Vehicle Industry, Studies in Conflict & Terrorism-2022

3. Michael A. Peters in his research paper (Declinism' and discourses of decline-the end of the war in Afghanistan and the limits of American power, Educational Philosophy and Theory, DOI: 10.1080/00131857.2021.1982694.

4. Afghanistan: Taliban Deprive Women of Livelihoods, Identity: Severe Restrictions, Harassment, Fear in Ghazni Province-18 January, 2022)

5. Kate Clark (Afghanistan's conflict in 2021 (2): Republic collapse and Taliban victory in the long-view of history. Afghanistan Analysts Network--30 Dec 2021.

6. Afghanistan: Taliban Kill, 'Disappear' Ex-Officials: Raids Target Former Police, Intelligence Officers- November 30, 2021

7. Qasim Jan, Yi Xie, Muhammad Habib Qazi, Zahid Javid Choudhary and Baha Ul Haq in their research paper (Examining the role of Pakistan's national curriculum textbook discourses on normalising the Taliban's violence in the USA's Post 9/11 war on terror in South Waziristan, Pakistan. British Journal of Religious Education-2022.

8. Eric Schmitt, "ISIS Branch Poses Biggest Immediate Terrorist Threat to Evacuation in Kabul", November 3, 2021, the New York Times

9. Clayton Sharb, Danika Newlee and the CSIS iDeas Lab in their joint work (Islamic State Khorasan (IS-K). Center for Strategic and International Studies-2018.

10. Mohamed Mokhtar Qandi in his paper (Challenges to Taliban Rule and Potential Impacts for the Region: Internal and external factors are weakening the Taliban, making the group's long term stability increasingly unlikely. Fikra Forum. The Washington Institute for Near East Policy-09 February 2022.

11. Amira Jadoon, Abdul Sayed and Andrew Mines in their research paper (The Islamic State Threat in Taliban Afghanistan: Tracing the Resurgence of Islamic State Khorasan. The Combating Terrorism Center at West Point. January 2022, Volum 15, Issue-1.

12. April 17, ISIS called on all fighters around the world to carry out "big and painful" attacks targeting officials and soldiers". Salam Times

13. Roshni Kapur in his paper (The Persistent ISKP Threat to Afghanistan: On China's Doorstep. Middle East Institute-January 6, 2022

14. Editor of Terrorism Monitor. Jacob Zenn in his article (Islamic State in Khorasan Province's One-Off Attack in Uzbekistan. Volium XX. Issue 9, 06 May 2022.

15. Amy Kazmin in her article (Isis-K insurgency jeopardises Taliban's grip on Afghanistan: New rulers accused of betraying Islam by jihadis intent on creating ideologically pure caliphate-October, 26, 2021.

16. Salman Rafi Sheikh in his article (Eight months on, Taliban's rule is far from stable: Resistance groups are mounting an increasingly potent challenge to the Taliban and may have Pakistan's clandestine support-Asia Times, May 2, 2022.

Chapter 6: Suicide Brigades, ISIS-K Military Strength and Taliban's Misrule in Afghanistan

1. Atal Ahmadzai. Dying to Live: The "Love to Death" Narrative Driving the Taliban's Suicide Bombings.

2. Amira Jadoon, Andrew Mines and Abdul Sayed in their research paper (The evolving Taliban-ISK rivalry, 07 Sep 2021, The Interpreter.

3. Global Witness research report

4. William A. Byrd and Javed Noorani. Industrial-Scale Looting of Afghanistan's Mineral Resources, 2017, the United States Institute of Peace.

5. BBC 11 October 2021

6. Niels Terpstra (2020) Rebel governance, rebel legitimacy, and external intervention: assessing three phases of Taliban rule in Afghanistan, Small Wars & Insurgencies,31:6, 1143-1173, DOI: 10.1080/09592318.2020.1757916-25 May 2020.

7. Asfandyar Mir. The ISIS-K Resurgence-08 October 2021

8. Asia Pacific Group on Money Laundering and Global Centre on Cooperative Security in its report (Financing and Facilitation of Foreign Terrorist Fighters

and Returnees in Southeast Asia," Asia Pacific Group on Money Laundering and Global Centre on Cooperative Security, November 2021.

9. Niamatullah Ibrahimi & Shahram Akbarzadeh in their research paper (Intra-Jihadist Conflict and Cooperation: Islamic State–Khorasan Province and the Taliban in Afghanistan, Studies in Conflict & Terrorism, DOI: 10.1080/1057610X.2018.1529367.

10. Sushant Sareen in his paper (The ISKP is Nothing but an Exaggerated Threat. SPECIAL Report. Of Observer Research Foundation: Afghanistan and the New Global (Dis)Order: Great Game and Uncertain Neighbours-December 2021.

11. Aman Bezreh, Chris Hitchcock, Jacob Berntson, Jen Wilton, Jennifer Dathan, Khalil Dewan, Leyla Slama, Michael Hart, Shaza Alsalmoni, Sophie Akram and Tim Hulse. Understanding the Rising Cult of Suicide Bomber. Action on Armed Violence AOAV.

Chapter 7: Al Qaeda, the Haqqni Terrorist Network, Lashkar-e-Taiba, Taliban and the Islamic State of Khorasan's Plundering of Mineral Resources in Afghanistan and their expedition Towards Central Asia

1. Analyst and expert, Ashok K. Behuria (2007) Fighting the Taliban: Pakistan at war with itself,Australian Journal of International Affairs, 61:4, 529-543, DOI: 10.1080/10357710701684963).

2. Cosmin Timofte in his paper. Unlikely Friends: What role would the USA play in the fight between ISIS K and the Taliban? The Institute of New Europe's Work-29 November 2021.

3. Hassan Abu Haniyeh in his commentary (Daesh's Organisational Structure-3 December 2014, Aljazeera Centre for Studied.

4. Expert and analyst Ellen Tveteraas "Department of Politics and International Relations, University of Oxford, Oxfordshire, United Kingdom" highlighted operational mechanism of the ISIS terrorist group in Iraq, and performance of Martyrdom Operatives Battalion (Katibat al-Istishadiin), and its associates in her paper (Under the Hood–Learning and Innovation in the Islamic State's Suicide Vehicle Industry. Studies in Conflict & Terrorism. 13 February, 2022.

5. Pepe Escobar. Who profits from Kabul suicide bombing? ISIS-Khorasan aims to prove to Afghans and to the outside world that the Taliban cannot secure the capital. 30 August, 2021

6. Michael Rubin in his commentary (Biden ignores Afghanistan at America's peril, The National Interest- April 28, 2022

7. Damon Mehl. Damon Mehl, CTC Sentinel, November 2018, Volume-11, Issue-10

8. Christian Bleuer. Chechens in Afghanistan: A Battlefield Myth That Will Not Die. 27 Jun 2016

9. Michael W. S. Ryan in his research paper (ISIS: The Terrorist Group That Would Be a State. U.S. Naval War College and Pepe Escobar (Who profits from the Kabul suicide bombing? ISIS-Khorasan aims to prove to Afghans and to the outside world that the Taliban cannot secure the capital. Asia Times-27 August 2021.

10. Dr. Sanchita Bhattacharya. The Taliban Financial Resources: Drug Trafficking, Illegal Mining, and Military Strength.

11. Global witness Press Release. 06 June 2016

12. Asad Mirza. For quick revenue, Afghan mining wealth is the best option for Taliban: A decade back some US geologists had calculated the mineral reserves in Afghanistan to be in excess of $1 trillion-14 March 2022.

13. Nik Martin (Afghanistan: Taliban to reap $1 trillion mineral wealth-18 August 2021

14. Tim McDonnell in his article (The Taliban now controls one of the world's biggest lithium deposits: Illegal mining of lapis lazuli, a gem, is a major source of revenue for the Taliban. December 28, 2021.

15. Christopher McIntosh and Ian Storey. 20 November 2019

16. Scholar and Lecturer Department of Social Sciences, Lahore Garrison University Pakistan, Dr. Yunis Khushi. A Critical Analysis of Factors and Implications of ISIS Recruitments and Concept of Jihad-Bil-Nikah-26 June 2017.

17. Rushni Kapur in her paper (The Persistent ISKP Threat to Afghanistan: On China's Doorstep, Middle East Institute--January 6, 2022

18. Assistant Professor and Research Faculty with Terrorism, Transnational Crime and Corruption Center (TraCCC) and the Schar School of Policy and Government at George Mason University. Dr. Mahmut Cengiz, in his paper (ISIS or al-Qaeda: Which Looms as the Greater Threat to Global Security? Small War Journal 01 October, 2022

Chapter 8: Arbitrary Power and a Loss of Fundamental Freedoms: A look at UNAMA's first major human rights report since the Taliban takeover. AAN Research Scholar Kate Clark

1. The other body still active is, of course, the International Committee of the Red Cross (ICRC), although its role is to work with the authorities and other conflict actors behind the scenes.

Chapter 9: Dying to Live: The "Love to Death" Narrative Driving the Taliban's Suicide Bombings. Atal Ahmadzai

1 This study conceptualizes "suicide mission" as a general term that refers to any type of suicide tactic that requires the death of the perpetrator for the success of the mission. The article, however, refers suicide bombings exclusively to

those suicide missions that use explosives attached to either human body or the vehicle to carry out the attack.

2   Pedahzur, Ami., Arie Perliger, and Leonard Weinberg. 'Altruism and Fatalism: The Characteristics of Palestinian Suicide Terrorists.' Deviant Behaviour 24 (2003): 405–23. https://doi.org/10.1080/713840227.

3   Pape, Robert. Dying to Win: The Strategic Logic of Suicide Terrorism. New York: Random House, 2005, p. 14.

4   Crenshaw, Martha. 'Explaining Suicide Terrorism: A Review Essay.' Security Studies 16, no. 1 (2007): 133–62. DOI: https://doi.org/10.1080/09636410701304580.

5   Horgan, John. The Psychology of Terrorism. London: Routledge, 2005.

6   For studies that are focused on suicide bombings in Middle East, see: Shakiki [44], Bloom [123], Pape [3], Moghadam [124], Moghadam [30], Hafez [14], Pedahzur, Perliger & Weinberg [2], Asad [107], Cohen [13], Merari [125], Brynen [126], Crenshaw [127], Schbley [128], Krueger and Maleckova [129], Post et al [130], Schweitzer [131], and Hicks & et al [132].

7   Semple, Michael. 'Rhetoric, Ideology, and Organizational Structure of the Taliban Movement.' Peaceworks, 102 (2014): 12.

8   Williams, Brian. 'Cheney Attack Reveals Taliban Suicide Bombing Patterns.' Terrorism Monitor 5, no. 4 (2007).

9   UNAMA. 'Suicide Attacks in Afghanistan (2001–2007).' United Nations Assistance Mission to Afghanistan, Kabul, 2007.

10 Rome, Henry. 'Revisiting the Problem from Hell: Suicide Terror in Afghanistan.' Studies in Conflict & Terrorism 36, no. 10 (2013): 819–38. DOI: https://doi.org/10.1080/1057610X.2013.823752.

11 Edwards, David. Caravan of Martyrs: Sacrifice and Suicide Bombing in Afghanistan. California: University of California Press, 2017.

12 These are several political theses on suicide bombings developed by various scholars. "Dying to live" is the thesis advanced by the author of the present study.

13 Cohen, Shuki. 'Mapping the Minds of Suicide Bombers using Linguistic Methods: The Corpus of Palestinian Suicide Bombers' Farewell Letters (CoPSBFL).' Studies in Conflict & Terrorism 39, no. 7–8 (2016): 749–780. DOI: https://doi.org/10.1080/1057610X.2016.1141005.

14 Hafez, Mohammed. 'Martyrdom and Mythology in Iraq: How Jihadists frame suicide terrorism in videos and biographies.' Terrorism and Political Violence 9 (2007): 95–115. DOI: https://doi.org/10.1080/09546550601054873.

15 Shuki, Cohen, 2016, op. cit.

16 For transparency and possible replication purposes of the study, the researcher has committed himself to make the corpus available upon request to bonafide researchers for these purposes. However, due to the nature of the content and its potential of unintentionally spreading and promoting violence, the corpus will not be made available on a public domain.

17 Braun, Virginia, & Victoria Clarke. 'Using Thematic Analysis in Psychology.' Qualitative Research in Psychology 3, no. 2 (2006): 77–101.

18 Macnair, Logan, & Richard Frank. '"To My Brothers in the West": A Thematic Analysis of Videos Produced by the Islamic State's al-Hayat Media Center.' Journal of Contemporary Criminal Justice 33, no. 3 (2017): 234–253. URL: https://doi. org/10.1177/1043986217699313.

19 Ibid., 18.

20 Khosravi, Shadi, Peter Kwantes, Natalia Derbentseva, & Laura Huey. 'Quantifying Salient Concepts Discussed in Social Media Content: An Analysis of Tweets Posted by ISIS Fangirls.' Journal of Terrorism Research 7, no. 2 (2016): 79–90. DOI: http://doi. org/10.15664/jtr.1241.

21 Goerzig, Carolin, & Khaled Al-Hashimi. Radicalization in Western Europe: Integration, Public Discourse, and Loss of Identity among Muslim Communities. New York: Routledge, 2015.

22 The Guardian. 'Taliban are back - and with a murderous vengeance'. June 7, 2003. URL: https://www.theguardian.com/world/2003/jun/08/afghanistan. lukeharding.

23 The New York Times. 'Threats and Responses: Afghanistan; Kabul Bombing Killed 4 German Soldiers and Injured 29.' July 08, 2003. URL: https://www. nytimes.com/2003/06/08/world/threats-responses-afghanistan-kabul-bombing-kills-4-german-soldiers-wounds-29.html.

24 It should be noted, however, that the first ever documented suicide bombing in the country was carried out by two Arab al-Qaeda operatives on September 9, 2001. The perpetrators, disguised as foreign journalists, assassinated the leader of the Northern Alliance, Ahmad Shah Masood, by detonating a bomb implanted inside a recording camera. Masood was resisting the Taliban's geographic expansion toward the northern parts of the country.

25 The repository is compiled and launched by the Norwegian Defence Research Establishment (FFI), in cooperation with the University of Oslo. URL: https://www.hf.uio.no/ikos/english/research/taliban-sources-repository/.

26 Semple, Michael, 2014, op. cit.

27 At this point, the CPOST database has become inaccessible for a number of years. As communicated to the author of this article by one of the project administrators, this is due to database renovation.

28 Chicago Project on Security and Terrorism (CPOST). 'Suicide Attack Database.' (Details; accessed April 26, 2016). URL: http://cpostdata.uchicago.edu/.

29 National Consortium for the Study of Terrorism and Responses to Terrorism (START), University of Maryland. (2019). The Global Terrorism Database (GTD) [Data file]. Accessed on November 24, 2020. URL: https://www.start.umd.edu/gtd.

30 Moghadam, Assaf. 'Motives for Martyrdom: Al-Qaida, Salafi Jihad, and the Spread of Suicide Attacks'. International Security 33, no. 3 (2009): 46–78. DOI: https://doi.org/10.1162/isec.2009.33.3.46.

31 Moghadam, Assaf, 2009, op. cit.

32 Williams, Brian, 2007, op. cit.

33 Barfield, Thomas. Afghanistan: A Cultural and Political History. New Jersey: Princeton University Press, 2010.

34 Habibi, Abdul Hai. Pashtu aw Pashtunwala [Pashtu and Pashtunwali]. Kandahar: Pashtu Farhangee Tollana, 1962.

35 Williams, Brian. 'Mullah Omar's Missiles: A Field Report on Suicide Bombers in Afghanistan'. Middle East Policy 15, no. 4 (2008): 26–46.

36 Semple, Michael, 2014, op. cit.

37 Rubin, Barnet. 'Saving Afghanistan'. Foreign Affairs 86, no. 1 (2007): 57–74, 76–78.

38 Khadim, Qayamudin. Pashtunwali. Quetta: Pashto Adabi Ghoorzang. 1952 [Reprinted in 2002].

39 Williams, Brian, 2008, op. cit.

40 Khadim, Qayamudin, 1952, op. cit.

41 Rzehak, Lutz. 'Doing Pashto: Pashtunwali as the Ideal of Honorable Behavior and Tribal Life among the Pashtuns'. Thematic Paper. Afghanistan Analysts Network, 2011.

42 Ergil, Doğu. 'Suicide Terrorism in Turkey'. Civil Wars 3, no. 1 (2000): 37–54. DOI: https://doi.org/10.1080/13698240008402430.

43 Kurz, Robert. and Charles Bartles. 'Chechen Suicide Bombers'. Journal of Slavic Military Studies 20 (2007): 529–547. DOI: https://doi.org/10.1080/13518040701703070.

44 Shakiki, Khahil. 'The View of Palestinian Society on Suicide Terrorism'. In: Countering Suicide Terrorism (Herzilya, Israel: The International Policy Institute for Counter-Terrorism), 2002.

45 Victoroff, Jeff. 'The Mind of the Terrorist: A Review and Critique of Psychological Approaches'. Journal of Conflict Resolution 49, no. 1 (2005): 3–42. URL: https://www.jstor.org/stable/30045097.

46 Friedland, Nehemia. 'Becoming a terrorist: Social and individual antecedents.' In Terrorism: Roots, Impact, Responses. New York: Praeger, 1992: 81–94.

47 Pedahzur et al. 2003, op. cit.

48 Post, Jerrold. Ehud Sprinzak, and Laurita Denny. 'The Terrorists in Their Own Words: Interviews with thirty-five Incarcerated Middle Eastern Terrorists'. Terrorism and Political Violence 1 (2003): 171–84. DOI: https://doi.org/10.10 80/09546550312331293007.

49 Sageman, Marc. Understanding Terror Networks. Philadelphia: University of Pennsylvania Press. 2004.

50 Hafez, Mohammed, 2007, op. cit.

51 Williams, Brian, 2008, op. cit.

52 Rzehak, Lutz, 2011, op. cit.

53 Clark, Kate. 'The Layha Calling the Taliban to Account: Appendix 1. The Taliban Codes of Conduct in English.' Thematic Report, Afghanistan Analyst Network, 2011.

54 Baryali, Ahmad Zeya.'!Seeking Martyrdom or Suicide?!]. 2013a. URL: http://www.nunn.asia/5301/.

55 Agha, Sayed Abu Qasim. Istish-haad or Suicide]. [Al-Heydaya Publishers], 2018. URL: https://alhedayat. com/1289-2/. [Note: this webpage does not exist anymore].

56 Abdul-Hameed, Atal. 2004. Martyrdom-Seeking Operations in Islam]. Translated from Yusuf Al-ayeri. Pakistan: Jihad Publications. 2004.

57 Ibn Taymiyya. Majmu` al-Fatawa Vols. 10, 20 & 28. Madina: Majma` al-Malik Fahd li-Taba`at al-Mushaf al-Sharif. 1995.

58 Baryali, Ahmad Zeya, 2013a, op. cit.

59 Istish-haad in the Arabic language is not a hyphenated term. The hyphen placed between the two parts of the term in the main text of this article is solely for pronunciation purposes.

60 It should be noted that the term used in the Quran for suicide is not "Intehar," but the phrase (killing oneself]. "Intehar" is a term from modern Arabic language.

61 Anonymous. Istish-haad is Jihad and Suicide is Vice. Nunn Asia, January 24, 2013.URL: https://www.nunn.asia/5970/.

62 Ibid., 61.

63 Seddiqi, Abdullah. Sacrificial Istish-haadi Attacks.] Kabull.com. March 2, 2017. URL:https://kabull. Com of Perspectives the from Intehar and haad-Istish.

64 Gulbadin,Hekmatyar. Ignorant Scholars. Nunn.Asia.com. February 21, 2018. URL: https://www.nunn.asia/116783/.

65 The".Zeya Ahmad, Baryali. decree of the Grand Imam of Al-Azhar on Istish-haadi attacks], Nunn Asia. March 13, 2013b. https://www.nunn.asia/6295/.

66 Afghan. Invaders, Religious Pressures, Decrees, and Sermons.] Islamic Emirates of Afghanistan. Da Jihad Ghazh, 2018. URL: https://shahamat1.com/?p=123866.

67 Fazli, Noon. Un-Islamic Decrees of Islamic Scholars.] Kabull.com. 2018. URL: https://kabull.com

68 Anonymous, 2013, op. cit.

69 Baryali, Ahmad Zeya, 2013a, op. cit.

70 Afghan, 2018, op. cit.

71 Fazli, Noon, 2018, op. cit.

72 Latif, Numan. Suicide bombers are Islamic Nuclear Bomb] Kabull.com, 2018. URL: https://com.kabull

73 Agha, Sayed Abu Qasim, 2018, op. cit.

74 Hamid, Sayed Wali. Exposing the Spell of the Witch!] NunnAsia, 2013. URL: https://www.nunn.asia/8029/.

75 Anonymous, 2013, op. cit.

76 A voice clip uploaded on YouTube of Mohammad Yasir Wardak, a prominent Taliban preacher and ideologue, who was reportedly killed later in 2014. See URL: https://youtu.be/G4xBFSdgPx8

77 Baryali, Ahmad Zeya. Sayyaf Khan. Istish-haad or Suicide.] Nunn Asia, 2012. URL: https://asia.nunn.www

78 Baryali, Ahmad Zeya, 2013a, op. cit.

79 (Quran 3:140) [Translation]:" ...that Allah may test those who believe, and that He may take martyrs from among you. And Allah likes not the transgressors".

80 Baryali, Ahmad Zeya, 2013a, op. cit.

81 Baryali, Ahmad Zeya, 2012, op. cit.

82 Anonymous, 2013, op. cit.

83 A preoperational proclamation clip of a teen Taliban suicide bomber that was uploaded on the Taliban's Al-Amara website. The video was

uploaded on YouTube on Sept. 28, 2018. URL: https://www.youtube.com/watch?v=2N27S8sh_qQ.

84 Part of a speech of a suicide bomber in a preoperational clip. URL: https://www.youtube.com/watch?v=B3I5C68JNaI.

86 Commission of the Cultural Affairs Islamic Emirate of Taliban. Eternal Life: Martyrdom Seeker Shukatullah (Hanzala)]. The date of production of the 22-minute video is not clear. The clip was redistributed by a Facebook account. See URL: https://www.facebook.com/354015902081916/videos/782909928724895/.

87 See the preoperational proclamation clip of a suicide bomber published on Taliban's Al-Hijrat website. In the clip, the bomber is shown to crash an explosive-laden vehicle reportedly into the motor convoy of foreign troops. The date of the attack is unknown, but the video clip was uploaded on January 20,, 2019. URL: https://www.youtube.com/watch?v=wpXZkTUwQZ4.

88 Commission of Cultural Affairs, Islamic Emirates of Afghanistan. The Caravan of the Heroes]. URL: http://alemara1.org/alemarah/index.php/news/.

89 Rapoport, Yossef & Shahab Ahmed. Ibn Taymiyya and His Times. Oxford: Oxford University Press, 2010.

90 Roshandel, Jalil & Sharon Chadha. Jihad and International Security. New York: Palgrave Macmillan. 2006.

91 Edwards, David, 2017, op. cit. p. 97.

92 Edwards, David, 2017, op. cit. p. 108.

93 Johnson, Thomas. 'Taliban Adaptations and Innovations.' Small Wars and Insurgencies 24:1 (2013): 3–27. URL: https://doi.org/10.1080/09592318.2013.740228.

94 Pakistan: Madrasas, Extremism and the Military. Rep. no. 36. International Crisis Group, 2002.

95 Gopal, Anand, & Alex Strick van Linschoten. 'Ideology in the Afghan Taliban: A New AAN Report'. Afghanistan Analysts Network. 2017.

96 Giustozzi, Antonio. Koran, Kalashnikov and Laptop: The Neo-Taliban Insurgency in Afghanistan. London. Hurst Publishers, 2007: p. 72.

97 Brahimi, Ali. 'The Taliban's Evolving Ideology. LSE Global Governance'. Working Paper WP 02/2010.

98 Gopal, Anand, & Alex Strick van Linschoten, 2017, op. cit.

99 Semple, Michael, 2014, op. cit.

100 Williams, Brian, 2007, op. cit.

101   Johnson, Thomas, & Chris Mason. 'Understanding the Taliban Insurgency in Afghanistan'. Orbis: A Journal of World Affairs 51, no. 1 (2007). DOI: https://doi.org/10.1016/j.orbis.2006.10.006.

102   Edwards, David, 2017, op. cit.

103   Edwards, David, 2017, op. cit., p. 19.

104   Sheikh, Mona. 'Sacred Pillars of Violence: Findings from a Study of the Pakistani Taliban'. Politics, Religion, and Ideology 13, no. 4 (2012): 439–54. URL: https://doi.org/10.1080/21567689.2012.725662.

105   Semple, Michael, 2014, op. cit.

106   Pape, Robert. 'The Strategic Logic of Suicide Terrorism'. American Political Science Review 97, no. 3 (2003): 343–61. URL:https://www.jstor.org/stable/3117613.

107   Talal, Asad. On Suicide Bombing. New York: Columbia University Press, 2007.

108   Ergil, Doğu, 2000, op. cit. Egril who studied the PKK suicide bombings argues that prolong subjugation, negligence, and persecution caused frustration among the members of the PKK which brought the group to resorting to suicide bombings. He claims that dying for the cause of independence and liberation is equal to Holy Scripture for the PKK members.

109   Bloom, Mia. Dying to Kill: The Allure of Suicide Terrorism. New York: Columbia University Press, 2005.

110   Hafez, Mohammad, 2007, op. cit.

111   Soufan, Ali. The black banners declassified: How torture derailed the war on terror after 9/11. New York: Norton, 2020, p. xxiv.

112   Talal, Asad, 2007, op. cit.

113   Durkheim, Emile. Suicide: A Study in Sociology, Trans. John Spaulding and George Simpson. Glenco: Free Press, 1951.

114   Johnson, Kathryn. "Durkheim Revisited: Why Do Women Kill Themselves?", Suicide and Life-Threatening Behavior, 9 (1979): 145–53.

115   Both authors conceptualized altruistic suicide missions as those committed as an act of duty for the collective benefits/satisfaction of the group and its members to which the suicide committing person belongs.

116   Semple, Michael, 2014, op. cit.

117   Strenski, Ivan. Why Politics cannot be separated from Religion. Oxford: Blackwell Publishing, 2010.

118   Fierke, Karin. 'Agents of Death: The Structural Logic of Suicide Terrorism and Martyrdom.' International Theory 1, no. 1 (2009): 155–184. URL: https://doi.org/10.1017/S1752971909000049.

119 Semple argues that the contents of the Taliban's preoperational proclamations—including the martyr's statement, the narration of the valedictory, the collage of pre-martyrdom shots of the martyr, the footage of the operation, as well as ballads—are selected to reinforce the martyrdom theme. By examining suicide bombings under the lens of structural logic, Fierke argues that while 'suicide bombings' and 'suicide terrorism' are the most prevalent terms used for the acts of human bombs, 'martyrdom operations' is the most-used term in the Arab World, the Middle East, and among Western Islamists.

120 Hafez, Mohammad, 2007, op. cit.

121 Ibid., 121.

122 Msellemu, Sengulo. 'From Kamikaze to Jihadist: What Are Its Causes?' Journal of Education and Practice 7, no. 2 (2016): 144.Msellemu argues that in the jihadist ideology, martyrdom does not signify an end of individual existence, but rather immortality in highly pleasurable circumstances.

123 Bloom, Mia. 'Palestinian Suicide Bombing: Public Support, Market Share, and Outbidding.' Political Science Quarterly 119, no. 1(2004): 61-88. URL: https://doi.org/10.2307/20202305.

124 Moghadam, Assaf. 'Palestinian Suicide Terrorism in the Second Intifada: Motivations and Organizational Aspects.' Studies in Conflict and Terrorism 26, no. 2 (2003): 65-92. https://doi.org/10.1080/10576100390145215.

125 Merari, Ariel. 'The Readiness to Kill and Die.' In: William Reich (Ed) Origins of Terrorism. Cambridge: Cambridge University Press, 1990: 192–207.

126 Brynen, Rex. 'The Dynamic of Palestinian Elite Formation.' Journal of Palestinian Studies 24, no. 3 (1995):31–43.

127 Crenshaw, Martha. 'Suicide Terrorism in Comparative Perspective.' In: Countering Suicide Terrorism (Herzliya, The International Policy Institute for Counter Terrorism), 2000: 21–30.

128 Schbley, Hammond. 'Torn between God, Family, and Money: The Changing Profile of Lebanon's Religious Terrorists.' Studies in Conflict & Terrorism 23 (2000):175-96. https://doi.org/10.1080/105761000412760.

129 Krueger, Alan. and Maleckova, Jitka. 'Education, poverty, political violence, and terrorism: Is there a connection?' Working Paper No. w9074, National Bureau of Economic Research, 2002. https://doi.org/10.3386/w9074.

130 Post, Jerrold., Sprinzak, Ehud., and Denny, Laurita. 2003. 'The Terrorists in Their Own Words: Interviews with Thirty-Five Incarcerated Middle Eastern Terrorists.' Terrorism and Political Violence 15 (2003):171-84. https://doi.org/10.1080/0954655031233 1293007.

131 Schweitzer, Yoram. 'The Rise and Fall of Suicide Bombings in the Second Intifada Yoram.' Strategic Assessment 30, no. 3 (2010): 39-48. https://

strategicassessment.inss.org.il/wp-content/uploads/antq/fe-3014381841. pdf.

132 Hicks, Madelyn., Dardagan, Hamit., Bagnall, Peter., Spagat, Michael., and Sloboda, John. 'Casualties in Civilians and Coalition Soldiers from Suicide Bombings in Iraq, 2003-10: a descriptive study.' Lancet 378, no. 9794 (2011)906-14. https://doi.org/10.1016/S0140-6736(11)61023-4.

Chapter 10: Tablighi Jamaat and its Role in the Global Jihad. South Asia Democratic Forum

Notes

1. Each Tablighi has to manage his/her own expenses for travel and dawah. 'They are encouraged to share in the cooking, cleaning, and other menial tasks that they would usually not engage in at home' (Pieri, 2015, p.63; Siddiqui, 2018, pp.98, 136).

2. It is reported that TJ 'does not maintain an account of its members, their names, addresses, profession, family, and other such details'. 'There is no card-holding cadre' and people can join or leave TJ regarding volition (Salam, 2020b).

3. TJ is guided by the following six key principles: '*Kalimah*: An article of faith in which the tabligh accepts that there is no god but Allah and the Prophet Muhammad is His messenger; *Salaat*: Five daily prayers that are essential to spiritual elevation, piety, and a life free from the ills of the material world; *Ilm and Dhikr*: The knowledge and remembrance of Allah conducted in sessions in which the congregation listens to preaching by the emir, performs prayers, recites the Quran and reads Hadith. The congregation will also use these sessions to eat meals together, thus fostering a sense of community and identity; *Ikram-i-Muslim*: The treatment of fellow Muslims with honor and deference; *Ikhlas-i-Niyat*: 'Reforming one's life in supplication to Allah by performing every human action for the sake of Allah and toward the goal of self-transformation'; *Tafrigh-i-Waqt*: 'The sparing of time to live a life based on faith and learning its virtues, following in the footsteps of the Prophet, and taking His message door-to-door for the sake of faith'.

4. The exact number is difficult to measure due to the absence of a formal registration.

5. Expert Patrick Sukhdeo states that TJ 'operates in every sense as a secret society...'.

6 Besides the Federal Bureau for the Protection of the Constitution (BfV) under the Ministry of the Interior, the most important intelligence authorities in Germany are the Federal Intelligence Service (BND) under the Federal Chancellery and the Military Counterintelligence Service (MAD) under the Ministry of Defence. The BfV is given authority to track any activities

by extremist groups that seek to foment ideological or religious strife domestically (Archick, K et. Al., 2006, p.n.n.).

7. State Bureaus for the Protection of the Constitution work independently of each other and independently of the BfV (Archick, K et. Al., 2006, p.n.n.).

8. Statement by the Bundesinnenminister Otto Schily zum Verfassungsschutzbericht 2004 am 17. Mai 2005 in Berlin, quoted in focus migration (2005, May). Deutschland: Verfassungsbericht 2004. Newsletter Ausgabe, 5/2005.

9. It is stated that 'considering the hard numbers, one can say that the Islamist extremist following increased by around 5 percent to a total of 28,020 individuals in 2019 (2018: 26,560)' (BMI, 2020b, p.26).

10. Verfassungsschutzbericht 2019 BMI, p.308, author's translation.

11. Verfassungsschutzbericht 2019 BMI, p.224, author's translation.

12. The LfVBW comes to a similar conclusion by questioning TJ's self-description as a religious, apolitical, and non-violent phenomenon. Instead, the intelligence agency comes to the conclusion that TJ must be classified as a 'extremist organisation' (IBW, 2012, p.67)

13. The LfVB further argues that the 'traditional prayer clothing and rules of conduct in everyday life, which are binding down to the last detail, are intended to express the absolute devotion to the Prophet Muhammad. These aspirations are necessarily disintegrating in non-Muslim societies, so that a lasting and serious turn to Western social orders, values and models of integration is not possible' (BSTMI, 2020).

14. This includes 'the subordination of women to men, the woman's duty of obedience to the man and the limited freedom of movement of women are postulated as well as their sexual availability' (MIKNW, 2010, p.109).

15. The Shura is supposed to function as an advisory committee 'to deal with all important matters including international congregations (ijtima)'.

16. Shah and Mushtaq are stating: 'The differences grew so much that several incidents of brawl occurred, and members and elders assaulted each other in London Markaz – also known as Masjid Ilyas and Abbey Mills Mosque. Tableeghi Jamaat and police sources have confirmed that the police were called about 13 times and four people were arrested on different occasions. A source said that a group of Tableeghi followers from Bangladesh and Indian Gujarat ganged up against the Tableeghi members from Pakistani background and other countries and as a result the Abbey Mills Mosque became a battleground'. 'The two factions now don't go to each other's mosques and security personnel are deputed at the gate of Ilyas Masjid to identify the members who come to the mosque to attend sermons'.

17. Verfassungsbericht Baden-Württemberg 2011, p.67, author's translation.

18. Case No. Az.: B 1 S 05.763, 24.11.2005.

19. Case No. Az.: 10 A 5681/04.

20. Verfassungsschutzbericht Freistaat Thüringen 2011, p.142, author's translation.

21. It is reported that TJ not only tolerates the use of its networks by extremists but also that individual Tablighis actively support extremist's trough the facilitation of contacts to Jihadist groups such as Al Qaeda and the Taliban – among others – to receive military training and/or serve as fighters.

22. Verfassungsschutzbericht des Landes Nordrhein-Westfalen für das Jahr 2012, p.128; author's translation.

23. Verfassungsschutzbericht 2005 BMI, p.194, author's translation.

24. This assessment of the German intelligence is strengthened by international observers. For example, after interviewing a Tablighi, Craig S. Smith highlights the causal role of such training courses not only for radicalising Muslims but also transforming them into militants: 'Tablighi-sponsored trips to Pakistan put young men in contact with fundamentalists of many stripes, including adherents of Salafism, a fundamentalist school of Islam whose radical fringe advocates war against non-Muslims'. Smith's interviewee also 'acknowledged that young men wishing to migrate from the Tablighi to more militant forms of Islam had no trouble finding their way' and 'it's easy to get into the jihadi network' since as a Tablighi you know where you can meet Salafists. Furthermore, the interviewee estimated that half of the Tablighis are being recruited by the Salafists.

25. Verfassungsschutzbericht 2005 BMI, p.226, author's translation.

26. Verfassungsschutzbericht 2005 BMI, p.194, author's translation.

27. Verfassungsbericht Baden-Württemberg 2011, p.67, author's translation.

28. TJ has a main presence in the Paris region, with a centre located in Saint-Denis (French Sénat, 2020a)

29. TJ fed on an emerging identity crisis among Muslim migrants and the major economic crisis following the oil shock of 1973 which created fragile socio-economic conditions. It is reported that not only urban but also rural Muslim populations are in the focus of TJ (DGSI, 2018, pp.4, 109).

30. The BfV states in its 2019 report (summary) that during the period of assessment, again a large number of anti-Semitic incidents motivated by Islamist extremism occurred. These incidents ranged from anti-Semitic speeches and sermons to anti-Jewish postings on social media and verbal or physical attacks on Jewish individuals. Antisemitism serves as an ideological link connecting all Islamist extremist movements, including TJ. The vast majority of Islamist extremist organisations operating in Germany holds anti-

Semitic ideas, which they disseminate through various channels (BMI, 2020b, pp.26, 27).

31. Rapport fait au nom de la commission d'enquête sur l'organisation et les moyens des services de l'État pour faire face à l'évolution de la menace terroriste après la chute de l'État islamique. [Report created in the name of the enquiry commission regarding the organisation and means available to the state so as to face terrorist threats following the fall of the Islamic State.]

32. These reports are based on Committee hearings with academic and non-academic researchers and other specialists.

33. For example, the stabbing attack on a soldier patrolling in La Defence, a business district in Paris in May 2013.

34. Dawah (literally 'call' or 'invitation') is understood as 'the propagation of the radical-Islamic ideology' (Mukhopadhyay, 2006, p.333). According to Siddiqi, TJ interprets the concept of Dawah 'as Allah's way of bringing believers to faith' which 'includes both activities with other people in one's own locality and missionary journeys to other places' (Siddiqi, 2018, p.2).

35. According to Mukhopadhyay, *exclusivism* 'denotes the trend of a general aloofness of Muslims in the European host societies. They have less interest in local and national politics and refuse to integrate into the mainstream of European societies. There exists among them, a general attitude towards their countries of residence as a temporary halt, from where they would eventually return.' (Mukhopadhyay, 2005, p.333).

    Parallelism he defines as 'the idea of establishing an alternate society, i.e., a transplanted version of their countries of origin with rituals, religious practices and mosques in a foreign land. If extended or as propagated by the global Islamic movements, this idea of parallelism may eventually lead to parallel Muslim societies (totally based on the literal interpretation of Islamic texts by these global Islamic movements) in a predominantly Christian setting. In the long run, such parallelism will result in greater division and ghettoisation in European societies solely on the basis of religion.' (Mukhopadhyay, 2005, p.333).

36. With the 'Hawala system' it is possible to deposit an amount in one country to be raised in another by an indicated person. The method functions on the 'basis of honor' and there are no records. Besides being hardly traceable (if at all), the Hawala system is vulnerable to misuse (infiltrations by criminals for money laundering) Marques, T., & Vilela, A. J., 2006, p.52). However, one must mention that TJ does maintain some bank accounts with the funds needed to carry out activities. On a more general note, regarding TJ's financial affairs, experts believe that the movement relies heavily on voluntary contributions (collection and contributions) of largely unknown amounts (Salam, 2020b; Siddiqui, 2018, p.136). There are also cases in which land or property are offered as donations. Construction work, community outreach

programmes and other types of developmental work are sponsored by wealthy supporters. It is reported that a large amount of contributions flow to TJ from Gulf countries so as to fund large congregations, the construction of mosques, and other activities (Salam, 2020b). Larger known patrons include Saudi Arabia and several among the Pakistani establishment.

37. COBA (Center for Information and Analysis) is a Moscow-based Russian non-profit organisation.

38. It is reported that in Russia TJ has been making inroads through underground cells. The movement's underground activities in the country have been noticed in Moscow, St. Petersburg and in the Muslim-dominated Republics of Bashkortostan, Tatarstan and Karachai-Cherkessia. In 2016, the Russian police busted several TJ underground cells. Cadres were detained and extremist literature as well as communication tools and electronic data storage devices were recovered. A few Tablighi cadres arrested in Moscow were planning to travel to Afghanistan and Pakistan for training in extremist camps. In one instance, a busted cell operated by Central Asian nationals also included Russian citizens. In August 2020, the Russian Federal Security Service's Directorate for Mordovia, in interaction with other law enforcing agencies, withheld a TJ cell for its extremist activities. TJ cell unearthed in St. Petersburg was run by a Tajik national suspected to be the head of a local HT cell. This is indicative of TJ's alliance with other extremist groups. Russia banned the group in 2009 for 'assistance to international terrorist organisations' and for actions 'aimed at the violation of the territorial integrity of Russia and religious discrimination of its citizens'.

39. The CSTO is a Russia-led military alliance of seven former Soviet states created in 2002. For more information see: Avedissian (2019).

40. For the original text, see: «The Tablighi Jamaat» movement: The Ideology and the Activity Specifics http://islam.dgu.ru/Stat/Islamoved percent202016-3-1. pdf

41. 12 Pakistanis, an Indian and a Bangladeshi.

42. According to Noivo (2010, pp.4-5), at least two persons of this group were members of TJ.

43. Mubin Shaikh is a former Tablighi, who joined a Jihadi group temporarily but later became engaged in the struggle against violent extremism (AFPC, 2012, p.7).

References

AFP (2020, April 9). Islamic missionary movement is blamed for spreading coronavirus in Asia after it held massive gatherings that have left hundreds of Muslims infected. Daily Mail.

https://www.dailymail.co.uk/news/article-8205135/Islamic-missionary-movement-blamed-spreading-coronavirus-Asia.html

AFPC (2012). Tablighi Jamaat. American Foreign Policy Council (AFPC).

Alexiev, A. (2011, March). The Wages of Extremism: Radical Islam's Threat to the West and the Muslim World. Hudson Institute.

https://www.hudson.org/content/researchattachments/attachment/875/ aalexievwagesofextremism032011.pdf

Alexiev, A. (2005). Tablighi Jamaat: Jihad's Stealthy Legions. Middle East Quarterly 12(5), 3-11.

https://www.meforum.org/686/tablighi-jamaat-jihads-stealthy-legions

Archick, K et. Al. (2006, July 24). European Approaches to Homeland Security and Counterterrorism. CRS Report for Congress.

https://fas.org/sgp/crs/homesec/RL33573.pdf

Avedissian, K. (2019, October 6). Fact Sheet: What is the Collective Security Treaty Organization? EVN Report, The Black Sea Trust for regional Cooperation. https://www.evnreport.com/understanding-the-region/fact-sheet-what-is-the-collective-security-treaty-organization

AVID (2007, October). The radical dawa in transition. The rise of Islamic neo-radicalisation in the Netherlands. General Intelligence and Security Service (AVID), Ministry of the Interior and Kingdom Relations, The Hague.

https://english.aivd.nl/binaries/aivd-en/documents/publications/2007/10/09/the-radical-dawa-in-transition/theradicaldawaintransition.pdf

AVID (2004, December). From dawa to jihad. The various threats from radical Islam to the democratic legal order. General Intelligence and Security Service (AVID), Ministry of the Interior and Kingdom Relations, The Hague. https://fas.org/irp/world/netherlands/dawa.pdf

Bastié, E. (2015, January 27). Islam radical: qu'est-ce que le mouvement tabligh. [Radical Islam: About the Tablighi Movement]. Le Figaro. https://www.lefigaro.fr/actualite-france/2015/01/27/01016-20150127ARTFIG00202-islam-radical-qu-est-ce-que-le-mouvement-tabligh.php

BBC (2013, May 26). Knife attack on soldier in Paris treated as terrorism. https://www.bbc.com/news/world-europe-22670697

Rougier Bernard, R. (2020). Les territoires conquis de l'islamisme. [Territories conquered by Islamism]. Presses Universitaires de France/ PUF).

BMI (2020a, July). Verfassungsschutzbericht 2019. [Constitutional Protection Report 2019]. Bundesamt für Verfassungsschutz, Bundesministerium des Innern, für Bau und Heimat (BMI).

https://brightsblog.files.wordpress.com/2008/11/2004.pdf.

BMI (2020b, July). Brief summary 2019 Report on the Protection of the Constitution. Facts and Trends. Bundesamt für Verfassungsschutz, Bundesminister des Innern, für Bau und Heimat (BMI)/Federal Ministry of the Interior,

Building and Community (BMI). Federal Office for the Protection of the Constitution (BfV). https://www.verfassungsschutz.de/en/public-relations/publications/annual-reports/annual-report-2019-summary

BMI (2012). Verfassungsschutzbericht 2011. [Constitutional Protection Report 2011]. Bundesamt für Verfassungsschutz, Bundesminister des Innern, für Bau und Heimat (BMI)/Federal Ministry of the Interior, Building and Community (BMI). Federal Office for the Protection of the Constitution (BfV). https://publikationen.uni-tuebingen.de/xmlui/bitstream/handle/10900/63256/vsb2011.pdf?sequence=1&isAllowed=y

BMI (2006, May). Verfassungsschutzbericht 2005. [Constitutional Protection Report 2005]. Bundesamt für Verfassungsschutz, Bundesminister des Innern, für Bau und Heimat (BMI) Federal Ministry of the Interior, Building and Community (BMI)/Federal Office for the Protection of the Constitution (BfV).

https://publikationen.uni-tuebingen.de/xmlui/bitstream/handle/ 10900/63244/Verfassungsschutzbericht_2005_de.pdf?sequence=1&isAllowed=y percent-20BMI percent202005 percent20Verfassungsschutzbericht percent202005"

https://publikationen.uni-tuebingen.de/xmlui/bitstream/handle/ 10900/63244/Verfassungsschutzbericht_2005_de.pdf?sequence=1&isAllowed=y percent-20BMI percent202005 percent20Verfassungsschutzbericht percent202005

BMI (2005, May). Verfassungsschutzbericht 2004. [Constitutional Protection Report 2004]. Bundesamt für Verfassungsschutz, Bundesminister des Innern, für Bau und Heimat (BMI).

https://brightsblog.files.wordpress.com/2008/11/2004.pdf

BSTMI (2020, April). Verfassungsschutzbericht 2019, Bayern. [Constitutional Protection Report 2019, Bavaria]. Bayrisches Staatsministerium des Inneren, für Sport und Integration (BSTMI)/The Bavarian Ministry of the Interior, Sport and Integration.

https://www.verfassungsschutz.bayern.de/mam/anlagen/vsb-2019_bf.pdf

BSTMI (2007, March). Verfassungsschutzbericht 2019, Bayern. [Constitutional Protection Report 2019, Bavaria]. Bayrisches Staatsministerium des Inneren, für Sport und Integration (BSTMI)/The Bavarian Ministry of the Interior, Sport and Integration.

https://www.yumpu.com/de/document/read/8144472/verfassungsschutzbericht-bayern-2006-bayerisches-landesamt-fur-Verfassungsschutzbericht Bayern 2006

Burton, F. & Stewart, S. (2008, January 23). Tablighi Jamaat: An Indirect Line to Terrorism. Worldview.

https://worldview.stratfor.com/article/tablighi-jamaat-indirect-line-terrorism

СОВА (2009, May 7). В России решением суда запрещена международная религиозная организация "Таблиги джамаат". [Russian Justice System banished the international religious organisation 'Tablighi Jamaat']. Center for Information and Analysis (СОВО/SOVA).

https://www.sova-center.ru/religion/news/extremism/counter-extremism/2009/05/d15947/

DGSI (2018). Rapport 2018. Etat des lieux de la pénétration de l'islam fondamentaliste en France. [Report 2018. State of play regarding the lodging of fundamentalist Islam in France]. Direction générale de la Sécurité intérieure/ General Directorate for Internal Security (DGSI).

http://www.guerredefrance.fr/Documents/ETATLIEUXISLAM2018.pdf

Duysheeva, R. (2019, May 20). Should Tablighi Jamaat be banned in Kyrgyzstan? Central Asian Bureau for Analytical Reporting (CABAR.asia), Institute for War and Peace Reporting.

https://cabar.asia/en/should-tablighi-jamaat-be-banned-in-kyrgyzstan

Finnegan, W. (2016, February 16). Last Days: Preparing for the Apocalypse in San Bernadino. The New Yorker.

http://www.newyorker.com/magazine/2016/02/22/preparing-for-apocalypse-in-san-bernardino

focus migration (2005, May). Deutschland: Verfassungsbericht 2004. [Germany: Constitutional Protection Report 2004]. Newsletter Ausgabe, 5/2005.

http://focus-migration.hwwi.de/Einzelansichten.1316.0.html?&tx_wilpubdb_pi1 percent5Barticle percent5D=236&cHash=20446b156249591b2c9067e77eec 6b81

Freedman, I. (2006). Gateway to Jihad: Tablighi Jama'at. The Center for Security Policy, Washington, D.C.

French Sénat (2020b, July 7). Rapport fait au nom de la commission d'enquête (1) sur les réponses apportées par les autorités publiques au développement de la radicalisation islamiste et les moyens de la combattre, No. 595, *Tome II : Comptes rendus des auditions et travaux de la commission d'enquête.* [Report created for the enquiry commission (1) regarding the responses advanced by authorities faced with the furthering of Islamic radicalisation and the means to be developed in this quest. N° 595, Volume II: A report of the auditions and workings of the enquiry committee]. French Sénat, Session Extraordinaire DE 2019-2020.

http://www.senat.fr/rap/r19-595-2/r19-595-21.pdf

French Sénat (2020a, July 7). Rapport fait au nom de la commission d'enquête (1) sur les réponses apportées par les autorités publiques au développement de la radicalisation islamiste et les moyens de la combattre, No. 595, *Tome I : Rapport.* [Report created for the enquiry commission (1) regarding the responses advanced by authorities faced with the furthering of Islamic radicalisation and the means to be developed in this quest. N° 595, Volume II: Report]. French Sénat, Session Extraordinaire DE 2019-2020.

http://www.senat.fr/rap/r19-595-1/r19-595-11.pdf

French Sénat (2018, July 4). Rapport fait au nom de la commission d'enquête (1) sur l'organisation et les moyens des services de l'État pour faire face à l'évolution de la menace terroriste après la chute de l'État islamique, No. 639. [Report created for the enquiry commission (1) regarding the means available to State services in their fight against the islamist threat following the fall of the Islamic State, N°639]. French Sénat, Session Extraordinaire DE 2017-2018.

https://www.senat.fr/rap/r17-639/r17-6391.pdf

Gaborieau, M. (1999). Transnational Islamic Movements: Tablighi Jama'at in Politics? ISIM Newsletter (International Institute for the Study of Islam in the Modern World),

https://www.researchgate.net/profile/Marc_Gaborieau/publication/277096388_Transnational_Islamic_Movements_Tablighi_Jama'at_in_Politics/links/5950e3f1aca27248ae461410/Transnational-Islamic-Movements-Tablighi-Jamaat-in-Politics.pdf

Goffman, E. 1961. Essays on the Social Situation of Mental Patients and Other Inmates. Anchor Books.

Hedges (2008, April). Tablighi Jamaat: The Premier Latent Network. Threat Convergence. Occasional Research Series. Washington, D.C.: The Fund for Peace.

https://css.ethz.ch/en/services/digital-library/publications/publication.html/93813

HHBI (2012, August). Hamburg Verfassungsschutzbericht 2011. [Hamburg: Constitutional Protection Report 2011]. Freie und Hansestadt Hamburg. Behörde für Inneres und Sport (HHBI). Landesamt für Verfassungsschutz (LfV).

https://www.hamburg.de/contentblob/3619106/   80b8befadd0897fc-f4180ae1b1d8da22/data/   verfassungsschutzbericht-2011-illustriert.pdf;jsessionid= EDC8D984B3A7E24C7B4720EE17767FEA.liveWorker2

Horstmann, A. (2007, April). The Inculturation of a Transnational Islamic Missionary Movement: Tablighi Jamaat al-Dawa and Muslim Society in Southern Thailand. Journal of Social Issues in Southeast Asia, Vol. 22, No. 1, pp.107-130.

https://www.jstor.org/stable/41308088?seq=1

Howenstein, N. (2006, October 12). Islamist Networks: The Case of Tablighi Jamaat. USIPeace Briefing. United States Institute of Peace (USIP).

https://www.usip.org/publications/2006/10/islamist-networks-case-tablighi-ja-maat

IBW (2012, April). Verfassungsbericht Baden-Württemberg 2011. [Constitutional Protection Report Baden-Württemberg 2011]. Innenministerium Baden-Württemberg (IBW).

https://www.km-bw.de/site/lfv/get/documents/IV.Dachmandant/Datenquelle/stories/public_files/vs-bericht_bw_2011/Vsbericht_BW_2011.pdf

Interfax (2020, August 10). Tablighi Jamaat literature found in mosques in Mordovia, activists detained. Interfax Religion.

http://www.interfax-religion.com/?act=news&div=15804

Interfax (2012, October 19). Work of 200 Tablighi Jamaat missionaries stopped in Kazakhstan in 2012 – senator. Interfax

https://interfax.com/newsroom/top-stories/53670/?sphrase_id=6640

Interfax (2012, July 2). Kyrgyzstan govt doing too little in fighting Islamist extremism – experts. Interfax Religion.

http://interfax-religion.com/?act=news&div=9483

Interfax (2009, August 3). Russian Supreme Court upholds banning Islamic organization as extremist. Interfax Religion.

http://www.interfax-religion.com/?act=news&div=6282

Javaid, A. (2017, January 20). NIA's study of arrested Indian ISIS fans busts common myths. Daily News & Analysis.

http://www.dnaindia.com/india/report-nia-s-study-of-arrested-indian-isis-fans-busts-common-myths-2294253

Jordán, J., & Wesley, R. (2006, March 9). The Madrid Attacks: Results of Investigations Two Years Later. Terrorism Monitor Volume: 4 Issue: 5, Jamestown Foundation.

https://jamestown.org/program/the-madrid-attacks-results-of-investigations-two-years-later/

Mandaville, P. (2010, September 15). Muslim Networks and Movements in Western Europe. Washington, DC: The Pew Forum on Religion & Public Life.

https://www..pewforum.org/2010/09/15/muslim-networks-and-movements-in-western-europe/

Marino, F. (2020, April 2). Tablighi Jamaat, an 'antechamber of terrorism' in Europe. ANI.

Marques, T., & Vilela, A. J. (2006, September 21). O mais polémico dos muçulmanos. [The most polemic Muslim]. SÁBADO, pp.51-52.

https://silo.tips/download/ogrupoislamicotablighjamaat-amazon-simple-storage-service-s3

MIKNW (2013, June). Verfassungsschutzbericht des Landes Nordrhein-Westfalen für das Jahr 2012. Pressefassung. [Constitutional Protection Report for the lands in Nordrhein-Westfalen in the year 2005. Statement to the Press]. Ministerium für Inneres und Kommunales des Landes Nordrhein-Westfalen.

https://www.ksta.de/blob/4791942/006f14ed391f22e95c91bb9fa5fdbfc0/verfassungschutzbericht-2012-data.pdf

MIKNW (2010, January). Verfassungsschutzbericht des Landes Nordrhein-Westfalen für das Jahr 2009. Pressefassung. [Constitutional Protection Report for the lands in Nordrhein-Westfalen in the year 2009. Statement to the Press]. Ministerium für Inneres und Kommunales des Landes Nordrhein-Westfalen.

http://www.gelsenzentrum.de/verfassungsschutzbericht_nrw_2009.pdf

Mukhopadhyay, A.R. (2005). Tabligh-e-Jama' at Under the Scanner of German Intelligence.

Strategic Analysis, Vol. 29, No. 2, April-June, Institute for Defence Studies and Analyses (IDSA).

https://idsa.in/system/files/strategicanalysis_armukhopadhyay_0605.pdf

Neumann, P.R., & Rogers, R. (2007). Recruitment and Mobilisation for the Islamist Militant Movement in Europe. King`s College London (Report commissioned by the Directorate General for Justice, Freedom and Security of the European Commission).

https://ec.europa.eu/home-affairs/sites/homeaffairs/files/doc_centre/ terrorism/ docs/ec_radicalisation_study_on_mobilisation_tactics_en.pdf

NMIS (2020, January). Verfassungsschutzbericht Niedersachsen 2019. [Constitutional Protection Report for Lower Saxony 2019]. Niedersächsisches Ministerium für Inneres und Sport (NMIS) – Verfassungsschutz.

https://www.mi.niedersachsen.de/startseite/service/publikationen/publikationen-63098.html

NMIS (2007). Verfassungsschutzbericht 2006 Niedersachen. [Constitutional Protection Report for Lower Saxony 2006]. Niedersächsisches Ministerium für Inneres und Sport (NMIS) – Verfassungsschutz.

https://verfassungsschutzberichte.de/niedersachsen/2006

Noivo, D. (2010). Jihadism in Portugal: Grasping a nebulous reality. ARI 113/2010 – 1/7/2010, Real Institudo Elcano.

http://www.realinstitutoelcano.org/wps/portal/rielcano_en/contenido?WCM_GLOBAL_CONTEXT=/elcano/elcano_in/zonas_in/ari113-2010

Pandey, M.C. (2020, April 16). ED lodges money laundering case against Tablighi Jamaat Markaz chief. India Today.

https://www.indiatoday.in/india/story/ed-lodges-money-laundering-case-against-tablighi-jamaat-s-markaz-chief-1667749-2020-04-16

Pieri, Z.P. (2015). Tablighi Jamaat and the quest for a London Mega Mosque. The Modern Muslim World. Palgrave Macmillan.

https://link.springer.com/chapter/10.1057 percent2F9781137464392_4

Pieri, Z.P. (2012, May 4). The Contentious Politics of Socio-Political Engagement: The Transformation of the Tablighi Jamaat in London. Doctoral Theses, University of Exeter.

https://ore.exeter.ac.uk/repository/handle/10036/3743

Pinto, M.d.C. (2012). An evaluation of the jihadist threat in Portugal. Journal of Policing, Intelligence and Counter Terrorism. Vol. 7, No. 2, October 2012, 115-133.

https://www.tandfonline.com/doi/abs/10.1080/18335330.2012.719094

Putra, Z.I. (2013). The Tablighi Jamaat Movement. Its Ideological Concept and Organizational Structure. Afkaruna, Vol.9, No.1 (Januari – Juni)

https://journal.umy.ac.id/index.php/afkaruna/article/view/26

Ragazzi, F. (2014). Towards "Policed Multiculturalism"? Counter-radicalization in France, the Netherlands and the United Kingdom Francesco Ragazzi. Les Etudes du CERI – n° 206 (September-December)

https://www.sciencespo.fr/ceri/sites/sciencespo.fr.ceri/files/Etude_206_anglais.pdf

Reetz, D. (2004) 'Keeping Busy on the Path of Allah: The Self-Organisation (Intizam) of the Tablighi Jamaat', In: *Islam in Contemporary South Asia (pp.295–305)*, ed. Daniela Bredi. Rome: Oriente Moderno.

RFE/RL (2013, February 26). Kazakhstan Bans Islamic Group. RadioFreeEurope/RadioLiberty.

https://www.rferl.org/a/kazakhstan-bans-tablighi-jamaat/24912890.html

Sachs, S. (2003, July 14). A Muslim Missionary Group Draws New Scrutiny in U.S. The New York Times

https://www.nytimes.com/2003/07/14/us/a-muslim-missionary-group-draws-new-scrutiny-in-us.html

Salam, Z. U. (2020b). Inside the Tablighi Jamaat. Harper Collins Publishers.

Salam, Z. U. (2020a, July 8). How the made-in-India Tablighi Jamaat became the largest organisation in Pakistan. The Print.

https://theprint.in/pageturner/excerpt/how-made-in-india-tablighi-jamaat-be-came-the-largest-organisation-in-pakistan/455990/.

Shah, M.A. & Mushtaq, W. (2018, August 14). Tableeghi Jamaat in Britain splits into two factions. The News International.

https://www.thenews.com.pk/print/354768-tableeghi-jamaat-in-britain-splits-into-two-factions

Siddiqi, B. (2018). Becoming 'Good Muslim'. The Tablighi Jamaat in the UK and Bangladesh. Singapore: Springer.

Sikand, Y. (2006). The Tablighi Jama'at and Politics: A Critical Re-Appraisal. The Muslim World, 96, pp.175–195.

https://onlinelibrary.wiley.com/doi/abs/10.1111/j.1478-1913.2006.00122.x

Sikand, Y. (2003, December). The Tablighi Jama'at and Politics. ISIM Newsletter 13, pp.42-43.

https://openaccess.leidenuniv.nl/bitstream/handle/1887/10073/newsl_13.pdf;sequence=1

Smith, C. S. (2005, April 28). Muslim Group in France Is Fertile Soil for Militancy. The New York Times.

https://www.nytimes.com/2005/04/28/world/europe/muslim-group-in-france-is-fertile-soil-for-militancy.html

The Sunday Telegraph (2006, August 20). Army of darkness.

https://www.pressreader.com/uk/the-sunday-tele-graph/20060820/281822869272359

TI (2012, July). Verfassungsschutzbericht Freistaat Thüringen 2011. [Constitutional Protection Report for Thüringia 2011]. Thüringer Innenministerium (TI).

https://www.thueringen.de/de/publikationen/pic/pubdownload1386.pdf

Timol, R. (2019). Structures of Organisation and Loci of Authority in a Glocal Islamic Movement: The Tablighi Jama'at in Britain. Religions 2019, 10 (10), 573; doi:10.3390/rel10100573

https://www.mdpi.com/2077-1444/10/10/573

Tremolet de Villers, V. (2020, January 6). Considered opinion: France's jihadists Ordinary Jihad. Newswire.

http://www.homelandsecuritynewswire.com/ordinary-jihad

Vidino, L. (2013, November). Jihadist Radicalization in Switzerland. CSS Studie. Center for Security Studies (CSS), ETH Zürich.

https://css.ethz.ch/en/services/digital-library/publications/publication.html/172401

Vilela, A. J., et. Al. (2006, September 21). Extremismo. Movimento Islâmico Controlado Em Portugal. SÁBADO, pp.48-50.

https://silo.tips/download/ogrupoislamicotablighjamaat-amazon-simple-storage-service-s3

Zahid, F. (2015). Tablighi Jamaat and its links with Islamist terrorism. Foreign Analysis, No 19. CENTER FRANÇAIS DE RESHERCHE SUR LE ENSEI-GNEMENT (CF2R).

https://cf2r.org/foreign/tablighi-jamaat-and-its-links-with-islamist-terrorism-2/

Chapter 11: Central Asian Extremist Groups, Kazakhstan and the Danger of Nuclear and Biological Terrorism

1. Scott Ritter. RT News, 28 April, 2020

2. Leonid Gusev. 01 February 2020

3. Radio Free Europe/Radio Liberty

4. The Diplomat, 20 September 2016, Uran Botobekov

5. Moscow Times, 03 April 2017 terrorist attack on the St. Petersburg metro station

6. Christopher McIntosh and Ian Storey, 20 November 2019

7. Simon Saradzhyan. Russia Matters, Simon Saradzhyan, August 06, 2019

8. Graham Allison. September/October 2004

9. October 2017, Columb Strack

10. Connor Dilleen. Asia Times-30 May 2019

11. Uran Botobekov. The Diplomat, January 10, 2017

12. Nick Mucerino. November 5, 2018

13. Dr. Yunis Khushi-June 26, 2017

14. The ISIS magazine Dabiq-May 2015

15. 25 March 2016, Daily Telegraph

16. Newsweek's Daily Beast blog provided another version of an overspill, already apparently happening in 2010

17. Leonid Gusev, an expert of Institute of International Studies, Moscow State Institute of International Relations of the Ministry of Foreign Affairs of the Russian Federation (MGIMO) has noted some consternating cooperative measures and planning's of the extremist groups of Central Asia.

18. Muhammad Wajeeh, a Research Associate at Department of Development Studies,COMSATS Institute of Information Technology, Abbottabad Pakistan in his research paper (Nuclear Terrorism: A Potential Threat to World's Peace and Security- JSSA Vol II, No. 2.

Chapter 12: The Islamic State, the Taliban, and Afghanistan's White Talc Mountains. The Global Witness Research Report

1 Details on the background of ISKP and their competition with the Taliban are set out later in the main text.

2. Who are the Taliban?', BBC News, May 26, 2016 http:// www.bbc.com/news/world-south-asia-11451718

3 Other estimates using different methodology (and estimates from the Taliban themselves) are in the same general area. Bill Roggio and Alexandra Gutowski, 'LWJ Map Assessment: Taliban controls or contests 45 percent of Afghan districts', Long War Journal, September 26, 2017 https://www.longwarjournal.org/ archives/2017/09/lwj-map-assessment-taliban-controls-or-contests-45-of-afghan-districts.php

4 See main text for details of the continued Taliban presence in areas such as Khogyani and Sherzad districts. Mujib Masha, 'Afghan ISIS Branch Makes Inroads in Battle Against Taliban', New York Times, October 13, 2017 https://www.nytimes.com/2015/10/14/world/asia/afghan-isis-branch-makes-inroads-in-battle-against-taliban.html; Caitlin Forrest, 'Afghanistan Partial Threat Assessment: November 22, 2016', Institute for the Study of War, November 23, 2016 www.understandingwar.org/backgrounder/afghanistan-partial-threat-assessment-november-22-2016; 'IS, Taliban fight for key towns in Nangarhar', Dawn, November 29, 2017 https:// www.dawn.com/news/1373507

5 Vera Bergengruen, 'Here's what the 'Mother of All Bombs' did for US fight in Afghanistan', Task and Purpose, April 29, 2017 http://taskandpurpose.com/moab-fight-afghanistan/

6 Borhan Osman, 'The Battle for Mamand: ISKP under strain, but not yet defeated', Afghanistan Analysts Network, May 23, 2017 https://www.afghanistan-analysts. org/the-battle-for-mamand-iskp-under-strain-but-notyet-defeated/; Jessica Purkiss and Abigail Fielding-Smith, 'Islamic State in Afghanistan: Is US assault working?', The Bureau of Investigative Journalism, July 28, 2017 https://www.thebureauinvestigates.com/stories/2017-07-28/islamic-state-in-afghanistan-us-military

7 See for example Borhan Osman, 'The Islamic State in 'Khorasan': How it began and where it stands now in Nangarhar', Afghanistan Analysts Network, July 27, 2016 https://www.afghanistan-analysts.org/the-islamic-state-in-khorasan-how-it-began-and-where-itstands-now-in-nangarhar/

8 Harleen Gambhir, 'ISIS in Afghanistan', Institute for the Study of War, December 3, 2015 http://www.understandingwar.org/sites/default/files/ISIS percent20in percent20 Afghanistan_2.pdf

9 Lizzie Dearden, 'Isis vs Islamic State vs Isil vs Daesh: What do the different names mean – and why does it matter?', The Independent, September 23, 2014

http:// www.independent.co.uk/news/world/middle-east/ isis-vs-islamic-state-vs-isil-vs-daesh-what-do-the-different-names-mean-9750629.html

10 The most comprehensive list of names was from the IMMAP Oasis software, which includes some geographic features but is mainly made up of settlement names.

11 Almost all our sources expressed prices in terms of Pakistani rupees.

12 'XE Currency Charts: USD to PKR,' XE.com http://www. xe.com/currencycharts/?from=USD&to=PKR&view=5Y

13 'XE Currency Charts: USD to AFN,' XE.com http://www.xe.com/currency charts/?from=USD&to=AFN&view=5Y

14 While two of our sources mentioned tourmaline or a mineral that could be tourmaline, they did not present it as a major focus for extraction, and other sources did not mention its presence.

15. See 'The Threat on the Ground', below.

16 'The Mineral Talc', Minerals.net, http://www.minerals. net/mineral/talc.aspx

17 'Talc', Etymology Online http://www.etymonline.com/ index.php?term=talc

18 'Talc: the softest mineral', Geology.com http://geology. com/minerals/talc. shtml

19 'Global Talc and Pyrophyllite Market Exhibits Slow Demand Growth', Ceramic Industry, December 1, 2014 https://www.ceramicindustry.com/articles/94359-global-talc-and-pyrophyllite-market-exhibits-slow-demand-growth

20 Ian Wilson, 'Global Talc Markets'

21 Mark Cocker, 'Summary for the Mineral Information Package for the Ghunday-Achin Magnesite and Talc Area of Interest', in Stephen G. Peters, Trude V.V. King, Thomas J. Mack, and Michael P. Chornack, 'Summaries of Important Areas for Mineral Investment and Production Opportunities of Nonfuel Minerals in Afghanistan', United States Geological Survey, 2011, p 1423 https:// pubs.usgs.gov/of/2011/1204/pdf/20A.pdf

22 'Minerals in Afghanistan: The Achin Magnesite Deposit', Ministry of Mines and Petroleum http://mom.gov.af/ Content/files/The percent20Achin percent20Magnesite percent20Deposit.pdf

23 'Chromite', Geology.com http://geology.com/minerals/ chromite.shtml

24 'Mineral Commodity Summaries: Chromium', United States Geological Survey, January 2018, pp 46-47 https://minerals.usgs.gov/minerals/pubs/commodity/ chromium/mcs-2018-chrom.pdf

25 Golnar Monetvalli, 'Afghanistan sees great white hope in marble sector', Reuters, April 21, 2010 https://www. reuters.com/article/us-afghanistan-marble-idUSTRE63K00C20100421; 'Marbles of Afghanistan', Ministry of

Mines and Petroleum of the Islamic Republic of Afghanistan, January 2014 http://www.mom.gov.af/ Content/files/MoMP_MARBLE_Midas_Jan_2014_ NEW. pdf

26 Sune Engel Rasmussen, 'Afghan government money reaching Taliban through marble trade', The Guardian, June 3, 2016 https://www.theguardian. com/global-development/2016/jun/03/afghan-government-money-taliban-marble-trade; 'Letter dated 9 June 2014 from the Chair of the Security Council Committee established pursuant to resolution 1988 (2011) addressed to the President of the Security Council', United Nations Security Council, June 10, 2014, pp 19-20 http://www.securitycouncilreport. org/atf/cf/   percent7B65BFCF9B-6D27-4E9C-8CD3-CF6E4FF96FF9 percent7D/s_2014_402.pdf

27 The movement headed by Abu Bakr al-Baghdadi generally refers to itself as the Islamic State, though other terms are often used. They include ISIS (the Islamic State in Iraq and Al-Shams, roughly corresponding the area known as the Levant), ISIL (the Islamic State in Iraq and the Levant), and Daesh (from the Arabic acronym for Islamic State – the term preferred by many observers who wish to avoid legitimising the movement, as it has negative connotations in Arabic). The movement's claim to represent a new Islamic Caliphate is abhorrent to many within Islam.

28 'Mapping the emergence of the Islamic State in Afghanistan', Long War Journal, March 5, 2015 https://www. longwarjournal.org/archives/2015/03/ mapping-the emergence-of-the-islamic-state-in-afghanistan.php

29 Historic Khorasan includes parts of Iran, Afghanistan and Turkmenistan, and some definitions of the term include Pakistan. Adam Taylor, 'The strange story behind the 'Khorasan' group's name', Washington Post, September 25, 2014 https://www.washingtonpost. com/news/worldviews/ wp/2014/09/25/the-strangestory-behind-the-khorasan-groups-name/?utm_ term=.6ac9453709a7; Seth Jones, James Dobbins, Daniel Byman, Christopher Chivvis, Ben Connable, Jeffrey Martini, Eric Robinson, and Nathan Chandler, 'Rolling back the Islamic State, RAND Corporation, 2017 p 153 https:// www.rand.org/content/dam/rand/ pubs/research_reports/RR1900/RR1912/ RAND_RR1912.pdf

30 Karen Leigh, Jason French and Jovi Juan, 'Islamic State and its affiliates', Wall Street Journal, 2017 http:// graphics.wsj.com/islamic-state-and-its-affiliates/

31 Some Islamic texts indicate that the army of true believers will gather in Khorasan before the apocalypse. Harleen Gambhir, 'ISIS in Afghanistan', p 2

32 Harleen Gambhir, 'ISIS in Afghanistan', p 2

33 It was not until September 2015 that ISKP began attacking Afghan government and international targets. Harleen Gambhir, 'ISIS in Afghanistan', p 3; Bill Roggio, 'Afghanistan's terrorist resurgence: Al Qaeda, ISIS, and beyond', Long War Journal, April 27, 2017 https://www. longwarjournal.

org/archives/2017/04/afghanistans-terrorist-resurgence-al-qaeda-isis-and-beyond.php

34   Harleen Gambhir, 'ISIS in Afghanistan', p 4; Lauren McNally, Alex Amiral, Marvin Weinbaum, and Antoun Issa, 'The Islamic State in Afghanistan: Examining its Threat to Stability', p 3

35   The Institute for the Study of War refers to commanders pledging allegiance from Kunar, Nangarhar, and Logar – presumably meaning defectors from the Taliban rather than TTP. As the United States Institute for Peace notes, ISKP appointed recruiters in nine other provinces beyond these core provinces. Four of these (Kunduz, Samangan, Sar-e Pol, and Faryab) are in northern Afghanistan: "perhaps a telling allocation of resources, and an indication that [ISKP]'s strategy is to recruit outside of traditional Taliban areas of influence and move northward from their current base along the Afghanistan-Pakistan (Af-Pak) border through northern Afghanistan into Central Asia." Casey Garret Johnson, 'The rise and stall of the Islamic State in Afghanistan', United States Institute for Peace, November 2016, p 3 https://www.usip.org/ publications/2016/11/rise-and-stall-islamic-state-afghanistan; Harleen Gambhir, 'ISIS in Afghanistan', p 4; Lauren McNally, Alex Amiral, Marvin Weinbaum, and Antoun Issa, 'The Islamic State in Afghanistan: Examining its Threat to Stability', Middle East Institute, May 2016, p 3 https://www.mei.edu/ sites/default/files/ publications/PF12_McNallyAmiral_ISISAfghan_web. pdf; Casey Garret Johnson, 'The rise and stall of the Islamic State in Afghanistan', United States Institute for Peace, November 2016, p 3

36   Other individual commanders had pledged loyalty or support to the Islamic State before July 2015, but statement in July 2015 from the IMU's spiritual leader Usman Ghazi was a formal commitment on behalf of the whole organisation. Edward Lemon, 'IMU pledges allegiance to Islamic State', Eurasianet, August 1, 2015 http://www.eurasianet.org/node/74471

37   Borhan Osman, 'Descent into chaos: Why did Nangarhar turn into an IS hub?', Afghanistan Analysts Network, September 27, 2016 https://www.afghanistan-analysts.org/descent-into-chaos-why-did-nangarhar-turn-into-an-is-hub/

38   A Russian estimate of 10,000 fighters overall is contested, while an American figure of 600 is likely out of date, even if it was not over-optimistic to begin with. Noor Zahid, 'A Look at Islamic State's Operations in Afghanistan', Voice of America, April 29, 2017 https:// www.voanews.com/a/a-look-at-is-operation-in-afghanistan/3831169.html; Lauren McNally, Alex Amiral, Marvin Weinbaum, and Antoun Issa, 'The Islamic State in Afghanistan: Examining its Threat to Stability', p 6; Casey Garret Johnson, 'The rise and stall of the Islamic State in Afghanistan', United States Institute for Peace, November 2016, p 2 https://www.usip.org/ publications/2016/11/rise-and-stall-islamic-state-afghanistan; 'Letter dated 9 May 2017 from the Chair of the Security Council Committee established pursuant to resolution 1988 (2011) addressed to the President of the Security Council', United Nations, May 25, 2017, p

12   http://www.un.org/en/ga/search/view_doc. asp?symbol=S/2017/409;
GulabuddinGhubar, 'Army Chief Rejects Russia's Figures On Daesh Fighters',
ToloNews, December 25, 2017 http://www.tolonews.com/ afghanistan/army-
chief-rejects-russia percentE2 percent80 percent99sfigures-daesh-fighters;
Ayaz Gul, 'US Military Rejects Russian Claims About Number of IS Fighters
in Afghanistan', Voice of America, February 24, 2018 https:// www.voanews.
com/a/us-military-rejects-russia-numbers-of-islamic-state-fighters-in-
afghanistan/4268999. html; Noor Zahid, 'A Look at Islamic State's Operations
in Afghanistan', Voice of America, April 29, 2017 https:// www.voanews.com/
a/a-look-at-is-operation-in-afghanistan/3831169.html

39   Harleen Gambhir, 'ISIS in Afghanistan', p 4; Casey Garret Johnson, 'The rise
and stall of the Islamic State in Afghanistan', United States Institute for Peace,
November 2016, pp 1-3 https://www.usip.org/publications/2016/11/rise-and-
stall-islamic-state-afghanistan

40   The NATO estimate is that 70 percent of ISKP fighters originated from the
TTP; the Afghan government estimate is that 80 percent of ISKP fighters are
Pakistani. 'IS in Afghanistan: How successful has the group been?', BBC ; 'The
rise and stall of the Islamic State in Afghanistan', United States Institute for
Peace, November 2016, p 2 https://www.usip.org/publications/2016/11/ rise-
and-stall-islamic-state-afghanistan.

41   Borhan Osman, 'Descent into chaos: Why did Nangarhar turn into an IS hub?',
Afghanistan Analysts Network, September 27, 2016 https://www.afghanistan-
analysts.org/descent-into-chaos-why-did-nangarhar-turn-into-an-is-hub/

42   Global Witness interview with Graeme Smith, UNAMA political officer,
February 2018; Christian Bleuer, 'Chechens in Afghanistan 1: A Battlefield
Myth That Will Not Die', Afghanistan Analysts Network, June 27, 2016 https://
www.afghanistan-analysts.org/chechens-in-afghanistan-1-a-battlefield-
myth-that-willnot-die/; 'French fighters appear with Islamic State in
Afghanistan', Agence France Presse, December 17, 2017 https://www.thelocal.
fr/20171210/french-fighters-appear-with-islamic-state-in-afghanistan

43   Within the ISIS structure, beneath the senior leadership is a Diwan [ministry]
for the "Administration of Distant Wilayat" [provinces], under which
ISKP would be organized. How ISIS Describes its Government Structure',
Stanford   University   http://interactive.   achariricenter.org/wp-content/
uploads/2016/07/ Structure-of-ISISFinal-1.pdf; 'IS in Afghanistan: How
successful has the group been?', BBC, February 27, 2017 http://www.bbc.
com/news/world-asia-39031000; Sune Engel Rasmussen and Zahra Nader,
'Iran Covertly Recruits Afghan Shias to Fight in Syria,' The Guardian, June
30, 2016, https://www.theguardian.com/ world/2016/jun/30/iran-covertly-
recruits-afghan-soldiers-to-fighting-syria

44   The July 2016 attack on a Shia rally in Kabul was claimed to be in retaliation
for Afghan Shias who have gone to fight in Syria on behalf of the Assad

government. The number of Afghans recruited from Afghanistan and Iran to fight for ISIS is Iraq and Syria is estimated to be anywhere from a few thousand to 20,000. 'IS in Afghanistan: How successful has the group been?', BBC, February 27, 2017 http://www.bbc. com/news/world-asia-39031000; Sune Engel Rasmussen and Zahra Nader, 'Iran Covertly Recruits Afghan Shias to Fight in Syria,' The Guardian, June 30, 2016, https://www.theguardian.com/world/2016/jun/30/ iran-covertly-recruits-afghan-soldiers-to-fight-in-syria

45   'Is Daesh really in Afghanistan?', TRT World, November 10, 2016 https://www.trtworld.com/magazine/ is-daesh-really-in-afghanistan--3692; Martin Sahak and Girish Gupta, 'Islamic State seizes new Afghan foothold after luring Taliban defectors', Reuters, December 1, 2017 https://uk.reuters.com/article/uk-afghanistan-islamic-state/islamic-state-seizes-new-afghan-foothold-after-luring-taliban-defectors-idUKKBN1DV3G3

46   Global Witness interview with Caitlin Forrest, March 2017

47   The ISIS statement accepting ISKP's allegiance in January 2015 also claimed ISKP had already submitted an overall military strategy to them. The spokesman was reportedly Abu Muhammad al-Adnani. Harleen Gambhir, 'ISIS in Afghanistan', p 4; Global Witness interview with an Islamic State commander, 2015

48   'Letter dated 9 May 2017 from the Chair of the Security Council Committee established pursuant to resolution 1988 (2011) addressed to the President of the Security Council', United Nations, May 25, 2017, p 12 http:// www.un.org/en/ga/search/view_doc.asp?symbol=S/2017/409

49   Caitlin Forrest, an analyst with the Institute for the Study of War, also reported that two groups are in contact, even if only by SMS. Brian Dodwell and Don Rassler, 'A View from the CT Foxhole: General John W. Nicholson', Combating Terrorism Center at West Point, February 22, 2017 https://ctc.usma.edu/posts/a-viewfrom-the-ct-foxhole-general-john-w-nicholson-commander-resolute-support-and-u-s-forces-afghanistan; Global Witness interview with Caitlin Forrest, Institute for the Study of War, Foundation for Defense of Democracies, March 21, 2017

50   Unlike the significant capture and reporting of Al Qaeda and ISIS documents over the decades as well as other analysis of their financial resourcing, no such documents has been publicly reported in the media or from other experts for ISKP that we are aware of. 'The Islamic State in Afghanistan', Middle East Institute, p 3; Harleen Gambhir, 'ISIS in Afghanistan', p 6

51   'Letter dated 11 January 2017 from the Chair of the Security Council Committee pursuant to resolutions 1267 (1999), 1989 (2011) and 2253 (2015) concerning Islamic State in Iraq and the Levant (Da'esh), Al-Qaida and associated individuals, groups, undertakings and entities addressed to the President of the Security Council', United Nations, January 13, 2017 http://

www.securitycouncilreport.org/atf/cf/ percent7B65BFCF9B-6D27-4E9C-8CD3-CF6E4FF96FF9 percent7D/s_2017_35.pdf

52 'Letter dated 9 May 2017 from the Chair of the Security Council Committee', United Nations

53 Caitlin Forrest says there is evidence that ISIS sends funds to ISKP forces in Zabul Province in Afghanistan, perhaps due to pre-existing relationships with the Islamic Movement of Uzbekistan (IMU) factions there that defected from Al Qaeda to ISKP. But it is unknown whether that applies to all ISKP groups, especially the core groups in Nangarhar. General Nicholson for his part also stated that some funds come from ISIS, claiming that ISKP "have had some financial difficulties, but there's still money getting through." Global Witness interview with Caitlin Forrest; Dodwell and Rassler, 'A View from the CT Foxhole'; 'Letter dated 9 May 2017 from the Chair of the Security Council Committee', United Nations

54 ISKP operates an FM radio station as well as internet propaganda and Facebook and Twitter accounts. 'IS in Afghanistan: How successful has the group been?', BBC; Thomas Joscelyn, 'US: 'Major' Islamic State media 'hub' destroyed in Nangarhar, Afghanistan', Long War Journal, June 17, 2017 https://www.longwarjournal. org/archives/2017/06/us-major-islamic-state-media-hub-destroyed-in-nangarhar-afghanistan.php

55 Harleen Gambhir, 'ISIS in Afghanistan', p 6

56 In early 2017 General Nicholson claimed that ISKP fighters are paid almost twice as much as their Taliban rivals. This was supported by our sources from Nangarhar and Logar. In Logar one Global Witness source alleged a salary of 70,000 Afghanis – more than $1,000 – was being paid to ISKP fighters, although the figure is worth treating with some scepticism given the implications for the funding of the group: it is possible this was just an initial sum that would fall away quickly after recruitment. In Nangarhar, a Global Witness source reported in 2016 that ISKP had "a lot of money – they give $600 a month salary for a soldier." This same figure was cited in a May 2017 UN report, although the salaries reportedly gradually fell back to parity with the Taliban after recruitment – and one ISKP commander reportedly estimated that his expenses per soldier were a much lower average of between $145 and $290 a month. Dodwell and Rassler, 'A View from the CT Foxhole'. Global Witness interview, mid-2016; Global Witness interview with Source T, late 2016; 'Letter dated 9 May 2017 from the Chair of the Security Council Committee established pursuant to resolution 1988 (2011) addressed to the President of the Security Council', United Nations, May 25, 2017, p 12 http://www.un.org/en/ga/search/view_doc. asp?symbol=S/2017/409; Franz Marty, 'Speaking to an Afghan Disciple of the Caliphate', The Diplomat, July 28, 2016 https://thediplomat.com/2016/07/speakingto-an-afghan-disciple-of-the-caliphate/

57 There are unconfirmed reports that some groups may in fact profit from the drugs trade. ISKP has officially banned poppy cultivation and drug sales, very publicly burned narcotics fields, and kidnapped some poppy farmers, and yet at least turning a blind eye to the drug trade may be a necessity. If this activity does take place, it does not seem to have been either condemned or condoned by the IS leadership overall. IS Senior Leadership and the IS franchise in Libya both reportedly engage in various forms of narcotics use and smuggling, so similar activities from ISKP would be plausible. Harleen Gambhir, 'ISIS in Afghanistan', p 6; Zarifi, 'Daesh Seizes 8 Nangarhar Farmers for Poppy Cultivation'; Osman, 'The Islamic State in "Khorasan"'; Allen et al., 'The Big Spin'; 'Turkey Seizes 11m Amphetamine Pills Used to Fuel Isis Fighters in Combat'.

58 Zakat is an Islamic tax raised on wealth, while Ushr is a form of Zakat charged on goods produced from land, including output from mines. It is charged at 5 percent (or 10 percent for the produce of unirrigated land). 'Zakat', Islamic Voice, December 1998 http://www.islamicvoice.com/ december.98/zakat. htm#MIN

59 One victim in Shinwar district of Nangarhar reportedly said that ISKP took "whatever they liked—goods in stores, our homes, our livestock, even our firewood." Another source noted, "They held people for ransom. They began to ask everyone, even teachers, for payments. They would say: 'We are mujahids, it is our right.'" An informed source from Nangarhar also said that ISKP would "take money from a person who was a little richer, they will beat him to the edge of death and detain them" – although another reported in contrast that "unlike the Taliban, [ISKP] do not take food and things from the people." Ali M. Latifi and Mohsin Khan Mohmand, 'When Islamic State Showed up in a Corner of Afghanistan, "Nothing Was Safe, Not Even the Cows"', Los Angeles Times, June 3, 2016 http://www. latimes.com/world/ asia/la-fg-afghanistan-daesh-advsnap-story.html; Ali M. Latifi and Mohsin Khan Mohmand, 'When Islamic State Showed up in a Corner of Afghanistan, "Nothing Was Safe, Not Even the Cows"'; Global Witness interview with an informed source from Nangarhar, late 2016; Global Witness interview with an informed source, mid-2016

60 Global Witness interview with Matt DuPée, April 2017

62 See US News and World Report article for a list of attacks up to the end of 2017. ISKP's claimed operations include an attack on a military hospital in March 2017 which killed at least 38, although an AAN analyst expressed some doubt that ISKP rather than the Taliban actually carried it out. More recent attacks claimed by ISKP have included an April 2018 suicide bombing against civilians waiting to register to vote which killed at least 52. Interview with Kate Clark, November 2017; 'IS in Afghanistan: How successful has the group been?', BBC; Global Witness interview with Matt DuPée, April 2017; Sayed Salahuddin, 'At least 52 Afghans killed in Kabul by suicide

bomber, health ministry says', Washington Post, April 22, 2018 https://www.
washingtonpost.com/world/at-least-31afghans-killed-in-kabul-by-suicide-
bomber-officialsays/2018/04/22/30174d76-4615-11e8-9072-f6d4bc32f223_
story.html?utm_term=.26b9a91f500e; 'A Look at Islamic State Attacks in
Afghanistan', Associated Press/U.S. News and World Report https://www.
usnews.com/news/world/articles/2017-12-28/a-lookat-islamic-state-attacks-
in-afghanistan; Hasib Danish Alikozai and Mohammad Habibzada, 'Afghan
General: Haqqani Network, Not IS, Behind Spike in Violence', Voice of
America, January 13, 2018 https://www.voanews.com/a/afghan-general-
haqqani-network-islamic-state/4206961.html ; Borhan Osman, 'A Black
Week in Kabul (2): Who are the most likely perpetrators?', Afghanistan
Analysts Network, June 7, 2017 https:// www.afghanistan-analysts.org/a-
black-week-in-kabul-2-who-are-the-most-likely-perpetrators;   Harleen
Gambhir, 'ISIS in Afghanistan', p 4; Lauren McNally, Alex Amiral, Marvin
Weinbaum, and Antoun Issa, 'The Islamic State in Afghanistan: Examining
its Threat to Stability', 2016, pp 3-4; Michael Safi, 'Isis militants disguised as
doctors kill 38 in Kabul hospital attack', The Guardian, March 8, 2017 https://
www.theguardian.   com/world/2017/mar/08/gunmen-dressed-as-doctors-
attack-military-hospital-in-kabul

63   Notorious reported incidents include the alleged beheading of women and
     children and the execution of village elders using explosives. An attack on the
     offices of the humanitarian NGO Save the Children in Jalalabad may or may
     not have been deliberately targeted at them. Global Witness interview with
     NGO security advisor in Kabul, February 2018; 'Death Toll Rises to 6 In Save
     The Children Attack In Jalalabad', Tolo News, January 25, 2018 http://www.
     tolonews.com/afghanistan/death-toll-rises-6-save-children-attack-jalalabad;
     Heather Barr, 'From the Taliban Frying Pan to the Islamic State Fire', Human
     Rights Watch, September 28, 2016 https://www.hrw.org/news/2016/09/28/
     taliban-frying-pan-islamic-state-fire; Mujib Mashal and Taimoor Shah,
     'Afghan Fighters Loyal to ISIS Beheaded 7 Hostages, Officials Say', New York
     Times, November 9, 2015 https://www.nytimes.com/2015/11/10/world/ asia/
     afghan-fighters-loyal-to-isis-beheaded-7-hostages-officials-say.html?_r=0;
     Lauren McNally, Alex Amiral, Marvin Weinbaum, and Antoun Issa, 'The
     Islamic State in Afghanistan: Examining its Threat to Stability', p 7; Shereena
     Qazi, 'Afghans protest 'beheadings of ethnic Hazara by ISIL', Al Jazeera,
     November   11,   2015   http://www.aljazeera.com/news/2015/11/afghans-
     protest-killings-hazara-isil-151110135854342.html;

64   Lauren McNally, Alex Amiral, Marvin Weinbaum, and Antoun Issa, 'The
     Islamic State in Afghanistan: Examining its Threat to Stability', p 8; Heather
     Barr, 'From the Taliban Frying Pan to the Islamic State Fire'; Mirren Gidda,
     'Why ISIS is failing to build a caliphate in Afghanistan', Newsweek, March 25,
     2017 http://www. newsweek.com/afghanistan-isis-taliban-caliphate-kabul-
     bombing-574198; 'ISIS in Afghanistan', p 4; Lauren McNally, Alex Amiral,
     Marvin Weinbaum, and Antoun Issa, 'The Islamic State in Afghanistan:

Examining its Threat to Stability', Middle East Institute, May 2016, pp 7-8 https://www.mei.edu/sites/default/files/publications/PF12_McNallyAmiral_ISISAfghan_web.pdf

65 ISKP claimed responsibility for a July 2016 bomb attack on a Hazara demonstration which killed at least 80 people, and for a December 2017 attack on a Shia cultural centre which killed at least 40. A March 2018 attack on a Hazara mosque killed at least 10. The Taliban have also targeted Hazaras in the past, but they have not made sectarian part of their official platform in the struggle against the current Afghan government. 'Hazaras and Afghan insurgent groups', Land Info, October 3, 2016 https://landinfo. no/asset/3483/1/3483_1.pdf ; Borhan Osman 'With an Active Cell in Kabul, ISKP Tries to Bring Sectarianism to the Afghan War', Afghanistan Analysts Network, October 19, 2016 https://www.afghanistan-analysts.org/with-an-active-cell-in-kabul-iskp-tries-to   bring-sectarianism-to-the-afghan-war/; Sune Engel Rasmussen, 'Isis claims responsibility for Kabul bomb attack on Hazara protesters', The Observer, July 24, 2016 https://www.theguardian. com/world/2016/jul/23/   hazara-minority-targeted-by-suicide-bombs-at-kabul-protest; Fahim Abed, Fatima Faizi and Mujib Mashal, 'Islamic State Claims Deadly Blast at Afghan Shiite Center', New York Times, December 28, 2017 https:// www.nytimes.com/2017/12/28/world/asia/afghanistan-suicide-attack.html; Emma Graham-Harrison and Haroon Janjua, 'Scores killed in Isis bombing of Kabul news agency and Shia centre', The Guardian, December 28, 2017 https://www.theguardian.com/world/2017/ dec/28/blast-afghan-news-agency-kabul-kills-dozens; Andrew Kramer. 'Hazaras Protest After an ISIS Attack Kills 10 in Kabul, New York Times, March 9, 2018 https://www. nytimes.com/2018/03/09/world/asia/suicide-attack-kabul-hazaras.html

66 By the end of 2015 the Taliban had liquidated ISKP-affiliated forces in Zabul and Logar, and a significant group led by former Taliban commanders in Farah. A combination of Taliban, government and international pressure also effectively eliminated the ISKP presence in Helmand. Borhan Osman, 'The Islamic State in 'Khorasan'

67 Dodwell and Rassler, 'A View from the CT Foxhole'

68 Borhan Osman, 'The Battle for Mamand: ISKP under strain, but not yet defeated'; Borhan Osman, 'Another ISKP leader "dead": Where is the group headed after losing so many amirs?', Afghanistan Analysts Network, July 23, 2017 https://www.afghanistan-analysts.org/ another-iskp-leader-dead-where-is-the-group-hea   ded-after-losing-so-many-amirs/

69 Borhan Osman, 'Another ISKP leader "dead": Where is the group headed after losing so many amirs?'

70 Jeff Seldin, 'Afghan Officials: Islamic State Fighters Finding Sanctuary in Afghanistan', Voice of America November 18, 2017 https://www. voanews.com/a/   afghan-officials-islamic-state-finds-sanctuary-in-

afghanistan/4122270.html; AnimeshRoul, 'Islamic State Gains Ground in Afghanistan as Its Caliphate Crumbles Elsewhere', Jamestown Foundation, January 26, 2018 https://jamestown.org/program/islamic-state-gains-ground-afghanistan-caliphate-crumbles-elsewhere/

71 The danger of ISKP organising attacks in the US should perhaps be treated with a certain caution as it appears to be based on a single statement made to an undercover FBI officer by a Canadian plotter, who said he "was in contact with an ISIS affiliate about obtaining official sanction of the planned attacks by the Khorasan Province, a branch of ISIS active in Pakistan." It is less clear how far ISKP's leadership is taking any active steps to organise such attacks themselves. Jennifer Cafarella, 'ISIS Plotting Attacks from Afghanistan', Institute for the Study of War, November 17, 2017 http://www. understandingwar.org/backgrounder/isis-plotting-attacks-afghanistan; 'Charges Unsealed Against Three Men for Plotting to Carry out Terrorist Attacks in New York City for ISIS in the Summer of 2016', United States Department of Justice, October 6, 2017 https://www.justice.gov/opa/pr/charges-unsealed-against-three-menplotting-carry-out-terrorist-attacks-new-york-city-isis

72 Sarah Almukhtar, 'How Much of Afghanistan Is Under Taliban Control After 16 Years of War With the U.S.?', New York times, August 23, 2017 https://www. nytimes. com/interactive/2017/08/23/world/asia/afghanistan-us-taliban-isis-control.html

73 The ISKP incursion into Jawzjan can be traced at least as far back as 2015, given that in late 2016 the Taliban reportedly launched an unsuccessful offensive against a local commander, QariHekmat, who had defected to ISKP the previous year. However, the tempo of their activities there seems to have increased since mid-2017. See lower in the main text for a discussion of ISKP links to mining in all the areas mentioned, and the resources involved. '34 provinces mines info', Pajhwok Afghan News, March 1, 2015 http://mines.pajhwok.com/ article-categories/34-provinces-mines-info; Obaid Ali, 'QariHekmat's Island: A Daesh enclave in Jawzjan?', Afghanistan Analysts Network, November 11, 2017 https://www.afghanistan-analysts.org/qari-hekmatsisland-a-daesh-enclave-in-jawzjan/; Jeff Seldin, 'Afghan Officials: Islamic State Fighters Finding Sanctuary in Afghanistan', Voice of America November 18, 2017 https://www.voanews.com/a/afghan-officials-islamic-state-finds-sanctuary-in-afghanistan/4122270.html; Khalid Zerai, 'Illegal logging, mining help bankroll militants in Kunar Province', Salaam Times, October 18, 2017 http://afghanistan.asia-news.com/en_GB/articles/cnmi_st/features/2017/10/18/feature-01; MatinSahak, 'Islamic State seizes new Afghan foothold after luring Taliban defectors', Reuters, December 1, 2017 https://www.reuters.com/article/us-afghanistan-islamic-state/islamic-state-seizes-new-afghan-foothold-after-luring-taliban-defectors-idUSKBN1DV3G5

74 See below in the main text for a discussion of the ISKP presence and mineral resources in these provinces.

75 Borhan Usman, 'The Islamic State in 'Khorasan': How it began and where it stands now in Nangarhar'

76 The fighting included ISKP fighters capturing and beheading ten Taliban commanders in June 2015. Lauren McNally, Alex Amiral, Marvin Weinbaum, and Antoun Issa, 'The Islamic State in Afghanistan: Examining its Threat to Stability', p 5; Borhan Usman, 'The Islamic State in 'Khorasan': How it began and where it stands now in Nangarhar'

77 The Taliban themselves acknowledged I March 2017 that "DehBala, Kot, Spin Ghar, Achin and Naziyan districts are 25 percent under Mujahideen control, 30 percent enemy and 45 percent under miscellaneous bandits". By "bandits" they presumably meant ISKP. AAN also noted that a significant ISKP presence also remained in the small district of Nazian. DehBala is also known as Haska Mina. 'HaskaMeyna District', Wikipedia, https://en.wikipedia. org/ wiki/Haska_Meyna_District; 'Afghanistan: The security situation in Nangarhar province', Landinfo, October 13, 2016 pp 11-14 https://landinfo. no/asset/3493/1/3493_1. pdf; Borhan Usman, 'The Islamic State in 'Khorasan': How it began and where it stands now in Nangarhar'; 'Percent of Country under the control of Mujahideen of Islamic Emirate', Voice of Jihad, March 26, 2017 https:// alemarah-english.com/?p=12443

78 See interview testimony below; Borhan Osman, 'The Battle for Mamand: ISKP under strain, but not yet defeated', Afghanistan Analysts Network, May 23, 2017 https://www.afghanistan-analysts.org/the-battle-formamand-iskp-under-strain-but-not-yet-defeated/; Jessica Purkiss and Abigail Fielding-Smith, 'Islamic State in Afghanistan: Is US assault working?', The Bureau of Investigative Journalism, July 28, 2017 https:// www.thebureauinvestigates. com/stories/2017-07-28/ islamic-state-in-afghanistan-us-military

79 There were seven US servicemen killed in Nangarhar in 2017. Chad Garland, 'Nangarhar is the deadliest Afghan province for US forces in the past year', Stars and Stripes, January 8, 2018 https://www.stripes.com/ news/nangarhar-is-the-deadliest-afghan-province-forus-forces-in-the-past-year-1.505390

80 Borhan Osman, 'The Battle for Mamand: ISKP under strain, but not yet defeated,' Ayaz Gul, 'IS Says It Has Captured E. Afghan District From Taliban', Voice of America, May 1, 2017 https://www.voanews.com/a/ islamic-state-claims-to-have-captured-district-from-rival-taliban-in-afghanistan/3833364.html;

81 That concern is shared by some diplomats. 'Saba: Daesh Seeking to Exploit Mines for Funding', Tolo News, June 8, 2015 http://www.tolonews.com/ business/saba-daesh-seeking-exploit-mines-funding; Global Witness interview with a senior official in a Western embassy, 2015

82 'Afghanistan: The security situation in Nangarhar province', Landinfo, October 13, 2016 pp 11-14 https:// landinfo.no/asset/3493/1/3493_1. pdf; Yousuf Zarifi, '11 Daesh fighters eliminated in Nangarhar drone raid',

Pajhwok Afghan News, September 6, 2017 https:// www.pajhwok.com/ en/2017/09/06/11-daesh-fighters-eliminated-nangarhar-drone-raid; Yousuf Zarifi, 'Daesh restricted to limited areas in Nangarhar', Pajwhok Afghan News, November 19, 2017 http://www. file.pajhwok.com/en/2017/11/19/ daesh-restricted-limited-areas-nangarhar; 'Dozens Killed In Daesh, Taliban Clash in Afghanistan's Nangarhar', Tasnim News, October 16, 2017 https:// www.tasnimnews.com/en/   news/2017/10/16/1547299/dozens-killed-in-daesh-taliban-clash-in-afghanistan-s-nangarhar; 'IS, Taliban fight for key towns in Nangarhar', Dawn, November 29, 2017 https://www.dawn.com/ news/1373507; Borhan Osman, 'The Islamic State in 'Khorasan'

83 Sune Engel Rasmussen, 'Devastation and a war that rages on: visiting the valley hit by the Moab attack', The Guardian, April 17, 2017 https://www. theguardian. com/world/2017/apr/17/moab-bomb-site-afghanistan

84 In late 2016 the source said that after ISKP captured two Taliban outposts and killed a prominent commander, the source said, "a lot of the Taliban became scared and fled the area." One of the Talebs who was reportedly killed was called Maulavi Abdul Salam, assassinated in the village of Khune Kalai. The source later reported that around April 2017 ISKP had taken over several more villages which had been in the hands of their rivals. Global Witness interview, late 2016; Global Witness interview, mid-2017

85 The source mentioned ISKP taking over mines in locations called Ruidod, Sherzad, Safed Koh, but they could not be identified on the map. Safed Koh is the Dari translation of Spinghar – the White Mountain – which can refer to the whole of the range on the Pakistan border with southern Nangarhar. Sherzad may have been a reference to the district of that name. In addition, there are two locations in Achin called Nargesai, one around 34.0732 North / 70.5556 East, and one at 34.0535 N / 70.6893 E. However, the first of these is in the area of the other mines mentioned by the sources, and fits the testimony. The satellite imagery does not appear to show any mines in the immediate vicinity of the second Nargesai. A village called Sangorai is marked on the best available maps (based on declassified Soviet military maps), but it appears to consist of a few houses a few hundred yards from the larger hamlet of Chaperai, and in fact on more modern satellite imagery no houses are visible in that specific location. It is of course still possible that the name has been applied to a larger mining area distinct from the village.

86 The source referred to the mineral as emerald, but also as 'like emerald.' They said it was found at Ai Tang, Nargesai, and Sangorai, but searches including on Mindat.org did not reveal any history of emeralds in Nangarhar (the Badel emerald mine which is sometimes listed appears to be in Kunar province). Tourmaline however can have a green colour and be easily be mistaken for emerald. See further mentions of emeralds in the main text for more details. Global Witness interviews, late 2016 and mid-2017

87 Global Witness interview, mid-2016

88 The source gave a rough date of early 2015 for the takeover of the mines by ISKP, which is about six months before the movement openly emerged to challenge the Taliban (although they were present in the area before this). But their recollection on dates in general was somewhat vague, as is often the case for sources of this nature. Global Witness interview, mid-2016

89 Global Witness interview, mid-2016

90 The source earlier said that in total nine different mines were in the hands of ISKP, but it was somewhat unclear if this referred to the number of mines he had more detailed information on, or the total number of mines across the wider local region. Global Witness interview, mid-2016' Global Witness interview, late 2016

91 An elder originally from Achin mentioned a 'blue stone' he called lapis being extracted in Ai Tang. Global Witness interview with an elder originally from Achin district, mid-2017

92 Based on data from the iMMAP OASIS software and satellite photos, locations of the places which were linked to three of the mining areas, Nargesai, Lagharjo, and Shne Kanda, are shown on our map, but the mines themselves were not necessarily immediately proximate to the villages in question. The source described these three mines as producing white marble. The location of Yanak, which he said also produced chromite, was unclear from the testimony. Global Witness interview, late 2016; Global Witness interview, mid-2016

93 Global Witness interview, mid-2016

94 Borhan Osman, 'The Battle for Mamand: ISKP under strain, but not yet defeated'

95 Global Witness interview, mid-2017

96 Yousuf Zarifi, 'Daesh rebels continue to get equipment: Achin residents', Pajhwok Afghan News, November 25, 2017 https://www.pajhwok.com/en/2017/11/25/ daesh-rebels-continue-get-equipment-achin-residents

97 Ayaz Gul, 'IS Says It Has Captured E. Afghan District From Taliban'; Thomas Joscelyn, 'Taliban and Islamic State clash in eastern Afghanistan', Long War Journal, May 1, 2017 https://www.longwarjournal.org/archives/2017/05/taliban-and-islamic-state-clash-in-eastern-afghanistan.php

98 The government claimed to have evicted Daesh from Tora Bora by the end of June. Borhan Osman, 'Another ISKP leader "dead": Where is the group headed after losing so many amirs?', Afghanistan Analysts Network, July 23, 2017 https://www.afghanistan-analysts. org/another-iskp-leader-dead-where-is-the-groupheaded-after-losing-so-many-amirs/ ; Rod Nordland and Fahim Abed, 'ISIS Captures Tora Bora, Once Bin Laden's Afghan Fortress', New York Times, June 14, 2017 https://www.nytimes.com/2017/06/14/world/asia/isis-captures-tora-bora-afghanistan.html;

99 ZiarYaad, 'Tora Bora Completely Cleared of Daesh: MoD', Tolo News, June 25, 2017 http://www.tolonews.com/afghanistan/tora-bora-completely-cleared-daesh-mod

100 The quote was from Source W. Global Witness interview with Source W, early 2018; Global Witness interview with Source X, early 2018.

101 Global Witness interview with Source W, early 2018; Global Witness interview with Source X, early 2018

102 Ahmed Sultan, 'Few clues on casualties at site of huge U.S. bomb in Afghanistan', Reuters, April 23, 2017 https://uk.reuters.com/article/uk-afghanistan-usa-bomb/few-clues-on-casualties-at-siteof-huge-u-s-bomb-in-afghanistan-idUKKBN17P0I6; Borhan Osman, 'The Battle for Mamand: ISKP under strain, but not yet defeated'; Global Witness interview with Source Z, early 2018; 'After the Dust Settles — Making Sense of the Non-sense', ALCIS, May 3, 2017 https:// stories.alcis.org/after-the-dust-settles-making-senseof-the-non-sense-c97da619a20f

103 ISKP still seem to be very much present in the area. Global Witness interview, mid-2017; Yousuf Zarifi, '7 Daesh rebels killed in Nangarhar airstrikes', Pajhwok Afghan News, March 16, 2018 https://www.pajhwok. com/en/2018/03/16/7-daesh-rebels-killed-nangarhar-airstrikes; 'Internecine rifts: 15 Daesh insurgents decapitated', Pajhwok Afghan News, November 23, 2017 https://www.pajhwok.com/en/2017/11/23/internecine-rifts-15-daesh-insurgents-decapitated

104 Global Witness interview, mid-2017. The source spoke of people mining 'aluminium', which seems fanciful – but could be plausible if it refers to people recovering scrap metal from the remains of the bomb itself.

105 One source claimed 'aluminium' was being mined at the site. That is profoundly improbably – but it is possible that locals were salvaging metal fragments left from bombing. Global Witness interview, mid-2017

106 Global Witness interview, late 2016.

107 Global Witness interview, mid-2017

108 Global Witness interview, late 2016

109 Global Witness interview, September 2016

110 Global Witness interview, late 2016

110 Global Witness interview, mid-2016

111 Global Witness interview, late 2016

112 Global Witness interview with an Afghan civil society researcher, February 2018

113 Global Witness interview, late 2016

114 We were not able to confirm the identity of this source, and there was some grounds for slight caution that he was in fact with ISKP, but other elements of the interview appeared credible. Global Witness interview with a purported ISKP official, mid-2017

115 Global Witness interview, late 2016

116 Global Witness interview, mid-2016; Global Witness interview, mid-2016.

117 Global Witness interview, late 2016.

118 The source also directly called the stones 'emeralds'. While mineral identifications by non-experts are often unreliable, the source's description of small green gemstones found in white rock is compatible with reports of emeralds in other mines. Some sources also mention emeralds found in white talc stone. However, searches including on Mindat.org did not reveal any clear history of emeralds in Nangarhar. The ancient Badel emerald mine is described variously as located in Nangarhar, Parwan and (most commonly) Kunar provinces: references which include a map have it in Kunar. Tourmaline can have a green colour, which could easily be mistaken for emerald. Global Witness interview, late 2016; 'The gemstone tourmaline', Minerals.net, http://www.minerals.net/gemstone/tourmaline_ gemstone.aspx ; 'Beryl (Var: Emerald) Sold', The Arkenstone http://www. irocks.com/minerals/specimen/12467; Mindat search, November 8, 2017 https:// www.mindat.org/minlocsearch.php?frm_id=mls&cform_is_ valid=1&cf_mls_ page=1&minname=emerald&region=afghanistan&sort= &submit_mls=Search; Selina Denman, 'Emeralds: The journey of a gem ', The National, May 1, 2014 https://www.thenational.ae/ lifestyle/emeralds-the-journey-of-a-gem-1.242915; 'Emerald on matrix', Mineral auctions https://www. mineralauctions.com/auctions/inventory-liquidation-auction-end-june-11-45/emerald-on-matrix-6920. html; 'Beryl var. Emerald on Talc from Badel Mine, Nangarhar, Afghanistan', Online Mineral Museum, http://www.johnbetts-fineminerals.com/jhbnyc/ mineralmuseum/picshow. php?id=49366; 'The Mineral Beryl', Minerals.net http://www.minerals.net/ mineral/ beryl.aspx; 'Badel Mine (Budel Mine), Narang District, Konar Province (Kunar Province; Konarh Province; Konarha Province; Nuristan), Afghanistan,' Mindat. org, https://www.mindat.org/loc-30624.html; 'Beryl from Badel Mine (Budel Mine), Narang District, Konar Province (Kunar Province; Konarh Province; Konarha Province; Nuristan), Afghanistan', Mindat.org https:// www.mindat.org/locentry-988391.html; G.J. Orris and J.D. Bliss, 'Mines and Mineral Occurrences of Afghanistan ', United States Geological Survey, 2002 https:// pubs.usgs.gov/of/2002/0110/pdf/of02-110. pdf; Global Witness interview, late 2016

119 Global Witness interview, mid-2016

120 Matt DuPée, an author and Afghan expert with the US Department of Defence, also reported that he "heard as well that [ISKP] is extracting directly." Global Witness interview with Matt DuPée, November 9, 2017

121 Global Witness interview, mid-2016.

122 Global Witness interview, late 2016

123 Global Witness interview, mid-2016

124 Global Witness interview, mid-2016

125 This counts the four sources who we directly interviewed and the sources who informed Matt DuPée and Borhan Usman.

126 DuPée reported that: "It looks like the activity has begun again, the taxation scheme [on minerals] is in place. The Afghan government in December 2016 was tracking more Taliban involvement in terms of taxation on talc – [but] by February 2017 we see data points on the Islamic State making money from talc. That time period from November 2016 to February 2017 – I think if we looked at the dynamics of what is happening, we would see both groups making a lot of money from both the exploitation and shipping of talc." DuPée's sources included locals, but he was unable to be more specific. Global Witness interviews with Matt DuPée, November 2017 and January 2018 In November 2017

127 Global Witness interview with Borhan Usman, late 2017

128 William Byrd and JavedNoorani, 'Industrial-Scale Looting of Afghanistan's Mineral Resources', United States Institute for Peace, June 2017, p 8 https:// www. usip.org/sites/default/files/2017-05/sr404-industrial-scale-looting-of-afghanistan-s-mineral-resources.

129 ZiarYad, 'Daesh, Taliban Plundering Mines, Destroying Forests In Nangarhar', Tolo News, April 3, 2017 http:// www.tolonews.com/afghanistan/provincial/ daesh-taliban-plundering-mines-destroying-forests-nangarhar

130 Global Witness interview with ISKP official, mid-2017

131 As we were unable to confirm the identities of the sources, there is some slight possibility that they were the same individual. The quote is from Marty's paraphrase of the conversation. Marty also reported that "the commander told me back in May 2016 that they did not have any financial problems at that time and did not need to do other work than fighting," which might be relevant to explaining why ISKP would not be interested in the potentially lucrative mines. Global Witness email correspondence with Franz Marty, January 20, 2018

132 Global Witness email correspondence with Franz Marty, January 19, 2018

133 Global Witness interview with a leading talc trader from Nangarhar province, mid-2017

134   Global Witness interview with local source from Shadal, mid-2017

135   Mansfield added that there were some reports in early 2018 that more locals were again being allowed into the mining areas. "My understanding is that things are back on line." Global Witness interview with Daniel Mansfield, January 18, 2018

136   Global Witness interview with a senior Afghan police official, February 2018

137   Global Witness interview, late 2016

138   Global Witness interview, mid-2017

139   Global Witness interview, mid-2017

140   Global Witness interview, mid-2016; Global Witness interview, late 2016. In late 2016 the source said that it was locals who did the work at the mines he knew of, and that "only the drivers are from outside." In the same interview however, the source said that: "the workers are 25 percent locals and 75 percent foreigners. Most of the locals escaped (…) some of those who left are in favour of them – the rest are foreigners." Global Witness interview, mid-2016; Global Witness interview, late 2016

141   The source spoke of foreigners who "would come and observe" the mining who were not labourers – but also that the extraction was done by both locals and foreigners. There is a small chance that this implies some uncertainty in their testimony over the presence of foreign labourers at all, but the most plausible explanation appears to be that they were highlighting that the visitors were not labourers. Global Witness interview, mid-2016.

142   None of our sources indicated such a route existed, and none was visible in the available satellite imagery. Borhan Osman, 'The Battle for Mamand: ISKP under strain, but not yet defeated', Afghanistan Analysts Network, May 23, 2017 https://www.afghanistan-analysts. org/the-battle-for-mamand-iskp-under-strain-butnot-yet-defeated/; 'Why Daesh chose Achin district as its base in Afghanistan', Pajhwok Afghan News, May 9, 2016 https://www.pajhwok.com/en/2016/05/09/whydaesh-chose-achin-district-its-base-afghanistan

143   Global Witness interview with a leading talc trader, mid-2017

144   Global Witness interview with a former senior police officer from Nangarhar, early 2018

145   The source referred to buying the minerals for Rs50,000 ($476) and sold it in the Korkhano area of Peshawar for Rs90,000-Rs130,000 ($857-$1,238), but there was some confusion whether it was per ton or for the whole load. There is also a possibility they carried talc. Global Witness interview with Source K, early 2018

146   Global Witness interview, late 2016 145 Global Witness interview, late 2016

147   A number of additional images in the missing time period do exist – mostly at lower resolution – but they were not among those Global Witness was able to access. One image from April 2015 was accessible, but was unusable because of 100 percent cloud cover.

Chapter 13: Salafism, Wahhabism, and the Definition of Sunni Islam. Rob J. Williams

1   Johnathan A.C. Brown, Hadith: Muhammad's Legacy in the Medieval and Modern World, (Oxford, One World Publications, 2009-11), 243.

2   Ibid.

3   Brown, 261.

4   Eyyup Said Kaya, "Continuity and Change in Islamic Law: The Concept of Maddhab and the Dimensions of Legal Disagreement in Hanafi Scholarship of the Tenth Century", in The Islamic School of Law: Evolution, Devolution, and Progress, eds. Peri Bearman, Rudolph Peters, and Frank E. Vogel, (Cambridge: Harvard University Press, 2005), 26-40.

5   Abdur Rahim, The Principles of Islamic Jurisprudence According to the Hanafi, Shafi'i, Maliki, and Hanbali Schools, (New Delhi, Kitab Bhavan: 1994), 15-34.

6   Ibid, 33-34.

7   Rudolph Peters, "What Does It Mean to be An Official Maddhab? Hanafism and the Ottoman Empire", in The Islamic School of Law: Evolution, Devolution, and Progress, eds. Peri Bearman, Rudolph Peters, and Frank E. Vogel, (Cambridge: Harvard University Press, 2005), 147-148

8.   Ibid.

9   Yassin Dutton, Original Islam: Malik and the maddhab of Madina (New York: Routledge, 2007), 69.

10   Ibid.

11   Alfonso Carmona, "The Introduction of Malik's Teachings in al-Andalus", in The Islamic School of Law: Evolution, Devolution, and Progress, eds. Peri Bearman, Rudolph Peters, and Frank E. Vogel, (Cambridge: Harvard University Press, 2005), 43.

12   Rahim, The Principles of Islamic Jurisprudence According to the Hanafi, Shafi'i, Maliki, and Hanbali Schools, 26.

13   Ibid, 78.

14   Dutton, Original Islam: Malik and the maddhab of Madina, 32-33.

15   Rahim, The Principles of Islamic Jurisprudence According to the Hanafi, Shafi'i, Maliki, and Hanbali Schools, 27.

16 Kemal A Faruki, "Al-Shafi'i's Agreements and Disagreements with the Hanafi and Maliki Schools", Islamic Studies 10, (1971): 129-131.

17 Ibid.

18 N. Calder, The Encyclopaedia of Islam, 2nd ed., s.v. "Usul al-fikh".

19 Ibid.

20 Rahim, 79.

21 Faruki, 135.

22 Ibid, 132.

23 Rahim, The Principles of Islamic Jurisprudence According to the Hanafi, Shafi'i, Maliki, and Hanbali Schools, 27.

24 Ibid, 28.

25 Ibid.

26 Abdul Hakim I. Al-Matroudi, The Hanbali School of Law and Ibn Taymiyyah: Conflict or Conciliation (London, Taylor and Francis, 2006), 34.

27 "Non-revealed" in this case means that it is a source of law coming from humans and not God.

28 Al-Matroudi, 33.

29 Ibid, 18-19.

30 Rahim, 28 and Algar, Wahhabism: A Critical Essay (Oneonta, Islamic Publications International, 2002), 2.

31 Brown, 243.

32 Ibid, 240.

33 Marilyn Waldman, The Encyclopedia Brittanica, 2017, s.v. "Islamic World", 49.

34 Ibid.

35 "The Omdurman Atrocity", Advocate of the Peace, vol. 60 no. 10 (1898), 222 and Winston Churchill, "The Battle of Omdurman, 1898," Fordham University Modern History Sourcebook, http://sourcebooks.fordham.edu/halsall/mod/1898churchill-omdurman.asp.

36 Wael Hallaq, "An Introduction to Islamic Law", (New York, Cambridge University Press, 2009), 85.

37 Ibid, 86. The idea that Muslim law is individual and arbitrary is far from true, as we will see in the subsequent paragraphs.

38 Ibid, 87.

39 Ibid, 87-88

40 Farine Zarinebaf, Crime & Punishment in Istanbul, 1700-1800, (Los Angeles: University of California Press, 2010), 176.

41 Ibid, 173-174.

42 Ibid.

43 Ibid, 165.

44 Ibid, 173-174.

45 Ibid, 169-170.

46 Ibid, 178.

47 A. Kevin Reinhardt, "Law", in Key Themes for the Study of Islam, ed. Jamal J. Elias (Oxford: OneWorld Publications, 2008), 222.

48 Wael Hallaq, "The Legal, the Political, and the Moral", in The Impossible State: Islam, Politics, and Modernity's Predicament (New York: Columbia University Press, 2013), 78, 93.

49 Bernard Weiss, "The Maddhab in Islamic Legal Theory", in The Islamic School of Law: Evolution, Devolution, and Progress, eds. Peri Bearman, Rudolph Peters, and Frank E. Vogel, (Cambridge: Harvard University Press, 2005), 1-9.

50 Ibid.

51 Ibid.

52 Ibid.

53 Ibid.

54 Hallaq, The Impossible State, 82.

55 Ibid, 83-84.

56 Zarinebaf, 173-174.

57 Brown, 243.

58 Ibid, 251.

59 Ibid, 253-254.

60 Ibid.

61 Ibid.

62 Ibid.

63 Marshall Hodgson, The Venture of Islam Volume 3: Gunpowder Empires and Modern Times, (Chicago: University of Chicago Press, 1974), 274.

64 Ibid.

65 Ibid.

66 Ibid, 256-257.

67 Ibid.

68 Ibid.

69 Ibid, 257-258.

70 Ibid, 258.

71 Ibid.

72 Joseph Lumbard, Islam, Fundamentalism, and the Betrayal of Tradition (World Wisdom, Inc., 2009), 68.

73 Algar, 47.

74 Ibid.

75 Ibid, 35.

76 Ibid, 1.

77   Algar, 30-31.

78 Ibid.

79 Ibid.

80 Ibid, 46.

81 Ibid, 19.

82 Ibid, 47.

83 Khaled M. Abou El Fadl, The Great Theft: Wrestling Islam from the Extremists, (HarperOne, 2007), 47.

84 Ibid, 48.

85 Ibid.

86 Algar, 35.

87 El Fadl, 46-47.

88 Ibid, 47.

89 Ibid.

90 Ibid, 48.

91 Algar, 24-25.

92 Ibid, 25.

93 Ibid, 26-27.

94 David Commins, The Wahhabi Mission and Saudi Arabia (I.B. Tauris, New York, 2006), 1.

95 Ibid, 1, 8-9.

96 Algar, 2.

97   Commins, 8.

98   Referred to as "al-Wahhab" from this point forward in the essay

99   Algar, 11-13.

100   Ibid, 7.

101   Ibid, 18.

102   Ibid, 18-19.

103   Ibid, 19.

104   Commins, 19.

105   Algar, 38-39.

106   Ibid, 40.

107   Ibid, 42.

108   Ibid.

109   Ibid, 48.

110   Ibid.

111   Ibid, 48-50.

112   Commins, 140.

113   Ibid, 141.

114   Ibid, 142.

115   Ibid, 148.

116   Ibid, 151-152.

117   Ibid, 152-153.

118   R. Kim Cragin, "Early History of al-Qai'da", The Historical Journal 51, no. 4 (2008): 1047, 1051.

119   Ibid, 1052-1054.

120   Ibid, 1056.

121   Eli Alschech, "The Doctrinal Crisis within the Salafi-Jihadi Ranks and the Emergence of Neo-Takfirism", Islamic Law and Society 21 (2014): 419-452.

122   Ibid.

123   Ibid, 421.

124   Ibid, 423.

125   Ibid, 423-424.

126   Ibid, 422.

127   Ibid, 439.

128   Ibid, 422.

129   Ibid, 426.

130   Ibid.

131   Ibid, 430-431.

132   Ibid, 423.

133   Ibid, 422.

134   Lumbard, 66.

135   Hodgson, 182.

136   Ibid, 182.

137   Ibid, 274.

References

Algar, Hamid. Wahhabism: A Critical Essay. Oneonta: Islamic Publications International, 2002.

Al-Matroudi, Abdul Hakim I. Hanbali School of Law and Ibn Taymiyyah: Conflict or Conciliation. London: Taylor and Francis, 2006.

Alschech, Eli. "The Doctrinal Crisis within the Salafi-Jihadi Ranks and the Emergence of Neo-Takfirism". Islamic Law and Society 21, (2014): 419-452.

Brown, Jonathan A. C. Hadith: Muhammad's Legacy in the Medieval and Modern World. Oxford: One World Publications, 2009.

Calder, N. The Encyclopaedia of Islam, 2nd ed., s.v. "Usul al-fikh".

Commins, David. The Wahhabi Mission and Saudi Arabia. New York: I.B. Tauris & Co., Ltd, 2006.

Churchill, Winston. "The Battle of Omdurman, 1898." Fordham University Modern History Sourcebook. http://sourcebooks.fordham.edu/halsall/mod/1898churchill-omdurman.asp.

Cragin, R Kim. "Early History of al-Qa'ida". The Historical Journal 51, no.4 (2008): 1047-1067.

El Fadl, Khaled M. Abou. The Great Theft: Wresting Islam from the Extremists. HarperOne, 2007.

Faruki, Kemal A. "Al-Shafi'i's Agreements and Disagreements with the Maliki and the Hanafi Schools". Islamic Studies 10, (1971): 127-136.

Hallaq, Wael. An Introduction to Islamic Law. New York: Cambridge University Press, 2009.

Hallaq, Wael. "The Legal, the Political, and the Moral". In The Impossible State: Islam, Politics, and Modernity's Predicament. New York: Columbia University Press, 2013.

Hodgson, Marshall. The Venture of Islam Volume 3: Gunpowder Empires and Modern Times. Chicago: University of Chicago Press, 1974.

Juergensmeyer, Mark. "How ISIS Will End." The Cairo Review of Global Affairs (Summer 2016): 1-19.

Kaya, Eyyup Said. "Continuity and Change in Islamic Law: The Concept of Maddhab and the Dimensions of Legal Disagreement in Hanafi Scholarship of the Tenth Century". In The Islamic School of Law: Evolution, Devolution, and Progress, edited by Peri Bearman, Rudolph Peters, and Frank E. Vogel, 26-40. Cambridge: Harvard University Press, 2005.

Lumbard, Joseph. "Chapter 2: The Decline of Knowledge and the Rise of Ideology in the Modern Islamic World". In Islam, Fundamentalism, and the Betrayal of Tradition. World Wisdom, Inc., 2009. "The Omdurman Atrocity." Advocate of the Peace, vol. 60 no. 10 (1898): 222.

Peters, Rudolph. "What Does It Mean to Be an Official Maddhab? Hanafism and the Ottoman Empire". In The Islamic School of Law: Evolution, Devolution, and Progress, edited by Peri Bearman, Rudolph Peters, and Frank E. Vogel, 147-158. Cambridge: Harvard University Press, 2005.

Rahim, Abdur. The Principles of Islamic Jurisprudence According to the Hanafi, Maliki, Shafi'i, and Hanbali Schools. New Delhi: Kitab Bhavan, 1994.

Reinhardt, A. Kevin. "Law". In Key Themes for the Study of Islam, edited by Jamal J. Elias, 220-244. Oxford: OneWorld Publications, 2010.

Waldman, Marilyn. The Encyclopedia Brittanica, 2017, s.v. "Islamic World".

Weiss, Bernard. "The Maddhab in Islamic Legal Theory". In The Islamic School of Law: Evolution, Devolution, and Progress, edited by Peri Bearman, Rudolph Peters, and Frank E. Vogel, 1-9. Cambridge: Harvard University Press, 2005.

Zarinebaf, Fariba. Crime & Punishment in Istanbul, 1700-1800. Los Angeles: University of California Press, 2010.

Chapter 14: Understanding PKK, Kurdish Hezbollah and ISIS Recruitment in Southeastern Turkey. Kerem Övet, James Hewitt and Tahir Abbas.

1   Süleyman Özeren, Murat Sever, Kamil Yılmaz, and Alper Sözer, "Whom Do They Recruit?: Profiling and Recruitment in the PKK/KCK," *Studies in Conflict & Terrorism* 37, no .4 (2014): 330.

2   Süleyman Özeren and Cécile Van De Voorde "Turkish Hizballah: A Case Study of Radical Terrorism," *International Journal of Comparative and Applied Criminal Justice* 30, no: 1 (2006): 84.

3   Doğu Eroğlu, *IŞİD Ağları: Türkiye'de Radikalleşme, Örgütleme, Lojistik* (İstanbul: İletişim Yayınları, 2018), 99–193.

4   Ebru E. Özbey, "Turkey's Fight Against Youth Radicalization: Small Steps on a Long Path," *Euromesco Policy Brief*, no. 78 (2018): 2.

5   HRW, *"Events of 2019,"* HRW (2020)

6   Mark Sedgwick, "The Concept of Radicalization as a Source of Confusion," *Terrorism and Political Violence* 22, no. 4 (2010).

7   KONDA, *"Kürt Meselesini Yeniden Düşünmek,"* KONDA (2010): 19.

8   KONDA, "Biz Kimiz? Toplumsal Yapı Araştırması," KONDA (2006): 16.

9   Gülay Kılıçaslan, "Forced Migration, Citizenship, and Space: The Case of Syrian Kurdish Refugees in İstanbul," *New Perspectives on Turkey* 54 (2016): 78.

10 TUİK, "Official Statistics Portal of Turkey," *Resmi İstatistik* (2018).

11 Bruce H. Rankin, "Economic Crises and the Social Structuring of Economic Hardship: The Impact of the 2001 Turkish Crisis," *New Perspectives on Turkey* 44 (2011): 29–34.

12 Ionnis N. Grigoriadis and Esra Dilek, "Struggling for the Kurdish Vote: Religion, Ethnicity and Victimhood in AKP and BDP/HDP Rally Speeches," *Middle Eastern Studies* 54, no. 2 (2018): 2–7.

13 Ibid. 20.

14 Onur Günay and Erdem Yörük, "Governing Ethnic Unrest: Political Islam and the Kurdish Conflict in Turkey," *New Perspectives on Turkey* 61 (2019): 27–33.

15 Ibid. 34–35.

16 Eroğlu, *IŞİD Ağları*, 86.

17 Michiel Leezenberg, "The Ambiguities of Democratic Autonomy: The Kurdish Movement in Turkey and Rojava," *Southeast European and Black Sea Studies* 16, no. 4 (2016): 671–690.

18 Mustafa E. Gurbuz, "Ideology in Action: Symbolic Localization of Kurdistan Workers' Party in Turkey," *Sociological Inquiry* 85, no. 1 (2015): 9.

19 Ibid.

20 Bahar Başer and Alpaslan Özerdem, "Conflict Transformation and Asymmetric Conflicts: A Critique of the Failed Turkish-Kurdish Peace Process," *Terrorism and Political Violence* (2019): 1.

21 ICG (International Crisis Group), "Turkey's PKK Conflict: A Visual Explainer," *Crisis Group* (2020).

22 Mehmet Kurt, *Kurdish Hizbullah in Turkey: Islamism, Violence and the State* (London: Pluto Press, 2017), 15–16.

23 Ibid., 22–24.

24 Ibid., 24–25.

25 Leyla Neyzi and Haydar Darıcı, "Generation in Debt: Family, Politics, and Youth Subjectivities in Diyarbakır," *New Perspectives on Turkey* 50 (2015): 59.

26 Ibid.

27 Kurt, *Kurdish Hizbullah in Turkey*, 39–55.

28 Bernard Haykel, "ISIS and al-Qaeda—What Are They Thinking? Understanding the Adversary," *The Annals of the American Academy of Political and Social Science* 668, no. 1 (2016): 77.

29 Eroğlu, *IŞİD Ağları*, 99-301; Ahmet S. Yayla, "Turkish ISIS and AQ Foreign Fighters: Reconciling the Numbers and Perception of the Terrorism Threat," *Studies in Conflict & Terrorism* 41, no. 7 (2019): 7.

30 Eroğlu, *IŞİD Ağları*, 99-193.

31 Ibid., 137-193.

32 Ibid. 164-180.

33 Richard Barrett, "Beyond the Caliphate: Foreign Fighters and the Threat of Returnees," *The Soufan Center* (2017): 16.

34 Metin Gürcan and Kerem Övet, "Combat Charities: New Phenomenon of the 21st Century or the Longstanding Reality of the Warfare?" *Bilge Strateji* 10, no. 18 (2018): 11.

35 Fevzi Kızılkoyun, "Türkiye'den YPG'ye 8 bin 500 militan," *Hürriyet*, Jun. 25, 2015, https://www.hurriyet.com.tr/dunya/turkiye-den-ypg-ye-8-bin-500-militan-29372989.

36 İçişleri Bakanlığı, "Basın Açıklaması," *İçişleri* (2016).

37 James A. Piazza, "Poverty, Minority Economic Discrimination, and Domestic Terrorism," *Journal of Peace Research* 48, no. 3 (2011).

38 James A. Piazza, "Types of Minority Discrimination and Terrorism," *Conflict Management and Peace Science* 29, no. 5 (2012).

39 James A. Piazza, "Repression and Terrorism: A Cross-National Empirical Analysis of Types of Repression and Domestic Terrorism," *Terrorism and Political Violence* 29, no. 1 (2017).

40 Ioana Emy Matesan, "Grievances and Fears in Islamist Movements: Revisiting the Link between Exclusion, Insecurity, and Political Violence," *Journal of Global Security Studies* 5, no. 1 (2020).

41 Johannes Karreth, Patricia Lynne Sullivan, and Ghazal Dezfuli, "Explaining How Human Rights Protections Change After Internal Armed Conflicts," *Journal of Global Security Studies* 5, no. 2 (2020): 259.

42 Ursula Daxecker, "Dirty Hands: Government Torture and Terrorism," *Journal of Conflict Resolution* 61, no. 6 (2017).

43 Halvard Buhaug, Lars Erik Cederman, and Jan Ketil Rød, "Disaggregating Ethno-Nationalist Civil Wars: A Dyadic Test of Exclusion Theory," *International Organization* 62, no. 3 (2008).

44 Lars Erik Cederman, Andreas Wimmer, and Brian Min, "Why Do Ethnic Groups Rebel? New Data and Analysis," *World Politics* 62, no. 1 (2010).

45 Lars Erik Cederman, Kristian Skrede Gleditsch, Idean Salehyan, and Julian Wucherpfennig, "Transborder Ethnic Kin and Civil War," *International Organization* 67, no. 2 (2013).

46 Vera Eccarius-Kelly, "Surreptitious Lifelines: A Structural Analysis of the FARC and the PKK," *Terrorism and Political Violence* 24, no. 2 (2012): 247.

47 Başer and Özerdem, "Conflict Transformation," 9.

48 Arie W. Kruglanski, Michele J. Gelfand, Jocelyn J. Bélanger, Anna Sheveland, Malkanthi Hetiarachchi, and Rohan Gunaratna, "The Psychology of Radicalization and Deradicalization: How Significance Quest Impacts Violent Extremism," *Advances in Political Psychology* 35, no. 1 (2014): 75.

49 Ibid.

50 Kurt, *Kurdish Hizbullah in Turkey*.

51 Eroğlu, *IŞİD Ağları*.

52 İsmail Saymaz, *Türkiye'de IŞİD*, (İstanbul: İletişim Yayıncılık, 2017).

53 Bejan Matur, *Dağın Ardına Bakmak* (İstanbul: Timaş Yayınları, 2011).

54 Canan Rojin Akın and Funda Danışman, *Bildiğin gibi değil - 90'larda Güneydoğu'da çocuk olmak* (Is tanbul: Metis Yayınları, 2011).

55 Nadire Mater, *Mehmed'in Kitabı* (İstanbul: Metis Yayınları, 1998).

56 HRW (Human Rights Watch), "Time For Justice: Ending Impunity for Killings and Disappearances in 1990s Turkey," *HRW* (2012).

57 Matur, *Dağın Ardına Bakmak*, 99.

58 Neyzi and Darıcı, "Generation in Debt."

59 Ibid., 67.

60 Karreth, Sullivan, and Dezfuli, "Explaining How Human Rights Protections Change."

61 Ibid., 259.

62 Daxecker, "Dirty Hands."

63 Cited in Naşit Tutar, *39. Koğuş [39th Ward]* (İstanbul: Dua Yayıncılık, 2007): 41.

64 TUİK, "Official Statistics Portal of Turkey."

65 Özge Biner, "Crossing the mountain and negotiating the border: Human smuggling in eastern Turkey," *New Perspectives on Turkey* 59 (2018): 97–98.

66 Eroğlu, *IŞİD Ağları*, 151.

67 Rankin, "Economic Crises."

68 Özeren, Sever, Yılmaz, and Sözer, "Whom Do They Recruit?," 328.

69 Piazza, "Poverty, Minority Economic Discrimination"; Piazza, "Types of Minority Discrimination."

70 Arda Bilgen, "The Southeastern Anatolia Project (GAP) Revisited: The Evolution of GAP over Forty Years," *New Perspectives on Turkey*, no. 58 (2018): 130.

71 TUİK, "Official Statistics Portal of Turkey."

72 Ibid.

73 Kurt, *Kurdish Hizbullah in Turkey*, 27.

74 Kruglanski, Gelfand, Bélanger, Sheveland, Hetiarachchi, and Gunaratna, "The Psychology of Radicalization."

75 Kılıçaslan, "Forced Migration, Citizenship, and Space," 82.

76 Leyla Şen, "Poverty Alleviation, Conflict and Power in Poor Displaced Households: A Study of the Views of Women in Diyarbakır," *New Perspectives on Turkey* 32 (2005): 118.

77 Ibid., 119.

78 Kruglanski, Gelfand, Bélanger, Sheveland, Hetiarachchi, and Gunaratna, "The Psychology of Radicalization."

79 Buhaug, Cederman, and Rød, "Disaggregating Ethno-Nationalist Civil Wars," 531.

80 Eccarius-Kelly, "Surreptitious Lifelines."

81 Cederman, Gleditsch, Salehyan, and Wucherpfennig, "Transborder Ethnic Kin."

82 For instance, Matesan, "Grievances and Fears."; Piazza, "Repression and Terrorism."

83 For instance, Kruglanski, Gelfand, Bélanger, Sheveland, Hetiarachchi, and Gunaratna, "The Psychology of Radicalization."

84 For instance, Daxecker, "Dirty Hands."

85 For instance, Piazza, "Poverty, Minority Economic Discrimination."; Piazza, "Types of Minority Discrimination."; Buhaug, Cederman, and Rød, "Disaggregating Ethno-Nationalist Civil Wars."; Cederman, Wimmer, and Min, "Why Do Ethnic Groups Rebel?"

86   Kruglanski, Gelfand, Bélanger, Sheveland, Hetiarachchi, and Gunaratna, "The Psychology of Radicalization."

87   Buhaug, Cederman, and Rød, "Disaggregating Ethno-Nationalist Civil Wars."

Chapter 15: Nuclear, Chemical and Biological Terrorism in Central Asia and Russia: Al Qaeda, the ISIS Affiliated Groups and Security of Sensitive Biological Weapons Facilities. Edward Lemon, Vera Mironova and William Tobey. Foreword by Simon Saradzhyan.

1   Saradzhyan, Simon and Monica Duffy Toft, "Islamic State and the Bolsheviks:Plenty in Common and Lessons to Heed," Russia Matters, Dec. 16, 2016, https://www. russiamatters.org/analysis/islamic-state-and-bolsheviks-plenty-common-and-lessons-heed.

2   Kramer, Andrew E. and Rukmini Callimachi, "ISIS Says It Killed 4 Cyclists in Tajikistan," The New York Times, July 30, 2018, https://www.nytimes. com/2018/07/30/world/asia/tajikistan-attack-cylists.html.

3   Nechepurenko, Ivan, "Suicide Bomber Attacks Chinese Embassy in Kyrgyzstan," The New York Times, Aug. 30, 2016, https://www.nytimes. com/2016/08/31/world/asia/bishkek-china-embassy-kyrgyzstan.html.

4   Global Terrorism Database, https://www.start.umd.edu/gtd/.

5   The European Commission's Radicalization Awareness Network estimated in a July 2017 report that more than 42,000 "foreign terrorist fighters" from over 120 countries had joined terrorist organizations in 2011-2016. See: https:// ec.europa.eu/home-affairs/sites/homeaffairs/files/ran_br_a4_m10_en.pdf.

6   According to the World Bank, the combined total population of Kazakhstan,Kyrgyzstan, Tajikistan, Turkmenistan and Uzbekistan for 2017 was just over 71.3 million out of a global population of more than 7.5 billion. See: http://databank.worldbank.org/data/reports.aspx?source=2&series=SP. POP.TOTL&country=.

7. "DataBank | World Development Indicators," The World Bank, 2018, http:// databank.worldbank.org/data/reports.aspx?source=2&series=SP.POP. TOTL&country=.

8   Spada, Andrea, "About 500-600 people originating from Kazakhstan fighting alongside ISIS," Islam Media Analysis, Apr. 11, 2017, http://www. islamedianalysis.info/about-500-600-people-originating-from-kazakhstan-fighting-alongside-isis/.

9   KNB: 150 Kazakhstantsev voyuyut v Sirii i Irake [NSC: 150 Kazakhstanis Fighting in Syria and Iraq]," Tengri News, June 29, 2015, https://tengrinews. kz/tv/novosti/obschestvo/4278/. This number comes from Kazakhstan's Committee of National Security, which estimated at the time that the fighters were accompanied by more than 200 wives, widows and children.

10   Matveeva, Anna, "Radicalisation and Violent Extremism in Kyrgyzstan: On the Way to the Caliphate?" The RUSI Journal, 163, (1), 2018, https://www.tandfonline.com/eprint/gXEVaGDNChmtBTJGUXJe/full. The paper's author cites official figures of 863 Kyrgyz citizens who had "left … for foreign fighting zones," including 185 women and 83 minors.

11   "Kyrgyzstan Apprehends ISIL Terrorist in Bishkek," FARS News Agency, July 23, 2016, http://en.farsnews.com/newstext.aspx?nn=13950502000746. Figure based on statements by Kyrgyz officials, with 205 women and children subtracted from the total of "over 500."

12   An estimated 200 women have been subtracted from the figures given in the cited articles: http://www2.unwomen.org/-/media/field office eca/attachments/publications/2017/iii_unw_eca_tajikistan chapter_final-02 final.pdf?la=en&vs=1241

13   Murodov, Abdumajid, "Peshgirii jalbi javonon ba tashkiloti terroristī vazifai jomeai shahrvandī niz hast [Civil Society Also Has a Role in Preventing Young People From Participating in Terrorist Groups]," Sadoi mardum, Nov. 15, 2018, http://sadoimardum.tj/ma-lisi-ol/peshgirii-albi-avonon-ba-tashkiloti-terrorist-vazifai-omeai-sha-rvand-niz-ast/.

14   "Vlasti Tadzhikistana ozabocheny vozvrascheniem "dzhikhadistov" iz Sirii [Authorities in Tajikistan Concerned by the Return of "Jihadists" From Syria]," Ozodlik,July 11, 2016, https://rus.ozodlik.org/a/28610097.html.

15   "Policy Briefing," International Crisis Group, Jan. 20, 2015, https://d2071andvip0wj.cloudfront.net/b72-syria-calling-radicalisation-in-central-asia.pdf.

16   Dyner, Anna, Arkadiusz Legieć and Kacper Rękawek, "Ready to Go? ISIS and Its Presumed Expansion into Central Asia," Polski Instytut Spraw Międzynarodowych (PISM), June 2015, https://www.pism.pl/files/?id_plik=20020.

17   Barrett, Richard, "Beyond the Caliphate: Foreign Fighters and the Threat of Returnees," The Soufan Center, October 2017, http://thesoufancenter.org/wp-content/ uploads/2017/11/Beyond-the-Caliphate-Foreign-Fighters-and-the-Threat-of-Returnees-TSC-Report-October-2017-v3.pdf. Russia Matters/U.S.-Russia Initiative to Prevent Nuclear Terrorism | Belfer Center for Science and International Affairs 37

18   "V ryadakh IGIL voyuyut okolo 200 grazhdan Uzbekistana [Around 200 Citizens of Uzbekistan Fighting for ISIS]," Regnum, Mar. 26, 2015, https://regnum.ru/ percent20 news/1908975.html.

19   Data from the EU Terrorism Situation and Trend reports (https://www.europol.europa.eu/activities-services/main-reports/eu-terrorism-situation-and-trend-report#fndtn-tabs-0-bottom-2) for 2014, 2015, 2016 and 2017.

20 By way of comparison, we were unable to find any reliable reports of Russian nationals' involvement in terrorist acts in the EU in the same time period. However, one IS-related terror attack (https://www.telegraph.co.uk/news/2018/05/12/knifeman-shot-dead-french-police-stabbing-several-people-paris/) in Paris in May 2018 involved a naturalized French citizen born in Russia's republic of Chechnya. (After the deadly knife attack, Chechen President Ramzan Kadyrov claimed (https://apostrophe.ua/news/world/ex-ussr/2018-05-13/krovavaya-reznya-v-parije-kadyirov-nashel-vinovatogo/129932) the 20-year-old assailant had not renewed his Russian passport, as he was supposed to and hence wasn't a Russian national.)

21 See https://www.europol.europa.eu/activities-services/main-reports/eu-terrorism-situation-and-trend-report#fndtn-tabs-0-bottom-2.

22 Global Terrorism Database, https://www.start.umd.edu/gtd/.

23 Priimark, Artur and Pavel Skrilnikov, "Bumerang radicalism vozvrashchyayetcyz iz Srednei Azii," Nezavisimaya Gazeta, April 19, 2017, http://www.ng.ru/facts/2017-04-19/9_419_bumerang.html.

24 Tsvetkova, Maria and Andrew Osborn, "Nanny who beheaded Russian girl cites revenge for Putin's Syria strikes," Reuters, March 3, 2016, https://www.reuters.com/article/us-russia-murder-child/nanny-who-beheaded-russian-girl-cites-revengefor-putins-syria-strikes-idUSKCN0W50OH.

25 "471: The Convert," This American Life, https://www.thisamericanlife.org/471transcript.

26 Shallwani, Pervaiz, Rebecca Davis O'Brien and Andrew Grossman, "Three Brooklyn Men Arrested and Accused of Plot to Join Islamic State," The Wall Street Journal, Feb. 25, 2015, https://www.wsj.com/articles/three-brooklyn-men-accused-ofplot-to-join-islamic-state-1424888001?mod=article_inline.

27 "Country Reports on Terrorism 2016 - Foreign Terrorist Organizations: Islamic Movement of Uzbekistan (IMU)," United States Department of State, July 19, 2017,https://www.refworld.org/docid/5981e3d7a.html.

28 Mitchell, Kirk, "Denver federal jury finds Uzbekistan refugee guilty of aiding terror group," The Denver Post, June 21, 2018, https://www.denverpost.com/2018/06/21/denver-jury-jamshid-muhtorov-guilty/.

29 At least one news report (https://www.theguardian.com/world/2014/jun/11/uzbek-militant-group-imu-karachi-airport-assault-pakistani-taliban-drone) put the number at 36; the BBC (https://www.bbc.com/news/world-asia-27790892) and later the U.S. State Department (https://www.state.gov/documents/organization/272488. pdf) put it at 39.

30 Guistozzi, Antonio and Anna Matveeva, "The Central Asian Militants: Cannon Fodder of Global Jihadism or Revolutionary Vanguard?" Small Wars and Insurgencies,29, (2), 2018, https://www.tandfonline.com/doi/abs/10.1080/09592318.2018.1433472

31 Donati, Jessica and Paul Sonne, "New York Attack Underlines Central Asia as Growing Source of Terrorism," The Wall Street Journal, Oct. 31, 2017, https://www.wsj.com/articles/new-york-attack-underlines-central-asia-as-growing-source-of-terrorism-1509508624.

32 Kranz, Michal, "Here's how the region the New York attacker immigrated from became fertile ground for terrorism," Business Insider, Nov. 1, 2017, https://www.businessinsider.com/central-asia-fertile-ground-for-terrorism-sayfullo-saipov-2017-11.

33 Matveeva, Anna, "Radicalisation and Violent Extremism in Kyrgyzstan: On thev Way to the Caliphate?" The RUSI Journal, 163, (1), 2018, https://www.tandfonline.com/eprint /gXEVaGDNChmtBTJGUXJe/full.

34 Tucker, Noah, "What Happens When Your Town Becomes an ISIS Recruiting Ground? Lessons from Central Asia about Vulnerability, Resistance and the Danger of Ignoring Injustice," Central Asia Program, July 2018. http://centralasiaprogram.org/wp-content/uploads/2018/06/Tucker-CAP-Paper-July-2018.pdf.

35 "Uzbek militant group IMU claims involvement in Karachi airport assault," The Guardian, June 11, 2014, https://www.theguardian.com/world/2014/jun/11/uzbek-militant-group-imu-karachi-airport-assault-pakistani-taliban-drone. 38 Jihadists from Ex-Soviet Central Asia: Where Are They? Why Did They Radicalize? What Next?

36 Weiss, Caleb, "State adds Uzbek jihadist group to terror list," Long War Journal, Mar. 22, 2018, https://www.longwarjournal.org/tags/imam-bukhari-jamaat. Weiss, Caleb, "Jihadists celebrate in key Idlib city after defeating Syrian regime," Long War Journal, Apr. 27, 2015, https://www.longwarjournal.org/archives/2015/04/jihadists-celebrate-in-key-idlib-city-after-defeating-syrian-regime.php. Paraszczuk, Joanna and Barno Anvar, "The Last Moments Of A Suicide Bomber In Syria," Radio Free Europe, Sep. 21, 2015, https://www.rferl.org/a/uzbek-suicide-bomber-syria/27260806.html.

37 Many observers have been skeptical about the IRPT's involvement. See Edward Lemon, "Violence in Tajikistan Emerges from within the State," CACI-Analyst,Sept. 23, 2015, https://cacianalyst.org/publications/analytical-articles/item/13279-violence-in-tajikistan-emerges-from-within-the-state.html.

38 Galdini, Franco and Zukhra Iakupbaeva, "The Strange Case of Jaysh al-Mahdi and Mr. ISIS: How Kyrgyzstan's Elites Manipulate the Threat of Terrorism," CERIA Briefs, 2016, http://centralasiaprogram.org/archives/10075.

39 Baizakova, Zhulduz and Roger N. McDermott, "Reassessing the Barriers to Islamic Radicalization in Kazakhstan," U.S. Army War College, July 29, 2015, https://apps.dtic.mil/dtic/tr/fulltext/u2/a621437.pdf.

40 On manipulation of the threat, see John Heathershaw and David Montgomery. "Islam, Secularism and Danger: A Reconsideration of the Link Between Religiosity,Radicalism and Rebellion in Central Asia." Religion, State and Society, 2016, 44, (3):192–218; Rustam Burnashev. 2014. "Why Islamists are not the most important regional security challenge for Central Asian states." In: Johan Norberg and Erika Holmquist, (ed.). ISAF's Withdrawal from Afghanistan - Central Asian Perspectives on Regional Security. Stockholm: Ministry of Defense.

41 "Tajikistan seizes momentum to tar opposition as terrorists," Eurasianet, Aug. 2, 2018, https://eurasianet.org/tajikistan-seizes-momentum-to-tar-opposition-as-terrorists.

42 "Tajikistan: A mystery Islamic State conversion for a hopeless young man," Eurasianet, July 31, 2018, https://eurasianet.org/tajikistan-a-mystery-islamic-stateconversion-for-a-hopeless-young-man.

43 Orazgaliyeva, Malika, "Kazakh President Declares June 9 as National Day of Mourning," The Astana Times, June 9, 2016, https://astanatimes.com/2016/06/kazakh-president-declares-june-9-as-national-day-of-mourning/.

44 "Country Reports on Terrorism 2016," United States Department of State, July 2017, https://www.state.gov/documents/organization/272488.pdf.

45 Weiser, Benjamin, "Bike Path Terrorism Suspect Seeks Plea Deal to Avoid Death Penalty," The New York Times, Jan. 17, 2018, https://www.nytimes.com/2018/01/17/nyregion/saipov-bike-path-terrorist-death-penalty.html.

46 For a discussion of the limits of our knowledge in the context of Central Asia, see John Heathershaw and David Montgomery. "Who Says Syria's Calling? Why It Is Sometimes Better to Admit That We Just Do Not Know," CEDAR Network, 17 February 2015, http://www.cedarnetwork.org/2015/02/17/who-says-syrias-calling-why-it-issometimes-better-to-admit-that-we-just-do-not-know-by-john-heathershaw-and-david-w-montgomery/

47 Matveeva, Anna and Antonio Giustozzi, "The Central Asian Militants: Cannon Fodder of Global Jihadism or Revolutionary Vanguard?" Small Wars & Insurgencies, 29, (2), 2018, https://www.tandfonline.com/doi/abs/10.1080/09592318.2018.1433472.

48 Roy, Olivier, "France's Oedipal Islamist Complex," Foreign Policy, Jan. 7, 2016,https://foreignpolicy.com/2016/01/07/frances-oedipal-islamist-complex-charlie-hebdo-islamic-state-isis/.

49 Roy, Olivier, "Who Are the New Jihadis?" The Guardian, April 13, 2017, https://www.theguardian.com/news/2017/apr/13/who-are-the-new-jihadis.

50 Nasritdinov, Emil, Zarina Urmanbetoeva, Kanatbek Murzakhililov and Mamatbek Myrzabaev, "Vulnerability and Resilience of Young People in Kyrgyzstan to Radicalization, Violence and Extremism: Analysis Across Six Domains," Research Institute for Islamic Studies, 2018; Elshimi , Mohammed

S. et al. "Understanding the Factors Contributing to Radicalisation Among Central Asian Labour Migrants in Russia," RUSI, Apr. 26, 2018, https://rusi.org/publication/occasional-papers/understanding-factors-contributing-radicalisation-among-central-asian

51   "Kyrgyzstan: Probe Forces' Role in June Violence," Human Rights Watch,Aug. 16, 2010, https://www.hrw.org/news/2010/08/16/kyrgyzstan-probe-forces-role-june-violence. Russia Matters/U.S.-Russia Initiative to Prevent Nuclear Terrorism | Belfer Center for Science and International Affairs 39

52   "Kyrgyzstan: Widening Ethnic Divisions in the South," International Crisis Group, Mar. 29, 2012, https://www.crisisgroup.org/europe-central-asia/central-asia/

kyrgyzstan/kyrgyzstan-widening-ethnic-divisions-south.

53   "Corruption Perceptions Index 2017," Transparency International, Feb. 21, 2018, https://www.transparency.org/news/feature/corruption_perceptions_index_2017.

54   "Worldwide Governance Indicators," The World Bank, 2018, http://info.worldbank.org/governance/wgi/index.aspx#reports.

55   Event transcript: "Sergey Abashin – Central Asian Migrants in Russia: Will There Be a Religious Radicalization?" Central Asia Program, George Washington University, Apr. 24, 2017, http://centralasiaprogram.org/archives/10989.

56   Lemon, Edward, "Pathways to Violent Extremism: Evidence from Tajik Recruits to Islamic State," The Harriman Magazine, May 2018, http://www.columbia.edu/cu/creative/epub/harriman/2018/summer/Pathways_to_Violent_Extremism.pdf; Nasritdinov, Emil, Zarina Urmanbetoeva, Kanatbek Murzakhililov and Mamatbek Myrzabaev,"Vulnerability and Resilience of Young People in Kyrgyzstan to Radicalization, Violence and Extremism: Analysis Across Six Domains," Research Institute for Islamic Studies, 2018.

57   Beissembayev, Serik, "Religious Extremism in Kazakhstan: From Criminal Networks to Jihad," The Central Asia Fellowship Papers, 15, 2013, http://centralasiaprogram.org/wp-content/uploads/2016/02/CAF-Paper-15-Serik-Beissembayev.pdf.

58   "'Congratulations, Your Brother's Become a Martyr': How Moscow's Migrant Workers Became Islamic State Fighters," Meduza, Apr. 27, 2015, https://meduza.io/en/feature/2015/04/27/congratulations-your-brother-s-become-a-martyr.

59   For two scholarly discussions of the linkages between sports and criminal violence in the former Soviet Union see "Criminal Networks in Georgia and Kyrgyzstan and Young Male Sportsmen" (2008) by Alexander Kupatadze (https://books.google.com/books?hl=en&lr=&id=xCW6nVReyAcC&oi=fnd&pg=PA170&dq=georgia+kyrgyzstan+sports+violence&ots=RBi_

pwek0M&sig=HMiFJBZAU-g1xScIVm9DBWab3vk#v =onepage&q=georgia percent20 kyrgyzstan percent20sports percent20violence&f=false) and "Violent Entrepreneurs: The Use of Force in the Making of Russian Capitalism" (2002) by Vadim Volkov.

60   "Why Did a Tajik Student & Mixed Martial-Arts Champ Die for IS in Iraq?"Radio Free Europe, Feb. 23, 2015, https://www.rferl.org/a/tajik-isis-fighter/26864323.html.

61   Naumkin, Vitaly, "Radical Islam in Central Asia: Between Pen and Rifle," Lanham, MD: Rowman & Littlefield, 2005.

62   Tucker, Noah, "What Happens When Your Town Becomes an ISIS Recruiting Ground? Lessons from Central Asia about Vulnerability, Resistance and the Danger of Ignoring Injustice," Central Asia Program, July 2018, http://centralasiaprogram.org/wp-content/uploads/2018/06/Tucker-CAP-Paper-July-2018.pdf; Lemon, Edward, "Daesh and Tajikistan: The Regime's (In) Security Policy," The RUSI Journal, 160:5, 68-76, https://rusi.org/publication/rusi-journal/daesh-and-tajikistan-regimes-insecurity-policy.

63   Mironova, Vera, Ekaterina Sergatskova and Karam Alhamad, "The Lives of Foreign Fighters Who Left ISIS: Why They Escaped and Where They Are Now," Foreign Affairs, Oct. 27, 2017, https://www.foreignaffairs.com/articles/2017-10-27/lives-foreignfighters-who-left-isis.

64   "Syria Calling: Radicalisation in Central Asia," International Crisis Group Europe and Central Asia Briefing, N°72, 2015, https://www.crisisgroup.org/europe-central-asia/central-asia/syria-calling-radicalisation-central-asia.

65   "Tajikistan pardons over 100 ex-militants in Syria, Iraq wars," PressTV, Feb. 8, 2018, http://www.presstv.com/Detail/2018/02/08/551716/Tajikistan-pardon-returnees-Iraq-Syria; Matveeva, Anna, "Radicalisation and Violent Extremism in Kyrgyzstan:On the Way to the Caliphate?" The RUSI Journal, 2018, 163, (1), https://www.tandfonline.com/eprint/gXEVaGDNChmtBTJGUXJe/full; https://eurasianet.org/s/kazakhstan-to-spend-840m-on-countering-religious-extremism.

66   Lang, Josef, "Exporting Jihad – Islamic terrorism from Central Asia." OSW Commentary, No. 236, April 12, 2017, https://www.osw.waw.pl/en/publikacje/osw-commentary/2017-04-12/exporting-jihad-islamic-terrorism-central-asia.

67   "Amaq Reports IS Fighter Behind Attack That Sparked Prison Riot in Tajikistan," SITE Intelligence Group, Nov. 8, 2018, https://ent.siteintelgroup.com/State-40 Jihadists from Ex-Soviet Central Asia: Where Are They? Why Did They Radicalize? What Next? ments/amaq-reports-is-fighter-behind-attack-that-sparked-prison-riot-in-tajikistan.html.

68   "Tajikistan admits to prison massacre," Eurasianet, Nov. 23, 2018, https://eurasianet.org/tajikistan-admits-to-prison-massacre.

69   Ibid.

70   Ratelle, Jean-Francois, "Terror Threat from Russian-Speaking Jihadists Won't End with World Cup, and the West Should Care," Russia Matters, June 13, 2018, https://www.russiamatters.org/analysis/terror-threat-russian-speaking-jihadists-wont-endworld-cup-and-west-should-care. The author focuses on Russian-speaking fighters, primarily from the North Caucasus, but many of his assessments may apply to Central Asians as well.

71   "Emomali Rakhmon: tadzhikskie boyevikik peremestilis' s Blizhnego Vostoka v Afganistan [Emomali Rahmon: Tajik Militants Have Moved from the Middle East to Afghanistan]," Radio Ozodi, May 12, 2018, https://rus.ozodi.org/a/29222903.html; "Official: 150 Kyrgyz Citizens Killed In Syria Fighting Alongside IS," RFE/RL, June, 28,2018,https://www.rferl.org/a/official-150-kyrgyz-citizens-killed-in-syria-fighting-alongsideis/29325374.html; "Cvishe 220 Grazhdan Kazakhstana Pogiblo v Boyevih Deistviyah na Blizhnyem Vostoke" [Over 220 Citizens of Kazakhstan Died in Fighting in the Middle East], BNews.Kz, Dec. 12, 2017, https://bnews.kz/ru/news/svishe_220_grazhdan_kazakhstana_pogiblo_v_boevih_deistviyah_na_blizhnem_vostoke

72   "'They deserve no mercy': Iraq deals briskly with accused 'women of Isis,'" The Guardian, May 22, 2018, https://www.theguardian.com/world/2018/may/22/ they-deserve-no-mercy-iraq-deals-briskly-with-accused-women-of-isis.

73   "Russian-Speaking Foreign Fights in Iraq and Syria," CSIS Report, December 2017, https://csis-prod.s3.amazonaws.com/s3fs-public/publication/180726_Russian_Speaking_Foreign_Fight.pdf?VyUdcO2D6TJdW_Zm4JkmIpRkJxoXEZU6

74   Lynch III, Thomas, Michael Bouffard, Kelsey King and Graham Vickowski, "The Return of Foreign Fighters to Central Asia: Implications for U.S. Counterterrorism Policy," Strategic Perspectives, 2016. 21.

75   Lemon, Edward, "To Afghanistan Not Syria? Islamic State Diverts Tajik Fighters South," Eurasia Daily Monitor, March 15, 2017, https://jamestown.org/program/afghanistan-not-syria-islamic-state-diverts-tajik-fighters-south/.

76   Ali, Obaid, "New Confusion About ISKP: A case study from Sar-e Pul," Afghanistan Analysts Network, Sep. 7, 2018, https://www.afghanistan-analysts.org/new-confusion-about-iskp-a-case-study-from-sar-e-pul/.

77   For an overview of ISKP's expansion and incorporation of Central Asian groups see Giustozzi, Antonio, The Islamic State in Khurasan, London: Hurst and Company, 2018, pp. 139-159.

78   Osman, Borhan, "ISKP's Battle for Minds: What are its Main Messages and Who Do They Attract?" Afghanistan Analysts Network, Dec. 12, 2016, https://

www. afghanistan-analysts.org/iskps-battle-for-minds-what-are-their-main-messages-andwho-do-they-attract/.

79 Obaid Ali, "Still Under the IS's Black Flag: Qari Hekmat's ISKP Island in Jawzjan after His Death by Drone," Afghanistan Analysts Network, 15 May 2018, https://www.afghanistan-analysts.org/still-under-the-iss-black-flag-qari-hekmats-iskp-islandin-jawzjan-after-his-death-by-drone/.

80 Borhan Osman, "ISKP's Battle for Minds: What are its Main Messages and Who Do They Attract?" Afghanistan Analysts Network, Dec. 12, 2016, https://www.afghanistan-analysts.org/iskps-battle-for-minds-what-are-their-main-messages-andwho-do-they-attract/.

81 Stepanova, Ekaterina, "The ISIS Factor in Afghanistan: How Much of a Challenge For Russia?" Bishkek Project, March 30, 2017, https://bishkekproject.com/memos/21.

82 "Russian General Says About 10,000 Militants Deployed in Afghanistan," Asia Plus, April 17, 2018, https://www.news.tj/en/news/world/20180417/russian-generalsays-about-10000-militants-deployed-in-afghanistan.

83 Lamothe, Dan, "Senior ISIS leader killed in northern Afghanistan, highlighting shifting militant allegiances," The Washington Post, April 9, 2018, https://www.washingtonpost.com/news/checkpoint/wp/2018/04/09/senior-isis-leader-killed-in-northern-afghanistan-highlighting-shifting-militant-allegiances/?utm_term=.da3aa49e1f98.

84 "Statement of General Joseph L. Votel on the Posture of U.S. Central Command," House Armed Services Committee Hearing, Feb. 27, 2018. Russia Matters/U.S.-Russia Initiative to Prevent Nuclear Terrorism | Belfer Center for Science and International Affairs 41

85 "Twenty-second report of the Analytical Support and Sanctions Monitoring Team submitted pursuant to resolution 2368 (2017) concerning ISIL (Daesh), Al-Qaida and associated individuals and entities," United Nations Security Council, July 16, 2018,http://www.un.org/en/ga/search/view_doc.asp?symbol=S/2018/705&referer=/english/&Lang=E.

86 Seldin, Jeff, "Afghan Officials: Islamic State Fighters Finding Sanctuary in Afghanistan," VOA News, Nov. 18, 2017, https://www.voanews.com/a/afghan-officials-islamic-state-finds-sanctuary-in-afghanistan/4122270.html.

87 Shalizi, Hamid, "Embassy, mosque attacks fuel fears ISIS bringing Iraq war to Afghanistan," Reuters, Aug. 2, 2017, https://www.reuters.com/article/us-afghanistan-islamic-state/embassy-mosque-attacks-fuel-fears-isis-bringing-iraq-war-to-afghanistan-idUSKBN1AI0V1.

88 "Country Reports on Terrorism 2015: Special Briefing," United States Department of State, June2,2016, https://web.archive.org/web/20160603121929/https:/www.state.gov/r/pa/prs/ps/2016/06/258013.htm.

89 Ali, Obaid, "Qari Hekmat's Island: A Daesh enclave in Jawzjan?" Afghanistan Analysts Network, Nov. 11, 2017, https://www.afghanistan-analysts.org/qari-hekmatsisland-a-daesh-enclave-in-jawzjan/.

90 Saeed Khan, August 2016; Sheikh Abdul Hasib, May 2017; Abu Saeed, July 2017.

91 Dickinson, Amanda, "How the Islamic State Got a Foothold in Afghanistan," The Washington Post, March 21, 2018, https://www.washingtonpost.com/news/worldviews/wp/2018/03/21/how-the-islamic-state-got-a-foothold-in-afghanistan/?noredirect=on&utm_term=.7967b4b66aa5.

92 Zahid, Farhan, "Islamic State Emboldened in Afghanistan," Terrorism Monitor, 16(12), https://jamestown.org/program/islamic-state-emboldened-in-afghanistan/.

93 Giustozzi, Anotonio, "Taliban and Islamic State: Enemies or Brothers in Jihad?" Center for Research and Policy Analysis, Dec. 14, 2017, https://www.crpaweb.org/single-post/2017/12/15/Enemies-or-Jihad-Brothers-Relations-Between-Taliban-and-Islamic-State.

94 Ibid.

95 Sharifi, Shoaib and Louise Adamou, "Taliban threaten 70 percent of Afghanistan, BBC finds," BBC, Jan. 31, 2018, https://www.bbc.com/news/world-asia-42863116.

96 Chughtai, Alia, "Afghanistan: Who controls what," Aljazeera, Oct. 19, 2018,https://www.aljazeera.com/indepth/interactive/2016/08/afghanistan-controls-160823083528213.html.

97 Almukhtar, Sarah, "How Much of Afghanistan Is Under Taliban Control After 16 Years of War With the U.S.?" The New York Times, Aug. 23, 2017, https://www.nytimes. com/interactive/2017/08/23/world/asia/afghanistan-us-taliban-isis-control.html.

98 "Quarterly Report on the Protection of Civilians in Armed Conflict: 1 January to 30 September 2018," United Nations Assistance Mission in Afghanistan, Oct. 10,2018, https://unama.unmissions.org/ sites/default/files/ unama_protection_of_civilians_in_armed_conflict_3rd_quarter_report_2018_10_oct.pdf.

99 Giustozzi, Anotonio, "Taliban and Islamic State: Enemies or Brothers in Jihad?" Center for Research and Policy Analysis, Dec. 14, 2017, https://www.crpaweb.org/single-post/2017/12/15/Enemies-or-Jihad-Brothers-Relations-Between-Taliban-and-Islamic-State.

100 Special thanks to Thomas Ruttig for confirming with Afghan sources that Moawiya was an ethnic Uzbek from Afghanistan, and not from Uzbekistan as suggested by earlier reporting in The Washington Post. (See https://www.

washingtonpost. com/news/checkpoint/wp/2018/04/09/senior-isis-leader-killed-in-northern-afghanistan-highlighting-shifting-militant-allegiances/.)

101 Rahim, Najim and Rod Nordland, "Taliban Surge Routs ISIS in Northern Afghanistan," The New York Times, Aug. 1, 2018, https://www.nytimes.com/2018/08/01/world/asia/afghanistan-taliban-isis.html.

102 "Quarterly Report on the Protection of Civilians in Armed Conflict: 1 January to 30 September 2018," United Nations Assistance Mission in Afghanistan, Oct. 10,2018, https://unama.unmissions.org/sites/default/files/unama_protection_of_civilians_in_armed_conflict_3rd_quarter_report_2018_10_oct.pdf.

103 "At Least 200 IS Fighters 'Surrender' In Afghanistan," Radio Free Europe, Aug.2, 2018, https://www.rferl.org/a/at-least-200-is-fighters-surrender-in-northern-fghanistan/29402416.html.

104 Musavi, Sayed Aref, "Jawzjan Governor Says Province 'Is Clear Of Daesh,'" Tolo News, Aug. 2, 2018, https://www.tolonews.com/afghanistan/jawzjan-governor-saysprovince-'-clear-daesh'.

105 Weiss, Caleb, "Foreign Islamic State fighters captured by Taliban in Jawzjan,"Long War Journal, Aug. 4, 2018, https://www.longwarjournal.org/archives/2018/08/foreign-islamic-state-fighters-captured-by-taliban-in-jawzjan.php.

106 "Emomali Rakhmon: tadzhikskie boyevikik peremestilis' s Blizhnego Vostoka v Afganistan [Emomali Rahmon: Tajik Militants Have Moved from the Middle East to Afghanistan]," Radio Ozodi, May 12, 2018, https://rus.ozodi.org/a/29222903.html.

107 "Kabul extradiroval grazhdanku Tadzhikistana s dvumya maloletnimi det'mi [Kabul Has Extradited a Tajik Woman with Two Small Children]," Radio Ozodi, May 6,2018, https://rus.ozodi.org/a/29210981.html.

108 Rakhmatzoda, Makhmuddzhon, "'Vernite syna domoy'. Kak 18-letniy migrant okazalsya v afganskom Nangarkhare ['Return my son home'. How an 18-year old migrant ended up in Nangarhar, Afghanistan]," Radio Ozodi, Jan. 26, 2018, https://rus.ozodi.org/a/28999437.html.

109 "How Former 'Islamic State' Militants Wind Up in Ukraine," Hromadske, Aug. 8,2017, https://en.hromadske.ua/posts/how-former-islamic-state-militants-wind-up-inukraine.

110 Barrett, Richard, "Beyond the Caliphate: Foreign Fighters and the Threat of Returnees," The Soufan Center, October 2017, http://thesoufancenter.org/research/beyond-caliphate/; Hegghammer, Thomas and Petter Nesser, "Assessing the Islamic State's Commitment to Attacking the West," Perspectives on Terrorism, 4(9), 2015,http://www.terrorismanalysts.com/pt/index.php/pot/article/view/440/html.

111   Sonmez, Gotkug, "Violent Extremism among Central Asians: The Istanbul, St. Petersburg, Stockholm, and New York City Attacks." CTC Sentinel, 10 (11), 2017; "Istanbul Nightclub Massacre Suspect Goes On Trial," Radio Free Europe, Dec. 11, 2017, https://www.rferl.org/a/uzbek-istanbul-nightclub-attack-islamic-state-trial-begins/28908886.html.

112   "Stockholm Attack Suspect Deported from Turkey in 2015 While on Way to Join ISIL in Syria," Hurriyet, 12 April 2017, http://www.hurriyetdailynews.com/stockholm-attack-suspect-deported-from-turkey-in-2015-while-on-way-to-join-isil-in-syria-111959.

113   "Tadzhiksky sled v terakte v Stokgolme" [Tajik Link in the Act of Terrorism in Stockholm], Radio Ozodi, 9 February 2018, https://rus.ozodi.org/a/29029512.html.

114   "Podozrevaemyy v terakte v Peterburge byl deportirovan iz Turtsii [Suspect in Petersburg terrorist attack had been deported from Turkey]," Radio Free Europe, Apr. 11, 2017, https://www.svoboda.org/a/28422548.html.

115   "Pravookhraniteli proveryayut dannye ob obuchenii terrorista Dzhalilova v ryadakh IG v Sirii [Law enforcement checking information about the training of the terrorist Jalilov in the ranks of ISIS in Syria]," TASS, Apr. 5, 2017, https://tass.ru/proisshestviya/4157978.

116   "St Petersburg bombing: Group says al-Qaeda chief ordered attack," BBC, Apr. 25, 2017, https://www.bbc.com/news/world-europe-39713324.

117   Solopov, Maksim, Amalia Zatari and German Petelin, "Terakt v Peterburge privyol k Abu Salakhu [Terrorist Act in St. Petersburg led to Abu Salah]," Gazeta.ru, Apr. 21, 2017, https://www.gazeta.ru/army/2017/04/21/10638311.shtml.

118   "St. Pete Metro Blast Suspect Received Money From Terrorist Group in Turkey," Sputnik News, Apr. 20, 2017, https://sputniknews.com/russia/201704201052820547-st-petersburg-metro-blast-suspect-money-turkey/.

119   Ratelle, Jean-Francois, "Terror Threat from Russian-Speaking Jihadists Won't End with World Cup, and the West Should Care," Russia Matters, June 13, 2018, https://www.russiamatters.org/analysis/terror-threat-russian-speaking-jihadists-wont-endworld-cup-and-west-should-care.

120   Najibullah, Farangis, "Life After Islamic State: Pardoned Tajik Militants Navigate Road to Reintegration," RFE/RL, Aug. 6, 2017, https://www.rferl.org/a/tajikistan-islamic-state-pardoned-militants-reintegration/28661770.html.

121   "More than 30 pardoned Tajiks have rejoined IS terror group, said Sughd chief police officer," Asia-Plus, Feb. 5, 2018, http://news.tj/en/news/tajikistan/security/20180205/more-than-30-pardoned-tajiks-have-rejoined-is-terror-group-saidsughd-chief-police-officer.

122 Kharzhaubayeva, Ainur, "Frontier Migration Between Kazakhstan and Russia: Russia Matters/U.S.-Russia Initiative to Prevent Nuclear Terrorism | Belfer Center for Science and International Affairs 43The Case of the West Kazakhstan," unpublished PhD dissertation, Charles University,Prague, 2013, p. 62,https://is.cuni.cz/webapps/zzp/download/140027754.

123 "2017 Report on Compliance with and Adherence to Arms Control, Nonproliferation, and Disarmament Agreements and Commitments," U.S. Department of State, https://www.state.gov/t/avc/rls/rpt/2017/270330. htm#CHEMICAL percent20WEAPONS percent20CONVENTION percent20(CWC).

124 "Poisoned Legacy," The Economist, July 9, 2015, https://www.economist.com/asia/ 2015/07/09/poisoned-legacy.

125 Tobey, William, "What Lies Beneath," Foreign Policy, April 30, 2012, https://foreignpolicy.com/2012/04/30/what-lies-beneath/.126 Ibid.

127 "Project Sapphire After Action Report," November 1994, declassified U.S. government document, https://nsarchive2.gwu.edu/NSAEBB/NSAEBB491/ docs/01 percent20- percent20After percent20Action percent20report percent20DTRA.pdf.

128 "GTRI Plans for FY2011," International Panel on Fissile Materials Blog, Feb. 5,2010, http://fissilematerials.org/blog/2010/02/gtri_plans_for_fy2011. html.

129 Miller, Judith, "Poison Island: A Special Report, at a Bleak Asian Site, Killer Germs Survive," The New York Times, June 2, 1999, p. A01, https://www. nytimes.com/1999/06/02/world/poison-island-a-special-report-at-bleak-asian-site-killergerms-survive.html.

130 Miller, Judith, William Broad, and Stephen Engelberg, Germs: Biological Weapons and America's Secret War, (New York: Simon and Schuster, 2001) pp. 165-67.

131 Budjeryn, Mariana, "Sen. Sam Nunn: 'We Have a Choice Between Cooperation or Catastrophe,'" Russia Matters, June 20, 2017, https://russiamatters.org/analysis/sen-sam-nunn-we-have-choice-between-cooperation-or-catastrophe.

132 Tobey, William, "What Lies Beneath," Foreign Policy, April 30, 2012, https://foreignpolicy.com/2012/04/30/what-lies-beneath/.

133 Butler, Kenley, "Weapons of Mass Destruction in Central Asia," Nuclear Threat Initiative, Oct. 1, 2002, https://www.nti.org/analysis/articles/weapons-mass-destruction-central-asia/.

134 Ibid.

135 Zhantikan, Timur, "Strengthening Security of Radioactive Sources in CentralAsia," slide presentation, May 24, 2017, https://inis.iaea.org/collection/NCLCollectionStore/_Public/48/078/48078661.pdf?r=1&r=1.

136 "Pathways to Cooperation," (Washington, DC: Nuclear Threat Initiative,November 2017), p. 18, https://www.nti.org/media/documents/Pathways_to_Cooperation_FINAL.pdf.

137 Binder, Marcus K., Jillian M. Quigley, Herbert F. Tinsley, "Islamic State Chemical Weapons: A Case Contained by Its Context," CTC Sentinel, March 2018, Vol. 11,Issue 3, p. 27, https://ctc.usma.edu/islamic-state-chemical-weapons-case-contained-context/138 Ibid., p. 30.

139 Quoted in David Albright and Sarah Burkhard, "Daesh Hype About Stealing Nuclear Weapons," Institute for Science and International Security, Oct. 2, 2015,pp. 1-2,https://isis-online.org/uploads/isis-reports/documents/Daesh_Hype_about_Nuclear_Weapons_Oct_2_2015-final1.pdf

140 Ibid.

141 Warrick, Joby and Loveday Morris, "How ISIS Nearly Stumbled on Ingredients for a 'Dirty Bomb'," The Washington Post, July 22, 2017, https://www.washingtonpost.com/world/national-security/how-isis-nearly-stumbled-on-the-ingredients-for-a-dirtybomb/2017/07/22/6a966746-6e31-11e7-b9e2-2056e768a7e5_story.html.

142 Bunn, Matthew, et al., "Advancing Nuclear Security: Evaluating Progress andSetting New Goals," Belfer Center for Science and International Affairs, March 2014, p.39, pp. 39-40, https://www.belfercenter.org/sites/default/files/legacy/files/advancingnuclearsecurity.pdf

143 Malashenko, Alexey and Alexey Staroshin, "The Rise of Nontraditional Islam in the Urals," Carnegie Moscow Center, Sept. 15, 2015, http://carnegie.ru/2015/09/30/rise-of-nontraditional-islam-in-urals-pub-61461

144 Ter, Marta and Ryskelki Satke, "Conditions for Central Asians in Russia Boost Radicalism," European Council on Foreign Relations, March 17, 2016, https://www.ecfr.eu/article/commentary_conditions_for_central_asians_in_russia_boost_radical-44 Jihadists from Ex-Soviet Central Asia: Where Are They? Why Did They Radicalize? What Next?ism_6034

145 Donnelly, D., Kovchegin, D., Mladineo, S., Ratz, L. and Roth, N., "Corrupting Nuclear Security: Potential Gaps and New Approaches to Insider Risk Mitigation," Institute for Nuclear Materials Management Paper, 2015, p. 3, https://www.belfercenter.   org/sites/default/files/files/publication/a525_1 percent20 percent281 percent29.pdf

146 Karim, Iskander, "Identifying Instability Pockets," School of Advanced Military Studies, U.S. Army Command and General Staff College, 2014, p. 11, http://www.dtic.mil/dtic/tr/fulltext/u2/a614169.pdf

147 "Four Russians Sentences for Smuggling Radioactive Sources Across the Russian Kazakh Border," ITAR-Tass, Jan. 23, 2008, https://www.nti.org/analysis/articles/four-russians-sentenced-smuggling-radioactive-sources-across-russian-kazakh-border/

148 "Russian-Speaking Foreign Fighters in Iraq and Syria: Assessing the Threat from (and to) Russia and Central Asia," Center for Strategic and International Studies, December 2017, https://csis-prod.s3.amazonaws.com/s3fs-public/publication/180726_Russian_ Speaking_Foreign_Fight.pdf?VyUdcO2D6TJdW_Zm4JkmIpRkJxoXEZU6.

Index

About the Author

Musa Khan Jalalzai is a journalist and research scholar. He has written extensively on Afghanistan, terrorism, nuclear and biological terrorism, human trafficking, drug trafficking, and intelligence research and analysis. He was an Executive Editor of the Daily Outlook Afghanistan from 2005-2011, and a permanent contributor in Pakistan's daily *The Post*, *Daily Times*, and *The Nation*, *Weekly the Nation*, (London). However, in 2004, US Library of Congress in its report for South Asia mentioned him as the biggest and prolific writer. He received Masters in English literature, Diploma in Geospatial Intelligence, University of Maryland, Washington DC, certificate in Surveillance Law from the University of Stanford, USA, and diploma in Counter terrorism from Pennsylvania State University, California, the United States.